Angela Gillespie

The book of oratory

Compiled for the use of colleges, academies, and the higher classes of select and

parish schools

Angela Gillespie

The book of oratory
Compiled for the use of colleges, academies, and the higher classes of select and parish schools

ISBN/EAN: 9783742892546

Manufactured in Europe, USA, Canada, Australia, Japa

Cover: Foto ©Paul-Georg Meister /pixelio.de

Manufactured and distributed by brebook publishing software (www.brebook.com)

Angela Gillespie

The book of oratory

THE METROPOLITAN FIFTH READER.

THE
BOOK OF ORATORY:

COMPILED FOR THE USE OF

COLLEGES, ACADEMIES,

AND THE

HIGHER CLASSES OF SELECT AND PARISH SCHOOLS,

By a Member of the Order of the Holy Cross.

NEW AND REVISED EDITION.

NEW YORK:
D. & J. SADLIER & CO., 31 BARCLAY STREET.
MONTREAL :—COR. NOTRE-DAME AND ST. FRANCIS XAVIER STS.
1871.

PREFACE.

The general principles which have guided the compilers of the Metropolitan Series are exemplified most fully in this the crowning volume of the series, and need not here be repeated. We present this volume as at once an advanced Reader and a manual for Elocution, in the highest classes in our academies and schools.

All are aware from how comparatively limited a circle the selections of Readers generally are made. In the present series there has been no limit, and resort has been had to sources hitherto almost untouched. This gives a novelty and a freshness to the selection that cannot fail to please both instructors and pupils. The pieces are especially adapted for the use which has led to their selection; that is, for delivery as exercises of elocution and oratory.

As this volume is intended for academies of both sexes, care has been taken to make it suitable for either. Young ladies are not expected, indeed, to become orators, or to enter the forum or senate chamber; yet as proper and elegant reading is almost impossible without a knowledge of the principles of elocution, and practise in delivery, elocution must form a branch of their education; and a suitable manual, such as we venture to say we here present, cannot fail to be appreciated.

New York, *August*, 1867.

CONTENTS.

PART I.—ELOCUTION.

	PAGE
PRINCIPLES AND DEFINITIONS	11
Exercises in Breathing	14
Gesture	14
THE VOCAL ORGANS	16
Articulation	17
THE VOICE	21
QUALITY OF VOICE	22
The Pure Quality	22
The Orotund Quality	23
The Guttural Quality	24
The Aspirate Voice	25
The Tremor Quality	25
VARIATIONS OF VOICE	27
Examples in Pitch	28
Examples in Force	30
Examples in Time	33
EMPHASIS	35
Examples in Emphatic Utterance	36
INFLECTION, CIRCUMFLEX, AND MONOTONE	37
Inflection	37
Circumflex	39
The Monotone	40
PAUSES	41
PERSONATION	44
THE STUDY OF EXPRESSION	48

PART II.—RHETORICAL.

1. Apostrophe to Water	*Judge Arrington*	51
2. Our Titles	*Miss A. A. Proctor*	53
3. English Operatives in Manufacturing Districts	*Southey*	54
4. The Miserere at Rome	*Headley*	56
5. St. Peter's	*Eustace*	58
6. Song of the Stars	*Bryant*	62
7. The Sea	*Wallace*	63
8. Burning of Moscow	*Alison*	65
9. The Parting of Marmion and Douglas	*Scott*	69
10. The Summer of Kings		72
11. Extempore or Sight Reading		75
12. The Campagna of Rome	*Ruskin*	76

CONTENTS.

			PAGE
13.	Monk Felix	*Longfellow*	76
14.	Description of the Ruins at Balbec	*Lamartine*	80
15.	The Convict Ship	*T. K. Hervey*	83
16.	Mountains	*William Howitt*	84
17.	Ireland and the Irish	*C. Edwards Lester*	86
18.	The Duellist's Honor	*Bishop England*	87
19.	Emotions on Returning to the United States, 1837	*Legaré*	89
20.	Afar in the Desert	*Pringle*	90
21.	Post Nummos Virtus	*Mt. Rev. Abp. Spalding*	92
22.	Grace Darling	*Wordsworth*	94
23.	The Church	*Macaulay*	97
24.	The Church—(*Concluded*)	*Ib.*	98
25.	The Crusaders Approach Jerusalem	*Tasso*	99
26.	The Suliote Mother	*Mrs. Hemans*	102
27.	The End of the Long Parliament	*Lingard*	103
28.	American Literature	*Grimke*	106
29.	Legend of St. Jodocus	*Translated from the German*	107
30.	The Poor Exile	*Lamennais*	109
31.	A Christmas Hymn	*Dommet*	110
32.	Baron Geramb	*Cardinal Wiseman*	112
33.	The Angels of Buena Vista	*Whittier*	114
34.	The Possession of Juba	*Newman*	118
35.	The Possession of Juba—(*Continued*)	*Ib.*	122
36.	The Possession of Juba—(*Concluded*)	*Ib.*	125
37.	Waiting for the May	*D. F. M'Carthy*	127
38.	Italy	*Wallace*	129
39.	The Tyrant and the Captive	*Adelaide A. Proctor*	130
40.	The Submarine Telegraph	*Cardinal Wiseman*	132
41.	The Human Voice	*Holmes*	134
42.	The Bell of Liberty	*Headley*	137
43.	The Just Man	*Giles*	140
44.	Summer Hymn	*From the German of Scheffler*	142
45.	The Christian Preacher	*Lamartine*	144
46.	What is Glory?	*Motherwell*	145
47.	Christendom	*Novalis*	146
48.	The Good Old Times	*Rev. J. M. Neale*	149
49.	Maryland	*Wm. Geo. Reed*	152
50.	The Female Martyr	*Whittier*	154
51.	American History	*Gulian C. Verplanck*	156
52.	Soggarth Aroon	*Banim*	158
53.	Summer's Farewell	*E. Cook*	160
54.	Rome Under Nero	*Munahan*	162
55.	Acre		164
56.	The Martyrs of Fatherland	*De Vere*	165
57.	The American Republic	*Judge Story*	167
58.	Don't Forget	*B. F. Taylor*	170
59.	The Penitent's Prayer	*Goëthe*	171
60.	The Church-Bell	*Cardinal Wiseman*	172
61.	The Bier that Conquered		173
62.	St. Bernard	*Montalembert*	175
63.	O for the Wings of the Wind to Wander L	*Judge Arrington*	178
64.	A Man Overboard	*Mitchell*	179
65.	The Fount of Song	*Miss Brown*	180
66.	Monasteries	*Hurter*	182

CONTENTS.

			PAGE
67.	Charity	O'Gorman	183
68.	The Peri's Song	Moore	185
69.	Floating Islands	Huc	186
70.	The Skylark	Hogg	188
71.	Revolutionists	Guizot	189
72.	The Aztec Empire	Prescott	190
73.	The Valley of Mexico	Ib.	192
74.	What is Poetry?	G. W. Prentice	193
75.	Our Neighbor	E. A. Starr	194
76.	The Angelus	Cardinal Wiseman	195
77.	Song of the Shirt	Hood	196
78.	The Press	Balmes	199
79.	Ruins of Copan and Palenque	Stephens	201
80.	The Spirit of Beauty	Dawes	203
81.	Man's Position in Creation	Faber	204
82.	The Acadians	D. MacLeod	207
83.	The Tyrolese	Wordsworth	209
84.	To the Memory of those who fell in the Rebellion of 1745	Collins	210
85.	The Gray Forest Eagle	S. B. Street	210
86.	Mother	Père Felix	213
87.	The Extra Train		214
88.	The Month of October in Italy	Cardinal Wiseman	217
89.	Coxcombry in Conversation	Cowper	219
90.	Henry IV's Apostrophe to Sleep	Shakspeare	220
91.	Success the Reward of Merit	Rev. F. S. Baker	221
92.	Alexander's Feast	Dryden	222
93.	The Silver-Bird's Nest	Miss H. F. Gould	223
94.	The Burial at Sea	Rev. J. M. Neale	224
95.	The Glove and the Lions	L. Hunt	225
96.	Modern Theories	Montalembert	226
97.	To-morrow is Saint Crispian	Shakspeare	228
98.	A Challenge to America	Punch	229
99.	The Wonderful "One-Hoss Shay"	Holmes	230
100.	Last Days of Peter Stuyvesant	Irving	234
101.	Steam	Punch	236
102.	Origin of the City of New York	Irving	237
103.	The Dismissal of General Von Poffenburgh	Ib.	238
104.	The Height of Ridiculous	Holmes	239
105.	Country Excursion	Dickens	240
106.	Country Excursion—(Concluded)	Ib.	243
107.	Sir Hudibras	Butler	246
108.	Modern Improvements	Halleck	247
109.	Squire Bull and his Son Jonathan	J. K. Paulding	248
110.	An Amusing Anecdote		251
111.	Fame	Joanna Baillie	252
112.	Life	Longfellow	253

PART III.—ORATORICAL.

1.	Oratory as an Art	Knowles	255
2.	The Study of Oratory in Greece and Rome	Wirt	256
3.	Oration on the Crown	Demosthenes	257
4.	Oration on the Crown—(Concluded)	Ib.	260

CONTENTS.

			PAGE
5.	Public Spirit of the Athenians	*Demosthenes*	261
6.	A Last Appeal	*Ib.*	262
7.	Cicero and Demosthenes Compared	*Fenelon*	264
8.	Catiline Denounced	*Cicero*	265
9.	Catiline Expelled	*Ib.*	267
10.	The Quarrel Scene from Julius Cæsar	*Shakspeare*	268
11.	Marc Antony's Oration	*Ib.*	272
12.	Against the Execution of Louis XVI.	*Virgniaud*	275
13.	The Rising of the Vendée	*Oroly*	277
14.	Lord Strafford's Defence		279
15.	Senatorial Denunciation of Richard Cromwell	*Sir Henry Vane*	281
16.	King John and Hubert	*Shakspeare*	283
17.	Strictures on William Pitt	*Sir Robert Walpole*	284
18.	Reply of William Pitt		286
19.	Hotspur	*Shakspeare*	288
20.	Repeal of the Stamp Act	*Lord Chatham*	290
21.	Reconciliation with America	*Earl of Chatham*	292
22.	The American War	*Fox*	294
23.	The Foreign Policy of Washington	*Ib.*	295
24.	"A Political Pause"	*Ib.*	297
25.	The American War Denounced	*William Pitt*	298
26.	On an Attempt to coerce him to Resign	*Ib.*	299
27.	Sectarian Tyranny, 1812	*Henry Grattan*	301
28.	Reply to the Duke of Grafton	*Thurlow*	302
29.	A Collision of Vices	*Canning*	303
30.	"Measures not Men"	*Ib.*	305
31.	Danger of Delay	*Lord Brougham*	306
32.	Parliamentary Reform	*Ib.*	308
33.	The Established Church in Ireland	*T. B. Macaulay*	311
34.	Satirical Extract from a Speech of Mr. Canning on the Address (1825)	*Canning*	313
35.	Declaration of Irish Rights	*Grattan*	315
36.	Reply to Mr. Flood, 1783	*Ib.*	317
37.	The Irish Parliament	*Ib.*	319
38.	The O'Kavanagh	*J. Augustus Shea*	321
39.	On American Taxation	*Burke*	322
40.	Enterprise of American Colonists	*Ib.*	324
41.	Pandemonium	*Ib.*	325
42.	Impeachment of Warren Hastings	*Ib.*	326
43.	Peroration to the Impeachment of Warren Hastings	*Ib.*	328
44.	Hyder Ali's Invasion of the Carnatic		330
45.	Marie Antoinette, Queen of Louis XVI.	*Burke*	333
46.	The Tithe Bills	*O'Connell*	334
47.	The Tail	*Ib.*	335
48.	Scenes of Our Youth	*Blackwood's Magazine*	336
49.	The Pillar Towers of Ireland	*D. F. M'Carthy*	338
50.	The Irish Disturbance Bill	*O'Connell*	340
51.	Religious Liberty	*Ib.*	342
52.	The Irish Soldier	*Curran*	343
53.	Laws for Ireland	*Grattan*	345
54.	National Independence	*Otis*	347
55.	The American Revolution	*Josiah Quincy*	349
56.	The Age of Washington	*Fisher Ames*	351
57.	Union and Liberty	*O. W. Holmes*	351

		PAGE
58. The Federal Constitution, 1787	*Franklin*	353
59. Dissolution of the National Compact	*Gouverneur Morris*	354
60. Washington's Sword and Franklin's Staff	*J. Q. Adams*	356
61. Liberty or Death	*Patrick Henry*	357
62. Liberty or Death—(*Concluded*)	*Ib.*	359
63. Return of British Fugitives, 1783	*Ib.*	360
64. Lafayette	*John Quincy Adams*	362
65. American Innovations	*James Madison*	365
66. The Eagle	*Percival*	366
67. The Prospect of War	*J. C. Calhoun*	368
68. Reply to Foot's Resolutions	*Robert Y. Hayne*	370
69. Song of Marion's Men	*Bryant*	373
70. Matches and Over-matches	*Webster*	375
71. The South during the Revolution	*Hayne*	377
72. The Federal Union	*Webster*	378
73. Peaceable Secession	*Ib.*	379
74. Free Trade	*Hayne*	381
75. Our Country	*Webster*	382
76. The State Constitution	*Judge Gaston*	384
77. The Folly of Disunion	*Ib.*	386
78. Party Spirit	*Ib.*	387
79. Factious Power	*Ib.*	388
80. The Permanence of American Liberty	*McDuffie*	389
81. New Territories	*Winthrop*	390
82. The Disinterestedness of Washington	*R. T. Paine*	392
83. Our Republic	*T. Ewing*	394
84. Liberty and Greatness	*Legaré*	395
85. Constitutional Changes	*John Randolph of Roanoke*	397
86. The Patriot's Courage	*Clay*	399
87. Honorable Ambition	*Ib.*	400
88. Aspirations for America	*C. M. Clay*	401
89. The Evils of War	*H. Clay*	403
90. Hohenlinden	*Campbell*	404
91. Valedictory Address to the Senate	*Clay*	406
92. Freedom of Discussion	*W. C. Preston*	409
93. The Mexican War	*T. Corwin*	412
94. Retributive Justice	*Ib.*	413
95. The Cause of the Union	*R. C. Winthrop*	415
96. Duty of American Citizens	*Douglas*	418
97. The Foundation of National Character	*Edward Everett*	419

PART IV.—MISCELLANEOUS.

1. On being found guilty of High Treason	*Robert Emmet*	421
2. Aaron Burr	*William Wirt*	430
3. Who is Blannerhassett?	*Ib.*	431
4. The Habeas Corpus Act	*Curran*	433
5. Curran's Appeal to Lord Avonmore	*Ib.*	435
6. Great Minds in their Relations to Christianity	*Erskine*	437
7. Guilt cannot Keep its Own Secret	*Daniel Webster*	439
8. An Appeal to the Jury	*Phillips*	441
9. Ireland	*T. F. Meagher*	442
10. Adherbal against Jugurtha	*Sallust*	443

CONTENTS.

			PAGE
11.	Alaric the Visigoth	*Everett*	446
12.	Speech of Salathiel in Favor of Resisting the Roman Power		449
13.	Extract from Roderick, the Last of the Goths	*Southey*	451
14.	Salathiel to Titus		451
15.	Sempronius' Speech for War	*Addison*	453
16.	Caius Marius to the Romans	*Paraphrase from Sallust*	453
17.	Brutus on the Death of Cæsar		455
18.	The Spartans' March	*Felicia Hemans*	456
19.	The Death of Leonidas	*Croly*	457
20.	The Flight of Xerxes	*Miss Jewsbury*	458
21.	Scipio to his Army	*Livy*	459
22.	Hannibal to his Army	*Ib.*	461
23.	Regulus to the Roman Senate		463
24.	Leonidas to his Three Hundred		465
25.	Speech of Galgacus to the Caledonians	*Tacitus*	467
26.	Titus Quintius against Quarrels between the Senate and the People	*Livy*	469
27.	Richard to the Princes of the Crusade	*Sir Walter Scott*	471
28.	Alfred the Great to his Men	*Knowles*	472
29.	The Battle	*Schiller*	473
30.	Before Vicksburg		476
31.	The Alarm—April 19, 1776	*Bancroft*	477
32.	Paul Revere's Ride	*Longfellow*	479
33.	Macbriar's Speech to the Scotch Insurgents	*Scott*	483
34.	Spanish War Song		484
35.	Spartacus to the Gladiators		485
36.	The Battle Hymn	*K. T. Körner*	488
37.	Flodden Field	*Scott*	489
38.	Flodden Field—(*Concluded*)	*Ib.*	492
39.	Edinburgh after Flodden	*William Edmondstoune Aytoun*	496
40.	The Light Brigade	*Tennyson*	499
41.	The Claims of Italy		501
42.	Napoleon to the Army of Italy		502
43.	Napoleon to the Soldiers at Fontainebleau	*Lamartine*	503
44.	Napoleon's Return	*Miss Wallace*	505
45.	The Soldier's Funeral	*Landon*	508
46.	Press On	*Park Benjamin*	509
47.	Death and the Warrior	*Hemans*	510
48.	King Richard's Meditation on Kings	*Shakspeare*	511
49.	Welcome to General Lafayette	*Edward Everett*	512
50.	Rolla's Address		513
51.	Address to the Sun	*Ossian*	514
52.	England's Doom	*Abp. Spalding*	515
53.	A National Monument to Washington	*R. C. Winthrop*	516
54.	Washington's Farewell to his Army	*Una*	518
55.	The Spirit of Democracy in America and in Europe	*Lacordaire*	520
56.	The Death of O'Connell	*W. H. Seward*	522
57.	The Execution of Montrose, 1645	*Aytoun*	523
57.*	A Storm at Sea	*Southey*	527
58.	How they Brought the Good News from Ghent	*R. Browning*	527
59.	Cato on the Soul's Immortality	*Addison*	530
60.	Marc Antony's Apostrophe to Cæsar's Body	*Shakspeare*	531
61.	Scene from Julius Cæsar	*Ib.*	533
62.	Peter Plymley's Letters	*Sydney Smith*	536

CONTENTS.

PAGE

63. The Reform Bill..................................*Sydney Smith* 538
64. Taxes the Price of Glory............................*Ib.* 540
65. The Union......................................*De Haes Janvier* 541
66. The Destiny of America...............................*Story* 542
67. Republics...*Legaré* 544
68. Cato's Speech over his Dead Son......................*Addison* 545
69. Who is there to Mourn?................................*Logan* 546
70. Black Hawk's Address to General Street....................... 548
71. The Indian Hunter................................*Longfellow* 549
72. Rights of the Indians defended.......................*Everett* 551
73. Lines to a Fallen Leaf..........................*Richard Ternan* 553
74. Dryburgh Abbey................................*Charles Swain* 554
75. Marius in Prison..................................*De Quincey* 559
76. Marius.......................................*Lydia Maria Child* 560
77. A Legend of Bregenz........................*Miss A. A. Proctor* 561
78. The Fire-Worshippers—(From "Lalla Rookh")...........*Moore* 567
79. The Irish Emigrant's Mother.....................*D. F. M'Carthy* 568
80. England's Present..................................*Ewing* 572
81. The Bible....................................*Donoso Cortes* 575
82. Influence of Pagan Classics on Religion...............*Gaume* 577
83. Pagan and Christian Classics..........................*Digby* 580
84. Christian Orators—Fathers of the Church........*Chateaubriand* 582
85. "Let the Waters be Gathered Together"..............*St. Basil* 584
86. "In the Beginning was the Word"......................*Ib.* 587
87. Letter of St. Basil, Describing his Hermitage, to St. Gregory Nazianzen..*St. Basil* 589
88. Thou art Beautiful, O Sea!.............................*Ib.* 590
89. Venerable Bede... 591
90. To the Christians of Rome................................. 592
91. Julian the Apostate....................................... 595
92. Martyrdom of St. Theodosia....................*Mrs. A. H. Dorsey* 597
93. St. Cecilia before the Roman Prefect....................... 599
94. The Second Coming of Jesus Christ........*St. Ephrem of Edessa* 603
95. My God! I Love Thee!..........................*St. Augustine* 608
96. Defence of Eutropius...........................*St. Chrysostom* 609
97. Supplication... 615
98. Appeal for the Crusaders, to the People of Franconia.
St. Bernard 617
99. Bossuet as an Orator.........................*Chateaubriand* 620
100. The Great Condé................................*Bossuet* 621
101. Christ our Light........................*De la Motte Fouqué* 623
102. Funeral Oration of Henrietta of England............*Bossuet* 625
103. Funeral Oration of the Duchess of Orleans..............*Ib.* 627
104. The Death of the Sinner.........................*Massillon* 629
105. On the Small Number of the Elect.......................*Ib.* 630
106. Exordium at St. Sulpice.......................*Père Bridaine* 632
107. Song of the Angels over the Skeptic's Conversion.
From an unpublished Poem by Judge Arrington 634
108. Character of Champlain................*Thomas D'Arcy McGee* 635
109. Heroism of the Hospital and the Prison.................*Ib.* 637
110. Mental and Moral Destitution of Deaf-Mutes............... 640
111. Paradise...*Faber* 642
112. The Song of the Cossack....................*Francis Mahony* 644
113. Ireland and the Irish........................*Henry Giles* 647

THE FIFTH READER.

PART I.
ELOCUTION.

PRINCIPLES AND DEFINITIONS.

WE define *Elocution* to be a knowledge of the principles which govern the outward expression of the inward workings of the mind. Science is knowledge systematized so as to be easily comprehended. The science of elocution, then, includes the whole theory of delivery. It is the embodying form or representative power of eloquence in speech. *Oratory* is the vital existence resulting from the perfect harmony and combination of *Elocution* and *Eloquence*.

We study elocution in order to improve in oral expression, and to cultivate every external grace or accomplishment with which the delivery of language should be accompanied—whether in reading, speaking, recitation, or extemporaneous discourse; and this is the art of elocution.

In our preparation for the delivery of thought, we must understand—

First. The vocal organs, and the muscles which act on them.

Second. The power of separate elements, and the meaning of the words to be read or spoken.

Third. We must be diligent in the practice or delivery of the best models of oratorical composition.

The right use of the *vocal organs* depends upon our knowledge of their relation to the body. *We must learn to sit properly, stand in an easy and graceful position*, and attend to the *management of the breath.*

The sitting position, for reading aloud and singing, may be learned from the cut.

SITTING POSTURE—PROPER AND IMPROPER.

Sit erect, with the head thrown back, that the chest may expand and contract freely in the operation of breathing. Place the feet upon the floor. Do not sit with the limbs crossed in reading, speaking, or singing.

The student should be careful to keep the body erect. A good voice depends upon it. An instrument, to produce a good tone, must be kept in tune.

---

[1] The celebrated Curran was accustomed to declaim the letters of Junius before a mirror; and the speech of Mark Antony over the body of Cæsar was an especial favorite. Though never satisfied with his rendering of the latter, he always recommended it to law-students.

The practice of *Position* and *Gesture* will prove a valuable aid in physical culture, and in acquiring a graceful address.

We have but two *Primary* positions of the feet.

First—The body rests on the right foot, the left a little advanced, left knee bent.

Second—The body rests on the left foot, right a little advanced, right knee bent.

FIRST POSITION.

SECOND POSITION.

We have two other positions, which are called *Secondary*. They are assumed in argument, appeal, or persuasion. The first secondary position is taken from the first primary, by advancing the unoccupied foot, and resting the body upon it, leaning forward, the *right* foot brought to its support.

THIRD POSITION, OR FIRST SECONDARY.

FOURTH POSITION, OR SECOND SECONDARY.

The second secondary position is the same as the first, the body resting upon the right foot.

In assuming these positions, all movements should be made with the utmost simplicity, avoiding "the stage strut and parade of the dancing-master."

Advance, retire, or change with ease, except when the action demands energy or marked decision. Adopt such positions only as consist of manly and simple grace, and change as the sentiment or subject changes, or as you address yourself to different parts of the audience. Avoid moving about, or "weaving," or moving the feet or hands while speaking.

EXERCISES IN BREATHING.

Deep breathing with the lips closed, inhaling as long as possible, and exhaling slowly, is very beneficial. Having inflated the lungs to their utmost capacity, form the breath into the element of long *o*, in its escape through the vocal organs. This exercise should be frequently repeated, as the voice will be strengthened thereby, and the capacity of the chest greatly increased. Do not raise the shoulders or the upper part of the chest alone when you breathe. Breathe as a healthy child breathes, by the expansion and contraction of the abdominal and intercostal muscles. Such breathing will improve the health, and be of great assistance in continuous reading or speaking. Great care is necessary in converting the breath into voice. Do not waste breath; use it economically, or hoarseness will follow. Much practice on the vocal elements, with all the varieties of pitch, then the utterance of words, then of sentences, and, finally, of whole paragraphs, is necessary in learning to use the breath, and in acquiring judgment and taste in vocalizing. Never speak when the lungs are exhausted. Keep them well inflated.

GESTURE.

It is understood that practice in the use of the hands and arms, to secure ease of movement and appropriateness in gesture, is the object to be gained in studying this part of Elocution. We have seen no system so complete as that given by Rev. Gilbert Austin in his Chironomia. For the present it may be sufficient to call attention to the *Sphere bounded by Circles.*

The human figure is supposed to be so placed within the sphere that the centre of the breast shall coincide with its centre.

The motions and positions of the arms are referred to and determined by these circles and their intersections.

The horizontal circles around the feet, breast, and above the head, denote the direction of the hand and arm in the practice. *First* use the right-hand palm up, in front; then at right angles with the body, gesticulating to the lower circle; then the same to the middle; then with energy to the upper circle. The

hand moves always from the side in curved lines, and expresses elevated and noble sentiments with the palm up, and repels or condemns with the palm outward or down. The stroke of gesture stops or rests upon the emphatic word. Now we may practise first with the right hand palm up, then the left; then the right-hand palm down, then the left; then both hands, palms up; then both, palms down—and we have forty-eight gestures. If we select an appropriate sentence for each, we have a most interesting and instructive *practice*. This system, if carefully followed after a good model from the living instructor, will secure freedom and grace in the movements of the hands and arms.

Professor Russell says: "The true speaker must have a true manner; the great attributes of genuine expression, in attitude and action, are *truth—firmness—*force—freedom and *propriety.*" To speak well, to gesticulate well, the orator must *stand well;* and much practice in position and gesture is necessary for *this.*

We know that gesture cannot be made by rule, in speaking; and, in the practice, mechanical precision is not to be enforced, though exactness and uniformity should be insisted upon.

Some insist that all gestures shall be made with the right hand and arm. We find no good authority either *ancient* or *modern,* for thus limiting the gesture.

THE VOCAL ORGANS.

THE LARYNX—ITS MUSCLES AND APPENDAGES.

HAVING learned how to stand, how to use the hands and arms, how to sit, and how to breathe, we now proceed to the *Vocal Organs* and their *use.*

At the root of the tongue lies a semilunar-shaped bone, which, from its resemblance to a certain Greek letter, is called the hyoid or u-like bone; and immediately from this bone arises a long cartilaginous tube, which extends to the lungs, and conveys the air backward and forward in the process of respiration. This tube is called the trachea, or windpipe; and the upper part of it, or that immediately connected with the hyoid bone, the larynx; and it is this upper part or larynx which constitutes the seat of the voice. The tube of the larynx is formed of five distinct cartilages, the largest and apparently lowermost of which, together with two other cartilages of a smaller size and power, form the ring or glottis, which is the aperture from the mouth into the larynx. The fourth cartilage lies immediately over the aperture, and closes it in the act of swallowing, so as to direct the food to the œsophagus, which leads to the stomach. These four cartilages or membranes are supported by a fifth, which constitutes their basis. The larynx is contracted and dilated in various ways, by different muscles, and the elasticity of its different coats. It is covered internally with a very sensitive, vascular, and mucous membrane, similar to the membrane of the mouth.

We see, then, that the *organ* of the voice is the *larynx, its muscles and appendages*, and the voice itself is *the sound of the air propelled through and striking against the sides of the glottis*, or opening into the mouth. The *modulation* of the voice depends upon the internal diameter of the glottis, its elasticity and mobility, and the force with which the air is propelled.

Speech is the modification of the voice into intelligible articulations in the cavity of the glottis itself, or in that of the mouth or the nostrils.

ARTICULATION.

Sheridan says: "A good articulation consists in giving every letter in a syllable its due proportion of sound, according to the most approved custom of pronouncing it; and in making such a distinction between the syllables of which words are composed, that the ear shall, without difficulty, acknowledge their number, and perceive at once to which syllable each letter belongs. Where these particulars are not observed the articulation is defective."

A good articulation may be acquired by carefully repeating aloud, and in a whisper, the elements of the language. These elements are divided into three classes—*Vocals, Sub-Vocals,* and *Aspirates*.

The vowels, or vocal sounds, are arranged in the following table for individual and class practice:

A long, as in ale, fate, state, lave, gale.
A short, as in at, hat, sat, mat, plaid, charity.
A Italian, as in arm, far, star, heart, mart.
A broad, as in all, fall, water.
{ *A long, before R,* as in fare, dare, rare, stare, air.
{ *A intermediate,* as in fast, branch, class, mastiff.

E long, as in eve, mete, speed, degree, theme.
E short, as in end, bend, leopard, special, yes
E like A long, before R, as in heir, their.

I long, as in ice, child, sky, smile, flight.
I short, as in it, pin, whip, cynic, ring.

O long, as in old, dome, bourne, more, poet, glow
O short, as in ox, not, got, fond, from, fossil.
O long, as in move, prove, food, remove.

U long, as in few, duty, music, tube.
U short, as in up, tub, must, rug, tongue, sum.
U middle, as in pull, push, puss, should.
U short and obtuse, as in burn, murmur.

Oi, as in oil, choice, noise, coin, toy, boil.
Ou, as in out, sound, town, thou, around.

Speak the word distinctly and then the element, exploding it with variety of force and on different notes of the scale. For flexibility of voice and good articulation, there is no better exercise than the utterance of the vowel elements with the different inflections, first rising, then falling, then the circumflexes. The practice of exploding the Vocal elements with a Consonant prefixed, first a Sub-Vocal Consonant, then an Aspirate, is of great value in acquiring control of the mouth, teeth, and lips.

Sub-Vocals or Vocal Consonants should be treated, in the practice, as the Vocals in the preceding table. They are

ELOCUTION. 19

formed by the vibration of the Vocal chords, modified by the organs of speech :

B, *as in* bat, bag, beet, babbler, beggar, bound.
D, *as in* dun, debt, dated, deed, need, did.
G, *as in* gun, gag, gog, gew-gaw, give.
J, *as in* jib, joy, judge, June, jury.
L, *as in* let, lull, wall, isle, lark, loll.
M, *as in* man, main, mound, mammon, drum.
N, *as in* nun, nay, noun, name.
Ng, *as in* sing, king, ring, flinging.
R (*trilled*), run, rap, Richard, France, round.
R, *as in* nor, far, border, appear, forbear, ear.
Th, *as in* thine, thus, thy, beneath, wreathe.
V, *as in* vent, valve, vine, veer, weave.
W, *as in* went, wall, one, woo, worn.
Y, *as in* yes, young, year, yawl, use, you.
Z, *as in* zeal, as, was, breeze, maze, arise.
Zh, or *Z*, *as in* azure, leisure, osier, vision.

Prolong the Sub-Vocal Consonants as follows : b———at d———un, and then pronounce the Sub-Vocal without uttering the word. Then give the Sub-Vocals with the inflections.

b′ b‵ d′ d‵ g′ g‵ j′ j‵ l′ l‵, etc.

The Aspirate Consonants should be repeated according to the table. Be careful not to waste breath, and utter them with no more power than they require in words :

F, *as in* fit, fame, fife, fanciful, futile, phantom.
H, *as in* hat, hope, hay, hap-hazard, hot-house.
K, *as in* kid, car, coil, king, talk, chasm, chorus.
P, *as in* pit, pin, pupil, piper, stop, steep, rapid.
S, *as in* suit, dose, sinless, science, steep, scene.
T, *as in* top, time, tune, matter, debt, titter, better.
Ch, *as in* chat, church, churn, child, satchel, chirp.
Sh, *as in* shun, shade, gash, rash, sash, mansion.
Th, *as in* thin, thank, thick, breath, thankful.
Wh, *as in* when, whit, whale, what, why, while, where.

The Elements, we repeat, afford a better exercise in Articulation than words connected to form sense. The drill on the Elements should form a daily exercise in all our primary schools. Change the pitch and force often in reciting them. The student will be well repaid for his trouble if he would study Webster's and Worcester's Dictionaries, especially the introduction in regard to the Elements of the English language.

If we give the Elements properly, we shall have no trouble with their combinations into words and sentences.

In exploding the vocals, be careful to breathe deeply, and use the whole of the upper part of the system, not confining the utterance to the upper part of the larynx, or to any one part of the vocal organs.

We here give a table of Cognates, which are produced by the same organs in a similar manner, and only differ in one being a half-tone, the other a whisper.

COGNATES.

ATONICS.			SUBTONICS.	
li*p*	*p*	. . . .	or*b*	*b*
*f*i*f*e	*f*	. . . .	*v*ase	*v*
*wh*ite	*wh*	. . . .	*w*ise	*w*
*s*ave	*s*	. . . .	*z*eal	*z*
*sh*ade	*sh*	. . . .	a*z*ure	*z*
*ch*arm	*ch*	. . . .	*j*oin	*j*
*t*ar*t*	*t*	. . . .	*d*i*d*	*d*
*th*ing	*th*	. . . .	TH is	TH
*k*in*k*	*k*	. . . .	*g*i*g*	*g*

THE VOICE.

VOICE is the sound of the breath, *propelled* through the larynx, striking against the glottis or opening into the mouth.

Its *modulation* depends upon the control of the larynx, the nternal diameter of the glottis, its elasticity and mobility, and the force with which the air is expelled.

To modulate or change the voice from one key to another, with proper degrees of power to each, as the subject demands, is as beautiful in its effect as it is difficult in its performance or acquirement.

The student should understand that the vocal organs may be developed and strengthened. If we have not passed through much practice in breathing, utterance of elements, and models in tone, we have no correct judgment in regard to the voice. Its power may be much increased, and its quality improved.

Poets, to produce variety, alter the structure of their verse, and rather hazard uncouthness and discord than sameness. Prose writers change the style, time, and structure of their periods, and sometimes throw in exclamations, and sometimes interrogatories, to rouse and keep alive the attention; but all this art is entirely thrown away, if the reader does not enter into the spirit of the author, and, by a similar kind of genius, render even variety itself more various; if he does not, by an alteration in his voice, manner, tone, gesture, loudness, softness, quickness, slowness, adopt every change of which the subject is susceptible.

We have never yet found a person who could not acquire proficiency in modulating the voice. It is the mind's instrument of communication. Some are obliged to practise more than others, but none need give up the work as useless.

QUALITY OF VOICE.

We should understand the different qualities of voice, and the ideas they express. We make two general divisions of Quality: PURE and IMPURE. These may again be subdivided into Pure Tone, deepened or Orotund Quality, Tremor Quality Guttural Quality, and Aspirate Quality.

The PURE QUALITY includes all Unemotional Utterances, Simple Narrations, Conversations, Joy, etc. It should be zealously cultivated.

EXAMPLES.

HOPE OF GOOD TIDINGS.

O Hope! sweet flatterer, whose delusive touch
Sheds on afflicted minds the balm of comfort:
Relieves the load of poverty; sustains
The captive bending with the weight of bonds,
And smooths the pillow of disease and pain;—
Send back the exploring messenger with joy,
And let me hail thee from that friendly grove.
Glover's Boadicea.

JOY EXPECTED.

Ah, Juliet! if the measure of thy joy
Be heap'd like mine, and that thy skill be more
To blazon it, then sweeten with thy breath
This neighbor air, and let rich music's tongue
Unfold the imagin'd happiness that both
Receive.
Romeo and Juliet.

JOY APPROACHING TO FOLLY.

Come, let us to the castle.—
News, friends; our wars are done, the Turks are drown'd
How does my old acquaintance of this isle?—
Honey, you shall be well desired in Cyprus,
I have found great love amongst them. O my sweet,
I prattle out of fashion, and I dote
In mine own comforts.
Othello.

Joy Approaching to Transport.

Oh! joy, thou welcome stranger, twice three years
I have not felt thy vital beam, but now
It warms my veins, and plays about my heart;
A fiery instinct lifts me from the ground,
And I could mount. *Dr. Young's Revenge.*

The OROTUND QUALITY is used in Sublime Exhortations, Apostrophe, Bold Declamation, and Animated Appeals.

EXAMPLES.

An Exhortation.

But wherefore do you droop? why look you sad?
Be great in act, as you have been in thought;
Let not the world see fear, and sad distrust
Govern the motion of a kingly eye:
Be stirring as the time; be fire with fire;
Threaten the threatener, and outface the brow
Of bragging horror: so shall inferior eyes,
That borrow their behavior from the great,
Grow great by your example, and put on
The dauntless spirit of resolution.
Away! and glisten like the god of war,
When he intendeth to become the field:
Show boldness and aspiring confidence.
What! shall they seek the lion in his den,
And fright him there? and make him tremble there?
O, let it not be said.—Forage and run
To meet displeasure farther from the doors,
And grapple with him ere he come so nigh.
 King John.

Definition of Eloquence.

When public bodies are to be addressed on momentous occasions, when great interests are at stake, and strong passions excited, nothing is valuable in speech farther than it is connected with high intellectual and moral endowments.

Clearness, force, and earnestness are the qualities which produce conviction. True eloquence, indeed, does not consist in speech; it cannot be brought from far. Labor and learning may toil for it, but they toil for it in vain: words and phrases may be marshalled in every way, but they cannot compass it: it must exist in the man, in the subject, and in the occasion. Affected passion, intense expression, the pomp of declamation, —all may aspire after it; they cannot reach it: it comes, if it come at all, like the outbreaking of a fountain from the earth, or the bursting forth of volcanic fires, with spontaneous, original, native force.—*Webster.*

The GUTTURAL QUALITY expresses Loathing, Contempt, Hatred, Revenge, Scorn, etc.

EXAMPLES.

ENVY AMOUNTING TO HATRED.

How like a fawning publican he looks!
I hate him for he is a Christian;
But more for that, in low simplicity,
He lends out money gratis, and brings down
The rate of usance here with us in Venice.
If I can catch him once upon the hip,
I will feed fat the ancient grudge I bear him.
He hates our sacred nation; and he rails,
Even there where merchants most do congregate,
On me, my bargains, and my well-won thrift,
Which he calls interest. Cursed be my tribe,
If I forgive him.   *Merchant of Venice.*

HATRED CURSING THE OBJECT HATED.

Poison be their drink!
Gall, worse than gall, the daintiest that they taste!
Their sweetest shade a grove of cypress-trees!
Their chiefest prospect, murthering basilisks!
Their softest touch, as smart as lizard's stings!

The ASPIRATE VOICE is used to express Fear, Horror, Remorse, and Despair.

EXAMPLES.

FEAR OF BEING DISCOVERED A MURDERER.

Alack! I am afraid they have awak'd,
And 'tis not done :—th' attempt, and not the deed,
Confounds us.—Hark!—I laid their daggers ready:
He could not miss 'em.—Had he not resembled
My father as he slept, I had done't. *Macbeth.*

HORROR AT A DREADFUL APPARITION.

How ill this taper burns!—Ha! who comes here?
I think it is the weakness of mine eyes
That shapes this monstrous apparition.
It comes upon me.—Art thou any thing?
Art thou some god, some angel, or some devil,
That mak'st my blood cold, and my hair to stare?
Speak to me, what thou art. *Julius Cæsar.*

TERROR BEFORE DREADFUL ACTIONS DESCRIBED.

Between the acting of a dreadful thing,
And the first motion, all the interim is
Like a phantasma, or a hideous dream:
The Genius, and the mortal instruments,
Are then in council; and the state of man,
Like a little kingdom, suffers then
The nature of an insurrection. *Julius Cæsar.*

The TREMOR QUALITY expresses Pity, Grief, Tenderness, etc.

EXAMPLES.

PITY FOR A DEPARTED FRIEND.

Alas, poor Yorick!—I knew him, Horatio: a fellow of infinite jest, of most excellent fancy: he hath borne me on his back a thousand times. And now, how abhorred my imagination is! my gorge rises at it: Here hung those lips that I have kissed I know not how oft. Where be your gibes now? Your gambols? Your songs? Your flashes of merriment, that were wont to set the table on a roar? Not one now, to mock your own grinning? Quite chop-fallen? Now, get you to my lady's chamber, and tell her, let her paint an inch thick, to this favor she must come; make her laugh at that.—*Hamlet.*

POOR LITTLE JIM.

The cottage was a thatched one, the outside old and mean,
But all within that little cot was wondrous neat and clean;
The night was dark and stormy, the wind was howling wild,
As a patient mother sat beside the death-bed of her child:
A little worn-out creature, his once bright eyes grown dim:
It was a collier's wife and child, they called him little Jim.

And oh! to see the briny tears fast hurrying down her cheek,
As she offered up the prayer, in thought, she was afraid to speak,
Lest she might waken one she loved far better than her life;
For she had all a mother's heart, had that poor collier's wife.
With hands uplifted, see, she kneels beside the sufferer's bed,
And prays that He would spare her boy, and take herself instead.

She gets her answer from the child: soft falls the words from him,
"Mother, the angels do so smile, and beckon little Jim,
I have no pain, dear mother, now, but oh! I am so dry,
Just moisten poor Jim's lips again, and, mother, don't you cry."
With gentle, trembling haste she held the liquid to his lip;
He smiled to thank her, as he took each little, tiny sip.

"Tell father, when he comes from work, I said good-night to him,
And, mother, now I'll go to sleep." Alas! poor little Jim!
She knew that he was dying; that the child she loved so dear,
Had uttered the last words she might ever hope to hear:
The cottage door is opened, the collier's step is heard,
The father and the mother meet, yet neither speak a word.

He felt that all was over, he knew his child was dead,
He took the candle in his hand and walked towards the bed;
His quivering lips gave token of the grief he'd fain conceal,
And see, his wife has joined him—the stricken couple kneel:
With hearts bowed down by sadness, they humbly ask of Him,
In heaven, once more, to meet again their own poor little Jim.

The emotions help to define the voices. It is difficult to separate these Qualities of Voice. Like the emotions, they shade into each other so much, that it requires long and patient study to express, with exactness, the ideas of an author.

VARIATIONS OF VOICE.

PITCH—FORCE—TIME.

THE voice depends, for expression, upon *Pitch*, which refers to the key-note, *Force*, which refers to the degree of loudness or volume, and *Time*, which refers to the rate of utterance or degree of rapidity with which words are uttered. We have anticipated these variations in the examples under Voice.

We mark three divisions of *Pitch: High*, as in shouting, or calling to persons at a distance, or giving commands; *Low*, as in solemn utterances, or emotions requiring the aspirate voice; and *Middle*, as in ordinary address and unimpassioned expressions.

The degrees of *Force* are almost without limit, but we make three general divisions: *Loud* and *full Force*, as in bold declamation and impassioned address; *Medium Force*, for unemotional utterances; and *Soft* or *gentle Force*, in pathetic or subdued emotions.

The time or movement of utterance depends upon the sentiments delivered, and the kinds are as numerous as the styles of thought, but we make three general divisions: *Quick, Moderate,* and *Slow;* or we might have quick and very quick, moderate and slow, and very slow.

EXAMPLES IN PITCH.

High pitch.
   Son.—HURRAH FOR FREEDOM'S JUBILEE!
      God bless our native land!
      And may *I* live to hold the boon
      Of *freedom* in my hand.

Moderate pitch.
   Father.—Well done, my boy, grow up and love
      The land that gave you birth,—
      A land where freedom loves to dwell,—
      A paradise on earth.

Low pitch.
We mustered at midnight,—in darkness we formed,—
And the whisper went round of a fort to be stormed:
But no drum-beat had called us, no trumpet we heard,
And no voice of command but our Colonel's low word—
          "Column, Forward!"

And out through the mist and the murk of the morn,
From the beaches of Hampton our barges were borne;
And we heard not a sound save the sweep of the oar,
Till the word of our Colonel came up from the shore—
          "Column, Forward!"

THE PILOT.

Moderate pitch.
   1. The waves are high, the night is dark,
      Wild roam the foaming tides,
   Dashing around the straining bark,
      As gallantly she rides.

High pitch.
     "Pilot! take heed what course you steer;
      Our bark is tempest-driven!"

Low pitch.
     "Stranger, be calm, there is no fear
      For him who trusts in Heaven!"

High pitch.
    2. "O pilot! mark yon thunder-cloud—
        The lightning's lurid rivers;
    Hark to the wind, 'tis piping loud—
        The mainmast bends and quivers!
    Stay, pilot, *stay*, and shorten sail,
        Our stormy trysail's riven!"

Low pitch.
    "Stranger, what matters calm or gale
        To him who trusts in Heaven?"

Moderate.
    3. Borne by the winds, the vessel flies
        Up to the thundering cloud;
    Now tottering low, the spray-winged seas
        Conceal the topmast shroud.

High pitch.
    "Pilot, the waves break o'er us fast,
        Vainly our bark has striven!"

Low pitch.
    "Stranger, the *Lord* can rule the blast—
        Go, put thy trust in Heaven!"

Moderate pitch, joyous.
    4. Good hope! good hope! one little star
        Gleams o'er the waste of waters;
    'Tis like the light reflected far
        Of Beauty's loveliest daughters;
    "Stranger, good hope He giveth thee,
        As He has often given;
    Then learn this truth—whate'er may be,
        To PUT THY TRUST IN HEAVEN!"

                              —*Cochran.*

Very high.
    "Young men, ahoy!"—

Moderate.
    "What is it?"—

Very high.
    "Beware! beware! The rapids are below you!"

EXAMPLES IN FORCE.

"THE BRIGADE" AT FONTENOY.—MAY 11, 1745.

Moderate force.

1. By our camp-fires rose a murmur,
   At the dawning of the day,
   And the tread of many footsteps
   Spoke the advent of the fray;
   And as we took our places,
   Few and stern were our words,
   While some were tightening horse-girths,
   And some were girding swords.

Moderate.

2. The trumpet-blast has sounded
   Our footmen to array—
   The willing steed has bounded
   Impatient for the fray—
   The green flag is unfolded,
   While rose the cry of joy—

Loud force.

   "Heaven speed dear Ireland's banner
   To-day at Fontenoy!"

Moderate.

3. We looked upon that banner,
   And the memory arose
   Of our homes and perished kindred,
   Where the Lee or Shannon flows;
   We looked upon that banner,
   And we swore to God on high
   To smite to-day the Saxon's might—

Loud force.

   To conquer or to die.

Full force.

4. Loud swells the charging trumpet—
   'Tis a voice from our own land—

God of battles—God of vengeance,
   Guide to-day the patriot's brand ;
There are stains to wash away—
   There are memories to destroy,
In the best blood of the Briton,
   To-day, at Fontenoy.

5. Plunge deep the fiery rowels
   In a thousand reeking flanks—
Down, chivalry of Ireland,
   Down on the British ranks.
Now shall their serried columns
   Beneath our sabres reel—
Through their ranks, then, with the war-horse—
   Through their bosoms with the steel.

6. With one shout for good King Louis,
   And the fair land of the vine,
Like the wrathful Alpine tempest,
   We swept upon their line.
Then rang along the battle-field
   Triumphant our hurrah,
And we smote them down, still cheering—
   "*Erin, slanthagal go bragh !*"[1]

Gentle force.

7. As prized as is the blessing
   From an aged father's lip—
As welcome as the haven
   To the tempest-driven ship—
As dear as to the lover
   The smile of gentle maid—
Is this day of long-sought vengeance
   To the swords of the Brigade.

---

[1] Ireland, the bright toast forever !

Loud force.
8. See their shattered forces flying,
   A broken, routed line—
See, England, what brave laurels
   For your brow to-day we twine.
Oh, thrice blessed the hour that witnessed
   The Briton turn to flee
From the chivalry of Erin
   And France's "*fleur de lis!*"

Gentle force.
9. As we lay beside our camp-fires,
   When the sun had passed away,
And thought upon our brethren
   Who had perished in the fray,

Moderate increase to the close.
   We prayed to God to grant us,
      And then we'd die with joy,
   One day upon our own dear land
      Like this of Fontenoy. —*Bartholomew Dowling.*

THE DYING SOLDIER.

Moderate force.
The crimson tide was ebbing, and the pulse grew weak and faint,
But the lips of that brave soldier scorned e'en now to make complaint;
"Fall in ranks!" a voice called to him,—calm and low was his reply:
"Yes, if I can, I'll do it—I will do it, though I die!"

Gentle force.
And he murmured, when the life-light had died out to just a spark,
"It is growing very dark, mother—growing very dark."

There were tears in manly eyes then, and manly heads were bowed,
Though the balls flew thick around them, and the cannons thundered loud;

They gathered round the spot where the dying soldier lay,
To catch the broken accents he was struggling then to say;
And a change came o'er the features where death had set
    his mark,
" It is growing very dark, mother—very, very dark."

Far away his mind had wandered to Ohio's hills and vales,
Where the loved ones watched and waited with that love that
    never fails ;
He was with them as in childhood, seated in the cottage door,
Where he watched the evening shadows slowly creeping on
    the floor :
Bend down closely, comrades, closely—he is speaking now,
    and hark !
" It is growing very dark, mother—very, very dark."

EXAMPLES IN TIME.

Very quick time.

1. Quick—man the boat! John, be quick! Get some water! Throw the powder overboard! "It cannot be reached." Jump into the boat, then! Shove off! There goes the powder! Thank Heaven, we are safe!

Moderate and quick.

2. At length, o'er Columbus, slow consciousness breaks,
   "LAND ! LAND !" cry the sailors; "LAND ! LAND !"—he
    awakes—
   He runs,—yes! behold it! it blesseth his sight!
   The land! oh! dear spectacle! transport! delight!

Very slow time.

3. The stars | shall fade away, ‖ the sun' himself |
   Grow dim with age, ‖ and Nature | sink' in years;
   But thou | shalt flourish' in immortal youth ‖
   Unhurt | amidst the war of elements, ‖
   The wreck of matter, ‖ and the crush of worlds !

Creation sleeps! || || 'tis as the general pulse of life |
Stood still || and Nature made a pause, ||
An awful pause, || || prophetic of her end!—

Quick time.
4. I come', I come'! Ye have called me long',
I come o'er the mountains with light and song!
Ye may trace my step o'er the wakening earth,
By the winds which tell of the violet's birth,
By the primrose stars in the shadowy grass
By the green leaves opening as I pass.

Moderate time.—Full force.
5. Upward,—onward! Fellow workmen!
  Ours the battle-field of life!
Ne'er a foot to foeman yielding,
  Pressing closer midst the strife!
Forward! in the strength of Manhood,—
  Forward! in the fire of Youth,—
Aim at something; ne'er surrender,—
  Arm thee in the mail of Truth!

Miller was a rough stone-mason;
  Shakespeare, Goldsmith, Keats, and Hood,
Franklin, Jerrold, Burns, and Gifford,
  Had to toil as we, for food.
Yes: these men with minds majestic,
  Sprang from ranks the rich call poor,
Cast a halo round brown labor,—
  Had to wrestle, fight, endure.

Forward, then! bright eyes are beaming;
  Fight, nor lose the conqueror's crown!
Stretch thy right hand, seize thy birthright,
  Take it, wear it, 'tis thine own!
Slay the giants which beset thee,
  Rise to manhood, glory, fame;
Take thy pen, and in the volume
  Of the gifted write thy name!

Slow time.

6. I thought that the course of the pilgrim to heaven
 Would be bright as the summer, and glad as the morn;
Thou show'dst me the path,—it was dark and uneven,
 All rugged with rock and tangled with thorn.

I dreamed of celestial reward and renown,
 I grasped at the triumph that blesses the brave
I asked for the palm-branch, the robe, and the crown,—
 I asked,—and Thou show'dst me a cross and a grave

Subdued and instructed, at length, to Thy will,
 My hopes and my longings I fain would resign;
Oh give me the heart that can wait and be still,
 Nor know of a wish or a pleasure but Thine.

There are mansions exempted from sin and from woe,
 But they stand in a region by mortals untrod;
There are rivers of joy, but they flow not below;
 There is rest, but it dwells in the presence of God.

EMPHASIS.

AS in pronunciation we mark certain syllables with stress of voice which we call *accent*, so in reading we distinguish certain words by stress of voice, which is called Emphasis. It is of three kinds, abrupt or radical, median or smooth, and vanishing Emphasis. By *radical*, we mean the sudden, emphatic force which is given to the first part of sound in speaking or reading; by *median*, that smooth or even sound applied to the middle of words; and *vanishing*, that last or ending sound. It is given with a sudden jerk or snap of the voice, on the last syllable of words in expressing Revenge, Scorn, Defiance, Anger, Contempt.

Sometimes we have the radical and vanishing emphasis united; we distinguish that emphasis as compound.

We append a few selections and extracts for practice in Emphasis, and, at the same time, would remind the student that this department of our subject cannot be learned from books. It is that natural variation in the utterance of sentences which exhibits thought, and gives the agreeable variety to the speech of those who understand its application. It is more than stress of voice. It requires feeling. The greatest emphasis is frequently exhibited when there is least voice. It is both expressive and impressive utterance.

To apply Emphasis correctly, in reading or speaking, it is necessary to understand thoroughly the sentiments uttered, and to enter fully into the spirit of them. This is the only suggestion or rule that we give for Emphasis, and we are assured that the student will rarely fail in its application, if he observe this rule.

Let the student enter into the spirit of each quotation and selection, and emphasis will take care of itself.

EXAMPLES IN EMPHATIC UTTERANCE.

1. Advance your standards, draw your willing swords!
Sound drums and trumpets, boldly and cheerfully!
God and St. George! Ireland and victory—

2. Where rests the sword?—where sleeps the brave?
Awake! Cecropia's ally save
From the fury of the blast!
Burst the storm Ghocis' walls—
Rise! or Greece forever falls;
Up! or Freedom breathes her last!

3. Strike for the sires who left you free!
Strike for their sakes who bore you!
Strike for your homes and liberty
And the Heaven you worship o'er you!

4. Villains! you did not threat when your vile daggers
   Hacked one another in the sides of Cæsar!
   You showed your teeth like apes, and fawned like hounds,
   And bowed like bondmen, kissing Cæsar's feet;
   Whilst damned Casca, like a cur, behind,
   Struck Cæsar on the neck.—Oh! flatterers!

5. Rejoice, you men of Angiers! ring your bells
   King John, your king and England's, doth approach!
   Open your gates and give the victors way!

INFLECTION, CIRCUMFLEX, AND MONOTONE.
INFLECTION.

BY Inflection we mean the axis, a slide of the voice on which the variety, force, and harmony of speaking turns. They are the great outlines of Pronunciation.

By the rising and falling inflection of the voice is not meant the pitch in which the whole word is pronounced, or that loudness or softness which may accompany any pitch; but the upward or downward slide which the voice makes, when the pronunciation of a word is finishing: and which may, therefore, not improperly be called the rising and falling inflection.

So important is a just mixture of these two inflections, that the moment they are neglected, our pronunciation becomes forceless and monotonous: *if the sense of a sentence require the voice to adopt the rising inflection, on any particular word, either in the middle or at the end of a phrase, variety and harmony demand the falling inflection on one of the preceding words, and, on the other hand, if emphasis, harmony, or a completion of sense, require the falling inflection on any word, the word immediately preceding, almost always, demands the rising inflection;* so that these inflections of voice are in an order nearly alternate.

These inflections depend upon the style of the composition or address, for their length. If the composition is to be read in pure voice, unimpassioned style, the inflections are moderately long. If grand, or sublime, or bold, requiring the orotund voice, the inflections will be long. If plaintive, or subdued, requiring the tremor voice, low pitch, or slow time, the inflection will be short.

If we understand the principle of utterence, that inflections alternate, we require to know which leads, and then the following cadence will take care of itself. We can decide which is the leading inflection by applying the following rule:

All complete or positive assertions have the *falling inflection* at the close. All incomplete, or negative sentences have the *rising inflection* at the close.

Sometimes the principal word, which has the emphasis and the inflection, will not be the closing word in the sentence.

EXAMPLES IN INFLECTIONS.

1. Count 1' 1` 2' 2` 3' 3` 4' 4` 5' 5` 6' 6`.
2. Elements a' a` e' e` i' i` o' o` u' u`.
3. As we cannot discern the shadow moving along the dial-plate', so the advances we make in knowledge are only perceivable by the distance` gone over.

4. How frightful the grave`! how deserted and drear`!
   With the howl of the storm-wind the creaks of the bier`,
   And the white bones all clattering` together.

5. How *peaceful*` the grave`! its quiet' how deep`!
   Its zephyrs breathe calmly`; and soft is its sleep;
   And flowers *perfume* it with ether.

6. When oceans roar, or thunders roll',
   May thoughts of THY *dread vengeance* shake my soul`!

7. Begone'! run to your houses, fall upon your knees,
Pray to the gods to intermit the plagues
That needs must light on this ingratitude'!

8. Can ministers still presume to expect support' in their infatuation'? Can Parliament be so dead to its dignity and its duty, as to give its support to measures thus obtruded and forcéd upon it'?¹

CIRCUMFLEX.

The Circumflex is a union of the inflections, and is of two kinds, *Rising* and *Falling*. It is governed by the same principle; that is, positive assertions of irony, raillery, etc., will have the falling Circumflex, and all negative assertions of double meaning will have the rising.

Doubt, pity, contrast, grief, supposition, comparison, irony, implication, sneering, raillery, scorn, reproach, and *contempt,* are expressed by them. Be sure and get the right *feeling* and *thought,* and you will find no difficulty in *expressing* them properly, if you have mastered the *voice.*

Both these circumflex inflections may be exemplified in the word *so,* in a speech of the Clown in Shakespeare's "As You Like It."

1. I knew when seven justices could not take up a quarrel; but when the parties were met themselves, one of them thought but of an If; as if you said sŏ, then I said sŏ. Oh hŏ! did you say sŏ? So they shook hands and were sworn friends.

---

¹ For further examples in inflection, study the varied selections in the body of the work. Accustom the ear to detect the difference between the inflection of the positive assertion of a fact, and the rising slide of indifference, doubt, or indecision.

HAMLET TO LAERTES.

2. Zounds! show me what thou'lt do: woul't *weep?* woul't *fig˘ht?* woul't fast? woul't *tear* thyself? I'll do it. Dost thou come here to *whine?* to outface *me,* with leaping in her *grave?* be buried *quick* with her, and so will *I;* and if thou prate of *moun˘tains,* let them throw MIL˘LIONS of acres on us, till our ground, singeing her pate against the burning *zone,* make *Ossa* like a *wart.* Nay, and thoul't mouthe, *I'll* rant as well as *thou.*

THE MONOTONE.

The Monotone is sameness of sound, arising from repeating the several words or syllables of a passage in one and the same general tone.

The Monotone is employed in the delivery of a passage that is solemn or sublime.

EXAMPLES.

1. Mān thāt īs bōrn ōf wōmān, īs ōf fēw dāys ānd fūll ōf trōuble. Hē cōmēth fōrth līke ā flōwēr, ānd īs cūt dōwn; hē flēēth ālsō ās ā shādōw, ānd cōntīnūēth nōt.

2. Mān dīēth, ānd wāstēth āwāy: yēā, mān gīvēth ūp thē ghōst, ānd whērē īs hē? Ās thē wātērs fāīl frōm thē sēā, ānd thē flōōd dēcāyēth ānd drīēth ūp, sō mān līēth dōwn, ānd rīsēth nōt; tīll thē hēāvēns bē nō mōrē, thēy shāll nōt āwāke, nōr bē rāīsēd ōut ōf thēīr slēēp.

3. Fōr thūs sāīth thē hīgh ānd lōfty ōne thāt īnhābītēth ētērnīty, whōse nāme īs Hōly, I dwēll īn thē hīgh ānd hōly plāce.

4. Lōrd, thōu hāst bēēn ōur dwēllīng-plāce īn āll gēnērātīōns. Bēfōre thē mōūntāīns wērē brōught fōrth, ōr ēvēr thōu hādst fōrmed thē ēārth ānd thē wōrld, ēvēn frōm ēvērlāstīng tō ēvērlāstīng, Thōu ārt Gōd.

5. In thoughts from the visions of the night, when dēēp slēēp fāllĕth on man, *fĕar* cāme upŏn mē and trĕmbling, which made āll my bŏnĕs to shāke. Then a spirit pāssed befŏre my fāce; the hāir of my flĕsh stŏŏd ŭp. It stood still; but I could not discĕrn the fŏrm thereof. An imāge wăs befŏre my eyĕs; there was sɪʟᴇɴᴄᴇ; and I hĕărd a vŏice săying, "Shăll mŏrtal măn bĕ mŏre jŭst thăn Gŏd? Shăll a măn bĕ mŏre pŭre than hĭs Măker'?"

6. *Hŏly!* ʜᴏʟʏ! HOLY *Lŏrd Gŏd* of Sābāŏth!

7. Blĕss the Lŏrd, O my sŏul; and all that is within me, bless his holy name!

PAUSES.

WE have seen that the art of Elocution is the application of that system of rules which teaches us to pronounce written composition with justness, energy, variety, and ease. Agreeably to this definition, reading may be considered as that species of delivery which not only expresses the sense of an author, so as barely to be understood, but which, at the same time, gives it all that force, beauty, delicacy, and variety of which it is susceptible; the first consideration depends upon *grammatical pauses* which separate clauses, sentences, and paragraphs, according to their sense—the last depends much upon rhetorical pauses which are introduced to give expression to the words of an author.

The length of pauses are not fixed and invariable, and so cannot be brought under precise rules. There are, however, a few general principles which may be safely observed as far as they have application.

One is, that the pause should be proportioned to the rate of utterance—the intervals of rest being comparatively long when the rate is slow, and short when it is quick.

RULES FOR RHETORICAL PAUSES.

RULE I. A long pause may be made before or after a word expressive of intense feeling.

Examples.

1. Banished | from Rome ! What's banished, but set free ?
2. And their young voices rose | A VENGEANCE CRY TO GOD !
3. And made | *me* | a poor orphan boy.
4. Stand—the ground's your own, my braves.
5. Ho ! | man the pumps.
6. Beware—beware—the rapids are below you.

RULE II. A slight pause should mark an ellipsis or omission of a word.

Examples.

1. Their palaces were houses not made with hands ; their diadems | crowns of glory.
2. To our faith we should add virtue ; and to virtue | knowledge ; and to knowledge | temperance ; and to temperance | patience ; and to patience | godliness ; and to godliness | brotherly kindness ; and to brotherly kindness | charity.

RULE III. After words, placed in opposition to each other, there should be a pause.

Examples.

1. The morn | was bright, but the eve | was clouded and dark.
2. Some | place the bliss in action, | some in ease ;
3. Those | call it pleasure, and contentment | these.

RULE IV. A pause is required between the parts of a sentence which may be transposed.

Examples.

1. With famine and death | the destroying angel came.
2. To whom | the Goblin, full of wrath, replied.
3. The pangs of memory are | to madness | wrought.

Rule V. Before and after an intervening phrase, there should be a short pause.

Examples.

1. A company of waggish boys were watching of frogs at the side of the pond, and still as any of them put up their heads, they would be pelting them down again with stones. "Children," (says one of the frogs,) "you never consider, that though this may be play to you, it is death to us."

2. I had letters from him (here I felt in my pockets) that exactly spoke the Czar's character, which I knew perfectly well.

Rule VI. Before conjunctions, or prepositions and similes, a pause is usually required.

Examples.

1. I have watched their pastimes | and their labors.
2. We must not yield | to their foolish entreaties.
3. He continued steadfast | like the spring-time.

Rule VII. There should be a pause before a verb in the infinitive mood, depending upon another verb.

Examples.

1. He daily strove | to elevate their condition.
2. Do not dare | to lay your hands on the Constitution.
3. I had hoped | to have had an opportunity to oblige so good a friend.

Rule VIII. Before the relative pronouns, who, which, that, and what, a pause is generally necessary.

Examples.

1. Let us look forward to the end of that century | which has commenced.
2. Spirit | that breathest through my lattice, thou |
   That cool'st the twilight of the sultry day.
3. His natural instinct discovers | what knowledge can perform.

4. There is not a great author here | who did not write for us ; not a man of science | who did not investigate for us. We have received advantages from every hour of toil | that ever made these great and good men weary.

RULE IX. An adjective placed after its noun, should be separated from it by a short pause.

Examples.
1. He was a man—contented, virtuous, and happy.
2. I behold its summit | noble and sublime.

RULE X. A pause is required after the nominative case, when it is emphatic or consists of more than one word.

Examples.
1. A remarkable affair | happened yesterday.
2. To be devoid of sense | is a terrible misfortune.
3. Industry is the guardian of innocence.[1]

PERSONATION.

WE mean, by Personation in Elocution, the change in the pitch-force movement and tone or quality of voice, from narrative or unimpassioned style to introduce a new character, or several characters. Several voices or speakers may be presented by observing certain peculiarities or changes in expression of countenance and voice.

EXAMPLES.

Narrative. And when Peter saw it he answered unto the people: "Ye men of Israel, why marvel ye at
Personation. this? or, why look ye so earnestly on us, as

---

[1] The student should be required to find examples of these pauses in the reading and speaking exercises, and recite the rules.

though by our own power or authority we had made this man to walk?" etc.

A Ship on Fire.

Narrative. All hands were called up. Buckets of water were dashed on the fire, but in vain. There were large quantities of resin and tar on board, and it was found useless to attempt to save the ship. The passengers rushed forward and inquired of the pilot:

Personation. Change the voice for passengers and pilot.

"How far are we from Buffalo?"

"Seven miles."

"How long before we can reach there?"

"Three-quarters of an hour at our present rate of steam."

"Is there any danger?"

"Danger! here—see the smoke bursting out—go forward if you would save your lives."

Narrative. Passengers and crew—men, women, and children—crowded the forward part of the ship. John Maynard stood at the helm. The flames burst forth in a sheet of fire; clouds of smoke arose. The captain cried out through his trumpet:

"John Maynard!"

Personation. "Aye, aye, sir!"

"Are you at the helm?"

"Aye, aye, sir!"

"How does she head?"

"South-east by east, sir."

"Head her south-east and run her on shore," said the captain.

Nearer, nearer, yet nearer, she approached the shore. Again the captain cried out:

"John Maynard!"

The response came feebly this time, "Aye, aye, sir!"

"Can you hold on five minutes longer, John?" he said.

"By God's help, I will."

The old man's hair was scorched from the scalp, one hand disabled, his knee upon the stanchion, and his teeth set, with his other hand upon the wheel, he stood firm as a rock. He beached the ship; every man, woman, and child was saved, as John Maynard dropped, and his spirit took its flight to its God.

The Power of Habit.

The voice should be changed to personate each speaker.

I remember once riding from Buffalo to the Niagara Falls, and said to a gentleman, "What river is that, sir?"

"That," said he, "is the Niagara River."

"Well, it is a beautiful stream," said I; "bright, and fair, and glossy; how far off are the rapids?"

"Only a mile or two," was the reply.

"Is it possible that only a mile from us we shall find the water in the turbulence which it must show when near the Falls?"

"You will find it so, sir." And so I found it; and the first sight of Niagara I shall never forget. Now, launch your bark on that Niagara River; it is bright, smooth, beautiful, and glassy. There is a ripple at the bow; the silver wake you leave behind adds to your enjoyment. Down the stream you glide, oars, sails, and helm in proper trim, and you set out on your pleasure excursion. Suddenly some one cries out from the bank, "Young men, ahoy!"

"What is it?"

"The rapids are below you!"

Laughter.

"Ha! ha! we have heard of the rapids, but we are not such fools as to get there. If we go too fast, then we shall up with the helm and steer to the shore; we will set the mast in the socket, hoist the sail, and speed to the land. Then on, boys; don't be alarmed; there is no danger."

Great force.

"Young men, ahoy there!"

"What is it?"

"The rapids are below you!"

THE SINKING CUMBERLAND.

We felt our vessel sinking fast,
   We knew our time was brief.
"Ho! man the pumps!" But those who worked,
   And fought not, wept with grief.

"Oh, keep us but an hour afloat!
   Oh, give us only time
To mete unto yon rebel crew
   The measure of their crime!"

From captain down to powder-boy
   No hand was idle then;
Two soldiers, but by chance aboard,
   Fought on like sailor-men.

"Up to the spar-deck! save yourselves!"
   Cried Selfridge. "Up, my men!
God grant that some of us may live
   To fight yon ship again!"

We turned,—we did not like to go;
   Yet staying seemed but vain,
Knee-deep in water; so we left;
   Some swore, some groaned with pain.

We reached the deck. There Randall stood:
   "Another turn, men,—so!"
Calmly he aimed his pivot-gun:
   "Now, Tenny, let her go!"

It did our sore hearts good to hear
   The song our pivot sang,
As, rushing on from wave to wave,
   The whirring bomb-shell sprang.

          Brave Randall leaped upon the gun,
              And waved his cap in sport;
Personation. "Well done! well aimed! I saw that shell
              Go through an open port."

Narrative. It was our last, our deadliest shot;
              The deck was overflown;
          The poor ship staggered, lurched to port,
              And gave a living groan.

          Down, down, as headlong through the waves
              Our gallant vessel rushed,
          A thousand gurgling watery sounds
              Around my senses gushed.

THE STUDY OF EXPRESSION.

The practice of reading or reciting aloud, selections containing different emotions and passions, secures variety of expression. The student should try to personate the passion, or enter so fully into the meaning of the quotation that he will vary the *pitch, force,* and *voice* to correspond with the emotion.

The organs of speech should be so disciplined as to adapt themselves naturally and easily to all the changes, even the most abrupt and frequent, that are required in continuous reading or speaking. This comprehends the particulars in the above analysis, and secures variety of *expression*, which is the great object to be gained by the student of elocution.

II.
READING LESSONS.

THE FIFTH READER.

PART II.
RHETORICAL.

1. APOSTROPHE TO WATER.

[The following, though ascribed to John B. Gough, is in truth an extract from a sketch of Paul Denton, the Texas missionary, by Charles Summerfield, the *nom de plume* of Judge Arrington, entitled "Paul Denton's Barbecue."

An invitation had been issued by the preacher to the rough Texans of some thirty years ago to attend a barbecue where there would be plenty to eat, and "the best of liquor."

The borderers came, found abundance of comestibles, but no liquor. In reply to their rude demand for it, Paul Denton burst into the following strain of inspired eloquence.]

LOOK at that, ye thirsty ones of earth! Behold it! See its purity! See how it glitters, as if a mass of liquid gems! It is a beverage that was brewed by the hand of the Almighty himself. Not in the simmering still or smoking fires, choked with poisonous gases, and surrounded by the stench of sickening odors and rank corruptions, doth our Father in Heaven prepare the precious essence of life, the pure cold water, but in the green glade and grassy dell, where the red deer wanders and the child loves to play! There God brews it, and down, down in the deepest valleys, where the fountains murmur and the rills sing; and high upon the tall mountain-tops, where the naked granite glitters like gold in the sun, where the storm-clouds brood and the thunder-storms crash; and away out on the billowy sea, where the hurricanes howl music, and the big waves roar the chorus, chanting the march of God—there He brews it, that beverage of life—health-giving water.

2. And everywhere it is a thing of beauty—gleaming in the dew-drop, singing in the summer rain, shining in the ice-gem, till the trees all seem turned into living jewels—spreading a golden veil over the setting sun, or a white gauze around the midnight moon—sporting in the cataract, sleeping in the glaciers, dancing in the hail showers—folding its bright curtain softly about the wintry world, and weaving the many-colored iris, that seraph's zone of the sky, whose woof is the sunbeam of heaven, all checkered over with celestial flowers by the mystic hand of rarefaction—still always it is beautiful, that blessed life-water! No poison bubbles on the brink! Its foam brings no sadness or murder; no blood-stains in its limpid glass; broken-hearted wives, pale widows, and starving orphans shed no tears in its depths; no drunkard's shrinking ghost, from the grave, curses it in words of eternal despair. Beautiful, pure, blessed, and glorious! give me forever the sparkling, cold water!   JUDGE ARRINGTON.

---

2. OUR TITLES.

ARE we not Nobles? we who trace
  Our Pedigree so high,
That God for us and for our race
  Created Earth and Sky,
And Light, and Air, and Time, and Space,
  To serve us, and then die.

RHETORICAL.

2. Are we not Princes? we who stand
   As heirs beside the Throne;
   We who can call the promised land
   Our Heritage, our own;
   And answer to no less command
   Than God's, and His alone.

3. Are we not Kings? Both night and day,
   From early until late,
   About our bed, about our way,
   A guard of Angels wait;
   And so we watch, and work, and pray
   In more than royal state.

4. Are we not holy? Do not start:
   It is God's sacred will
   To call us Temples set apart
   His Holy Ghost may fill:
   Our very food ...... Oh Hush, my heart,
   Adore *It* and be still!

5. Are we not more? Our life shall be
   Immortal and divine;
   The nature Mary gave to Thee,
   Dear Jesus, still is Thine;—
   Adoring in Thy Heart I see
   Such blood as beats in mine.

6. O God, that we can dare to fail,
   And dare to say we must!
   O God, that we can ever trail
   Such banners in the dust,
   Can let such starry honors pale,
   And such a Blazon rust!

7 Shall we upon such Titles bring
    The taint of sin and shame?
   Shall we, the children of the King
    Who hold so grand a claim,
   Tarnish by any meaner thing,
    The glory of our name?   Miss A. A. Proctor.

---

8. ENGLISH OPERATIVES IN MANUFACTURING DISTRICTS.

[Southey, the late Poet Laureate of England, and the able Reviewer, is also the author of an interesting work, in prose, entitled "Espriella's Letters," from which we take the following touching picture of the actual state of English operatives. It forms a forcible contrast to the immense wealth which the work of these unpaid, untaught laborers yields to the kingdom of Great Britain.]

THEY are deprived in childhood of all instruction and all enjoyment; of the sports in which childhood instinctively indulges; of fresh air by day, and of natural sleep by night. Their health, physical and moral, is alike destroyed; they die of diseases induced by unremitting task-work, by confinement in the impure atmosphere of crowded rooms, by the particles of metallic or vegetable dust which they are continually inhaling; or they live to grow up without decency, without comfort, and without hope; without morals, without religion, and without shame; and bring forth slaves, like themselves, to tread in the same path of misery. The dwellings of the laboring manufacturers are in narrow streets and lanes, blockaded up from light and air; crowded together, because every inch of land is of such value that room for light and air cannot be afforded them.

2. In Manchester, a great proportion of the poor lodge in cellars, damp and dark, where every kind of filth is suffered to accumulate, because no exertions of domestic care can ever make such homes decent. Those places are so many hotbeds of infection, and the poor in large towns are rarely or

never without an infectious fever among them; a plague of their own, which leaves the habitations of the rich, like a Goshen of cleanliness and comfort, unvisited.

3. Wealth flows into the country; but how does it circulate there? Not equally and healthfully through the whole system; it sprouts into wens and tumors, and collects in aneurisms, which starve and palsy the extremities. The Government, indeed, raises millions as easily as it raised thousands in the days of Elizabeth; the metropolis is six times the size that it was a century ago. . . .

4. A thousand carriages drive about the streets of London, where three generations ago there were not a hundred; a thousand hackney-coaches are licensed in the same city, where, at the same distance of time, there was not one; they whose grandfathers dined at noon from wooden trenchers, and from the produce of their own farms, sit down by the light of waxen tapers to be served upon silver, and to partake of delicacies from the four quarters of the globe. But the numbers of the poor and the sufferings of the poor have continued to increase.

5. When the poor can contribute no longer to their own support, they are removed to what is called the workhouse. I cannot express to you the feeling of hopelessness and dread with which all the decent poor look to this wretched termination of a life of labor. To this place all vagrants are sent for punishment; unmarried women with child go here to be delivered; and poor orphans and base-born children are brought up here till they are of age to be apprenticed off; the other inmates are those unhappy people who are utterly helpless;— parish idiots and madmen, the blind, and the palsied, and the old, who are fairly worn-out.

6. It is not in the nature of things that the superintendents of such institutions as these should be gentle-hearted, when the superintendence is undertaken merely for the salary Whatever kindness of disposition they may bring with them to the task, is soon warped by continual contact with great de-

pravity and suffering. The management of children who grow up without one natural affection, where there is none to love them, and, consequently, none whom they can love, would alone be sufficient to sour a happier disposition than is usually brought to the government of a workhouse. To this society of wretchedness the laboring poor of England look as their last resting-place on this side of the grave; and, rather than enter abodes so miserable, they endure the severest privations as long as it is possible to exist.

7. We talk of the liberty of the English, and they talk of their own liberty; but *there is no liberty in England for the poor.* They are no longer sold with the soil, it is true; but they cannot quit the soil, if there be any probability or suspicion that age or infirmity may disable them. If, in such a case, they endeavor to remove to some situation where they hope more easily to maintain themselves—where work is more plentiful or provisions cheaper—the overseers are alarmed; the intruder is apprehended, as if he were a criminal, and sent back to his own parish!

8. Wherever a pauper dies, that parish must be at the cost of his funeral; instances, therefore, have not been wanting of wretches in the last stage of disease having been hurried away in an open cart upon straw, and dying upon the road! Nay, even women in the very pains of labor have been driven out, and have perished by the way-side, because the birth-place of the child would be its parish!

SOUTHEY.

---

4. THE MISERERE AT ROME.

THE night on which our Saviour is supposed to have died, is selected for this service. The Sistine Chapel is dimly lighted, to correspond with the gloom of the scene shadowed forth. ...

2. The ceremonies commenced with the chanting of the La-

mentations. Thirteen candles, in the form of an erect triangle, were lighted up in the beginning, representing the different moral lights of the ancient Church of Israel. One after another was extinguished as the chant proceeded, until the last and brightest one at the top, representing *Christ*, was put out.

3. As they one by one slowly disappeared in the deepening gloom, a blacker night seemed gathering over the hopes and fate of man, and the lamentation grew wilder and deeper. But as the Prophet of prophets, the Light, the Hope of the world, disappeared, the lament suddenly ceased. Not a sound was heard amid the utter darkness.

4. The catastrophe was too awful, and the shock too great, to admit of speech. He who had been lamenting in mournful notes the recent decease of the good and great, seemed struck utterly dumb at this bitterest woe. Stunned and stupefied, he could not contemplate the mighty disaster. I never felt a heavier pressure on my heart than at this moment.

5. The chapel was packed in every inch of it, even out of the door far back into the ample hall, and yet not a sound was heard. I could hear the breathing of the mighty multitude, and amid it the suppressed half-drawn sigh. Like the chanter, each man seemed to say, "Christ is gone; we are orphans—all orphans!"

6. The silence at length became too painful. I thought I should shriek out in agony, when suddenly a low wail, so desolate and yet so sweet, so despairing and yet so tender, like the last strain of a broken heart, stole slowly out from the distant darkness and swelled over the throng, that the tears rushed unbidden to my eyes, and I could have wept like a child for sympathy.

7. It then died away, as if the grief were too great for the strain. Fainter and fainter, like the dying tone of a lute, it sunk away, as if the last sigh of sorrow was ended, when suddenly there burst through the arches a cry so piercing and shrill that it seemed not the voice of song, but the language

of a wounded and dying heart in its last agonizing throb. The multitude swayed to it like the forest to the blast.

8. Again it ceased, and broken sobs of exhausted grief alone were heard. Then all the choir joined in the piteous lament, and seemed to weep with the weeper. After a few notes they paused again, and that sweet, melancholy voice mourned on alone.

9. Its note is still in my ear. I wanted to see the singer. It seemed as if such sounds could come from nothing but a broken heart. Oh! how unlike the joyful, the triumphant anthem that swept through the same chapel on the morning that symbolized the resurrection!

HEADLEY.

5. ST. PETER'S.

FROM the bridge and *Castle of St. Angelo*, a wide street conducts in a direct line to a square, and that square presents at once the court or portico, and part of the Basilica. When the spectator approaches the entrance of this court, he views four rows of lofty pillars *sweeping* on to the right and left in a bold semicircle.

2. In the centre of the area formed by this immense colonnade, an Egyptian obelisk, of one solid piece of granite, ascends to the height of one hundred and thirty feet; two perpetual fountains, one on each side, play in the air, and fall in spray round the basins of porphyry that receive them.

3. Before him, raised on three successive flights of marble steps, he beholds the majestic front of the Basilica itself, extending four hundred feet in length, and towering to the elevation of one hundred and eighty. This front is supported by a single row of Corinthian pillars and pilasters, and adorned with an attic, a balustrade, and thirteen colossal statues.

4. Far behind and above it, rises the matchless Dome, the justly-celebrated *wonder of Rome* and *of the world*. The colon-

nade of coupled pillars that surround and strengthen its vast base, the graceful attic that surmounts this colonnade, the bold and expansive swell of the dome itself, and the pyramid seated on a cluster of columns, and bearing the ball and cross to the skies, all perfect in their kind, form the most magnificent and singular exhibition that the human eye perhaps ever contemplated. On each side, a lesser cupola, rising proudly, reflects the grandeur, and adds not a little to the majesty of the principal dome.

5. The interior corresponds perfectly with the grandeur of the exterior, and fully answers the expectations, however great, which so magnificent an entrance must have raised. Five lofty portals open into the portico or vestibulum, a gallery in dimensions and decorations equal to the most spacious cathedrals.

6. It is four hundred feet in length, seventy in height, and fifty in breadth, paved with variegated marble, covered with a gilt vault, adorned with pillars, pilasters, mosaic, and basso-relievos, and terminated at both ends by equestrian statues, one of Constantine, the other of Charlemagne.

7. A fountain at each extremity supplies a stream sufficient to keep a reservoir always full, in order to carry off every unseemly object, and perpetually refresh and purify the air and the pavement. Opposite the five portals of the vestibule are the five doors of the church; three are adorned with pillars of the finest marble; that in the middle has valves of bronze.

8. As you enter, you behold the most extensive hall ever constructed by human art, expanded in magnificent perspective before you; advancing up the nave, you are delighted with the beauty of the variegated marble under your feet, and with the splendor of the golden vault over your head. The lofty Corinthian pilasters with their bold entablature, the intermediate niches with their statues, the arcades with the graceful figures that recline on the curves of their arches, charm your eye in succession as you pass along.

9. But how great your astonishment when you reach the

foot of the altar, and standing in the centre of the church contemplate the four superb vistas that open around you; and then raise your eyes to the dome, at the prodigious elevation of four hundred feet, extended like a firmament over your head, and presenting, in glowing mosaic, the companies of the just, the choirs of celestial spirits, and the whole hierarchy of heaven arrayed in the presence of the Eternal, whose "throne, high raised above all height," crowns the awful scene.

10. When you have feasted your eye with the grandeur of this unparalleled exhibition in the whole, you will turn to the parts, the ornaments, and the furniture, which you will find perfectly corresponding with the magnificent form of the temple itself. Around the dome rise four other cupolas, small indeed when compared to its stupendous magnitude, but of great boldness when considered separately; six more, three on either side, cover the different divisions of the aisles, and six more of greater dimensions canopy as many chapels, or, to speak more properly, as many churches.

11. All these inferior cupolas are like the grand dome itself, lined with mosaics; many, indeed, of the master-pieces of painting which formerly graced this edifice, have been removed and replaced by mosaics which retain all the tints and beauties of the originals, impressed on a more solid and durable substance. The aisles and altars are adorned with numberless antique pillars, that border the church all around, and form a secondary and subservient order.

12. The variegated walls are, in many places, ornamented with festoons, wreaths, angels, tiaras, crosses, and medallions representing the effigies of different pontiffs. These decorations are of the most beautiful and rarest species of marble, and often of excellent workmanship. Various monuments rise in different parts of the church; but, in their size and accompaniments, so much attention has been paid to general as well as local effect, that they appear rather as parts of the original plan, than posterior additions. Some of these are much admired for their groups and exquisite sculpture, and form

very conspicuous features in the ornamental part of this noble temble.

13. The high altar stands under the dome, and thus as it is the most important, so it becomes the most striking object. In order to bring it out in strong relief and full effect, according to the ancient custom still retained in the patriarchal churches at Rome, and in most of the cathedrals in Italy, a lofty canopy rises above it, and forms an intermediate break or repose for the eye between it and the immensity of the dome above.

14. The form, materials, and magnitude of this decoration are equally astonishing. Below the steps of the altar, and of course some distance from it, at the corners, on four massive pedestals, rise four twisted pillars fifty feet in height, and support an entablature which bears the canopy itself topped with a cross. The whole soars to the elevation of one hundred and thirty-two feet from the pavement, and, excepting the pedestals, is of Corinthian brass; the most lofty massive work of that, or of any other metal, now known.

15. But this brazen edifice, for so it may be called, notwithstanding its magnitude, is so disposed as not to obstruct the view by concealing the chancel and veiling the *Cathedra* or *Chair* of St. Peter. This ornament is also of bronze, and consists of a group of four gigantic figures, representing the four principal Doctors of the Greek and Latin churches, supporting the patriarchal chair of St. Peter. The chair is a lofty throne elevated to the height of seventy feet from the pavement; a circular window tinged with yellow throws from above a mild splendor around it, so that the whole not unfitly represents the pre-eminence of the Apostolic See, and is acknowledged to form a most becoming and majestic termination to the first of Christian temples.

EUSTACE.

6. SONG OF THE STARS.

WHEN the radiant morn of creation broke,
And the world in the smile of God awoke,
And the empty realms of darkness and death
Were moved through their depths by His mighty breath;
And orbs of beauty, and spheres of flame,
From the void abyss by myriads came,
In the joy of youth, as they darted away,
Through the widening wastes of space to play,
Their silver voices in chorus rung,
And this was the song that the bright ones sung:

2. Away, away, through the wide, wide sky,
The fair blue fields that before us lie:
Each sun with the worlds that round us roll,
Each planet poised on her turning pole,
With her isles of green, and her clouds of white,
And her waters that lie like fluid light.

3. For the Source of Glory uncovers his face,
And the brightness o'erflows unbounded space;
And we drink, as we go, the luminous tides,
In our ruddy air and our blooming sides;
Lo! yonder the living splendors play;—
Away, on your joyous path away!

4. Look, look, through our glittering ranks afar,
In the infinite azure, star after star,
How they brighten and bloom as they swiftly pass!
How the verdure runs o'er each rolling mass:
And the path of the gentle winds are seen,
When the small waves dance, and the young woods lean.

5.   And see, where the brighter day-beams pour,
　　How the rainbows hang in the sunny shower!
　　And the morn and the eve, with their pomp of hues,
　　Shift o'er the bright planets and shed their dews!
　　And, 'twixt them both, o'er the teeming ground,
　　With her shadowy cone, the night goes round.

6.   Away, away!—in our blossoming bowers,
　　In the soft air wrapping these spheres of ours,
　　In the seas and fountains that shine with morn,
　　See, love is brooding, and life is born,
　　And breathing myriads are breaking from night,
　　To rejoice, like us, in motion and light.

7.   Glide on in your beauty, ye youthful spheres!
　　To weave the dance that measures the years;
　　Glide on in the glory and gladness sent
　　To the farthest wall of the firmament;
　　The boundless, visible smile of Him,
　　To the veil of whose brow our lamps are dim.

BRYANT.

7. THE SEA.

HA! exclaimed I, as I sprang upon the broad beach of the Mediterranean, and my spirit drank the splendid spectacle of light and life that spread before me—what a relief it is to escape from the straining littleness and wearisome affectation of men, to the free, majestic, and inspiring sea—to listen to his stern, exalted voice—to watch the untrammeled swell of these pure waters, till the pulse of our own heart beats in sympathetic nobleness—to behold it heave in untiring energy—changing momently in form, changing never in impression!

2. What joy is it to be sure that *here* there is nothing coun-

terfeit—nothing feigned—nothing artificial! Feeling, here, grapples with what will never falter; imagination here may spread its best-plumed wings, but will never outstrip the real There is here none of that fear which never leaves the handicraft of art—the fear of penetrating beneath the surface of beauty. Here man feels his majesty by feeling his nothingness; for the majesty of man lies in his conceptions, and the conception of self-nothingness is the grandest we can have. That small and noxious passion-mist, which we *call* our soul, is driven without; and our TRUE soul—the soul of the universe, which we are—enters into us.

3. The spirit which rests like a vapor visibly upon the bosom of the waters, is a presence and a pervading power; and the breath which it exhales is life, and love, and splendid strength. Nothing in nature renders back to man the full and instant sympathy which is accorded by the Mighty Being who thus reposes mildly in the generous grandeur of His glorious power. We may love the forms of the trees, the colors of the sky, and the impressive vastness of the hills; but we can never animate them with a soul of life, and persuade ourselves that they experience the feeling which they cause.

4. But the sea, as its countenance shows its myriad mutations with the variety and rapidity of the passions which sport through the breast of man, seems truly to return the emotion which is breathed towards him; and fellowship and friendship—yea, and personal affection—are the sentiments which his gambols rouse in the spectator's heart. The flashing smiles that sparkle in his eye—are they not his happy thoughts? and the ripples that flit their scouring dance over his breast—are they not feelings of delight that agitate his frame?

5. Whether I am amid mountains or on plains, there is not an hour in which my existence is not haunted by the remembrance of the ocean. It abides beside me like a thought of my mind;—it occupies my total fancy;—I ever seem to stand

before it. And I know that whenever it shall fare so ill with me in the world that comfort and consolation can no longer be found in it, I have a paraclete beside the shelving beach who will give the consolation man withholds. The strong, thick wind which comes from it will be full of life; the petty tumult of care will be shamed by the gigantic struggle of the elements, and subside to peace. What can be more noble or more affecting than the picture of the old priest, who, wronged by the Grecian king—his calm age fired with passion—retires along the shore of the sounding sea, and soothes his breast ere he invokes the god? "Thoughts like those are medicined best by nature."

6. I have never stood by the banks of the ocean thus superbly fringed with curling waves, and listened to that strange, questionable, echoed roar, without an emotion altogether supernatural. That moan—that wail of the waters—which comes to the ear, borne on the wind in the stillness of evening, sounds like the far-off complaint of another world, or the groan of our own world's innermost spirit. Like some of the unearthly music of Germany, when heard for the first time, it startles a feeling in the secret mind which has never before been wakened in this world, giving us assurance of another life, and the strongest proof that our soul is essentially immortal.

WALLACE.

---

8. BURNING OF MOSCOW.

[In Alison's History of Europe during the French Revolution, we find the following graphic description of the burning of Moscow—which took place in Napoleon's Russian expedition in 1812—one of the most striking historical episodes on record; whether we regard it in the magnitude of its preparation, the immense number of its forces, the horrors of the retreat, or the terrible sufferings of the soldiers.]

THE sight of the grotesque towers and venerable walls of the Kremlin first revived the Emperor's imagination, and rekindled those dreams of Oriental conquest which from his earliest years had floated in his mind. His followers, dispersed over the vast extent of the city, gazed with astonishment on the sumptuous palaces of the nobles and the gilded domes of the churches.

2. The mixture of architectural decoration and shady foliage, of Gothic magnificence and Eastern luxury, excited the admiration of the French soldiers, more susceptible than any other people of impressions of that description. Evening came on: with increasing wonder the French troops traversed the central parts of the metropolis, recently so crowded with passengers; but not a living creature was to be seen to explain the universal desolation. It seemed like a city of the dead.

3. Night approached: an unclouded moon illuminated those beautiful palaces—those vast hotels, those deserted streets; all was still—the silence of the tomb. The officers broke open the doors of some of the principal mansions in search of sleeping quarters. They found every thing in perfect order: the bedrooms were fully furnished, as if guests were expected; the drawing-rooms bore the marks of having been recently inhabited; even the work of the ladies was on the tables, the keys in the wardrobes; but not an inmate was to be seen. By degrees a few of the lowest class of slaves emerged, pale and trembling, from the cellars, showed the way to the sleeping apartments, and laid open every thing which these sumptuous mansions contained; but the only account they could give was, that the inhabitants had fled, and that they alone were left in the deserted city.

4. But the terrible catastrophe soon commenced. On the night of the 13th September, 1812, a fire broke out in the Exchange, behind the Bazaar, which soon consumed that noble edifice, and spread through a considerable part of the crowded streets in the vicinity. This, however, was but the prelude to more extended calamities.

5. At midnight on the 15th, a bright light was seen to illuminate the northern and western parts of the city; and the sentinels on duty at the Kremlin soon saw that the splendid

buildings in those quarters were in flames. The wind changed repeatedly in the night; but to whatever quarter it veered the conflagration extended itself; fresh fires were every instant seen breaking out in all directions; and Moscow soon exhibited the appearance of a sea of flame agitated by the wind. The French soldiers, drowned in sleep, or overcome by intoxication, were incapable of arresting its progress; and burning fragments, floating through the hot air, began to fall on the roofs and courts of the Kremlin. The fury of an autumnal tempest added to the horrors of the scene; it seemed as if the wrath of Heaven had combined with the vengeance of man to destroy the invaders in the city they had conquered.

6. But it was during the night of the 18th and 19th that the conflagration attained its greatest violence. Then the whole city was wrapped in flames; and volumes of fire of various colors ascended to the heavens in many places, diffusing a prodigious light on all sides, and an intolerable heat. These masses of flame threw out a frightful hissing noise, and loud explosions, the effect of the vast stores of oil, tar, resin, spirits, and other combustible materials, with which the greater part of the warehouses were filled.

7. Large pieces of canvas, unrolled from the outside of the buildings by the violence of the heat, floated on fire through the air, and sent down a flaming shower, which spread the conflagration in quarters the most remote from those where it originally commenced. The wind, previously high, was raised by the sudden rarefaction of the air, produced by the heat, to a perfect hurricane. The howling of the tempest drowned even the roar of the conflagration; the whole heavens were filled with the whirl of the masses of smoke and flame, which rose on all sides and made midnight as bright as day; while even the bravest hearts, subdued by the sublimity of the scene, and the feeling of human impotence in the midst of such elemental strife, sank and trembled in silence.

8. The return of day did not diminish the terrors of the con-

flagration. An immense crowd of people, who had taken refuge in the cellars or vaults of buildings, came forth as the flames reached the dwellings; the streets were filled with multitudes flying in every direction with the most precious articles of furniture; while the French army, whose discipline this fearful event had entirely dissolved, assembled in drunken crowds, and loaded themselves with the spoils of the city. Never in modern times had such a scene been witnessed. The men were loaded with valuable furniture and rich goods, which often took fire as they were carried along, and which they were obliged to throw down to save themselves.

9. Women had sometimes two or three children on their backs, and as many led by the hand, while, with trembling steps and piteous cries, they sought their devious way through the labyrinth of flame. Many old men, unable to walk, were drawn on hurdles, or wheelbarrows, by their children and grandchildren, while their burned beards and smoking garments showed with what difficulty they had been rescued from death.

10. French soldiers, tormented by hunger and thirst, and released from all discipline by the horrors that surrounded them, not content with the booty in the streets, rushed headlong into the burning houses to ransack their cellars for wine and spirits, and beneath the ruins great numbers perished miserably, the victims of intemperance and the flames. Meanwhile the fire, fanned by the tremendous gale, advanced with frightful rapidity, devouring alike, in its course, the palaces of the great, the temples of religion, and the cottages of the poor.

11. For thirty-six hours the conflagration continued at its height, and in that time about nine-tenths of the city was destroyed. The remainder, abandoned to pillage and deserted by the inhabitants, offered no resources for the army. Moscow had been conquered, but the victors had gained only a heap of ruins.

12. Imagination cannot conceive the horrors into which the people who could not abandon their houses were plunged by this unparalleled sacrifice. Bereft of every thing, they wandered among the ruins, eagerly searching for missing relatives; the wrecks of former magnificence were ransacked equally by the licentious soldiery and the suffering natives, while numbers rushed in from the neighboring country to share in the general license.

13. The most precious furniture, splendid jewelry, East Indian and Turkish stuffs, stores of wine and brandy, gold and silver plate, rich furs, gorgeous hangings of silk and satin, were spread about in promiscuous confusion, and became the prey of the least intoxicated among the multitude. A frightful tumult succeeded to the stillness which had reigned in the city when the French troops first entered it. The cries of the pillaged inhabitants, the coarse imprecations of the soldiers, were mingled with the lamentations of those who had lost parents, children, their all, in the conflagration. Pillage became universal; the ruins were covered with motley groups of soldiers, peasants, and marauders of all countries and aspects, seeking for the valuable articles they once contained.

ALISON.

---

9. THE PARTING OF MARMION AND DOUGLAS.

[The following is a spirited account of the parting between the fearless and noble Scottish Earl Douglas and the base English Lord Marmion, whom Douglas, in obedience to his sovereign's orders, had received into his castle. But, while Douglas had granted him the hospitality of his roof and table, yet the scorn he felt for him he did not seek to disguise, in the cold welcome he gave Marmion and his suite.]

THE train without the castle drew,
And Marmion stopped to bid adieu.
"Though something I might plain," he said,
"Of cold respect to stranger guest,
Sent hither by your king's behest,

While in Tantallon's towers I staid,
Part we in friendship from your land,
And, noble earl, receive my hand."

2. But Douglas round him drew his cloak,
Folded his arms, and thus he spoke:
"My manors, halls, and bowers shall still
Be open, at my sovereign's will,
To each one whom he lists, howe'er
Unmeet to be the owner's peer.
My castles are my king's alone,
From turret to foundation-stone;
The hand of Douglas is his own,
And never shall in friendly grasp
The hand of such as Marmion clasp."

3. Burned Marmion's swarthy cheek like fire,
And shook his very frame for ire.
   "And this to me!" he said;
"An' 'twere not for thy hoary beard,
Such hand as Marmion's had not spared
   To cleave the Douglas' head.
And first I tell thee, haughty peer,
He, who does England's message here,
Although the meanest in her State,
May well, proud Angus, be thy mate:
And, Douglas, now I tell thee here,
   Even in thy pitch of pride,
Here in thy hold, thy vassals near
(Nay, never look upon your lord,
And lay your hands upon your swords),
   I tell thee thou'rt defied!
And if thou saidst I am not peer
To any lord in Scotland here,
Lowland or Highland, far or near,
   Lord Angus, thou hast lied."

4. On the Earl's cheek the flash of rage
O'ercame the ashen hue of age.
Fierce he broke forth: "And dar'st thou then
To beard the lion in his den,
 The Douglas in his hall?
And hop'st thou hence unscathed to go?
No! by St. Bride of Bothwell, no!
Up drawbridge, grooms! what, warder, ho!
 Let the portcullis fall."

5. Lord Marmion turned,—well was his need,—
And dashed the rowels in his steed,
Like arrow through the archway sprung;
The ponderous grate behind him rung;
To pass there was such scanty room,
The bars, descending, raised his plume.

6. The steed along the drawbridge flies,
Just as it trembled on the rise;
Nor lighter does the swallow skim
Along the smooth lake's level brim:
And when Lord Marmion reached his band,
He halts, and turns with clinchéd hand,
And shout of loud defiance pours,
And shook his gauntlet at the towers.
"Horse! horse!" the Douglas cried, "and chase!"
 But soon he reined his fury's pace:
"A royal messenger he came,
Though most unworthy of the name;
A letter forged! St. Jude to speed!
Did ever knight so foul a deed?
St. Mary mend my fiery mood,
Old age ne'er cools the Douglas' blood.
I thought to slay him where he stood.
'Tis pity of him, too," he cried;

"Bold can he speak and fairly ride,—
I warrant him a warrior tried."
With this his mandate he recalls,
And slowly seeks his castle's halls.   Scott.

---

10. THE SUMMER OF KINGS.

I WAS one evening on the Ohio, when the river was swollen with recent rains. The current was passing quickly, but with a placidity which reminded me of the old proverb, that "smooth water runs deep." It was early in May. The sky was pale. Thin clouds, with softened outlines, and mingling gently with one another, were moving towards the north. There was something in the air which, if not vivifying, if not genial, was quieting.

2. It was an evening when good hearts might have been touched with great tenderness, if not with mournfulness. Not with the mournfulness which comes from anguish, and pervades our nature as if with faint pulsations of a subsiding struggle, but with that mournfulness which accompanies the recollections of home, and is tempered and sweetened and lit up with the love of old scenes and faces, and the hope of seeing them once more.

3. From the various incidents that were going on in the boat about me, and the varying features of the scene through which we were gliding, I turned to one object, which, far more forcibly than the rest, attracted my attention. It was a sycamore-tree—a noble-looking tree; noble in its proportions, noble in its profusion, noble in its promise.

4. And the birds were in it, on its topmost branches, striking out their wings and uttering their quick notes of joy Oh! with what a sweet thrill came forth the liquid song from that waving, sparkling foliage, and how confident it made the looker-on, that the tree from which it gushed 'in a thousand mingling streams, would stand and flourish, and put forth its

beauty, and rejoice in the fragrant breath of the summer, and stoutly defy the shock of winter for years to come!

5. It was a dream. I looked downward; the roots were stripped. The earth had been loosened from them, and they glistened like bones, whitened as they were with the water which tumbled through them, and about them, and over them. One hold alone it seemed to have. But the sleepless element was busy upon that; even as I looked the soft mould slipped in flakes from the solitary stay which held the tree erect.

6. And there it stood, full of vigor, full of beauty, full of festive life; full of promise, with a grave a fathom opened at its feet. The next flood, and the last link must give way. And down must come that lord of the forest, with all his honors, with all his strength, with all his mirth; and the remorseless river shall toss him to the thick slime, and then fling him up again, tearing his tangled finery, and bruising and breaking his proud limbs until two thousand miles below, on some stagnant swamp, tired of the dead prey, the wild pursuer, chafed and foaming from the chase, shall cast a shapeless log ashore.

7. "Such," said I, "shall be the fate of the European kings. It is now summer with them. The sunbeams gild the domes of their palaces; the helmets, with crimson manes, burn along those white lines within which legions, countless as that of Xerxes, are encamped."

8. Prayers are going on in a pavilion on the field. It is the camp near Olmutz. Elsewhere are bridal feasts. There are pennons of silk and flowers fresh with luscious fragrance. Beauty is clustered there in snowy vesture, and the princes and warriors of the cities are plumed and harnessed for the field.

9. And there are senators and counsellors of state, and doctors of the law, and ministers of police and other functionaries, assembled likewise in holiday costume. The market-places, and the public squares, and all the public offices, are decked out with floral wreaths, and painted shields, and pendent

flags. And there are gay processions through the streets, and market-choruses, and barges with carved and gilded prows and silken awnings fringed and tasselled richly, all laden with revelry, gliding up and down the river.

10. The sun goes down, yet the sky is bright—brighter than at noon. There is a broad avenue walled on either side, and arched with fire. There are fountains of fire, pillars of fire, temples of fire ("temples of immortality," they call them), arches of fire, pyramids of fire. The fable of the phœnix is more than realized. Above that mass and maze of flames, an eagle, feathered with flames, spreads his gigantic wings, and mounts and expands, until tower, and dome, and obelisk are spanned.

11. Visions of Arabian Nights visit the earth again. The wealth and wonders of Nineveh are disentombed. The festival costs one million sixteen hundred francs; all done to order. It is summer with the kings; aye, summer with the kings. Bright leaves are upon and life and song are among them: but death is at the root. The next flood and the proud lord shall be uprooted and the waters shall beat him away; when they have stripped him of his finery they shall fling him in upon the swamp to rot. Such shall be the fate of the European kings, European aristocracies, European despotisms. Who will lament it? Who would avert it?

12. What though it is now summer with the kings? What though the evil ones have been exalted, and the perjured have been named holy, and the blood of the people is mixed with the wine of the princes, and illuminations bewilder the memory of those who mourn, and the gibbet is disguised in lamps and flowers and the relics of imperial wars, and the desolate laugh hysterically in their intoxication, and the reign of the wicked is a jubilee, and he spreadeth himself like a green bay-tree, and his power is supreme? What recks it? It shall pass like the dream of the drunkard.

11. EXTEMPORE OR SIGHT READING.

TO read a piece the first time with a good, distinct, and deliberate articulation, pronouncing the words with boldness and force, and at the same time with propriety and elegance, distinguishing the more significant words by a natural, forcible, and varied emphasis, and the subordinate words with a proper degree of accent; together with a just variety of pause and cadence, accompanied by the emotions and passions, with their correspondent tones, looks, and gestures, the reader must be in possession of these requisites to do it well.

2. In the former part of this work these requisites are to be found; and if the reader has studied them carefully, with those relating to the inflections and modulations of the voice, ne may then attempt to read at sight the following sections, commencing with the shortest and easiest pieces in each of the selections, and progressing gradually to the most difficult.

3. To read well at sight is a difficult performance; but it can be accomplished by daily practice; the same as a skilful musician or well-trained amateur, after long, laborious practice, performing a piece of music the first time, can throw into it all the spirit, feeling, expression, and pathos imaginable. This fine accomplishment, from its very difficulty of acquirement, is perhaps the highest excellence of a reader; and the time and labor bestowed in its acquirement will richly repay him in the pleasure he will afford those who may hear him read.

4. To render sight-reading perfectly easy, if the reader will cast his eye a little beyond the point at which he is reading, this exercise will enable him to anticipate the sense of what follows, and in time he will be able to take into his mind a whole clause or sentence at a glance of the eye.

12. THE CAMPAGNA OF ROME.

PERHAPS there is no more impressive scene on earth than the solitary extent of the Campagna of Rome under evening light. Let the reader imagine himself for a moment withdrawn from the sounds and motion of the living world, and sent forth alone into this wild and wasted plain. The earth yields and crumbles beneath his feet, tread he ever so lightly, for its substance is white, hollow, and carious, like the dusty wreck of the bones of men. The long-knotted grass waves and tosses feebly in the evening wind, and the shadows of its motion shake feverishly along the banks of rivers that lift themselves to the sunlight. Hillocks of mouldering earth heave around him, as if the dead beneath were struggling in their sleep; scattered blocks of black stones—four-square remnants of mighty edifices, not one left upon another—lie upon them to keep them down.

2. A dull, poisonous haze stretches level along the desert, vailing its spectral wrecks of mossy ruins, on whose rents the red light rests like dying fire on defiled altars. The blue ridge of the Alban Mount lifts itself against a solemn space of green, clear, quiet sky. Watch-towers of dark clouds stand steadfastly along the promontories of the Apennines. From the plain to the mountains, the shattered aqueducts, pier beyond pier, melt into the darkness like shadowy and countless troops of funeral mourners passing from a nation's grave.

RUSKIN.

13. MONK FELIX.

[In this poem, Longfellow has given in sweet rhythm one of the touching old legends of the Middle Ages.]

ONE morning all alone,
   Out of his convent of gray stone,
Into the forest older, darker, grayer,
 His lips moving as if in prayer,

His head sunken upon his breast
As in a dream of rest,
Walked the Monk Felix. All about
The broad, sweet sunshine lay without,
Filling the summer air;
And within the woodlands as he trod,
The twilight was like the truce of God
With worldly woe and care.

2. Under him lay the golden moss;
And above him the boughs of the hemlock trees
Waved, and made the sign of the cross,
And whispered their Benedicites;
And from the ground
Rose an odor, sweet and fragrant,
Of the wild-flowers and the vagrant
Vines that wandered,
Seeking the sunshine round and round;
These he heeded not, but pondered
On the volume in his hand,
A volume of St. Augustine,
Wherein he read of the unseen
Splendors of God's great town
In the unknown land,
And, with his eyes cast down,
In humility he said:
"I believe, O God,
What herein I have read,
But, alas! I do not understand!"

3. And lo! he heard
The sudden singing of a bird,
A snow-white bird, that from a cloud
Dropped down,
And among the branches brown
Sat singing

So sweet, and clear, and loud,
It seemed a thousand harp-strings ringing.
And the Monk Felix closed his book,
And long, long,
With rapturous look,
He listened to the song,
And hardly breathed or stirred,
Until he saw, as in a vision,
The land of Elysian,
And in the heavenly city heard
Angelic feet
Fall on the golden flagging of the street.
And he would fain have caught the wondrous bird,
But strove in vain;
For it flew away, away,
Far over hill and dell,
And instead of its sweet singing
He heard the convent bell
Suddenly in the silence ringing
For the service of noonday.
And he retraced
His pathway homeward, sadly and in haste.

4. In the convent there was a change!
He looked for each well-known face,
But the faces were new and strange;
New figures sat in the oaken stalls,
New voices chanted in the choir;
Yet the place was the same place,
The same dusty walls
Of cold gray stone;
The same cloisters, and belfry, and spire.

5. A stranger and alone
Among that brotherhood
The Monk Felix stood.

RHETORICAL.

"Forty years," said a friar,
"Have I been prior
Of this convent in the wood;
But for that space,
Never have I beheld thy face!"

6. The heart of the Monk Felix fell;
And he answered with submissive tone,
"This morning after the hour of Prime
I left my cell,
And wandered forth alone,
Listening all the time
To the melodious singing
Of a beautiful white bird,
Until I heard
The bells of the convent ringing
Noon from their noisy towers.
It was as if I dreamed;
For what to me had seemed
Moments only, had been hours!"

7. "Years!" said a voice close by.
It was an aged monk who spoke,
From a bench of oak
Fastened against the wall;
He was the oldest monk of all.
For a whole century
Had he been there,
Serving God in prayer,
The meekest and humblest of his creatures.
He remembered well the features
Of Felix, and he said,
Speaking distinct and slow:
"One hundred years ago,
When I was a novice in this place,
There was here a monk full of God's grace,

Who bore the name
Of Felix, and this man must be the same."

8 And straightway
They brought forth to the light of day
A volume old and brown,
A huge tome, bound
In brass and wild boar's hide,
Wherein was written down
The names of all who had died
In the convent since it was edified.
And there they found,
Just as the old monk said,
That on a certain day and date,
One hundred years before,
Had gone forth from the convent gate
The Monk Felix, and never more
Had entered that sacred door.
He had been counted among the dead!
And they knew, at last,
That such had been the power
Of that celestial and immortal song,
A hundred years had passed,
And had not seemed so long as a single hour!

LONGFELLOW.

14. DESCRIPTION OF THE RUINS AT BALBEC.

WE rose with the sun, whose first rays struck on the temples of Balbec, and gave to those mysterious ruins that *éclat* which his brilliant light ever throws over scenes which it illuminates. Soon we arrived, on the northern side, at the foot of the gigantic walls which surround those beautiful remains. A clear stream, flowing over a bed of granite, murmured around the enormous blocks of stone, fallen from the top of the wall, which obstructed its course. Beautiful sculptures were half concealed in the limpid stream. We passed the rivulet by an arch formed by these fallen remains, and mounting a narrow breach, were soon lost in admiration of the scene which surrounded us.

2. At every step a fresh exclamation of surprise broke from our lips. Every one of the stones of which that wall was composed was from eight to ten feet in length, by five or six in breadth, and as much in height. They rest, without cement, one upon the other, and almost all bear the mark of Indian or Egyptian sculpture. At a single glance, you see that these enormous stones are not placed in their original site—that they are the precious remains of temples of still more remote antiquity, which were made use of to encircle this colony of Grecian and Roman citizens.

3. When we reached the summit of the breach, our eyes knew not to what object first to turn. On all sides were gates of marble, of prodigious height and magnitude; windows or niches, fringed with the richest friezes; fallen pieces of cornices, of entablatures, or capitals, thick as the dust beneath our feet; magnificent vaulted roofs above our heads; every where a chaos of confused beauty, the remains of which lay scattered about, or piled on each other in endless variety. So prodigious was the accumulation of architectural remains, that it defies all attempts at classification, or conjecture of the kind of buildings to which the greater part of them had belonged.

4. After passing through this scene of ruined magnificence, we reached an inner wall, which we also ascended; and from its summit the view of the interior was yet more splendid. Of much greater extent, far more richly decorated than the outer circle, it presented an immense platform, the level surface of which was frequently broken by the remains of still more elevated pavements, on which temples to the sun, the object of adoration at Balbec, had been erected. All around that platform were a series of lesser temples, or chapels, decorated with niches, admirably engraved, and loaded with sculptured ornaments, to a degree that appeared excessive to those

who had seen the severe simplicity of the Parthenon or the Coliseum.

5. But how prodigious the accumulation of architectural riches in the middle of an Eastern desert! Combine in imagination the temple of Jupiter Stator, and the Coliseum at Rome, of Jupiter Olympius, and the Acropolis at Athens, and you will yet fall short of that marvellous assemblage of admirable edifices and sculptures. Many of the temples rest on columns seventy feet in height, and seven feet in diameter, yet composed only of two or three blocks of stone, so perfectly joined together that to this day you can barely discern the lines of their junction. Silence is the only language which befits man when words are inadequate to convey his impressions. We remained mute with admiration, gazing on the eternal ruins.

6. The shades of night overtook us while we yet rested in amazement at the scene by which we were surrounded. One by one they enveloped the columns in their obscurity, and added a mystery the more to that magical and mysterious work of time and man. We appeared, as compared with the gigantic mass and long duration of these monuments, as the swallows which nestle a season in the crevices of the capitals, without knowing by whom, or for whom, they have been constructed.

7. The thoughts, the wishes, which moved these masses, are to us unknown. The dust of marble which we tread beneath our feet knows more of it than we; but it cannot tell us what it has seen; and in a few ages the generations which shall come in their turn to visit our monuments, will ask, in like manner, wherefore we have built and engraved. The works of man survive his thought. Movement is the law of the human mind; the definite is the dream of his pride and his ignorance. LAMARTINE.

15. THE CONVICT SHIP.

MORN on the waters! and purple and bright,
Bursts on the billows the flushing of light;
O'er the glad waves, like a child of the sun,
See! the tall vessel goes gallantly on;
Full to the breeze she unbosoms her sail,
And her pennon streams onward, like hope, in the gale;
The winds come around her, in murmur and song,
And the surges rejoice as they bear her along;
See! she looks up to the golden-edged clouds,
And the sailor sings gayly aloft in the shrouds.

2. Onward she glides, amid ripple and spray,
O'er the rough waters,—away, and away!
Bright as the visions of youth, ere they part,
Passing away like a dream of the heart!
Who,—as the beautiful pageant sweeps by,
Music around her, and sunshine on high,—
Pauses to think, amid glitter and glow,
Oh! there are hearts that are breaking below!

3. Night on the waves!—and the moon is on high,
Hung, like a gem, on the brow of the sky,
Treading its depths in the power of her might,
And turning the clouds, as they pass her, to light!
Look to the waters!—asleep on their breast,
Seems not the ship like an island of rest?
Bright and alone on the shadowy main,
Like a heart-cherished home on some desolate plain!

4. Who,—as she smiles in the silvery light,
Spreading her wings on the bosom of night,
Alone on the deep, as the moon in the sky,
A phantom of beauty,—could deem with a sigh,

That so lovely a thing is the mansion of sin,
And that souls that are smitten, lie bursting within ?

5. Who,—as he watches her silently gliding,—
Remembers that wave after wave is dividing
Bosoms that sorrow and guilt could not sever,—
Hearts which are parted and broken for ever?
Or deems that he watches, afloat on the wave,
The death-bed of hope, or the young spirit's grave ?

6. 'Tis thus with our life, while it passes along,
Like a vessel at sea, amidst sunshine and song !
Gayly we glide, in the gaze of the world,
With streamers afloat, and with canvas unfurled ;
All gladness and glory, to wandering eyes,
Yet chartered by sorrow, and freighted with sighs ;
Fading and false is the aspect it wears,
As the smiles we put on, just to cover our tears ;
And the withering thoughts which the world cannot know,
Like heart-broken exiles, lie burning below ;
While the vessel drives on to that desolate shore,
Where the dreams of our childhood are vanished and o'er.

T. K. HERVEY.

16. MOUNTAINS.

THANKS be to God for mountains ! The variety which they impart to the glorious bosom of our planet were no small advantage ; the beauty which they spread out to our vision in their woods and waters ; their crags and slopes, their clouds and atmospheric hues, were a splendid gift ; the sublimity which they pour into our deepest souls from their majestic aspects ; the poetry which breathes from their streams, and dells, and airy heights, from the sweet abodes, the garbs and manners of their inhabitants, the songs and legends which have awoke in them, were a proud heritage to imaginative minds; but what are all these when the thought comes, that without mountains the spirit of man must have bowed to the brutal and the base, and probably have sunk to the monotonous level of the unvaried plain?

2. When I turn my eyes upon the map of the world, and behold how wonderfully the countries where our faith was nurtured, where our liberties were generated, where our philosophy and literature, the fountains of our intellectual grace and beauty, sprang up, were as distinctly walled out by God's hand with mountain ramparts, from the eruptions and interruptions of barbarism, as if at the especial prayer of the early fathers of man's destinies, I am lost in an exalting admiration.

3. Look at the bold barriers of Palestine! see how the infant liberties of Greece were sheltered from the vast tribes of the uncivilised north by the heights of Hæmus and Rhodope! behold how the Alps describe their magnificent crescent, inclining their opposite extremities to the Adriatic and Tyrrhine Seas, locking up Italy from the Gallic and Teutonian hordes till the power and spirit of Rome had reached their maturity, and she had opened the wide forest of Europe to the light, spread far her laws and language, and planted the seeds of many mighty nations!

4. Thanks to God for mountains! Their colossal firmness seems almost to break the current of time itself; the geologist in them searches for traces of the earlier world; and it is there, too, that man, resisting the revolutions of lower regions, retains through innumerable years his habits and his rights. While a multitude of changes have remoulded the people of Europe; while languages, and laws, and dynasties, and creeds, have passed over it like shadows over the landscape, the children of the Celt and the Goth, who fled to the mountains a thousand years ago, are found there now, and show us in face and figure, in language and garb, what their fathers were; show us a fine contrast with the modern tribes dwelling below and around them; and show us, moreover, how adverse is the spirit of the mountain to mutability, and that there the fiery heart of freedom is found for ever. WILLIAM HOWITT.

17. IRELAND AND THE IRISH

[C. E. Lester is wide and expansive in his writings, generous in his feelings, and truly American in his mind and heart. His view of "Ireland under English Oppression," in his admirable work entitled "Condition and Fate of England," is one of the most eloquent essays in the English language.]

IRELAND still has an existence as a nation. She has her universities and her literature. She is still the "Emerald Isle of the Ocean." An air of romance and chivalry is around her. The traditionary tales that live in her literature invest her history with heroic beauty. But she has no need of these. Real heroes, the O'Neils, the O'Briens, and the Emmets, will be remembered as long as self-denying patriotism and unconquerable valor are honored among men.

2. In every department of literature she will take her place. Where is the wreath her shamrock does not adorn? Where the muse that has not visited her hills? Her harp has ever kindled the soul of the warrior and soothed the sorrows of the broken-hearted. It has sounded every strain that can move the human heart to greatness or to love. Whatever vices may stain her people, they are free from the crime of voluntary servitude. The Irishman is the man last to be subdued. Possessing an elasticity of character that will rise under the heaviest oppression, he wants only a favorable opportunity and a single spark to set him in a blaze.

3. The records of religious persecutions in all countries have nothing more hideous to offer to our notice than the Protestant persecutions of the Irish Catholics. On them, all the devices of cruelty were exhausted. Ingenuity was taxed to devise new plans of persecution, till the machinery of penal iniquity might almost be pronounced perfect. The great Irish chieftains and landlords were purposely goaded into rebellion, that they might be branded as traitors and their lands confiscated for the benefit of English adventurers. Such was the course adopted towards Earl Desmond, a powerful chief of Munster; such also was the treatment of O'Neil. When

Queen Elizabeth heard of the revolt of the latter, she remarked to her courtiers: "It would be better for her servants, as there would be estates enough for them all."

4. This single expression of Elizabeth reveals the entire policy of the English Government towards Ireland. That injured country was the great repast at which every monarch bade his lords sit down and eat. After they had gorged their fill, the remains were left for those who came after. Tranquillity succeeded these massacres, but it was the tranquillity of the grave-yard. The proud and patriotic Irishmen were folded in the sleep of death, and the silence and repose around their lifeless corpses were called *peace*.

"They made a solitude,
And called it peace."

5. Often a great chief, possessed of large estates, was purposely driven by the most flagrant injustice and insults into open rebellion, that he might be branded as a traitor, and his rich possessions, by confiscation, revert to the English vampyres that so infested the land. Every cruelty and outrage that can dishonor our nature was perpetrated in these unjust wars by English leaders and English soldiers. Cities were sacked, villages burned, and the helpless and the young slaughtered by thousands. A record of these scenes of crime and blood we cannot furnish. It is written, however, on every foot of Irish soil, and in the still living memories of many an Irish heart. C. EDWARDS LESTER.

18. THE DUELLIST'S HONOR.

HONOR is the acquisition and preservation of the dignity of our nature: that dignity consists in its perfection; that perfection is found in observing the laws of our Creator; the laws of the Creator are the dictates of reason and of religion: that is, the observance of what He teaches us by the natural light of our own minds, and by the special revelations of His will manifestly given. They both concur in teaching us that individuals have not the dominion of their own lives; otherwise, no suicide would be a criminal. They concur in teaching us that we ought to be amenable to the laws of the society of which we are members; otherwise, morality and honor would be consistent with the violation of law and the disturbance of the social system.

2. They teach us that society cannot continue to exist where the public tribunals are despised or undervalued, and the redress of injuries withdrawn from the calm regulation of public justice, for the purpose of being committed to the caprice of private passion, and the execution of individual ill-will; therefore, the man of honor abides by the law of God, reveres the statutes of his country, and is respectful and amenable to its authorities. Such, my friends, is what the reflecting portion of mankind has always thought upon the subject of honor. This was the honor of the Greek; this was the honor of the Roman; this the honor of the Jew; this the honor of the Gentile; this, too, was the honor of the Christian, until the superstition and barbarity of Northern devastators darkened his glory and degraded his character.

3. Man, then, has not power over his own life; much less is he justified in depriving another human being of life. Upon what ground can he who engages in a duel, through the fear of ignominy, lay claim to courage? Unfortunate delinquent! Do you not see by how many links your victim was bound to a multitude of others? Does his vain and idle resignation of his title to life absolve you from the enormous claims which society has upon you for his services—his family for that support, of which you have robbed them without your own enrichment?

4. Go, stand over that body; call back that soul which you have driven from its tenement; take up that hand which your pride refused to touch, not one hour ago. You have, in your pride and wrath, usurped *one* prerogative of God. You have inflicted death. At least, in mercy, attempt the exorcise of

another; breathe into those distended nostrils—let your brother be once more a living soul! Merciful Father! how powerless are we for good, but how mighty for evil! Wretched man! he does not answer—he cannot rise. All your efforts to make him breathe are vain. His soul is already in the presence of your common Creator! Like the wretched Cain, will you answer, "Am I my brother's keeper?"

5. Why do you turn away from the contemplation of your own honorable work? Yes, go as far as you will, still the admonition will ring in your ears: *It was by your hand he fell!* The horrid instrument of death is still in that hand, and the stain of blood upon your soul. Fly, if you will—go to that house which you have filled with desolation. It is the shriek of his widow—they are the cries of his children—the broken sobs of his parent; and, amidst the wailings, you distinctly hear the voice of imprecation on your own guilty head! Will your *honorable* feelings be content with this? Have you *now* had abundant and gentlemanly satisfaction?

BISHOP ENGLAND.

---

19. EMOTIONS ON RETURNING TO THE UNITED STATES, 1837.

SIR, I dare not trust myself to speak of my country with the rapture which I habitually feel when I contemplate her marvellous history. But this I will say—that on my return to it, after an absence of only four years, I was filled with wonder at all I saw and all I heard.

2. What is to be compared with it? I found New York grown up to almost double its former size, with the air of a great capital, instead of a mere flourishing commercial town, as I had known it. I listened to accounts of voyages of a thousand miles in magnificent steamboats on the waters of those great lakes, which, but the other day, I left sleeping in the primeval silence of nature, in the recesses of a vast wilderness; and I felt that there is a grandeur and a majesty in this irresistible onward march of a race, created, as

I believe, and elected, to possess and people a Continent, which belong to few other objects, either of the moral or material world.

3. We may become so much accustomed to such things that they shall make as little impression upon our minds as the glories of the heavens above us; but, looking on them, lately, as with the eye of the stranger, I felt, what a recent English traveller is said to have remarked, that, far from being without poetry, as some have vainly alleged, our whole country is one great poem.

4. Sir, it is so; and if there be a man that can think of what is doing, in all parts of this most blessed of all lands, to embellish and advance it—who can contemplate that living mass of intelligence, activity and improvement, as it rolls on, in its sure and steady progress, to the uttermost extremities of the West—who can see scenes of savage desolation transformed, almost with the suddenness of enchantment, into those of fruitfulness and beauty, crowned with flourishing cities, filled with the noblest of all populations—if there be a man, I say, that can witness all this, passing under his very eyes, without feeling his heart beat high, and his imagination warmed and transported by it, be sure, sir, that the raptures of song exist not for him; he would listen in vain to Tasso or Camoëns, telling a tale of the wars of knights and crusaders, or of the discovery and conquest of another hemisphere.

LEGARÉ.

20. AFAR IN THE DESERT.

[This piece is characterized by great feeling and high descriptive powers.]

AFAR in the desert I love to ride,
With the silent Bush boy alone by my side,
When the sorrows of life the soul o'ercast,
And sick of the present I cling to the past,
When the eye is suffused with regretful tears,
From the fond recollections of former years,

And shadows of things that have long since fled
Flit over the brain like the ghosts of the dead;
Bright visions of glory that vanished too soon;
Day-dreams that departed ere manhood's noon;
Attachments by fate or by falsehood reft,
Companions of early days, lost or left.
And my native land—whose magical name
Thrills to the heart like electric flame;
The home of my childhood, "the haunts of my prime,"
All the passions and scenes of that rapturous time
When the feelings were young and the world was new,
Like the fresh flowers of Eden unfolding to view;
All—all now forsaken—forgotten—foregone—
And I,—a poor exile, remembered of none.
My high aims abandoned—my good acts undone,—
Aweary of all that is under the sun.
With that sadness of heart, that no stranger can scan,
I fly to the desert—afar from man.

2. Afar in the desert I love to ride
With the silent Bush boy alone by my side.
When the wild turmoil of this wearisome life,
With its scenes of corruption, oppression, and strife,—
The proud man's frown, and the base man's fear—
The scorner's laugh, and the sufferer's tear,—
And malice, and meanness, and falsehood, and folly,
Dispose me to musing and sad melancholy;
When my bosom is full, and my thoughts are high,
And my soul is sick with the bondsman's sigh,
Oh! then there is freedom, and joy, and pride,
Afar in the desert alone to ride!
There is rapture to vault on the champing steed,
And to bound away with the eagle's speed,
With the death-fraught firelock in my hand—
The only law of the desert land!

3. Afar in the desert I love to ride,
With the silent Bush boy alone by my side.
Away—away from the dwellings of men,
By the wild deer's haunt, by the buffalo's glen;
By valleys remote, where the oribi plays,
Where the gnu, the gazelle, and the hartébeest graze—
Where the kuder and eland unhunted recline,
By the skirts of gray forest o'erhung with wild vine;
Where the elephant browses at peace in his wood,
And the river-horse gambols, unscared in the flood,
Where the fleet-footed ostrich, over the waste,
Speeds like a horseman who travels in haste,
Hieing away to the home of her rest,
Where she and her mate have scooped their nest,
Far hid from the pitiless plunderer's view,
In the pathless depths of the parched karroo.

4. And here while the night winds round me sigh,
And the stars burn bright in the midnight sky,
As I sit apart by the desert stone,
Like Elijah at Horeb's cave alone,
A still, small voice comes through the wild
(Like a father consoling his fretful child),
Which banishes bitterness, wrath, and fear;
Saying: "Man is distant, but God is near." PRINGLE.

21. POST NUMMOS VIRTUS.

AVARICE is the besetting sin of the age. Ours is, emphatically, the enlightened age of *dollars and cents!* Its motto is: POST NUMMOS VIRTUS;—MONEY FIRST, VIRTUE AFTERWARDS! Utilitarianism is the order of the day. Every thing is estimated in dollars and cents. Almost every order and profession—our literature, our arts, and our sciences—all worship in the temple of Mammon.

2. The temple of God is open during only *one* day in the week; that of mammon is open during *six*. Every thing smacks of gold. The fever of avarice is consuming the very heart's blood of our people. Hence that restless desire to grow suddenly rich; hence that feverish agitation of our population; hence broken constitutions and premature old age. If we have not discovered the philosopher's stone, it has surely not been for want of the seeking. If every thing cannot now be turned into gold, it is certainly not for want of unceasing exertions for this purpose.

3. We have even heard of churches having been built on speculation! And if the traveller from some distant clime should chance suddenly to enter one of our *fashionable* meeting-houses; if he should look at its splendidly-cushioned seats, on which people are seen comfortably lolling, and then glance at the naked walls, and the utter barrenness of all religious emblems and associations in the interior of the building, he would almost conclude that he had entered, by mistake, into some finely-furnished lecture-room, where the ordinary topics of the day were to be discussed.

4. And if he were informed that this edifice had been erected and furnished by a joint-stock company on shares, and that these shrewd speculators looked confidently to the income from the rent of the seats as a return for their investment, his original impression would certainly not be weakened. But the conclusion would be irresistible, if he were told still farther, that, in order to secure a good attendance of the rich and fashionable, the owners of the stock had taken the prudent precaution to engage, at a high salary, some popular and eminent preacher! Those who have watched closely the signs of the times, will admit that this is not a mere fancy sketch, and that it is not even exaggerated.

5. Alas! alas! for the utilitarianism, or rather materialism, of our boasted age of enlightenment! In such a condition of things, can we wonder at the general prevalence of religious indifference, and of unblushing infidelity? As in the days of

Horace, our children are taught to calculate, but not to pray. They learn arithmetic, but not religion.

6. The mischievous maxim, that children must grow up without any distinctive religious impressions, and then, when they have attained the age of discretion, must choose a religion for themselves, is frightfully prevalent amongst us. This maxim is about as wise as would be that of the agriculturist who should resolve to permit his fields to lie neglected in the spring season, and to become overgrown with weeds and briers, under the pretext that, when summer would come, it would be time enough to scatter over them the good seed! It amounts to this: human nature is corrupt and downward in its tendency; let it fester in its corruption, and become confirmed in its rottenness; and then it will be time enough to apply the remedy, or, rather, human nature will then react and heal itself.   Mt. Rev. Abp. Spalding.

22. GRACE DARLING.

IT was in the Fall of 1838, during a terrific storm, that a noble British steamer was wrecked upon the dangerous reefs of Longstone Island, and all night long a portion of the crew clung to the shattered vessel, with fearful waves dashing over them. Rocks and dangerous islets lay between them and the nearest shore, and around these a sea was raging, through which it did not seem possible any boat could pass. The Longstone lighthouse was a mile distant. At daybreak the keeper saw the terrible state of the shipwrecked, but feared to expose himself to certain destruction by going to their aid, until the earnest entreaties of his young daughter, Grace, determined him to make the attempt, and nine persons were rescued by the aid of an old man and a young woman.

2. This heroic deed shot a thrill of sympathy and admiration throughout all Europe. The lonely lighthouse became

the centre of attraction to thousands of travellers; but Grace, preserving her natural modesty and simplicity, pursued her former quiet domestic duties as quietly as if nothing had happened. She had many advantageous offers of marriage, but declined them all, saying she would not leave her parents while they lived. But God did not leave her to them three years after the event which identified her name with courage and heroism of the highest order: she died of consumption.

ALL night the storm had raged, nor ceased, nor paused,
When, as day broke, the maid, through misty air,
Espies far off a wreck, amid the surf,
Beating on one of those disastrous isles—
Half of a wreck; half—no more; the rest
Had vanished, swallowed up with all that there
Had for the common safety striven in vain,
Or thither thronged for refuge. With quick glance,
Daughter and sire through optic glass discern
Clinging about the remnant of this ship
Creatures, how precious in the maiden's sight,
For whom, belike, the old man grieves still more
Than for their fellow-sufferers, engulfed
Where every parting agony is hushed,
And hope and fear mix not in open strife.

2. "But courage, father! let us out to sea—
A few may yet be saved." The daughter's words,
Her earnest tone and look beaming with faith,
Dispels the father's doubts:
* * * * *
Together they put forth, father and child!
Each grasps an oar, and struggling on they go—
Rivals in effort; and a like intent
Here to elude and there surmount, they watch
The billows lengthening, mutually crossed
And shattered, and regathering their might

As if the tumult, by the Almighty's will,
Were in the conscious sea roused and prolonged,
That woman's fortitude—so tried, so proved—
May brighten more and more!

8.   True to the mark,
They stem the current of that perilous gorge,
Their arms still strengthening with the strengthening heart,
Though danger, as the wreck is neared, becomes
More imminent. Not unseen do they approach;
And rapture with varieties of fear
Incessantly conflicting, thrills the frames
Of those who, in that dauntless energy,
Foretaste deliverance; but the least perturbed
Can scarcely trust his eyes, when he perceives
That of the pair—tossed on the waves to bring
Hope to the hopeless, to the dying life—
One is a woman, a poor earthly sister;
Or, be the visitant other than she seems,
A guardian spirit, sent from pitying Heaven,
In woman's shape.

4.   But why prolong the tale,
Casting meek words amid a host of thoughts
Armed to repel them? Every hazard faced,
And difficulty mastered, with resolve
That no one breathing should be left to perish,
This last remainder of the crew are all
Placed in the little boat, then o'er the deep
Are safely borne, landed upon the beach,
And in fulfilment of God's mercy, lodged
Within the sheltering lighthouse.

5.   Shout, ye waves,
Send forth a song of triumph. Waves and winds
Exult in this deliverance wrought through faith

In Him whose providence your rage hath served!
Ye screaming sea-mews, in the concert join!
And would that some immortal voice—a voice
Fully attuned to all that gratitude
Breathes out from floor or couch, through pallid lips
Of the survivors—to the clouds might beat—
Blended with praise of that parental love,
Beneath whose watchful eye the maiden grew
Pious and pure; modest, and yet so brave;
Though young, so wise; though weak, so resolute—
Might carry to the clouds and to the stars,
Yea, to celestial choirs, Grace Darling's name!
WORDSWORTH.

28. THE CHURCH.

THERE is not, and there never was, on this earth, a work of human policy so well deserving of examination as the Roman Catholic Church. The history of that Church joins together the two great ages of human civilization. No other institution is left standing which carries the mind back to the times when the smoke of sacrifice rose from the Pantheon, and when camelopards and tigers bounded in the Slavian amphitheatre.

2. The proudest royal houses are but of yesterday when compared with the line of the Supreme Pontiffs. That line we trace back in an unbroken series from the Pope who crowned Napoleon, in the nineteenth century, to the Pope who crowned Pepin in the eighth; and far beyond the time of Pepin the august dynasty extends, till it is lost in the twilight of fable. The republic of Venice came next in antiquity. But the republic of Venice was modern when compared with the Papacy; and the republic of Venice is gone, and the Papacy remains. The Papacy remains not in decay, not a mere antique, but full of life and youthful vigor.

3. The Catholic Church is still sending forth to the farther

ends of the world missionaries as zealous as those who landed in Kent with Augustin; and still confronting hostile kings with the same spirit with which she confronted Attila. The number of her children is greater than in any former age. Her acquisitions in the New World have more than compensated her for what she has lost in the Old. Her spiritual ascendency extends over the vast countries which lie between the plains of Missouri and Cape Horn; countries which, a century hence, may not improbably contain a population as large as that which now inhabits Europe.

4. The members of her community are certainly not fewer than one hundred and fifty millions; and it will be difficult to show that all the other Christian sects united amount to a hundred and twenty millions. Nor do we see any sign which indicates that the term of her long dominion is approaching.

5. She saw the commencement of all the governments and of all the ecclesiastical establishments that now exist in the world; and we feel no assurance that she is not destined to see the end of them all. She was great and respected before the Saxon had set foot on Britain—before the Frank had passed the Rhine—when Grecian eloquence still flourished at Antioch—when idols were still worshipped in the temple of Mecca. And she may still exist in undiminished vigor when some traveller from New Zealand shall, in the midst of a vast solitude, take his stand on a broken arch of London Bridge to sketch the ruins of St. Paul's. MACAULAY.

---

24. THE CHURCH—(CONTINUED.)

IS it not strange that in the year 1799 even sagacious observers should have thought that at length the hour of the Church of Rome had come? An infidel power ascendant—the Pope dying in captivity—the most illustrious prelates of France living in a foreign country on Protestant alms—the noblest edifices which the munificence of former ages had consecrated to the worship of God turned into temples of victory, or into banqueting-houses for political socities, or into Theophilanthropic chapels—such signs might well be supposed to indicate the approaching end of that long domination.

2. But the end was not yet. Again doomed to death, the milk-white hind was fated not to die. Even before the funeral rites had been performed over the ashes of Pius the Sixth, a great reaction had commenced, which, after the lapse of more than forty years, appears to be still in progress. Anarchy had its day. A new order of things rose out of confusion—new dynasties, new laws, new titles; and amidst them emerged the ancient religion. The Arabs had a fable that the great pyramid was built by the antediluvian kings, and alone of all the works of men, bore the weight of the flood.

3. Such was the fall of the Papacy. It had been buried under the great inundation, but its deep foundations had remained unshaken; and when the waters abated, it appeared alone amidst the ruins of a world which had passed away. The republic of Holland was gone, and the empire of Germany, and the Great Council of Venice, and the old Helvetian League, and the House of Bourbon, and the Parliaments and aristocracy of France.

4. Europe was full of young creations—a French empire, a kingdom of Italy, a Confederation of the Rhine. Nor had the late events affected only the territorial limits and political institutions. The distribution of property, the composition and spirit of society, had, through great part of Catholic Europe, undergone a complete change. But the unchangeable Church was still there. MACAULAY.

25. THE CRUSADERS APPROACH JERUSALEM.

THE purple morning left her crimson bed,
   And donned her robes of pure vermilion hue;
Her amber locks she crowned with roses red,
   In Eden's flowery gardens gathered new;

When through the camp a murmur shrill was spread,
　"Arm! arm!" they cried: "Arm! arm!" the trumpets blew;
Their merry noise prevents the joyful blast.
　So hum small bees before their swarms they cast.

2. Their Captain rules their courage, guides their heat;
　Their forwardness he stays with gentle rein;
And yet more easy, haply, were the feat,
　To stop the current near Charybdis' main,
Or calm the blustering winds on mountains great,
　Than fierce desires of warlike hearts restrain:
He rules them yet, and ranks them in their haste,
　For well he knows disordered speed makes waste.

3. Feathered their thoughts, their feet in wings were dight;
　Swiftly they marched, yet were not tired thereby,
For willing minds make heaviest burdens light:
　But when the gliding sun was mounted high,
Jerusalem, behold! appeared in sight:
　Jerusalem they view, they see, they spy.
Jerusalem with merry noise they greet,
　With joyful shouts and acclamations sweet.

4. As when a troop of jolly sailors row
　Some new-found land and country to descry;
Through dangerous seas, and under stars unknown,
　Thrall to the faithless waves and trothless sky;
If once the wishéd shore begin to show,
　They all salute it with a joyful cry,
And each to other show the land in haste,
　Forgetting quite their pains and perils past.

5. To that delight which their first sight did breed,
　That pleaséd so the secret of their thought,
A deep repentance did forthwith succeed,
　That reverend feet and trembling with it brought,

Scantily they durst their feeble eyes dispread
  Upon that town where Christ was sold and bought,
Where for our sins He, faultless, suffered pain,
  There where He died, and where He lived again.

6. Soft words, low speech, deep sobs, sweet sighs, salt tears,
  Rose from their breasts with joy and pleasure mixed;
For thus fears he, the Lord aright that fears;
  Fear on devotion, joy on faith is fixt;
Such noise their passion makes, as when one hears
  The hoarse sea-waves roar, hollow rocks betwixt;
Or, as the winds in hoults and shady greaves
  A murmur makes among the boughs and leaves.

7. Their naked feet trod on the dusty way,
  Following th' ensample of their zealous guide;
Their scarfs, their crests, their plumes, and feathers gay,
  They quickly doft, and willing laid aside;
Their molten hearts their wonted pride allay
  Along their watery cheeks warm tears down slide,
And then such secret speech as this they used,
  While to himself each one himself accused:

8. "Flower of goodness, Root of lasting bliss,
  Thou Well of life, whose streams were purple blood,
That flowéd here, to cleanse the foul amiss
  Of sinful man, behold this brinish flood,
That from my melting heart distilléd is;
  Receive in gree these tears, O Lord, so good,
For never wretch with sin so over-gone,
  Had fitter time, or greater cause to moan."

TASSO.

26. THE SULIOTE MOTHER.

SHE stood upon the loftiest peak,
   Amidst the clear blue sky:
A bitter smile was on her cheek,
   And a dark flash in her eye.

2 "Dost thou see them, boy?—through the dusky pines,
Dost thou see where the foeman's armor shines?
Hast thou caught the gleam on the conqueror's crest?
My babe, that I cradled on my breast!
Wouldst thou spring from thy mother's arms with joy
That sight hath cost thee a father, boy!"

3.   For in the rocky strait beneath
      Lay Suliote, sire and son;
    They had heapéd high the piles of death,
      Before the pass was won.

4. "They have crossed the torrent, and on they come!
Woe for the mountain hearth and home!
There, where the hunter laid by his spear,
There, where the lyre hath been sweet to hear,
There, where I sang thee, fair babe, to sleep,
Naught but the blood-stain our trace shall keep!"

5.   And now the horn's loud blast was heard,
      And now the cymbal's clang,
    Till even the upper air was stirred,
      As cliff and hollow rang.

6. "Hark! they bring music, my joyous child!
What saith the trumpet to Suli's wild?
Doth it light thine eye with so quick a fire,
As if at a glace of thine arméd sire?
Still! be thou still! there are brave men low,—
Thou wouldst not smile couldst thou see him now!"

7.   But nearer came the clash of steel,
          And louder swelled the horn,
          And farther yet the tambour's peal
             Through the dark pass was borne.

8. "Hear'st thou the sound of their savage mirth?—
    Boy, thou wert free when I gave thee birth,—
    Free, and how cherished my warrior's son!
    He, too, hath blessed thee, as I have done!
    Aye, and unchain'd must his loved ones be—
    Freedom, young Suliote, for thee and me!"

9.   And from the arrowy peak she sprung,
          And fast the fair child bore:
          A vail upon the wind was flung,
             A cry, and all was o'er!   MRS. HEMANS.

---

27. THE END OF THE LONG PARLIAMENT.

AT this eventful moment, big with the most important consequences both to himself and his country, whatever were the workings of Cromwell's mind, he had the art to conceal them from the eyes of the beholders. Leaving the military in the lobby, he entered the Parliament House, and composedly seated himself on one of the outer benches. His dress was a plain suit of black cloth, with gray worsted stockings. For a while he seemed to listen with interest to the debate; but when the speaker was going to put the question, he whispered to Harrison, "This is the time; I must do it;" and, rising, put off his hat to address the house.

2. At first his language was decorous and even laudatory. Gradually he became more warm and animated. At last he assumed all the vehemence of passion, and indulged in personal vituperation. He charged the members with self-seeking

and profaneness, with the frequent denial of justice, and numerous acts of oppression; with idolizing the lawyers, the constant advocates of tyranny; with neglecting the men who had bled for them in the field, that they might gain the Presbyterians, who had apostatized from the cause; and with doing all this in order to perpetuate their own power, and to replenish their own purses. But their time was come; the Lord had disowned them; He had chosen more worthy instruments to perform His work.

3. Here the orator was interrupted by Sir Peter Wentworth, who declared that he had never heard language so unparliamentary,—language, too, the more offensive, because it was addressed to them by their own servant, whom they had made what he was. At these words, Cromwell put on his hat, and, springing from his place, exclaimed, "Come, come, sir, I will put an end to your prating!" For a few seconds, apparently in the most violent agitation, he paced forward and backward, and then stamping on the floor, added, "You are no Parliament! I say you are no Parliament! Bring them in, bring them in!" Instantly the door opened, and Colonel Worsley entered, followed by more than twenty musketeers.

4. "This," cried Sir Henry Vane, "is not honest; it is against morality and common honesty."—"Sir Henry Vane," replied Cromwell; "O, Sir Henry Vane! The Lord deliver me from Sir Henry Vane! He might have prevented this. But he is a juggler, and has not common honesty himself!" From Vane he directed his discourse to Whitelock, on whom he poured a torrent of abuse; then pointing to Chaloner, "There," he cried, "sits a drunkard;" and afterwards selecting different members in succession, he described them as dishonest and corrupt livers, a shame and scandal to the profession of the Gospel. Suddenly, however, checking himself, he turned to the guard, and ordered them to clear the house. At these words, Colonel Harrison took the Speaker by the hand, and led him from the chair; Algernon Sydney was next compelled to quit his seat; and the other members, eighty in number, on

the approach of the military, rose and moved towards the door.

5. Cromwell now resumed his discourse. "It is you," he exclaimed, "that have forced me to do this. I have sought the Lord both day and night, that He would rather slay me than put me on the doing of this work." Alderman Allen took advantage of these words to observe that it was not yet too late to undo what had been done; but Cromwell instantly charged him with peculation, and gave him into custody. When all were gone, fixing his eye on the mace, "What," said he, "shall we do with this fool's bauble? Here, carry it away." Then taking the act of dissolution from the clerk, he ordered the doors to be locked, and, accompanied by the military, returned to Whitehall.

6. That afternoon the members of the Council assembled in their usual place of meeting. Bradshaw had just taken the chair, when the Lord-General entered, and told them that if they were there as private individuals, they were welcome; but if as the Council of State, they must know that the Parliament was dissolved, and with it also the Council. "Sir," replied Bradshaw, with the spirit of an ancient Roman, "we have heard what you did at the House this morning, and, before many hours, all England will know it. But, sir, you are mistaken to think that the Parliament is dissolved. No power under heaven can dissolve them but themselves; therefore take you notice of that."

7. After this protest they withdrew. Thus, by the parricidal hands of its own children, perished the Long Parliament, which, under a variety of forms, had, for more than twelve years, defended and invaded the liberties of the nation. It fell without a struggle or a groan, unpitied and unregretted. The members slunk away to their homes, where they sought by submission to purchase the forbearance of their new master; and their partisans—if partisans they had—reserved themselves in silence for a day of retribution, which came not before Cromwell slept in his grave. LINGARD.

28. AMERICAN LITERATURE.

WE cannot honor our country with too deep a reverence; we cannot love her with an affection too pure and fervent; we cannot serve her with an energy of purpose or a faithfulness of zeal too steadfast and ardent. And what is our country? It is not the East, with her hills and her valleys, with her countless sails, and the rocky ramparts of her shores. It is not the North, with her thousand villages, and her harvest-home, with her frontiers of the lake and the ocean. It is not the West, with her forest-sea and her inland isles, with her luxuriant expanses, clothed in the verdant corn, with her beautiful Ohio and her majestic Missouri. Nor is it yet the South, opulent in the mimic snow of the cotton, in the rich plantations of the rustling cane, and in the golden robes of the rice-field. What are these but the sister families of one greater, better, holier family—our country?

2. If, indeed, we desire to behold a literature like that which has sculptured, with such energy of expression, which has painted so faithfully and vividly the crimes, the vices, the follies of ancient and modern Europe; if we desire that our land should furnish for the orator and the novelist, for the painter and the poet, age after age, the wild and romantic scenery of war; the glittering march of armies, and the revelry of the camp; the shrieks and blasphemies, and all the horrors of the battle-field; the desolation of the harvest, and the burning cottage; the storm, the sack, and the ruin of cities; if we desire to unchain the furious passions of jealousy and selfishness, of hatred, revenge, and ambition, those lions that now sleep harmless in their den; if we desire that the lake, the river, the ocean, should blush with the blood of brothers; that the winds should waft from the land to the sea, from the sea to the land, the roar and the smoke of battle; that the very mountain-tops should become altars for the sacrifice of brothers;—if we desire that these, and such as these—the elements, to an incredible extent, of the literature of the Old

World—should be the elements of our literature, then, but then only, let us hurl from its pedestal the majestic statue of our Union, and scatter its fragments over all our land. But, if we covet for our country the noblest, purest, loveliest literature the world has ever seen, such a literature as shall honor God and bless mankind ; a literature whose smiles might play upon an angel's face, whose "tears would not stain an angel's cheek ;" then let us cling to the union of these States, with a patriot's love, with a scholar's enthusiasm, with a Christian's hope.

3. In her heavenly character, as a holocaust self-sacrificed to God ; at the height of her glory, as the ornament of a free, educated, peaceful, Christian people, American literature will find that the intellectual spirit is her very tree of life, and that union her garden of paradise. GRIMKE.

---

29. LEGEND OF ST. JODOCUS.

IN trial of his servant's truth,
  One day came begging, as a youth
Of humble mien, in garments poor,
The Lord, to St. Jodocus' door.

2. "Give to him," St. Jodocus said ;
"Open, good steward, thy store of bread."
"Here's but one loaf, my master, see,
Left for our dog, and thee, and me."

3. "Yet give to him," the abbot cried,
"For us the Lord will still provide."
The sullen butler said no more,
But cut the loaf in pieces four.

4. "One for the abbot, one for me,
One for our dog, and one for thee,"

Unkindly to the youth he said,
And handed him his share of bread.

5. Again, in semblance yet more poor,
The Lord came to our abbot's door;
"Give, still," the good Jodocus said,
" Give him my little share of bread;
For us the good God still will care."
And now he gives the abbot's share.

6. A hungered came the Lord again,
Nor asked he the third time in vain;
"Give now, O steward, thy little bit—
God will provide."—He yielded it.

7. More destitute and blind and lame,
The Lord yet for the fourth time came;
"Give," said Jodocus, "give again;
Doth not the dog's piece still remain?
For He who doth the ravens feed
Will not forget us in our need."

8. The steward gives, the beggar goes;
Then through the air a clear voice rose:
"Thou true disciple of thy Lord,
Great is thy faith,—take thy reward;
As thou believedst it should be,
So shall it happen unto thee."

9. The steward went to the open door—
Lo! onward towards the nearest shore
Four heavy-laden ships are borne,
With bread and fruit and wine and corn.

10. He to the strand runs joyfully,
And there no sailor can he see;

But to the shore a white wave rolled,
On which these words were traced in gold:

11. "Four ships are sent with large supply,
By Him who hears the raven's cry;
He sends them to the abbot good,
Who, this day, four times gave Him food.

12. "One, for the good man's self is sent;
Another for his dog is meant;
One for the steward is coming in;
One for the Sender's needy kin."

TRANSLATED FROM THE GERMAN.

80. THE POOR EXILE.

[There are few pages in any language of deeper feeling or more touching pathos than this exquisite episode from the French. To appreciate it fully, it should be read in the original.]

MAY Heaven guide the poor exile! He goes wandering over the earth.

2. I have passed through various countries; their inhabitants have seen me, and I have seen them, but we have not known each other. The exile is everywhere alone! When, at the close of day, I saw the smoke of some cottage rise from the bosom of a valley, I said, "Happy is he who returns at evening to his fireside, and seats himself among those he loves!" The exile is everywhere alone!

3. Whence come these clouds driven by the storm? It drives me along like them. But what matters it? The exile is everywhere alone! These trees are noble, these flowers are beautiful; but they are not the flowers nor trees of my country; to me they say nothing. The exile is everywhere alone! This stream flows gently over the meadow, but its murmur is not that which my childhood heard. To me it recalls no remembrances. The exile is everywhere alone!

4. These songs are sweet; but the sorrows and the joys which they awake are not my sorrows nor my joys. The exile is everywhere alone! I have been asked, Why weepest thou? but when I have told my tale, no one wept: for no one understood me. The exile is everywhere alone! I have seen old men surrounded by children, as the olive by its branches; but none of those old men called me his son; none of those children called me his brother. The exile is everywhere alone!

5. I have seen young girls smile, with a smile as pure as the dawn, on him they had chosen for a husband; but not one smiled on me. The exile is everywhere alone! I have seen young men heart to heart embrace each other as if they held in common but one existence; but not one pressed my hand. The exile is everywhere alone! There are friends, wives, fathers, brothers, only in one's own country. The exile is everywhere alone!

6. Poor exile! cease to lament. Every one is banished like thyself; every one beholds father, mother, wife, friend, pass away and vanish. Our country is not here below; man seeks for it here in vain; that which he mistakes for it is only a resting-place for a night.

7. Heaven guide the poor exile. He goes wandering over the earth. LAMENNAIS.

---

81. A CHRISTMAS HYMN.

IT was the calm and silent night!—
   Seven hundred years and fifty-three
Had Rome been growing up to might,
   And now was queen of land and sea!
No sound was heard of clashing wars,
   Peace brooded o'er the hushed domain;
Apollo, Pallas, Jove and Mars
   Held undisturbed their ancient reign,
     In the solemn midnight,
        Centuries ago!

2. 'Twas in the calm and silent night!
   The senator of haughty Rome
Impatient urged his chariot's flight,
   From lordly revel rolling home.
Triumphal arches, gleaming, swell
   His breast with thoughts of boundless sway;
What recked the Roman what befell
   A paltry province far away,
      In the solemn midnight,
         Centuries ago?

3. Within that province far away
   Went plodding home a weary boor;
A streak of light before him lay,
   Fallen through a half-shut stable door
Across his path. He paused, for naught
   Told what was going on within;
How keen the stars, his only thought;
   The air how calm, and cold, and thin,
      In the solemn midnight,
         Centuries ago!

4. O, strange indifference!—low and high
   Drowsed over common joys and cares;
The earth was still, but knew not why;
   The world was listening—unawares!
How calm a moment may precede
   One that shall thrill the world forever!
To that still moment none would heed,
   Man's doom was linked, no more to sever,
      In the solemn midnight,
         Centuries ago!

5. It is the calm and solemn night!
   A thousand bells ring out, and throw
Their joyous peals abroad, and smite
   The darkness, charmed and holy now!

> The night that erst no shame had worn,
>   To it a happy name is given;
> For in that stable lay, new-born,
>   The peaceful Prince of earth and heaven,
>   In the solemn midnight,
>   Centuries ago!
>
> DOMNIE.

---

82. BARON GERAMB.

THOSE whose memory does not carry back beyond the days of Waterloo may have found, in Moore's politico-satirical poems, mention of a person enjoying a celebrity similar to that possessed more lately by a French count resident in London, as a leader of fashion, remarkable at the same time for wit and accomplishments. Such was the Baron Geramb, in the days when George the Third was king. But some may possibly remember a higher renown gained by him beyond that of having his last *bon-mot* quoted in the morning papers.

2. Being an alien, though neither a conspirator nor an assassin, he was ordered to leave the country, and refused. He barricaded his house, and placarded it with the words, "Every Englishman's house is his castle," in huge letters. He bravely stood a siege of some duration against the police of those days, and crowds around the house; till at length, whether starved out by a stern blockade, or overreached by Bow Street strategy, he either yielded at discretion, or was captured through want of it, and was forthwith transferred to a foreign shore.

3. So ends the first chapter of the public life of the gallant and elegant Baron Geramb, the charm of good society, to which by every title he belonged. What became of him after this? Did that society, on losing sight of him, ask any more? Probably few of those who had been entertained by his cleverness, or amused by his freaks, ever gave him another thought; and a commentator on Thomas Moore encountering the "whiskers of Geramb" in one of his verses, might be at a

loss to trace the history of their wearer. Certainly those ornaments of his countenance would have lent but slight assistance in tracing him in after-life.

4. Many years later, in the reign of Gregory the Sixteenth, let the reader suppose himself to be standing on the small plateau shaded by the ile which fronts the Franciscan convent above Castle Gandolfo. He is looking down on the lovely lake which takes its name from that, through an opening in the oaken screen, enjoying the breeze of an autumn afternoon. He may see issuing from the convent-gate a monk not of his fraternity, but clothed in the white Cistercian habit; a man of portly dimensions, bestriding the humblest but most patriarchal of man-bearing animals selected of hundreds, his rider used to say, to be in just proportion to the burden.

5. If the stranger examines him, he will easily discern, through the gravity of his look, not only a nobleness of countenance, and through the simplicity of his habit, not merely a gracefulness of demeanor which speaks the highly-bred gentleman, but even visible remains of the good-humored, kind-hearted, and soldierly courtier. There lurks in his eye a sparkling gleam of wit suppressed, or disciplined into harmless coruscations. Once, when I met him at Albano, he had brought as a gift to the English Cardinal Acton a spirited sketch of himself and his "Gallant Gray" rolling together in the dust.

6. When I called on him at his convent he showed me an imperial autograph letter, just received, announcing to him the gallantry and wounds of his son, fighting in Circassia, and several other royal epistles written in the pleasant tone of friend to friend. Yet he is thoroughly a monk of the strictest order known in the Church, living in a cell without an object of luxury near him, sleeping on a straw bed, occupied in writing, reading, meditating on holy things, devout in prayer, edifying in conversation. Among other works of his overflowing with piety is one peculiarly tender, "My Saviour's Tomb."

7. The good old monk had been to Jerusalem, and had manifested his affections by a novel and exquisite prodigality, borrowed in idea from a certain woman who had been a sinner in the city. He anointed the sepulchre of our Lord with the most costly of perfumes, the attargul, or otto of roses, as we call it, so that the whole house was filled with its fragrance. Such is the Père Geramb; such the second chapter of his known life. What had been the intermediate hidden stage?

8. When expelled, happily for him, from England, he very soon fell into the enemy's hands, I know not how. But he happened to be cast into the same prison, I think Vincennes, where the good Cardinal de Gregorio was also in bonds. He was first struck by the patience and virtues of his fellow-captive, and gradually entered into conversation with him. The result was a change of heart and a change of life. Liberty soon put the sincerity of both to the severest test. Baron Geramb remained attached to the land of his captivity: in it he joined the fervent and austere life of La Trappe. After some years he was sent to Rome as resident procurator of the order, where I had the pleasure of knowing him. Several amusing anecdotes mingle with his memory, to show how even in his sackcloth and ashes lived his wonted fire. CARDINAL WISEMAN.

---

83. THE ANGELS OF BUENA VISTA.

I.

SPEAK and tell us, our Ximena, looking northward far away,
O'er the camp of the invaders, o'er the Mexican array,
Who is losing? who is winning? are they far or come they near?
Look abroad, and tell us, sister, whither rolls the storm we hear.

II.

"Down the hills of Angostura still the storm of battle rolls;
Blood is flowing, men are dying; God have mercy on their souls!"

Who is losing? who is winning?—"Over hill and over plain,
I see but smoke of cannon clouding through the mountain rain."

III.

Holy Mother! keep our brothers! Look, Ximena, look once more:
'Still I see the fearful whirlwind rolling darkly as before,
Bearing on, in strange confusion, friend and foeman, foot and horse,
Like some wild and troubled torrent sweeping down its mountain course."

IV.

Look forth once more, Ximena! "Ah! the smoke has rolled away;
And I see the Northern rifles gleaming down the ranks of gray.
Hark! that sudden blast of bugles! there the troop of Minon wheels;
There the Northern horses thunder, with the cannon at their heels.

V.

"Jesu, pity! how it thickens! now retreat and now advance!
Right against the blazing cannon shivers Puebla's charging lance!
Down they go, the brave young riders; horse and foot together fall;
Like a ploughshare in the fallow, through them ploughs the Northern ball."

VI.

Nearer came the storm and nearer, rolling fast and frightful on:
Speak, Ximena, speak and tell us, who has lost and who has won?
"Alas! alas! I know not; friend and foe together fall;
O'er the dying rush the living: pray, my sisters, for them all!"

VII.

"Lo! the wind the smoke is lifting: Blessed Mother, save my
    brain!
I can see the wounded crawling slowly out from heaps of slain:
Now they stagger, blind and bleeding; now they fall, and
    strive to rise;
Hasten, sisters, haste and save them, lest they die before our
    eyes!

VIII.

"Oh, my heart's love! oh, my dear one! lay thy poor head on
    my knee;
Dost thou know the lips that kiss thee? Canst thou hear me?
    canst thou see me?
Oh, my husband, brave and gentle! Oh, my Bernal, look once
    more
On the blessèd cross before thee! Mercy! mercy! all is o'er!"

IX.

Dry thy tears, my poor Ximena; lay thy dear one down to rest;
Let his hands be meekly folded, lay the cross upon his breast;
Let his dirge be sung hereafter, and his funeral Masses said;
To-day, thou poor bereaved one, the living ask thy aid.

X.

Close beside her, faintly moaning, fair and young, a soldier lay,
Torn with shot and pierced with lances, bleeding slow his life
    away;
But, as tenderly before him, the lorn Ximena knelt,
She saw the Northern eagle shining on his pistol-belt.

XI.

With a stifled cry of horror straight she turned away her head
With a sad and bitter feeling looked she back upon her dead;
But she heard the youth's low moaning, and his struggling
    breath of pain,
And she raised the cooling water to his parching lips again.

XII.

Whispered low the dying soldier, pressed her hand and faintly smiled:
Was that pitying face his mother's? did she watch beside her child?
All his stranger words with meaning her woman's heart supplied;
With her kiss upon his forehead, "Mother!" murmured he, and died!

XIII.

"A bitter curse upon them, poor boy, who led thee forth,
From some gentle sad-eyed mother, weeping lonely in the North!"
Spake the mournful Mexic woman as she laid him with her dead,
And turned to soothe the living, and bind the wounds which bled.

XIV.

Look forth once more, Ximena! "Like a cloud before the wind
Rolls the battle down the mountain, leaving blood and death behind;
Ah! they plead in vain for mercy; in the dust the wounded strive;
Hide your faces, holy angels! Oh, thou Christ of God, forgive!"

XV.

Sink, oh night, among thy mountains! let the cool, gray shadows fall;
Dying brothers, fighting demons, drop thy curtain over all!
Through the thickening winter twilight wide apart the battle rolled;
In its sheath the sabre rested, and the cannon's lips grew cold.

XVI.

But the noble Mexic women still their holy task pursued,
Through that long, dark night of sorrow, worn faint and lacking food:
Over weak and suffering brothers with a tender care they hung,
And the dying foeman blessed them in a strange and Northern tongue.

XVII.

Not wholly lost, oh Father! is this evil world of ours;
Upward, through its blood and ashes, spring afresh the Eden flowers;
From its smoking hell of battle, Love and Pity send their prayer,
And still thy white-winged angels hover dimly in our air!

WHITTIER.

---

84. THE POSSESSION OF JUBA.

[This chapter from Callista has been considered by able critics not to be surpassed in its way by any thing in the English language. Among the writers of pure kingly English, Dr. Newman stands unrivalled. We prefer giving the entire description in three lessons, rather than to take extracts, which would destroy the effect of the piece.]

"WELL, my precious boy," said the old woman, "the choicest gifts of great Cham be your portion! You had excellent sport yesterday, I'll warrant. The rats squeaked, eh? and you beat the life out of them. That scoundrel sacristan, I suppose, has taken up his quarters below." "You may say it," answered Juba. "The reptile! he turned righ about, and would have made himself an honest fellow, when it couldn't be helped." "Good, good!" returned Gurta, as if she had got something very pleasant in her mouth: "Ah! that is good! but he did not escape on that score, I do trust."

2. "They pulled him to pieces all the more cheerfully," said Juba. "Pulled him to pieces, limb by limb, joint by joint, eh?"

answered Gurta. "Did they skin him?—did they do any thing to his eyes, or his tongue? Any how, it was too quickly, Juba. Slowly, leisurely, gradually. Yes, it's like a glutton to be quick about it. Taste him, handle him, play with him,—that's luxury! but to bolt him,—faugh!"

3. "Cæso's slave made a good end," said Juba: "he stood up for his views, and died like a man." "The gods smite him! but he has gone up,—up;" and she laughed. "Up to what they call bliss and glory;—such glory! but he's out of their domain, you know. But he did not die easy?" "The boys worried him a good deal," answered Juba: "but it's not quite in my line, mother, all this. I think you drink a pint of blood morning and evening, and thrive on it, old woman. It makes you merry; but it's too much for my stomach."

4. "Ha, ha, my boy!" cried Gurta; "you'll improve in time, though you make wry faces, now that you're young. Well, and have you brought me any news from the capitol? Is any one getting a rise in the world, or a downfall? How blows the wind? Are there changes in the camp? This Decius, I suspect, will not last long." "They all seem desperately frightened," said Juba, "lest they should not smite your friends hard enough, Gurta. Root and branch is the word. They'll have to make a few Christians for the occasion, in order to kill them: and I almost think they're about it," he added, thoughtfully. "They have to show that they are not surpassed by the rabble. 'Tis a pity Christians are so few, isn't it, mother?"

5. "Yes, yes," she said; "but we must crush them, grind them, many or few; and we shall, we shall! Callista's to come." "I don't see they are worse than other people," said Juba; "not at all, except that they are commonly sneaks. If Callista turns, why should not I turn too, mother, to keep her company, and keep your hand in?"

6. "No, no, my boy," returned the witch, "you must serve my master. You are having your fling just now, but you will buckle to in good time. You must one day take some work

with my merry men. Come here, child," said the fond mother, "and let me kiss you."

7. "Keep your kisses for your monkeys, and goats, and cats," answered Juba: "they're not to my taste, old dame. Master! my master! I won't have a master! I'll be nobody's servant. I'll never stand to be hired, nor cringe to a bully, nor quake before a rod. Please yourself, Gurta; I'm a free man. You're my mother by courtesy only."

8. Gurta looked at him savagely. "Why, you're not going to be pious and virtuous, Juba? A choice saint you'll make! You shall be drawn for a picture." "Why shouldn't I, if I choose?" said Juba. "If I must take service, willy, nilly, I'd any day prefer the others to that of your friend. I've not left the master to take the man." "Blaspheme not the great gods," she answered, "or they'll do you a mischief yet." "I say again," insisted Juba, "if I must lick the earth, it shall not be where your friend has trod. It shall be in my brother's fashion, rather than in yours, Gurta."

9. "Agellius!" she shrieked out with such disgust, that it is wonderful she uttered the name at all. "Ah! you have not told me about him, boy. Well, is he safe in the pit, or in the stomach of an hyena?" "He's alive," said Juba; "but he has not got it in him to be a Christian. Yes, he's safe with his uncle."

10. "Ah! Jucundus must ruin him, debauch him, and then we must make away with him. We must not be in a hurry," said Gurta, "it must be body and soul." "No one shall touch him, craven as he is," answered Juba. "I despise him, but let him alone." "Don't come across me," said Gurta, sullenly "I'll have my way. Why, you know I could smite you to the dust, as well as him, if I chose."

11. "But you have not asked me about Callista," answered Juba. "It is really a capital joke, but she has got into prison for certain, for being a Christian. Fancy it! they caught her in the streets, and put her in the guard-house, and have had her up for examination. You see they want a Christian for

the nonce; it would not do to have none such in prison; so they will flourish with her till Decius bolts from the scene."

12. "The furies have her!" cried Gurta: "she is a Christian, my boy: I told you so, long ago." "Callista a Christian!" answered Juba; "ha! ha! She and Agellius are going to make a match of it, of some sort or other. They're thinking of other things than paradise." "She and the old priest, more likely, more likely," said Gurta. "He's in prison with her,— in the pit, as I trust." "Your master has cheated you for once, old woman," said Juba.

13. Gurta looked at him fiercely, and seemed waiting for his explanation. He began singing:

"She wheedled and coaxed, but he was no fool;
He'd be his own master, he'd not be her tool;
Not the little black moor should send him to school.

"She foamed and she cursed,—'twas the same thing to him;
She laid well her trap; but he carried his whim,—
The priest scuffled off, safe in life and in limb."

14. Gurta was almost suffocated with passion. "Cyprianus has not escaped, boy?" she asked at length. "I got him off," said Juba, undauntedly. A shade, as of Erebus, passed over the witche's face; but she remained quite silent. "Mother, I am my own master," he continued. "I must break your assumption of superiority. I'm not a boy, though you call me so. I'll have my own way. Yes, I saved Cyprianus. You're a blood-thirsty old hag! Yes, I've seen your secret doings. Did not I catch you the other day practising on that little child? You had nailed him up by hands and feet against the tree, and were cutting him to pieces at your leisure, as he quivered and shrieked the while. You were examining or using his liver for some of your black purposes. It's not in my line; but you gloated over it; and when he wailed, you wailed in mimicry. You were panting with pleasure."

15. Gurta was still silent, and had an expression on her face, awful from the intensity of its malignity. She had uttered a

low, piercing whistle. "Yes!" continued Juba, "you revelled in it. You chattered to the poor babe, when it screamed, as a nurse to an infant. You called it pretty names, and squeaked out your satisfaction each time you stuck it. You old hag! I'm not of your breed, though they say I am of your blood. I don't fear you," he said, observing the expression of her countenance; "I don't fear the immortal devil!" and he continued his song:

> "She beckoned the moon, and the moon came down;
> The green earth shrivelled beneath her frown;
> But a man's strong will can keep his own."

16. While he was talking and singing, her call had been answered from the hut. An animal of some wonderful species had crept out of it, and proceeded to creep and crawl, moeing and twisting as it went, along the trees and shrubs which rounded the grass-plot. When it came up to the old woman, it crouched at her feet, and then rose up upon its hind legs and begged. She took hold of the uncouth beast and began to fondle it in her arms, muttering something in its ear. At length, when Juba stopped for a moment in his song, she suddenly flung it right at him, with great force, saying, "Take that!" She then gave utterance to a low, inward laugh, and leaned herself back against the trunk of a tree under which she was sitting, with her knees drawn up almost to her chin.

NEWMAN.

---

85. THE POSSESSION OF JUBA—(CONTINUED).

THE blow seemed to act on Juba as a shock on his nervous system, both from its violence and its strangeness. He stood still for a moment, and then, without saying a word, he turned away, and walked slowly down the hill, as if in a maze. Then he sat down. . . . . .

2. In an instant up he started again with a great cry, and

began running at the top of his speed. He thought he heard a voice speaking in him; and, however fast he ran, the voice, or whatever it was, kept up with him. He rushed through the underwood, trampling and crushing it under his feet, and scaring the birds and small game which lodged there. At last, exhausted, he stood still for breath, when he heard it say loudly and deeply, as if speaking with his own organs, "You cannot escape from yourself!" Then a terror seized him; he fell down and fainted away.

3. When his senses returned, his first impression was of something in him not himself. He felt it in his breathing; he tasted it in his mouth. The brook which ran by Gurta's encampment had by this time become a streamlet, though still shallow. He plunged into it; a feeling came upon him as if he ought to drown himself, had it been deeper. He rolled about in it, in spite of its flinty and rocky bed. When he came out of it, his tunic sticking to him, he tore it off his shoulders, and let it hang round his girdle in shreds, as it might. The shock of the water, however, acted as a sedative upon him, and the coolness of the night refreshed him. He walked on for a while in silence.

4. Suddenly the power within him began uttering, by means of his organs of speech, the most fearful blasphemies; words embodying conceptions which, had they come into his mind, he might indeed have borne with patience before this, or uttered in bravado, but which now filled him with inexpressible loathing, and a terror to which he had hitherto been quite a stranger. He had always in his heart believed in a God, but he now believed with a reality and intensity utterly new to him. He felt it as if he saw Him; he felt there was a world of good and evil beings. He did not love the good, or hate the evil; but he shrank from the one, and he was terrified at the other; and he felt himself carried away, against his will, as the prey of some dreadful, mysterious power, which tyrannized over him.

5. The day had closed—the moon had risen. He plunged into

the thickest wood, and the trees seemed to him to make way for him. Still they seemed to moan and to creak as they moved out of their place. Soon he began to see that they were looking at him, and exulting over his misery. They, of an inferior nature, had had no gift to abuse and lose; and they remained in that honor and perfection in which they were created. Birds of the night flew out of them, reptiles slunk away; yet soon he began to be surrounded, wherever he went, by a circle of owls, bats, ravens, crows, snakes, wild-cats, and apes, which were always looking at him, but somehow made way, retreating before him, and yet forming again, and in order, as he marched along.

6. He had passed through the wing of the forest which he entered, and penetrated into the more mountainous country. He ascended the heights; he was a taller, stronger man than he had been; he went forward with a preternatural vigor, and flourished his arms with the excitement of some vinous or gaseous intoxication. He heard the roar of the wild beasts echoed along the woody ravines which were cut into the solid mountain rock, with a reckless feeling as if he could cope with them.

7. As he passed the dens of the lion, leopard, hyena, jackal, wild-boar, and wolf, there he saw them sitting at the entrance, or stopping suddenly as they prowled along, and eyeing him, but not daring to approach. He strode along from rock to rock, and over precipices, with the certainty and ease of some giant in Eastern fable. Suddenly a beast of prey came across him; in a moment he had torn up by the roots the stump of a wild vine-plant, which was near him, had thrown himself upon his foe before it could act on the aggressive, had flung it upon its back, forced the weapon into its mouth, and was stamping on its chest. He knocked the life out of the furious animal; and crying "Take that!" tore its flesh, and, applying his mouth to the wound, sucked a draught of its blood. NEWMAN.

26. THE POSSESSION OF JUBA—(Continued).

HE has passed over the mountain, and has descended its side. Bristling shrubs, swamps, precipitous banks, rushing torrents, are no obstacle to his course. He has reached the brow of a hill, with a deep placid river at the foot of it, just as the dawn begins to break. It is a lovely prospect, which every step he takes is becoming more definite and more various in the daylight. Masses of oliander, of great beauty, with their red blossoms, fringed the river and tracked out its course into the distance. The bank of the hill below him, and on the right and left, was a maze of fruit-trees, about which nature, if it were not the hand of man, had had no thought except that they should be altogether there.

2. The wild olive, the pomegranate, the citron, the date, the mulberry, the peach, the apple, and the walnut, formed a sort of spontaneous orchard. Across the water groves of palm-trees waved their long and graceful branches in the morning breeze. The stately and solemn ilex, marshalled into long avenues, showed the way to substantial granges or luxurious villas. The green turf or grass was spread out beneath, and here and there flocks and herds were emerging out of the twilight and growing distinct upon the eye.

3. Elsewhere the ground rose up into sudden eminences crowned with chestnut woods, or with plantations of cedar and acacia, or wildernesses of the cork-tree, the turpentine, the carooba, the white poplar, and the Phœnician juniper; while overhead ascended the clinging tendrils of the hop, and an underwood of myrtle clothed their stems and roots. A profusion of wild-flowers carpeted the ground far and near.

4. Juba stood and gazed till the sun rose opposite to him, envying, repining, hating, like Satan looking in upon Paradise. The wild mountains or the locust-smitten tract would have better suited the tumult of his mind. It would have been a relief to him to have retreated from so fair a scene, and to have retraced his steps; but he was not his own master, and was

hurried on. Sorely against his determined strong resolve and will, crying out and protesting and shuddering, the youth was forced along into the fulness of beauty and blessing with which he was so little in tune.

5. With rage and terror he recognized that he had no part in his own movements, but was a mere slave. In spite of himself he must go forward, and behold a peace and sweetness which witnessed against him. He dashed down through the thick grass, plunged into the water, and, without rest or respite, began a second course of aimless toil and travail through the day.

6. The savage dogs of the villages howled and fled from him as he passed by; beasts of burden, on their way to market, which he overtook or met, stood still, foamed and trembled; the bright birds, the blue jay and golden oriole, hid themselves under the leaves and grass; the storks, a religious and domestic bird, stopped their sharp clattering note from the high tree or farm-house turret, where they had placed their nests; the very reptiles skulked away from his shadow, as if it were poisonous. The boors who were at their labor in the fields suspended it to look at one whom the Furies were lashing and whirling on. Hour passed after hour, the sun attained its zenith, and then declined, but this dreadful compulsory race continued.

7. O, what would he have given for one five minutes of oblivion, of slumber, of relief from the burning thirst which now consumed him! But the master within him ruled his muscles and his joints, and the intense pain of weariness had no concomitant of prostration of strength. Suddenly he began to laugh hideously; and he went forward dancing and singing loud, and playing antics. He entered a hovel, made faces at the children, till one of them fell into convulsions, and he ran away with another; and, when some country people pursued him, he flung the child in their faces, saying, "Take that!" and said he was Pentheus, King of Thebes, of whom he had never heard, about to solemnize the orgies of Bacchus, and he

began to spout a chorus of Greek, a language he had never learnt or heard spoken.

8. Now it is evening again, and he has come up to a village grove, where the rustics were holding a feast in honor of Pan. The hideous brutal god, with yawning mouth, horned head, and goat's feet, was placed in a rude shed, and a slaughtered lamb, decked with flowers, lay at his feet. The peasants were frisking before him, boys and women, when they were startled by the sight of a gaunt, wild, mysterious figure, which began to dance too. He flung and capered about with such vigor that they ceased their sport to look on, half with awe and half as a diversion.

9. Suddenly he began to groan and to shriek, as if contending with himself, and willing and not willing some new act; and the struggle ended in his falling on his hands and knees, and crawling like a quadruped towards the idol. When he got near his attitude was still more servile; still groaning and shuddering, he laid himself flat on the ground, and wriggled to the idol as a worm, and lapped up with his tongue the mingled blood and dust which lay about the sacrifice. And then again, as if Nature had successfully asserted her own dignity, he jumped up high in the air, and, falling on the god, broke him to pieces, and scampered away out of pursuit, before the lookers-on recovered from the surprise.

NEWMAN.

---

87. WAITING FOR THE MAY.

[Denis Florence M'Carthy, an Irish barrister of an ancient family, and born about 1820, ranks among the best living poets and most elegant writers of Ireland. Besides "Ballads, Poems, and Lyrics," he has enriched English literature, with some of the noblest translations we possess, especially from Calderon. He is, we believe, a barrister, and is also Professor of Poetry in the Catholic University of Ireland.]

AH! my heart is weary waiting,
    Waiting for the May—
Waiting for the pleasant rambles,

Where the fragrant hawthorn brambles,
　　With the woodbine alternating,
　　　　Scent the dewy way.
Ah! my heart is weary waiting,
　　　　Waiting for the May.

2. Ah! my heart is sick with longing,
　　　　Longing for the May—
Longing to escape from study
To the fair young face and ruddy,
　　And the thousand charms belonging
　　　　To the summer's day.
　Ah! my heart is sick with longing,
　　　　Longing for the May.

3. Ah! my heart is sore with sighing,
　　　　Sighing for the May—
Sighing for their sure returning
When the summer-beams are burning,
　　Hopes and flowers that dead or dying
　　　　All the winter lay.
　Ah! my heart is sore with sighing,
　　　　Sighing for the May.

4. Ah! my heart is pained with throbbing,
　　　　Throbbing for the May—
Throbbing for the seaside billows,
Or the water-wooing willows,
　　Where in laughing and in sobbing
　　　　Glide the streams away.
　Ah! my heart is pained with throbbing,
　　　　Throbbing for the May.

5. Waiting, sad, dejected, weary,
　　　　Waiting for the May.
Spring goes by with wasted warnings—

> Moonlit evenings, sunbright mornings—
> Summer comes, yet dark and dreary
> Life still ebbs away—
> Man is ever weary, weary,
>   Waiting for the May!
>
> D. F. M'CARTHY.

---

88. ITALY.

AN era it is in the life of any man, when, for the first time, he crosses the Alps. A sympathy is touched and developed that shall vibrate and expand forever. Upon that soil we learn that Imagination and Sentiment are the Italian elements of our nature. All things seem ideal, poetic, visionary. Splendors that the northern world knows only by half—heavenly flashes that fade before they can be felt, here are natural and permanent. From the valleys and plains of Italy summer is never entirely withdrawn, and winter seems but a tardier spring.

2. Elsewhere we have glimpses of her life in conservatories, and when we enter the guarded retreats, where orange-trees, and olives, and myrtles are garnered up as creating around them a kind of sacred soul-life, we say, "This is like Italy." Its atmosphere is fragrance, its soil is beauty, its canopy a glory unimaginable. Its air is a prism to turn the common light into enchantment. What melodies of color—violet, rose, purple—roll along its steeps! Yet the true fascination of Italy is of the soul; and the features of the scene enjoy our devotion on account of the Spirit that looks out from them, and which they typify.

3. It is the clime of Art,—the temple of the sacraments of the material transfigured into the spiritual; of the perpetual marriage of the formal with the divine. Life, thought, passion, manners, all things, partake of an æsthetic quality. An ethereal stream of ideal sentiment seems to float over the

land and refract all perceptions, feelings, and objects into beautiful outlines and hues.

4. It is the land of Antiquity, the school of History, the home of the Past. No time is recorded when Italy stood not foremost in the annals; a scene where great things were thought and wrought. Etruscan, Roman, Pontifical,—these civilizations have succeeded one another, and no later one has effaced vestiges of that which preceded it. All now dwell together; and the face of the land is a self-registering chronicle of all that has been felt and done upon its surface. Here, under the calm, grave eye of the venerable Past, the Present moves modestly and with self-distrust.

5. Here you may stand in the religious presence of the Older Days, and imbibe a temper which is more than wisdom. The active, the stirring, the destructive we leave behind when we cross the mountains. Existence here is moral, consultative, intellectual. It seems like an Elysium, where life is fancied, and interests notional; the blissful future state of an existence gone by, where shadowy forms rehearse in silent show the deeds that once resounded, or elsewhere resound. It is a land where all is ruin; but where ruin itself is more splendid, more permanent, and more vital than the freshest perfections of other countries.   WALLACE.

---

89. THE TYRANT AND THE CAPTIVE.

IT was midnight when I listened,
   And I heard two Voices speak;
One was harsh, and stern, and cruel,
   And the other soft and weak:
Yet I saw no Vision enter,
   And I heard no steps depart,
Of this tyrant and his captive—
   Fate it might be and a *Heart*.

2. Thus the stern Voice spake in triumph:
"I have shut your life away
From the radiant world of nature,
And the perfumed light of day.
You, who loved to steep your spirit
In the charm of Earth's delight,
See no glory of the daytime,
And no sweetness of the night."

3. But the soft Voice answered calmly:
"Nay, for when the March winds bring
Just a whisper to my window,
I can dream the rest of Spring;
And to-day I saw a swallow
Flitting past my prison bars,
And my cell has just one corner
Whence at night I see the stars."

4. But its bitter taunt repeating,
Cried the harsh Voice: "Where are they,
All the friends of former hours,
Who forget your name to-day?
All the links of love are shattered,
Which you thought so strong before;
And your very heart is lonely,
And alone, since loved no more."

5. But the low Voice spoke still lower:
"Nay, I know the golden chain
Of my love is purer, stronger,
For the cruel fire of pain:
They remember me no longer,
But I, grieving here alone,
Bind their souls to me forever
By the love within my own."

6. But the Voice cried: "Once remember
  You devoted soul and mind
To the welfare of your brethren,
  And the service of your kind.
Now, what sorrow can you comfort?
  You, who lie in helpless pain,
With an impotent compassion
  Fretting out your life in vain."

7. "Nay;" and then the gentle answer
  Rose more loud, and full, and clear:
"For the sake of all my brethren,
  I thank God that I am here!
Poor had been my Life's best efforts,
  Now I waste no thought or breath—
For the prayer of those who suffer
  Has the strength of Love and Death."

ADELAIDE A. PROCTOR.

---

40. THE SUBMARINE TELEGRAPH.

HITHERTO there seems to have been above earth but little or no obstacle to the enterprise of man; and yet he has often been balked in his attempts to pass from one land to another. In his panting impatience to communicate with his fellow-man wherever he might be found, or in obedience to that supreme law which commands him to go forth and people the earth, he has endeavored to track his way to its remotest regions—he has dived into the darkest of its valleys, and there groped his way amidst the stones of the torrent, to create a path beyond the chains of mountains that seemed to shut him in.

2. He has climbed as high as it was possible for all his breathless vigor to bear him, until at length he has come to the snow-built pyramids on the summit of the mountain

or the impassable glacier; and then he has turned its flank, and with wonderful perseverance has made his way into the opposite region. But who ever thought till now of at once plunging into the very depths of the ocean, without the power of seeing a single step beyond him; almost beyond the power of the fathoming-line to reach, to a depth, as we have been told, as great as the height of the highest mountains explored but by a few individuals? And there he has ventured to trace his path, and has traced it without deviation, and without yielding to any, however formidable, obstacles.

3. He has made that path bury itself deep into the very undermost of the valleys of that unseen region; he has made it to ascend its steepest precipices—to cross its highest mountains—to pass down again; till thus by an effort of perseverance, the like of which the world has never witnessed, the two continents have been moored safe to one another—moored so safe by this little metallic hawser, as no other power, no amount of "inky blots and rotten parchment bonds," or protocols of treaties, could ever have done.

4. And what is the result of this mighty work? Why, the Greek used to boast of his fire, which would burn under the sea, and which, attached to the keel of a ship, would destroy it in the midst of the sea; and we know how the power of electricity has been similarly employed to explode mines high into the air and cause the sacrifice of hundreds of human lives.

5. But this little spark which we are now sending under the ocean—this flash of lightning which passes from shore to shore—this fire which burns inextinguishable below the depths of the mighty waters, may truly be considered, if it were not too sacred an expression to use—to be the flame of that love and of that charity between the two nations of which the sacred text says, that "many waters shall not extinguish it, and floods shall not overwhelm it." Yes; I have no hesitation in saying, that it is time now for the American eagle to let go those lightnings which it is represented as grasping in its

talons, and let them drop into the ocean, and they will cross it safely and come to us, not accompanied with any roar of thunder, but murmuring the words of softest peace.

CARDINAL WISEMAN.

---

41. THE HUMAN VOICE.

I GRIEVE to say it, but our people, I think, have not generally agreeable voices. The marrowy organisms, with skins that shed water like the backs of ducks, with smooth surfaces neatly padded beneath, and velvet linings to their singing-pipes, are not so common among us as that other pattern of humanity with angular outlines and plain surfaces, arid integuments, hair like the fibrous covering of a cocoanut in gloss and suppleness as well as color, and voices at once thin and strenuous,—acidulous enough to produce effervescence with alkalis, and stridulous enough to sing duets with the katydids.

2. I think our conversational soprano, as sometimes overheard in the cars, arising from a group of young persons, who may have taken the train at one of our great industrial centres, for instance,—young persons of the female sex, we will say, who have bustled in full-dressed, engaged in loud strident speech, and who, after free discussion, have fixed on two or more double seats, which having secured, they proceed to eat apples and hand round daguerreotypes,—I say, I think the conversational soprano, heard under these circumstances, would not be among the allurements the old enemy would put in requisition, were he getting up a new temptation of St. Anthony.

3. There are sweet voices among us, we all know, and voices not musical, it may be, to those who hear them for the first time, yet sweeter to us than any we shall hear until we listen to some warbling angel in the overture to that eternity of blissful harmonies we hope to enjoy. But why should I

tell lies? If my friends love me, it is because I try to tell the truth. I never heard but two voices in my life that frightened me by their sweetness. . . . They made me feel as if there might be constituted a creature with such a chord in her voice to some string in another's soul, that, if she but spoke, we would leave all and follow her, though it were into the jaws of Erebus.

4. Our only chance to keep our wits is, that there are so few natural chords between others' voices and this string in our souls, and that those which at first may have jarred a little, by-and-by come into harmony with it. But I tell you this is no fiction. You may call the story of Ulysses and the Sirens a fable, but what will you say to Mario and the poor lady who followed him?

5. Whose were those two voices that bewitched me so? They both belonged to German women. One was a chambermaid, not otherwise fascinating. The key of my room at a certain great hotel was missing, and this Teutonic maiden was summoned to give information respecting it. The simple soul was evidently not long from her mother-land, and spoke with sweet uncertainty of dialect.

6. But to hear her wonder and lament and suggest, with soft, liquid inflexions, and low, sad murmurs, in tones as full of serious tenderness for the fate of the lost key as if it had been a child that had strayed from its mother, was so winning, that, had her features and figure been as delicious as her accents,—if she had looked like the marble Clytie, for instance, why, all I can say is . . . I was only going to say that I should have drowned myself. For Lake Erie was close by, and it is so much better to accept asphyxia, which takes only three minutes by the watch, than a *mésalliance*, that lasts fifty years to begin with, and then passes along down the line of descent (breaking out in all manner of boorish manifestations of feature and manner, which, if men were only as short-lived as horses, could be readily traced back through the square-roots and the cube-roots of the family

stem on which you have hung the armorial bearings of the De Champignons or the De la Morues, until one came to beings that ate with knives and said "Haow?"), that no person of right feeling could have hesitated for a single moment.

7. The second of the ravishing voices I have heard was, as I have said, that of another German woman.—I suppose I shall ruin myself by saying that such a voice could not have come from any Americanized human being. . . . It had so much *woman* in it,—*muliebrity*, as well as *femineity;*—no self-assertion, such as free suffrage introduces into every word and movement; large, vigorous nature, running back to those huge-limbed Germans of Tacitus, but subdued by the reverential training and tuned by the kindly culture of fifty generations. Sharp business habits, a lean soil, independence, enterprise, and east winds, are not the best things for the larynx.

8. Still you hear noble voices among us,—I have known families famous for them,—but ask the first person you meet a question, and ten to one there is a hard, sharp, metallic, matter-of-business clink in the accents of the answer, that produces the effect of one of those bells which small tradespeople connect with their shop-doors, and which spring upon your ear with such vivacity, as you enter, that your first impulse is to retire at once from the precincts.

9. ——Ah, but I must not forget that dear little child I saw and heard in a French hospital. Between two and three years old. Fell out of a chair and snapped both thigh-bones. Lying in bed, patient, gentle. Rough students round her, some in white aprons, looking fearfully business-like; but the child placid, perfectly still. I spoke to her, and the blessed little creature answered me in a voice of such heavenly sweetness, with that reedy thrill in it which you have heard in the thrush's even-song, that I hear it at this moment, while I am writing, so many, many years afterwards.—

"*C'est tout somme un serin*,"¹ said the French student at my side.

10. These are the voices which struck the key-note of my conceptions as to what the sounds we are to hear in heaven will be, if we shall enter through one of the twelve gates of pearl. There must be other things besides aërolites that wonder from their own spheres to ours; and when we speak of celestial sweetness or beauty, we may be nearer the literal truth than we dream.

11. If mankind generally are the shipwrecked survivors of some pre-Adamitic cataclysm, set adrift in these little open boats of humanity to make one more trial to reach the shore, —as some grave theologians have maintained,—if, in plain English, men are the ghosts of dead devils who have "died into life" (to borrow an expression from Keats), and walk the earth in a suit of living rags which lasts three or fourscore summers,—why, there must have been a few good spirits sent to keep them company, and these sweet voices I speak of must belong to them. HOLMES.

42. THE BELL OF LIBERTY.

[This is an admirable description of the first peal that announced the declaration of the United Colonies to be free and independent of all British control.]

THE representatives of the people assembled in solemn conclave, and long and anxiously surveyed the perilous ground on which they were treading. To recede was now impossible; to go on seemed fraught with terrible consequences. The result of the long and fearful conflict that must follow was more than doubtful. For twenty days Congress was tossed on a sea of perplexity.

2. At length, Richard Henry Lee, shaking off the fetters that galled his noble spirit, arose on the 7th of June, and in a

---

¹ Just like a canary-bird.

clear, deliberate tone, every accent of which rang to the farthest extremity of the silent hall, proposed the following resolution:

"*Resolved*, That these United Colonies are, and ought to be, free and independent States, and all political connection between us and the States of Great Britain is, and ought to be, totally dissolved."

3. John Adams, in whose soul glowed the burning future, seconded the resolution in a speech so full of impassioned fervor, thrilling eloquence, and prophetic power, that Congress was carried away before it, as by a resistless wave. The die was cast, and every man was now compelled to meet the dreadful issue. The resolution was finally deferred till the 1st of July, to allow a committee, appointed for that purpose, to draft a Declaration of Independence.

4. When the day arrived, the Declaration was taken up, and debated article by article. The discussion continued for three days, and was characterized by great excitement. At length, the various sections having been gone through with, the next day, July 4th, was appointed for final action. It was soon known throughout the city; and in the morning, before Congress assembled, the streets were filled with excited men, some gathered in groups, engaged in eager discussion, and others moving towards the State House.

5. All business was forgotten in the momentous crisis which the country had now reached. No sooner had the members taken their seats than the multitude gathered in a dense mass around the entrance. The bell-man mounted to the belfry, to be ready to proclaim the joyful tidings of freedom as soon as the final vote had passed. A bright-eyed boy was stationed below to give the signal.

6. Around the bell, brought from England, had been cast more than twenty years before the prophetic motto:

"PROCLAIM LIBERTY THROUGHOUT ALL THE LAND UNTO ALL THE INHABITANTS THEREOF."

Although its loud clang had often sounded over the city, the proclamation engraved on its iron lip had never yet been spoken aloud. It was expected that the final vote would be taken without delay, but hour after hour wore on, and no report came from that mysterious hall where the fate of a continent was in suspense.

7. The multitude grew impatient; the old man leaned over the railing, straining his eyes downward, till his heart misgave him, and hope yielded to fear. But at length, at about two o'clock, the door of the hall opened, and a voice exclaimed, "It has passed." The word leaped like lightning from lip to lip, followed by huzzas that shook the building. The boy-sentinel turned to the belfry, clapped his hands, and shouted, "Ring! ring!"

8. The desponding bell-man, electrified into life by the joyful news, seized the iron tongue, and hauled it backward and forward with a clang that startled every heart in Philadelphia like a bugle-blast. "Clang! clang!" the Bell of Liberty resounded on, higher, and clearer, and more joyous, blending in its deep and thrilling vibrations, and proclaiming in loud and long accents over all the land the motto that encircled it.

9. Glad messengers caught the tidings as they floated out on the air, and sped off in every direction to bear them onward. When they reached New York, the bells rang out the glorious news, and the excited multitude, surging hither and thither, at length gathered around the Bowling Green, and seizing the leaden statue of George III., which stood there, tore it into fragments. These were afterwards run into bullets, and hurled against his majesty's troops.

10. When the Declaration arrived in Boston, the people gathered to old Faneuil Hall to hear it read; and as the last sentence fell from the lips of the reader, a loud shout went up, and soon from every fortified height and every battery the thunder of cannon re-echoed the joy. HEADLEY.

43. THE JUST MAN.

A JUST man is always simple. He is a man of direct aims and purposes; there is no complexity in his motives, and, thence, there is no jarring or discordancy in his character. He wishes to do right, and in most cases he does it; he may err, but in most cases it is by mistake of judgment, and not by perversity of intention. The moment his judgment is enlightened, his action is corrected. Setting before himself always a clear and worthy end, he will never pursue it by any concealed or unworthy means.

2. We may carry our remarks, for illustration, both into private and into public life. Observe such a man in his home, there is a charm about him, which no artificial grace has ever had the power to bestow; there is a sweetness, I had almost said, a music, in his manners, which no sentimental refinement has ever given. His speech, ever fresh from purity and rectitude of thought, controls all that are within its hearing, with an unfelt, yet a resistless sway. Faithful to every domestic trust, as to his religion and his God, he would no more prove recreant to any loyalty of home, than he would blaspheme the Maker in whom he believes, or than he would forswear the heaven in which he hopes.

3. Fidelity and truth to those bound by love and nature to his heart, are to him most sacred principles; they throb in the last recesses of his moral being, they are embedded in the life of his life; and to violate them, or even think of violating them, would seem to him as a spiritual extermination, the suicide of his soul. Nor is such a man unrewarded, for the goodness he so largely gives is largely paid back to him again; and though the current of his life is transparent, it is not shallow; on the contrary, it is deep and strong. The river that fills its channel glides smoothly along in the power of its course; it is the stream which scarcely covers the ruggedness of its bed, that is turbulent and noisy.

4. With all this gentleness, there is exceeding force; with

all this meekness, there is imperative command; but the force is the force of wisdom, and the command is the command of love. And, yet, the authority which rules so effectually, never gathers an angry or an irritable cloud over the brow of the ruler; and this sway, which admits of no resistance, does not oppress one honest impulse of nature, one movement of the soul's high freedom, one bound of joy from the heart's unbidden gladness, in the spirit of the governed.

5. Take this character into public life. Place him before the people as the candidate for their legislative suffrages; he is there for no selfish ambition, and, willing to be most loyal to his country, he will be no traitor to his conscience. Place him in the legislative assembly to which these willing suffrages send him, he maintains inviolate the trust given to him; with a brave eloquence he maintains the rights of the citizens; with a grave dignity he maintains the privileges of the senator. Place him in the council of the executive magistrate, and no favor can win him, and no danger appal; indifferent to office and fearless of power, he will assert the highest right, and he will stand by it, whatever be the cost.

6. Place him on the bench of justice, no prejudice can approach him, no passion can move him. Nothing can ruffle the august placidity of his soul, except it be the stirrings of a gracious pity. Unmoved he sits, while all around him heaves; he listens not to popular clamor, he cares not for the scowl of power; and, while he is guardian, no corruption shall sully the fountain of justice, and no obstruction shall impede its stream. Place him in the presence of a tyrant; call upon him for his opinion, let life or death hang on the result, he will not speak rashly, but he will not speak falsely.

7. Let the tyrant cajole and fondle, it avails not; let the tyrant rail and threaten, it is still as vain; let wife entreat, let children hang upon his neck, let friends beseech, let multitudes implore, he meets affection with affection; he weeps while others weep; but, fixed as the rock in the ocean, the tempest may crash about his head, and the waves strike

against his breast, his foundation based unchangeably on the centre of eternal right, his head majestically erect, gloriously lifted up to heaven, bends not before the shock, and his breast receives the tempest only to shiver it.

8. Place him in the dungeon; shut him in from the fair earth and the open sky; wrench him from the delights of home; let him be loaded with years; let him be enfeebled by sickness; let him be wearied with confinement; let life hang by the finest thread that ever held a spirit from its God,— the unwavering faith of a true man upholds him, and his hope remains undimmed, and his peace remains unbroken.

9. Call him from the dungeon to his doom, he goes rejoicing to the scaffold; he looks cheerfully on the axe; he faces death almost with gayety; he forgives his enemies; he pities his destroyers; he wishes good to all men; he gives a moment to silent prayer; he meekly lays his head upon the block;—then, there is the echo of a blow that sends a soul to heaven. This character is not imaginary; it is real, it is practicable. The original is Sir Thomas More, of England. GILES.

---

44. SUMMER HYMN.

[Scheffler, who wrote under the name "Angelus," holds a distinguished rank among the poets of sacred subjects in Germany. The glories of sunrise, the soft radiance of the mellow moon, the tints of the spring flowers, the silvery stream, the notes of the nightingale, the sound of the lute in which he reads the reflected beauty of their Creator, have a peculiar and inexpressible charm, as in the writings of Angelus.]

EARTH has nothing sweet or fair,
Lovely forms or beauties rare,
But before my eyes they bring
Christ, of beauty source and spring.

2. When the morning paints the skies,
When the golden sunbeams rise,
Then my Saviour's form I find
Brightly imaged on my mind.

3. When the day-dreams pierce the night,
Oft I think on Jesu's light;
Think how bright that light will be,
Shining through eternity.

4. When, as moonlight softly steals,
Heaven its thousand eyes reveals,
Then I think who made their light
Is a thousand times more bright.

5. When I see in spring-time gay,
Fields their varied tints display,
Wakes the awful thought in me—
What must their Creator be?

6. If I trace the fountain's source,
Or the brooklet's devious course,
Straight my thoughts to Jesus mount,
As the best and purest fount.

7. Sweet the song the night-bird sings,
Sweet the lute, with quivering strings;
Far more sweet than every tone
Are the words, Maria's Son.

8. Sweetness fills the air around,
At the echo's answering sound;
But more sweet than echo's fall
Is to me the Bridegroom's call.

9. Lord of all that's fair to see!
Come, reveal Thyself to me;
Let me, 'mid Thy radiant light,
See Thine unveiled glories bright.

10. Let Thy Deity profound
    Me in heart and soul surround;
    From my soul its idols chase,
    Wean'd from joys of time and place.

11. Come, Lord Jesus! and dispel
    This dark cloud in which I dwell;
    Thus to me the power impart,
    To behold Thee as Thou art.

FROM THE GERMAN OF SCHEFFLER.

45. THE CHRISTIAN PREACHER.

["The dignity and grandeur of the office of the Christian preacher have never been more eloquently described than in Lamartine's magnificent sketch of Bossuet."—POTTER.]

OF all the eminences which a mortal may reach upon earth, the highest to a man of talent is incontestably the sacred pulpit. If this individual happens to be Bossuet—that is to say, if he unites in his person conviction to inspire the commanding attitude, purity of life to enhance the power of truth, untiring zeal, an air of imposing authority, celebrity which commands respectful attention, episcopal rank which consecrates, aye, which gives holiness of appearance, genius which constitutes the divinity of speech, reflective power which marks the mastery of intelligence, sudden bursts of eloquence which carry the minds of listeners by assault, poetic imagery which adds lustre to truth—a deep, sonorous voice which reflects the tone of the thoughts—silvery locks, the paleness of strong emotion, the penetrating glance and expressive mouth—in a word, all the animated and well-varied gestures which indicate the emotions of the soul—if such a man issues slowly from his self-concentrated reflection, as from some inward sanctuary—if he suffers himself to be gradually, by excitement, like the eagle, the first heavy flapping of whose wings can scarcely produce air enough to carry him aloft; if he at length respires freely, and takes flight; if he no longer feels the pulpit beneath his feet; if he draws in a full breath of the Divine Spirit, and pours forth from this lofty height to his hearers the inspiration which comes to them as the word of God—this being is no longer individual man; he becomes an organ of the Divine will, a prophetic voice.

2. And what a voice! A voice which is never hoarse, broken, soured, irritated, or troubled by the worldly and passionate struggles of interest peculiar to the time; a voice which, like that of the thunder in the clouds, or the organ in the cathedral, has never been any thing but the medium of power and Divine persuasion to the soul; a voice which only speaks to kneeling auditors; a voice which is listened to in profound silence, to which none reply save by an inclination of the head or by falling tears—those mute applauses of the soul! a voice which is never refuted or contradicted, even when it astonishes or wounds; a voice, in fine, which does not speak in the name of opinion, which is variable; nor in the name of philosophy, which is open to discussion; nor in the name of country, which is local; nor in the name of regal supremacy, which is temporal; nor in the name of the speaker himself, who is an agent transformed for the occasion; but which speaks, in the name of God, an authority of language unequalled upon earth, and against which the lowest murmur is impious and the smallest opposition a blasphemy.

LAMARTINE.

46. WHAT IS GLORY?

[These graceful and expressive lines contain a profusion of illustrations crowded into a brief space, each preserving its own individuality, and none repeating the idea presented by any of those preceding it.]

"WHAT is glory? What is fame?
The echo of a long-lost name;
A breath—an idle hour's brief talk,
The shadow of an arrant naught;

A flower that blossoms for a day,
            Dying next morrow;
A stream that hurries on its way,
            Singing of sorrow;
The last drop of a bootless shower,
Shed on a sear and leafless bower;
A rose stuck in a dead man's breast—
This is the world's fame, at the best!

2. "What is fame? and what is glory?
A dream—a jester's lying story,
To tickle fools withal, or be
A theme for second infancy;
A joke scrawled on an epitaph,
A grin at death's own ghastly laugh;
A visioning that tempts the eye,
But mocks the touch—nonentity;
A rainbow, substanceless as bright,
            Flitting forever,
O'er hill-top to more distant height,
            Nearing us never;
A bubble blown by fond conceit,
In very sooth itself to cheat;
The witch-fire of a frenzied brain,
A fortune that to lose were gain;
A word of praise, perchance of blame,
The wreck of a time-bandied name—
Ah! this is Glory! this is Fame!"

                          MOTHERWELL.

---

47. CHRISTENDOM.

[Novalis belonged to that brilliant society, consisting of Tieck, the two Schlegels, and Stolberg, which, at the commencement of the present century, exerted so powerful an influence in arresting the progress of that literary Paganism which Lessing, Goethe, and others had encouraged and promoted.

Novalis possessed wonderful versatility of genius, and his style is remarkable for poetical richness and variety. In the midst of the irreligious spirit that pervaded Germany, he caught a glimpse of the glories which radiate from the sanctuary of the Church—when he was snatched away by the pitiless hand of death.]

THOSE were the brilliant and glorious times, when Europe formed one Christian country, when one Christendom inhabited this civilized portion of the globe; and one common interest bound together the most remote provinces of this widely-extended spiritual empire. Without great secular possessions, one head guided and united the great political powers. A numerous corporation, to which every one had access, stood in subordination to this head and executed its mandates, and zealously strove to consolidate its salutary power. Every member of this order was universally respected.

2. A filial confidence attached men to their instructions. How serenely could each one perform his daily task, when by these holy men a secure futurity was prepared for him, and every transgression was forgiven, and every dark passage of life was blotted out and effaced! They were the experienced pilots on the great unknown sea, under whose guidance we might safely disregard all storms, and confidently expect a secure landing on the coast of our true country.

3. The most savage and impetuous passions were compelled to bend with awe and submission to their words. Peace went out from them. They preached nothing but love for the holy, marvellous Virgin of Christianity, who, endowed with a heavenly power, was prepared to rescue every believer from the most fearful dangers.

4. They spake of long-departed men of God, who, by their ttachment and fidelity to that blessed Mother and her divine Child, had withstood the temptations of the world, had attained unto heavenly honors, and were now become tutelary and beneficent powers to their brethren on earth, willing helpers in their wants, intercessors for human frailty, and efficacious friends to humanity at the throne of God.

5. With what serenity of mind did men leave the beautiful

assemblies in those churches, which were adorned with heart-stirring pictures, filled with the sweetest odors, and enlivened by a holy and exalting music! In them were gratefully preserved, in costly vessels, the sacred relics of these venerable servants of God. And in these churches, too, glorious signs and miracles attested as well the efficacious beneficence of these happy saints, as the Divine goodness and omnipotence.

6. In the same way as tender souls preserve locks of hair, or autographs of their departed loves, and nourish thereby the sweet flame of affection, down to the reuniting hour of death; so men then gathered with pious assiduity whatever had belonged to those holy souls, and every one esteemed himself happy who could possess, or even touch, such consoling relics.

7. Here and there the grace of heaven lighted down on some favored image or tombstone. Thither men flocked from all countries to proffer their fair donations, and brought back in return those celestial gifts—peace of mind and health of body.

8. This powerful but pacific society zealously labored to make all men participators in its beautiful faith, and sent forth its missionaries to announce everywhere the gospel of life, and make the kingdom of heaven the only kingdom of this world.

9. At the court of the head of the Church the most prudent and the most venerable men in Europe were assembled. Thither all treasures flowed; the destroyed Jerusalem had avenged herself, and Rome had become Jerusalem—the holy abode of God's government on earth.

10. Princes submitted their disputes to the arbitration of the common Father of Christendom, willingly laid down at his feet their crowns and their regal pomp, and esteemed it a glory to become members of the great clerical fraternity, and pass the evening of their lives in divine contemplation within the walls of a cloister.

11. How very beneficial, how well adapted to the exigencies of human nature were these religious institutions, is proved

by the vigorous expansion of all human energies—by the harmonious development of all moral and intellectual faculties which they promoted—by the prodigious height which individuals attained to in every department of art and science—and by the universally prosperous condition of trade, whether in intellectual or material merchandise, throughout the whole extent of Europe, and even to the remotest India!

NOVALIS.

48. THE GOOD OLD TIMES.

[Rev. J. M. Neale is a Puseyite clergyman. The following extracts from his late work, "Hierologus," apply with much force to the state of England at the present time.]

I.

OH! the good old times of England, ere in her evil day,
   From their Holy Faith, and her ancient rites, her people fell away;
When her gentlemen had hands to give, and her yeomen hearts to feel;
And they raised full many a bead-house, but never a bastile;
And the poor they honored, for they knew that He who for us bled,
Had seldom, when He came on earth, whereon to lay His head;
And by the poor man's dying bed the holy pastor stood,
To fortify the parting soul with that celestial Food.

II.

And in the mortal agony the priest ye might behold,
Commending to his Father's hands a sheep of his own fold;
And, when the soul was fled from earth, the Church could do yet more;
For the chanting priests came slow in front, and the Cross went on before,
And o'er the poor man's pall they bade the sacred banner wave,
To teach her sons that Holy Church hath victory o'er the grave;

But times and things are alter'd now, and Englishmen begin
To class the beggar with the knave, and poverty with sin.

III.

We shut them up from tree and flower, and from the blesséd sun;
We tear in twain the hearts that God in wedlock had made one—
The hearts that beat so faithfully, reposing side by side,
For fifty years of weal and woe, from eve till morning-tide;
No gentle nun with her comfort sweet, no friar standeth nigh,
With ghostly strength and holy love, to close the poor man's eye;
But the corpse is thrown into the ground, when the prayers are hurried o'er,
To rest in peace a little while, and then make way for more!

IV.

We mourn not for abbey lands, e'en pass they as they may!
But we mourn because the tyrant found a richer spoil than they;
He cast away, as a thing defiled, the remembrance of the just,
And the relics of the martyrs he scattered to the dust;
Yet two, at least, in their holy shrines, escaped the spoiler's hand;
And S. Cuthbert and S. Edward might alone redeem a land!
And still our litanies ascend like incense, as before;
And still we hold the one full faith Nicæa taught of yore.

V.

And still our children, duly plunged in the baptismal flood
Of water and the Holy Ghost, are made the Sons of God;
And still our solemn festivals from age to age endure,
And wedded troth remains as firm, and wedded love as pure

And many an earnest prayer ascends from many a hidden spot;
And England's Church is Catholic, though England's self be not!
England of Saints! the hour is come—for nigher it may be
Than yet I deem, albeit that day I may not live to see,

VI.

When all thy commerce, all thy arts, and wealth, and power, and fame,
Shall melt away at thy most need, like wax before the flame;
Then shalt thou find thy truest strength, thy martyrs' prayers above:
Then shalt thou find thy truest wealth, their holy deeds of love;
And thy Church, awaking from her sleep, come glorious forth at length,
And in sight of angels and of men, display her hidden strength.
Again shall long processions sweep through Lincoln's Minster pile;
Again shall banner, cross, and cone, gleam through the incensed aisle.

VII.

And the faithful dead shall claim their part in the Church's thoughtful prayer,
And the daily sacrifice to God be duly offered there;
And tierce, and nones, and matins, shall have each their holy lay;
And the Angelus at Compline shall sweetly close the day.
England of Saints, the peace will dawn, but not without the fight;
So, come the contest, when it may, and God defend the right!

REV. J. M. NEALE.

49. MARYLAND.

[Mr. Reed was a brilliant lawyer and eloquent orator of Maryland. The following extract is from an impressive address delivered on the anniversary of the landing of Lord Baltimore and his colony on the green shores of the St. Mary's River.]

THE land of Mary, so named at the instance of Henrietta Maria, was to receive, in its sheltered seclusion, the suffering brethren in the faith of the youthful queen. But the exactions of the Penal Code so impoverished the Catholics of England and Ireland, from among whom the first emigrants were collected, that it was only at an immense expense, out of his private fortune, which had, as yet, through causes already alluded to, remained intact, that the proprietary was enabled to equip, under the conduct of his brother, who seems to have been eminently fitted for the trust, an expedition of about two hundred gentlemen, including their domestics.

2. With equal piety and taste, he denominates "The Ark," the stout ship that was to bear this family from the devastation of the ancient world, with the sacred traditions of primeval times, to the green bosom of a new earth. Her light consort is named "The Dove," and the voyagers prepare to leave their home.

3. Their home! What a tale of sorrow is concentrated in that single word! a sensual utilitarianism had not then subdued the best feelings of the heart and philosophized the expatriation of a family, down to the cold calculations of expediency that direct the migration of a commercial firm. The country had trampled and spurned them, but it was reserved for modern times to hear, that "to make us love our country, our country must be lovely." Oh no! such is not the language of truth and nature.

4. We love our country, because it is our country, maugre the malice or misrule of man! God has, for wise purposes, implanted in our bosoms the principle of attachment. We love through the blest necessity of loving, ere we can well dis-

tinguish good from evil. Like the climbing plants, our affections must cling to something, and they twine around the objects of our early associations with a tenacity that no violence can ever tear away. They may wither through neglect; they may be blighted by unkindness; but the tender grasp of their first luxuriance only stiffens in death.

5. And the Pilgrims of Maryland, what had they to leave? They were mostly, as I have stated, of the well-born of the land, honorable through long descent, and the constancy with which themselves had adhered to the faith of their fathers. They and their progenitors had sealed their devotion to it, not always, perhaps, in that physical martyrdom which rouses manhood, which is sustained by the countenance and prayers of admiring and sympathizing friends, or the proud consciousness that its firmness animates some fainting brother; no! like those unheeded and unpitied martyrs, who bleed and burn in the secret cells of the heart, cut off from all earthly sources of sympathy and consolation, they had endured in poverty and distress, in contempt and obscurity; but still they failed not—

—"Unshaken, unseduced, unterrified,
Their constancy they kept, their love, their zeal;
Nor number nor example with them wrought,
To swerve from truth, or change their constant mind."

And dear to them was the fair land they were to leave, with its hallowed associations, its old family recollections, its memorials of the friendship strong as death, that had suffered with them, often in spite of temptation or prejudice.

6. Above all, it was England with her white cliffs, her verdant meads, her "mossed trees that had outlived the eagle;" her ocean breezes, vocal with the language of Chaucer and Spenser, of Dryden and Shakespeare, and "all-accomplished Surrey;" the "royal throne of Alfred," and the sainted Edward; the nursing land of chivalry; of a third Edward, of a Black Prince, of the men of Crecy, Poictiers, and Agincourt, the Nevilles, the Chandos, the Staffords, the Cliffords, the Spencers, the Talbots—the men who sought the shock of nations as they

did the fierce pastime of the tourney—who bowed in confession, and knelt at Mass, and received their incarnate God, sheathed in the armor that might coffin their corpses ere the sun went down; England, rich in monuments of the free jurisprudence of her early Catholic times—the work of her Bractons, her Britons, her Fortescues; rich in the monuments of her old Catholic charity—her churches, before which modern imitation sits down abashed and despairing; her cities of colleges, whose scholars once were armies; richer in the virtue of her saints, her Beckets, her Mores, her Fishers, and the countless array whose names, though unhonored on earth, are registered in the Book of Life, and whose blood pleads louder to heaven than the prayers of her Sibthorpes and her Spencers, for the return to Christian unity of the beautiful land it has made holy!

WM. GEO. REED.

50. THE FEMALE MARTYR.

[Mary G——, aged eighteen, a "Sister of Charity," died in one of our Atlantic cities during the prevalence of the Asiatic cholera, while in voluntary attendance on the sick.]

FOR thou wast one in whom the light
Of Heaven's own love was kindled well,
Enduring with a martyr's might,
Through every day and wakeful night,
Far more than words may tell:
Gentle, and meek, and lowly, and unknown—
Thy mercies measured by thy God alone!

2. Where many hearts were failing,—where
The throngful street grew foul with death,
O, high-souled martyr!—thou wast there
Inhaling from the loathsome air
Poison with every breath,
Yet shrinking not from offices of dread
For the wrung dying, and the unconscious dead.

3. And, where the sickly taper shed
   Its light through vapors, damp, confined,
   A new Electra by the bed
   Of suffering human-kind !
   Pointing the spirit, in its dark dismay,
   To that pure hope which fadeth not away.

4. Innocent teacher of the high
   And holy mysteries of Heaven !
   In mute and awful sympathy,
   As thy low prayers were given ;
   And the o'erhovering Spoiler wore, the while,
   An angel's features—a deliverer's smile !

5. A blesséd task ! and worthy one
   Who, turning from the world, as thou,
   Before life's pathway had begun
   To leave its spring-time flower and sun,
   Had sealed her early vow ;
   Giving to God her beauty and her youth,
   Her pure affections and her guileless truth.

6. Earth may not claim thee. Nothing here
   Could be for thee a meet reward ;
   Thine is a treasure far more dear—
   Eye hath not seen it, nor the ear
   Of living mortal heard,—
   The joys prepared—the promised bliss above—
   The holy presence of Eternal Love !

7. Sleep on in peace. The earth has not
   A nobler name than thine shall be.
   The deeds by martial manhood wrought,
   The lofty energies of thought,
       The fire of poesy—
   These have but frail and fading honors ;—thine
   Shall Time unto Eternity consign.

8. Yea, and when thrones shall crumble down,
   And human pride and grandeur fall,—
   The herald's line of long renown—
   The mitre and the kingly crown—
      Perishing glories all!
   The pure devotion of thy generous heart
   Shall live in Heaven, of which it was a part.

                                        WHITTIER.

---

51. AMERICAN HISTORY.

THE study of the history of most other nations fills the mind with sentiments not unlike those which the American traveller feels on entering the venerable and lofty cathedral of some proud old city of Europe. Its solemn grandeur, its vastness, its obscurity, strike awe to the heart. From the richly-painted windows, filled with sacred emblems and strange antique forms, a dim religious light falls around. A thousand recollections of romance, poetry, and legendary story come thronging in upon him. He is surrounded by the tombs of the mighty dead, rich with the labors of ancient art, and emblazoned with the pomp of heraldry.

2. What names does he read upon them? Those of princes and nobles, who are now remembered only for their vices; and of sovereigns at whose death no tears were shed, and whose memories lived not an hour in the affection of their people. There, too, he sees other names, long familiar to him for their guilty or ambitious fame. There rest the blood-stained soldier of fortune, the orator who was ever the ready apologist of tyranny—great scholars, who were the pensioned flatterers of power,—and poets who profaned the high gift of genius to pamper the vices of a corrupted court.

3. Our history, on the contrary, like that poetical temple of fame, reared by the imagination of Chaucer. and decorated by the taste of Pope, is almost exclusively dedicated to the memory of the truly great. Or, rather, li . the Pantheon of

Rome, it stands in calm and severe beauty amid the ruins of ancient magnificence and "the toys of modern state." Within, no idle ornament encumbers its simplicity. The pure light of heaven enters from above, and sheds an equal and serene radiance around.

4. As the eye wanders about its extent, it beholds the unadorned monuments of brave and good men who have bled or toiled for their country; or it rests on votive tablets inscribed with the names of the best benefactors of mankind.

> "Patriots are here, in Freedom's battle slain;
> Priests whose long lives were closed without a stain;
> Bards worthy him who breathed the poet's mind;
> Founders of arts that dignify mankind;
> And lovers of our race, whose labors gave
> Their names a memory that defies the grave."

5. We have been repeatedly told, and sometimes, too, in a tone of affected impartiality, that the highest praise which can fairly be given to the American mind is that of possessing an enlightened selfishness; that, if the philosophy and talents of this country, with all their effects, were forever swept into oblivion, the loss would be felt only by ourselves; and that if to the accuracy of this general charge the labors of Franklin present an illustrious, it is still but a solitary exception.

6. If Europe has hitherto been wilfully blind to the value of our example, and the exploits of our sagacity, courage, invention, and freedom, the blame must rest with her, and not with America. Is it nothing for the universal good of mankind to have carried into successful operation a system of self-government, uniting personal liberty, freedom of opinion, and eqality of rights, with national power and dignity, such as had before existed only in the Utopian dreams of philosophers? Is it nothing, in moral science, to have anticipated, in sober reality, numerous plans of reform in civil and criminal jurisprudence, which are, but now, received as plausible theories by the politicians and economists of Europe?

7. Is it nothing to have been able to call forth on every emergency, either in war or in peace, a body of talents always equal to the difficulty? Is it nothing to have, in less than a half-century, exceedingly improved the sciences of political economy, of law, and of medicine, with all their auxiliary branches; to have enriched human knowledge by the accumulation of a great mass of useful facts and observations, and to have augmented the power and the comforts of civilized man, by miracles of mechanical invention? Is it nothing to have given the world examples of disinterested patriotism, of political wisdom, of public virtue; of learning, eloquence, and valor, never exerted save for some praiseworthy end?

8. LAND OF LIBERTY! thy children have no cause to blush for thee. What though the arts have reared few monuments among us, and scarce a trace of the Muse's footstep is found in the paths of our forests, or along the banks of our rivers; yet our soil has been consecrated by the blood of heroes, and by great and holy deeds of peace. Its wide extent has become one vast temple and hallowed asylum, sanctified by the prayers and blessings of the persecuted of every sect, and the wretched of all nations.

9. LAND OF REFUGE! LAND OF BENEDICTIONS! Those prayers still arise, and they still are heard: May peace be within thy walls, and plenteousness within thy palaces! May there be no decay, nor leading into captivity, and no complaining in thy streets! May truth flourish out of the earth, and righteousness look down from heaven! GULIAN C. VERPLANCK.

---

52. SOGGARTH AROON.

[These lines, full of deep tenderness, graphically and touchingly depict the reverential and affectionate feeling that, through all trials and long generations, has existed in the heart of the Irish peasant for his Soggarth Aroon—*priest dear*.]

A M I the slave they say,
     Soggarth Aroon,
Since you did show the way
     Soggarth Aroon?
Their slave no more to be,
While they would work with me,
Ould Ireland's slavery,
     Soggarth Aroon?

2. Why not her poorest man,
     Soggarth Aroon,
Try and do all he can,
     Soggarth Aroon,
Her commands to fulfil,
Of his own heart and will,
Side by side with you still,
     Soggarth Aroon?

3. Loyal and brave to you,
     Soggarth Aroon,
Yet be no slave to you,
     Soggarth Aroon;
Nor, out of fear to you,
Stand up so near to you—
Och! out of fear to you,
     Soggarth Aroon.

4. Who, in the winter's night,
     Soggarth Aroon,
When the could blast did bite,
     Soggarth Aroon,
Came to my cabin-door,
And on my earthen flure
Knelt by me sick and poor,
     Soggarth Aroon?

5. Who on the marriage-day,
   Soggarth Aroon,
  Made the poor cabin gay
   Soggarth Aroon?
  And did both laugh and sing,
  Making our hearths to ring,
  At the poor christening,
   Soggarth Aroon?

6. Who as friend only met,
   Soggarth Aroon,
  Never did flout me yet,
   Soggarth Aroon?
  And, when my eye was dim,
  Gave while his eye did brim
  What I should give to him,
   Soggarth Aroon?

7. Och! you, and only you,
   Soggarth Aroon,
  And for this I was true to you,
   Soggarth Aroon;
  In love they'll never shake,
  When, for ould Ireland's sake,
  We a true part did take,
   Soggarth Aroon.

53. SUMMER'S FAREWELL.

WHAT sound is that? 'Tis Summer's farewell,
   In the breath of the night-wind sighing;
The chill breeze comes like a sorrowful dirge
   That wails o'er the dead and dying.
The sapless leaves are eddying round
   On the path which they lately shaded;

The oak of the forest is losing its robe,
  The flowers have fallen and faded.
All that I look on but saddens my heart,
To think that the lovely so soon must depart.

2. Yet, why should I sigh? Other Summers will come,
  Joys like the past one bringing;
Again will the vine bear its blushing fruit;
  Again will the birds be singing:
The forest will put forth its "honors" again;
  The rose be as sweet in its breathing;
The woodbine will climb round the lattice-frame,
  As wild and rich in its wreathing.
The hives will have honey, the bees will hum,
Other flowers will spring, other Summers will come.

3. They will, they will; but oh! who can tell
  Whether I may live on till their coming?
This spirit sleeps too soundly then
  To awake with the warbling or humming.
This cheek now pale may be paler far
  When the Summer's next sun is glowing;
The cherishing rays may gild with light
  The grass on my grave-turf glowing:
The earth may be glad, but worms and gloom
May dwell with me in the silent tomb!

4. And few would weep in the beautiful world
  For the fameless one who had left it;
Few would remember the form cut off,
  And mourn the stroke that cleft it:
Many might keep my name on their lips,
  Pleased while that name degrading;
My follies and sins alone would live,
  A theme for their cold upbraiding.
Oh! what a change in my spirit's dream
May there be ere the Summer's sun next shall beam!

E. Cook.

54. ROME UNDER NERO.

AUGUSTUS is no more; but still the folds and fringes of his mantle hang over the marble city. The freshness of his works of taste and magnificence in every one of his "fourteen regions" is yet undimmed, though soon to be marred by the flames and the smoke of Nero's conflagration. Rome reclines with ease and beauty in the mellow sunset of her fairest day of refinement and elegant letters. The golden age is not yet all gone.

2. The enchantment, not yet all dispelled, lingers awhile around temple and triumphal arch, amphitheatre and colonnade. While poetry, eloquence, and the fine arts are slowly and not ungracefully sinking to rest on their own heaped-up trophies, the altars of Venus, and Hebe, and Bacchus are fain to break beneath the rich offerings sent thither by high and low, from every "region" of the city, and from the suburbs.

3. How every remnant of the urbane manliness of yore is softening away into Greek sentimentality and Oriental luxuriousness! Pleasure, with both her hands, flings perfumes and roses over the mansions that crown the hills, and among the suburban and inter-mountain crowds over whom swell up every day unwonted forms and numbers of circuses of great vastness, and most luxurious baths: all through the day-long leisure of equestrian youth, a mimicry of Grecian sports stirs along the once warlike Campus Martius.

4. To sounds of soothing music processions of fancifully-decorated victims pace the solemn way to the almost untrodden temples. The Roman knight smiles languidly on his train of white slaves that troop along in pairs, or cluster in groups along his usual progress to an imperial bath, or one of his own delicious villas. The gravity and power of the Senate have vanished, still the stately retinue is borne homeward with hollow pomp.

5. Ever and anon from the gates and walls of the city come

outbursts of boisterous joy; it is the prætorian guard, whose revelries send back their echoes far across to the Palatine, that palace hill that still glows on through the long night; amid the effulgence streaming out from Nero's banquet-halls, and the golden saloons of his gay and dissolute court.

6. Yet loudly and fiercely resounds throughout all the gayety and dissipations of the city a cry that was first caught up at the theatres : " *To the lions with the Christians! The Christians to the lions!"*

7. Peter had lifted up his voice, but a short time before, in the patrician street, and in the mansion of the Senator Pudens, and he had with simplicity and earnestness told equestrian and plebeian, in the heart of Rome—as he had told the Israelites from beyond the Tiber—of Him who loved us all even unto death !

8. A loud laugh from all sides first met these words of "foolishness ;" yet some there were, Gentiles as well as Jews, who at once followed Peter, and for twenty-five years, day after day, brought around him new groups of believers. First converts of the holy Church of Rome, towards them the laugh of scorn is soon turned into cries of rage and sentence of death. High or low, young or old, it matters not, they must away from any share in the glory, the festivities, or the enjoyments of Rome, as soon as suspected of being followers of Christ.

9. They are ever driven away from the face of day itself, and must hasten out into some of the caverns and sand-pits yawning along the roads, or in the fields outside the city, and look through their dark windings and intricacies underground, for some temporary place of refuge for themselves and their household, and some uncontaminated burial-place for their martyred brethren.

10. Forty years since the crucifixion of man's Redeemer have not yet gone by—Rome yet shines in the faintly altering brightness of the golden age—and behold ! the first chapel and tomb in the catacombs are already lighted up with Catholic rites—the Litany of Sepulchral Inscriptions, commonly ending

"with dread and tears," is already begun—the first dates in the calendar of the Roman martyrology are already fixed ; and in Rome, the capital and mistress of the heathen world, the contest for the dominion of Rome—the empire of the world— is already fierce and hot between the foes of God and man, and the divine Spouse of Christ.

11. Soon shall the engagement spread through the provinces, and the field of battle become as vast, and the trophies that ornament the triumph of the victorious party become as numerous, as all the nations and tribes of earth. MANAHAN.

---

55. ACRE.

["The city of Acre was the first seat of the sovereignty of the Knights of Malta."]

BEAUTIFUL as it is, in our own day, it was yet more beautiful when, seven centuries ago, it was the Christian's capital of the East. Its snow-white palaces sparkled like jewels against the dark woods of Carmel, which rose towards the south. To the east there stretched away the glorious plain, over which the eye might wander till it lost itself in the blue outlines of hills on which no Christian eye could gaze unmoved ; for they hid in their bosoms the village of Nazareth and the waters of Tiberius, and had been trodden all about by One whose touch had made them holy ground.

2. That rich and fertile plain, now marshy and deserted, but then a very labyrinth of fields and vineyards, circled Acre to the north ; but there the eye was met by a new boundary— the sunny summits of a lofty mountain range, whose bases were covered with cedar ; while all along the lonely coast broke blue waves of that mighty sea whose shores are the empires of the world. And there lay Acre among her gardens; the long rows of her marble houses, with their flat roofs, forming terraces odorous with orange-trees, and rich with flowers of a thousand hues, which silken awnings shaded from the sun.

3. You might walk from one end of the city to the other on these terraced roofs, and never once descend into the streets; and the streets themselves were wide and airy, their shops brilliant with the choicest merchandise of the East, and thronged with the noblest chivalry of Europe.

4. It was the gayest, gallantest city in existence; its gilded steeples stood out against the mountains or above the horizon of those bright waters that tossed and sparkled in the flood of southern sunshine, and in the fresh breeze that kissed them from the west; every house was rich with painted glass; for this art, as yet rare in Europe, is spoken of by all writers as lavishly employed in Acre, and was perhaps first brought from thence by the Crusaders. Every nation had its street, inhabited by its own merchants and nobles, and no less than twenty crowned heads kept up within the city walls their palaces and courts.

5. The Emperor of Germany, and the kings of England and France, Sicily, Spain, Portugal, Denmark, and Jerusalem, had each their residence there; while the Templars and the Teutonic Order had establishments as well as the Hospitallers, and on a scarcely less sumptuous scale.

---

56. THE MARTYRS OF FATHERLAND.

WOE, woe to tyrants! Who are they?
    Whence come they? Whither are they sent?
Who gave them first their baleful sway
    O'er ocean, isle, and continent?
Wild beasts they are, ravening for aye;
Vultures that make the world their prey;
Pests ambushed in the noontide day;
Ill stars of ruin and dismay.
We heard them coming from afar;
Heard, and rushed into the war:
We kissed our fathers' graves,
And rushed to meet our Country's foes.

2. I trembled when the strife began—
    Woman (was I), my clasp'd hands trembled
    With ill-timed weakness ill dissembled;
But now beyond the strength of man,
    My strength has in a moment grown,
And I no more my griefs deplore
    Than doth a shape of stone.
And dost thou (tyrant) make thy boast then, of their lying
    All cold upon the mountain and the plain,
    My sons whom thou hast slain?
And that no tears nor sighing
    Can raise their heads again?

3. My sons not vainly have died,
For ye your country glorified!
Each moment as in death ye bowed,
    On high your martyred souls ascended;
Yea, soaring in perpetual cloud,
    This earth with heaven ye blended.
A living chain in death ye wove;
And, rising, raised our world more near those worlds above!

4. They perish idly? they in vain?
When not a sparrow to the plain
Drops uncared for! Tyrant! they
Are radiant with eternal day!
And if, unseen, on us they turn
Those looks that make us inly burn,
And swifter through our pulses flow
The bounding blood, their blood below!

5. How little cause have those for fear
Whose outward forms alone are here!
How nigh are they to heaven, who there
Have stored their earliest, tenderest care!

Whate'er was ours of erring pride,
This agony hath sanctified.
Our destined flower thy blasts but tear
Its sacred seed o'er earth to bear!
O'er us the storm hath passed, and we
Are standing here immovably
Upon the platform of the Right.   DE VERE.

57. THE AMERICAN REPUBLIC.

WHEN we reflect on what has been and what is, how is it possible not to feel a profound sense of the responsibilities of this Republic to all future ages? What vast motives press upon us for lofty efforts! What brilliant prospects invite our enthusiasm! What solemn warnings at once demand our vigilance and moderate our confidence! The Old World has already revealed to us, in its unsealed books, the beginning and the end of all marvellous struggles in the cause of Liberty.

2. Greece! lovely Greece! "the land of scholars and the nurse of arms," where sister republics, in fair processions, chanted the praise of liberty and the good, where and what is she? For two thousand years the oppressors have bound her to the earth. Her arts are no more. The last sad relics of her temples are but the barracks of a ruthless soldiery; the fragments of her columns and her palaces are in the dust, yet beautiful in ruins.

3. She fell not when the mighty were upon her. Her sons united at Thermopylæ and Marathon; and the tide of her triumph rolled back upon the Hellespont. She was conquered by her own factions—she fell by the hands of her own people. The man of Macedonia did not the work of destruction. It was already done by her own corruptions, banishments, and dissensions. Rome! republican Rome! whose eagles glanced in the rising and setting sun,—where and

what is she? The Eternal City yet remains, proud even in her desolation, noble in her decline, venerable in the majesty of religion, and calm as in the composure of death.

4. The malaria has but travelled in the parts won by the destroyers. More than eighteen centuries have mourned over the loss of the empire. A mortal disease was upon her before Cæsar had crossed the Rubicon; and Brutus did not restore her health by the deep probings of the senate-chamber. The Goths, and Vandals, and Huns, the swarms of the North, completed only what was begun at home. Romans betrayed Rome. The legions were bought and sold, but the people offered the tribute-money.

5. And where are the republics of modern times, which cluster around immortal Italy? Venice and Genoa exist but in name. The Alps, indeed, look down upon the brave and peaceful Swiss, in their native fastnesses; but the guarantee of their freedom is in their weakness, and not in their strength. The mountains are not easily crossed, and the valleys are not easily retained.

6. When the invader comes, he moves like an avalanche, carrying destruction in his path. The peasantry sink before him. The country, too, is too poor for plunder, and too rough for a valuable conquest. Nature presents her eternal barrier on every side, to check the wantonness of ambition. And Switzerland remains with her simple institutions, a military road to climates scarcely worth a permanent possession, and protected by the jealousy of her neighbors.

7. *We* stand the latest, and if *we* fall, probably the last experiment of self-government by the people. We have begun it under circumstances of the most auspicious nature. We are in the vigor of youth. Our growth has never been checked by the oppression of tyranny. Our Constitutions never have been enfeebled by the vice or the luxuries of the world. Such as we are, we have been from the beginning: simple, hardy, intelligent, accustomed to self-government and self-respect.

8. The Atlantic rolls between us and a formidable foe. Within our own territory, stretching through many degrees of latitude, we have the choice of many products, and many means of independence. The government is mild. The press is free. Religion is free. Knowledge reaches, or may reach, every home. What fairer prospects of success could be presented? What means more adequate to accomplish the sublime end? What more is necessary than for the people to preserve what they themselves have created?

9. Already has the age caught the spirit of our institutions. It has already ascended the Andes, and snuffed the breezes of both oceans. It has infused itself into the life-blood of Europe, and warmed the sunny plains of France and the lowlands of Holland. It has touched the philosophy of Germany and the North, and, moving onward to the South, has opened to Greece the lesson of her better days.

10. Can it be that America, under such circumstances, should betray herself? That she is to be added to the catalogue of republics, the inscription upon whose ruin is, "They were, but they are not!" Forbid it, my countrymen! forbid it, Heaven! I call upon you, fathers, by the shades of your ancestors, by the dear ashes which repose in this precious soil, by all you are, and all you hope to be, resist every project of disunion; resist every attempt to fetter your consciences, or smother your public schools, or extinguish your system of public instruction.

11. I call upon you, mothers, by that which never fails in woman, the love of your offspring, to teach them, as they climb your knees, or lean on your bosoms, the blessings of liberty. Swear them at the altar, as with their baptismal vows, to be true to their country, and never forsake her. I call upon you, young men, to remember whose sons you are—whose inheritance you possess. Life can never be too short, which brings nothing but disgrace and oppression. Death never comes too soon, if necessary, in defence of the liberties of our country.   JUDGE STORY.

58. DON'T FORGET.

OLD LETTERS! Don't you love, sometimes, to look over old letters? Some of them are dim with years, and some are dim with tears. Here is one now, the burden of which is, "Don't forget;" the device on the seal is "Don't forget;" and the writer thereof went, winters ago, to "the narrow beds of peace." But surely she needn't have written it, for we can't forget if we would.

2. "Don't forget!" They are common words; we hear them, perhaps use them every day; and yet how needless, we may almost say, how meaningless they are! What is it we forget? That which was forgotten and set down in the tablets of memory long ago; set down, we may not remember where, we may not remember when, but it is there still. Remove with the palm of Time the inscriptions upon marble—eat out with its "corroding tooth" the lettering upon brass, but that thing forgotten remains unobliterated.

3. Some breath may whirl back the leaves of memory to its page—in some hour an epitome of its contents may be unrolled before us. Every thought consigned to memory is immortal; its existence runs parallel with the mind that conceives and the heart that cradled it. "Don't forget!" We cannot forget. Earth is full of strains Lethean of man's invention, but the past is with him still.

4. New days, new hopes, new loves arise; but "pleasant, yet mournful to the soul is the memory of joys that are past." Our eyes are dazzled with the clear of the present, but dimmed with the clouds of the past. Ride as we will on the swiftest billow of to-morrow, we are never out of sight of yesterday. There it stands still, with a tearful, gentle light, like some pale Pleiad through the rack of the storm.

5. "Don't forget!" Ah! the science that could teach men to forget would be more welcome than all the trickery of Mnemonics. When the heart beats sadder, and the tide of life runs slower, how the Yesterdays come drifting down to

waiting Age—waiting for Him who enters hall and hovel, unbidden and unstayed.

6 "Don't forget!" Alas! who does not remember? Even Ocean itself, busy as it is in laving from its shores all records of the past, is the great memory of the natural world. Clarence's dream was no fiction, and its treasures glitter, and whiten, and sway amid the groves of red coral. But even the Sea is not oblivious, for "the sea shall give up its dead."

B. F. TAYLOR.

---

59. THE PENITENT'S PRAYER.

["There has seldom been any thing written more exquisitely tender or containing more of the true poetry of nature and religion than the simple prayer of Margaret by the great poet of Germany, Goëthe."—*Dublin Review.*]

MOTHER benign,
   Look down on me!
     No grief like thine;
Thou who dost see,
In his death-agony,
     Thy Son divine,

In faith unto the Father
  Dost thou lift up thine eyes;
In faith unto the Father
  Dost pray with many sighs.

The sword is piercing thine own soul, and thou in pain dost pray
That the pangs which torture Him, and are thy pangs, may pass away.

    And who my wound can heal,
    And who the pain can feel,
      That rends asunder brain and bone?

How my poor heart, within me aching,
Trembles and yearns, and is forsaken—
　　Thou knowest it—thou alone!

Where can I go? where can I go?
Everywhere woe! woe! woe!
　　Nothing that does not my own grief betoken!
And, when I am alone,
I moan, and moan, and moan,
　　And am heart-broken!

The flowers upon my window-sill,
　Wet with my tears since dawn they be;
All else were sleeping, while I was weeping,
　Praying and choosing flowers for thee.

Into my chamber brightly
　Came the early sun's good-morrow!
On my mother's bed, unsightly,
　I sate up in my sorrow.

Oh, in this hour of death, and the near grave,
Look on me, then, and save!
Look on me with that countenance benign.
Never was grief like thine—
Look down, look down on mine! 　　　Goëthe.

---

60. THE CHURCH-BELL.

OF all musical instruments, it is by far the grandest, solemn or deep, or shrill and clear; or, still better, with both combined in a choral peal, it is the only instrument whose music can travel on the winds, can heave in noble swells upon the breeze, and can out-bellow the storm. It alone speaks to heaven as to earth, and scatters abroad its sounds, till in the distance they seem to come but by fragments and broken notes.

2. Every other instrument creeps on earth, or sends its sounds skimming over its surface; but this pours it out from above, like the shower, or the light, or whatever comes from the higher regions to benefit those below. Indeed, it seems to call out from the middle space which heavenly messengers would occupy, to make proclamation to man; condescending to an inferior sphere, but not wholly deigning to soil themselves with earth; high enough to command, low enough to be understood.

3. The Levite trumpet had something startling and military in it, that spoke of alarms and human passions; every other vocal instrument belongs to the world (excepting, perhaps, the noble organ, too huge and too delicately constructed for out of doors), and associates itself with profane amusements; but the solemn old bell has refused to lend itself for any such purpose, and as it swings to and fro, receiving its impulses from the temple of God below, talks of nothing but sacred things, and now reproves the laggard, and now cheers the sorrowful, and now chides the over-mirthful.

Cardinal Wiseman.

---

61. THE BIER THAT CONQUERED.

[The highly dramatic scene of The O'Donnell, when dying of the wounds he had received in battle, having heard that his great rival, O'Neill, demanded hostages, is admirably rendered in the following spirited stanzas.]

LAND which the Norman would make his own!
   (Thus sang the bard 'mid a host overthrown,
While their white cheeks some on the clench'd hand propp'd,
And from some the life-blood scarce heeded dropp'd,)
There are men in thee that refuse to die,
And that scorn to live while a foe stands by

2. O'Donnell lay sick with a grievous wound;
   The leech had left him; the priest had come;
   The clan sat weeping upon the ground,
   Their banners furl'd and their minstrels dumb.

3. Then spoke O'Donnell, the king: "Although
   My hour draws nigh, and my dolors grow;
   And although my sins I have now confess'd,
   And desire in the land my charge to rest,
   Yet leave this realm, nor will I, nor can,
   While a stranger treads on her, child or man.

4. "I will languish no longer a sick man here:
   My bed is grievous; build up my Bier.
   The white robe a king wears over me throw;
   Bear me forth to the field where he camps—your foe,
   With the yellow torches and dirges low,
   The heralds his challenge have brought and fled:
   The answer they bore not I bear instead.
   My people shall fight my pain in sight,
   And I shall sleep well when their wrongs stand right."

5. Then the clan to the words of their Chief gave ear,
   And they fell'd great oak-trees and built a bier;
   Its plumes from the eagle's wing were shed,
   And the wine-black samite above it they spread,
   Inwoven with sad emblems and texts divine,
   And the braided bud of Tyrconnell's pine,
   And all that is meet for the great and brave
   When past are the measured years God gave,
   And a voice cries "Come," from the waiting grave.

6. When the bier was ready, they laid him thereon
   And the army forth bare him with wail and moan;
   With wail by the sea-lakes and rock abysses;
   With moan through the vapor-trailed wildernesses;

And men sore wounded themselves drew nigh,
And said, "We will go with our king and die;"
And women wept as the pomp pass'd by.
The sad, yellow torches far off were seen;
No war-note peal'd through the gorges green;
But the black pines echo'd the mourners' keen.

7. "What," said the Invader, "that pomp in sight?
They sue for pity, they shall not win."
But the sick king sat on the bier upright,
And said, "So well! I shall sleep to-night:
Rest here, my couch, and my peace begin."

8. Then the war-cry sounded—"Bataillah Aboo!"
And the whole clan rush'd to the battle-plain:
They were thrice driven back, but they form'd anew,
That an end might come to their king's great pain.
'Twas a people, not army, that onward rush'd;
'Twas a nation's blood from their wounds that gush'd:
Bare-bosom'd they fought, and with joy were slain,
Till evening their blood fell fast like rain;
But a shout swell'd up o'er the setting sun,
And O'Donnell died, for the field was won.

9. So they buried their king upon Aileach's shore:
And in peace he slept—O'Donnell More.

---

62. ST. BERNARD.

[In the "Monks of the West," from which this sketch is taken, Montalembert has penned one of the freshest tributes ever paid to Liberty. And he has portrayed, in the most brilliant and true colors, how men adopted and persevered in the monastic state, not from a spirit of sacrifice, nor for the good of their kind, nor through a disgust for the troubles of life, but from a love of the state itself.]

ALL acknowledge Saint Bernard to be a great man and a man of genius; he exercised over his age an influence that has no parallel in history; he reigned by eloquence, courage, and virtue. More than once he decided the future of nations and of crowns. At one time he held, as it were, in his hands the destiny of the Church. He knew how to move Europe, and precipitate it upon the East; he completely vanquished Abelard, the precursor of modern Rationalism. All the world knows it, and all the world says it; all, with one voice, place him by the side of Ximenes, Richelieu, and Bossuet.

2. But this is not sufficient. If he was, and who can doubt it? a great orator, a great writer, and a great person, it was almost without his knowing it, and always in opposition to his own wish. He was, and above all wished to be, something else; he was a monk and he was a saint; he lived in a cloister and he worked miracles.

3. The Church has defined and canonized the sanctity of Bernard; history is charged with the mission of relating his life, and of explaining the wonderful influence he exercised over his contemporaries.

4. But in studying the life and epoch of this great man, who was a monk, we find that the Popes, Bishops, and Saints, who were the bulwark and honor of Christian society, all, or almost all, like Bernard, came from the monastic orders. Who then were these monks, and whence did they come, and what had they done, up to this period, to make them occupy so high a place in the destiny of the world?

5. These questions we must solve before going farther. And we must do more; for in trying to judge of the age in which Saint Bernard lived, we find that it is impossible to explain or comprehend it, if we do not recognize that it was animated by the same breath which vivified an anterior epoch, of which it is only the direct and faithful continuation.

6. If the twelfth century bowed before the genius and virtue of Saint Bernard, it was because the eleventh century had been regenerated and penetrated with the virtue and

genius of another monk, Gregory VII.; and we could not comprehend either the epoch or the action of Bernard, when apart from the salutary crisis which the one had prepared and rendered possible for the other; and never would a simple monk have been heard and obeyed as Bernard was, if his uncontested greatness had not been preceded by the struggles, the trials, and the posthumous victories of that other monk, who died six years before the birth of our Saint.

7. It must then be characterized, not only by a conscientious view of the pontificate of the greatest of the Popes, taken from the ranks of the monks, but also by passing in review the entire period which unites the last combats of Gregory with the first efforts of Bernard;—and, while keeping this in view, describe the most important and most glorious struggle in which the Church was ever engaged—in which the monks were the first in sufferings as in honors.

8. And even this is not sufficient. Far from being the founders of monastic orders, Gregory VII. and Bernard were only their offsprings, in common with so many thousands of their contemporaries. When these great men took so wondrous a part in them, these institutions had existed more than five centuries.

9. To understand their origin, and to appreciate their nature and services, we must go back to another Gregory—to Saint Gregory the Great—the first Pope who left the cowl for the tiara; or back still farther, to Saint Benedict, the legislator and patriarch of the monks of the West. We must at least cast a glance, during these five centuries, upon the superhuman efforts made by these legion of monks to subdue, pacify, discipline, and purify twenty barbarous nations, and successively transform them into Christian nations. MONTALEMBERT.

68. O FOR THE WINGS OF THE WIND TO WANDER!

[The following breathings of the heart are full of poetical beauty, and testify that if the author turned his attention as assiduously to the Court of the Muses as to the civil courts of the land, he would stand as high as a poet as he now stands at the bar as an eloquent and profound lawyer.]

O FOR the wings of the wind to wander
   Farther than the sun in the zenith shines,
Over the peaks of the paradise yonder,
   Richer in gems than a million mines!
Up where the maidenly moon is beaming,
The face of a snow-white angel seeming,
Or queen of the sinless angels dreaming,—
   Love by the light of her starry shrines.

2. O for the speed of a spirit's pinions,
   Soaring like thought from a burning brain;
Soaring from sorrow in sin's dominions,
   Realms where the pitiless passions reign!
O, but to flee from the fiend that chases
Hope to the home of the charnel places,
Lurid with lights of the faded faces,
   Beauty that never shall bloom again.

3. Why should I shiver beside the dim river
   Which the feet of Christ have coasted before?
For the angel of death alone can deliver
   Grief-laden souls that are yearning to soar.
O for the faith all my darkness to brighten;
O for the faith all the demons to frighten;
O for the love that all terror can lighten—
   Mary, sweet Mother, I ask for no more!

JUDGE ARRINGTON.

64. A MAN OVERBOARD.

IT is a dreadful night! The passengers are clustered, trembling, below. Every plank shakes; and the oak ribs groan, as if they suffered with their toil. The hands are all aloft; the captain is forward shouting to the mate in the cross-trees, and I am clinging to one of the stanchions, by the binnacle

2. The ship is pitching madly, and the waves are toppling up, sometimes as high as the yard-arm, and then dipping away with a whirl under our keel, that makes every timber in the vessel quiver. The thunder is roaring like a thousand cannons; and, at the moment, the sky is cleft with a stream of fire, that glares over the tops of the waves, and glistens on the wet deck and the spars,—lighting up all so plain, that I can see the men's faces in the main-top, and catch glimpses of the reefers on the yard-arm, clinging like death; then all is horrible darkness.

3. The spray spits angrily against the canvas; the waves crash against the weather-bow like mountains; the wind howls through the rigging, or, as a gasket gives way, the sail, bellying to leeward, splits like the crack of a musket. I hear the captain in the lulls, screaming out orders; and the mate in the rigging, screaming them over, until the lightning comes, and the thunder, deadening their voices as if they were chirping sparrows.

4. In one of the flashes, I see a hand upon the yard-arm lose his foothold, as the ship gives a plunge; but his arms are clinched around the spar. Before I can see any more the blackness comes, and the thunder, with a crash that half deafens me. I think I hear a low cry, as the mutterings die away in the distance; and at the next flash of lightning, which comes in an instant, I see upon the top of one of the waves alongside, the poor reefer who has fallen. The lightning glares upon his face.

5. But he has caught at a loose bit of running-rigging, as he fell; and I see it slipping off the coil upon the deck. I shout

madly, "Man overboard!" and catch the rope, when I can see nothing again. The sea is too high, and the man too heavy for me. I shout, and shout, and shout, and feel the perspiration starting in great beads from my forehead, as the line slips through my fingers.

6. Presently the captain feels his way aft, and takes hold with me; and the cook comes, as the coil is nearly spent, and we pull together upon him. It is desperate work for the sailor; for the ship is drifting at a prodigious rate; but he clings like a dying man.

7. By-and-by, at a flash, we see him on a crest, two oars' length away from the vessel. "Hold on, my man!" shouts the captain. "For God's sake, be quick!" says the poor fellow; and he goes down in a trough of the sea. We pull the harder, and the captain keeps calling to him to keep up courage, and hold strong. But, in the hush, we can hear him say, "I can't hold out much longer; I'm most gone!"

8. Presently we have brought the man where we can lay hold of him, and are only waiting for a good lift of the sea to bring him up, when the poor fellow groans out, "It's no use; I can't. Good-by!" And a wave tosses the end of the rope clean upon the bulwarks. At the last flash, I see him going down under the water.

MITCHELL.

---

65. THE FOUNT OF SONG.

WHERE flows the fount whose living streams
    Are heard in every clime—
Whose voice hath mingled with the dreams
    Of far-departed time?
Is it where Grecian fanes lie hid
    Among the olives dim,
Or the Nile beside the pyramid,
    Sends up its ceaseless hymn?

2. Alas! by old Castilian wave
   The muses meet no more,
Nor breaks from Delphi's mystic cave
   The prophet voice of yore:
Old Egypt's river hath forgot
   The Theban glory gone;
And the land of Homer knows him not,—
   Yet still that fount flows on!

3. The sacred fount of song, whose source
   Is in the poet's soul,
Though living laurels crown its course
   All-glorious to the goal;
Yet who can tell what desert part
   Its earliest springing nursed?
As from the glacier's icy heart
   The mightiest rivers burst!

4. *Perchance the wind that woke the lyre*
   Was but a blighting blast
That sear'd with more than tempest's ire
   The verdure where it passed.
Perchance the fire that seemed divine
   On ruined altars shone,
Or glowed like that Athenian shrine,
   For deity unknown.

5. It is not Fame, with all her spells,
   Could wake the spirit's springs,
Or call the music forth that dwells
   Amid its hidden strings;
For evermore, through sun and cloud,
   To the first fountain true,
It flows—but oh! ye soulless crowd,
   It never sprang for you!

6. The wild-bird sings in forest far,
   Where foot may never be;
The eagle meets the morning star,
   Where none his path may see.
So many a gifted heart hath kept
   Its treasures unrevealed,—
A spring whose depth in silence slept,
   A fount forever sealed!

7. Woe for the silent oracles
   That went with all their lore!
For the world's early wasted wells,
   Whose waters flow no more!
Yet one remains no winter's wrath
   Can bind, or summer dry;
For, like our own, its onward path
   Is to eternity.

Miss Brown.

66. MONASTERIES.

[An extract from "Institutions, Manners, and Customs of the Middle Age," by Dr. Hurter, of Switzerland, one of the most profound, comprehensive minds, and erudite scholars of the day.]

ON the ancestral grave—on the spot where a nobleman had selected the place of rest for his family—on the foundation of the modest church out of the wooden cell of the hermit—there, where the waves had given back to the afflicted father the child they had snatched away, arose the structure wherein daily were to ascend canticles of praise to the Eternal, and thanksgiving for redemption, or, which even sometimes were to expiate the murders and crimes of a former robber's cave, or convert the accursed place of execution into an abode of blessings.

2. That age considered it indeed as a glory and a happiness to put in force such pious resolutions; nay, vanity might often

be tempted to purchase, by such donations, the praises of posterity. Yet the more pious sense of those times protested against any feelings of ostentation or ambition attaching to works which sprang from Divine inspiration, out of pure zeal for religion, from a regard to the perishableness of all earthly things, from the wish of sowing a seed in time for eternity, and of there laying up a portion of one's treasure, and obtaining one day a hundred-fold reward.

3. The prince believed that out of the transitory goods of this world he might procure for himself a mansion in heaven. One who had been rescued from imminent danger, sought to attest by such foundations his gratitude to the Almighty in a manner the most acceptable.

4. A nobleman who had wandered long amid the turmoils of an agitated life could better understand, in the evening of his days, the value of monastic quiet and seclusion. The service of her eternal Master offered to the noble lady greater charms than all the vanities of the world; and the baron sought, by means of such establishments, to reduce to subordination the rebellious spirit of his vassals.

5. The sorrow of deeply-afflicted parents at the death of the loved ones of their heart, induced them to offer up to the Almighty a sacrifice of thanksgiving as soon as they were enabled to inter their bodies. HURTER.

67. CHARITY.

[The following is an extract from an eloquent appeal for the sufferers in the South, delivered in New York, in the winter of 1866-7.]

BUT the age of Chivalry is gone. All things—kingdoms, cities, systems, habits—wear out and perish. So wrote Edmund Burke in that noble passage where all the chivalry of his own high nature flashed out in anger at the insult that France, degraded into rationalism, had cast on a fair and innocent woman—Marie Antoinette. He was right. France will never be able to cleanse from its escutcheon the stain of that murdered lady's blood. "The age of chivalry is gone; that of sophisters, economists, and calculators has succeeded." Progress, the Juggernaut of our idolatry, crushes under its remorseless wheels many a harmless superstition, a kindly tradition, and gracious habit of the past.

2. Woman asks not loyalty now-a-days. The dignified submission, the tender regard for her sex and weakness, the homage of the heart with which every man, not wholly debased, delights to regard her, she slights and repudiates, and demands instead liberty and equality. Be it so. The world does move. War acknowledges now no truce of God, no holydays; and, by a queer coincidence, many of the bloodiest battles of modern times have been fought on Sunday. There is small immunity for vine-dresser or olive-grower now, and we can fancy what short work a foraging party would make of the shepherd and his flock.

3. Our improved projectiles spare neither shrine nor spire; and modern reason would laugh at the superstition which would spare a foe because he had sought asylum by the altar or the cross. The world has moved. Relieved of ancient restraint, war has resumed all its pagan ferocity, with the additional improvements in the machinery for killing which modern inventiveness has devised. A more complete disregard of the immemorial rights of war, of courtesy, of chivalry, of Christianity—a harder insensibility to the waste of human life have never been shown than by the armies of the civilized nations within the last twenty years.

4. Witness the sack of Kertch, an unfortified, ungarrisoned city, in the Crimean war; the "loot" in China; the devilish vengeance wreaked on the Sepoys, blown into atoms from the cannon's mouth; the wholesale devastation of Poland; the atrocities inflicted on Crete to-day—these are some of the instances of superior civilization of which our nineteenth century—our golden age of knowledge and enlightenment—exhibits to an admiring world. Cromwell, the merciless hero of

the Puritans, has found an eulogist. Frederick of Prussia has a Carlyle to recommend him. When shall full justice be done to Alaric, and Attila be recognized as the pacificator and benefactor of mankind?

5. But modern philosophers have devised a happy knack of dealing with all disasters not their own, and lull themselves into contentment with the easy conviction that "whatever is, is best"—a very consoling creed. Nay, I perceive that a too sensitive philanthropy hesitates to relieve human suffering from a fear lest such suffering should be the result of error and sin, and every attempt to mitigate it should thwart the vengeful designs of an angry God. Far from us, oh! far from us, be this impious thought!

6. The God we serve is not Jupiter, grasping the red lightning of destruction; not Mars, the avenging and triumphant; not Pallas Athene, all armed, the personification of reason—cold, pitiless, severe; our heaven is no Valhalla, where round the celestial festive board only conquerors are seated. We pray to "our Father," and we are his children, white men, black men, red men—they that dwell in the palace or languish in the jail, all living on His bounty and hopeful of His mercy and forgiveness. With us Charity is not a matter of reason, or calculation, or sentiment, but of duty and religion; and to our charity no barrier can be known; nor can any difference of race, or creed, or language, or color, exclude any sufferer from his right to a place in the great brotherhood of man. O'GORMAN.

---

68. THE PERI'S SONG.

ONE morn a Peri at the gate
  Of Eden stood disconsolate;
    And as she listened to the springs
  Of life within, like music flowing,
    And caught the light upon her wings
  Through the half-open portal glowing,

She wept to think her recreant race
Had ever lost so bright a place.

2. "How happy!" exclaimed this child of air,
"Are the holy spirits who wander there,
   Mid flowers that never shall fade or fall!
Though mine are the gardens of earth and sea,
And the stars themselves have flowers for me,
   One blossom of heaven outblooms them all.

3. "Though sunny the lake of cool Chasmere,
With its plane-tree isle reflected clear,
   And sweetly the founts of that valley fall;
Though bright are the waters of Sing-su-Hay,
And the golden floods that thitherward stray:
Yet oh! 'tis only the blest can say,
   How the waters of heaven outshine them all!

4. "Go, wing thy flight from star to star,
From world to luminous world, as far
   As the universe spreads its flaming wall:
Take all the pleasures of all the spheres,—
And multiply each through endless years,—
   One minute of heaven is worth them all."

MOORE.

69. FLOATING ISLANDS.

[Every one has read of the singular device of "Floating Islands" of the Chinese, to which the necessities of an overcrowded population have driven this ingenious and industrious race. The Abbé Huc, in his interesting work, "The Chinese Empire," encountered a number of these curious structures in the course of his wonderful missionary duties in the Celestial Empire.]

WE passed several floating islands, those curious productions of Chinese ingenuity which no other people seem to have thought of. These islands are enormous rafts, generally constructed of bamboos, which resist the decomposing influence of the water for a long time. Upon the raft is laid a tolerably thick bed of vegetable soil; and, thanks to the patient labors of a few families of aquatic agriculturists, the astonished traveller beholds a whole colony lying on the surface of the water,—pretty houses with their gardens, as well as fields and plantations of every sort. The inhabitants of these farms appear to enjoy peace and abundance.

2. During the leisure time which is not occupied by the culture of their rice-fields, they employ themselves in fishing, which is at the same time a pastime and a source of profit; and often, after gathering a crop of grain from the surface of the lake, they cast their nets and bring up a harvest of fish from its depths; for these waters teem with creatures fit for the use of man. Many birds, particularly swallows and pigeons, build their nests in these floating isles, and enliven the peaceful and poetic solitude.

3. Towards the middle of the lake one of these islands on its way took up a fresh position. It moved very slowly, though there was a good deal of wind, and large sails were attached to the houses as well as to each corner of the island; the inhabitants, men, women, and children, lent their strength to aid its progress, by working at large oars; but their efforts did not seem materially to increase the speed at which they moved. However, these peculiar mariners do not probably trouble themselves about delay, as they are sure of sleeping on land, at whatever pace they may go.

4. Their migrations are often without any apparent motive. Like the Mongols in their vast prairies, they wander at will; but, more fortunate than these latter, they have constructed for themselves a little solitude in the midst of civilization, and unite the charms of a nomade life to the advantages of a sedentary abode.

5. These floating islands are to be found on all of the great lakes of China, and at first sight present an enchanting picture of happiness and plenty, whilst it is impossible not to

admire the ingenious industry of these Chinese, so singular in all their proceedings. But when you consider the cause of their construction, the labor and the patience necessary for their creation by people unable to find a corner of the solid earth on which to establish themselves, the smiling picture assumes a darker tint, and the mind endeavors vainly to penetrate the future of a race so numerous that the land will no longer hold it, and which has sought a resting-place on the surface of the waters. Hua.

---

70. THE SKYLARK.

BIRD of the wilderness,
 Blithesome and cumberless,
Sweet be thy matin o'er moorland and lea!
 Emblem of happiness,
 Blessed is thy dwelling-place,—
Oh, to abide in the desert with thee!
 Wild is thy lay, and loud,
 Far in the downy cloud,
Love gives it energy, love gave it birth.
 Where, on thy dewy wing,
 Where art thou journeying?
Thy lay is in heaven, thy love is on earth.

2. O'er fell and fountain sheen,
 O'er moor and mountain green,
O'er the red streamers that herald the day;
 Over the cloudlet dim,
 Over the rainbow's rim,
Musical cherub, soar, singing away!
 Then, when the gloaming comes,
 Low in the heather blooms,
Sweet will thy welcome and bed of love be!
 Emblem of happiness,
 Blest is thy dwelling-place,—
Oh, to abide in the desert Hogg.

71 REVOLUTIONISTS.

["The futility of the regicide plea—the iniquity which stamps the judicial murder of Charles I., and the ruin which temporary success in crime is sure to bring down on its authors—is ably exhibited in the following extract from Guizot's masterly essay on the Revolution in England."—*Dublin Review.*]

REVOLUTIONISTS, even the ablest, are short-sighted. Intoxicated by passion, or governed by the necessity of the moment, they foresee not that what constitutes to-day their triumph, will be their condemnation to-morrow. The execution of Charles I. delivered up to the Republicans and to Cromwell, England stricken with stupor. But the Republic and Cromwell, wounded by that very blow which they had struck, held, from that very day, but a violent transitory dominion, stamped with that seal of supreme iniquity, which devotes to certain ruin governments even the strongest and most successful.

2. The judges of Charles I. set every engine at work to divest their act of that fatal character, and to represent it as a divine judgment, which they had the mission to execute. Charles, they said, had aimed at absolute power, and upheld the civil war. Many rights had been violated, and much blood spilled by his orders, or with his knowledge. On him they cast the whole responsibility of tyranny and of civil war ; from him they demanded reckoning of all the liberties that had been trampled under foot, and of all the blood that had been shed ;—a crime without a name, which his death could alone expiate.

3. But the conscience of a people, even when it is seized with trouble and consternation, cannot be so beguiled. Others besides the king had filled the country with oppression and blood-shed. If the king had violated the rights of his sujects—the rights of royalty, ancient also, inscribed also in the statute-book, necessary also to the maintenance of the public liberties, had been equally violated, assailed, and infringed. He had, indeed, made war, but in self-defence.

4. Who is ignorant that at the very moment when he had decided on war, it was preparing against him, in order to force him, after so many concessions, to abandon whatever yet remained of his power and prerogatives—the last remnants of the legal government of the country? And now when the king was conquered, he was judged, he was condemned without law, contrary to all laws, for acts which no law had ever foreseen, or qualified as crimes, which the conscience neither of the king nor of the people had ever dreamed of considering as falling under the jurisdiction of men, or of being punishable at their hands.

5. How would every soul have swelled with indignation, had the obscurest citizen been treated in this manner, and been put to death for crimes defined by an *ex post facto* law, and by pretended judges, yesterday his enemies, to-day his rivals, to-morrow his heirs! And what would not have been attempted against the least of Englishmen, was perpetrated on the King of England, on the head of the English Church as well as the State, on the representative and the symbol of all authority, order, law, justice, of all that in human society borders on the limit, and awakens the idea of the Divine attributes!

GUIZOT.

72. THE AZTEC EMPIRE.

[Some of the horrible abominations prevalent among the Aztecs, at the time of the conquest of Mexico by Cortez, are here graphically described by Prescott.]

THE amount of victims immolated on its accursed altars would stagger the faith of the least scrupulous believer. Scarcely any author pretends to estimate the yearly sacrifice throughout the empire at less than twenty thousand, and some carry the number as high as fifty. On great occasions, as the coronation of a king, or the consecration of a temple, the number becomes still more appalling. At the dedication of the great temple Huitzilopotchli, in 1486, the prisoners who, for some years, had been reserved for the purpose, were drawn from all quarters of the capital. They were ranged in files, forming a procession nearly two miles long. The ceremony consumed several days, and seventy thousand captives are said to have perished at the shrine of this terrible deity.

2. One fact may be considered certain. It was customary to preserve the skulls of the sacrificed in buildings appropriated to the purpose. The companions of Cortez counted one hundred and thirty-six thousand of these edifices. . . . Indeed, the great object of war with the Aztecs was quite as much to gather victims for their sacrifices as to extend their empire. Hence it was that an enemy was never slain in battle, if there was a chance to take him alive. To this circumstance the Spaniards repeatedly owed their own preservation. When Montezuma was asked why he had suffered the republic of Tlascala to maintain her independence on his borders, he replied, "that she might furnish him with victims for his gods."

3. The Aztecs not only did not advance the condition of their vassals, but, morally speaking, they did much to degrade it. How can a nation where human sacrifice prevails, and especially when combined with cannibalism, further the work of civilization? How the interests of humanity be consulted, where a man is lowered to the rank of the brutes that perish? The influence of the Aztecs introduced their gloomy superstitions into lands, before it or where it was not established in any great strength. The example of the capital was contagious; and as the latter increased in opulence, the religious celebrations were conducted with still more terrible magnificence; in the same manner as the gladiatorial shows of the Romans increased in pomp with the increasing splendor of the capital.

4. Men became familiar with scenes of horror, and the most loathsome abominations; women and children, the whole nation, became familiar with and assisted at them. The heart was hardened; the manners were made ferocious. The feeble light of civilization, transmitted from a milder race, was grow-

ing fainter and fainter, as thousands and thousands of miserable victims, through the empire, were yearly fattened in its cages, sacrificed on its altars, dressed and served at its banquets. The whole land was converted into a vast human shamble. The empire of the Aztecs did not fall before its time.

PRESCOTT.

78. THE VALLEY OF MEXICO.

[The annals of history record few feats of greater daring and bravery than those by which a handful of Spaniards, led on by the noble Cortez, subdued an immense empire, and placed the banner of Castile on the loftiest pinnacle, Tenochtitlan.]

THEY had not advanced far, when, turning an angle of the Sierra, they suddenly came upon a view which more than compensated for the toils of the preceding day. It was the Valley of Mexico, or Tenochtitlan, as more commonly called by the natives, which, with its picturesque assembly of water, woodland, and cultivated plains, its shining cities and shadowy hills, was spread out like some gay and gorgeous panorama before them. In the highly rarefied atmosphere of these upper regions, even remote objects have a brilliancy of coloring, and a distinctness of outline, which seems to annihilate distance.

2. Stretching far away at their feet, were seen noble forests of oak, sycamore, and cedar, and far beyond yellow fields of maize and the towering maguey, intermingled with orchards and blooming gardens; for flowers, in such demand for their religious festivals, were even more abundant in this populous valley than in other parts of Anahuac.

3. In the centre of the great basin were beheld the lakes, occupying then a much larger portion of its surface than at present; their borders thickly studded with towns and hamlets; and in the midst, like some Indian empress, with her coronal of pearls, the fair city of Mexico, with her white towers and pyramidal temples, reposing, as it were, on the bosom of the waters, the far-famed Venice of the Aztecs.

4. High over all rose the royal hill of Chapultepec, the residence of the Mexican monarchs, crowned with the same grove of gigantic cypresses, which at this day fling their broad shadows over the land. In the distance, beyond the blue waters of the lake, nearly screened by the intervening foliage, was seen a shining speck, the rival city of Tezcuco; and still farther on, the dark belt of Porphyry, girdling the valley round like a rich setting, which nature had devised for the fairest of her jewels. PRESCOTT.

74. WHAT IS POETRY?

WHAT is poetry? A smile, a tear, a glory, a longing after the things of eternity. It lives in all created existences —in man, and every object that surrounds him. There is poetry in the gentle influences of love and affliction, in the quiet broodings of the soul over the memories of early years, and in the thoughts of glory that chain our spirits to the gates of Paradise.

2. There is poetry, too, in the harmonies of nature. It glitters in the wave, the rainbow, the lightning and the star; its cadence is heard in the thunder and the cataract—its softer tones go sweetly up from the thousand voice-harps of wind, and rivulet, and forest; the cloud and the sky go floating over us to the music of its melodies, and its ministers to heaven from the mountains of the earth and the untrodden shrines of ocean.

3. There is not a moonlight ray that comes down upon stream or hill, not a breeze calling from its blue air-throne to the birds of the summer valleys, or sounding through midnight rains its low and mournful dirge over the perishing flowers of spring, not a cloud bathing itself like an angel-vision in the rosy gushes of autumn twilight, not a rock glowing in the yellow starlight, as if dreaming of the Eden-land, but is full of the beautiful influences of poetry. It is the soul

of being. The earth and heavens are quickened by its spirit; and the heavings of the great deep, in tempest and in calm, are but its secret and mysterious breathings.

G. W. PATRICK.

75. OUR NEIGHBOR.

SET it down gently at the altar rail,
   The faithful, agéd dust, with honors meet;
Long have we seen that pious face so pale
   Bowed meekly at her Saviour's bless'd feet.

2. These many years her heart was hidden where
   Nor moth, nor rust, nor craft of man could harm;
The blue eyes, seldom lifted save in prayer,
   Beamed with her wished-for heaven's celestial calm.

3. As innocent as childhood's was the face,
   Though sorrow oft had touched that tender heart;
Each trouble came as winged by special grace,
   And resignation saved the wound from smart.

4. On bead and crucifix her fingers kept,
   Until the last, their fond, accustomed hold;
"My Jesus," breathed the lips; the raised eyes slept,
   The placid brow, the gentle hand, grew cold.

5. The choicely ripening cluster, lingering late
   Into October on its shrivelled vine,
Wins mellow juices which in patience wait
   Upon those long, long days of deep sunshine.

6. Then set it gently at the altar rail,
   The faithful, agéd dust, with honors meet;
How can we hope, if such as she can fail
   Before the eternal God's high judgment-seat?

E. A. STARR.

76. THE ANGELUS.

THE bell, at the appointed hour, gives the signal; and upon it every occupation, be it of study or recreation, is suspended. The solitary student in his cell puts down his pen, and turns to his little domestic memorials of piety, picture, or crucifix, and joins his absent brethren in prayer.

2. The professor pauses in his lecture, and, kneeling at the head of his class, leads the way to their responses. The little knot engaged in cheerful talk or learned disputation, drop their mirth or their cunning instruments of fence, and contend more pleasantly in the verses of that angelic prayer. Nay, even the sport and play of youth and childhood are interrupted, to give a few moments to more serious thoughts.

3. Well might the Angelus bell have inscribed upon it, "At evening, morn, and noon, I will call out, and give the angelic annunciation." For this is truly the order of the ecclesiastical day; and in southern countries of more Catholic atmosphere, of the civil. With first vespers comes in the festival; and the *Ave Maria*, with its clattering peal, rings in the new day. We own we like it. We love not the old day to slip away from us, and the new one to steal in, "like a thief in the night," upon our unconscious being, at the hour when ghosts walk, and when nature, abroad and within us, most awfully personates death.

4. We like the day to die even as a good Christian would wish, with a heaven of mild splendor above, enriched in hues as its close approaches; with golden visions and loved shapes, however fantastically, floating in clouds around, with whispered prayer, and a cheering passing-bell, and the comfort that when gloom has overspread all, a new, though unseen, day, has risen to the spirit; that the vigil only has expired, that so the festival day may break. Then, when we awake once to sense and consciousness, let the joyful peal arouse us, with the first dawn of day and reason, to commemorate that Mystery which alone has made the day worth living; and

greet, with the natural, the spiritual Sun, the Day-spring from on high that rose on benighted man, and chased away the darkness and the shadow of death wherein he sate.

5. Who does not see and feel the clear analogy? And who will neglect, if it be brought thus to his memory, to shield himself behind the ample measure of this grace, against "the arrow flying in the day," in its sharp and well-aimed temptations? At these eventful periods will the Angelus bell call out to us aloud, and make the joyful Annunciation, speaking in angel's words and angel's tones, to the gladsome, to the anxious, and to the weary heart; gladsome at morn, anxious at noon, weary at eve.

6. Truly it was a heavenly thought that suggested the appointment of both time and thing. For what can chime so well with the first of those feelings and its season, as the glorious news that "the Lord's angel" hath brought to earth such tidings as his? What can suit the second better than to speak resignation in Mary's words: "Behold thy servant, or handmaid,"—"Be it done unto me according to Thy word?" What can refresh the third, and cast forward bright rays into the gloom of approaching night, more than the thought that God's own Eternal Word dwelleth ever amongst us, our comforter and help?   CARDINAL WISEMAN.

---

77. SONG OF THE SHIRT.

[An able critic says of this song, that its great merit is its truthfulness. The cracked, tuneless voice, trembling under its burden of sorrows, now shrunk down into the whispers of weakness, and now shuddering up into the laughter of despair. In the centre of this true tragedy its author has, with a skilful and sparing hand, dropped a pun or two and conceit or two, and these quibbles are precisely what make you quake—"every tear hinders needle and thread." He knew that, to deepen the deepest woe of humanity, it is the best way to show it in the lurid light of mirth; that there is a sorrow too deep for tears—too deep for sighs—but none too deep for smiles, and that the *aside of* and laughter of an idiot might accompany and serve to aggravate the anguish of a god.]

WITH fingers weary and worn,
　　With eyelids heavy and red,

A woman sat, in unwomanly rags,
  Plying her needle and thread:
Stitch! stitch! stitch!
  In poverty, hunger, and dirt,
And still, with a voice of dolorous pitch,
  She sang the "Song of the Shirt."

2. Work! work! work!
  While the cock is crowing aloof!
And work—work—work,
  Till the stars shine through the roof!
It's oh! to be a slave,
  Along with the barbarous Turk,
Where woman has never a soul to save,
  If this is Christian work!

3. Work—work—work—
  Till the brain begins to swim!
Work—work—work,
  Till the eyes are heavy and dim!
Seam, and gusset, and band,
  Band, and gusset, and seam,
Till over the buttons I fall asleep,
  And sew them on in a dream!

4. Oh! men, with sisters dear!
  Oh! men, with mothers and wives!
It is not linen you're wearing out,
  But human creatures' lives!
Stitch—stitch—stitch,
  In poverty, hunger, and dirt,
Sewing at once a double thread—
  A shroud as well as a shirt.

5. But why do I talk of Death,
  That Phantom of grisly bone?

I hardly fear his terrible shape,
  It seems so like my own!—
It seems so like my own,
  Because of the fasts I keep:
O God! that bread should be so dear,
  And flesh and blood so cheap!

6. Work—work—work!
    My labor never flags;
  And what are its wages? A bed of straw,
    A crust of bread,—and rags,—
  That shatter'd roof—and this naked floor—
    A table—a broken chair—
  And a wall so blank, my shadow I thank
    For sometimes falling there!

7. Work—work—work!
    From weary chime to chime!
  Work—work—work,
    A prisoner's work for crime!
  Band, and gusset, and seam,
    Seam, and gusset, and band,
  Till the heart is sick, and the brain benumb'd,
    As well as the weary hand.

8. Work—work—work!
    In the dull December light,
  And work—work—work,
    When the weather is warm and bright:
  While underneath the eaves
    The brooding swallows cling,
  As if to show me their sunny backs,
    And twit me with the Spring.

9. Oh! but to breathe the breath
    Of the cowslip and primrose sweet,

With the sky above my head,
  And the grass beneath my feet :
For only one short hour
  To feel as I used to feel,
Before I knew the woes of want,
  And the walk that costs a meal !

10. Oh ! but for one short hour !
  A respite, however brief !
No blesséd leisure for Love or Hope,
  But only time for Grief !
A little weeping would ease my heart ;
  But in their briny bed
My tears must stop, for every drop
  Hinders needle and thread !

11. With fingers weary and worn,
  With eyelids heavy and red,
A woman sat, in unwomanly rags,
  Plying her needle and thread ;—
Stitch ! stitch ! stitch !
  In poverty, hunger, and dirt,
And still with a voice of dolorous pitch—
Would that its tone could reach the rich !—
  She sang this "Song of the Shirt." Hood.

78. THE PRESS.

THE Press was inaugurated by the publication of the Bible ; it has descended to the language of Billingsgate ; thus music, painting, poetry, have sprung up in the temples, and have strayed to the tavern and to the house of iniquity. But as the vilest poets have not been able to tarnish the glory of Homer, of Virgil, and of Tasso, and as the discordant sounds of a wretched musical instrument detract nothing from the magic notes of Mozart and Rossini; as the prodigies of Michael Angelo and of Raphael are in nowise impaired by the ridiculous imitations of sign-board painters, so the Press should lose nothing of its value on account of the follies and excesses wherein it has been rendered an accomplice.

2. Let us never confound abuse with use; if it were necessary to destroy the latter to restrain the former, but little would remain to us on the face of the earth. What is it that man does not abuse? He abuses his intellect, his will, all the faculties of his soul, his senses, his body, his fortune, his reputation, his relations with other men; all, in fact, that is under his control. There is no evil to which the abuse of good may not lead; to bury a sword in an innocent heart is to abuse the instrument and the hand; it is to turn from their object two valuable agents which Heaven has allowed us to provide for our happiness.

3. The influence of the Press has extended over all branches of human learning; it has acted in extremes the most remote from each other; there is no point which has not felt its irresistible power. Religion, society, politics, science, literature, and the fine arts, have all experienced the effects of this wonderful invention. It has everywhere acquired titles to gratitude, and everywhere it has left subjects of recrimination and complaint.

4. But from the very fact that the new agent was of universal application, it followed that we might always expect to find evil along with the good. The same sun that enlightens, fertilizes, and embellishes the earth, sometimes burns up our fields, poisons the marshes, and lets loose the pestilential vapors which scatter broadcast desolation and death.

5. If religion has many evils to deplore, it has new triumphs to engrave upon its annals; if it is true that the Press has greatly favored the diffusion of error, it is not the less true that, with its aid, religious knowledge has elevated itself to an extent that could scarcely have been reached without this discovery. The Press has doubtless contributed to prepare our

epoch for skepticism and incredulity; but the very contradictions which have sprung up against the faith have shown more and more the solidity of its foundations, and have placed at its service a treasure of learning and science, which probably it would never have possessed but for this powerful vehicle of human thought. BALMEZ.

---

79. RUINS OF COPAN AND PALENQUE.

[These ruins exist in the interior of Guatemala, in Central America.]

WE returned to the base of the pyramidal structure, and ascended by regular stone steps, in some places forced apart by bushes and saplings, and in others thrown down by the growth of large trees, while some remained entire. In parts they were ornamented with sculptured figures and rows of death's-heads. Climbing over the ruined top, we reached a terrace overgrown with trees, and, crossing it, descended by stone steps into an area so covered with trees, that at first we could not make out its form, but which, on clearing the way with the machete, we ascertained to be a square, and with steps on all sides almost as perfect as those of the Roman amphitheatre.

2. The steps were ornamented with sculpture, and on the south side, about half-way up, forced out of its place by roots, was a colossal head, evidently a portrait. We ascended these steps, and reached a broad terrace a hundred feet high, overlooking the river, and supported by the wall which we had seen from the opposite bank. The whole terrace was covered with trees, and, even at this height from the ground, were two gigantic cibas, or wild cotton-trees of India, above twenty feet in circumference, extending their half-naked roots fifty or a hundred feet around, binding down the ruins, and shading them with their wide-spreading branches.

3. We sat down on the very edge of the wall, and strove in vain to penetrate the mystery by which we were surrounded.

Who were the people that built this city? In the ruined cities of Egypt, even in the long-lost Petra, the stranger knows the story of the people whose vestiges are around him. America, say historians, was peopled by savages; but savages never reared these structures, savages never carved these stones. We asked the Indians who made them, and their dull answer was, "Quien sabe?" "Who knows?"

4. There were no associations connected with the place, none of those stirring recollections which hallow Rome, Athens, and

> "The world's great mistress on the Egyptian plain;"

but architecture, sculpture, and painting, all the arts which embellish life, had flourished in this overgrown forest; orators, warriors, and statesmen, beauty, ambition, and glory, had lived and passed away, and none knew that such things had been, or could tell of their past existence. Books, the records of knowledge, are silent on this theme.

5. The city was desolate. It lay before us like a shattered bark in the midst of the ocean, her masts gone, her name effaced, her crew perished, and none to tell whence she came, to whom she belonged, how long on her voyage, or what caused her destruction; her lost people to be traced only by some fancied resemblance in the construction of the vessel, and, perhaps, never to be known at all. The place where we sat, was it a citadel from which an unknown people had sounded the trumpet of war? or a temple for the worship of the God of peace? or did the inhabitants worship the idols made with their own hands, and offer sacrifices on the stones before them?

6. All was mystery—dark, impenetrable mystery; and every circumstance increased it. In Egypt, the colossal skeletons of gigantic temples stand in the unwatered sands in all the nakedness of desolation; here an immense forest shrouded the ruins, hiding them from sight, heightening the impression and moral effect, and giving an intensity and almost wildness to the interest.

7. There were the remains of cultivated, polished, and peculiar people, who had passed through all the stages incident to the rise and fall of nations; reached their golden age, and perished, entirely unknown. The links which connected them with the human family were severed and lost; and these were the only memorials of their footsteps upon earth. We lived in the ruined palace of their kings; we went up to their desolate temples and fallen altars; and, wherever we moved, we saw the evidences of their taste, their skill in arts, their wealth and power.

8. In the midst of desolation and ruin, we looked back to the past, cleared away the gloomy forest, and fancied every building perfect, with its terraces and pyramids, its sculptured and pointed ornaments, grand, lofty, and imposing, and overlooking an immense inhabited plain. We called back into life the strange people who gazed at us in sadness from the walls; pictured them in fanciful costumes and adorned with plumes of feathers, ascending the terraces of the palace, and the steps leading to the temples, and often we imagined a scene of unique and gorgeous beauty and magnificence.

9. In the romance of the world's history, nothing ever impressed me more forcibly than the spectacle of this great and lovely city, overturned, desolate, and lost; discovered by accident, overgrown with trees for miles around, and without even a name to distinguish it. Apart from every thing else, it was a mourning witness to the world's mutations. STEPHENS.

---

80. THE SPIRIT OF BEAUTY.

THE Spirit of Beauty unfurls her light,
And wheels her track in a joyous flight;
I know her track through the balmy air,
By the blossoms that cluster and whiten there;
She leaves the tops of the mountains green,
And gems the valley with crystal sheen.

2. At morn I know where she rested at night,
   For the roses are gushing with dewy light;
   Then she mounts again, and round her flings
   A shower of light from her crimson wings;
   Till the spirit is drunk with the music on high,
   That silently fills it with ecstasy.

3. At noon she hies to a cool retreat,
   Where bowering elms over waters meet;
   She dimples the wave where the green leaves dip,
   As it smilingly curls like a maiden's lip,
   When her tremulous bosom would hide, in vain,-
   From her lover, the hope that she loves again.

4. At eve she hangs o'er the western sky,
   Dark clouds for a glorious canopy,
   And round the skirts of their deepen'd fold
   She paints a border of purple and gold,
   Where the lingering sunbeams love to stay,
   When their god in his glory has passed away.

5. She hovers round us at twilight hour,
   When her presence is felt with the deepest power;
   She silvers the landscape and crowds the stream
   With shadows that flit like a fairy dream;
   Then wheeling her flight through the gladdened air,
   The Spirit of Beauty is *everywhere*.   DAWES.

---

81. MAN'S POSITION IN CREATION.

THE first feature to be noticed in the condition of this creature, man, is his want of power. Not only is his health uncertain, but at his best estate his strength is very small. Brute matter resists him passively. He cannot lift great weights of it, nor dig deep into it. Even with the help of the most ingenious machinery and the united labor of multitudes he can do little but scratch the surface of the planet, without being able to alter the expression of one of its lineaments. Fire and water are both his masters. His prosperity is at the mercy of the weather.

2. Matter is baffling and ruining him somewhere on the earth at all hours of day and night. He has to struggle continually to maintain his position, and then maintains it with exceeding difficulty. Considering how many thousands of years the race of man has inhabited the world, it is surprising how little control he has acquired over diseases, how little he knows of them, how much less he can do to alleviate them. Even in his arts and sciences there are strangely few things which he can reduce to certainty.

3. His knowledge is extremely limited, and is liable to the most humiliating errors and the most unexpected mistakes. He is in comparative ignorance of himself, of his thinking principle, of the processes of his immaterial soul, of the laws of its various faculties, or of the combinations of mind and matter. Metaphysics, which should rank next to religion in the scale of sciences, are a proverb for confusion and obscurity. Infinite longings perpetually checked by a sense of feebleness, and circumscribed within the limits of a narrow prison,—this is a description of the highest and most aspiring moods of man.

4. Such is the condition of our man if we look at him in his solitary dignity as lord of the creation. But even this is too favorable a representation of him. His solitary dignity is a mere imagination. On the contrary, he is completely mixed up with the crowd of inferior creatures, and in numberless ways dependent upon them. If left to himself, the ponderous earth is simply useless to him. Its maternal bosom contains supplies of minerals and gases, which are meant for the daily sustaining of human life. Without them this man would die in torture in a few days; and yet by no chemistry can he get hold of them himself and make them into food.

5. He is simply dependent upon plants. They alone can make the earth nutritious to him, whether directly as food themselves, or indirectly by their support of animal life. And they do this by a multitude of hidden processes, many of which, perhaps the majority, are beyond the explanation of human chemistry. Thus he is at the mercy of the vegetable world. The grass that tops his grave, which fed him in his life, now feeds on him in turn.

6. In like manner is he dependent upon the inferior animals. Some give him strength to work with, some warm materials to clothe himself with, some their flesh to eat or their milk to drink. A vast proportion of mankind have to spend their time, their skill, their wealth, in waiting upon horses and cows and camels, as if they were their servants, building houses for them, supplying them with food, making their beds, washing and tending them as if they were children, and studying their comforts.

7. More than half the men in the world are perhaps engrossed in this occupation at the present moment. Human families would break up, if the domestic animals ceased to be members of them. Then, as to the insect world, it gives us a sort of nervous trepidation to contemplate it. The numbers of insects, and their powers, are so terrific, so absolutely irresistible, that they could sweep every living thing from the earth and devour us all within a week, as if they were the fiery breath of a destroying angel.

8. We can hardly tell what holds the lightning-like speed of their prolific generations in check. Birds of prey, intestine war, man's active hostility,—these, calculated at their highest, seem inadequate to keep down the insect population, whose numbers and powers of annoyance yearly threaten to thrust us off our own planet. It is God Himself who puts an invisible bridle upon these countless and irresistible legions, which otherwise would lick us up like thirsty fire. FABER.

82. THE ACADIANS.

THEY were Bretons originally, these Acadians, and from that land, and from illustrious La Vendée, whose warriors went to battle with the sacred Heart of Mary, white embroidered, upon their breasts, they brought their fidelity to the Queen of Angels, far over the troubled Atlantic, to the wild and ice-bound shores of Cape Breton. They made those deserts blossom; the valleys of that boreal and breeze-swept land stood thick with golden corn; sixty thousand head of horned cattle soon grazed upon the pastures tilled by their careful and industrious hands.

2. The flax which they cultivated and the flocks which they reared, spun and woven by the nimble fingers of their pious women, clothed the Acadian farmers. Each family was well able to provide for its own wants, so that there were no poor, and little barter. The blessing of paper money had not lighted upon them, and they had little or no use for the slight stock of gold and silver which they possessed. They kept as clear of the court of justice as they did of the trader's exchange.

3. The elders of the villages settled all slight quarrels; they carried the greater to the priest. He drew their public acts, recorded their wills, kept them instructed in the law of God, consecrated their lives by Sacraments, kept vivid in their souls devotion to Mary Immaculate. His salary was the twenty-seventh part of the harvest — always more than he needed, for there were no poor. "Misery was wholly unknown, and benevolence anticipated the demands of poverty."

4. The Acadian married young, chose his own partner for life, and she brought him her portion in flocks and herds. When the union had been determined on, the whole community built the young couple a house, broke up the lands about it, supplied them with life's necessaries for a twelvemonth, and bade them God-speed. The population numbered eighteen

thousand souls. And when their sun was at its serenest the storm came down.

5. In 1762 this charge was brought against them: "that the Council were fully convinced of their strict attachment to the French king, and their readiness at all times to take part with and assist him." This was the cloud, and from it the lightning soon fell. In the Octave of Our Lady's Seven Sorrows, September 17, they stood upon the shore surrounded with bayonets which were to drive them, if resisting, into the vessels prepared for their deportation. Their houses, churches, barns, and mills, had been given to the flames—two hundred and fifty-three of these burning at once in a single settlement, five hundred lying in ashes in another. Some fled and perished in the woods, some made good their escape, most of them submitted to the force employed.

6. Back from the cold beach about a mile stood the Church of Our Lady of Acadie. There they gathered for the last time, while Father Reynal offered the Holy Mysteries for them Then they marched slowly out, weeping, telling their beads chanting the Litanies of the Blessed Virgin, singing hymns to her eternal Son and her. All the way from that chapel to the shore the mourning procession passed through the kneeling ranks of their wild weeping mothers and wives, of their sisters and little children; and when the men had passed, these rose and followed to the ships. And so, driven aboard, they passed away over the strange seas, in that Octave of Our Lady of Sorrows.

7. The sun went down. Such of the poor women as were left found shelter where they could for themselves and their children, and the provincial soldiery stood in their ranks upon the sands, alone in a once beautiful and fertile country, "without a foe to subdue, or a population to protect. But the volumes of smoke," says the Protestant historian, "which the half-expiring embers emitted, while they marked the site of the peasant's cottage, bore testimony to the extent of the work of destruction. For several successive evenings the

cattle gathered round the smoking ruins, as if in expectation of the return of their masters, and all night long the faithful watchdogs howled over the scene of desolation, and mourned alike the hand that had fed and the house that had sheltered them."

8. All these sad victims were sown, like wild-flower seeds, by chance as it were, all along the North American coast from Maine to Louisiana. No regard was paid to family ties: daughters were separated from their mothers, wives from husbands, and little children from their families.

X. D. MacLeod.

88. THE TYROLESE.

[The Tyrolese from their Alpine heights are represented as returning this proud answer to the insulting demands of unconditional surrender to the French invaders. If their own mountains had spoken, they could not have replied more majestically.]

THE land we, from our fathers, had in trust,
And to our children will transmit, or die;
This is our maxim, *this* our piety,
And God and Nature say that it is just:
That which we *would* perform in arms we *must!*
We read the dictate in the infant's eye,
In the wife's smile; and in the placid sky,
And at our feet amid the silent dust
Of them that were before us. *Sing aloud*
OLD SONGS—the precious music of the heart!
Give, herds and flocks, your voices to the wind,
While we go forth, a self-devoted crowd,
With weapons in the fearless hand, to assert
Our virtue, and to vindicate mankind.

WORDSWORTH.

84. TO THE MEMORY OF THOSE WHO FELL IN THE REBELLION OF 1745.

[These stanzas are full of the most delicate and exquisite imagery and deep pathos.]

HOW sleep the brave who sink to rest
With all their country's wishes bless'd!
When Spring, with dewy fingers cold,
Returns to deck their hallowed mould,
She there shall dress a sweeter sod
Than Fancy's feet have ever trod.

2. By fairy hands their knell is rung,
By forms unseen their dirge is sung;
There Honor comes, a pilgrim gray,
To bless the turf that wraps their clay;
And Freedom shall a while repair
To dwell, a weeping hermit there. — COLLINS.

85. THE GRAY FOREST EAGLE.

WITH storm-daring pinion and sun-gazing eye,
The Gray Forest Eagle is king of the sky!
Oh! little he loves the green valley of flowers,
Where sunshine and song cheer the bright summer hours;
For he hears in those haunts only music, and sees
But rippling of waters, and waving of trees;
There the red-robin warbles, the honey-bee hums,
The timid quail whistles, the shy partridge drums;

2 And if those proud pinions, perchance, sweep along,
There's a shrouding of plumage, a hushing of song;
The sunlight falls stilly on leaf and in moss,
And there's naught but his shadow black gliding across;
But the dark, gloomy gorge, where down plunges the foam
Of the fierce rock-lashed torrent, he claims as his home;

There he blends his keen shriek with the roar of the flood,
And the many-voiced sounds of the blast-smitten wood ;
3. From the fir's lofty summit, where morn hangs its wreath,
He views the mad water's white writhing beneath :
On a limb of that moss-bearded hemlock far down,
With bright azure mantle and gay mottled crown,
The kingfisher watches, while o'er him his foe,
The fierce hawk, sails circling, each moment more low ;
Now poised are those pinions and pointed that beak,
His dread swoop is ready, when hark! with a shriek
4. His eyeballs red blazing, high bristling his crest,
His snake-like neck arch'd, talons drawn to his breast,
With the rush of the wind-gust, the glancing of light,
The Gray Forest Eagle shoots down in his flight ;
One blow of those talons, one plunge of that neck,
The strong hawk hangs lifeless, a blood-dripping wreck ;
And as dives the free kingfisher, dart-like on high
With his prey soars the eagle, and melts in the sky.

* * * * * * * * *

5. Time whirls round his circle, his years roll away,
But the Gray Forest Eagle minds little his sway ;
The child spurns its buds for youth's thorn-hidden bloom,
Seeks manhood's bright phantoms, finds age and a tomb ;
But the eagle's eye dims not, his wing is unbowed,
Still drinks he the sunshine, still scales he the cloud !
The green tiny pine shrub points up from the moss,
The wren's foot would cover it, tripping across ;
6. The beechnut down dropping would crush it beneath,
But 'tis warm'd with heaven's sunshine and fann'd by its breath ;
The seasons fly past it, its head is on high,
Its thick branches challenge each mood of the sky ;
On its rough bark the moss a green mantle creates,
And the deer from his antlers the velvet down grates :
Time withers its roots, it lifts sadly in air
A trunk dry and wasted, a top jagged and bare,

7. Till it rocks in the soft breeze, and crashes to earth,
   Its brown fragments strewing the place of its birth.
   The eagle has seen it up-struggling to sight,
   He has seen it defying the storm in its might,
   Then prostrate, soil-blended, with plants sprouting o'er,
   But the Gray Forest Eagle is still as of yore.
   His flaming eye dims not, his wing is unbow'd,
   Still drinks he the sunshine, still scales he the cloud!

8. He has seen from his eyrie the forest below,
   In bud and in leaf, robed with crimson and snow,
   The thickets, deep wolf-lairs, the high crag his throne,
   And the shriek of the panther has answer'd his own.
   He has seen the wild red man the lord of the shades,
   And the smoke of his wigwams curl'd thick in the glades;
   He has seen the proud forest melt breath-like away,
   And the breast of the earth lying bare to the day:

9. He sees the green meadow-grass hiding the lair,
   And his crag-throne spread naked to sun and to air;
   And his shriek is now answer'd, while sweeping along,
   By the low of the herd and the husbandman's song;
   He has seen the wild red man swept off by his foes,
   And he sees dome and roof where those smokes once arose;
   But his flaming eye dims not, his wing is unbow'd,
   Still drinks he the sunshine, still scales he the cloud!

10. An emblem of Freedom, stern, haughty, and high,
    Is the Gray Forest Eagle, that king of the sky!
    It scorns the bright scenes, the gay places of earth—
    By the mountain and torrent it springs into birth;
    There, rock'd by the whirlwind, baptized in the foam,
    It's guarded and cherish'd, and there is it's home!

A. B. Street.

86. MOTHER.

[Père Felix, of Paris, is one of the most brilliant orators of the day.]

THE word *Mother* is the first which the heart pronounces, even without ever having learnt it. In the language of every nation it expresses the first respiration of the heart. Those who love to explore the mysteries of human language, concealed in the folds of even the simplest words, say wonderful things of this one phrase, *My Mother*. Whatever may be the cause, the perfume it exhales never passes away; the word *My Mother* preserves a charm that ever lingers around the heart. Man may become deaf to every word, insensible to every name; but there is still one word he comprehends, one name that ever vibrates—*My Mother*.

2. Man may forget all; even God; but he never forgets his mother. Amid the greatest ruins of his heart, this image always stands erect. Above all, when years have passed since we lost her; when our life is already on the decline, and the descending sun casts the lengthened shadow of our past days before us, we seem to see in its sombre shade an image crowned with pure light, which years embellish in proportion as they withdraw it from us; and under the charm of a remembrance always fresh and full of youth, our heart in its secret recesses cries out, "My mother! Ah, yes, it is my mother!" With this thought the heart seems to find a perpetual youth. Our most secret souvenirs, hidden, perhaps, from even our most intimate friends, preserve a charm which is perpetuated and multiplied as our days increase.

3. Whence comes the mysterious charm attached to this word?—Charm incomparable, surviving all that dies during our life—strong and vigorous, resting in the heart until the end? Ah, gentlemen, it is because this word is the most natural and lively expression of a something in our hearts for which we can find none similar. This something, permit me to name it here—because it is impossible in the purely human order to find for it a sense more legitimate, purer, and more

sacred, than that which our subject imposes upon it;—this something, whence comes this word, Mother—the perfume which embalms it—is *Love.*

4. On this earth the mother is the sweetest personification of love; her face bears the most beautiful smile of love, because her heart guards its richest treasure. The maternal heart is the birth-place of the love which forms the foundation of our life.
Père Félix.

---

87. THE EXTRA TRAIN.

AT a quiet country station, where flowers climbing beneath the windows, hanging their heads languidly in the summer's heat—where, during the intervals of business, a warm repose reigns over the place—in a small room opening from the sunny platform, a telegraph lad sits before his idle instrument. He has so little to do that, to keep himself from dozing in the sultry stillness, he is playing at marbles—superior marbles, a new purchase, and their click, as he gives many a well-directed aim, is the only sound on the air.

2. But hark! another sound comes from the distance, a shrill, faint whistle, and a hum, swelling into a continuous, increasing roar. A train is coming. Well, let it come. It is an extra train, and it don't stop here; it may bang away. And bang away it does, with a wild scream, shaking the windows and platform of the station as it rattles through, and making the marbles dance out of their scientific positions. The lad pauses, to watch, through the open door, the flitting carriages and white-glancing faces of the passengers, and then resumes his game.

3. Again there is silence, until, after a warning gurgled from its deep throat, the clock strikes—Three. He glances listlessly up; then, as if the fingers were pointed with a stern and solemn warning, suddenly utters a dreadful cry,

and with both arms flung up, rushes, like a little maniac, out on the platform. The station-master, coming leisurely down a side-path, sees him, and runs forward. "I didn't signal—I didn't signal, and the up-train is just due!" cries the boy.

4. "My God!" The man fairly staggers, appalled by the frightful peril. If the up-train is punctual to its time, and has left the next station, where, according to some late agreement, it ought to have been detained until this train (run on for some casual purpose) had passed, they must inevitably meet, and a catastrophe ensue. There was a tunnel on the line. May God be merciful this day!

5. The alarm is quickly raised, and officials start from various corners. Now the signals work with frantic speed. After a breathless pause, the needle quivers with the response—the up-train *has* passed the next station, and is on its way, unconscious of danger; so clearly there is nothing to do but prepare for the worst.

6. Men, with grave faces, hurry down the line. A surgeon, and then another, appears on the scene; the few inhabitants of the neighborhood, suspending every employment, gather, with straining eyes, on the little bridge which spans the rails; and all this time the poor negligent lad, kicked indignantly by a dozen feet, stands shivering and crying on the platform.

* * * * *

7. "Well, we had not *that* to bear in my young days," said Father Lawrence, as the train, after tearing, with a desperate shriek, into subterraneous gloom, and rattling, quivering, in darkness, relieved only by an occasional gleam of light from an occasional crevice overhead, at length emerged into the fair sunshine, and triumphantly screamed to the fields which it cast behind it.

8. The old gentleman laughs, though rather nervously; for, though on the line pretty often, he can never get quite used to this way of travelling, never overcome a horror of those

underground passages. Selwyn, also, feels a strange uneasiness creeping over him, and, to escape it, shows a willingness to converse. There is more good-will between them that moment than there has been during their two hours' unbroken journey.

9. "We had a very different way of travelling in those days," resumed the priest. "It was safety versus speed then; but the saying is reversed by this generation. It is altogether too clever for a loiterer like me."

10. Selwyn replied, "What, do you regret the good old High-flier so long? His neck is broken, and will never be set again, depend upon it. But I also must own a sneaking attachment to him, for the sake of old times. To a gay young dog as I was, there was something pleasant about travelling in those days, what with the bright company you often met outside, the jolly coachman with his inexhaustible stories, and the hundred incidents you had time to notice on the road. Yet I must say I would not like to coach it to London now. The improvements which we grumble at are useful to you and me, sir, after all."

11. "What's that?" A piercing whistle, sharply repeated and answered—a curious movement—a hoarse call or two. Something is going wrong. Down claps every window, and heads look anxiously out. The peril is instantly understood. *We are on the same line with an approaching train.*

12. Such a scene of confusion as follows, such rapid, dismal whistles, such heart-rending screams of distress as rise from those flying carriages, may we never hear or see again. Some of the doors are burst open, and the frenzied occupants leap out, to be left, writhing and ghastly, on the road. "Keep in—keep in—see! we have still a chance for life."

13. By a special providence, the trains sighted each other at a good distance. The men have turned off the steam, and stand, white and breathless, in a terrible calculation—slacken perceptibly—we slide onward—good God! we meet!—No! Our lingering impetus carries us within six yards of each

other, and there, with laboring vapor bursting from every outlet, face to face, we stop.

14. We stop, but are in imminent danger, for other trains are closely due, and if the irregularity has not been already rectified, our destruction is certain. The casual train has made the least way—it must go back, and we must follow. Slowly we follow, as, with retrograding movement, it slowly goes, a belching monster, whose murderous crash has been arrested, but whose hot breath still snorts at us in rage and menace.

15. What's that! A man in the next compartment, unable to bear the suspense, and trusting to the slow movement of the train, has jumped out; he lies with a dislocated neck, so keep quiet there, if you value your safety: we keep quiet, in such prayer as terror can make: we proceed without new danger; and presently,—passing men who stand and seem to cheer,—passing an engine with a tail of carriages, which has arrived, and been detained for us,—passing beneath the crowded bridge, we glide into the station.

16. The casual train slides off into safety, and we pause before a throng of anxious faces on the platform. Our stoker jumps down—heavy beads are standing on his forehead. "*Six yards between us and eternity!*" he shouts, with an outstretched arm. "SIX YARDS BETWEEN US AND ETERNITY!" He is a God-fearing man from that hour.

---

88. THE MONTH OF OCTOBER IN ITALY.

THE month of October in Italy is certainly a glorious season. The sun has contracted his heat, but not his splendor; he is less scorching, but not less bright. As he rises in the morning, he dashes sparks of radiance over awaking nature, as an Indian prince, upon entering his presence-chamber, flings handfuls of gems and gold into the crowd; and the mountains seem to stretch forth their rocky heads, and the woods to wave their lofty arms, in eagerness to catch his royal largess.

2. And after careering through a cloudless sky, when he reaches his goal, and finds his bed spread with molten gold on the western sea, and canopied above with purple clouds, edged with burnished yet airy fringes, more brilliant than Ophir supplied to the couch of Solomon, he expands himself into a huge disk of most benignant radiance, as if to bid farewell to his past course; but soon sends back, after disappearing, radiant messengers from the world he is visiting and cheering, to remind us he will soon come back and gladden us again.

3. If less powerful, his ray is certainly richer and more active. It has taken months to draw out of the sapless, shrivelled vine-stem, first green leaves, then crisp, slender tendrils, and last, little clusters of hard, sour berries; and the growth has been provokingly slow. But now the leaves are large and mantling, and worthy in vine countries to have a name of their own; and the separated little knots have swelled up into luxurious bunches of grapes. And of these some are already assuming their bright amber tint, while those which are to glow in rich imperial purple are passing rapidly to it, through a changing opal hue, scarcely less beautiful.

4. It is pleasant then to sit in a shady spot, on a hillside, and look ever and anon, from one's book, over the varied and varying landscape. For, as the breeze sweeps over the olives on the hillside, and turns over their leaves, it brings out from them light and shade, for their two sides vary in sober tint; and as the sun shines, or the cloud darkens, on the vineyards, in the rounded hollows between, the brilliant web of unstirring vine-leaves displays a yellower or browner shade of its delicious green.

5. Then, mingle with these the innumerable other colors that tinge the picture, from the dark cypress, the duller ilex, the rich chestnut, the reddening orchard, the adust stubble, the melancholy pine—to Italy what the palm-tree is to the East—towering above the box, and the arbutus, and laurels of villas,

and these scattered all over the mountain, hill, and plain, with fountains leaping up, and cascades gliding down, porticoes of glittering marble, statues of bronze and stone, painted fronts of rustic dwellings, with flowers innumerable, and patches of greensward; and you have a faint idea of the attractions which, for this month, as in our days, used to draw out the Roman patrician and knight, from what Horace calls the clatter and smoke of Rome, to feast his eyes upon the calmer beauties of the country. — CARDINAL WISEMAN.

---

89. COXCOMBRY IN CONVERSATION.

THE emphatic speaker dearly loves to oppose,
In contact inconvenient, nose to nose,
As if the gnomon on his neighbor's phiz,
Touch'd with a magnet, had attracted his.
His whisper'd theme, dilated and at large,
Proves, after all, a wind-gun's airy charge,—
An extract of his diary,—no more,—
A tasteless journal of the day before.

2. He walk'd abroad, o'ertaken in the rain,
Call'd on a friend, drank tea, stepped home again,
Resumed his purpose, had a world of talk
With one he stumbled on, and lost his walk.
I interrupt him with a sudden bow,—
"Adieu, dear sir! lest you should lose it now."

3. I cannot talk with civet in the room—
A fine puss gentleman, that's all perfume;
His odoriferous attempts to please
Perhaps might prosper with a swarm of bees;
But we that make no honey, though we sting,—
Poets,—are sometimes apt to maul the thing.

4. A graver coxcomb we may sometimes see,
Quite as absurd, though not so light as he;

A shallow brain behind a serious mask,
An oracle within an empty cask.
The solemn fop;—significant and budge,
A fool with judges, amongst fools a judge;
He says but little, and that little said
Owes all its weight, like loaded dice, to lead.
5. His wit invites you, by his looks, to come;
But when you knock, it never is at home:
'Tis like a parcel sent you by the stage,
Some handsome present, as your hopes presage;
'Tis heavy, bulky, and bids fair to prove
An absent friend's fidelity and love,—
But when unpack'd, your disappointment groans
To find it stuffed with brickbats, earth, and stones.

COWPER.

90. HENRY IV.'S APOSTROPHE TO SLEEP.

HOW many thousands of my poorest subjects
Are at this hour asleep! O Sleep, O gentle Sleep,
Nature's soft nurse, how have I frighted thee,
That thou no more wilt weigh my eyelids down,
And steep my senses in forgetfulness!
2. Why rather, Sleep, liest thou in smoky cribs,
Upon uneasy pallets stretching thee,
And hush'd with buzzing night-flies to thy slumber,
Than in the perfumed chambers of the great,
Under the canopies of costly state,
And lull'd with sounds of sweetest melody?
Oh thou dull god, why liest thou with the vile,
In loathsome beds; and leav'st the kingly couch,
A watch-case, or a common 'larum-bell?
3 Wilt thou, upon the high and giddy mast,
Seal up the ship-boy's eyes, and rock his brains
In cradle of the rude, imperious surge,
And in the visitation of the winds,

> Who take the ruffian billows by the top,
> Curling their monstrous heads, and hanging them
> With deafening clamors in the slippery shrouds
> That, with the hurly, death itself awakes?
>
> 4. Canst thou, O partial Sleep! give thy repose
> To the wet sea-boy in an hour so rude;
> And, in the calmest and most stillest night,
> With all appliances and means to boot,
> Deny it to a king? Then, happy low, lie down!
> Uneasy lies the head that wears a crown.
>
> SHAKSPEARE.

91. SUCCESS THE REWARD OF MERIT.

DISAPPOINTED authors and artists often talk as if they were the victims of the world's stupidity or malice; as if men were unable or unwilling to appreciate them. Now, I know it is said that such things have been. There have been men of rare promise, but of a sensitive nature, who have been crushed by coldness and neglect, or by the hard and unfair criticism with which their first attempts were met. But this is far from being a common thing. The world likes to be amused and pleased. It is really interested in having something to praise.

2. This being so, how is it possible for a man of real merit to remain long unrecognized? Who can imagine that the great masterpieces of painting, or the great poems that have come down to us from the past, *could* have failed to excite the admiration of men? In fact, human judgment, when you take its suffrages over wide tracts and through the lapse of ages, is infallible. In a particular place it may be warped by passion; in a particular time it may conform to an artificial standard; but give it time and room, and it is sure with unerring accuracy to detect the true.

3. It is as far as possible, then, from being the case that celebrated authors or celebrated artists have become great by

accident. There may have been favorable circumstances. There were undoubtedly great gifts of nature; but there was also deep study and painful, persevering toil. I have been told that the manuscripts of a distinguished English poet show so many erasures that scarcely a line remains unaltered. The great cathedrals of Europe were the fruit of life-long labor. And these are but instances of a general rule.

4. We go into the workshops in which some of the beautiful articles of merchandise are manufactured, and see a great fire and hear the clank of machinery, and men are hurrying to and fro, stained with dust and sweat. Now something like this has been going on to give birth to these beautiful creations in letters and arts which have delighted the world. There has been a great fire in the furnace of the brain, and each faculty of the mind has toiled to do its part, and there have been many blows with the pen, the pencil, or the chisel, until the beautiful conception is complete. Such men are successful, because they deserve it. The approbation of the world did not create their success, it only recognized it.

Rev. F. S. Baker.

---

92. ALEXANDER'S FEAST.

[This poem, of which we give but an extract, is considered the lyric masterpiece of English poetry, exemplifying as it does all the capabilities of our language, in the use of every figure of speech. The measures change in every couplet; there are scarce two lines alike in accentuation, yet the whole seems as spontaneous as the cries of alarm and consternation excited by the bacchanal orgies described.]

NOW strike the golden lyre again,
   A louder yet, and yet a louder strain;
Break his bands of sleep asunder,
And rouse him like a rattling peal of thunder.
   Hark! hark! the horrid sound
     Has raised up his head,
     As awaked from the dead,
   And amazed he stares around.

2. Revenge! revenge! Timotheus cries;
   See the furies arise;
   See the snakes that they rear,
   How they hiss in the air,
   And the sparkles that flash from their eyes.
     Behold the ghastly band,
     Each a torch in his hand!
   These are Grecian ghosts, that in battle are slain,
     And unburied remain,
   Inglorious on the plain;
   Give the vengeance due
   To the valiant crew!

3. Behold how they toss their torches on high—
   How they point to the Persian abodes
   And glittering temples of the hostile gods!
   The princes applaud with a furious joy,
   And the king seized a flambeau, with zeal to destroy;
     Thais led the way,
     To light him to his prey,
   And, like another Helen, fired another Troy.
                                              DRYDEN.

93. THE SILVER-BIRD'S NEST.

["We were shown a beautiful specimen of the ingenuity of birds a few days since. It was a bird's-nest made entirely of silver wires, beautifully woven together. The nest was found on a sycamore-tree. It was the nest of a hanging-bird, and the material was probably obtained from a soldier's epaulet which it had found."]

A STRANDED soldier's epaulet,
   The water's cast ashore,
A little wingéd rover met,
   And eyed it o'er and o'er.
The silver bright so pleased her sight,
   On that lone, idle vest,
She knew not why she should deny
   Herself a silver nest.

2. The shining wire she peck'd and twirl'd,
   Then bore it to her bough,
  Where on a flowery twig 'twas curl'd—
   The bird can show you how;
  But when enough of that bright stuff
   The cunning builder bore
  Her house to make, she would not take,
   Nor did she covet, more.

3. And when the little artisan,
   While neither pride nor guilt
  Had entered in her pretty plan,
   Her resting-place had built;
  With here and there a plume to spare
   About her own light form,
  Of these, inlaid with skill, she made
   A lining soft and warm.

4. But, do you think the tender brood
   She fondled there, and fed,
  Were prouder when they understood
   The sheen about their bed?
  Do you suppose that ever rose,
   Of higher powers possess'd,
  Because they knew they peep'd and grew
   Within a silver nest?   Miss H. F. Gould.

94. THE BURIAL AT SEA.

[The author of this extract, singularly beautiful in thought and expression, is an Anglican clergyman of England, a popular, pure, and poetical writer.]

IT was that of one who, after seeking for health in a more genial climate, was returning to England, in the hope of lying among her own people. But we yet wanted three days of making our own land, when it pleased God to call her to himself.

2. It was a still summer evening that I committed her to the deep. The sea was calm and peaceful; the sun almost rested his broad, red disk upon the waters, forming a path of glory to himself upon the ocean like a road for happy spirits to a better world; the soft hills of Portugal were blue in the distance, the air was mild and balmy. It was just the scene that seemed as if the world had never known and never could know grief; and there, while the vessel was held on and off, were the mourners' clustering round the gangway.

3. There were the weather-beaten sailors, with some feeling even in their iron countenances; there was the union-jack, the only mark of respect we could give; then came the solemn service, and at the sad words, " *We therefore commit her body to the deep,*" the splash of the waters, and the gurgling of the waves over that which was committed to their trust—not given to their possession. For who but could feel that to be Christian burial, when the waves had been stilled and trodden by our Redeemer, when the bodies of so many of his saints have been committed to them, and when one day they must of necessity give up their dead?

Rev. J. M. Neale.

95. THE GLOVE AND THE LIONS.

KING FRANCIS was a hearty king, and loved a royal sport,
And one day, as his lions fought, sat looking on the court;
The nobles fill'd the benches round, the ladies by their side,
And 'mongst them sat the Count de Lorge, with one for whom he sigh'd:
And truly 'twas a gallant thing to see that crowning show,
Valor and love, and a king above, and the royal beasts below.

II.

Ramp'd and roar'd the lions, with horrid laughing jaws;
They bit, they glared, gave blows like beams, a wind went with their paws;

With wallowing might and stifled roar, they roll'd on one
    another,
Till all the pit, with sand and mane, was in a thund'rous
    smother;
The bloody foam above the bars came whizzing thro' the air:
Said Francis then, "Faith! gentlemen, we're better here than
    there!"

III.

De Lorge's love o'erheard the king, a beauteous lively dame,
With smiling lips and sharp bright eyes, which always seem'd
    the same;
She thought,—The Count my lover is brave as brave can be;
He surely would do wondrous things to show his love of me.
Kings, ladies, lovers, all look on! the occasion is divine!
I'll drop my glove, to prove his love: great glory will be mine!

IV.

She dropp'd her glove, to prove his love, then look'd at him
    and smiled;
He bow'd, and in a moment leap'd among the lions wild.
The leap was quick, return was quick—he has regain'd the
    place,—
Then threw the glove—but not with love—right in the lady's
    face.
"By Heaven!" cried Francis, "rightly done!" and he rose
    from where he sat:
"No love," quoth he, "but vanity, sets love a task like that!"
                                                 L. HUNT.

---

96. MODERN THEORIES.

[Extract from a brilliant and eloquent speech delivered in the National Assembly of France, 1848.]

ALL the novel doctrines of our day, all modern theories, tend to an immoderate thirst of enjoyment, and to a spirit of aversion for and revolt against social authority. Yes, all the anti-social tendencies that threaten our country, may be summed up in those two words, *enjoyment* and *contempt*. In the first place, enjoyment not only of one's own property, but of another's property; at least what has heretofore been termed the property of others.

2. Here I beg leave to place before you the authorities on which my assertion rests; and I shall do so without the slightest intention to wound the feelings of others, but merely for the purpose of discussion. I will call your attention to a certain number of axioms or expressions put forth by eminent socialists, which imply that desire of enjoyment to which I have alluded.

3. At the Luxembourg, the working classes were told that they ought to aspire to the highest degree—the maximum of enjoyment. Another orator has declared on this very floor, "The people tell you, through me, that they wish no longer to be poor, and will not be so any longer." It has been said by a third, that the want of the present day was a paradise on earth. Thus you see the idea of enjoyment is everywhere predominant.

4. Other aspirants after the same end endeavor to make labor attractive, and thus destroy the very notion of labor in the popular mind. Instead of its being an obligation, a warning, a punishment, a remedy for the soul of man, it is represented as an enjoyment and a right. At the same time, the notion of self-sacrifice and self-devotion is set aside, and that of happiness is substituted in its place.

5. A man is said to have attained his end upon earth when he has risen to a state of happiness; not, indeed, that moral happiness which consists in the performance of duty and the acquisition of merit, and which necessarily supposes sacrifice and self-devotion, but a happiness which is altogether material.

6. This is the end held out to mankind in general, and to the French nation in particular. And, in addition to this thirsting after a material and immoderate enjoyment, the

people are taught to despise and to resist all kind of authority. This rebellious disposition is not a spirit of liberty, but a spirit of revolt, which threatens as much danger, if not more, to a republican government, as to any other kind of power.

7. In fact, authority is an essential element in a republic as well as in a monarchy; but the idea of authority is now-a-lays materially impaired among those classes, which threaten the social existence of France. The people are very willing to obey laws which they find to their taste; but to obey the law because it is law, to obey the magistrate because he is the magistrate, is an idea which is fast becoming extinct in the mind of the French people. — MONTALEMBERT.

---

97. TO-MORROW IS SAINT CRISPIAN.

[Before the battle of Agincourt, several of the officers were discouraged by the fewness of their soldiers. The Duke of Westmoreland wishes but "one ten thousand of those men who were that day idle were there to help them." The king, Henry V., replies:]

WHAT'S he that wishes so?
    My cousin Westmoreland? No, my fair cousin;
The fewer men, the greater share of honor.
God's will! I pray thee, wish not one man more.
. . . Oh, do not wish one more.
Rather proclaim it, Westmoreland, through our host,
That he which hath no stomach to this fight,
Let him depart; his passport shall be made,
And crowns for coming put into his purse.
This day is called the Feast of Crispian:
He that outlives this day, and comes safe home,
Will stand on tiptoe when this day is named.

2. He that shall live this day, and see old age,
   Will yearly on the vigil feast his neighbors,
   And say: To-morrow is Saint Crispian.

1   . . . Then shall our names,
Familiar in his mouth as household words,—
Harry the king, Bedford and Exeter,
Warwick and Talbot, Salisbury and Glo'ster,—
Be in their flowing cups freshly remember'd;
This story shall the good man teach his son;
And Crispin Crispian shall ne'er go by,
From this day to the ending of the world,
But we in it shall be remembered;
We few, we happy few, we band of brothers.

SHAKSPEARE.

98. A CHALLENGE TO AMERICA.

LET us quarrel, American kinsmen. Let us plunge into war. We have been friends too long. We have too highly promoted each other's wealth and prosperity. We are too plethoric; we want depletion: to which end let us cut one another's throats.

2. Let us sink, burn, kill, and destroy—with mutual energy; sink each other's shipping, burn each other's arsenals, destroy each other's property at large. We will bombard your towns, and you shall bombard ours—if you can. Let us ruin each other's commerce as much as possible, and that will be a considerable some.

3. Let our banks break while we smite and slay one another; let our commercial houses smash right and left in the United States and the United Kingdom. Let us maim and mutilate one another; let us make of each other miserable objects, cripples, halt, and blind, adapted for the town's end, to beg during life.

4. Come, let us render the wives of each other widows, and the mothers childless, and cause them to weep rivers of tears, amounting to an important quantity of "water privilege."

5. The bowl of wrath, the devil's punch-bowl, filled high,

filled high as possible, share we with one another. This, with shot and bayonets, will be good in your insides and in my inside—in the insides of all of us brethren.

6. Oh, how good it is—oh, how pleasant it is, for brethren to engage in internecine strife! What a glorious spectacle we Christian Anglo-Saxons, engaged in the work of mutual destruction—in the reciprocation of savage outrages—shall present to the despots and the fiends!

7. How many dollars will you spend? How many pounds sterling shall we? How much capital we shall sink on either side—on land as well as in the sea! How much we shall have to show for it in corpses and wooden legs!—never ask what other return we may expect for the investment.

8. So, then, American kinsmen, let us fight; let us murder and ruin each other. Let demagogues come hot from their conclave of evil spirits, "cry havoc, and let slip the dogs of war," and do you be mad enough to be those mad dogs, and permit yourselves to be hounded upon us by them. PUNCH.

---

99. THE WONDERFUL "ONE-HOSS SHAY."

A LOGICAL POEM.

[This witty and humorous poem is illustrative of New England character. The words italicised are spelt in such a way as to indicate certain peculiarities of pronunciation sometimes heard among the uneducated in New England.]

HAVE you heard of the wonderful one-*hoss shay,*
That was built in such a logical way
It ran a hundred years to a day,
And then, of a sudden, it—Ah, but stay,
I'll tell you what happened, without delay;
Scaring the parson into fits,
Frightening people out of their wits—
Have you ever heard of that, I say?

2. Seventeen Hundred and Fifty-five,
Georgius Secundus was then alive—
Snuffy old drone from the German hive!
That was the year when Lisbon town
Saw the earth open and gulp her down;
And Braddock's army was done so brown,
Left without a scalp to its crown.
It was on the terrible Earthquake-day
That the Deacon finished the one-*hoss shay*

3. Now, in building of chaises, I tell you what,
There is always, somewhere, a weakest spot—
In hub, tire, felloe, in spring or thill,
In panel or crossbar, or floor, or sill,
In screw, bolt, thoroughbrace—lurking still,
Find it somewhere you must and will—
Above or below, or within or without—
And that's the reason, beyond a doubt,
A chaise breaks down, but does n't wear out.

4. But the Deacon swore—(as Deacons do,
With an "*I dew vum*" or an "*I tell yeou*")—
He would build one *shay* to beat the *taown*
'*N' the keounty 'n' all the kentry raoun'*;
It should be so built that it *couldn'* break *daown:*
"*Fur*," said the Deacon, "'*t's* mighty plain
That the *weakes' place mus' stan'* the strain;
'*N'* the way *t' fix it, uz,* I maintain,
      Is ouly *jest*
T' make that place *uz* strong *uz* the rest."

5. So the Deacon inquired of the village folk
Where he could find the strongest oak,
That could n't be split, nor bent, nor broke—
That was for spokes, and floor, and sills:
He sent for lancewood to make the thills;

The crossbars were ash, from the straightest trees;
The panels of white-wood, that cuts like cheese,
But lasts like iron for things like these;
The hubs of logs from the "Settler's *ellum*"—
Last of its timber—they could n't sell 'em;

6. Never an axe had seen their chips,
And the wedges flew from between their lips,
Their blunt ends frizzled like celery tips;
Step and prop-iron, bolt and screw,
Spring, tire, axle, and linchpin too,
Steel of the finest, bright and blue;
Thoroughbrace, bison-skin, thick and wide;
Boot, top, dasher, from tough old hide,
Found in the pit where the tanner died.
That was the way he "put her through."
"There!" said the Deacon, "*naow she'll dew!*"

7. Do! I tell you, I rather guess
She was a wonder, and nothing less!
Colts grew horses, beards turned gray,
Deacon and deaconess dropped away;
Children and grandchildren—where were they?
But there stood the stout old one-*hoss shay*,
As fresh as on Lisbon-earthquake-day!

8. Eighteen Hundred—it came, and found
The Deacon's masterpiece strong and sound.
Eighteen hundred, increased by ten—
"*Hahnsum kerridge*" they called it then.
Eighteen hundred and twenty came;—
Running as usual—much the same.
Thirty and forty at last arrive;
And then came Fifty—and Fifty-five.

9. Little of all we value here
Wakes on the morn of its hundredth year,
Without both feeling and looking queer.

RHETORICAL.

In fact, there's nothing that keeps its youth,
So far as I know, but a tree and truth.
(This is a moral that runs at large:
Take it.—You're welcome.—No extra charge.)

10. First of November—the Earthquake-day;
There are traces of age in the one-*hoss shay*,
A general flavor of mild decay,
But nothing local, as one may say.
There could n't be—for the Deacon's art
Had made it so like in every part
That there was n't a chance for one to start.
For the wheels were just as strong as the thills,
And the floor was just as strong as the sills,
And the panels just as strong as the floor,
And the whipple-tree neither less nor more,
And the back crossbar as strong as the fore,
And spring, and axle, and hub encore.
And yet, as a whole, it is past a doubt
In another hour it will be worn out!

11. First of November, 'Fifty-five!
This morning the parson takes a drive.
Now, small boys, get out of the way!
Here comes the wonderful one-*hoss shay*,
Drawn by a rat-tailed, ewe-necked bay.
"*Huddup!*" said the parson.—Off went they!

12. The parson was working his Sunday text,—
Had got to *fifthly*, and stopped perplexed
At what the—Moses—was coming next.
All at once the horse stood still,
Close by the *meet'n'-house* on the hill.
—First a shiver, and then a thrill,
Then something decidedly like a spill—
And the parson was sitting upon a rock,

At half-past nine by the *meet'n'-house clock—*
Just the hour of the Earthquake shock!

13. What do you think the parson found,
When he got up and stared around?
The poor old chaise in a heap or mound,
As if it had been to the mill and ground!
You see, of course, if you're not a dunce,
How it went to pieces all at once—
All at once, and nothing first—
Just as bubbles do when they burst.
End of the wonderful one-*hoss* *shay*.
Logic *is* Logic. That's all I say.

HOLMES.

100. LAST DAYS OF PETER STUYVESANT.

IN process of time, the old Governor, like all other children of mortality, began to exhibit tokens of decay. Like an aged oak, which, though it has long braved the fury of the elements, and still retains its gigantic proportions, yet begins to shake and groan with every blast—so was it with the gallant Peter; for though he still bore the port and semblance of what he was in the days of his hardihood and chivalry, yet did age and infirmity begin to sap the vigor of his frame—but his heart, that most unconquerable citadel, still triumphed unsubdued.

2. With matchless avidity would he listen to every article of intelligence concerning the battles between the English and Dutch—still would his pulse beat high whenever he heard of the victories of De Ruyter—and his countenance lower, and his eyebrows knit, when fortune turned in favor of the English. At length, as on a certain day he had just smoked his fifth pipe, and was napping after dinner in his arm-chair, conquering the whole British nation in his dreams, he was suddenly aroused by a fearful ringing of bells, rattling of drums, and roaring of cannon, that put all his blood in a ferment.

3. But when he learned that these rejoicings were in honor of a great victory obtained by the combined English and French fleets over the brave De Ruyter and the younger Von Tromp, it went so much to his heart that he took to his bed, and in less than three days was brought to death's door by a violent cholera morbus! But, even in this extremity, he still displayed the unconquerable spirit of Peter *the Headstrong;* holding out to the last gasp with the most inflexible obstinacy against a whole army of old women, who were bent upon driving the enemy out of his bowels, after a true Dutch mode of defence, by inundating the seat of war with catnip and pennyroyal.

4. While he thus lay, lingering on the verge of dissolution, news was brought him that the brave De Ruyter had suffered but little loss—had made good his retreat—and meant once more to meet the enemy in battle. The closing eye of the old warrior kindled at the words—he partly raised himself in bed—a flash of martial fire beamed across his visage—he clenched his withered hand, as if he felt within his gripe that sword which waved in triumph before the walls of Fort Christina, and, giving a grim smile of exultation, sank back upon his pillow and expired.

5. Thus died Peter Stuyvesant, a valiant soldier—a loyal subject—an upright Governor, and an honest Dutchman—who wanted only a few empires to desolate to have been immortalized as a hero!

6. His funeral obsequies were celebrated with the utmost grandeur and solemnity. The town was perfectly emptied of its inhabitants, who crowded in throngs to pay the last sad honors to their good old Governor. All his sterling qualities rushed in full tide upon their recollections, while the memory of his foibles and his faults had expired with him. The ancient burghers contended who should have the privilege of bearing the pall; the populace strove who should walk nearest to the bier—and the melancholy procession was closed by a number of gray-headed negroes, who had wintered and summered in

the household of their departed master for the greater part of a century.

7. With sad and gloomy countenances the multitude gathered around the grave. They dwelt with mournful hearts on the sturdy virtues, the signal services, and the gallant exploits of the brave old worthy. They recalled with secret upbraidings their own factious opposition to his government; and many an ancient burgher, whose phlegmatic features had never been known to relax, nor his eyes to moisten, was now observed to puff a pensive pipe, and the big drop to steal down his cheek, while he muttered, with affectionate accent and melancholy shake of the head, "Well den!—Hardkoppig Peter ben gone at last!" IRVING.

---

101. STEAM.

OVER the billows and over the brine,
 Over the water to Palestine!
Am I awake, or do I dream?
Over the Ocean to Syria by steam!
My say is *sooth* by this right hand
  A steamer brave
  Is on the wave,
Bound, positively, for the Holy Land!
 Godfrey of Boulogne, and thou,
Richard, lion-hearted king,
  Candidly inform us, now,
   Did you ever?
   No, you never
Could have fancied such a thing.

2. Never such vociferations
  Entered your imaginations
   As the ensuing—

"Ease her, stop her!"
"Any gentleman for Joppa?"
"'Mascus, 'Mascus?" "Ticket, please, Sir."
"Tyre or Sidon?" "Stop her, ease her!"
"Jerusalem, 'lem! 'lem!"—"Shur! Shur!"
"Back her!" "Stand clear, I say, old file!"
"What gent or lady's for the Nile,
Or Pyramids?" "Thebes! Thebes! Sir!"
"Steady!" "Now where's that party for Engedi?"

3. Pilgrims holy, Red Cross Knights,
 Had you e'er the least idea,
Even in your wildest flights,
 Of a steam trip to Judea?
What next marvel time will show,
 It is difficult to say—
"Buss," perchance, to Jericho;
 "Only sixpence all the way!"
Cabs in Solyma may ply,
 'Tis not an unlikely tale;
And from Dan the tourist hie
 Unto Beersheba by rail.
        PUNCH.

---

102. ORIGIN OF THE CITY OF NEW YORK.

THE sage Oloffe dreamed a dream—and lo, the good St. Nicholas came riding over the tops of the trees in that self-same wagon wherein he brings his yearly presents to children, and he came and descended hard by where the heroes of Communipaw had made their late repast.

2. And the shrewd Van Kortlandt knew him by his broad hat, his long pipe, and the resemblance which he bore to the figure on the bow of the Goede Vrouw. And he lit his pipe by the fire and sat himself down and smoked; and as he

smoked, the smoke from his pipe ascended into the air, and spread like a cloud overhead.

3. And Oloffe bethought him, and he hastened and climbed up to the top of one of the tallest trees, and saw that the smoke spread over a great extent of country—and as he considered it more attentively, he fancied that the great volume of smoke assumed a variety of marvellous forms, where in dim obscurity he saw shadowed out palaces, and domes, and lofty spires, all of which lasted but a moment, and then faded away, until the whole rolled off, and nothing but the green woods were left.

4. And when St. Nicholas had smoked his pipe, he twisted it in his hat-band, and laying his finger beside his nose, gave the astonished Van Kortlandt a very significant wink, then mounting his wagon, he returned over the tree-tops and disappeared. And Van Kortlandt awoke from his sleep greatly instructed, and he aroused his companions and related to them his dream, and he interpreted it that it was the will of St. Nicholas that they should settle down and build the city here.

5. And that the smoke of the pipe was a type how vast should be the extent of the city; inasmuch as the volumes of its smoke should spread over a wide extent of country. And they all with one voice assented to this interpretation excepting Mynheer Ten Broeck, who declared the meaning to be that it should be a city wherein a little fire should occasion a great smoke, or, in other words, a very vaporing little city—both which interpretations have come strangely to pass!   IRVING.

---

103. THE DISMISSAL OF GENERAL VON POFFENBURGH.

THE vigilant Peter the Headstrong was not to be deceived. Sending privately for the commander-in-chief of all the armies, and having heard all his story, garnished with the customary pious oaths, protestations, and ejaculations—"Harkee, comrade," cried he, "though by your own account you are the most brave, upright, and honorable man in the whole province, yet do you lie under the misfortune of being damnably traduced and immeasurably despised.

2. "Now, though it is certainly hard to punish a man for his misfortunes, and though it is very possible you are totally innocent of the crimes laid to your charge, yet as Heaven, at present, doubtless for some wise purpose, sees fit to withhold all proofs of your innocence, far be it from me to counteract its sovereign will. Besides, I cannot consent to venture my armies with a commander whom they despise, or to trust the welfare of my people to a champion whom they distrust.

3. "Retire, therefore, my friend, from the irksome toils and cares of public life with this comforting reflection—that if guilty, you are but enjoying your just reward—and if innocent, you are not the first great and good man who has most wrongfully been slandered and maltreated in this wicked world—doubtless to be better treated in a better world, where there shall be neither error, calumny, nor persecution. In the mean time, let me never see your face again, for I have a horrible antipathy to the countenances of unfortunate great men like yourself."

Irving.

---

104. THE HEIGHT OF RIDICULOUS.

I WROTE some lines, once on a time,
   In wondrous merry mood,
And thought, as usual, men would say
   They were exceeding good.

2. They were so queer, so very queer,
   I laugh'd as I would die;
Albeit in the general way
   A sober man am I.

3. I call'd my servant, and he came;
   How kind it was of him,

To mind a slender man like me,
　　He of the mighty limb!

4. "These to the printer," I exclaimed,
　　And in my humorous way,
I added (as a trifling jest),
　　"There'll be the deuce to pay."

5. He took the paper, and I watched,
　　And saw him peep within;
At the first line he read, his face
　　Was all upon the grin.

6. He read the next; the grin grew broad,
　　And shot from ear to ear;
He read the third; a chuckling noise
　　I now began to hear.

7. The fourth, he broke into a roar;
　　The fifth, his waistband split;
The sixth, he burst five buttons off,
　　And tumbled in a fit.

8. Ten days and nights, with sleepless eye,
　　I watched that wretched man,
And since, I never dare to write
　　As funny as I can.　　　　　HOLMES.

---

105. COUNTRY EXCURSION.

[An amusing extract, describing the efforts of Mr. Pickwick and his three friends to ride and drive.]

MR. PICKWICK found that his three companions had risen, and were waiting his arrival to commence breakfast, which was ready laid in tempting display. They sat down to the meal; and broiled ham, eggs, tea, coffee, and sundries, began to disappear with a rapidity which at once bore testimony to the excellence of the fare, and the appetites of its consumers.

2. "Now about Manor Farm," said Mr. Pickwick. "How shall we go?" "We had better consult the waiter, perhaps," said Mr. Tupman; and the waiter was summoned accordingly. "Dingley Dell, gentlemen?—Fifteen miles, gentlemen—cross road.—Post-chaise, sir?" "Post-chaise won't hold more than two," said Mr. Pickwick. "True, sir—beg your pardon, sir.—Very nice four-wheel chaise, sir—seat for two behind—one in front for the gentleman that drives—oh! beg your pardon, sir—that'll only hold three."

3. "What's to be done?" said Mr. Snodgrass. "Perhaps one of the gentlemen like to ride, sir?" suggested the waiter, looking towards Mr. Winkle; "very good saddle-horses, sir—any of Mr. Wardle's men coming to Rochester, bring 'em back, sir." "The very thing," said Mr. Pickwick. "Winkle, will you go on horseback?"

4. Now Mr. Winkle did entertain considerable misgivings, in the very lowest recesses of his own heart, relative to his equestrian skill; but, as he would not have them even suspected on any account, he at once replied with great hardihood, "Certainly. I should enjoy it of all things." Mr. Winkle had rushed upon his fate; there was no resource. "Let them be at the door by eleven," said Mr. Pickwick. "Very well, sir," replied the waiter.

5. The waiter retired; the breakfast concluded; and the travellers ascended to their respective bedrooms, to prepare change of clothing, to take with them on their approaching expedition. Mr. Pickwick had made his preliminary arrangements, and was looking over the coffee-room blinds at the passengers in the street, when the waiter entered, and announced that the chaise was ready—an announcement which the vehicle itself confirmed, by forthwith appearing before the coffee-room blinds aforesaid.

6. It was a curious little green box on four wheels, with a low place like a wine-bin for two behind and an elevated perch for one in front, drawn by an immense brown horse, displaying great symmetry of bone. An hostler stood near it, holding by the bridle another immense horse—apparently a near relative of the animal in the chaise—ready saddled for Mr. Winkle.

7. "Bless my soul!" said Mr. Pickwick, as they stood upon the pavement while the coats were being put in. "Bless my soul! who's to drive? I never thought of that." "Oh! you, of course," said Mr. Tupman. "Of course," said Mr. Snodgrass. "I!" exclaimed Mr. Pickwick. "Not the slightest fear, sir," interposed the hostler. "Warrant him quiet, sir; a hinfant in arms might drive him." "He don't shy, does he?" inquired Mr. Pickwick. "Shy, sir?—he wouldn't shy if he was to meet a vagin-load of monkeys, with their tails burnt off."

8. The last recommendation was indisputable. Mr. Tupman and Mr. Snodgrass got into the bin; Mr. Pickwick ascended to his perch, and deposited his feet on a floor-clothed shelf "erected beneath it, for that purpose." "Now, shiny Villiam," said the hostler to the deputy-hostler, "give the gen'lm'n the ribbins." "Shiny Villiam"—so called, probably, from his sleek hair and oily countenance—placed the reins in Mr. Pickwick's left hand; and the upper hostler thrust a whip into his right.

9. "Woo!" cried Mr. Pickwick, as the tall quadruped evinced a decided inclination to back into the coffee-room window. "Wo-o!" echoed Mr. Tupman and Mr. Snodgrass, from the bin. "Only his playfulness, gen'lm'n," said the head-hostler, encouragingly; "jist kitch hold on him, Villiam." The deputy restrained the animal's impetuosity, and the principal ran to assist Mr. Winkle in mounting. "Tother side, sir, if you please." "Blowed if the gen'lm'n worn't a gettin' up on the wrong side," whispered a grinning post-boy to the inexpressibly gratified waiter.

10. Mr. Winkle, thus instructed, climbed into his saddle with about as much difficulty as he would have experienced in getting up the side of a first-rate man-of-war. "All right?" inquired Mr. Pickwick, with an inward presentiment that it was all wrong. "All right," replied Mr. Winkle, faintly. "Let 'em go," cried the hostler. "Hold him in, sir;" and away went the chaise and the saddle-horse, with Mr. Pickwick on the box of the one, and Mr. Winkle on the back of the other, to the delight and gratification of the whole inn-yard.

106. COUNTRY EXCURSION—(Continued).

"WHAT makes him go sideways?" said Mr. Snodgrass in the bin to Mr. Winkle in the saddle. "I can't imagine," replied Mr. Winkle. His horse was going up the street in the most mysterious manner—side first, with his head towards one side of the way, and his tail to the other.

2. Mr. Pickwick had no leisure to observe either this, or any other particular, the whole of his faculties being concentrated in the management of the animal attached to the chaise, who displayed various peculiarities, highly interesting to a by-stander, but by no means equally amusing to any one seated behind him. Besides constantly jerking his head up in a very unpleasant and uncomfortable manner, and tugging at the reins to an extent which rendered it a matter of great difficulty for Mr. Pickwick to hold them, he had a singular propensity for darting suddenly every now and then to the side of the road, then stopping short, and then rushing forward for some minutes at a speed which it was wholly impossible to control.

3. "What *can* he mean by this?" said Mr. Snodgrass, when the horse had executed this manœuvre for the twentieth time. "I don't know," replied Mr. Tupman; "it *looks* very like shying, don't it?" Mr. Snodgrass was about to reply, when he was interrupted by a shout from Mr. Pickwick.

4. "Woo!" said that gentleman, "I have dropped my whip." "Winkle," cried Mr. Snodgrass, as the equestrian came trotting up on the tall horse, with his hat over his ears, and shaking all over, as if he would shake to pieces, with the violence of the exercise. "Pick up the whip, there's a good fellow." Mr. Winkle pulled at the bridle of the tall horse till he was black in the face; and having at length succeeded in stopping him, dismounted, handed the whip to Mr. Pickwick, and, grasping the reins, prepared to remount.

5. Now whether the tall horse, in the natural playfulness of his disposition, was desirous of having a little innocent recreation with Mr. Winkle, or whether it occurred to him that he could perform the journey as much to his own satisfaction without a rider as with one, are points upon which, of course, we can arrive at no definitive and distinct conclusion. By whatever motives the animal was actuated, certain it is that Mr. Winkle had no sooner touched the reins, than he slipped them over his head, and darted backwards to their full length.

6. "Poor fellow," said Mr. Winkle, soothingly,—"poor fellow—good old horse." The "poor fellow" was proof against flattery: the more Mr. Winkle tried to get near him, the more he sidled away; and, notwithstanding all kinds of coaxing and wheedling, there were Mr. Winkle and the horse going round and round each other for ten minutes, at the end of which time each was at precisely the same distance from the other as when they first commenced—an unsatisfactory sort of thing under any circumstances, but particularly so in a lonely road, where no assistance can be procured.

7. "What am I to do?" shouted Mr. Winkle, after the dodging had been prolonged for a considerable time. "What am I to do? I can't get on him!" "You had better lead him till we come to a turnpike," replied Mr. Pickwick from the chaise. "But he won't come," roared Mr. Winkle. "Do come and hold him."

8. Mr. Pickwick was the very personation of kindness and

humanity: he threw the reins on the horse's back; and having descended from his seat, carefully drew the chaise into the hedge, lest any thing should come along the road, and stepped back to the assistance of his distressed companion, leaving Mr. Tupman and Mr. Snodgrass in the vehicle.

9. The horse no sooner beheld Mr. Pickwick advancing towards him, with the chaise-whip in his hand, than he exchanged the rotary motion in which he had previously indulged for a retrograde movement of so very determined a character that it at once drew Mr. Winkle, who was still at the end of the bridle, at a rather quicker rate than fast walking, in the direction from which they had just come. Mr. Pickwick ran to his assistance; but the faster Mr. Pickwick ran forward, the faster the horse ran backward.

10. There was a great scraping of feet, and kicking up of the dust; and at last Mr. Winkle, his arms being nearly pulled out of their sockets, fairly let go his hold. The horse paused, stared, shook his head, turned round, and quietly trotted home to Rochester, leaving Mr. Winkle and Mr. Pickwick gazing on each other with countenances of blank dismay. A rattling noise at a little distance attracted their attention. They looked up. "Bless my soul!" exclaimed the agonized Mr. Pickwick, "there's the other horse running away!"

11. It was but too true. The animal was startled by the noise, and the reins were on his back. The result may be guessed. He tore off with the four-wheeled chaise behind him, and Mr. Tupman and Mr. Snodgrass in the four-wheeled chaise. The heat was a short one. Mr. Tupman threw himself into the hedge, Mr. Snodgrass followed his example; the horse dashed the four-wheeled chaise against a wooden bridge, separated the wheels from the body, and the bin from the perch, and finally stood stock-still to gaze upon the ruin he had made.

12. The first care of the two unspilt friends was to extricate their unfortunate companions from their bed of quickset—a

process which gave them the unspeakable satisfaction of discovering that they had sustained no injury beyond sundry rents in their garments and various lacerations from the brambles. The next thing to be done was to unharness the horse. This complicated process having been effected, the party walked slowly forward, leading the horse among them, and abandoning the chaise to its fate. — DICKENS.

---

107. SIR HUDIBRAS.

[In this most witty poem Hudibras, a Republican officer during the period of the Commonwealth in England, is represented as sallying out for the entire reformation of the kingdom. Before giving an account of his doughty exploits, his character is thus described:]

HE was in logic a great critic,
Profoundly skill'd in analytic:
He could distinguish and divide
A hair 'twixt south and southwest side;
On either which he would dispute,
Confute, change hands, and still confute;
He'd run in debt by disputation,
And pay with ratiocination:

2. All this by syllogism true,
In mood and figure he would do.
For rhetoric he could not ope
His mouth, but out there flew a trope;
And when he happen'd to break off
I' th' middle of his speech, or cough,
H' had hard words ready to show why,
And tell what rules he did it by;

3. Else when with greatest art he spoke,
You'd think he talk'd like other folk;
For all a rhetorician's rules
Teach nothing but to name his tools.

But when he pleased to show 't, his speech
In loftiness of sound was rich;
A Babylonish dialect,
Which learned pedants much affect;

4. It was a party-color'd dress
Of patch'd and piebald languages;
'Twas English, cut on Greek and Latin,
Like fustian, heretofore, on satin.
In mathematics he was greater
Than Tycho Brahe or Erra Pater;
For he, by geometric scale,
Could take the size of pots of ale;

5. Resolve by signs and tangents straight,
If bread and butter wanted weight;
And wisely tell what hour o' th' day
The clock does strike by algebra.
Besides, he was a shrewd philosopher,
And had read every text and gloss over;
Whate'er the crabbed'st author hath,
He understood b' implicit faith;

6. Whatever skeptic could inquire for,
For every why he had a wherefore;
Knew more than forty of them do,
As far as words and terms could go;
All which he understood by rote,
And, as occasion served, would quote;
No matter whether right or wrong,
They might be either said or sung. BUTLER.

---

108. MODERN IMPROVEMENTS.

[The following is a fine example of irony.]

WE owe the ancients something. You have read
Their works, no doubt—at least, in a translation;
Yet there was argument in what he said,
I scorn equivocation or evasion,

And own, it must, in candor, be confess'd,
They were an ignorant set of men at best.

2. 'Twas their misfortune to be born too soon
   By centuries, and in the wrong place, too;
They never saw a steamboat or balloon,
   Velocipede, or Quarterly Review;
Or wore a pair of Back's black satin breeches,
Or read an almanac, or C———n's speeches.

3. In short, in every thing we far outshine them—
   Art, science, taste, and talent; and a stroll
Through this enlightened city would refine 'em
   More than ten years' hard study of the whole
Their genius has produced, of rich and rare—
God bless the corporation and the mayor!

4. And on our City Hall a justice stands;
   A neater form was never made of board;
Holding majestically in her hands
   A pair of steelyards and a wooden sword,
And looking down with complaisant civility—
Emblem of dignity and durability.   HALLECK.

---

109. SQUIRE BULL AND HIS SON JONATHAN.

JOHN BULL was a choleric old fellow, who held a good manor in the middle of a great mill pond, and which, by reason of its being quite surrounded by water, was generally called *Bullock Island*. Bull was an ingenious man, an exceedingly good blacksmith, a dexterous cutler, and a notable weaver and pot-baker besides. He also brewed capital porter, ale, and small-beer, and was, in fact, a sort of Jack-of-all-trades, and good at each. In addition to these, he was a hearty fellow, an excellent bottle-companion, and *passably* honest as times go.

2. But what tarnished all these qualities was a very quarrelsome, overbearing disposition, which was always getting him into some scrape or other. The truth is, he never heard of a quarrel going on among his neighbors but his fingers itched to be in the thickest of them; so that he was hardly ever seen without a broken head, a black eye, or a bloody nose. Such was Squire Bull, as he was commonly called by the country people, his neighbors—one of those odd, testy, grumbling, boasting old codgers, that never get credit for what they are, because they are always pretending to be what they are not.

3. The Squire was as tight a hand to deal with in doors as out. Sometimes treating his family as if they were not the same flesh and blood, when they happened to differ with him in certain matters. One day he got into a dispute with his youngest son Jonathan, who was familiarly called *Brother Jonathan*, about whether churches ought to be called churches or meeting-houses, and whether steeples were not an abomination.

4. The Squire, either having the worst of the argument, or being naturally impatient of contradiction (I can't tell which), fell into a great passion, and swore he would physic such notions out of the boy's noddle. So he went to some of his *doctors*, and got them to draw up a prescription made up of *thirty-nine different articles*, many of them bitter enough to some palates. This he tried to make Jonathan swallow, and finding he made villainous wry faces, and would not do it, fell upon him and beat him like fury.

5. After this he made the house so disagreeable to him, that Jonathan, though as hard as a pine-knot, and as tough as leather, could bear it no longer. Taking his gun and axe, he put himself in a boat, and paddled over the mill-pond to some new lands to which the Squire pretended some sort of claim,

intending to settle them and build a meeting-house without a steeple as soon as he grew rich enough.

6. When he got over, Jonathan found the land was quite in a state of nature, covered with wood, and inhabited by nobody but wild beasts. But being a lad of mettle, he took his axe on one shoulder and his gun on the other, marched into the thickest of the wood, and clearing a place, built a log cabin. Pursuing his labors, and handling his axe like a notable woodsman, he, in a few years, cleared the land, which he laid out into *thirteen good farms;* and building himself a fine frame house, about half finished, began to be quite snug and comfortable.

7. But Squire Bull, who was getting old and stingy, and, besides, was in want of money, on account of his having lately been made to pay swinging damages for assaulting his neighbors and breaking their heads—the Squire, I say, finding that Jonathan was getting well to do in the world, began to be very much troubled about his welfare; so he demanded that Jonathan should pay him a good rent for the land which he had cleared and made good for something.

8. He trumped up I know not what claim against him, and, under different pretences, managed to pocket all Jonathan's honest gains. In fact, the poor lad had not a shilling left for holiday occasions; and, had it not been for the filial respect he felt for the old man, he would certainly have refused to submit to such impositions. But, for all this, in a little time Jonathan grew up to be very large of his age, and became a tall, stout, double-jointed, broad-footed cub of a fellow, awkward in his gait, and simple in his appearance, but showing a lively, shrewd look, and having the promise of great strength when he should get his full growth.

9. He was rather an odd-looking chap, in truth, and had many queer ways. Like the old Squire, he was apt to be blustering and saucy; but in the main was a peaceable sort of careless fellow, that would quarrel with nobody if you only let him alone. While Jonathan was outgrowing his strength,

Bull kept on picking his pockets of every penny he could scrape together; till at last one day, when the Squire was even more than usually pressing in his demands, which he accompanied with threats, Jonathan started up in a furious passion, and threw the *tea-kettle* at the old man's head.

10. The choleric Bull was hereupon exceedingly enraged; and after calling the poor lad an undutiful, ungrateful, rebellious rascal, seized him by the collar, and forthwith a furious scuffle ensued. This lasted a long time; for the Squire, though in years, was a capital boxer, and of most excellent bottom. At last, however, Jonathan got him under; and before he would let him up, made him sign a paper, giving up all claims to the farms, and acknowledging the fee-simple to be in Jonathan forever.

J. K. PAULDING.

110. AN AMUSING ANECDOTE.

OF Stuart, the American painter, this amusing anecdote is related. He had put up at an inn, and his companions were desirous, by putting roundabout questions, to find out his calling or profession. Stuart answered, with a grave face and serious tone, that he sometimes dressed gentlemen's and ladies' hair. At that time, high-cropped pomatumed hair was all the fashion.

2. "You are a hair-dresser, then?" "What," said he, "do I look like a barber?" "I beg your pardon, sir, but I inferred it from what you said. If I mistook you, may I take the liberty to ask what you are, then?" "Why, I sometimes brush a gentleman's coat or hat, and sometimes adjust a cravat."

3. "Oh, you are a valet, then, to some nobleman?" "A valet! Indeed, sir, I am not. I am not a servant. To be sure, I make coats and waistcoats for gentlemen." "Oh, you are a tailor?". "A tailor! do I look like a tailor? I assure you, I never handled a goose, other than a roasted one."

4. By this time they were all in a roar. "What are you,

then?" said one. "I'll tell you," said Stuart. "Be assured, all I have said is literally true. I dress hair, brush hats and coats, adjust a cravat, and make coats, waistcoats, and breeches, and likewise boots and shoes, at your service."

5. "Oh, ho! a boot and shoemaker, after all!" "Guess again, gentlemen. I never handled boot or shoe, but for my own feet and legs; yet all I have told you is true." "We may as well give up guessing." "Well, then, I will tell you, upon my honor as a gentleman, my *bona fide* profession. I get my bread by making faces."

6. He then screwed his countenance, and twisted the lineaments of his visage, in a manner such as Samuel Foote or Charles Matthews might have envied. His companions, after loud peals of laughter, each took credit to himself for having suspected that the gentleman belonged to the theatre, and they all knew he must be a comedian by profession; when, to their utter astonishment, he assured them that he was never on the stage, and very rarely saw the inside of a play-house, or any similar place of amusement. They all now looked at each other in utter amazement.

7. Before parting, Stuart said to his companions: "Gentlemen, you will find that all I have said of my various employments is comprised in these few words: *I am a portrait painter*. If you will call at my place in London, I shall be ready and willing to brush you a coat or hat, dress your hair *à la mode*, supply you, if in need, with a wig of any fashion or dimensions, accommodate you with boots or shoes, give you ruffles or cravat, and make faces for you."

---

111. FAME.

OH, who shall lightly say that fame
   Is nothing but an empty name,
While in that sound there is a charm,
The nerves to brace, the heart to warm;

As, thinking of the mighty dead,
  The young from slothful couch will start,
And vow, with lifted hands outspread,
  Like them to act a noble part?

2. Oh, who shall lightly say that fame
Is nothing but an empty name,
When, but for those, our mighty dead,
  All ages past a blank would be?
Sunk in Oblivion's murky bed—
  A desert bare—a shipless sea!
They are the distant objects seen,
The lofty marks of what hath been.

3. Oh, who shall lightly say that fame
Is nothing but an empty name,
When memory of the mighty dead
  To earth-worn pilgrim's wistful eye
The brightest rays of cheering shed,
  That point to immortality?   JOANNA BAILLIE.

112. LIFE.

TELL me not, in mournful numbers,
  "Life is but an empty dream!"
For the soul is dead that slumbers,
  And things are not what they seem.

2. Life is real! Life is earnest!
  And the grave is not its goal:
"Dust thou art, to dust returnest,"
  Was not spoken of the soul.

3. Not enjoyment, and not sorrow,
  Is our destined end or way;

But to act, that each to-morrow
Find us further than to-day.

4. Art is long, and time is fleeting;
And our hearts, though stout and brave,
Still, like muffled drums, are beating
Funeral marches to the grave.

5. In the world's broad field of battle,
In the bivouac of Life,
Be not like dumb, driven cattle;
Be a hero in the strife!

6. Trust no Future, howe'er pleasant;
Let the dead Past bury its dead;
Act—act in the living present,—
Heart within, and God o'erhead!

7. Lives of great men all remind us
We can make our lives sublime,
And, departing, leave behind us
Footprints on the sands of Time;—

8. Footprints, that perhaps another,
Sailing o'er life's solemn main,
A forlorn and shipwrecked brother,
Seeing, shall take heart again.

9. Let us, then, be up and doing,
With a heart for any fate;
Still achieving, still pursuing,
Learn to labor and to wait! LONGFELLOW.

PART III.
ORATORICAL.

1. ORATORY AS AN ART.

ONE cause of our not excelling in oratory is our neglecting to cultivate the art of speaking,—of speaking our own language. We acquire the power of expressing our ideas almost insensibly; we consider it as a thing natural to us; we do not regard it as an art; but it is an art, a difficult art, an intricate art; and our ignorance of that circumstance, or our omitting to give it due consideration, is the cause of our deficiency.

2. In the infant just beginning to articulate, you will observe every inflection that is recognized in the most accurate treatise on elocution; you will observe, further, an exact proportion in its several cadences, and a speaking expression in its tones. I say, you will observe these things in almost every infant. Select a dozen men, men of education, erudition; ask them to read a piece of animated composition. You will be fortunate if you find one in the dozen that can raise or depress his voice, inflect or modulate it, as the variety of the subject requires.

3. What has become of the inflections, the cadences, and the modulation of the infant? They have not been exercised; they have been neglected; they have never been put into the hands of the artist, that he might apply them to his proper use; they have been laid aside, spoiled, abused; and ten to one they will never be good for any thing. If we consider the

very early period at which we begin to exercise the faculty of speech, and the frequency with which we exercise it, it must be a subject of surprise that so few excel in oratory. In any enlightened community, you will find numbers skilled in some particular science or art, to the study of which they do not apply themselves till they had almost arrived at the stage of manhood.

4. Yet with regard to the powers of speech—those powers which the very second year of our existence generally calls into action, the exercise of which goes on at our sports, our studies, our walks, our very meals, and which is never long suspended, except at the hour of refreshing sleep—with regard to those powers, how few surpass their fellow-creatures of common information and moderate attainments! how very few desire distinction! how rarely does one attain eminence!

5. In common conversation, observe the advantage which the fluent speaker enjoys over the man that hesitates and stumbles in discourse. With half his information, he has twice his importance; he commands the respect of his auditors; he instructs and gratifies them. In the general transaction of business, the same superiority attends him. He communicates his views with clearness, precision, and effect; he carries his point by his mere readiness; he concludes his treatise before another man has set about it. Does he plead the cause of friendship? how happy is his friend! Of charity? how fortunate is the distressed! Should he enter the legislature of his country, he proves himself the people's bulwark.

KNOWLES.

---

2. THE STUDY OF ORATORY IN GREECE AND ROME.

IN the ancient Republics of Greece and Rome oratory was a necessary branch of a finished education. A much smaller proportion of the citizens were educated than among us; but of these a much larger number became orators. No man could hope for distinction or influence and yet slight this art. The commanders of their armies were orators as well as soldiers, and ruled as well by their rhetorical as by their military skill.

2. There was no trusting with them, as with us, to a natural facility, or the acquisition of an accidental fluency by actual practice. But they served an apprenticeship to the art. They passed through a regular course of instruction in schools. They submitted to long and laborious discipline. They exercised themselves frequently both before equals and in the presence of teachers, who criticized, repined, rebuked, excited emulation, and left nothing undone which art and perseverance could accomplish. The greatest orators of antiquity, so far from being favored by natural tendencies—except, indeed, in their high intellectual endowments—had to struggle against natural obstacles; and, instead of growing up spontaneously to their unrivalled eminence, they forced themselves forward by the most discouraging artificial process.

3. Demosthenes combated an impediment in speech, an ungainliness of gesture, which at first drove him from the forum in disgrace. Cicero failed at first through weakness of lungs and an excessive vehemence of manner, which wearied his hearers and defeated his own purpose. These defects were conquered by study and discipline. He exiled himself from home, and during his absence in various lands, passed not a day without a rhetorical exercise, seeking the masters who were most severe in criticism, as the surest means of leading him to the perfection at which he aimed. WIRT.

---

8. ORATION ON THE CROWN.

[This has been ever regarded by the ablest critics as the greatest speech of the greatest orator. It is virtually a justification of the orator's whole public life, and derives additional interest from being the last great speech delivered in Athens. It was occasioned by the following event: After the battle of Cheronea the Athenians appointed Demosthenes to superintend the repairs in the fortifications of their city. A portion of the expense incurred he paid from his private fortune. In acknowledgment for this, Ctesiphon proposed that a golden crown be voted to him. Æschines maintained that the proposal was illegal, and brought suit nominally against Ctesiphon, but in reality to crush Demosthenes—his speech was a great effort. But Demosthenes' reply was overwhelming. Ctesiphon was triumphantly acquitted and Æschines went into banishment to Rhodes, where he opened a school of rhetoric. He once read Demosthenes' oration to his pupils. Upon their expressing their admiration, he said, "Ah, what would you have thought had you heard the lion himself?"]

BUT, if I am accused for what I have actually done, how would it have been if, through my hard bargaining, the States had gone off and attached themselves to Philip, and he had become master at the same time of Eubœa, Thebes, and Byzantium? What think ye these impious men would have said or done? Said, doubtless, that the States were abandoned—that they wished to join us and were driven away—that he had got command of the Hellespont by the Byzantines, and become master of the corn trade of Greece—that a heavy neighbor-war had, by means of the Thebans, been brought into Attica—that the sea had become unnavigable by the excursion of pirates from Eubœa!

2. All this would they have said, sure enough, and a great deal besides. A wicked, wicked thing, O Athenians, is a calumniator always—every way spiteful and fault-finding. But this creature is a reptile by nature, that from the beginning never did any thing honest or liberal; a very ape of a tragedian, village Œnomaus, counterfeit orator.

3. What advantage has your eloquence been to your country? Now do you speak to us about the past? As if a physician should visit his patient and not order or prescribe any thing for the disease, but on the death of any one, when the last ceremonies were performing, should follow him to the grave and expound how, if the poor fellow had done this and that, he never would have died! Idiot! do you speak now?

4. Even the defeat—if you exult in that which should make you groan—you accursed one!—by nothing that I have done

will it appear to have befallen us. Consider it thus, O Athenians. From no embassy, on which I was commissioned by you, did I ever come away defeated by the ambassadors of Philip—neither from Thessaly nor from Ambracia, nor from the kings of Thrace, nor from Byzantium, nor from any other place, nor on the last recent occasion from Thebes; but where his ambassadors were vanquished with argument, he came with arms and carried the day.

5. And for this you call me to account; and are not ashamed to jeer the same person for cowardice, whom you require single-handed to overcome the might of Philip—and that too by words. For what else had I at command? Certainly not the spirit of each individual, nor the fortune of the army, nor the conduct of the war, for which you would make me accountable—such a blunderer are you!

6. Yet, understand me. Of what a statesman must be responsible, I deprecate it not. What are his functions? To observe things in the beginning, to foresee and foretell them to others. This I have done: again, wherever he finds delays, backwardness, ignorance, jealousies, vices, inherent and unavoidable in communities, to contract them into the narrowest compass; on the other hand, to promote unanimity, friendship, and zeal in the discharge of duty.

7. All this, too, I have performed; and no one can discover the least neglect on my part. Ask any man by what means Philip achieved his successes, and he will answer, "By his army, and by bribing and corrupting men in power." Well, your forces were not under my command or control; so that I cannot be questioned by any thing done in that department.

8. But, by refusing the price of corruption, I have overcome Philip; for, as the offerer of a bribe, if it be accepted, has vanquished the taker, so the person who refuses it, and is not corrupted, has vanquished the person offering. Therefore is the commonwealth undefeated as far as I am concerned.

DEMOSTHENES.

4. ORATION ON THE CROWN—(Continued).

[Of the following extract, Lord Brougham says: "The fame of this noble passage is great and universal. It is of a beauty and a force made for all time and all places."]

OF this base and infamous conspiracy and profligacy—or rather, O Athenians, if I am to speak in earnest of this betrayal of Grecian liberty—Athens is by all mankind acquitted, owing to my counsels; and I am acquitted by you. Then do you ask me, Æschines, by what I claim to be honored? I will tell you. Because, while all the statesmen in Greece, beginning with yourself, have been corrupted, formerly by Philip, and now by Alexander, me, neither opportunity, nor fair speeches, nor large promises, nor hope, nor fear, nor any thing else, could tempt nor induce to betray aught that I considered just and beneficial to my country.

2. Whatever I have advised my fellow-citizens, I have never advised like you, men, leaning as in a balance to the side of profit; all my proceedings have been those of a soul upright, honest, and incorrupt; intrusted with affairs of greater magnitude than any of my contemporaries, I have administered them all honestly and faithfully. Therefore do I claim to be honored.

3. As to this fortification, for which you ridiculed me—for the well and fosse—I regard them as deserving thanks and praise, and so they are; but I place them nowhere near my acts of administration. Not with stones, nor with bricks, did I fortify Athens; nor is this the ministry on which I most pride myself. Would you view my fortifications aright? You will find arms, and States, and posts, and harbors; and galleys, and horses, and men for their defence. These are the bulwarks with which I protected Attica as far as was possible by human wisdom: with these I fortified our territories, not the circle of Piræus nor the city alone. Nay, more, I was not beaten by Philip in estimates or preparations; far from it;

but the generals and forces of the allies were overcome by his fortune. Where are the proofs of this? They are plain and evident.

DEMOSTHENES.

5. PUBLIC SPIRIT OF THE ATHENIANS.

[In the speeches against Philip, the eloquence of Demosthenes fused th Athenians, as it were, into one common unit. The whole assembly became as one man—and had but one voice. LET US MARCH AGAINST PHILIP. LET US FIGHT FOR OUR LIBERTIES. LET US CONQUER OR DIE!]

THE Athenians never were known to live contented in a slavish though secure obedience to unjust and arbitrary power. No; our whole history is a series of gallant contests for pre-eminence: the whole period of our national existence has been spent in braving dangers, for the sake of glory and renown. And so highly do you esteem such conduct, as characteristic of the Athenian spirit, that those of your ancestors who were most eminent for it, are ever the most favorite objects of your praise. And with reason: for, who can reflect, without astonishment, on the magnanimity of those men who resigned their lands, gave up their city, and embarked in their ships, rather than live at the bidding of a stranger?

2. The Athenians of that day looked out for no speaker, no general, to procure them a state of easy slavery. They had the spirit to reject even life, unless they were allowed to enjoy that life in freedom. For it was a principle fixed deeply in every breast, that man was not born to his parents only but to his country. And mark the distinction. He who regards himself as born only to his parents, waits in passive submission for the hour of his natural dissolution. He who considers that he is the child of his country, also volunteers to meet death rather than behold that country reduced to vassalage; and thinks those insults and disgraces which he must endure in a state enslaved, much more terrible than death.

3. Should I attempt to assert that it was I who inspired you

with sentiments worthy of your ancestors, I should meet the just resentment of every hearer. No: it is my point to show that such sentiments are properly your own; that they were the sentiments of my country long before my days. I claim but my share of merit in having acted on such principles during every part of my administration. He, then, who condemns every part of my administration,—he who directs you to treat me with severity, as one who hath involved the State in terrors and dangers,—while he labors to deprive me of present honors, robs you of the applause of all posterity. For, if you now pronounce that my public conduct hath not been right, it must be thought that you yourselves have acted wrong, not that you owe your present state to the caprice of fortune. But it cannot be.

4. No, my countrymen, it cannot be that you here acted wrong in encountering danger bravely for the liberty and safety of all Greece. No! I swear it by the spirits of our sires, who rushed upon destruction at Marathon!—by those who stood arrayed at Platæa!—by those who fought the sea-fight at Salamis!—by the men of Artemisium!—by the others, so many and so brave, who now rest in our public sepulchres!—all of whom their country judged worthy of the same honor; all, I say, not those only who were victorious. And with reason: what was the part of gallant men, they all performed. Their success was such as the Supreme Ruler of the universe dispensed to each. DEMOSTHENES.

---

6. A LAST APPEAL.

O MY countrymen, you must be firmly convinced in your minds, that Philip is at war with our State, and has broken the peace; that, while he is inimical and hostile to the whole of Athens, to the ground of Athens, and, I may add, to the gods of Athens (may they exterminate him!), there is nothing which he strives and plots against so much as our

Constitution, nothing in the world that he is so anxious about as its destruction. And thereunto he is driven in some sort by necessity.

2. Consider. He wishes for empire: and believes you to be his only opponents. He has been a long time injuring you, as his own conscience best informs him; for by means of your possessions, which he is able to enjoy, he secures all the rest of his kingdom: had he given up Amphipolis and Potidæa, he would not have deemed himself safe even in Macedonia. He knows, therefore, both that he is plotting against you, and that you are aware of it; and, supposing you to have common sense, he judges that you detest him as you ought.

3. Besides these important considerations, he is assured that, though he become master of every thing else, nothing can be safe for him while you are under popular government: should any reverse ever befall him (and many may happen to man), all who are now under constraint will come for refuge to you. For you are not inclined yourselves to encroach and usurp dominion; but famous rather for checking the usurper than depriving him of his conquests, ever ready to molest the aspirants for empire, and vindicate the liberty of all nations. He would not like that a free spirit should proceed from Athens, to watch the occasions of his weakness; nor is such reasoning foolish or idle.

4. First, then, you must assume that he is an irreconcilable enemy of our Constitution and democracy; secondly, you must be convinced that all his operations and contrivances are designed for the injury of our State. None of you can be so silly as to suppose that Philip covets those miseries in Thrace (for what else can one call Drongilus, and Cabyle, and Mastira, and the places which he is said now to occupy?), and that to get possession of them he endures hardships, and winters, and the utmost peril, but covets not the harbors of Athens, the docks, the galleys, the silver-mines, the revenues of such value, the place and the glory—never may he or any other man obtain these by the conquest of our city!—or that

he will suffer you to keep these things, while, for the sake of the barley and the millet in Thracian caverns, he winters in the midst of horrors. Impossible. The object of that and every other enterprise of Philip is to become master here.

5. You have quitted, O Athenians, the position in which your ancestors left you; you have been persuaded by these politicians, that to stand foremost of the Greeks, to keep a permanent force, and redress injured nations, is all vanity and idle expense; you imagine that to live in quiet, to perform no duty, to abandon one thing after another, and let strangers seize on all, brings with it a marvellous welfare and abundant security. By such means a stranger has advanced to the post which you ought to have occupied, has become prosperous and great, and made large conquests: naturally enough.

6. A prize there was—noble, great, and glorious—one for which the mightiest States were contending all along; but as the Lacedæmonians were humbled, the Thebans had their hands full through the Phocian war, and we took no regard; he carried it off without competition. The result has been to others terror, to him a vast alliance and extended power; while difficulties so many and so distressing surround the Greeks, that even advice is not easy to be found.

DEMOSTHENES.

---

7. CICERO AND DEMOSTHENES COMPARED.

TO me Demosthenes seems superior to Cicero. I yield to no one in my admiration of the latter. He adorns whatever he touches. He lends honor to speech. He uses words as no one else can use them. His versatility is beyond description. He is even concise and vehement when disposed to be so,—as against Catiline, against Verres, against Antony. But we detect the embellishments in his discourses. The art is marvellous, but it is not hidden. The orator does not, in his concern for the Republic, forget himself, nor does he allow himself to be forgotten.

2. Demosthenes, on the contrary, seems to lose all consciousness of himself, and to recognize only his country. He does not seek the beautiful; he unconsciously creates it. He is superior to admiration. He uses language as a modest man uses his garment—for a covering. He thunders, he lightens; he is like a torrent hurrying all before it. We cannot criticize him, for we are in the sweep of his influence. We think on what he says, not on how he says it. We lose sight of the speaker; we are occupied only with his subject.

FENELON.

---

8. CATILINE DENOUNCED.

[Cicero, the greatest of the Roman orators, was born 106 B. C. As an orator he ranks next to Demosthenes. The rapidity with which he composed his immortal discourses, notwithstanding the multiplicity and importance of the business which oppressed him, did not prevent him bestowing on his style a perfection so uncommon, that it is as easy to understand his Orations as it is difficult, and perhaps even impossible, to translate them well. The Orations against Catiline and Verres are masterpieces of denunciatory eloquence. Having taken part against Antony, Cicero was proscribed. He was murdered by a party of soldiers headed by Popilius Lænas, whose life he had formerly saved by his eloquence. He perished in his sixty-fourth year.]

HOW long, O Catiline, wilt thou abuse our patience? How long also shall thy madness elude us? Whither will thy ungovernable audacity impel thee? Could neither the nightly garrison of the citadel, nor the watch of the city, nor the general consternation, nor the congress of all good men, nor this strongly-fortified place where the Senate is held, nor the enraged countenances of those senators, deter thee from thy impious designs? Dost thou not perceive that thy counsels are all discovered? Thinkest thou that there are any of us ignorant of thy transactions the past night, the place of rendezvous, thy collected associates?

2. Alas, the times! alas, the public morals! The Senate understands all this. The Consul sees it, yet the traitor lives!

Lives? Aye, and truly confronts us here in council—takes part in our deliberations—and, with his measuring eye, marks out each man of us for slaughter! And we all this while, strenuous that we are, think that we have amply discharged our duties to the State if we but *shun* this madman's sword and fury!

3. Long since, O Catiline, ought the Consul to have ordered thee to execution, and brought upon thine own head the ruin thou hast been meditating against others! There was that virtue once in Rome, that a wicked citizen was held more execrable than the deadliest foe. We have a law still, Catiline, for thee! Think not that we are powerless because forbearing. We have a decree—though it rests among our archives, like a sword in the scabbard—a decree by which thy life would be made to pay the forfeit of thy crimes.

4. And should I order thee to be instantly seized and put to death, I make just doubt whether all good men would not think it done rather too late, than any man too cruelly. But for good reasons I will yet defer the blow long since deserved. *Then* I will doom thee when no man is found so lost, so wicked, nay, so like thyself, but shall confess that it was justly dealt. While there is one man that dares defend thee, live! But thou shalt live so beset, so surrounded, so scrutinized, by the vigilant guards that I have placed around thee, that thou shalt not stir a foot against the Republic without my knowledge.

5. There shall be eyes to detect thy slightest movement, and ears to catch thy lowest whisper, of which thou shalt not dream. The darkness of night shall not cover thy treason—the walls of privacy shall not stifle its voice. Baffled on all sides, thy most secret counsels clear as noonday, what canst thou now have in view? Proceed, plot, conspire as thou wilt there is nothing you can contrive, nothing you can propose, nothing you can attempt, which I shall not know, hear, and promptly understand. Thou shalt soon be made aware that I am even more active in providing for the preservation of the State, than thou in plotting its destruction!   CICERO.

9. CATILINE EXPELLED.

AT length, Romans, we are rid of Catiline! We have driven him forth, drunk with fury, breathing mischief, threatening to revisit us with fire and sword. He is gone; he is fled; he has escaped; he has broken away. No longer, within the very walls of the city, shall he plot her ruin. We have forced him from secret plots into open rebellion. The bad citizen is now the avowed traitor. His flight is the confession of his treason! Would that his attendants had not been so few!

2. Be speedy, ye companions of his dissolute pleasures; be speedy, and you may overtake him before night, on the Aurelian road. Let him not languish, deprived of your society. Haste to join the congenial crew that compose his army; *his* army, I say,—for who doubts that the army under Manlius expect Catiline for their leader? And such an army! Outcasts from honor, and fugitives from debt; gamblers and felons; miscreants, whose dreams are of rapine, murder, and conflagration!

3. Against these gallant troops of your adversary, prepare, O Romans, your garrisons and armies; and first, to that maimed and battered gladiator oppose your consuls and generals; next, against that miserable outcast horde, lead forth the strength and flower of all Italy!

4. On the one side chastity contends; on the other, wantonness: here purity, there pollution; here integrity, there treachery; here piety, there profaneness; here constancy, there age; here honesty, there baseness; here continence, there lust; in short, equity, temperance, fortitude, prudence, struggle with iniquity, luxury, cowardice, rashness; every virtue with every vice; and, lastly, the contest lies between well grounded hope and absolute despair. In such a conflict, were even human aid to fail, would not the immortal gods empower such conspicuous virtue to triumph over such complicated vice?

CICERO.

10. THE QUARREL SCENE FROM JULIUS CÆSAR.

Enter Cassius, Trebonius, Titinius, Pindarus.

Cas. Most noble brother, you have done me wrong.
Bru. Judge me, you gods! Wrong I mine enemies?
And if not so, how should I wrong a brother?
Cas. Brutus, this sober form of yours hides wrongs;
And when you do them,—
Bru. Cassius, be content:
Speak your griefs softly—I do know you well:—
Before the eyes of both our armies here,
Which should perceive nothing but love from us,
Let us not wrangle: Bid them move away;
Then in my tent, Cassius, enlarge your griefs,
And I will give you audience.
Cas. Pindarus,
Bid your commanders lead their chargers off
A little from this ground. [*Exeunt* Pindarus.
Bru. Metellus, do the like:— [*Exeunt* Metellus.
And let no man
Come to our tent, till we have done our conference. [*Exeunt*

Scene II.—*The tent of Brutus.*

Enter Cassius *and* Brutus.

Cas. That you have wrong'd me doth appear in this:
You have condemn'd and noted Lucius Pella,
For taking bribes here of the Sardinians;
Wherein, my letters, praying on his side,
Because I knew the man, were slighted off.
Bru. You wrong'd yourself to write in such a case.
Cas. In such a time as this, it is not meet
That every nice offence should bear its comment.
Bru. Let me tell you, Cassius, you yourself
Are much condemn'd to have an itching palm;

To sell and mart your offices for gold
To undeservers.

Cas. I an itching palm!
You know that you are Brutus that speak this,
Or, by the gods, this speech were else your last.

Bru. The name of Cassius honors this corruption,
And chastisement doth therefore hide its head.

Cas. Chastisement!

Bru. Remember March—the ides of March remember!
Did not great Julius bleed for justice' sake?
What villain touch'd his body, that did stab,
And not for justice? What, shall one of us,
That struck the foremost man of all this world,
But for supporting robbers—shall we now
Contaminate our fingers with base bribes,
And sell the mighty space of our large honors
For so much trash as may be graspéd thus?
I had rather be a dog, and bay the moon,
Than such a Roman.

Cas. Brutus, bay not me;
I'll not endure it: I am a soldier, I,
Older in practice, abler than yourself
To make conditions.

Bru. Go to; you're not Cassius.

Cas. I am.

Bru. I say you are not.

Cas. Urge me no more: I shall forget myself:
Have mind upon your health, tempt me no further.

Bru. Away, slight man!

Cas. Is't possible?

Bru. Hear me, for I will speak.
Must I give way and room to your rash choler?
Shall I be frighted when a madman stares?

Cas. Ye gods! ye gods! Must I endure all this?

Bru. [*Nearer.*] All this? ay, more!—Fret till your proud
       heart break.—

Go, show your slaves how choleric you are,
And make your bondmen tremble: Must I budge?
Must I observe you? Must I stand and crouch
Under your testy humor? By the gods,
You shall digest the venom of your spleen,
Though it do split you; for, from this day forth,
I'll use you for my mirth—yea, for my laughter—
When you are waspish.

Cas. Is it come to this?

Bru. You say you are a better soldier;
Let it appear so; make your vaunting true,
And it shall please me well: for mine own part,
I shall be glad to learn of noble men.

Cas. You wrong me, every way you wrong me, Brutus;
I said an older soldier, not a better:
Did I say better?

Bru. If you did, I care not.

Cas. When Cæsar lived, he durst not thus have moved me.

Bru. Peace, peace: you durst not so have tempted him.

Cas. I durst not?

Bru. No.

Cas. What! durst not tempt him?

Bru. For your life you durst not.

Cas. Do not presume too much upon my love;
I may do that I shall be sorry for.

Bru. You have done that you should be sorry for.
There is no terror, Cassius, in your threats;
For I am arm'd so strong in honesty,
That they pass by me as the idle wind,
Which I respect not. I did send to you
For certain sums of gold, which you denied me;
For I can raise no money by vile means;
No, Cassius, I had rather coin my heart,
And drop my blood for drachms, than to wring
From the hard hands of peasants their vile trash,
By any indirection. I did send

To you for gold to pay my legions,
Which you denied me: Was that done like Cassius?
Should I have answer'd Caius Cassius so?
When Marcus Brutus grows so covetous,
To lock such rascal counters from his friends,
Be ready, gods, with all your thunderbolts:
Dash him to pieces!

Cas. I denied you not!

Bru. You did.

Cas. I did not:—He was but a fool
That brought my answer back.—Brutus hath rived my heart·
A friend should bear his friend's infirmities;
But Brutus makes mine greater than they are.

Bru. I do not till you practise them on me.

Cas. You love me not.

Bru. I do not like your faults.

Cas. A friendly eye could never see such faults.

Bru. A flatterer's would not, though they do appeal
As huge as high Olympus.

Cas. Come, Antony, and young Octavius, come,
Revenge yourselves alone on Cassius,
For Cassius is aweary of the world:
Hated by one he loves; braved by his brother;
Check'd like a bondman: all his faults observed,
Set in a note-book, learn'd and conn'd by rote,
To cast into my teeth. Oh, I could weep
My spirit from mine eyes!—There is my dagger,
And here my naked breast; within, a heart
Dearer than Plutus' mine, richer than gold:
If that thou be'st a Roman, take it forth;
I, that denied thee gold, will give my heart:
Strike as thou didst at Cæsar: for I know,
When thou didst hate him worst, thou lov'dst him better
Than ever thou lov'dst Cassius.

Bru. Sheathe your dagger;
Be angry when you will, it shall have scope;

Do what you will, dishonor shall be humor.
Oh, Cassius, you are yoked with a lamb
That carries anger, as a flint bears fire;
Who, much enforced, shows a hasty spark,
And straight is cold again.

Cas. Hath Cassius lived
To be but mirth and laughter to his Brutus,
When grief and blood ill-temper'd vexeth him?

Bru. When I spoke that, I was ill-tempered too.

Cas. Do you confess so much? Give me your hand.
[*Both embrace.*

Bru. And my heart, too.

Cas. Oh Brutus!—

Bru. What's the matter?

Cas. Have you not love enough to bear with me,
When that rash humor which my mother gave me,
Makes me forgetful?

Bru. Yes, Cassius; and henceforth,
When you are over-earnest with your Brutus,
He'll think your mother chides, and leave you so.

SHAKSPEARE.

11. MARC ANTONY'S ORATION.

FRIENDS, Romans, countrymen, lend me your ears;
I come to bury Cæsar, not to praise him.
The evil that men do lives after them;
The good is oft interred with their bones;
So let it be with Cæsar. The noble Brutus
Hath told you, Cæsar was ambitious;
If it were so, it was a grievous fault;
And grievously hath Cæsar answered it.

1. Here, under leave of Brutus and the rest—
   (For Brutus is an honorable man,
   So are they all, all honorable men)—
   Come I to speak in Cæsar's funeral.

He was my friend, faithful and just to me:
But Brutus says he was ambitious;
And Brutus is an honorable man.
He hath brought many captives home to Rome,
Whose ransoms did the general coffers fill:
Did this in Cæsar seem ambitious?

3. When that the poor have cried, Cæsar hath wept:
Ambition should be made of sterner stuff—
Yet Brutus says, he was ambitious;
And Brutus is an honorable man.
You all did see that, on the Lupercal,
I thrice presented him a kingly crown,
Which he did thrice refuse: was this ambition?
Yet Brutus says he was ambitious;
And, sure, he is an honorable man!

4. I speak not to disprove what Brutus spoke,
But here I am to speak what I do know.
You all did love him once, not without cause;
What cause withholds you then to mourn for him?
O judgment, thou art fled to brutish beasts,
And men have lost their reason!—Bear with me:
My heart is in the coffin there with Cæsar,
And I must pause till it come back to me.

5. But yesterday, the word of Cæsar might
Have stood against the world: now lies he there,
And none so poor to do him reverence.
O masters! if I were disposed to stir
Your hearts to mutiny and rage,
I should do Brutus wrong and Cassius wrong,
Who, you all know, are honorable men:
I will not do them wrong; I rather choose
To wrong the dead, to wrong myself, and you,
Than I will wrong such honorable men.

6. But here's a parchment, with the seal of Cæsar;
I found it in his closet, 'tis his will:
Let but the commons hear his testament,

Which, pardon me, I do not mean to read,
And they would go and kiss dead Cæsar's wounds,
And dip their napkins in his sacred blood:
Yea, beg a hair of him for memory,
And, dying, mention it within their wills,
Bequeathing it, as a rich legacy,
Unto their issue.—

7. If you have tears, prepare to shed them now.
You all do know this mantle; I remember
The first time ever Cæsar put it on;
'Twas on a summer's evening, in his tent,—
That day he overcame the Nervii:—
Look, in this place, ran Cassius' dagger through:
See what a rent the envious Casca made:
Through this the well-beloved Brutus stabb'd;
And, as he pluck'd his cursed steel away,
Mark how the blood of Cæsar followed it,
As rushing out of doors, to be resolv'd
If Brutus so unkindly knock'd, or no!

8. For Brutus, as you know, was Cæsar's angel:
Judge, O you gods, how dearly Cæsar loved him!
This was the most unkindest cut of all:
For when the noble Cæsar saw him stab,
Ingratitude, more strong than traitors' arms,
Quite vanquished him: then burst his mighty heart
And, in his mantle muffling up his face,
Even at the base of Pompey's statua,
Which all the while ran blood, great Cæsar fell.

9. O, what a fall was there, my countrymen!
Then I, and you, and all of us fell down,
Whilst bloody treason flourish'd over us.—
O, now you weep; and, I perceive, you feel
The dint of pity: these are gracious drops;
Kind souls! What, weep you, when you but behold
Our Cæsar's vesture wounded? Look you here.
Here is himself, marr'd as you see, with traitors.—

10. Good friends, sweet friends, let me not stir you up
To such a sudden flood of mutiny.
They that have done this deed are honorable;
What private griefs they have, alas! I know not,
That made them do it: They are wise and honorable:
And will, no doubt, with reasons answer you.
I come not, friends, to steal away your hearts·
I am no orator, as Brutus is;
But as you know me all, a plain, blunt man,
That love my friend: and that they know full well
That gave me public leave to speak of him;
11. For I have neither wit, nor words, nor worth,
Action, nor utterance, nor the power of speech
To stir men's blood. I only speak right on;
I tell you that which you yourselves do know;
Show you sweet Cæsar's wounds, poor dumb mouths,
And bid them speak for me: But, were I Brutus,
And Brutus Antony, there were an Antony
Would ruffle up your spirits, and put a tongue
In every wound of Cæsar that should move
The stones of Rome to rise and mutiny!

SHAKSPEARE.

12. AGAINST THE EXECUTION OF LOUIS XVI.

[Vergniaud, the most eloquent orator of the celebrated party known as the Girondists during the French Revolution, was born in 1749; executed in 1793. His speech at the opening of the Assembly for the trial of Louis XVI. produced the greatest sensation on his hearers, of all parties, even the most reckless; Robespierre himself, thunder-struck by his earnest and persuasive eloquence, remained silent, and did not attempt to reply to it.]

IT is said that it behooves the Convention to show courage sufficient to pass judgment on the king, without calling on the opinion of the people for its support. Courage! It required courage to attack Louis XVI. in the height of his power. Does it require as much to send Louis vanquished and disarmed to execution?

2. A soldier entered the prison of Marius with the intention of murdering him. Terrified at the sight of his victim, he fled without daring to strike. Had this soldier been a member of a senate, do you suppose he would have hesitated to vote the death of a tyrant? What courage do you find in the performance of an act of which a coward would be capable?

3. Have you not heard in this place and elsewhere men crying out, "If bread is dear, the cause of it is in the Temple?" If we are shocked every day by the sight of beggary, the cause of it is in the Temple.

4. And yet those who hold this language well know that the dearness of bread, the want of circulation in provisions, the maladministration of the armies, and the indigence whose sight afflicts us, spring from other causes than those in the Temple.

5. What, then, are their designs? Who will guarantee that these same men, who are continually striving to degrade the Convention, and who might possibly have succeeded if the majesty of the people which resides in it could depend on their perfidies; that those same men who are everywhere proclaiming that a new revolution is necessary—who are declaring this or that section in a state of permanent insurrection; who say that when the Convention succeeded Louis we only changed tyrants, and that we want another 10th of August; that these same men who talked of nothing but plots, deaths, traitors, proscriptions; who insist in their meetings and in their writings that a *Defender* ought to be appointed for the Republic, and that nothing but a chief can save it;—who, say, will guarantee to me that these very men will not, fter the death of Louis, cry out with greater violence than ever, "If bread is dear, the cause of it is in the Convention! if money is scarce, if our armies are scantily supplied, the cause of this is in the Convention!" VERGNIAUD.

13. THE RISING OF THE VENDEE.

[La Vendée is a district on the western coast of France, the inhabitants of which were royalists, and fought bravely against the revolutionary government in France, 1793.]

I.

IT was a Sunday morning, and sweet and pure the air,
And brightly shone the Summer sun upon the day of prayer
And silver-sweet the village bells o'er mount and valley tolled,
And in the Church of St. Florent were gathered young and old,
When rushing down the woodland hill, in fiery haste was seen,
With panting steed and bloody spur, a noble Angevine;
And bounding on the sacred floor, he gave his fearful cry,
"Up! up for France! the time is come for France to live or die!"

II.

"Your queen is in the dungeon; your king is in his gore;
O'er Paris waves the flag of death, the fiery tri-colour;
Your nobles in their ancient halls are hunted down and slain;
In convent cells and holy shrines the blood is poured like rain.
The peasant's vine is rooted up, his cottage given to flame;
His son is to the scaffold sent, his daughter sent to shame.
With torch in hand and hate in heart, the rebel host is nigh.
Up! up for France! the time is come for France to live or die!"

III.

That live-long night the horn was heard from Orleans to Anjou,
And poured from all their quiet fields our shepherds bold an true.
Along the pleasant banks of Loire shot up the beacon-fires,
And many a torch was blazing bright on Luçon's stately spires
The midnight cloud was flushed with flame, that hung o'er Parthenay;
The blaze that shone o'er proud Brissac was like the breaking day,

Till east, and west, and north and south, the loyal beacons shone
Like shooting stars from haughty Nantes to sea-begirt Olonne.

IV.

And through the night, on horse and foot, the sleepless summons flew,
And morning saw the Lily-flag wide-waving o'er Poitou.
And many an ancient musketoon was taken from the wall,
And many a jovial hunter's steed was harnessed in the stall,
And many a noble's armory gave up the sword and spear,
And many a bride, and many a babe, was left with kiss and tear,
And many a homely peasant bade farewell to his old dame,
As in the days when France's king unfurled the Oriflamme.

V.

There, leading his bold marksmen, rode the eagle-eyed Lescure,
And dark Stofflet, who flies to fight as an eagle to his lure ;
And fearless as the lion roused, but gentle as the lamb,
Came marching at his people's head the great and good Bonchamp ;
Charette, where honor was the prize, the hero sure to win ;
And there, with Henri Quatre's plume, young Rochejacquelein;
And there, in peasant garb and speech—the terror of the foe—
A noble, made by Heaven's own hand, the great Cathelineau.

VI.

We marched by tens of thousands, we marched by day and night,
The Lily-standard in our front, like Israel's holy light.
Around us rushed the rebels, as the wolf upon the sheep—
We burst upon their columns as a lion roused from sleep ;
We tore their bayonets from their hands, we slew them at their guns ;
Their boasted horsemen fled like chaff before our forest sons.

That night we heaped their baggage high their lines of dead between,
And in the centre blazed to heaven their blood-dyed guillotine!

VII.

In vain they hid their heads in walls; we rushed on stout Thouar;
What cared we for shot or shell, for battlement or bar?
We burst its gates; then like a wind we rushed on Fontenay;
We saw its flag with morning light—'twas ours by setting day;
We crushed like ripened grapes Montreuil, we bore down old Vihiers;
We charged them with our naked breasts, and took them with a cheer.
We'll hunt the robbers through the land, from Seine to sparkling Rhone;
Now, "Here's a health to all we love—our kiny shall have his own!"

Croly.

14. LORD STRAFFORD'S DEFENCE.

[Lord Strafford, an ardent supporter of Charles I., was impeached, and finally beheaded in consequence, by the House of Commons, towards the close of the reign of that unfortunate monarch. His defence was characterized by a depth of passion, breaking forth at times in passages of startling power or tenderness, which we find only in the highest class of oratory. The pathos of the conclusion has been much admired, and if we go back in imagination to the scene as presented at Westminster Hall—the once proud Earl, standing amid the wreck of his fortunes, with that splendid Court around him, which lately bowed submissive to his will; with his humbled monarch looking on from behind the screen that concealed his person, unable to interpose or arrest the proceedings; with that burst of tenderness at the thought of earlier days, and of his wife, the Lady Arabella Hollis, "that saint in heaven," to whose memory he had always clung amid the power and splendor of later life; with his body bowed down under the pressure of intense physical suffering, and his strong spirit utterly subdued, and poured out like water in that startling cry, "My Lords, *my Lords*, my Lords: Something more I had intended to say, but my voice and my spirit fail me,"—we cannot but feel that there are few passages of equal tenderness and power in the whole range of English eloquence. We are strongly reminded of Shakspeare's delineation of Wolsey, under similar circumstances, in some of the most pathetic scenes which poetry has ever depicted.]

MY LORDS, be pleased to give that regard to the peerage of England, as never to expose yourselves to such novel points, such constructive interpretations of law. If there must be a trial of wits, let the subject-matter be something else than the lives and honor of peers! It will be wisdom for yourselves and your posterity to cast into the fire these bloody and mysterious volumes of constructive and arbitrary treason, as the primitive Christians did their books of curious arts, and betake yourselves to the plain letter of the law and the statute, which telleth what is and what is not treason, without being ambitious to be more learned in the art of killing than our forefathers. These gentlemen tell us that they speak in defence of the Commonwealth against their arbitrary treason!

2. It is now full two hundred and forty years since any man was touched for this alleged crime to this height before myself. Let us not awaken those sleeping lions to our destruction, by taking up a few musty records that have lain by the walls for so many ages, forgotten or neglected.

3. My Lords, what is my present misfortune may be forever yours. It is not the smallest part of my grief that not the crime of treason, but my other sins, which are exceeding many, have brought me to this bar; and, except your Lordships' wisdom provide against it, the shedding of my blood may make way for the tracing out of yours. You, your estates, your posterity, lie at the stake.

4. For my poor self, if it were not for your Lordships' interest, and the interest of a saint in heaven, who hath left me here two pledges on earth (at this his breath stopped, and he shed tears abundantly in mentioning his wife), I should never take the pains to keep up this ruinous cottage of mine. It is loaded with such infirmities, that in truth I have no great pleasure to carry it about with me any longer. Nor could I

ever leave it at a fitter time than this, when I hope that the better part of the world would perhaps think that by my misfortunes I had given a testimony of my integrity to my God, my king, and my country. I thank God, I count not the afflictions of the present life to be compared to that glory which is to be revealed in the time to come!

5. My Lords! my Lords! my Lords! something more I had intended to say, but my voice and my spirit fail me. Only I do in all humility and submission cast myself down at your Lordships' feet, and desire that I may be a beacon to keep you from shipwreck. Do not put such rocks in your own way, which no prudence, no circumspection can eschew or satisfy but by your utter ruin!

6. And so, my Lords, even so with all tranquillity of mind, I submit myself to your decision. And whether your judgment in my case— I wish it were not the case of you all—be for life or for death, it shall be righteous in my eyes, and shall be received with a *Te Deum laudamus*—we give God the praise.

---

15. SENATORIAL DENUNCIATION OF RICHARD CROMWELL.

[Sir Henry Vane was born in England, 1612. He was the fourth Governor of the Colony of Massachusetts. In 1662 he was executed for high treason, on Malvern Hill, England. The remarkable speech, of which we give a brief extract, did not fail in its effects—Richard Cromwell never appeared in public after it was delivered. "This impetuous torrent," says one of Vane's biographers, "swept every thing before it. Oratory, genius, and the spirit of liberty never achieved a more complete triumph. It broke, and forever, the power of Richard and his party."]

MR. SPEAKER: Among all the people of the universe, I know none who have shown so much zeal for the liberty of their country as the English at this time have done;—they have, by the help of Divine Providence, overcome all obstacles, and have made themselves free. We have driven away the hereditary tyranny of the House of Stuart, at the expense of much blood and treasure, in hopes of enjoying hereditary liberty, after having shaken off the yoke of kingship; and there is not a man among us who could have imagined that any person would be so bold as to dare to attempt the ravishing from us that freedom which cost us so much blood and so much labor.

2. But so it happens, I know not by what misfortune, we are fallen into the error of those who poisoned the Emperor Titus to make room for Domitian; who made away Augustus that they might have Tiberius; and changed Claudius for Nero. I am sensible these examples are foreign from my subject, since the Romans in those days were buried in lewdness and luxury, whereas the people of England are now renowned all over the world for their great virtue and discipline; and yet,—suffer an idiot, without courage, without sense,—nay, without ambition,—to have dominion in a country of liberty!

3. One could bear a little with Oliver Cromwell, though, contrary to his oath of fidelity to the Parliament, contrary to his duty to the public, contrary to the respect he owed that venerable body from whom he received his authority, he usurped the Government. His merit was so extraordinary, that our judgments, our passions, might be blinded by it. He made his way to empire by the most illustrious actions; he had under his command an army that had made him a conqueror, and a people that had made him their general.

4. But, as for Richard Cromwell, his son, who is he? what are his titles? We have seen that he had a sword by his side; but did he ever draw it? And, what is of more importance in this case, is *he* fit to get obedience from a mighty nation, who could never make a footman obey him? Yet, we must recognize this man as our king, under the style of Protector!—a man without birth, without courage, without conduct! For my part, I declare, sir, it shall never be said that I made such a man my master! SIR HENRY VANE.

16. KING JOHN AND HUBERT.

[This speech, where King John takes Hubert aside and tempts him to undertake the murder of the king's fair young nephew, Prince Arthur, is a most admirable exercise on the lower tones of the voice. It exhibits a sort of descending, or anti-climax, the words, *a grave*, being pronounced in the lowest tones we can command. It must be delivered in an earnest whisper; but as this whisper must be heard by the entire audience, great force must be added to these low tones. None but good readers and the best orators can do this well; but these notes are of great importance, and in the hands of a well-practiced speaker or reader, they are a source of much pleasing variety.]

K. John. Come hither, Hubert. O, my gentle Hubert,
We owe thee much; within this wall of flesh
There is a soul counts thee her creditor,
And with advantage means to pay thy love.
And, my good friend, thy voluntary oath
Lives in this bosom, dearly cherished.
Give me thy hand, I had a thing to say—
But I will fit it with some better time.
By heav'n, Hubert, I'm almost ashamed
To say what good respect I have of thee.
 Hub. I am much bounden to your majesty
 K. John. Good friend, thou hast no cause to say so yet,
But thou shalt have—and creep time ne'er so slow,
Yet it shall come for me to do thee good:
I had a thing to say,—but let it go;
The sun is in the heav'n, and the proud day,
Attended with the pleasures of the world,
Is all too wanton and too full of gauds
To give me audience. If the midnight bell
Did with his iron tongue and brazen mouth
Sound one unto the drowsy race of night;
If this same were a churchyard where we stand,
And thou possessed with a thousand wrongs;
Or if that thou couldst see me without eyes,
Hear me without thine ears, and make reply
Without a tongue, using conceit alone,

Without eyes, ears, and harmful sound of words
Then in despite of broad-eyed, watchful day,
I would into thy bosom pour my thoughts.
But, ah! I will not—yet I love thee well,
And by my troth, I think thou lov'st me well.

Hub. So well, that what you bid me undertake,
Though that my death were adjunct to my act,
By heav'n I'd do it.

K. John. Do I not know that thou wouldst?
Good Hubert, Hubert, Hubert, throw thine eye
On yon young boy: I'll tell thee what, my friend,
He is a very serpent in my way,
And wheresoe'er this foot of mine doth tread,
He lies before me. Dost thou understand me?
Thou art his keeper.

Hub. And I'll keep him so,
That he shall not offend your majesty.

K. John. Death.

Hub. My lord?

K. John. A grave.

Hub. He shall not live.

K. John. Enough.
I could be merry now. Hubert, I love thee;
Well, I'll not say what I intend for thee:
Remember.
SHAKSPEARE.

17. STRICTURES ON WILLIAM PITT.

SIR, I was unwilling to interrupt the course of this debate, while it was carried on with calmness and decency, by men who do not suffer the ardor of opposition to cloud their reason, or transport them to such expressions as the dignity of this assembly does not admit. I have hitherto deferred to answer the gentleman who declaimed against the bill with such fluency of rhetoric, and such vehemence of gesture,— who charged the advocates for the expedients now proposed with having no regard to any interest but their own, and with making laws only to consume paper, and threatened them with the defection of their adherents, and the loss of their influence, upon this new discovery of their folly and their ignorance.

2. Nor, sir, I do now answer him for any other purpose than to remind him how little the clamors of rage and the petulancy of invectives contribute to the purposes for which this assembly is called together; how little the discovery of truth is promoted, and the security of the nation established, by pompous diction and theatrical emotions. Formidable sounds and furious declamation, confident assertions and lofty periods, may affect the young and inexperienced; and, perhaps, the gentleman may have contracted his habits of oratory by conversing more with those of his own age than with such as have had more opportunities of acquiring knowledge, and more successful methods of communicating their sentiments.

3. If the heat of his temper, sir, would suffer him to attend to those whose age and long acquaintance with business give them an indisputable right to deference and superiority, he would learn, in time, to reason rather than declaim, and to prefer justness of argument, and an accurate knowledge of facts, to sounding epithets and splendid superlatives, which may disturb the imagination for a moment, but which leave no lasting impression on the mind.

4. He will learn, sir, that to accuse and to prove are very different; and that reproaches, unsupported by evidence, affect only the character of him that utters them. Excursions of fancy and flights of oratory are, indeed, pardonable in young men, but in no other; and it would surely contribute more, even to the purpose for which some gentlemen appear to speak (that of depreciating the conduct of the administration), to prove the inconvenience and injustice of this bill, than barely to assert them, with whatever magnificence of language, or appearance of zeal, honesty, or compassion.

SIR ROBERT WALPOLE.

18. REPLY OF WILLIAM PITT—1741.

[William Pitt, first Earl of Chatham, has generally been regarded as the most powerful orator of modern times. He certainly ruled the British Senate as no man has ever ruled over a great deliberative assembly. His success, no doubt, was in part owing to extraordinary personal advantages. Such was the power of his eye that he often cowed down an antagonist in the midst of is speech, and threw him into utter confusion by a glance of scorn or contempt. Whenever he rose to speak his countenance glowed with animation. His voice was clear and full. His lowest whisper was distinctly heard; his middle notes were of exceeding sweetness; and when he elevated his voice to its highest pitch, the house was completely filled with the rich volume of sound. The effect was awful, except when he wished to cheer and animate,— then he had spirit-stirring notes which were perfectly irresistible. The first sound of his voice in the following reply is said to have terrified Sir R. Walpole, who exclaimed, "We must muzzle that terrible cornet of horse." Sir Robert offered to promote Mr. Pitt in the army provided he gave up his seat in Parliament. Every speech of Lord Chatham is worth the attention of the student of oratory.]

SIR,—The atrocious crime of being a young man, which the honorable gentleman has, with such spirit and decency, charged upon me, I shall neither attempt to palliate nor deny, but content myself with wishing that I may be one of those whose follies may cease with their youth, and not of that number who are ignorant in spite of experience. Whether youth can be imputed to man as a reproach, I will not, sir, assume the province of determining; but surely age may become justly contemptible if the opportunities which it brings have passed away without improvement, and vice appears to prevail when passions have subsided.

2. The wretch who, after having seen the consequences of a thousand errors, continues still to blunder, and whose age has only added obstinacy to stupidity, is surely the object of either abhorrence or contempt, and deserves not that his gray hairs should secure him from insult. Much more, sir, is he to be abhorred, who, as he has advanced in age, has receded from virtue, and becomes more wicked with less temptation; who prostitutes himself for money which he cannot enjoy, and spends the remainder of his life in the ruin of his country.

3. But youth, sir, is not my only crime, I have been accused of acting a theatrical part. A theatrical part may either imply some peculiarities of gesture or a dissimulation of my real sentiments, and an adoption of the opinions and languages of other men. In the first sense, sir, the charge is too trifling to be confuted, and deserves only to be mentioned to be despised.

4. I am at liberty, like every other man, to use my own language; and though, perhaps, I may have some ambition to please this genleman, I shall not lay myself under any restraint, nor very solicitously copy his direction or his mien, however matured by age, or modeled by experienced. If any man shall, by charging me with theatrical behavior, imply that I utter any sentiments but my own, I shall treat him as a calumniator and a villain, nor shall any protection shelter him from the treatment he deserves. I shall, on such an occasion, without scruple, trample upon all those forms with which wealth and dignity intrench themselves, nor shall any thing but age restrain my resentment—age, which always brings one privilege, that of being insolent and supercilious without punishment.

5. But with regard, sir, to those whom I have offended, I am of opinion that if I had acted a borrowed part, I would have avoided their censure. But the heat that offended them is the ardor of conviction, that zeal for the service of my country which neither hope nor fear shall influence me to suppress. I will not sit unconcerned while my liberty is invaded, nor look in silence upon public robbery. I will exert my endeavors at whatever hazard to repel the aggression, and drag the thief to justice, whoever may partake of their plunder. And if the honorable gentleman—

6. [At this point Mr. Pitt was called to order by Mr. Wynnington, who went on to say: "No diversity of opinion can justify the violation of decency and the use of rude and violent expressions, dictated only by resentment, and uttered without regard to—" Here Mr. Pitt called to order and proceeded thus :]

7. Sir, if this be to preserve order, there is no danger of indecency from the most licentious tongues. For what calumny can be more atrocious, what reproach more severe, than that of speaking with regard to any thing but truth. Order may sometimes be broken by passion or inadvertency, but will hardly be re-established by a monitor like this, who cannot govern his own passions while he is restraining the impetuosity of others.

8. Happy would it be for mankind if every one knew his own province. We should not then see the same man at once a criminal and a judge; nor would this gentleman assume the right of dictating to others what he has not learned himself. That I may return in some degree the favor he intends me, I will advise him never hereafter to exert himself on the subject of order; but whenever he feels inclined to speak on such occasions, to remember how he has now succeeded, and condemn in silence what his censures will never amend.

---

19. HOTSPUR.

[This scene, where Hotspur, fresh from the field of his daring exploits, vindicates himself from the charge of refusing to give up the prisoners of war, should be declaimed very rapidly, harshly, and sometimes with interruption and hesitation, as if the speaker were unable to give it sufficient force. The voice assumes the highest tone it can command consistently with force and boldness—though sometimes the low and forcible tone is used to express anger with uncommon energy.]

MY liege, I did deny no prisoners,
But I remember when the fight was done,
When I was dry with rage and extreme toil,
Breathless and faint, leaning upon my sword,
Came there a certain lord, neat, trimly dress'd,
Fresh as a bridegroom; and his chin, new reap'd,
Show'd like a stubble land at harvest home:
2. He was perfumed like a milliner;
And 'twixt his finger and his thumb he held

A pouncet-box, which ever and anon
He gave his nose, and took 't away again;—
Who, therewith angry when it next came there,
Took it in snuff—and still he smiled and talk'd,
And as the soldiers bore dead bodies by,
He call'd them untaught knaves, unmannerly,
To bring a slovenly unhandsome corse
Betwixt the wind and his nobility.

3. With many holiday and lady terms,
He question'd me; among the rest demanded
My prisoners, in your majesty's behalf.
I then, all smarting with my wounds being cold,
To be so pester'd with a popinjay,
Out of my grief and my impatience
Answer'd neglectingly, I know not what,

4. He should, or should not;—for he made me mad,
To see him shine so brisk, and smell so sweet,
And talk so like a waiting gentlewoman,
Of guns, and drums, and wounds (heaven save the mark!)
And telling me the sovereign'st thing on earth
Was parmacity for an inward bruise;
And that it was great pity, so it was,
That villanous saltpetre should be digg'd
Out of the bowels of the harmless earth,

5. Which many a good tall fellow had destroy'd
So cowardly; and but for these vile guns
He would himself have been a soldier.
This bold, unjointed chat of his, my lord,
I answer'd indirectly as I said,
And I beseech you, let not his report
Come current for an accusation
Betwixt my love and your high majesty.

SHAKSPEARE.

20. REPEAL OF THE STAMP ACT.

[Lord Chatham is justly endeared to every American for his eloquent appeals in their behalf against the aggressions of the Mother Country. Feeble and decripit as he had become, he forgot his age and sufferings. He stood forth in the presence of the whole empire to arraign as a breach of the Constitution every attempt to tax a people who had no representative in Parliament. It was the era of his sublimest efforts in oratory. He denounced the war with a prophetic sense of the shame and disaster attending such a conflict. His voice rang throughout every town and hamlet in the Colonies, and when he proclaimed in Parliament: "I rejoice that America has resisted!" millions of hearts on this side of the Atlantic swelled with a prouder determination of resisting even to the end.]

SIR,—A charge is brought against gentlemen sitting in this house of giving birth to sedition in America. Several have spoken their sentiments with freedom against this unhappy act,—and that freedom has become their crime. Sorry I am to hear the liberty of speech in this house imputed as a crime. But the imputation shall not discourage me.

2. The gentleman tells us, America is obstinate; America is almost in open rebellion. I rejoice that America has resisted! Three millions of people so dead to all the feelings of liberty as voluntarily to let themselves be made slaves would have been fit instruments to make slaves of all the rest.

3. I come not here armed at all points with law cases and acts of Parliament, with statute-books doubled down in dogs' ears, to defend the cause of liberty. I would not debate a particular point of law with the gentleman. I know his abilities. But, for the defence of liberty, upon a general principle, upon a constitutional principle, it is a ground on which I stand firm—on which I dare meet any man.

4. The gentleman boasts of his bounties to America. Are not those bounties intended finally for the benefit of this kingdom? If they are not, he has misapplied the national treasures. He asks, When were the Colonies emancipated? I desire to know when they were made slaves! But I dwell not upon words.

5. I will be bold to affirm that the profits of Great

Britain from the trade of the Colonies, through all its branches, are two millions a year. This is the fund that carried you triumphantly through the last war. This is the price America pays for her protection. And shall a miserable financier come, with a boast that he can fetch a peppercorn into the exchequer, by the loss of millions to the nation?*

6. A great deal has been said, without doors, of the power, of the strength of America. It is a topic that ought to be cautiously meddled with. In a good cause, the force of this country can crush America to atoms. I know the valor of your troops; I know the skill of your officers.

7. But on this ground,—on the Stamp Act, when so many here will think it a crying injustice,—I am one who will lift up my hands against it. In such a cause, even your success would be hazardous. America, if she fell, would fall like the strong man. She would embrace the pillars of the State, and pull down the Constitution along with her. Is this your boasted peace? To sheathe the sword, not in its scabbard, but in the bowels of your countrymen?

8. Will you quarrel with yourselves, now the whole house of Bourbon is united against you? While France disturbs your fisheries in Newfoundland, embarrasses your slave-trade to Africa, and withholds from your subjects in Canada their property stipulated by treaty? while the ransom for Manillas is denied by Spain?

9. The Americans have been wronged. They have been driven to madness by injustice. Will you punish them for the madness you have occasioned? Rather let prudence and temper come first from this side! I will undertake for America that she will follow the example.

"Be to her faults a little blind;
Be to her virtues very kind."

Let the Stamp Act be repealed; and let the reason for the re-

---

* Mr. Nugent had said that a peppercorn in acknowledgment of the right to tax America was of more value than millions without it.

peal—*because the Act was founded on erroneous principles*—be assigned. Let it be repealed absolutely, totally, and immediately!
LORD CHATHAM.

21. RECONCILIATION WITH AMERICA.

[In regard to this speech, we find in the diary of Josiah Quincy, jr., the following memorandum: "Attended the debates in the House of Lords. Good fortune gave me one of the best places for hearing, and taking a few minutes. Lord Chatham rose like Marcellus. His language, voice, and gesture, were more pathetic than I ever saw or heard before, at the Bar or Senate. He seemed like an old Roman Senator, rising with the dignity of age, yet speaking with the fire of youth." Dr. Franklin, who was also present at the debate, said of this speech, that "he had seen, in the course of his life, sometimes eloquence without wisdom, and often wisdom without eloquence; in the present instance, he saw both united, and both, as he thought, in the highest degree possible."]

AMERICA, my Lords, cannot be reconciled to this country — she ought not to be reconciled—till the troops of Britain are withdrawn. How can America trust you, with the bayonet at her breast? How can she suppose that you mean less than bondage or death? I therefore move that an address be presented to his majesty, advising that immediate orders be dispatched to General Gage, for removing his majesty's forces from the town of Boston.

2. The way must be immediately opened for reconciliation. It will soon be too late. An hour now lost in allaying ferments in America may produce years of calamity. Never will I desert for a moment the conduct of this weighty business. Unless nailed to my bed by the extremity of sickness I will pursue it to the end. I will knock at the door of this sleeping and confounded ministry, and will, if possible, rouse them to a sense of their danger.

3. I contend not for indulgence, but for justice, to America. What is our right to persist in such cruel and vindictive acts against a loyal, respectable people? They say you have no right to tax them without their consent. They say truly

Representation and taxation must go together; they are inseparable. I therefore urge and conjure your lordships immediately to adopt this conciliating measure.

4. If illegal violences have been, as it is said, committed in America, prepare the way—open the door of possibility—for acknowledgment and satisfaction; but proceed not to such coercion—such proscription: cease your indiscriminate inflictions; amerce not thirty thousand; oppress not three millions; irritate them not to unappeasable rancor, for the fault of forty or fifty. Such severity of injustice must forever render incurable the wounds you have inflicted.

5. What though you march from town to town, from province to province? What though you enforce a temporary and local submission; how shall you secure the obedience of the country you leave behind you in your progress? How grasp the dominion of eighteen hundred miles of continent, populous in numbers, strong in valor, liberty, and the means of resistance?

7. The spirit which now resists your taxation, in America, is the same which formerly opposed loans, benevolences and ship-money, in England;—the same spirit which called all England on its legs, and, by the Bill of Rights, vindicated the English Constitution;—the same spirit which established the great fundamental essential maxim of your liberties, *that no subject of England shall be taxed but by his own consent.*

8. This glorious Whig spirit animates three millions in America, who prefer poverty, with liberty, to gilded chains and sordid affluence; and who will die in defence of their rights as men. What shall oppose this spirit, aided by the congenial flame glowing in the breast of every Whig in England! "'Tis liberty to liberty engaged," that they will defend themselves, their families, and their country. In this great cause they are immovably allied: it is the alliance of God and nature,—immutable, eternal,—fixed as the firmament of Heaven.

EARL OF CHATHAM.

32. THE AMERICAN WAR.

[CHARLES JAMES FOX, born in England, 1729; died, 1762. His style of oratory has been compared by some critics to Demosthenes'. In his language Mr. Fox studied simplicity, strength, and boldness. "Give me an elegant Latin word," said he, "and a homely Saxon one, and I will choose the latter." Another of his sayings was this: "Did the speech read well when reported; if so it was a bad one." These two remarks give us the secret of his style as an orator.

The life of Fox has this lesson for young men: that early habits of recklessness and vice can hardly fail to destroy the influence of the most splendid abilities and the most humane and generous dispositions.]

WE are charged with expressing joy at the triumphs of America. True it is that, in a former session, I proclaimed it as my sincere opinion, that if the ministry had succeeded in their first scheme on the liberties of America, the liberties of this country would have been at an end. Thinking this, as I did, in the sincerity of an honest heart, I rejoiced at the resistance which the ministry had met to their attempt. That great and glorious statesman, the late Earl of Chatham, feeling for the liberties of his native country, thanked God that America had resisted.

2. But, it seems, "all the calamities of the country are to be ascribed to the wishes, and the joy, and the speeches, of opposition." Oh, miserable and unfortunate ministry! Oh, blind and incapable men! whose measures are framed with so little foresight, and executed with so little firmness, that they not only crumble to pieces, but bring on the ruin of their country, merely because one rash, weak, or wicked man, in the House of Commons, makes a speech against them!

3. But who is he who arraigns gentlemen on this side of the House with causing, by their inflammatory speeches, the misfortunes of their country? The accusation comes from one whose inflammatory harangues have led the nation, step by step, from violence to violence, in that inhuman, unfeeling system of blood and massacre, which every honest man must detest, which every good man must abhor, and every wise man condemn!

4. And this man imputes the guilt of such measures to those who had all along foretold the consequences; who had prayed, entreated, and supplicated, not only for America, but for the credit of the nation and its eventual welfare, to arrest the hand of power, meditating slaughter, and directed by injustice!

5. What was the consequence of the sanguinary measures recommended in those bloody, inflammatory speeches? Though Boston was to be starved, though Hancock and Adams were proscribed, yet at the feet of these very men the Parliament of Great Britain was obliged to kneel, flatter, and cringe; and, as it had the cruelty at one time to denounce vengeance against these men, so it had the meanness afterwards to implore their forgiveness.

6. Shall he who called the Americans "Hancock and his crew,"—shall he presume to reprehend any set of men for inflammatory speeches? It is this accursed American war that has led us, step by step, into all our present misfortunes and national disgraces.

7. What was the cause of our wasting forty millions of money, and sixty thousand lives? The American war! What was it that produced the French rescript and a French war? The American war! What was it that produced the Spanish manifesto and Spanish war? The American war! What was it that armed forty-two thousand men in Ireland with the arguments carried on the points of forty thousand bayonets? The American war! For what are we about to incur an additional debt of twelve or fourteen millions? This accursed, cruel, diabolical American war! Fox.

---

28. THE FOREIGN POLICY OF WASHINGTON.

HOW infinitely superior must appear the spirit and principles of General Washington, in his late address to Congress, compared with the policy of modern European courts!

Illustrious man!—deriving honor less from the splendor of his situation than from the dignity of his mind! Grateful to France for the assistance received from her, in that great contest which secured the independence of America, he yet did not choose to give up the system of neutrality in her favor.

2. Having once laid down the line of conduct most proper to be pursued, not all the insults and provocations of the French minister, Genet, could at all put him out of his way, or bend him from his purpose. It must, indeed, create astonishment, that, placed in circumstances so critical, and filling a station so conspicuous, the character of Washington should never once have been called in question;—that he should, in no one instance, have been accused either of improper insolence, or of mean submission, in his transactions with foreign nations.

3. It has been reserved for him to run the race of glory without experiencing the smallest interruption to the brilliancy of his career. The breath of censure has not dared to impeach the purity of his conduct, nor the eye of envy to raise its malignant glance to the elevation of his virtues. Such has been the transcendent merit and the unparalleled fate of this illustrious man!

4. How did he act when insulted by Genet? Did he consider it as necessary to avenge himself for the misconduct or madness of an individual, by involving a whole continent in the horrors of war? No; he contented himself with procuring satisfaction for the insult, by causing Genet to be recalled; and thus, at once, consulted his own dignity and the interests of his country.

5. Happy Americans! while the whirlwind flies over one quarter of the globe, and spreads everywhere desolation, you remain protected from its baneful effects by your own virtues, and the wisdom of your government. Separated from Europe by an immense ocean, you feel not the effect of those prejudices and passions which convert the boasted seats of civilization into scenes of horror and bloodshed. You profit by the

folly and madness of the contending nations, and afford, in your more congenial clime, an asylum to those blessings and virtues which they wantonly contemn, or wickedly exclude from their bosom!

6. Cultivating the arts of peace under the influence of freedom, you advance, by rapid strides, to opulence and distinction; and if, by any accident, you should be compelled to take part in the present unhappy contest,—if you should find it necessary to avenge insult, or repel injury,—the world will bear witness to the equity of your sentiments and the moderation of your views; and the success of your arms will, no doubt, be proportioned to the justice of your cause! Fox.

24. "A POLITICAL PAUSE."

SAYS the honorable gentleman: "But we must pause!" What! must the bowels of Great Britain be torn out— her best blood be spilt—her treasures wasted—that you may make an experiment? Put yourselves, O! that you would put yourselves on the field of battle, and learn to judge of the sort of horrors that you excite.

2. In former wars a man might, at least, have some feeling, some interest, that served to balance in his mind the impressions which a scene of carnage and of death must inflict. But if a man were present now at the field of slaughter, and were to inquire for what they were fighting,—"Fighting!" would be the answer; "they are not fighting; they are pausing."

3. "Why is that man expiring? Why is that other writhing with agony? What means this implacable fury?" The answer must be,—"You are quite wrong, sir; you deceive yourself—they are not fighting—do not disturb them—they are merely pausing! This man is not expiring with agony— that man is not dead—he is only pausing!

4. "Lord help you, sir! they are not angry with one another: they have now no cause of quarrel; but their country

thinks that there should be a pause. All that you see, sir, is nothing like fighting—there is no harm, nor cruelty, nor bloodshed in it, whatever; it is nothing more than a political pause! It is merely to try an experiment—to see whether Bonaparte will not behave himself better than heretofore; and in the mean time we have agreed to a pause, in pure friendship!"

5. And is this the way, sir, that you are to show yourselves the advocates of order? You take up a system calculated to uncivilize the world—to destroy order—to trample on religion—to stifle in the heart, not merely the generosity of noble sentiment, but the affections of social nature; and in the prosecution of this system, you spread terror and devastation all around you.
Fox.

---

25. THE AMERICAN WAR DENOUNCED.

[Mr. Pitt was the second son of the great Lord Chatham. He entered Parliament at the age of twenty-two, and became virtually leader of the House and Prime Minister at twenty-four. As a debater, his speeches are logical and argumentative. They are stamped with the strongest marks of originality. His eloquence, occasionally rapid, electric, and vehement, was always chaste, winning, and persuasive—not awing into acquiescence, but arguing into conviction. Unallured by dissipation and unswayed by pleasure, he never sacrificed the national treasure to one, nor the national interest to the other. With Chatham, Burke, and Fox, Pitt stands, by universal consent, at the head of British eloquence.]

GENTLEMEN have passed the highest eulogiums on the American war. Its justice has been defended in the most fervent manner. A noble lord, in the heat of his zeal, has called it a holy war. For my part, although the honorable gentleman who made this motion, and some other gentlemen, have been, more than once, in the course of the debate, severely reprehended for calling it a wicked and accursed war, I am persuaded, and would affirm, that it was a most accursed, wicked, barbarous, cruel, unnatural, unjust, and diabolical war!

2. It was conceived in injustice; it was nurtured and

brought forth in folly; its footsteps were marked with blood, slaughter, persecution, and devastation;—in truth, every thing which went to constitute moral depravity and human turpitude were to be found in it. It was pregnant with misery of every kind.

3. The mischief, however, recoiled on the unhappy people of this country, who were made the instruments by which the wicked purposes of the authors of the war were effected. The nation was drained of its best blood, and of its vital resources of men and money. The expense of the war was enormous,—much beyond any former experience.

4. And yet, what has the British nation received in return? Nothing but a series of ineffective victories, or severe defeats;—victories celebrated only by a temporary triumph over our brethren, whom we would trample down and destroy; victories, which filled the land with mourning for the loss of dear and valued relatives, slain in the impious cause of enforcing unconditional submission, or with narratives of the glorious exertions of men struggling in the holy cause of liberty, though struggling in the absence of all the facilities and advantages which are in general deemed the necessary concomitants of victory and success.

5. Where was the Englishman, who, on reading the narratives of those bloody and well-fought contests, could refrain from lamenting the loss of so much British blood spilt in such a cause; or from weeping, on whatever side victory might be declared? WILLIAM PITT.

---

26. ON AN ATTEMPT TO COERCE HIM TO RESIGN.

[Certain resolutions were passed by the House of Commons, in 1784, for the removal of his Majesty's ministers, at the head of whom was Mr. Pitt. These resolutions, however, his Majesty had not thought proper to comply with. A reference having been made to them, Mr. Pitt spoke as follows, in reply to Mr. Fox:]

CAN any thing that I have said, Mr. Speaker, subject me to be branded with the imputation of preferring my personal situation to the public happiness? Sir, I have declared, again and again, Only prove to me that there is any reasonable hope—show me but the most distant prospect—that my resignation will at all contribute to restore peace and happiness to the country, and I will instantly resign.

2. But, sir, I declare, at the same time, I will not be induced to resign as a preliminary to negotiation. I will not abandon this situation, in order to throw myself upon the mercy of that right honorable gentleman. He calls me now a mere nominal minister, the mere puppet of secret influence.

3. Sir, it is because I will not become a mere nominal minister of his creation,—it is because I disdain to become the puppet of that right honorable gentleman,—that I will not resign; neither shall his contemptuous expressions provoke me to resignation: my own honor and reputation I never will resign.

4. Let this house beware of suffering any individual to involve his own cause, and to interweave his own interests, in the resolutions of the House of Commons. The dignity of the house is forever appealed to. Let us beware that it is not the dignity of any set of men. Let us beware that personal prejudices have no share in deciding these great constitutional questions.

5. The right honorable gentleman is possessed of those enchanting arts whereby he can give grace to deformity. He holds before your eyes a beautiful and delusive image; he pushes it forward to your observation; but, as sure as you embrace it, the pleasing vision will vanish, and this fair phantom of liberty will be succeeded by anarchy, confusion, and ruin to the Constitution. For, in truth, sir, if the constitutional independence of the crown is thus reduced to the very verge of annihilation, where is the boasted equipoise of the Constitution?

6. Dreadful, therefore, as the conflict is, my conscience, my duty, my fixed regard for the Constitution of our ancestors,

maintain me still in this arduous situation. It is not any proud contempt, or defiance of the constitutional resolutions of this house,—it is no personal point of honor,—much less is it any lust of power, that makes me still cling to office. The situation of the times requires of me—and, I will add, the country calls aloud to me—that I should defend this castle; nd I am determined, therefore, I WILL defend it!

WILLIAM PITT.

---

27. SECTARIAN TYRANNY, 1812.

WHENEVER one sect degrades another on account of religion, such degradation is the tyranny of a sect. When you enact that, on account of his religion, no Catholic shall sit in Parliament, you do what amounts to the tyranny of a sect. When you enact that no Catholic shall be a sheriff, you do what amounts to the tyranny of a sect. When you enact that no Catholic shall be a general, you do what amounts to the tyranny of a sect.

2. There are two descriptions of laws,—the municipal law, which binds the people, and the law of God, which binds the Parliament and the people. Whenever you do any act which is contrary to His laws, as expressed in His work, which is the world, or in His book, the Bible, you exceed your right; whenever you rest any of your establishments on that excess, you rest it on a foundation which is weak and fallacious; whenever you attempt to establish your government, or your property, or your Church, on religious restrictions, you establish them on that false foundation, and you oppose the Almighty; and though you had a host of mitres on your side, you banish God from your ecclesiastical constitution, and freedom from your political.

3. In vain shall men endeavor to make this the cause of the Church; they aggravate the crime, by the endeavor to make their God their fellow in the injustice. Such rights are

the rights of ambition; they are the rights of conquest; and, in your case, they have been the rights of suicide. They begin by attacking liberty; they end by the loss of empire!

HENRY GRATTAN.

---

28. REPLY TO THE DUKE OF GRAFTON.

[The Duke of Grafton had reproached Lord Thurlow (High Chancellor of England), with his plebeian extraction and his recent admission to the peerage. Lord Thurlow rose from the woolsack and advanced slowly towards the place from which the chancellor generally addresses the house; then fixing on the duke the look of Jove when he grasps the thunder, he said in a loud tone of voice, "I am amazed at the attack which the noble lord has made upon me." Then raising his voice—"Yes, my lords, I am amazed," etc. The effect of this speech, both within the house and out of it, was prodigious. It gave Lord Thurlow an ascendency, which no chancellor had ever possessed; it invested him in public opinion with a character of independence and honor, and this, though he was ever on the unpopular side of politics, made him always popular with the people.]

I AM amazed at the attack the noble duke has made on me. Yes, my lords, I am amazed at his grace's speech. The noble duke cannot look before him, behind him, or on either side of him, without seeing some noble peer who owes his seat in this house to his successful exertions in the profession to which I belong. Does he not feel that it is as honorable to owe it to these, as to being the accident of an accident?

2. To all these noble lords the language of the noble duke is as applicable and insulting as it is to myself. But I do not fear to meet it single and alone. No one venerates the peerage more than I do: but, my lords, I must say, that the peerage solicited me, not I the peerage.

3. Nay, more: I can say, and will say, that as a peer of Parliament, as Speaker of this right honorable house, as keeper of the great seal, as guardian of his majesty's conscience, as lord high chancellor of England, nay, even in that character alone in which the noble duke would think it an affront to be

considered,—as A MAN, I am at this moment as respectable,—I beg leave too add,—I am at this time as much respected, as the proudest peer I now look down upon. THURLOW.

29. A COLLISION OF VICES.

[GEORGE CANNING, born in London, 1770.—His father was of Irish descent. In 1827 he became Prime Minister. The Duke of Wellington, Mr. Peel, and nearly all his Tory colleagues, threw up their places at once out of hostility to Catholic emancipation, which they saw must prevail if he remained in office—the very two men who, two years after, under the strong compulsion of public sentiment carried that same emancipation through both houses of Parliament! But they sacrificed Mr. Canning before they could be made to do it. Mr. Canning is considered the best model among our orators of the adorned style. No English speaker used the keen, brilliant weapon of wit so long, so often, and so effectively as Mr. Canning. His eloquence was persuasive and impassioned, his reasoning clear and logical, his manner graceful, and his expression winning.]

MY honorable and learned friend began by telling us that, after all, hatred is no bad thing in itself. "I hate a Tory," says my honorable friend; "and another man hates a cat; but it does not follow that he would hunt down the cat, or I the Tory."

2. Nay, so far from it, hatred, if it be properly managed, is, according to my honorable friend's theory, no bad preface to a rational esteem and affection. It prepares its votaries for a reconciliation of differences; for lying down with their most inveterate enemies, like the leopard and the kid in the vision of the prophet.

3. This dogma is a little startling, but it is not altogether without precedent. It is borrowed from a character in a play, which is, I dare say, as great a favorite with my learned friend as it is with me,—I mean the comedy of the Rivals; in which Mrs. Malaprop, giving a lecture on the subject of marriage to her niece (who is unreasonable enough to talk of liking, as a necessary preliminary to such a union), says, "What have you to do with your likings and your preferences, child? Depend upon it, it is safest to begin with a little

aversion. I am sure I hated your poor dear uncle like a blackamoor before we were married; and yet, you know, my dear, what a good wife I made him."

4. Such is my learned friend's argument, to a hair. But finding that this doctrine did not appear to go down with the house so glibly as he had expected, my honorable and learned friend presently changed his tack, and put forward a theory, which, whether for novelty or for beauty, I pronounce to be incomparable; and, in short, as wanting nothing to recommend it but a slight foundation in truth.

5. "True philosophy," says my honorable friend, "will always continue to lead men to virtue by the instrumentality of their conflicting vices. The virtues, where more than one exists, may live harmoniously together; but the vices bear mortal antipathy to one another, and, therefore, furnish to the moral engineer the power by which he can make each keep the other under control."

6. Admirable! but, upon this doctrine, the poor man who has but one single vice must be in a very bad way. No fulcrum, no moral power, for effecting his cure! Whereas, his more fortunate neighbor, who has two or more vices in his composition, is in a fair way of becoming a very virtuous member of society. I wonder how my learned friend would like to have this doctrine introduced into his domestic establishment.

7. For instance, suppose that I discharge a servant because he is addicted to liquor, I could not venture to recommend him to my honorable and learned friend. It might be the poor man's only fault, and therefore clearly incorrigible; but, if I had the good fortune to find out that he was also addicted to stealing, might I not, with a safe conscience, send him to my learned friend with a strong recommendation, saying, "I send you a man whom I know to be a drunkard; but I am happy to assure you he is also a thief: you cannot do better than employ him; you will make his drunkenness counteract his thievery."

CANNING.

80. "MEASURES NOT MEN."

IF I am pushed to the wall, and forced to speak my opinion, I have no disguise nor reservation:—I do think that this is a time when the administration of the government ought to be in the ablest and fittest hands; I do not think the hands in which it is now placed answer to that description.

2. I do not pretend to conceal in what quarter I think that fitness most eminently resides; I do not subscribe to the doctrines which have been advanced, that in times like the present, the fitness of individuals for their political situation is no part of the consideration to which a member of Parliament may fairly turn his attention.

3. I know not a more solemn or important duty that a member of Parliament can have to discharge, than by giving at fit seasons a free opinion upon the character and qualities of public men. Away with the cant of "measures, not men!" the idle supposition that it is the harness, and not the horses, that draw the chariot along!

4. No, sir; if the comparison must be made, if the distinction must be taken, men are every thing, measures comparatively nothing. I speak, sir, of times of difficulty and danger; of times when systems are shaken, when precedents and general rules of conduct fail.

5. Then it is, that not to this or that measure,—however prudently devised, however blameless in execution,—but to the energy and character of individuals, a State must be indebted for its salvation. Then it is that kingdoms rise or fall in proportion as they are upheld, not by well-meant endeavors (laudable though they may be), but by commanding, overawing talents,—by able men.

6. And what is the nature of the times in which we live? Look at France, and see what we have to cope with, and consider what has made her what she is. A man! You will tell me that she was great, and powerful, and formidable before the days of Bonaparte's government, that he found in her

great physical and moral resources; that he had but to turn them to account. True, and he did so.

7. Compare the situation in which he found France with that to which he has raised her. I am no panegyrist of Bonaparte; but I cannot shut my eyes to the superiority of his talents, to the amazing ascendency of his genius. Tell me not of his measures and his policy. It is his genius, his character that keeps the world in awe.

8. Sir, to meet, to check, to curb, to stand up against him, we want arms of the same kind. I am far from objecting to the large military establishments which are proposed to you. I vote for them, with all my heart. But, for the purpose of coping with Bonaparte, one great, commanding spirit is worth them all.

CANNING.

---

81. DANGER OF DELAY.

[So completely had Lord Brougham wrought up his own feelings and those of his hearers at the close of this speech, that it was nothing strained or unnatural—it was in fact almost a matter of course—for him to sink down upon one of his knees at the table where he stood, when he uttered the last words—"*I supplicate you*, reject not this bill." But the sacrifice was too great for that proud nobility. It was rejected by a majority of *forty-one*, of whom *twenty-one* belonged to the board of bishops of the Established Church.]

MY Lords, I do not disguise the intense solicitude which I feel for the event of this debate, because I know full well that the peace of the country is involved in the issue. I cannot look without dismay at the rejection of the measure. But grievous as may be the consequences of a temporary defeat—temporary it can only be; for its ultimate and even speedy success is certain. Nothing can now stop it.

2. Do not suffer yourselves to be persuaded that even if the present ministers were driven from the helm, any one could steer you through the troubles which surround you without reform. But our successors would take up the task under circumstances far less auspicious. Under them you would be

fain to grant a bill compared with which the one we now proffer you is moderate indeed.

3. Hear the parable of the Sibyl; for it conveys a wise and wholesome moral. She now appears at your gate, and offers you mildly the volumes—the precious volumes of wisdom and peace. The price she asks is reasonable; to restore the franchise, which without any bargain you ought voluntarily to give; you refuse her terms—her moderate terms—she darkens the porch no longer.

4. But soon, for you cannot do without her wares, you call her back; again she comes, but with diminished treasures; the leaves of the book are in part torn away by lawless hands—in part defaced with characters of blood. But the prophetic maid had risen in her demands—it is Parliament by the year—it is vote by the ballot—it is suffrage by the million!

5. From this you turn away indignant, and for the second time she departs. Beware of her third coming: for the treasure you must have, and what price she may next demand who shall tell? It may even be the mace which rests upon that woolsack. What may follow your course of obstinacy, if persisted in, I cannot take upon me to predict, nor do I wish to conjecture.

6. But this I know full well, that as sure as man is mortal, and to err is human, justice deferred enhances the price at which you must purchase safety and peace; nor can you expect to gather in another crop than they did who went before you, if you persevere in their utterly abominable husbandry, of sowing injustice and reaping rebellion.

7. But among the awful considerations that now bow down my mind, there is one which stands pre-eminent above the rest. You are the highest judicature in the realm; you sit here as judges, decide all causes, civil and criminal, without appeal. It is a judge's first duty never to pronounce sentence, in the most trifling case, without hearing. Will you make this the exception?

8. Are you really prepared to determine but not to hear the mighty cause upon which a nation's hopes and fears hang? You are. Then beware of your decision! Rouse not, I beseech you, a peace-loving, but resolute people: alienate not from your body the affections of a whole empire.

9. As your friend, as the friend of my order, as the friend of my country, as the faithful servant of my sovereign, I counsel you to assist with your utmost efforts in preserving the peace and upholding and perpetuating the constitution. Therefore I pray and exhort you not to reject this measure. By all you hold most dear—by all the ties that bind every one of us to our common order and to our common country, I solemnly adjure you—I warn you—I implore you—yea, on my bended knees, I supplicate you—reject not this bill.

LORD BROUGHAM.

---

82. PARLIAMENTARY REFORM.

[Lord Brougham, born in Edinburgh, 1779.—He was appointed Lord Chancellor in 1830. The bill on Parliamentary Reform, after having passed the Commons with a large majority, was taken to the House of Lords, the greater number of whom were known to be bitterly opposed to the measure. The great body of the nation were equally resolved that it should pass: petitions came in by thousands from every part of the kingdom, and the feeling seemed universal "*through* Parliament, or *over* Parliament, it must be carried." For five nights it was discussed in the House of Lords with "a skill, force, and variety of argument, which for historical, constitutional, and classical information, was never surpassed." Lord Brougham reserved himself for the fifth night, and after Lord Eldon had spoken, with all the weight of his age and authority, against the bill, the Lord Chancellor came down from the woolsack, to reply in the most powerful speech of the kind that had ever been delivered in the House of Lords. For the characteristics of his oratory, see the article on "Canning and Lord Brougham." In the following extract a rare opportunity is afforded for rhetorical effect. The *time* is slow, utterance distinct at the beginning. Pure voice, which, as the student advances to the parable, will increase in force and quality to the orotund—not the climax of orotund until the student comes to the last paragraph. Then with great earnestness, begin *slow*, with much feeling in the utterance—and as you near the close, orotund climax—slow time—high pitch—long pauses—as if the feeling was almost overpowering. Close with elevated, imploring gestures.]

THOSE portentous appearances, the growth of later times, those figures that stalk abroad, of unknown stature and strange form—unions of leagues, and musterings of men in myriads, and conspiracies against the exchequer—whence do they spring, how come they to haunt our shores? What power engendered these uncouth shapes, what multiplied the monstrous births till they people the land? Trust me, the same power which called into frightful existence, and armed with resistless force the Irish volunteers, 1782—the same power which rent in twain your empire, and raised up thirteen republics—the same power which created the Catholic Association, and gave it Ireland for its portion.

2. What power is that? Justice denied—rights withheld—wrongs perpetrated—the force which common injuries lend to millions—the wickedness of using the sacred trust of government as a means of indulging private caprice—the idiocy of treating Englishmen like the children of the South Sea Islands—the frenzy of believing, or making believe, that the adults of the nineteenth century can be led like children, or driven like barbarians!

3. This it is that has conjured up the strange sights at which we now stand aghast! And shall we persist in the fatal error of combating the giant progeny instead of extirpating the execrable parent? Good God! Will men never learn wisdom, even from their own experience? Will they never believe until it be too late, that the surest way to prevent immoderate desires being formed, aye, and unjust demands being forced, is to grant in due season the moderate requests of justice?

4. You stand, my lords, on the brink of a great event; you are in the crisis of a whole nation's hopes and fears. An awful importance hangs over your decision. Pause ere you plunge! There may not be any retreat! It behooves you to shape your conduct by the mighty occasion. They tell you not to be afraid of personal consequences in discharging your duty. I, too, would ask you to banish all fears; but above

all, that most mischievous, most despicable fear—the fear of being thought afraid.

5. If you won't take counsel from me, take example from the statesman-like conduct of the noble duke (Wellington), while you also look back, as you may with satisfaction, upon your own. He was told, and you were told, that the impatience of Ireland for equality of civil rights was partial, the clamor transient, likely to pass away with its temporary occasion, and that yielding to it would be conceding to intimidation.

6. I recollect hearing this topic urged within this hall in 1828; less regularly I heard it than I have now done, for I belonged not to your number—but I heard it urged in the self-same terms. The burden of the cry was: It is no time for concession; the people are turbulent, and the association dangerous. That summer passed, and the ferment subsided not; autumn came, but brought not the precious fruit of peace—on the contrary, all Ireland was convulsed with the unprecedented conflict which returned the great chief of the Catholics to sit in a Protestant Parliament.

7. Winter bound the earth in chains, but it controlled not the popular fury, whose surge, more deafening than the tempest, lashed the frail bulwarks of law founded upon injustice. Spring came; but no ethereal mildness was its harbinger or followed in its train: the Catholics became stronger by every month's delay, displayed a deadlier resolution, and proclaimed their wrongs in a tone of louder defiance than before. And what course did you, at this moment of greatest excitement, and peril, and menace, deem it most fitting to pursue?

8. Eight months before you had been told how unworthy it would be to yield when men clamored and threatened. No change had happened in the interval, save that the clamors were become far more deafening, and the threats, beyond comparison, more overbearing. What, nevertheless, did your lordships do? Your duty: for you despised the cuckoo-note of the season, "Be not intimidated." You granted all that the Irish demanded, and you saved your country.

9. Was there in April a single argument advanced which had not held good in July? None, absolutely none, except the new height to which the danger of long delay had risen, and the increased vehemence with which justice was demanded; and yet the appeal to your pride, which had prevailed in July, was in vain made in April, and you wisely and patriotically granted what was asked, and ran the risk of being supposed to yield through fear. But the history of Catholic claims conveys another important lesson.

10. Though in right, and policy, and justice, the measure of relief could not be too ample, half as much as was received with little gratitude when so late wrung from you, would have been hailed, twenty years before, with delight; and even the July preceding the measure would have been received as a boon freely given, which, I fear, was taken with but sullen satisfaction in April as a right long withheld.

11. Yet, blessed be God, the debt of justice, though tardily, was at length paid, and the noble duke won by it civic honors, which rival his warlike achievements in lasting brightness—than which there can be no higher praise. What, if he had still listened to the topics of intimidation and inconsistency which had scared his predecessors? He might have proved his obstinacy, and Ireland would have been sacrificed.

LORD BROUGHAM.

---

83. THE ESTABLISHED CHURCH IN IRELAND.

OF all the institutions now existing in the civilized world, the Established Church of Ireland seems to me the most absurd. Is there any thing else like it? Was there ever any thing else like it? The world is full of ecclesiastical establishments. But such a portent as this Church of Ireland is nowhere to be found.

2. Look round the continent of Europe. Ecclesiastical establishments from the White Sea to the Mediterranean,

ecclesiastical establishments from the Wolga to the Atlantic; but nowhere the church of a small minority enjoying exclusive establishment.

3. Look at America! There you have all forms of Christianity, from Mormonism—if you call Mormonism Christianity—to Romanism. In some places you have the voluntary system. In some you have several religions connected with the State. In some you have the solitary ascendency of a single church.

4. But nowhere, from the Arctic Circle to Cape Horn, do you find the church of a small minority exclusively established. In one country alone—in Ireland alone—is to be seen the spectacle of a community of eight millions of human beings, with a church which is the church of only eight hundred thousand!

5. Two hundred and eighty-five years has this church been at work. What could have been done for it in the way of authority, privileges, endowments, which has not been done? Did any other set of bishops and priests in the world ever receive so much for doing so little?

6. Nay, did any other set of bishops and priests in the world ever receive half as much for doing twice as much? And what have we to show for all this lavish expenditure? What, but the most zealous Roman Catholic population on the face of the earth? On the great, solid mass of the Roman Catholic population you have made no impression whatever. There they are, as they were ages ago, ten to one against the members of your Established Church. Explain this to me. I speak to you, the zealous Protestants on the other side of the house. Explain this to me on Protestant principles.

7. If I were a Roman Catholic, I could easily account for the phenomenon. If I were a Roman Catholic, I should content myself with saying that the mighty hand and the outstretched arm had been put forth, according to the promise, in defence of the unchangeable Church; that He, who, in the old time, turned into blessings the curses of Balaam, and smote

the host of Sennacherib, had signally confounded the arts and the power of heretic statesmen.

8. But what is the Protestant to say? Is this a miracle, that we should stand aghast at it? Not at all. It is a result which human prudence ought to have long ago foreseen, and long ago averted. It is the natural succession of effect to cause. A church exists for moral ends. A church exists to be loved, to be reverenced, to be heard with docility, to reign in the understandings and hearts of men. A church which is abhorred is useless, or worse than useless; and to quarter a hostile church on a conquered people, as you would quarter a soldiery, is, therefore, the most absurd of mistakes.

T. B. MACAULAY.

---

84. SATIRICAL EXTRACT FROM A SPEECH OF MR. CANNING ON THE ADDRESS (1825).

[Satire demands a good-natured, dignified earnestness; rising or falling circumflexes on emphatic words depending upon positive or negative utterances of irony or satire. The second sentence in the extract below affords a fine opportunity for these circumflexes. In the quotation the voice should be raised, and the quotation uttered as if a particular point was to be made. All "Dennis's" speeches should be given with a foolish assurance—which always produces exactly the opposite conclusion from what is intended. Then, in the application, apply the circumflexes.—See Remarks on Inflection and Circumflex.]

I NOW turn to that other part of the honorable and learned gentleman's (Mr. Brougham) speech, in which he acknowledges his acquiescence in the passages of the Address, echoing the satisfaction felt at the success of the liberal commercial principles adopted by this country, and at the steps taken for recognizing the new States of America.

2. It does happen, however, that the honorable and learned gentleman, being not unfrequently a speaker in this house, nor very concise in his speeches, and touching occasionally, as he proceeds, on almost every subject within the range of his imagination, as well as making some observations on

the matters on hand, and having at different periods proposed and supported every innovation of which the law or constitution of the country is susceptible,—it is impossible to innovate, without appearing to borrow from him.

3. Either, therefore, we must remain forever locked up as in a northern winter, or we must break our way out by some mode already suggested by the honorable and learned gentleman: and then he cries out, "Ah, I was there before you! That is what I told you to do; but, as you would not do it then, you have no right to do it now."

4. In Queen Anne's reign there lived a very sage and able critic, named Dennis, who in his old age was the prey of a strange fancy, that he had himself written all the good things in all the good plays that were acted. Every good passage that he met with in any author he insisted was his own. "It is none of his," Dennis would always say; "it is mine."

5. He went one day to see a new tragedy. Nothing particularly good, to his taste, occurred, till a scene in which a great storm was represented. As soon as he had heard the thunder rolling overhead, he exclaimed, "That's my thunder!" So it is with the honorable and learned gentleman—*it's all his thunder!* It will henceforth be impossible to confer any boon, or make any innovation, but he will claim it as *his thunder*.

6. But it is due to him to acknowledge that he does not claim every thing. He will be content with the exclusive merit of the liberal measures relating to trade and commerce. Not desirous of violating his own principles, by claiming a monopoly of foresight and wisdom, he kindly throws overboard to my honorable and learned friend (Sir J. Mackintosh) near him, the praise of South America.

7. I should like to know whether, in some degree, *this* also is not his thunder. He thinks it right in itself; but, lest we should be too proud if he approved our conduct *in toto*, he thinks it wrong in point of time. I differ from him essentially: for, if I pique myself on any thing in this affair, it is on the time.

8. That, at some time or other, States which had separated themselves from the mother-country, should be admitted to the rank of independent nations is a proposition to which no possible dissent could be given. The whole question was one of time and mode.

9. There were two modes: one a reckless and headlong course, by which we might have reached our object at once, but at the expense of drawing upon us consequences not lightly to be incurred; the other was more strictly guarded in point of principle; so that, while we pursued our own interests, we took care to give no just cause of offence to other powers, while we acted in obedience to a sound and enlightened policy.   CANNING.

---

85. DECLARATION OF IRISH RIGHTS.

[Henry Grattan, born in Dublin, 1746; died, 1820. The history of this great man, from his entrance into the Irish Parliament, in 1775, down to its extinction, is the history of Ireland's most splendid epoch. He achieved her triumph, established her rights, and, at the hazard of his life, confronted her enemies. "His voice penetrated the recesses of the treasury, and peculation ceased. He revealed the abuses against the Church, and religion blessed him. He disdained the gold, and defied the vengeance of the Castle and its power, and its minions cowered before him. Every measure which tended to the dignity or prosperity of Ireland, he either originated or advanced. Free trade, legislative independence, and final judicature, head a list of boons and triumphs exclusively his own; and he was an earnest of the entire emancipation of Catholics from the shameful and outrageous disabilities imposed on them by English *liberality* and *tolerance*."]

SIR, I have entreated an attendance on this day, that you might, in the most public manner, deny the claim of the British Parliament to make law for Ireland, and with one voice lift up your hands against it. England now smarts under the lesson of the American war; her enemies are a host, pouring upon her from all quarters of the earth; her armies are dispersed; the sea is not hers; she has no minister, no ally, no admiral, none in whom she long confides, and no general whom she has not disgraced; the balance of her fate is in the hands of Ireland; you are not only her last connection,—you are the only nation in Europe that is not her enemy.

2. Let corruption tremble; but let the friends of liberty rejoice at these means of safety, and this hour of redemption. You have done too much not to do more; you have gone too far not to go on; you have brought yourselves into that situation in which you must silently abdicate the rights of your country, or publicly restore them. Where is the freedom of trade? Where is the security of property? Where is the liberty of the people?

3. I therefore say, nothing is safe, satisfactory, or honorable, nothing except a declaration of rights. What! are you, with three hundred thousand men at your back, with charters in one hand and arms in the other, afraid to say you are a free people? If England is a tyrant, it is you who have made her so; it is the slave that makes the tyrant, and then murmurs at the master whom he himself has constituted.

4. The British minister mistakes the Irish character; had he intended to make Ireland a slave, he should have kept her a beggar. There is no middle policy: win her heart by the restoration of her rights, or cut off the nation's right hand; greatly emancipate, or fundamentally destroy. We may talk plausibly to England, but so long as she exercises a power to bind this country, so long are the nations in a state of war; the claims of the one go against the liberty of the other, and the sentiments of the latter go to oppose those claims to the last drop of her blood.

5. The English opposition, therefore, are right; mere trade will not satisfy Ireland. They judge of us by other great nations; by the nation whose political life has been a struggle for liberty,—America! They judge of us with a true knowledge and just deference for our character; that a country enlightened as Ireland, chartered as Ireland, armed as Ireland, and injured as Ireland, will be satisfied with nothing less than liberty.

6. I might, as a constituent, come to your bar and demand my liberty. I do call upon you, by the laws of the land and their violation, by the instruction of eighteen centuries, by the arms, inspiration, and providence of the present moment, tell us the rule by which we shall go; assert the law of Ireland; declare the liberty of the land. I will not be answered by a public lie in the shape of an amendment; neither, speaking for the subject's freedom, am I to hear of faction.

7. I wish for nothing but to breathe, in this our island, in common with my fellow-subjects, the air of liberty. I have no ambition, unless it be the ambition to break your chain, and contemplate your glory. I never will be satisfied so long as the meanest cottager in Ireland has a link of the British chain clanking to his rags. He may be naked,—he shall not be in iron.

8. And I do see the time is at hand, the spirit is gone forth, the declaration is planted; and though great men should apostatize, yet the cause will live; and though the public speaker should die, yet the immortal fire shall outlast the organ which conveyed it, and the breath of liberty, like the word of the holy man, will not die with the prophet, but survive him.

GRATTAN.

86. REPLY TO MR. FLOOD, 1783.

[At the time of this speech in the Irish Parliament, Flood and Grattan, although previously friends, stood before the British public as rival leaders. A bitter animosity had arisen between them; and Grattan having unfortunately led the way in personality, by speaking of his opponent's "affectation of infirmity," Flood replied with great asperity, denouncing Grattan as "a mendicant patriot," who, "bought by his country for a sum of money, then sold his country for prompt payment." He also sneered at Grattan's "aping the style of Lord Chatham." To these taunts Grattan replied in a speech, an abridgment of which we here give.]

IT is not the slander of an evil tongue that can defame me. I maintain my reputation in public and in private life. No man, who has not a bad character, can ever say that

I deceived. No country can call me a cheat. But I will suppose such a public character. I will suppose such a man to have existence. I will begin with his character in his political cradle, and I will follow him to the last stage of political dissolution.

2. I will suppose him, in the first stage of his life, to have been intemperate; in the second, to have been corrupt; and in the last, seditious; that, after an envenomed attack on the persons and measures of a succession of viceroys, and after much declamation against their illegalities and their profusion, he took office, and became a supporter of government, when the profusion of ministers had greatly increased, and their crimes multiplied beyond example.

3. With regard to the liberties of America, which were inseparable from ours, I will suppose this gentleman to have been an enemy decided and unreserved; that he voted against her liberty, and voted, moreover, for an address to send four thousand Irish troops to cut the throats of the Americans; that he called these butchers "armed negotiators," and stood with a metaphor in his mouth and a bribe in his pocket, a champion against the rights of America, — of America, the only hope of Ireland, and the only refuge of the liberties of mankind.

4. Thus defective in every relationship, whether to constitution, commerce, and toleration, I will suppose this man to have added much private improbity to public crimes; that his probity was like his patriotism, and his honor on a level with his oath. He loves to deliver panegyrics on himself. I will interrupt him and say:

5. Sir, you are much mistaken if you think that your talents have been as great as your life has been reprehensible. You began your parliamentary career with an acrimony and personality which could have been justified only by a supposition of virtue; after a rank and clamorous opposition, you became, on a sudden, *silent;* you were silent for seven years; you were silent on the greatest questions, and you were silent for money!

6. You supported the unparalleled profusion and jobbing of Lord Harcourt's scandalous ministry. You, sir, who manufacture stage thunder against Mr. Eden for his anti-American principles,—you, sir, whom it pleases to chant a hymn to the immortal Hampden;—you, sir, approved of the tyranny exercised against America,—and you, sir, voted four thousand Irish troops to cut the throats of the Americans fighting for their freedom, fighting for your freedom, fighting for the great principle, *liberty!*

7. But you found, at last, that the court had bought, but would not trust you. Mortified at the discovery, you try the sorry game of a trimmer in your progress to the acts of an incendiary; and observing, with regard to prince and people, the most impartial treachery and desertion, you justify the suspicion of your sovereign by betraying the government, as you had sold the people.

8. Such has been your conduct, and at such conduct every order of your fellow-subjects have a right to exclaim! The merchant may say to you, the constitutionalist may say to you, the American may say to you,—and I, I now say, and say to your beard, sir,—you are not an honest man!

GRATTAN.

87. THE IRISH PARLIAMENT.

THE Parliament of Ireland!—of that assembly I have a parental recollection. I sate by her cradle,—I followed her hearse! In fourteen years she acquired for Ireland what you did not acquire for England in a century,—freedom of trade, independency of the legislature, independency of the judges, restoration of the final judicature, repeal of a perpetual mutiny bill, *habeas corpus* act, *nullum tempus* act,—a great work!

2. You will exceed it, and I shall rejoice. I call my coun-

trymen to witness, if in that business I have compromised the claims of my country, or temporized with the power of England; but there was one thing which baffled the effort of the patriot, and defeated the wisdom of the Senate,—it was the folly of the theologian!

3. When the Parliament of Ireland rejected the Catholic petition, and assented to the calumnies then uttered against the Catholic body, on that day she voted the Union: if you should adopt a similar conduct, on that day you will vote the separation. Many good and pious reasons you may give; many good and pious reasons *she* gave; and she lies THERE, with her many good and pious reasons!

4. That the Parliament of Ireland should have entertained prejudices, I am not astonished; but that you,—that you, who have as individuals and as conquerors, visited a great part of the globe, and have seen men in all their modifications, and Providence in all her ways,—that you, now, at this time of day, should throw up dikes against the Pope, and barriers against the Catholic, instead of uniting with that Catholic to throw up barriers against the French, this surprises; and, in addition to this, that you should have set up the Pope in Italy, to tremble at him in Ireland; and, further, that you should have professed to have placed yourself at the head of a Christian, not a Protestant league, to defend the civil and religious liberty of Europe, and should deprive of their civil liberty one-fifth of yourselves, on account of their religion,—this—this surprises me!

5. This proscriptive system you may now remove. What the best men in Ireland wished to do, but could not do, you may accomplish. Were it not wise to come to a good understanding with the Irish now? The franchises of the Constitution!—your ancestors were nursed in that cradle. The ancestors of the petitioners were less fortunate.

6. The posterity of both, born to new and strange dangers,—let them agree to renounce jealousies and proscriptions, in order to oppose what, without that agreement, will over

power both. Half Europe is in battalion against us, and we are devoting one another to perdition on account of mysteries,—when we should form against the enemy, and march!

GRATTAN.

88. THE O'KAVANAGH.

THE Saxons had met, and the banquet was spread,
And the wine in fleet circles the jubilee led;
And the banners that hung round the festal that night,
Seemed brighter by far than when lifted in fight.

II.

In came the O'Kavanagh, fair as the morn,
When earth to new beauty and vigor is born;
They shrank from his glance, like the waves from the prow,
For nature's nobility sat on his brow.

III.

Attended alone by his vassal and bard—
No trumpet to herald, no clansmen to guard—
He came not attended by steed or by steel:
No danger he knew, for no fear did he feel.

IV.

In eye and on lip his high confidence smiled—
So proud, yet so knightly—so gallant, yet mild;
He moved like a god through the light of that hall,
And a smile, full of courtliness, proffered to all.

V.

"Come pledge us, lord chieftain! come pledge us!" they cried;
Unsuspectingly free to the pledge he replied;
And this was the peace-branch O'Kavanagh bore—
"The friendships to come, not the feuds that are o'er!"

VI.

But, minstrel, why cometh a change o'er thy theme?
Why sing of red battle—what dream dost thou dream?
Ha! "Treason!" 's the cry, and "Revenge!" is the call,
As the swords of the Saxon surrounded the hall!

VII.

A kingdom for Angelo's mind! to portray
Green Erin's undaunted avenger that day;
The far-flashing sword, and the death-darting eye,
Like some comet commissioned with wrath from the sky.

VIII.

Through the ranks of the Saxon he hewed his red way—
Through lances, and sabres, and hostile array;
And, mounting his charger, he left them to tell
The tale of that feast, and its bloody farewell.

IX.

And now on the Saxons his clansmen advance,
With a shout from each heart, and a soul in each lance:
He rushed, like a storm, o'er the night-covered heath,
And swept through their ranks, like the angel of death.

X.

Then hurrah! for thy glory, young chieftain, hurrah!
Oh! had we such lightning-souled heroes to-day,
Again would our "sunburst" expand in the gale,
And Freedom exult o'er the green Innisfail!

J. Augustus Shea.

---

89. ON AMERICAN TAXATION.

[Burke is the greatest of Irish statesmen, and unsurpassed as a writer; by universal consent he stands equal to Lord Chatham. As an orator, he derived little advantage from personal qualifications; his voice and delivery were not good, but the extent and variety of his powers in debate were greater than that of any other orator in ancient or modern times. When he rose to give his speech on American taxation, the evening was far advanced; the debate was dull, and many of the members had withdrawn to neighboring rooms. The first sentences of his wonderful exordium awakened universal attention: the report of what was going on spread in every direction, and the members came crowding back until the hall was crowded to overflowing, and it resounded throughout the speech with the loudest expressions of applause. Lord Townsend exclaimed, at the close of one of those powerful passages in which the speech abounds: "Heavens, what a man is this! Where could he acquire such transcendent powers?" Col. Barre, in the fervor of his excitement, declared that if it could be written out he would nail it on every church door in the kingdom. Gov. Johnston said "It was fortunate for the noble lords (North and Germaine) that spectators had been excluded during the debate, for if any had been present they would have excited the people to tear the noble lords in pieces on their way home."]

COULD any thing be a subject of more just alarm to America, than to see you go out of the plain high road of finance, and give up your most certain revenues and your clearest interests, merely for the sake of insulting your colonies? No man ever doubted that the commodity of tea could bear an imposition of three-pence. But no commodity will bear three-pence, or will bear a penny, when the general feelings of men are irritated, and two millions of men are resolved not to pay.

2. The feelings of the colonies were formerly the feelings of Great Britain. Theirs were formerly the feelings of Mr. Hampden, when called upon for the payment of twenty shillings. Would twenty shillings have ruined Mr. Hampden's fortune? No! but the payment of half twenty shillings, on the principle it was demanded, would have made him a slave!

3. It is the weight of that preamble, of which you are so fond, and not the weight of the duty, that the Americans are unable and unwilling to bear. You are, therefore, at this moment, in the awkward situation of fighting for a phantom; a quiddity; a thing that wants, not only a substance, but even a name; for a thing which is neither abstract right, nor profitable enjoyment.

4. They tell you, sir, that your dignity is tied to it. I know not how it happens, but this dignity of yours is a terrible incumbrance to you; for it has of late been ever at war with your interest, your equity, and every idea of your policy

Show the thing you contend for to be reason, show it to be common sense, show it to be the means of obtaining some useful end, and then I am content to allow it what dignity you please. But what dignity is derived from the perseverance in absurdity, is more than I ever could discern!

5. Let us, sir, embrace some system or other before we end this session. Do you mean to tax America, and to draw a productive revenue from thence? If you do, speak out: name, fix, ascertain this revenue; settle its quantity; define its objects; provide for its collection; and then fight, when you have something to fight for. If you murder, rob; if you kill, take possession: and do not appear in the character of madmen, as well as assassins,—violent, vindictive, bloody, and tyrannical, without an object. But may better counsels guide you!

BURKE.

---

40. ENTERPRISE OF AMERICAN COLONISTS.

FOR some time past, Mr. Speaker, has the Old World been fed from the New. The scarcity which you have felt would have been a desolating famine, if this child of your old age,—if America,—with a true filial piety, with a Roman charity, had not put the full breast of its youthful exuberance to the mouth of its exhausted parent.

2. Turning from the agricultural resources of the colonies, consider the wealth which they have drawn from the sea by their fisheries. The spirit in which that enterprising employment has been exercised ought to raise your esteem and admiration. Pray, sir, what in the world is equal to it? Pass by the other parts, and look at the manner in which the people of New England have of late carried on the whale fishery.

3. While we follow them among the tumbling mountains of ice, and behold them penetrating into the deepest frozen recesses of Hudson's Bay and Davis' Straits, while we are looking for them beneath the Arctic Circle, we hear that they have pierced into the opposite region of Polar cold, that they are at

the antipodes, and engaged under the frozen serpent of the South.

4. Falkland Island, which seemed too remote and romantic an object for the grasp of national ambition, is but a stage and resting-place in the progress of their victorious industry. Nor is the equinoctial heat more discouraging to them than the accumulated winter of both the Poles. We know that while some of them draw the line and strike the harpoon on the coast of Africa, others run the longitude, and pursue their gigantic game, along the coast of Brazil.

5. No sea but what is vexed by their fisheries. No climate that is not witness to their toils. Neither the perseverance of Holland, nor the activity of France, nor the dexterous and firm sagacity of English enterprise, ever carried this most perilous mode of hardy industry to the extent to which it has been pushed by this recent people; a people who are still, as it were, but in the gristle, and not yet hardened into the bone, of manhood.

6. When I contemplate these things,—when I know that the colonies in general owe little or nothing to any care of ours, and that they are not squeezed into this happy form by the constraints of a watchful and suspicious government, but that, through a wise and salutary neglect, a generous nature has been suffered to take her own way to perfection,—when I reflect upon these effects, when I see how profitable they have been to us, I feel all the pride of power sink, and all presumption in the wisdom of human contrivances melt, and die away within me. My rigor relents. I pardon something to the spirit of liberty.

BURKE.

41. PANDEMONIUM.

SINCE I had the honor, I should say, the dishonor, of sitting in this house, I have been witness to many strange, many infamous transactions. What can be your intention in attacking all honor and virtue. Do you mean to bring all men to a level with yourselves, and to extirpate all honor and independence! Perhaps you imagine a vote will settle the whole controversy.

2. Alas! you are not aware that the manner in which your vote is procured is a secret to no man. Listen: for if you are not totally callous, if your consciences are not seared, I will speak daggers to your souls, and wake you to all the hell of guilty recollection. I will follow you with whips and stings, through every maze of your unexampled turpitude, and plant thorns under the rose of ministerial approbation.

3. You have flagrantly violated justice and the law of the land, and opened a door for anarchy and confusion. After assuming an arbitrary dominion over law and justice, you issue orders, warrants, and proclamations, against every opponent, and send prisoners to your Bastile all those who have the courage and virtue to defend the freedom of their country.

4. But it is in vain that you hope by fear and terror to extinguish the native British fire. The more sacrifices, the more martyrs you make, the more numerous the sons of liberty will become. They will multiply like the hydra, and hurl vengeance on your heads. Let others act as they will; while I have a tongue, or an arm, they shall be free.

5. And that I may not be a witness of these monstrous proceedings, I will leave the house; nor do I doubt but every independent, every honest man, every friend to England, will follow me. These walls are unholy, baleful, deadly, while a prostitute majority holds the bolt of parliamentary power, and hurls its vengeance only upon the virtuous. To yourselves, therefore, I consign you. Enjoy your *pandemonium!*

BURKE.

---

49. IMPEACHMENT OF WARREN HASTINGS.

[This speech has been characterized as the greatest intellectual effort ever made before the Parliament of Great Britain. Burke astonished even those who were most intimately acquainted with him by the vast extent of his reading, the variety of his resources, the minuteness of his information, and the lucid order in which he arranged the whole for the support of his subject. All India was present to the eye of his mind, from the halls where suitors laid gold and perfume at the feet of sovereigns, to the wild moor where the Arab camps were pitched; from the bazaars humming like beehives with the crowd of buyers and sellers, to the jungle where the lonely courier shakes his bunch of iron rings to scare away the hyenas. When Burke described the cruelties inflicted upon the natives, a convulsive shudder ran throughout the whole assembly. His descriptions were more vivid, more harrowing, more horrific than human utterance on either fact or fancy, perhaps, ever formed before. The bosoms of his auditors became convulsed with passion, and those of more delicate organs swooned away. Mr. Hastings, in describing the scene afterwards, said, "For half an hour I looked up at the orator in a revery of wonder, and actually felt myself to be the most culpable man on earth."]

MY Lords, I do not mean now to go further than just to remind your lordships of this—that Mr. Hastings' government was one whole system of oppression, of robbery of individuals, of spoliation of the public, and of suppression of the whole system of the English Government, in order to vest in the worst of the natives all the power that could possibly exist in any government; in order to defeat the ends which all governments ought, in common, to have in view. In the name of the Commons of England, I charge all this villainy upon Warren Hastings, in this last moment of my application to you.

2. My lords, what is it that we want here, to a great act of national justice? Do we want a cause, my lords? You have the cause of oppressed princes, of undone women of the first rank, of desolated provinces, and of wasted kingdoms.

3. Do you want a criminal, my lords? When was there so much iniquity ever laid to the charge of any one?—No, my lords, you must not look to punish any other such delinquent from India. Warren Hastings has not left substance enough in India to nourish such another delinquent.

4. My lords, is it a prosecutor you want? You have before you the Commons of Great Britain as prosecutors; and I believe, my lords, that the sun, in his beneficent progress round the world, does not behold a more glorious sight than

that of men, separated from a remote people by the material bounds and barriers of nature, united by the bond of a social and moral community ;—all the Commons of England resenting, as their own, the indignities and cruelties that are offered to all the people of India.

5. Do we want a tribunal? My lords, no example of antiquity, nothing in the modern world, nothing in the range of human imagination, can supply us with a tribunal like this. We commit safely the interests of India and humanity into your hands. Therefore, it is with confidence that, ordered by the Commons,

6. I impeach Warren Hastings, Esquire, of high crimes and misdemeanors.

7. I impeach him in the name of the Commons of Great Britain, in Parliament assembled, whose parliamentary trust he has betrayed.

8. I impeach him in the name of all the Commons of Great Britain, whose national character he has dishonored.

9. I impeach him in the name of the people of India, whose laws, rights, and liberties, he has subverted ; whose properties he has destroyed ; whose country he has laid waste and desolate.

10. I impeach him in the name and by virtue of those eternal laws of justice which he has violated.

11. I impeach him in the name of human nature itself, which he has cruelly outraged, injured, and oppressed, in both sexes, in every age, rank, situation, and condition of life.

BURKE.

---

43. PERORATION TO THE IMPEACHMENT OF WARREN HASTINGS.

[This speech lasted four days. It was in the darkest season of the French Revolution—a few days before the fall of Robespierre, when the British empire was agitated with conflicting passions, and fears were entertained by many of secret conspiracies to overthrow the government. To these things Burke referred at the close of his peroration, which has a grandeur and solemnity becoming the conclusion of such a trial.]

MY Lords, I have done! The part of the Commons is concluded! With a trembling hand, we consign the product of these long, *long* labors to your charge. *Take it!* TAKE IT! It is a sacred trust! Never before was a cause of such magnitude submitted to any human tribunal!

2. My lords, at this awful close, in the name of the Commons, and surrounded by them, I attest the retiring, I attest the advancing generations, between which, as a link in the chain of eternal order, we stand.

3. We call this nation, we call the world, to witness, that the Commons have shrunk from no labor; that we have been guilty of no prevarications; that we have made no compromise with crime; that we have not feared any odium whatsoever, in the long warfare which we have carried on with the crimes, the vices, the exorbitant wealth, the enormous and overpowering influence of Eastern corruption.

4. A business which has so long occupied the councils and tribunals of Great Britain, cannot possibly be hurried over in the course of vulgar, trite, and transitory events. Nothing but some of those great revolutions that break the traditionary chain of human memory, and alter the very face of nature itself, can possibly obscure it. My lords, we are all elevated to a degree of importance by it. The meanest of us will, by means of it, become more or less *the concern of posterity*.

5. My lords, your house yet stands; it stands, a great edifice; but, let me say, it stands in the midst of ruins—in the midst of ruins that have been made by the greatest moral earthquake that ever convulsed and shattered this globe of ours. My lords, it has pleased Providence to place us in such a state, that we appear every moment to be on the verge of some great mutation.

6. There is one thing, and one thing only, that defies mutation—that which existed before the world itself. I mean JUSTICE: that justice which, emanating from the Divinity, has a place in the breast of every one of us, given us for our guide with regard to ourselves, and with regard to others; and

which will stand after this globe is burned to ashes, our advocate or our accuser before the great Judge, when He comes to call upon us for the tenor of a well-spent life.

7. My lords, the Commons will share in every fate with your lordships. There is nothing sinister which can happen to you, in which we are not involved. And if it should so happen that your lordships, stripped of all the decorous distinctions of human society, should, by hands at once base and cruel, be led to those scaffolds and machines of murder upon which great kings and glorious queens have shed their blood, amid the prelates, the nobles, the magistrates who supported their thrones, may you in those moments feel that consolation which I am persuaded they felt in the critical moments of their dreadful agony! * * *

8. My lords, if you must fall, may you so fall! But if you stand—and stand I trust you will, together with the fortunes of this ancient monarchy; together with the ancient laws and liberties of this great and illustrious kingdom—may you stand as unimpeached in honor as in power! May you stand, not as a substitute for virtue; may you stand, and long stand, the terror of tyrants; may you stand, the refuge of afflicted nations; may you stand, a sacred temple for the perpetual residence of inviolable JUSTICE! .
BURKE.

---

44. HYDER ALI'S INVASION OF THE CARNATIC.

[This is taken from Burke's great speech on the "Nabob of Arcot's Debts," in which for nearly five hours this unrivaled orator poured out his feelings with an ardor and impetuosity which he had never before equaled. In rhetorical address, vivid painting, lofty declamation, bitter sarcasm, and withering invective it surpasses all his other speeches. His description of Hyder Ali sweeping over the Carnatic with fire and sword is the most eloquent passage he ever produced. Lord Brougham has pronounced this speech "by far the best of all Mr. Burke's orations."]

WHEN at length Hyder Ali found that he had to do with men who either would sign no convention, or whom no treaty and no signature could bind, and who were the determined enemies of human intercourse itself, he decreed to make the country possessed by these incorrigible and predestinated criminals a memorable example to mankind.

2. He resolved, in the gloomy recesses of a mind capacious of such things, to leave the whole Carnatic an everlasting monument of vengeance, and to put perpetual desolation as a barrier between him and those against whom the faith which holds the moral elements of the world together was no protection. He became at length so confident of his force, so collected in his might, that he made no secret whatsoever of his dreadful resolution.

3. Having terminated his disputes with every enemy and every rival, who buried their mutual animosities in their common detestation against the creditors of the Nabob of Arcot, he drew from every quarter whatever a savage ferocity could add to his new rudiments in the arts of destruction; and compounding all the materials of fury, havoc, and desosation into one black cloud, he hung for a while on the declivities of the mountains.

4. While the authors of all these evils were idly and stupidly gazing on this menacing meteor, which blackened all their horizon, it suddenly burst, and poured down the whole of its contents upon the plains of the Carnatic. Then ensued a scene of woe, the like of which no eye had seen, no heart conceived, and which no tongue can adequately tell.

5. All the horrors of war before known or heard of were mercy to that new havoc. A storm of universal fire blasted every field, consumed every house, destroyed every temple.

6. The miserable inhabitants, flying from their flaming villages, in part were slaughtered; others, without regard to sex, to age, to the respect of rank, or sacredness of function; fathers torn from children, husbands from wives, enveloped in a whirlwind of cavalry, and, amid the goading spears of drivers and the trampling of pursuing horses, were swept into captivity, in an unknown and hostile land.

7. Those who were able to evade this tempest fled to the walled cities, but, escaping from fire, sword, and exile, they fell into the jaws of famine. The alms of the settlement (Madras), in this dreadful exigency, were certainly liberal, and all was done by charity that private charity could do ; but it was a people in beggary; it was a nation which stretched out its hands for food.

8. For months together these creatures of sufferance, whose very excess and luxury in their most plenteous days had fallen short of the allowance of our austerest fasts, silent, patient, resigned, without sedition or disturbance, almost without complaint, perished by a hundred a day in the streets of Madras; every day seventy at least laid their bodies in the streets, or on the glacis of Tanjore, and expired of famine in the granary of India.

9. I was going to awake your justice towards this unhappy part of our fellow-citizens, by bringing before you some of the circumstances of this plague of hunger. Of all the calamities which beset and waylay the life of man, this comes the nearest to our heart, and is that wherein the proudest of us all feels himself to be nothing more than he is. But I find myself unable to manage it with decorum.

10. These details are of a species of horror so nauseous and disgusting ; they are so degrading to the sufferers and to the hearers ; they are so humiliating to human nature itself, that, on better thoughts, I find it more advisable to throw a pall over this hideous object, and to leave it to your general conceptions.

11. For eighteen months, without intermission, this destruction raged from the gates of Madras to the gates of Tanjore ; and so completely did these masters in their art, Hyde Ali and his more ferocious son (Tippoo Saib), absolve themselves of their impious vow, that when the British armies traversed, as they did, the Carnatic, for hundreds of miles in all directions, through the whole line of their march they did not see one man—not one woman—not one child—not one

four-footed beast of any description whatever! One dead, uniform silence reigned over the whole region.

---

45. MARIE ANTOINETTE, QUEEN OF LOUIS XVI.

IT is now sixteen or seventeen years since I saw the Queen of France, then the Dauphiness, at Versailles; and surely never lighted on this orb, which she hardly seemed to touch, a more delightful vision. I saw her just above the horizon, decorating and cheering the elevated sphere she just began to move in—glittering like the morning-star, full of life, and splendor, and joy.

2. Oh, what a revolution! and what a heart must I have to contemplate, without emotion, that elevation and that fall! Little did I dream, when she added titles of veneration to that enthusiastic, distant, respectful love, that she should ever be obliged to carry the sharp antidote against disgrace concealed in that bosom; little did I dream that I should have lived to see such disasters fallen upon her in a nation of gallant men, in a nation of men of honor and of cavaliers.

3. I thought ten thousand swords must have leaped from their scabbards to avenge even a look that threatened her with insult. But the age of chivalry is gone. That of sophisters, economists, and calculators has succeeded; and the glory of Europe is extinguished forever! Never, never more shall we behold that generous loyalty to rank and sex, that proud submission, that dignified obedience, that subordination of the heart, which kept alive, even in servitude itself, the spirit of an exalted freedom.

4. The unbought grace of life, the cheap defence of nations, the nurse of manly sentiment and heroic enterprise is gone! It is gone, that sensibility of principle, that chastity of honor, which felt a stain like a wound, which inspired courage while it mitigated ferocity, and ennobled whatever it touched, and under which vice itself lost half its evil by losing all its grossness.

BURKE.

46. THE TITHE BILLS.

[An able British reviewer gives the following able criticism of O'Connell, as an orator:

O'Connell was successful alike at the bar, in the senate, and before assembled thousands of his fellow-citizens and fellow-countrymen, exhibiting an almost solitary instance of eminence in the various modifications of style necessary for his different audiences. O'Connell occupies one of the highest stations among modern orators. The whole course of his eloquence, as well in Parliament as out of doors, is rapid and sonorous, and whenever he spoke he bends, or sways, or alarms, or soothes, at pleasure, the passions of his hearers. He was master of the eloquence which sometimes tears up all before it like a whirlwind or at other times steals imperceptibly upon the senses and probes to the bottom of the heart—eloquence which engrafts opinions that are new, and eradicates the old. In graphic and heart-rending descriptions of scenes, whether of weal or of woe, O'Connell surpassed all competitors. Most soul-stirring was the debate on the Irish tithe bill, when he thus depicted the scenes of blood that had been perpetrated in Ireland, 1835.]

THE tithe bills were continued; laws passed, with some cessation from time to time, but the innate sense of injustice, the conviction of wrong, arising from the payment of a sinecure Protestant clergy by a Catholic population, overturned the boundaries of law; broke asunder the parchment chains of the acts of Parliament; the dungeons were filled, the convict ship was crowded, even the scaffold was reared, and blood has been shed in oceans, but shed in vain.

2. Is it not time to put an end to such scenes of atrocity? Blood is flowing still; even now, is not Rathcormac red with human gore? I do not mean to canvass the merits of this melancholy event, which is under progress of legal inquiry; but two magistrates, who are implicated in the matter, have presided over the investigation.

3. A poor woman has been examined. Have honorable members read her statement? The mother was with her child in the morning. After the affray, she went out to look for her son. The first body she turned over she shouted for joy. Why? Because human blood had been spilled? Because the life of a human being had been sacrificed? Ah! no; but because it happened not to have been her son.

4. She had a similar shout of joy looking in the countenance of the second murdered man; but the third was her son; from that moment her eyeballs became as coals of fire, and she did not shed a single tear. That woman's tears have not yet begun to flow. When is she to have redress? She is to have no redress, and the cause of her woe, the grand evil, s still to remain in Ireland.

5. We are still to follow up the old cause, giving new acts of Parliament, but no new principle, no new spirit unknown to our predecessors, and leaving all the evils of the tithe system substantially untouched and in full operation. What does it signify whether the designation be tithe or tithe composition, or land tax, or rent charge; magical as names are supposed to be, will that verbal magic do away with the intolerable, interminable injustice of the impost, so obnoxious in itself?

O'CONNELL.

---

47. THE TAIL.

[In one of O'Connell's speeches he remarked that "It is consistent with the genius and disposition of my country to mix merriment with woe, and the sound of laughter is often heard while the soul is wrung with bitter anguish, and the tear of sorrow dims the cheek." In accordance with this national characteristic, he occasionally gave vent to the most ludicrous remarks, as when, in his great speech on the Reform Bill, he laughingly described the desertion of Lord Stanley and his followers from the ranks of the Reformers.]

WHAT are we to call the section of the house over which the noble lord (Stanley) presides? It is not a party;—that he denies; it is not a faction;—that would be a harsher title. I will give it a name. We ought to call it "the Tail."

2. How delightful would it be to see it walking in St. James' Street to-morrow,—to see the noble lord strutting proudly with his sequents behind with a smile passing over his countenance,—something like, as Curran said, "a silver plate on a coffin," while the right honorable member for Cumberland (Sir James Graham) made one of its lustiest links,—not held by

the Cockermouth crutch, but supported by his detestation of all coalition.

3. Yes, sir, this is the ridiculous combination of supports by which the right honorable baronet (Sir Robert Peel) is this night saved. How is he to be saved? By the Tories? Oh, no! By the Whigs? Oh, no! the genuine Whigs have not gone over yet.

4. Whatever becomes of speculation for places, where no negotiation for places has as yet been entered into—whatever becomes of future perspects, of difficulties not over and subdued, of kindness thrown out and courtesies offered, and protection held over these unfortunate orphans—the ministers as we call them—whatever becomes of their party, the true Whig, the true Reformer, the true friend of liberty will stand firm; and I doubt much that the right honorable baronet's protection, with that of his noble friend, the noble lord, and the sequents which he may carry with him, will avail those over whom it is extended:

> "Down thy hill, romantic Ashbourne, glides
> The Derby Dilly, with its six insides!"
>
> O'CONNELL.

---

48. SCENES OF OUR YOUTH.

["I came to the place of my birth, and said, 'The friends of my youth, where are they?' an echo answered, 'Where are they?'"]

LONG years had elapsed since I gazed on the scene,
Which my fancy still robed in its freshness of green—
The spot where, a schoolboy, all thoughtless, I stray'd,
By the side of the stream, in the gloom of the shade.

II.

I thought of the friends who had roam'd with me there,
When the sky was so blue, and the flowers were so fair—
All scatter'd!—all sunder'd by mountain and wave,
And some in the silent embrace of the grave!

III.

I thought of the green banks, that circled around,
With wild-flowers, and sweetbrier, and eglantine crown'd;

I thought of the river, all quiet and bright
As the face of the sky on a blue summer night.

IV.

And I thought of the trees, under which we had stray'd,
Of the broad leafy bows, with their coolness of shade;
And I hoped, though disfigured, some token to find
Of the names and the carvings impress'd on the rind.

V.

All eager, I hasten'd the scene to behold,
Render'd sacred and dear by the feelings of old;
And I deem'd that, unalter'd, my eye should explore
This refuge, this haunt, this Elysium of yore.

VI.

'Twas a dream!—not a token or trace could I view
Of the names that I loved, of the trees that I knew:
Like the shadows of night at the dawning of day,
"Like a tale that is told," they had vanish'd away.

VII.

And methought the lone river, that murmur'd along,
Was more dull in its motion, more sad in its song,
Since the birds that had nestled and warbled above,
Had all fled from its banks, at the fall of the grove.

VIII.

I paused; and the moral came home to my heart:
Behold how of earth all the glories depart!
Our visions are baseless; our hopes but a gleam;
Our staff but a reed; and our life but a dream.

IX.

Then, oh, let us look—let our prospects allure—
To scenes that can fade not, to realms that endure,
To glories, to blessings, that triumph sublime
O'er the blightings of change, and the ruins of time.

BLACKWOOD'S MAGAZINE.

49. THE PILLAR TOWERS OF IRELAND.

THE pillar towers of Ireland, how wondrously they stand
By the lakes and rushing rivers through the valleys of
  our land;
In mystic file, through isle, they lift their heads sublime,
These gray old pillar temples, these conquerors of time.

II.

Beside these gray old pillars, how perishing and weak
The Roman's arch of triumph, and the temple of the Greek,
And the gold domes of Byzantium, and the pointed Gothic
  spires!
All are gone, one by one, but the temples of our sires!

III.

The column with its capital, is level with the dust;
And the proud halls of the mighty and the calm homes of
  the just;
For the proudest works of man, as certainly, but slower,
Pass like the grass at the sharp scythe of the mower!

IV.

But the grass grows again when in majesty and mirth,
On the wing of the spring comes the Goddess of the Earth;
But for man in this world no spring-tide e'er returns
To the labors of his hands or the ashes of his urns!

V.

Two favorites hath Time—the pyramids of Nile,
And the old mystic temples of our own dear isle;
As the breeze o'er the seas, where the halcyon has its nest,
Thus time o'er Egypt's tombs and the temples of the West!

VI.

The names of their founders have vanished in the gloom,
Like the dry branch in the fire or the body in the tomb;

But to-day, in the ray, their shadows still they cast—
These temples of forgotten gods—these relics of the past!

VII.

Around these walls have wandered the Briton and the Dane—
The captives of Armorica, the cavaliers of Spain—
Phœnician and Milesian, and the plundering Norman Peers—
And the swordsmen of brave Brian, and the chiefs of later years!

VIII.

How many different rites have the gray old temples known!
To the mind what dreams are written in these chronicles of stone!
What terror and what error, what gleams of love and truth,
Have flashed from these walls since the world was in its youth!

IX.

Here blazed the sacred fire, and, when the sun was gone,
As a star from afar to the traveller it shone;
And the warm blood of the victim* have these gray old temples drunk,
And the death-song of the Druid and the matin of the Monk.

X.

Here was placed the holy chalice that held the sacred wine,
And the gold cross from the altar, and the relics from the shrine,
And the mitre shining brighter with its diamonds than the East,
And the crosier of the Pontiff, and the vestments of the Priest!

XI.

Where blazed the sacred fire, rung out the vesper bell,—
Where the fugitive found shelter, became the hermit's cell;

And hope hung out its symbol to the innocent and good,
For the Cross o'er the moss of the pointed summit stood!

XII.

There may it stand forever, while this symbol doth impart
To the mind one glorious vision, or one proud throb through
    the heart;
While the breast needeth rest may the gray old temples last,
Bright prophets of the future, as preachers of the past!
D. F. M'CARTHY.

50. THE IRISH DISTURBANCE BILL.

[The annals of political eloquence offer no example of a triumph like that gained by the eloquence of O'Connell, when he wrenched from England the first instalment of long-deferred justice in the Act of Catholic Emancipation.]

I DO not rise to fawn or cringe to this house. I do not rise to supplicate you to be merciful towards the nation to which I belong—towards a nation which, though subject to England, yet is distinct from it. It is a distinct nation: it has been treated as such by this country, as may be proved by history, and by seven hundred years of tyranny.

2. I call upon this house, as you value the liberty of England, not to allow the present nefarious bill to pass. In it are involved the liberties of England, the liberty of the press, and of every other institution dear to Englishmen.

3. Against the bill I protest in the name of the Irish people, and in the face of heaven. I treat with scorn the puny and pitiful assertions that grievances are not to be complained of, that our redress is not to be agitated! for, in such cases, remonstrances cannot be too strong, agitation cannot be too violent, to show to the world with what injustice our fair claims are met, and under what tyranny the people suffer.

4. There are two frightful clauses in this bill. The one which does away with trial by jury, and which I have called upon you to baptize: you call it a *court-martial,—*

a mere nickname; I stigmatize it as a *revolutionary tribunal*. What, in the name of heaven, is it, if it is not a revolutionary tribunal?

5. It annihilates the trial by jury; it drives the judge from his bench,—the man who, from experience, could weigh the nice and delicate points of a case,—who could discriminate between the staightforward testimony and the suborned evidence,—who could see, plainly and readily, the justice or injustice of the accusation.

6. It turns out this man who is free, unshackled, unprejudiced,—who has no previous opinions to control the clear exercise of his duty. You do away with that which is more sacred than the throne itself; that for which your king reigns, your lords deliberate, your commons assemble.

7. If ever I doubted before of the success of our agitation for repeal, this bill, this infamous bill, the way in which it has been received by the house, the manner in which its opponents have been treated, the personalities to which they have been subjected, the yells with which one of them has this night been greeted,—all these things dissipate my doubts, and tell me of its complete and early triumph.

8. Do you think those yells will be forgotten? Do you suppose their echo will not reach the plains of my injured and insulted country; that they will not be whispered in her green valleys, and heard from her lofty hills?

9. Oh, they will be heard there! Yes; and they will not be forgotten. The youth of Ireland will bound with indignation; they will say, "We are eight millions; and you treat us thus, as though we were no more to your country than the isle of Guernsey or of Jersey!"

10. I have done my duty; I stand acquitted to my conscience and my country; I have opposed this measure throughout; and I now protest against it as harsh, oppressive, uncalled for, unjust; as establishing an infamous precedent by retaliating crime against crime; as tyrannous, cruelly and vindictively tyrannous. O'CONNELL.

51. RELIGIOUS LIBERTY.

CAN any thing be more absurd and untenable than the argument of the learned gentleman, when you see it stripped of the false coloring he has given to it? First, he alleges that the Catholics are attached to their religion with a bigoted zeal. I admit the zeal, but I utterly deny the bigotry.

2. He proceeds to insist that these feelings, on our part, justify the apprehensions of Protestants. The Catholics, he says, are alarmed for their Church ; why should not the Protestants be alarmed, also, for theirs ? The Catholic desires safety for his religion; why should not the Protestant require security for his? Hence, he concludes that, merely because the Catholic desires to keep his religion free, the Protestant is thereby justified in seeking to enslave it.

3. He says that our anxiety for the preservation of our Church vindicates those who deem the proposed arrangement necessary for the protection of *theirs ;*—a mode of reasoning perfectly true, and perfectly applicable, if we sought any interference with, or control over, the Protestant Church,—if we asked or required that a single Catholic should be consulted upon the management of the Protestant Church, or of its revenues or privileges.

4. But the fact does not bear him out ; for we do not seek nor desire, nor would we accept of, any kind of interference with the Protestant Church. We disclaim and disavow any kind of control over it. We ask not, nor would we allow, any Catholic authority over the mode of appointment of their clergy. Nay, we are quite content to be excluded forever from even advising his majesty with respect to any matter relating to or concerning the Protestant Church,—its rights, its properties, or its privileges.

5. I will, for my own part, go much further ; and I do declare, most solemnly, that I would feel and express equal, if not stronger repugnance, to the interference of a Catholic with

the Protestant Church, than that I have expressed and do feel to any Protestant interference with ours.

6. In opposing their interference with us, I content myself with the mere war of words. But, if the case were reversed, —if the Catholic sought this control over the religion of the Protestant,—the Protestant should command my heart, my tongue, my arm, in opposition to so unjust and insulting a measure.

7. So help me God! I would, in that case, not only feel for the Protestant, and speak for him, but I would fight for him, and cheerfully sacrifice my life in defence of the great principle for which I have ever contended—the principle of universal and complete religious liberty! O'CONNELL.

---

52. THE IRISH SOLDIER.

[JOHN PHILPOT CURRAN, born in Ireland, 1750. Although his senatorial eloquence stands deservedly high, yet it was entirely eclipsed by his brilliant reputation at the bar. "There never lived a greater advocate," says Phillips. "His eloquence was copious, rapid, and ornate, and his powers of winning beyond expression." In his boyhood he had an impediment in his utterance, for which reason his schoolmates called him "Stuttering Jack Curran." But, with an energy that should be imitated by all who seek to become great orators, he employed every means to correct his elocution and render it perfect, by speaking very slowly, to correct his defective utterance; and he most carefully committed to memory, and was never tired repeating aloud the most celebrated orations. The following extract is from one of his speeches in the Irish Senate, at the time of the war between England and France:]

THE present is the most awful and important crisis that Ireland ever saw, considering the actual state of the nation, of the empire, and of the war in which we are engaged. As to the original motives of the war, it is not the time to inquire into them; they are lost in the events: if they had been as pure as they have been represented, how much is it to be regretted that the issue has proved only that it is not in mortals to command success.!

2. The armies of Europe have poured into the field, and surrounded the devoted region of France on every side; but, far

from achieving their purpose, they have only formed an iron hoop about her, which, instead of quelling the fury of her dissensions, has compressed their spring into an irresistible energy, and forced them into coaction.

3. During its progress we saw the miserable objects for whom it was undertaken consumed in nameless thousands, in the different quarters of Europe, by want, and misery, and despair; or expiring on the scaffold, or perishing in the field.

4. We have seen the honest body of the British manufacturer tumbled into the common grave with the venal carcass of the Prussian hireling; we have seen the generous Briton submit to the alliance of servitude and venalty, and submit to it in vain. The sad vicissitudes of each successive campaign have been marked by the defeat of our armies and triumphs of our enemies, and the perfidy of our allies.

5. What was the situation of the contending parties at the beginning of the contest? England, with Spain, with Austria, with Prussia, with Holland, with Ireland on her side; while France had to count the revolt of Toulon, the insurrection of La Vendée, the rebellion of Lyons, and her whole eastern territory in the hands of her enemies.

6. How direful the present reverse! England exhausted, Holland surrendered, Austria wavering, Prussia fled, and Spain fainting in the contest; while France, triumphant and successful, waves a military and triumphant sceptre over an extent of territory that stretches from the ocean and the Rhine to the Pyrenees and the ocean.

7. I will not dwell upon this miserable picture; I will only observe that, during this long succession of disaster and defeat, Ireland alone, of all the allies Great Britain has, neither trafficked, nor deceived, nor deserted.

8. The present distresses of her people attest her liberality of her treasure, while the bones of her enemies and of her children, bleaching upon all the plains of Europe, attest the brilliancy of her courage and the steadfastness of her faith.

CURRAN.

53. LAWS FOR IRELAND.

[The best efforts of English speakers which have been preserved, read tamely compared with Grattan's, abounding as the latter do with fulminating bursts of the most brilliant eloquence. His oration on the declaration of Irish Rights conveys the best idea of his genius as an orator. The following is one of the most eloquent perorations that can be found in any nation or age:

AND as any thing less than liberty is inadequate to Ireland, so is it dangerous to Great Britain. We are too near the British nation, we are too conversant with her history, we are too much fired by her example, to be any thing less than her equal; any thing less, we should be her bitterest enemies— an enemy to that power which smote us with her mace, and to that constitution from whose blessings we were excluded; to be ground as we have been by the British nation, bound by her parliament, plundered by her crown, threatened by her enemies, insulted with her protection, while we returned thanks for her condescension, is a system of meanness and misery which has expired in our determination, as I hope it has in her magnanimity.

2. Do not tolerate that power which blasted you for a century, that power which shattered your loom, banished your manufactures, dishonored your peerage, and stopped the growth of your people; do not, I say, be bribed by an export of woollen, or an import of sugar, and permit that power which has thus withered the land to remain in your country and have existence in your pusillanimity.

3. Do not suffer the arrogance of England to imagine a surviving hope in the fears of Ireland; do not send the people to their own resolves for liberty, passing by the tribunals of justice and the high court of parliament; neither imagine that, by any formation of apology, you can palliate such a commission to your hearts, still less to your children, who will sting you with their curses in your grave for having interposed between them and their Maker, robbing them of an immense occasion, and losing an opportunity which you did not create, and can never restore.

4. Hereafter, when these things shall be history—your age of thraldom and poverty, your sudden resurrection, commercial redress, and miraculous armament—shall the historian stop at liberty, and observe, that here the principal men among us fell into mimic trances of gratitude—they were awed by a weak ministry, and bribed by an empty treasury; and when liberty was within their grasp, and the temple opened her folding-doors, and the arms of the people clanged, and the zeal of the nation urged and encouraged them on, that they fell down, and were prostituted at the threshold.

5. I might, as a constituent, come to your bar and demand my liberty. I do call upon you, by the laws of the land and their violation, by the instruction of eighteen counties, by the arms, inspiration, and providence of the present moment, tell us the rule by which we shall go—assert the law of Ireland—declare the liberty of the land.

6. I will not be answered by a public lie in the shape of an amendment; neither, speaking for the subjects' freedom, am I to hear of faction. I wish for nothing but to breathe, in this our island, in common with my fellow-subjects, the air of liberty. I have no ambition, unless it be the ambition to break your chain, and contemplate your glory.

7. I never will be satisfied so long as the meanest cottager in Ireland has a link of the British chain clanking to his rags; he may be naked, he shall not be in iron; and I do see the time is at hand, the spirit has gone forth, the declaration is planted; and though great men should apostatize, yet the cause will live; and though the public speaker should die, yet the immortal fire shall outlast the organ which conveyed it, and the breath of liberty, like the word of the holy man, will not die with the prophet, but survive him.

8. I shall move you, "That the King's most excellent Majesty, and the Lords and Commons of Ireland, are the only power competent to make laws to bind Ireland." GRATTAN.

54. NATIONAL INDEPENDENCE.

[JAMES OTIS, born in Massachusetts, 1725; died, 1783. He became famous in the struggle for Independence, as the bold and brilliant advocate of colonial rights.]

ENGLAND may as well dam up the waters of the Nile with bulrushes, as to fetter the step of Freedom, more proud and firm in this youthful land, than where she treads the sequestered glens of Scotland, or crouches herself among the magnificent mountains of Switzerland. Arbitrary principles, like those against which we now contend, have cost one king of England his life—another his crown—and they may yet cost a third his most flourishing colonies.

2. We are two millions—one-fifth fighting men. We are bold and vigorous, and we call no man master. To the nation from whom we are proud to derive our origin, we were ever, and we ever will be, ready to yield unforced assistance; but it must not, and it never can be extorted.

3. Some have sneeringly asked, "Are the Americans too poor to pay a few pounds on stamped paper?" No! America, thanks to God and herself, is rich. But the right to take ten pounds, implies the right to take a thousand; and what must be the wealth that avarice, aided by power, cannot exhaust.

4. True, the spectre is now small; but the shadow he casts before him is huge enough to darken all this fair land. Others, in sentimental style, talk of the immense debt of gratitude which we owe to England. And what is the amount of this debt? Why, truly, it is the same that the young lion owes to the dam which has brought it forth on the solitude of the mountain, or left it amid the winds and storms of the desert.

5. We plunged into the wave, with the great charter of freedom in our teeth, because the faggot and torch were behind us. We have waked this new world from its savage lethargy; forests have been prostrated in our path; towns and cities have grown up suddenly as the flowers of the

tropics; and the fires in our autumnal woods are scarcely more rapid than the increase of our wealth and population.

6. And do we owe all this to the kind succor of the mother-country? No! we owe it to the tyranny that drove us from her—to the pelting storms which invigorated our helpless infancy. But perhaps others will say, "We ask no money from your gratitude—we only demand that you should pay your own expenses."

7. And who, I pray, is to judge of their necessity? Why, the king (and, with all due reverence to his sacred majesty, he understands the real wants of his distant subjects as little as he does the language of the Choctaws). Who is to judge concerning the frequency of these demands? The ministry. Who is to judge whether the money is properly expended? The cabinet behind the throne. In every instance, those who take are to judge for those who pay.

8. If this system is suffered to go into operation, we shall have reason to esteem it a great privilege that rain and dew do not depend upon parliament; otherwise they would soon be taxed and dried. But thanks to God, there is freedom enough left upon earth to resist such monstrous injustice.

9. The flame of liberty is extinguished in Greece and Rome, but the light of its glowing embers is still bright and strong on the shores of America. Actuated by its sacred influence, we will resist unto death. But we will not countenance anarchy and misrule.

10. The wrongs that a desperate community have heaped upon their enemies, shall be amply and speedily repaired. Still, it may be well for some proud men to remember, that a fire is lighted in these colonies, which one breath of their king may kindle into such fury that the blood of all England can not extinguish it.

OTIS.

55. THE AMERICAN REVOLUTION

[Among the men whose character and genius had an acknowledged influence on the events immediately preceding the Revolution, was JOSIAH QUINCY. His name is associated with those of Otis, Adams, and other distinguished men whose talents and bravery led to the Declaration of Independence. The pathos of his eloquence, the boldness of his invectives, and the impressive vehemence with which he arraigned the measures of the British ministry inflamed the zeal and animated the resentment of the colonists.]

WHEN we speak of the glory of our fathers, we mean not that vulgar renown to be attained by physical strength, nor yet that higher fame to be acquired by intellectual power. Both often exist without lofty thought, or pure intent, or generous purpose. The glory which we celebrate was strictly of a moral and religious character; righteous as to its ends; just as to its means.

2. The American Revolution had its origin neither in ambition, nor avarice, nor envy, nor in any gross passion; but in the nature and relation of things, and in the thence resulting necessity of separation from the parent State. Its progress was limited by that necessity.

3. During the struggle our fathers displayed great strength and great moderation of purpose. In difficult times, they conducted with wisdom; in doubtful times, with firmness; in perilous, with courage; under oppressive trials, erect; amid great temptations, unseduced; in the dark hour of danger, fearless; in the bright hour of prosperity, faithful.

4. It was not the instant feeling and pressure of the arm of despotism that roused them to resist, but the *principle* on which that arm was extended. They could have paid the *stamp-tax*, and the *tea-tax*, and other impositions of the British Government, had they been increased a thousand-fold. Bu payment acknowledged the *right;* and they spurned the consequences of that acknowledgment.

5. In spite of those acts they could have lived, and happily; and bought, and sold, and got gain, and been at ease But

they would have held those blessings on the tenure of dependence on a foreign and distant power; at the mercy of a king, or his minions; or of councils in which they had no voice, and where their interests could not be represented, and were little likely to be heard. They saw that their prosperity in such case would be precarious, their possessions uncertain, their ease inglorious.

6. But, above all, they realized that those burdens, though light to them, would, to the coming age, to us, their posterity, be heavy, and probably insupportable. Reasoning on the inevitable increase of interested imposition, upon those who are without power and have none to help, they foresaw that, sooner or later, desperate struggles must come.

7. They preferred to meet the trial in their *own times*, and to make the sacrifices in their *own persons*. They were willing *themselves* to endure the toil, and to incur the hazard, that we and our descendants, their posterity, might reap the harvest and enjoy the increase.

8. Generous men! Exalted patriots! Immortal statesmen! For this deep moral and social affection, for this elevated self-devotion, this noble purpose, this bold daring, the multiplying myriads of your posterity, as they thicken along the Atlantic coast, from the St. Croix to the Mississippi, as they spread backwards to the lakes, and from the lakes to the mountains, and from the mountains to the western waters, shall, on this day (the 4th of July), annually, in all future time, as we at this hour, come up to the temple of the Most High, with song, and anthem, and thanksgiving, and choral symphony, and hallelujah, to repeat your NAMES; to look steadfastly on the brightness of your glory; to trace its spreading rays to the points from which they emanate; and to seek, in your character and conduct, a practical illustration of public duty, in every occurring social exigence. JOSIAH QUINCY.

56. THE AGE OF WASHINGTON.

["The speeches of AMES are characterized by a felicity and smoothness of expression, and by a well-tempered animation which adapts them in a very peculiar degree to the exercise of being declaimed."]

GREAT generals have arisen in all ages of the world, and, perhaps, most in those of despotism and darkness. In times of violence and convulsion, they rise, by the force of the whirlwind, high enough to ride in it, and direct the storm.

2. Like meteors, they glare on the black clouds with a splendor, which, while it dazzles and terrifies, makes nothing visible but the darkness. The fame of heroes is, indeed, growing vulgar; they multiply in every long war; they stand in history, and thicken in their ranks, almost as undistinguished as their own soldiers.

3. But such a chief magistrate as Washington appears like the pole-star in a clear sky, to direct the skillful statesman. His presidency will form an epoch, and be distinguished as the age of Washington.

4. Like the milky way, it whitens along its allotted portion of the hemisphere. The latest generations of men will survey, through the telescope of history, the space where so many virtues blend their rays, and delight to separate them into groups and distinct virtues.

5. As the best illustration of them, the living monument, to which the first of patriots would have chosen to consign his fame, it is my earnest prayer to Heaven, that our country may subsist, even to that late day, in the plenitude of its liberty and happiness, and mingle its mild glory with Washington's.
FISHER AMES.

57. UNION AND LIBERTY.

FLAG of the heroes who left us their glory,
  Borne through our battle-field's thunder and flame,
Blazoned in song and illumined in story,
  Wave o'er us all who inherit their fame!

Up with our banner bright,
Sprinkled with starry light,
Spread its fair emblems from mountain to shore;
While through the sounding sky,
Loud rings the nation's cry,—
Union and Liberty!—one evermore!

II.

Light of our firmament, guide of our nation,
Pride of her children, and honored afar,
Let the wide beams of thy full constellation
Scatter each cloud that would darken a star!

III.

Empire unsceptred! what foe shall assail thee,
Bearing the standard of Liberty's van?
Think not the God of thy fathers shall fail thee,
Striving with men for the birthright of man!

IV.

Yet, if by madness and treachery blighted,
Dawns the dark hour when the sword thou must draw,
Then, with the arms of thy millions united,
Smite the bold traitors to Freedom and Law!

V.

Lord of the universe! shield us and guide us,
Trusting Thee always, through shadow and sun!
Thou hast united us, who shall divide us?
Keep us, oh keep us, the Many in One!
Up with our banner bright,
Sprinkled with starry light,
Spread its fair emblems from mountain to shore;
While through the sounding sky,
Loud rings the nation's cry,—
Union and Liberty!—one evermore!

O. W. Holmes.

58. THE FEDERAL CONSTITUTION, 1787.

[The following is strongly marked by the leading traits of FRANKLIN'S character,—his liberality, practical wisdom, and spirit of compromise.]

SIR, I agree to this Constitution, with all its faults—if they are such—because I think a general government necessary for us, and there is no form of government but what may be a blessing to the people, if well administered; and I believe, further, that this is likely to be well administered for a course of years, and can only end in despotism, as other forms have done before it, when the people shall become so corrupted as to need despotic government, being incapable of any other.

2. I doubt, too, whether any other convention we can obtain may be able to make a better Constitution. For, when you assemble a number of men, to have the advantage of their joint wisdom, you inevitably assemble with those men all their prejudices, their passions, their errors of opinion, their local interests, and their selfish views. From such an assembly can a perfect production be expected?

3. It, therefore, astonishes me, sir, to find this system approaching so near to perfection as it does; and I think it will astonish our enemies, who are waiting with confidence to hear that our counsels are confounded, like those of the builders of Babel, and that our States are on the point of separation, only to meet hereafter for the purpose of cutting one another's throats.

4. Thus I consent, sir, to this Constitution, because I expect no better, and because I am not sure that this is not the best. The opinions I have had of its errors I sacrifice to the public good. I have never whispered a syllable of them abroad. Within these walls they were born, and here they shall die.

5. If every one of us, in returning to his constituents, were to report the objections he has had to it, and endeavor to gain partisans in support of them, we might prevent its being generally received, and thereby lose all the salutary effects

and great advantages resulting naturally in our favor among foreign nations, as well as among ourselves, from our real or apparent unanimity.

6. Much of the strength and efficacy of any government, in procuring and securing happiness to the people, depends on opinion—on the general opinion of the goodness of that government, as well as of the wisdom and integrity of its governors.

7. I hope, therefore, that, for our own sakes, as a part of the people, and for the sake of our posterity, we shall act heartily and unanimously in recommending this Constitution, wherever our influence may extend, and turn our future thoughts and endeavors to the means of having it well administered.
FRANKLIN.

59. DISSOLUTION OF THE NATIONAL COMPACT.

[GOUVERNEUR MORRIS, born in New York, 1752; died, 1818. He was a Delegate to the Continental Congress from New York, and subsequently represented that State in the Senate of the United States, before which body he delivered a succession of brilliant speeches on the vital necessity of preserving the Union. Of one of these speeches we give the following extract:]

WHAT will be the situation of these States, organized as they now are, if, by the dissolution of our national compact, they be left to themselves? What is the probable result? We shall either be the victims of foreign intrigue, and, split into factions, fall under the domination of a foreign power, or else, after the misery and torment of a civil war, become the subjects of an usurping military despot.

2. What but this compact, what but this specific part of it, can save us from ruin? The judicial power, that fortress of the Constitution, is now to be overturned. With honest Ajax, I would not only throw a shield before it,—I would build around it a wall of brass.

3. But I am too weak to defend the rampart against the host of assailants. I must call to my assistance their good

sense, their patriotism, and their virtue. Do not, gentlemen, suffer the rage of passion to drive Reason from her seat! If this law be indeed bad, let us join to remedy the defects. Has it been passed in a manner which wounded your pride, or roused your resentment?

4. Have, I conjure you, the magnanimity to pardon that offence! I entreat, I implore you, to sacrifice those angry passions to the interests of our country. Pour out this pride of opinion on the altar of patriotism. Let it be an expiating libation for the weal of America. Do not, for God's sake, do not suffer that pride to plunge us all into the abyss of ruin!

5. Indeed, indeed, it will be but of little, very little, avail, whether one opinion or the other be right or wrong; it will heal no wounds, it will pay no debts, it will rebuild no ravaged towns. Do not rely on that popular will which has brought us frail beings into political existence. That opinion is but a changeable thing. It will soon change. This very measure will change it. You will be deceived.

6. Do not, I beseech you, in a reliance on a foundation so frail, commit the dignity, the harmony, the existence of our nation, to the wild wind! Trust not your treasure to the waves. Throw not your compass and your charts into the ocean. Do not believe that its billows will waft you into port. Indeed, indeed, you will be deceived!

7. Cast not away this only anchor of our safety. I have seen its progress. I know the difficulties through which it was obtained: I stand in the presence of Almighty God, and of the world; and I declare to you, that, if you lose this charter, never,—no, never, will you get another! We are now, perhaps, arrived at the parting point. Here, even here, we stand on the brink of fate. Pause—pause!—for Heaven's sake, pause! GOUVERNEUR MORRIS.

60. WASHINGTON'S SWORD AND FRANKLIN'S STAFF.

[From an address in the United States House of Representatives, on the reception of these memorials by Congress.]

THE sword of Washington! The staff of Franklin! Oh, sir, what associations are linked in adamant with these names! Washington, whose sword was never drawn but in the cause of his country, and never sheathed when wielded in his country's cause! Franklin, the philosopher of the thunderbolt, the printing-press, and the ploughshare!

2. What names are these in the scanty catalogue of the benefactors of human kind! Washington and Franklin! What other two men, whose lives belong to the eighteenth century of Christendom, have left a deeper impression of themselves upon the age in which they lived, and upon all after time?

3. Washington, the warrior and the legislator! In war, contending, by the wager of battle, for the independence of his country, and for the freedom of the human race,—ever manifesting, amidst its horrors, by precept and by example, his reverence for the laws of peace, and for the tenderest sympathies of humanity; in peace, soothing the ferocious spirit of discord, among his own countrymen, into harmony and union, and giving to that very sword, now presented to his country, a charm more potent than that attributed, in ancient times, to the lyre of Orpheus.

4. Franklin! The mechanic of his own fortune; teaching in early youth, under the shackles of indigence, the way to wealth, and, in the shade of obscurity, the path to greatness; in the maturity of manhood, disarming the thunder of its terrors, the lightning of its fatal blast; and wresting from the tyrant's hand the still more afflictive sceptre of oppression; while descending into the vale of years, traversing the Atlantic Ocean, braving, in the dead of winter, the battle and the breeze, bearing in his hand the charter of independence, which

he had contributed to form, and tendering from the self-created nation to the mightiest monarchs of Europe, the olive-branch of peace, the mercurial wand of commerce and the amulet of protection and safety to the man of peace, on the pathless ocean, from the inexorable cruelty and merciless rapacity of war.

5. And, finally, in the last stage of life, with fourscore winters upon his head, under the torture of an incurable disease, returning to his native land, closing his days as the chief magistrate of his adopted commonwealth, after contributing by his counsels, under the presidency of Washington, and recording his name, under the sanction of devout prayer, invoked by him to God, to that Constitution under the authority of which we are here assembled, as the representatives of the North American people, to receive, in their name and for them, these venerable relics of the wise, the valiant, and the good founders of our great confederated Republic—these sacred symbols of our golden age.

6. May they be deposited among the archives of our government! And may every American who shall hereafter behold them, ejaculate a mingled offering of praise to that Supreme Ruler of the universe, by whose tender mercies our Union has been hitherto preserved, through all the vicissitude and revolutions of this turbulent world ; and of prayer for the continuance of these blessings, by the dispensations of Providence, to our beloved country, from age to age, till time shall be no more !   J. Q. ADAMS.

---

61. LIBERTY OR DEATH.

[This speech was delivered by PATRICK HENRY before the Virginia Convention of Delegates, 1775. When he took his seat at the close, no murmur of applause was heard. The effect was too deep. After a trance of a moment, several members started from their seats. The cry, "To arms!" seemed to quiver on every lip, and gleam from every eye. Richard H. Lee arose and supported Mr. Henry with spirit and elegance ; but his melody was lost amidst the agitation of that ocean which the master spirit of the storm had lifted up on high. The supernatural voice still sounded in their ears. They heard in every pause the cry of "Liberty or Death!" They became impatient of speech. Their souls were on fire for action. "The speeches of Patrick Henry are uniformly pervaded by an impassional glow, by a strength and point of language, and by a convenient structure of the sentences which make them of great service for a pupil in declaiming."]

MR. PRESIDENT, it is natural for man to indulge in the illusions of hope. We are apt to shut our eyes against a painful truth, and listen to the song of that siren till she transforms us into beasts. Is it the part of wise men, engaged in the great and arduous struggle for liberty? Are we disposed to be of the number of those, who, having eyes, see not, and having ears hear not, the things which so nearly concern their temporal salvation? For my part, whatever anguish of spirit it may cost, I am willing to know the whole truth, and to provide for it.

2. I have but one lamp, by which my feet are guided; and that is the lamp of experience. I know of no way of judging of the future, but by the past. And, judging by the past, I wish to know, what there has been in the conduct of the British ministry, for the last ten years, to justify those hopes with which gentlemen have been pleased to solace themselves and the house?

3. Is it that insidious smile, with which our petition has been lately received? Trust it not, sir; it will prove a snare to your feet. Suffer not yourselves to be betrayed with a kiss. Ask yourselves how this gracious reception of our petition comports with those warlike preparations which cover our waters and darken our land.

4. Are fleets and armies necessary to a work of love and reconciliation? Have we shown ourselves so unwilling to be reconciled, that force must be called in to win back our love? Let us not deceive ourselves, sir. These are the implements of war and subjugation—the last arguments to which kings resort. I ask, gentlemen, sir, what means this martial array, if its purpose be not to force us to submission? Can gentlemen assign any other motive for it?

5. Has Great Britain any other enemy in this quarter of the world, to call for all this accumulation of navies and armies? No, sir, she has none. They are meant for us; they can be meant for no other. They are sent over to bind and rivet upon us those chains which the British ministers have been so long forging.

6. And what have we to oppose them? Shall we try argument? Sir, we have been trying that for the last ten years. Have we any thing new to offer on the subject? Nothing. We have held the subject up in every light of which it is capable; but it has been all in vain. Shall we resort to entreaty and humble supplication? What terms shall we find which have not been already exhausted? Let us not, I beseech you, sir, deceive ourselves longer.

7. Sir, we have done every thing that could be done, to avert the storm which is now coming on. We have petitioned—we have remonstrated—we have supplicated—we have prostrated ourselves before the throne, and have implored its interposition to arrest the tyrannical hands of the ministry and parliament. Our petitions have been slighted; our remonstrances have produced additional violence and insult; our supplications have been disregarded; and we have been spurned, with contempt, from the foot of the throne. PATRICK HENRY.

62. LIBERTY OR DEATH—(Continued).

THEY tell us, sir, that we are weak—unable to cope with so formidable an adversary. But when shall we be stronger? Will it be the next week, or the next year? Will it be when we are totally disarmed; and when a British guard shall be stationed in every house? Shall we gather strength by irresolution and inaction? Shall we acquire the means of effectual resistance by lying supinely on our backs, and hugging the delusive phantom of hope, until our enemies shall have bound us hand and foot?

2. Sir, we are not weak, if we make a proper use of those means which the God of nature hath placed in our power. Three millions of people, armed in the holy cause of liberty, and in such a country as that which we possess, are invincible by any force which our enemy can send against us. Besides, sir, we shall not fight alone. There is a just God who presides over the destinies of nations, and who will raise up friends to fight our battles for us.

3. The battle, sir, is not to the strong alone,—it is to the active, the vigilant, the brave. Besides, sir, we have no election! If we were base enough to desire it, it is now too late to retire from the contest. There is no retreat—but in submission and slavery! Our chains are forged. Their clanking may be heard on the plains of Boston. The war is inevitable—and let it come! I repeat it, sir, let it come!

4. It is in vain, sir, to extenuate the matter. Gentlemen may cry peace, peace—but there is no peace! The war is actually begun! The next gale that sweeps from the north will bring to our ears the clash of resounding arms!

5. Our brethren are already in the field. Why stand we here idle? What is it that gentlemen wish? What would they have? Is life so dear, or peace so sweet, as to be purchased at the price of chains and slavery? Forbid it, Heaven! I know not what course others may take, but as for me—give me liberty, or give me death! PATRICK HENRY

---

63. RETURN OF BRITISH FUGITIVES, 1782.

I VENTURE to prophesy, there are those now living who will see this favored land amongst the most powerful on earth,—able, sir, to take care of herself, without resorting to that policy which is always so dangerous, though sometimes unavoidable, of calling in foreign aid.

2. Yes, sir, they will see her great in arts and in arms,—her golden harvests waving over fields of immeasurable extent,

her commerce penetrating the most distant seas, and her cannon silencing the vain boasts of those who now proudly affect to rule the waves.

3. But, sir, you must have *men*,—you cannot get along without them. Those heavy forests of valuable timber, under which your lands are groaning, must be cleared away. Those vast riches which cover the face of your soil, as well as those which lie hid in its bosom, are to be developed and gathered only by the skill and enterprise of men.

4. Your timber, sir, must be worked up into ships, to transport the productions of the soil from which it has been cleared. Then, you must have commercial men and commercial capital, to take off your productions, and find the best markets for them abroad. Your great want, sir, is the want of men; and these you must have, and will have speedily, if you are wise.

5. Do you ask how you are to get them? Open your doors, sir, and they will come in! The population of the Old World is full to overflowing. That population is ground, too, by the oppressions of the governments under which they live. Sir, they are already standing on tiptoe upon their native shores, and looking to your coasts with a wistful and longing eye.

6. They see here a land blessed with natural and political advantages, which are not equalled by those of any other country upon earth;—a land on which a gracious Providence hath emptied the horn of abundance,—a land over which peace hath now stretched forth her white wings, and where content and plenty lie down at every door.

7. Sir, they see something still more attractive than all this. They see a land in which Liberty hath taken up her abode,—that liberty whom they had considered as a fabled goddess, existing only in the fancies of poets. They see here a real divinity,—her altars rising on every hand, throughout these happy States; her glories chanted by three millions of tongues, and the whole region smiling under her blessed influence.

8. Sir, let but this, our celestial goddess, Liberty, stretch forth her fair hand towards the people of the Old World,—tell

them to come, and bid them welcome,—and you will see them pouring in from the North, from the South, from the East, and from the West. Your wilderness will be cleared and settled, your deserts will smile, your ranks will be filled, and you will soon be in a condition to defy the powers of any adversary.

9. But gentlemen object to any accession from Great Britain, and particularly to the return of the British refugees. Sir, I feel no objection to the return of those deluded people. They have, to be sure, mistaken their own interests most wofully; and most wofully have they suffered the punishment due to their offences.

10. But the relations which we bear to them, and to their native country, are now changed. Their king hath acknowledged our independence; the quarrel is over, peace hath returned, and found us a free people. Let us have the magnanimity, sir, to lay aside our antipathies and prejudices, and consider the subject in a political light.

11. Those are an enterprising, moneyed people. They will be serviceable in taking off the surplus produce of our lands, and supplying us with necessaries, during the infant state of our manufactures. Even if they be inimical to us in point of feeling and principle, I can see no objection, in a political view, in making them tributary to our advantage. And, as I have no prejudices to prevent my making this use of them, so, sir, I have no fear of any mischief that they can do us. Afraid of *them!*—What, sir, shall *we*, who have laid the proud British *lion* at our feet, now be afraid of *his whelps?*

PATRICK HENRY.

64. LAFAYETTE.

[JOHN QUINCY ADAMS was not merely a statesman, but, as Professor of Oratory, his lectures are able productions, and evince the vigor of a mind thoroughly conversant with the subject it investigates. The following is an extract from Mr. Adams's finished oration on the life and character of Lafayette, delivered before Congress in 1834:]

PRONOUNCE him one of the first men of his age, and you have yet not done him justice. Try him by that test to which he sought in vain to stimulate the vulgar and selfish spirit of Napoleon; class him among the men who, to compare and seat themselves, must take in the compass of all ages; turn back your eyes upon the records of time; summon, from the creation of the world to this day, the mighty|dead of every age and every clime,—and where, among the race of merely mortal men, shall one be found who, as the benefactor of his kind, shall claim to take precedence of Lafayette?

2. There have doubtless been in all ages men whose discoveries or inventions in the world of matter, or of mind, have opened new avenues to the dominion of man over the material creation; have increased his means or his faculties of enjoyment; have raised him in nearer approximation to that higher and happier condition, the object of his hopes and aspirations in his present state of existence.

3. Lafayette discovered no new principle of politics or of morals. He invented nothing in science. He disclosed no new phenomenon in the laws of nature. Born and educated in the highest order of feudal nobility, under the most absolute monarchy of Europe; in possession of an affluent fortune, and master of himself and of all his capabilities, at the moment of attaining manhood the principle of republican justice and of social equality took possession of his heart and mind, as if by inspiration from above.

4. He devoted himself, his life, his fortune, his hereditary honors, his towering ambition, his splendid hopes, all to the cause of Liberty. He came to another hemisphere, to defend her. He became one of the most effective champions of our independence; but, that once achieved, he returned to his own country, and thenceforward took no part in the controversies which have divided us.

5. In the events of our Revolution, and in the forms of policy which we have adopted for the establishment and perpetuation of our freedom, Lafayette found the most perfect form

of government. He wished to add nothing to it. He would gladly have abstracted nothing from it. Instead of the imaginary Republic of Plato, or the Utopia of Sir Thomas More, he took a practical existing model in actual operation here, and never attempted or wished more than to apply it faithfully to his own country.

6. It was not given to Moses to enter the promised land; but he saw it from the summit of Pisgah. It was not given to Lafayette to witness the consummation of his wishes in the establishment of a Republic and the extinction of all hereditary rule in France. His principles were in advance of the age and hemisphere in which he lived. . . . The prejudices and passions of the people of France rejected the principle of inherited power in every station of public trust, excepting the first and highest of them all; but there they clung to it, as did the Israelites of old to the savory deities of Egypt. . . . .

7. When the principle of hereditary dominion shall be extinguished in all the institutions of France; when government shall no longer be considered as property transmissible from sire to son, but as a trust committed for a limited time, and then to return to the people whence it came; as a burdensome duty to be discharged, and not as a reward to be abused; — then will be the time for contemplating the character of Lafayette, not merely in the events of his life, but in the full development of his intellectual conceptions, of his fervent aspirations, of the labors, and perils, and sacrifices of his long and eventful career upon earth; and thenceforward till the hour when the trump of the Archangel shall sound, to announce that time shall be no more, the name of Lafayette shall stand enrolled upon the annals of our race high on the list of pure and disinterested benefactors of mankind.

JOHN QUINCY ADAMS.

65. AMERICAN INNOVATIONS.

[JAMES MADISON, who served two terms as President of the United States, was a Virginian by birth. As a writer and a statesman, he stands among the first of his times.]

WHY is the experiment of an extended Republic to be rejected, merely because it may comprise what is new? Is it not the glory of the people of America, that while they have paid a decent regard to the opinions of former times and other nations, they have not suffered a blind veneration for antiquity, for custom, or for names, to overrule the suggestions of their own good sense, the knowledge of their own situation, and the lesson of their own experience?

2. To this manly spirit, posterity will be indebted for the possession, and the world for the example, of the numerous innovations displayed on the American theatre, in favor of private rights and public happiness.

3. Had no important step been taken by the leaders of the Revolution, for which a precedent could not be discovered,— no government established, of which an exact model did not present itself,—the people of the United States might, at this moment, have been numbered among the melancholy victims of misguided councils; must, at best, have been laboring under the weight of some of those forms which have crushed the liberties of the rest of mankind.

4. Happily for America,—happily, we trust, for the whole human race,—they pursued a new and more noble course. They accomplished a Revolution which has no parallel in the annals of human society. They reared the fabric of governments which have no model on the face of the globe. They formed the design of a great confederacy, which it is incumbent on their successors to improve and perpetuate.

5. If their works betray imperfections, we wonder at the fewness of them. If they erred most in the structure of the Union, this was the most difficult to be executed; this is the work which has been new modelled by the act of your con-

vention, and it is that act on which you are now to deliberate
and to decide.   JAMES MADISON.

66. THE EAGLE.

BIRD of the broad and sweeping wing!
　　Thy home is high in heaven,
Where wide the storms their banners fling,
　　And the tempest clouds are driven.
Thy throne is on the mountain top;
　　Thy fields—the boundless air;
And hoary peaks, that proudly prop
　　The skies—thy dwellings are.

II.

Thou sittest like a thing of light,
　　Amid the noontide blaze:
The midway sun is clear and bright—
　　It cannot dim thy gaze.
Thy pinions to the rushing blast
　　O'er the bursting billow spread,
Where the vessel plunges, hurry past,
　　Like an angel of the dead.

III.

Thou art perch'd aloft on the beetling crag,
　　And the waves are white below,
And on, with a haste that cannot lag,
　　They rush in an endless flow.
Again, thou hast plumed thy wing for flight
　　To lands beyond the sea,
And away like a spirit wreath'd in light,
　　Thou hurriest wild and free.

IV.

Thou hurriest o'er the myriad waves,
　　And thou leavest them all behind;

Thou sweepest that place of unknown graves,
   Fleet as the tempest wind.
When the night storm gathers dim and dark,
   With a shrill and boding scream,
Thou rushest by the foundering bark,
   Quick as a passing dream.

V.

Lord of the boundless realm of air!
   In thy imperial name,
The hearts of the bold and ardent dare
   The dangerous path of fame.
Beneath the shade of thy golden wings,
   The Roman legions bore,
From the river of Egypt's cloudy springs
   Their pride, to the polar shore.

VI.

For thee they fought, for thee they fell,
   And their oath was on thee laid;
To thee the clarions raised their swell,
   And the dying warrior pray'd.
Thou wert, through an age of death and fears,
   The image of pride and power,
Till the gather'd rage of a thousand years
   Burst forth in one awful hour.

VII.

And then, a deluge of wrath it came,
   And the nations shook with dread;
And it swept the earth till its fields were flame,
   And piled with the mingled dead.
Kings were roll'd in the wasteful flood,
   With the low and crouching slave;
And together lay, in a shroud of blood,
   The coward and the brave.

VIII.

And where was then thy fearless flight?
  "O'er the dark mysterious sea,
To the lands that caught the setting light,
  The cradle of Liberty.
There, on the silent and lonely shore,
  For ages I watch'd alone,
And the world, in its darkness, ask'd no more
  Where the glorious bird had flown.

IX.

"But then came a bold and hardy few,
  And they breasted the unknown wave;
I caught afar the wandering crew;
  And I knew they were high and brave.
I wheel'd around the welcome bark,
  As it sought the desolate shore;
And up to heaven, like a joyous lark,
  My quivering pinions bore.

X.

"And now that bold and hardy few
  Are a nation wide and strong,
And danger and doubt I have led them through,
  And they worship me in song;
And over their bright and glancing arms
  On field and lake and sea,
With an eye that fires, and a spell that charms,
  I guide them to victory."

PERCIVAL.

---

67. THE PROSPECT OF WAR.

[J. C. CALHOUN, born in South Carolina, 1782; died, 1850.—"The eloquence of Mr. Calhoun," said Webster, "was a part of his intellect. It grew out of the qualities of his mind, and was plain, strong, terse, condensed, concise. Rejecting ornament, his force consisted in the plainness of his propositions, in the closeness of his logic, and in the strength and energy of his manner." A distinguished contemporary statesman, Wilde, gives the following analysis of Calhoun's oratory:—"With a genius eminently metaphysical, he applied to politics his habits of analysis, abstraction, and condensation, and thus gave to the problems of government something of that grandeur which the higher mathematics have borrowed from astronomy. The wings of his mind were rapid, but capricious, and there were times when the light which flashed from them as they passed, glanced like a mirror in the sun, only to dazzle th beholder. Engrossed with his subject, careless of his words, his loftier flights of eloquence were sometimes followed by colloquial or provincial barbarisms But, though often incorrect, he was always fascinating. Language, with him, was merely the scaffolding of thought, employed to raise a dome, which, like Angelo's, he suspended in the heavens.]

WE are told of the danger of war. We are ready to acknowledge its hazard and misfortune, but I cannot think that we have any extraordinary danger to apprehend,—at least, none to warrant an acquiescence in the injuries we have received. On the contrary, I believe no war would be less dangerous to internal peace, or the safety of the country.

2. In speaking of Canada, the gentleman from Virginia introduced the name of Montgomery with much feeling and interest. Sir, there is danger in that name to the gentleman's argument. It is sacred to heroism! It is indignant of submission! It calls our memory back to the time of our Revolution,—to the Congress of 1774 and 1775.

3. Suppose a speaker of that day had risen and urged all the arguments which we have heard on this occasion; had told *that* Congress, "Your contest is about the right of laying a tax; the attempt on Canada has nothing to do with it; the war will be expensive; danger and devastation will overspread our country, and the power of Great Britain is irresistible?" With what sentiment, think you, would such doctrines have been received?

4. Happy for us, they had no force at that period of our country's glory. Had such been acted on, this hall would never have witnessed a great people convened to deliberate for the general good; a mighty empire, with prouder prospects than any nation the sun ever shone on, would not have risen

in the West. No! we would have been vile, subjected colonies; governed by that imperious rod which Britain holds over her distant provinces.

5. The gentleman is at a loss to account for what he calls our hatred to England. He asks, How can we hate the country of Locke, of Newton, Hampden, and Chatham; a country having the same language and customs with ourselves, and descended from a common ancestry?

6. Sir, the laws of human affections are steady and uniform. If we have so much to attach us to that country, powerful, indeed, must be the cause which has overpowered it. Yes, sir; there is a cause strong enough. Not that occult, courtly affection which he has supposed to be entertained for France; but continued and unprovoked insult and injury,—a cause so manifest, that the gentleman had to exert much ingenuity to overlook it.

7. But, in his eager admiration of that country, he has not been sufficiently guarded in his argument. Has he reflected on the cause of that admiration? Has he examined the reasons of our high regard for her Chatham?

8. It is his ardent patriotism, his heroic courage, which could not brook the least insult or injury offered to his country, but thought that her interest and honor ought to be vindicated, be the hazard and expense what they might. I hope, when we are called on to admire, we shall also be asked to imitate.

J. C. CALHOUN.

68. REPLY TO FOOT'S RESOLUTIONS.

[ROBERT HAYNE's powers of oratory first became conspicuous in an address which he delivered on the anniversary of the independence of America, in 1812, before the officers and soldiers of Fort Moultrie. The purity of style and depth of pathos he evinced in this address won the applause of his hearers, and widely extended his reputation. It was exalted still more when his career in the Senate began, and his speeches on the Tariff in 1824, and on the Bankrupt Bill, are justly famous. But the most celebrated are those delivered in the great debate on Mr. Foot's resolutions. Of the last of these, as able writer has said. "As an effort of intellect, it will rank among the highest in the annals of American eloquence."—"He had a copious and ready elocution, flowing at will in a strong and steady current, and rich in the material which constitutes argument." In fine, Nature had lavished upon him all those gifts of person and mind which fascinate the stranger, and at the same time rendered his influence so powerful over those with whom he came in contact in the various walks of life. "The speeches of Mr. Hayne may be classed among the most admirable specimens of eloquence for declamatory discipline which have ever emanated from our National Councils."]

THE gentleman from Massachusetts, in reply to my remarks on the injurious operations of our land system on the prosperity of the West, pronounced an extravagant eulogium on the paternal care which the Government had extended towards the West, to which he attributed all that was great and excellent in the present condition of the new States.

2. The language of the gentleman on this topic fell upon my ears like the almost forgotten tones of the Tory leaders of the British Parliament at the commencement of the American Revolution. They, too, discovered that the colonies had grown great under the fostering care of the mother-country; and I must confess, while listening to the gentleman, I thought the appropriate reply to his argument was to be found in the remark of a celebrated orator made on that occasion: "They have grown great in spite of your protection."

3. . . . . Sir, let me tell that gentleman, that the South repudiates the idea that a pecuniary dependence on the Federal Government is one of the legitimate means of holding the States together. A moneyed interest in the Government is essentially a base interest; and just so far as it operates to bind the feelings of those who are subjected to it, to the Government—just so far as it operates in creating sympathies and interests that would not otherwise exist—is it opposed to all the principles of free government, and at war with virtue and patriotism. . . . .

4. The honorable gentleman from Massachusetts has gone out of his way to pass a high eulogium on the State of Ohio. In the most impassioned tones of eloquence, he described her majestic march to greatness. He told us that, having already

left all the other States far behind, she was now passing by Virginia and Pennsylvania, and about to take her station by the side of New York.

5. To all this, sir, I was disposed most cordially to respond When, however, the gentleman proceeded to contrast the State of Ohio with Kentucky, to the disadvantage of the latter, I listened to him with regret; and when he proceeded further to attribute the great, and, as he supposed, acknowledged superiority of the former in population, wealth, and general prosperity, to the policy of Nathan Dane, of Massachusetts, which had secured to the people of Ohio a population of freemen, I will confess that my feelings suffered a revulsion, which I am now unable to describe in any language sufficiently respectful towards the gentleman from Massachusetts.

6. Did that gentleman, sir, when he formed the determination to cross the Southern border, in order to invade the State of South Carolina, deem it prudent or necessary to enlist under his banners the prejudices of the world, which, like Swiss troops, may be engaged in any cause, and are prepared to serve under any leader? Did he desire to avail himself of those remorseless allies, the passions of mankind, of which it may be more truly said than of the savage tribes of the wilderness, "that their known rule of warfare is an indiscriminate slaughter of all ages, sexes, and conditions?"

7. Or was it supposed, sir, that, in an unpremeditated and unprovoked attack upon the South, it was advisable to begin by a gentle admonition of our supposed weakness, in order to prevent us from making that firm and manly resistance due to our own character and our dearest interest?

8. Was the significant hint of the weakness of slaveholding States, when contrasted with the superior strength of free States, like the glare of the weapon, half drawn from its scabbard, intended to enforce the lessons of prudence and patriotism which the gentleman has resolved, out of his abundant generosity, gratuitously to bestow upon us?

9. I know it has been supposed by certain ill-informed per-

sons that the South exists only by the protection and countenance of the North. . . . . There is a spirit which, like the father of evil, is constantly "walking to and fro about the earth, seeking whom it may devour;" it is the spirit of false philanthropy. The persons whom it possesses leave their own affairs, and neglect their own duties, to regulate the affairs and duties of others. Theirs is the task to feed the hungry and clothe the naked of other lands, while they thrust the naked, famished, and shivering beggar from their own doors— to instruct the heathen, while their own children want the bread of life.

10. It is a spirit which has long been busy with the slaves of the South, and is even now displaying itself in vain efforts to drive the Government from its wise policy in relation to the Indians. . . . . Do gentlemen value the Union at so low a price that they will not even make one effort to bind the States together with the chord of affection? Is this the spirit in which this Government is to be administered? If so, let me tell you, the seeds of dissolution are already sown, and our children will reap the bitter fruit. ROBERT Y. HAYNE.

69. SONG OF MARION'S MEN.

OUR band is few, but true and tried,—
  Our leader frank and bold;
The British soldier trembles
  When Marion's name is told.
Our fortress is the good green wood,
  Our tent the cypress-tree;
We know the forest round us,
  As seamen know the sea.
We know its walls of thorny vines,
  Its glades of reedy grass,
Its safe and silent islands
  Within the dark morass.

2. Woe to the English soldiery
   That little dread us near!
   On them shall light, at midnight,
   A strange and sudden fear:
   When, waking to their tents on fire,
   They grasp their arms in vain,
   And they who stand to face us
   Are beat to earth again;
   And they who fly in terror deem
   A mighty host behind,
   And hear the tramp of thousands
   Upon the hollow wind.

3. Then sweet the hour that brings release
   From danger and from toil:
   We talk the battle over,
   And share the battle's spoil.
   The woodland rings with laugh and shout,
   As if a hunt were up;
   And woodland flowers are gathered
   To crown the soldier's cup.
   With merry songs we mock the wind
   That in the pine-top grieves,
   And slumber long and sweetly,
   On beds of oaken leaves.

4. Well knows the fair and friendly moon
   The band that Marion leads—
   The glitter of their rifles,
   The scampering of their steeds.
   'Tis life to guide the fiery barb
   Across the moonlight plain;
   'Tis life to feel the night-wind
   That lifts his tossing mane.
   A moment in the British camp—
   A moment—and away,

Back to the pathless forest,
    Before the peep of day.

5. Grave men there are by broad Santee,
    Grave men with hoary hairs;
  Their hearts are all with Marion,
    For Marion are their prayers.
  And lovely ladies greet our band,
    With kindliest welcoming,
  With smiles like those of summer,
    And tears like those of spring.
  For them we wear these trusty arms,
    And lay them down no more,
  Till we have driven the Briton
    Forever from our shore.

BRYANT.

---

70. MATCHES AND OVER-MATCHES.

[The reply to Colonel Hayne, of South Carolina, in 1830, was one of WEBSTER's greatest congressional speeches. This gentleman had indulged in personalities against Mr. Webster, and in a very authoritative manner enunciated his views of "Nullification." The reply, in beauty, strength, and perspicuity of style, in sound logic, keen sarcasm, true patriotism, and lofty eloquence, has scarcely its equal in the English language. A distinguished member of Congress, Mr. Wilde of Georgia, says of Webster, that his deep thoughts, forcible expressions, short sentences, calm, cold, collected manner, air of dignity, deep, sepulchral, unimpassioned voice, which in the early part of his career gave promise of his future greatness,—were fully realized in after life. His sarcasms were peculiar to him, "they seemed to be emanations from the spirit of the icy ocean—or frozen mercury, becoming caustic as red-hot iron." In comparing him with American orators, he is considered inferior to Preston in pathos, he lacks the electric rapidity and fire of Calhoun, and the versatile graces of Clay.]

MATCHES and over-matches! Those terms are more applicable elsewhere than here, and fitter for other assemblies than this. Sir, the gentleman seems to forget where and what we are. This is a Senate; a Senate of equals; of men of individual honor and personal character, and of absolute independence.

We know no masters; we acknowledge no dictators. This is a hall for mutual consultation and discussion; not an arena for the exhibition of champions.

2. I offer myself, sir, as a match for no man; I throw the challenge of debate at no man's feet. But, then, sir, since the honorable member has put the question, in a manner that calls or an answer, I will give him an answer; and I tell him, that, holding myself to be the humblest of the members here, I yet know nothing in the arm of his friend from Missouri, either alone, or when aided by the arm of his friend from South Carolina, that need deter even me from espousing whatever opinions I may choose to espouse, from debating whenever I may choose to debate, or from speaking whatever I may see fit to say on the floor of the Senate.

3. Sir, when uttered as matter of commendation or compliment, I should dissent from nothing which the honorable member might say of his friend. Still less do I put forth any pretensions of my own. But, when put to me as matter of taunt, I throw it back, and say to the gentleman that he could possibly say nothing less likely than such a comparison to wound my pride of personal character. The anger of its tone rescued the remark from intentional irony, which, otherwise, probably, would have been its general acceptation.

4. But, sir, if it be imagined that, by this mutual quotation and commendation; if it be supposed that, by casting the characters of the drama, assigning to each his part,—to one, the attack; to another, the cry of onset;—or, if it be thought that, by a loud and empty vaunt of anticipated victory, any laurels are to be won here; if it be imagined, especially, that any or all these things shall shake any purpose of mine,—I can tell the honorable member, once for all, that he is greatly mistaken, and that he is dealing with one of whose temper and character he has yet much to learn.

5. Sir, I shall not allow myself, on this occasion,—I hope on no occasion,—to be betrayed into any loss of temper; but if provoked, as I trust I never shall allow myself to be, into

crimination and recrimination, the honorable member may, perhaps, find that in that contest there will be blows to take, as well as blows to give; that others can state comparisons as significant, at least as his own; and that his impunity may, perhaps, demand of him whatever powers of taunt and sarcasm he may possess. I commend him to a prudent husbandry of his resources. WEBSTER.

71. THE SOUTH DURING THE REVOLUTION

IF there be one State in the Union, Mr. President (and I say it not in a boastful spirit), that may challenge comparison with any other for a uniform, zealous, ardent, and uncalculating devotion to the Union, that State is South Carolina.

2. Sir, from the very commencement of the Revolution up to this hour, there is no sacrifice, however great, she has not cheerfully made; no service she has ever hesitated to perform. She has adhered to you in your prosperity; but in your adversity she has clung to you with more than filial affection.

3. No matter what was the condition of her domestic affairs, though deprived of her resources, divided by parties, or surrounded by difficulties, the call of the country has been to her as the voice of God. Domestic discord ceased at the sound, every man became at once reconciled to his brethren, and the sons of Carolina were all seen crowding together to the temple, bringing their gifts to the altar of their common country.

4. What, sir, was the conduct of the South during the Revolution? Sir, I honor New England for her conduct in that glorious struggle. But great as is the praise which belongs to her, I think at least equal honor is due to the South. They espoused the quarrel of their brethren with a generous zeal, which did not suffer them to stop to calculate their interest in the dispute.

5. Favorites of the mother-country, possessed of neither ships nor seamen to create commercial rivalship, they might

have found in their situation a guarantee that their trade would be forever fostered and protected by Great Britain. But, trampling on all considerations, either of interest or of safety, they rushed into the conflict, and, fighting for principle, periled all in the sacred cause of freedom.

6. Never was there exhibited, in the history of the world, higher examples of noble daring, dreadful suffering, and heroic endurance, than by the Whigs of Carolina, during the Revolution.

7. The whole State, from the mountains to the sea, was overrun by an overwhelming force of the enemy. The fruits of industry perished on the spot where they were produced, or were consumed by the foe. The "plains of Carolina" drank up the most precious blood of her citizens! Black and smoking ruins marked the places which had been the habitations of her children.

8. Driven from their homes into the gloomy and almost impenetrable swamps, even there the spirit of liberty survived, and South Carolina, sustained by the example of her Sumpters and her Marions, proved by her conduct, that, though her soil might be overrun, the spirit of her people was invincible.

HAYNE.

---

72. THE FEDERAL UNION.

I PROFESS, sir, in my career hitherto, to have kept steadily in view the prosperity and the honor of the whole country, and the preservation of the Federal Union. I have not allowed myself to look beyond the Union, to see what might lie hidden in the dark recess behind. I have not coolly weighed the chances of preserving liberty, when the bonds that unite us together shall be broken asunder.

2. I have not accustomed myself to hang over the precipice of disunion, to see whether, with my short sight, I can fathom the depths of the abyss below; nor could I regard him as

a safe counsellor in the affairs of this government, whose thoughts should be mainly bent on considering, not how the Union should be preserved, but how tolerable might be the condition of the people when it shall be broken up and destroyed.

3. While the Union lasts, we have high, exciting, gratifying prospects spread out before us, for us and our children. Beyond that, I seek not to penetrate the vail. God grant, that, in my day, at least, that curtain may not rise! God grant, that on my vision never may be opened what lies behind!

4. When my eyes shall be turned to behold, for the last time, the sun in heaven, may I not see him shining on the broken and dishonored fragments of a once-glorious Union; on States dissevered, discordant, belligerent; on a land rent with civil feuds, or drenched, it may be, in fraternal blood!

5. Let their last feeble and lingering glance rather behold the gorgeous ensign of the republic, now known and honored throughout the earth, still full high advanced, its arms and trophies streaming in their original lustre, not a stripe erased or polluted, nor a single star obscured, bearing for its motto no such miserable interrogatory as,—*What is all this worth?* nor those other words of delusion and folly,—*Liberty first, and Union afterward;* but everywhere spread all over in characters of living light, blazing on all its ample folds as they float over the sea, and over the land, and in every wind under the whole heavens, that other sentiment, dear to every true American heart,—LIBERTY AND UNION, NOW AND FOREVER, ONE AND INSEPARABLE! WEBSTER.

---

73. PEACEABLE SECESSION.

SIR, he who sees these States now revolving in harmony around a common centre, and expects to see them quit their places and fly off without convulsion, may look the next hour to see the heavenly bodies rush from their spheres, and jostle against each other in the realms of space, without causing the crush of the universe.

2. There can be no such thing as a peaceable secession. Peaceable secession is an utter impossibility. Is the great Constitution under which we live, covering this whole country, is it to be thawed and melted away by secession, as the snows on the mountain melt under the influence of a vernal sun, disappear almost unobserved, and run off?

3. No, sir! No, sir! I will not state what might produce the disruption of the Union: but, sir, I see, as plainly as I see the sun in heaven, what that disruption itself must produce; I see that it must produce war, and such a war as I will not describe, *in its twofold character.*

4. Peaceable secession!—peaceable secession! The concurrent agreement of all the members of this great republic to separate! A voluntary separation, with alimony on one side and on the other. Why, what would be the result? Where is the line to be drawn? What States are to secede? What is to remain America? What am I to be? An American no longer? Am I to become a sectional man, a local man, a separatist, with no country in common with the gentlemen who sit around me here, or who fill the other House of Congress?

5. Heaven forbid! Where is the flag of the republic to remain? Where is the eagle still to tower?—or is he to cower, and shrink, and fall to the ground? Why, sir, our ancestors—our fathers and our grandfathers, those of them that are yet living amongst us, with prolonged lives—would rebuke and reproach us; and our children and our grandchildren would cry out shame upon us, if we, of this generation, should dishonor these ensigns of the power of the government and the harmony of that Union, which is every day felt among us with so much joy and gratitude.

6. What is to become of the army? What is to become of the navy? What is to become of the public lands? How is any one of the thirty States to defend itself?

7. Sir, we could not sit down here to-day, and draw a line of separation that would satisfy any five men in the country. There are natural causes that would keep and tie us together; and there are social and domestic relations which we could not break if we would, and which we should not if we could.

WEBSTER.

---

74. FREE TRADE.

SIR, next to the Christian religion, I consider free trade, in its largest sense, as the greatest blessing that can be conferred upon any people. Hear, sir, what Patrick Henry, the great orator of Virginia, whose soul was the very temple of freedom, says on this subject:

2. "Why should we fetter commerce? If a man is in chains, he droops and bows to the earth, because his spirits are broken; but let him *twist the fetters from his legs*, and he will stand erect.

3. "Fetter not commerce! Let her be free as air. She will range the whole creation, and return on the four winds of heaven to bless the land with plenty."

4. But it has been said that free trade would do very well if all nations would adopt it; but, as it is, every nation must protect itself from the effect of restriction by countervailing measures.

5. I am persuaded, sir, that this is a great, a most fatal error. If retaliation is resorted to for the honest purpose of producing a redress of grievance, while adhered to no longer than there is a hope of success, it may, like war itself, be sometimes just and necessary. But if it have no such object, "it is the unprofitable combat of seeing which can do the other most harm."

6. The case can hardly be conceived in which permanent restrictions, as a measure of retaliation, could be profitable. In every possible situation, a trade, whether more or less

restricted, is profitable, or it is not. This can only be decided by experience; and if the trade be left to regulate itself, water would not more naturally seek its level than the intercourse adjust itself to the true interest of the parties.

7. Sir, as to this idea of the regulation by government of the pursuits of men, I consider it as a remnant of barbarism, disgraceful to an enlightened age, and inconsistent with the first principles of rational liberty. I hold government to be utterly incapable, from its position, of exercising such a power wisely, prudently, or justly.

8. Are the rulers of the world the depositaries of its collected wisdom? Sir, can we forget the advice of a great statesman to his son: "Go, see the world, my son, that you may see with how little wisdom mankind is governed."

9. And is our own government an exception to this rule, or do we not find here, as everywhere else, that

"Man, proud man,
Dressed in a little brief authority,
Plays such fantastic tricks before high heaven,
As make the angels weep?"

HAYNE.

---

75. OUR COUNTRY.

THIS lovely land, this glorious liberty, these benign institutions (the dear purchase of our fathers), are ours: ours to enjoy, ours to preserve, ours to transmit; generations past, and generations to come, hold us responsible for this trust. Our fathers from behind admonish us with their anxious parental voices; posterity calls out to us from the bosom of the future; the world turns hither with its solicitous eye; all, all conjure us to act wisely and faithfully in this relation which we sustain.

2. We can never, indeed, pay the debt which is upon us; but, by virtue, by morality, by religion, by the cultivation of every good habit, we may hope to enjoy the blessings through our day, and to leave them unimpaired to our children. Let

us feel deeply how much of what we are and what we possess, we owe to this liberty and these institutions of government.

3. Nature has, indeed, given us a soil which yields bounteously to the hand of industry; the mighty and fruitful ocean is before us, and the skies over our head shed health and vigor. But what are lands and seas, and skies, to civilized man, without society, without knowledge, without morals, without religious culture? and how can these be enjoyed in all their excellence, but under the protection of wise institutions and a free government?

4. There is no American who does not at this moment, and at every moment, experience in his own condition, and in the condition of the most near and dear to him, the influence and benefits of this liberty, of these institutions. Let us, then, acknowledge the blessing; let us feel it deeply and powerfully; let us cherish a strong affection for it, and resolve to maintain and perpetuate it. The blood of our fathers, let it not have been shed in vain; the great hope of posterity, let it not be blasted.

5. The striking attitude, too, in which we stand to the world around us, cannot be altogether omitted. Neither individuals nor nations can perform their part well, until they understand and appreciate all the duties belonging to it. It is not to inflate national vanity, nor to swell a light and empty feeling of self-importance, but it is that we may judge justly of our situation, and of our duties, that I earnestly urge the consideration of our position and our character among the nations of the earth.

6. It cannot be denied but by those who would dispute against the sun, that with America, and in America, a new era commences in human affairs. This era is distinguished by free representative government, by entire religious liberty, by improved systems of national intercourse, by a newly awakened and unconquerable spirit of inquiry, and by diffusion of knowledge among the community, such as has been before altogether unheard of and unknown. America! Amer-

ica! our country, our dear native land, is inseparably connected, fast bound up in fortune and by fate, with these great interests. If they fall, we fall with them. If they stand, it will be because we have upheld them. — WEBSTER.

76. THE STATE CONSTITUTION.

[Hon. WILLIAM GASTON was born in South Carolina, 1778. His Congressional career was of unsurpassed brilliancy. As a profound jurist he was also eminent among the great legal minds of our country. But his greatest praise was in his profoundly religious life. No political or judicial business ever prevented him from observing every duty of a zealous, practical Christian.]

SIR, I am opposed, out and out, to any interference of the State with the opinions of its citizens, and more especially with their opinions on religious subjects. The good order of society requires that actions and practices injurious to the public peace and public morality should be restrained, and but a moderate portion of practical good sense is required to enable the proper authorities to decide what conduct is really thus injurious.

2. But to decide on the truth or error, on the salutary or pernicious consequences of opinions, requires a skill in dialectics, a keenness of discernment, a forecast and comprehension of mind, and, above all, an exemption from bias, which do not ordinarily belong to human tribunals.

3. The preconceived opinions of him who is appointed to try become the standard by which the opinions of others are measured, and as these correspond with, or differ from his own, they are pronounced true or false, salutary or pernicious. Let the Arminian pass on the doctrines of the high Calvinist, and he will have no hesitation in branding them as utterly destructive of the distinctions between right and wrong, and leading to the subversion of all morality.

4. Let the Calvinist determine on the soundness and the tendencies of the Arminian faith, and he will have little diffi-

culty in arraigning it for blasphemy, as stripping the Almighty of His essential attributes, and setting up man as independent of God, and needing not His grace. Law is the proper judge of action, and reward or punishment its proper sanction.

5. Reason is the proper umpire of opinion, and argument and discussion its only fit advocates. To denounce opinions by law is as silly, and unfortunately much more tyrannical, as it would be to punish crime by logic. Law calls out the force of the community to compel obedience to its mandates. To operate on opinion by law is to enslave the intellect and oppress the soul—to reverse the order of nature and make reason subservient to force.

6. But of all the attempts to arrogate unjust dominion, none is so pernicious as the efforts of tyrannical men to rule over the human conscience. Religion is exclusively an affair between man and his God. If there be any subject upon which the interference of human power is more forbidden than on all others it is on religion. Born of Faith,—nurtured by Hope,—invigorated by Charity,—looking for its rewards in a world beyond the grave,—it is of heaven, heavenly.

7. The evidence on which it is founded, and the sanctions by which it is upheld are addressed solely to the understanding and the purified affections. Even He from whom cometh every pure and perfect gift, and to whom religion is directed as its author, its end, and its exceeding great reward, imposes no coercion on His children. He causes His sun to shine alike on the believer and the unbeliever and His dews to fertilize equally the soil of the orthodox and the heretic.

8. No earthly gains or temporal privations are to influence their judgment here, and it is reserved until the last day for the just Judge of all the earth to declare who have criminally refused to examine or to credit the evidences which were laid before them.

9. But civil rulers thrust themselves in and become God's avengers, under a pretended zeal for the honor of His house and the propagation of His revelation—

"Snatch from his hand the balance and the rod;
Rejudge his justice—are the gods of God,"

to define faith by edicts, statutes, and constitutions; deal out largesses to accelerate conviction, and refute unbelief and heresy by the unanswerable logic of pains and penalties.

10. Let not religion be abused for this impious tyranny—religion has nothing to do with it. Nothing can be conceived more abhorrent to the spirit of true religion, than the hypocritical pretensions of kings, princes, and magistrates to uphold her holy cause by their unholy violence.

JUDGE GASTON.

77. THE FOLLY OF DISUNION.

THREATS of resistance, secession, separation, have become common as household words, in the wicked and silly violence of public declaimers. The public ear is familiarized, and the public mind will soon be accustomed to the detestable suggestions of DISUNION!

2. Calculations and conjectures, what may the East do without the South, and what may the South do without the East; sneers, menaces, reproaches, and recriminations, all tend to the same fatal end! What can the East do without the South? What can the South do without the East?

3. They may do much; they may exhibit to the curiosity of political anatomists, and the pity and wonder of the world, the "*disjecta membra*," the sundered and bleeding limbs of a once gigantic body instinct with life, and strength, and vigor. They can furnish to the philosophic historian another melancholy and striking instance of the political axiom, that all republican confederacies have an inherent and unavoidable tendency to dissolution.

4. They will present fields and occasions for border wars, for leagues and counter-leagues, for the intrigues of petty statesmen, the struggles of military chiefs, for confiscations,

insurrections, and deeds of darkest hue. They will gladden the hearts of those who have proclaimed that men are not fit to govern themselves, and shed a disastrous eclipse on the hopes of rational freedom throughout the world.

5. Solon, in his code, proposed no punishment for parricide treating it as an impossible crime. Such, with us, ought to be the crime of political parricide—the dismemberment of our "fatherland." GASTON.

78. PARTY SPIRIT.

PARTIES and party men may deserve reprobation for their selfishness, their violence, their errors, or their wickedness. They may do our country much harm. They may retard its growth, destroy its harmony, impair its character, render its institutions unstable, pervert the public mind, and deprave the public morals. These are, indeed, evils, and sore evils; but the principle of life remains, and will yet struggle, with assured success, over these temporary maladies.

2. Still we are great, glorious, united and free; still we have a name that is revered abroad, and loved at home—a name which is a tower of strength to us against foreign wrong, and a bond of internal union and harmony—a name which no enemy pronounces but with respect, and which no citizen hears but with a throb of exultation.

3. Still we have that blessed Constitution, which, with all its pretended defects, and all its alleged violations, has conferred more benefit on man than ever yet flowed from any other institution—which has established justice, insured domestic tranquillity, provided for the common defence, promoted the general welfare, and which, under God, if we be true to ourselves, will insure the blessings of liberty to us and our posterity.

4. Surely, such a country and such a Constitution have claims upon you, my friends, which cannot be disregarded. I

entreat and adjure you, then, by all that is near and dear to you on earth, by all the obligations of patriotism, by the memory of your fathers, who fell in the great and glorious struggle, for the sake of your sons, whom you would not have to blush for your degeneracy, by all your proud recollections of the past, and all the fond anticipations of the future renown of our nation—preserve that country, uphold that Constitution.

5. Resolve that they shall not be lost while in your keeping, and may God Almighty strengthen you to perform that vow!
GASTON.

79. FACTIOUS POWER.

[On the subject of the Loan Bill of twenty-five millions, Mr. Calhoun, in the course of his speech in favor of this bill, had reflected quite severely on what he termed the factious opposition to the Administration, which might be salutary to a monarchy, but was highly inappropriate in a government so republican as ours.]

IF this doctrine were then to be collected from the history of the world, can it now be doubted, since the experience of the last twenty-five years? Go to France—once revolutionary, now imperial France—and ask her whether factious power or intemperate opposition be the more fatal to freedom and happiness.

2. Perhaps at some moment, when the eagle eye of her master is turned away, she may whisper to you to behold the demolition of Lyons, or the devastation of La Vendée. Perhaps she will give you a written answer.

3. Draw near the fatal lamp-post, and by its flickering light read it as traced in characters of blood that flowed from the guillotine,—"Faction is a demon—faction out of power is a demon enchained—faction vested with the attributes of rule is a Moloch of destruction!"

4. In this question I assuredly have a very deep interest, but it is the interest of the citizen only. My public career, I hope, will not continue long. Should it please the Disposer of

events to permit me to see the great interest of this nation confided to men who will secure its rights by firmness, moderation, and impartiality abroad, and at home cultivate the arts of peace, encourage honest industry in all its branches, dispense equal justice to all classes of the community, and thus administer the Government in the true spirit of the Constitution, as a trust for the people, not as the property of a party, it will be to me utterly unimportant by what political epithet they may be characterized.

5. As a private citizen, grateful for the blessings I may enjoy, and yielding a prompt obedience to every legitimate demand that can be made upon me, I shall rejoice, as far as my little sphere may extend, to foster the same dispositions among those who surround me. GASTON.

---

80. THE PERMANENCE OF AMERICAN LIBERTY.

THE election of a chief magistrate by the mass of the people of an extensive community was, to the most enlightened nations of antiquity, a political impossibility. Destitute of the art of printing, they could not have introduced the representative principle into their political systems, even if they had understood it. In the very nature of things, that principle can only be coextensive with popular intelligence.

2. In this respect, the art of printing, more than any invention since the creation of man, is destined to change and elevate the political condition of society. It has given a new impulse to the energies of the human mind, and opens new and brilliant destinies to modern republics, which were utterly unattainable by the ancients. The existence of a country population, scattered over a vast extent of territory, as intelligent as the population of the cities, is a phenomenon which was utterly and necessarily unknown to the free States of antiquity.

3. All the intelligence which controlled the destiny and upheld the dominion of republican Rome, was confined to the

walls of the great city. Even when her dominion extended beyond Italy to the utmost known limits of the inhabited world, the city was the exclusive seat both of intelligence and empire.

4. Without the art of printing, and the consequent advantages of a free press, that habitual and incessant action of mind upon mind, which is essential to all human improvement, could no more exist, among a numerous and scattered population, than the commerce of disconnected continents could traverse the ocean without the art of navigation.

5. Here, then, is the source of our superiority, and our just pride as a nation. The statesmen of the remotest extremes of the Union can converse together, like the philosophers of Athens, in the same portico, or the politicians of Rome, in the same forum. Distance is overcome, and the citizens of Georgia and of Maine can be brought to co-operate in the same great object, with as perfect a community of views and feelings, as actuated the tribes of Rome, in the assemblies of the people.

6. It is obvious that liberty has a more extensive and durable foundation in the United States than it ever has had in any other age or country. By the representative principle—a principle unknown and impracticable among the ancients—the whole mass of society is brought to operate, in constraining the action of power, and in the conservation of public liberty.

McDuffie.

---

81. NEW TERRITORIES.

SIR, the territories which have come under our guardianship are, in my judgment, of more worth than to be made the mere make-weights in the scales of sectional equality. They are entitled to another sort of consideration, than to be cut up, and partitioned off, like trodden-down Poland, in order to satisfy the longings and appease the jealousies of surrounding States.

2. They are—they ought certainly—to be disposed of and regulated by us, with a primary regard to the prosperity and welfare of those who occupy them now, and those who are destined to occupy them hereafter, and not with the selfish view of augmenting the mere local power or pride of any of us.

3. Mr. Chairman, I see in the territorial possessions of this Union the seats of new States, the cradles of new commonwealths, the nurseries, it may be, of new republican empires. I see in them the future abodes of our brethren, our children, and our children's children, for a thousand generations.

4. I see, growing up within our borders, institutions upon which the character and condition of a vast multitude of the American family, and of the human race, in all time to come, are to depend. I feel that, for the original shaping and moulding of these institutions, you and I, and each one of us who occupy these seats, are in part responsible. And I cannot omit to ask myself, what shall I do, that I may deserve the gratitude and the blessing, and not the condemnation and the curse, of that posterity, whose welfare is thus in some degree committed to my care?

5. Here, then, sir, I bring these remarks to a close. I have explained, to the best of my ability, the views which I entertain of the great questions of the day. Those views may be misrepresented hereafter, as they have been heretofore; but they cannot be misunderstood by any one who desires, or who is even willing, to understand them.

6. One tie, however, I am persuaded, still remains to us all—a common devotion to the union of these States, and a common determination to sacrifice every thing but principle to its preservation. Our responsibilities are indeed great. This vast republic, stretching from sea to sea, and rapidly outgrowing every thing but our affections, looks anxiously to us, this day, to take care that it receives no detriment.

7. Nor is it too much to say, that the eyes and the hearts of the friends of constitutional freedom throughout the world are

at this moment turned eagerly here—more eagerly than ever before—to behold an example of successful republican institutions, and to see them come out safely and triumphantly from the fiery trial to which they are now subjected.

8. I have the firmest faith that these eyes and these hearts will not be disappointed. I have the strongest belief that the isions and phantoms of disunion which now appal us, will soon ie remembered only like the clouds of some April morning, or "the dissolving views" of some evening spectacle. I have the fullest conviction that this glorious republic is destined to outlast all—all at either end of the Union, who may be plotting against its peace, or predicting its downfall.

> "Fond, impious man! think'st thou yon sanguine cloud,
> Raised by thy breath, can quench the orb of day?
> To-morrow, it repairs its golden flood,
> And warms the nations with redoubled ray!"

9. Let us proceed in the settlement of the unfortunate controversies in which we find ourselves involved, in a spirit of mutual conciliation and concession; let us invoke fervently upon our efforts the blessings of that Almighty Being who is "the author of peace and the lover of concord." And we shall still find order springing out of confusion, harmony evoked from discord, and peace, union, and liberty once more reassured to our land! WINTHROP.

---

82. THE DISINTERESTEDNESS OF WASHINGTON.

TO the pen of the historian must be resigned the more arduous and elaborate tribute of justice to those efforts of heroic and political virtue, which conducted the American people to peace and liberty. The vanquished foe retired from our shores, and left to the controlling genius who repelled them the gratitude of his own country, and the admiration of the world.

2. The time had now arrived which was to apply the touch stone to his integrity—which was to assay the affinity of his

principles to the standard of immutable right. On the one hand, a realm, to which he was endeared by his services, almost invited him to empire; and on the other, the liberty to whose protection his life had been devoted, was the ornament and boon of human nature.

3. Washington could not depart from his own great self. His country was free—he was no longer a general. Sublime spectacle! more elevating to the pride of virtue than the sovereignty of the globe united to the sceptre of ages!

4. Enthroned in the hearts of his countrymen, the gorgeous pageantry of prerogative was unworthy the majesty of his dominion. That effulgence of military character which in ancient states has blasted the rights of the people whose renown it had brightened, was not here permitted, by the hero from whom it emanated, to shine with so destructive a lustre. Its beams, though intensely resplendent, did not wither the young blossoms of our independence; and liberty, like the burning bush, flourished unconsumed by the glory which surrounded it.

5. To the illustrious founder of our republic was it reserved to exhibit the example of a magnanimity that commanded victory—of a moderation that retired from triumph. Unlike the erratic meteors of ambition, whose flaming path sheds a disastrous light on the pages of history, his bright orb, eclipsing the luminaries among which it rolled, never portended "fearful change" to religion, nor from its "golden tresses" shook pestilence on empire.

6. What to other heroes has been glory, would to him have been disgrace. To his intrepidity it would have added no honorary trophy, to have waded, like the conqueror of Peru, through the blood of credulous millions, to plant the standard of triumph at the burning mouth of a volcano. To his fame it would have erected no auxiliary monument, to have invaded, like the ravager of Egypt, an innocent though barbarous nation, to inscribe his name on the pillar of Pompey.

R. T. Paine.

88. OUR REPUBLIC.

[THOMAS EWING has filled with honor some of the most important posts in the Union. At the bar of the Supreme Court, and in the Senate Hall, he holds a distinguished place as a powerful and brilliant orator.]

SIR, our republic has long been a theme of speculation among the savans of Europe. They profess to have cast its horoscope, and fifty years was fixed upon by many as the utmost limit of its duration. But those years passed by, and beheld us a united and happy people; our political atmosphere agitated by no storm, and scarce a cloud to obscure the serenity of our horizon; all of the present was prosperity; all of the future, hope.

2. True, upon the day of that anniversary two venerated fathers of our freedom and of our country fell; but they sank calmly to rest, in the maturity of years and in the fulness of time; and their simultaneous departure on that day of jubilee, for another and a better world, was hailed by our nation as a propitious sign, sent to us from Heaven.

3. Wandering the other day in the alcoves of the library, I accidentally opened a volume containing the orations delivered by many distinguished men on that solemn occasion, and I noted some expressions of a few who now sit in this hall, which are deep fraught with the then prevailing, I may say universal, feeling.

4. It is inquired by one, "Is this the effect of accident or blind chance, or has that God, who holds in his hand the destiny of nations and of men, designed these things as an evidence of the permanence and perpetuity of our institutions?"

5. Another says, "Is it not stamped with the seal of divinity?" And a third, descanting on the prospects, bright and glorious, which opened on our beloved country, says, "Auspicious omens cheer us."

6. Yet it would have required but a tinge of superstitious gloom to have drawn from that event darker forebodings of that which was to come. In our primitive wilds, where the

order of nature is unbroken by the hand of man; there, where majestic trees arise, spread forth their branches, live out their age, and decline; sometimes will a patriarchal plant, which has stood for centuries the winds and storms, fall when no breeze agitates a leaf of the trees that surround it.

7. And when, in the calm stillness of a summer's noon, the solitary woodsman hears on either hand the heavy crash of huge, branchless trunks, falling by their own weight to the earth whence they sprang, prescient of the future, he foresees the whirlwind at hand, which shall sweep through the forest, break its strongest stems, upturn its deepest roots, and strew in the dust its tallest, proudest heads. But I am none of those who indulge in gloomy anticipation. I do not despair of the republic.

8. My trust is strong that the gallant ship, in which all our hopes are embarked, will yet outride the storm; saved alike from the breakers and billows of disunion, and the greedy whirlpool—the all-engulfing maelstrom of executive power, that unbroken, if not unharmed, she may pursue her prosperous voyage far down the stream of time; and that the banner of our country, which now waves over us so proudly will still float in triumph—borne on the wings of heaven, fanned by the breath of fame, every stripe, bright and unsullied, every star fixed in its sphere, ages after each of us now here shall have ceased to gaze on its majestic folds forever.

T. Ewing.

---

84. LIBERTY AND GREATNESS.

THE name of "Republic" is inscribed upon the most imperishable monuments of the human race; and it is probable that it will continue to be associated, as it has been in all past ages, with whatever is heroic in character, sublime in genius, and elegant and brilliant in the cultivation of arts and letters.

2. What land has ever been visited with the influences of

liberty, that did not flourish like the spring? What people has ever worshipped at her altars, without kindling with a loftier spirit, and putting forth nobler energies?

3. Where she has ever acted, her deeds have been heroic. Where she has ever spoken, her eloquence has been triumphant and sublime.

4. We live under a form of government, and in a state of ociety, to which the world has never yet exhibited a parallel. Is it then nothing to be "free?" How many nations, in the whole annals of human kind, have proved themselves worthy of being so? Is it nothing that we are Republicans?

5. Were all men as enlightened, as brave, as proud as they ought to be, would they suffer themselves to be insulted with any other title? Is it nothing that so many independent sovereignties should be held together in such a confederacy as ours?

6. What does history teach us of the difficulty of instituting and maintaining such a polity, and of the glory that ought to be given to those who enjoy its advantages in so much perfection, and on so grand a scale?

7. Can any thing be more striking and sublime, than the idea of an Imperial Republic, spreading over an extent of territory, more immense than the empire of the Cæsars, in the accumulated conquests of a thousand years—without prefects, proconsuls, or publicans—founded in the maxims of common sense—employing within itself no arms but those of reason—and known to its subjects only by the blessings it bestows and perpetuates, yet capable of directing against a foreign foe all the energies of a military despotism,—a Republic, in which men are completely insignificant, and *principles* and *laws* exercise, throughout its vast domain, a peaceful and irresistible sway, blending, in one divine harmony, such various habits and conflicting opinions, and mingling, in our institutions, the light of philosophy with all that is dazzling in the associations of heroic achievement, extended dominion, and formidable power?   LEGARÉ.

85. CONSTITUTIONAL CHANGES.

[No speeches commanded greater attention in Congress, or were more universally read at the period of their delivery, than those of this brilliant and eccentric Virginia statesman. He was a skilful debater, a ripe scholar, profoundly versed in the politics of our own country, and intimately familiar with the history of others. Few speakers in any age were more thoroughly master of all the beauty, strength, and delicacy of the English language. Many of his speeches abound in sharp flashes of sarcasm; keen and cutting as a bright Toledo blade, his satire was universally feared.]

SIR, I see no wisdom in making this provision for future changes. You must give governments time to operate on the people, and give the people time to become gradually assimilated to their institutions. Almost any thing is better than this state of perpetual uncertainty.

2. A people may have the best form of government that the wit of man ever devised; and yet, from its uncertainty alone, may, in effect, live under the worst government in the world. Sir, how often must I repeat, that *change* is not *reform?* I am willing that this new Constitution shall stand as long as it is possible for it to stand, and that, believe me, is a very short time.

3. Sir, it is vain to deny it. They may say what they please about the old Constitution—the defect is not there. It is not in the form of the old edifice, neither in the design nor the elevation: it is in the *material*—it is in the people of Virginia. To my knowledge, that people are changed from what they have been.

4. The four hundred men who went out to David were *in debt*. The partisans of Cæsar were *in debt*. The fellow-laborers of Catiline were *in debt*. And I defy you to show me a desperately indebted people anywhere who can bear a regular, sober government.

5. I throw the challenge to all who hear me. I say that the character of the good old Virginia planter—the man who owned from five to twenty slaves, or less, who lived by hard work, and who paid his debts—is passed away.

6. A new order of things is come. The period has arrived of living by one's wits—of living by contracting debts that one cannot pay—and above all, of living by office-hunting.

7. Sir, what do we see? Bankrupts—branded bankrupts—giving great dinners—sending their children to the most expensive schools—giving grand parties—and just as well received as anybody in society.

8. I say, that in such a state of things the old Constitution was too good for them; they could not bear it. No, sir—they could not bear a freehold suffrage and a property representation.

9. I have always endeavored to do the people justice—but I will not flatter them—I will not pander to their appetite for change. I will do nothing to provide for change. I will not agree to any rule of future apportionment, or to any provision for future changes called amendments to the Constitution.

10. They who love change—who delight in public confusion—who wish to feed the caldron, and make it bubble—may vote if they please for future changes. But by what spell—by what formula are you going to bind the people to all future time?

11. You may make what entries upon parchment you please. Give me a Constitution that will last for half a century—that is all I wish for. No Constitution that you can make will last the one-half of half a century.

12. Sir, I will stake any thing short of my salvation, that those who are malcontent now, will be more malcontent three years hence than they are at this day. I have no favor for this Constitution.

13. I shall vote against its adoption, and I shall advise all the people of my district to set their faces—ay—and their shoulders against it. But if we are to have it, let us not have it with its death-warrant in its very face, with the sardonic grin of death upon its countenance.

JOHN RANDOLPH OF ROANOKE.

86. THE PATRIOT'S COURAGE.

[One of HENRY CLAY's ablest contemporaries in the Senate says of this great statesman: "He was indeed eloquent. All the world knows that. He held the keys to the hearts of his countrymen, and turned the wards within them with a skill attained by no other master." Some of his noblest oratorical efforts were delivered in favor of the recognition of the South American Republics, the independence of Greece, and the war with Great Britain, in 1812. His style of oratory was heightened by all the charms of a voice of sustained sweetness and a heart full of chivalrous courtesy.]

THERE is a sort of courage which, I frankly confess it, I do not possess, a boldness to which I dare not aspire, a valor which I cannot covet. I cannot lay myself down in the way of the welfare and happiness of my country. That I cannot, I have not the courage to do.

2. I cannot interpose the power with which I may be invested, a power conferred, not for my personal benefit, nor for my aggrandizement, but for my country's good, to check her onward march to greatness and glory. I have not courage enough. I am too cowardly for that.

3. I would not, I dare not, in the exercise of such a trust, lie down, and place my body across the path that leads my country to prosperity and happiness. This is a sort of courage widely different from that which a man may display in his private conduct and personal relations.

4. Personal or private courage is totally distinct from that higher and nobler courage which prompts the patriot to offer himself a voluntary sacrifice to his country's good. Apprehensions of the imputation of the want of firmness sometimes impel us to perform rash and inconsiderate acts. It is the greatest courage to be able to bear the imputation of the want of courage.

5. But pride, vanity, egotism, so unamiable and offensive in private life, are vices which partake of the character of crimes, in the conduct of public affairs. The unfortunate victim of these passions cannot see beyond the little, petty, contemptible circle of his own personal interests. All his

thoughts are withdrawn from his country, and concentrated on his consistency, his firmness, himself.

6. The high, the exalted, the sublime emotions of a patriotism which, soaring towards heaven, rises far above all mean, low, or selfish things, and is absorbed by one soul-transporting thought of the good and the glory of one's country, are never felt in his impenetrable bosom.

7. That patriotism which, catching its inspirations from the immortal God, and leaving at an immeasurable distance below all lesser, grovelling, personal interests and feelings, animates and prompts to deeds of self-sacrifice, of valor, of devotion, and of death itself—that is public virtue; that is the noblest, the sublimest of all public virtues! CLAY.

---

87. HONORABLE AMBITION.

[Extract from his speech in favor of compromise.]

I HAVE been accused of *ambition* in presenting this measure —*ambition—inordinate ambition.* If I had thought of myself *only,* I should have never brought it forward. I know well the perils to which I expose myself; the risk of alienating faithful and valued friends, with but little prospect of making new ones, if any new ones could compensate for the loss of those we have long tried and loved; and the honest misconception both of friends and foes.

2. *Ambition?* If I had listened to its soft and seducing whispers; if I had yielded myself to the dictates of a cold, calculating, and prudential policy, I would have stood still and unmoved. I might even have silently gazed on the raging storm, enjoyed its loudest thunders, and left those who are charged with the care of the vessel of State to conduct it as they could.

3. I have been, heretofore, often unjustly accused of ambition. Low, grovelling souls, who are utterly incapable of elevating themselves to the higher and nobler duties of pure

patriotism,—beings who, forever keeping their own selfish ends in view, decide all public measures by their presumed influence on their aggrandizement,—judge me by the venal rule which they prescribe to themselves.

4. I have given to the winds those false accusations, as I consign that which now impeaches my motives. I have no desire for office, not even the highest. The most exalted is but a prison, in which the incarcerated incumbent daily receives his cold, heartless visitants, marks his weary hours, and is cut off from the practical enjoyment of all the blessings of genuine freedom.

5. I am no candidate for any office in the gift of the people of these States, united or separated; I never wish, never expect to be. Pass this bill, tranquillize the country, restore confidence and affection in the Union, and I am willing to go home to Ashland, and renounce public service forever.

6. I should there find, in its groves, under its shades, on its lawns, midst my flocks and herds, in the bosom of my family, sincerity and truth, attachment and fidelity, and gratitude, which I have not always found in the walks of public life.

7. Yes, I have *ambition:* but it is the *ambition* of being the humble instrument, in the hands of Providence, to reconcile a divided people; once more to revive concord and harmony in a distracted land,—the pleasing *ambition* of contemplating the glorious spectacle of a free, united, prosperous, and fraternal people! CLAY.

88. ASPIRATIONS FOR AMERICA.

WHILE the Union lasts, amid these fertile, verdant fields, these ever-flowing rivers, these stately groves, this genial, healthful clime, this Old Kentucky land,—hallowed by the blood of our sires, endeared by the beauty of her daughters, illustrious by the valor and eloquence of her sons, the centre of a most glorious empire, guarded by a cordon of

States garrisoned by freemen, girt round by the rising and setting seas,—we are the most blessed of all people.

2. Let the Union be dissolved,—let that line be drawn, where be drawn it must, and we are a border State: in time of peace, with no outlet to the ocean, the highway of nations,— a miserable dependency; in time of war, the battle-ground of more than Indian warfare, of civil strife and indiscriminate slaughter!

3. When, worse than Spanish provinces, we shall contend, not for glory and renown, but, like the aborigines of old, for a contemptible life and miserable subsistence! Let me not see it! Among those proud courts and lordly coteries of Europe's pride, where, fifty years ago, we were regarded as petty provinces, unknown to ears polite, let me go forth great in the name of an American citizen.

4. Let me point them to our statesmen and the laws and governments of their creation; the rapid growth of political science; the monuments of their fame, now the study of all Europe. Let them look at our rapidly increasing and happy population; see our canals, and turnpikes, and railroads, stretching over more space than combined Britain and Europe have reached by the same means.

5. Let them send their philanthropists to learn of our penitentiary systems, our schools, and our civil institutions. Let them behold our skill in machinery, in steamboat and ship-building,—hail the most gallant ship that breasts the mountain wave, and she shall wave from her flagstaff the stars and stripes.

6. These are the images which I cherish; this the nation which I honor; and never will I throw one pebble in her track, to jostle the footsteps of her glorious march!

C. M. CLAY.

89. THE EVILS OF WAR.

WAR, pestilence, and famine, by the common consent o mankind, are the three greatest calamities which can befall our species ; and war, as the most direful, justly stands foremost and in front. Pestilence and famine, no doubt for wise although inscrutable purposes, are inflictions of Providence, to which it is our duty, therefore, to bow with obedience, humble submission, and resignation. Their duration is not long, and their ravages are limited. They bring, indeed, great affliction, while they last, but society soon recovers from their effects.

2. War is the voluntary work of our own hands, and whatever reproaches it may deserve, should be directed to ourselves. When it breaks out, its duration is indefinite and unknown,—its vicissitudes are hidden from our view. In the sacrifice of human life, and in the waste of human treasure,—in its losses and in its burdens,—it affects both belligerent nations, and its sad effects of mangled bodies, of death, and of desolation, endure long after its thunders are hushed in peace.

3. War unhinges society, disturbs its peaceful and regular industry, and scatters poisonous seeds of disease and immorality, which continue to germinate and diffuse their baneful influence long after it has ceased. Dazzling by its glitter, pomp, and pageantry, it begets a spirit of wild adventure and romantic enterprise, and often disqualifies those who embark in it, after their return from the bloody fields of battle, for engaging in the industrious and peaceful vocations of life.

4. History tells the mournful tale of conquering nations and conquerors. The three most celebrated conquerors, in the civilized world, were Alexander, Cæsar, and Napoleon. The first, after ruining a large portion of Asia, and sighing and lamenting that there were no more worlds to subdue, met a premature and ignoble death. His lieutenants quarrelled and warred with each other as to the spoils of his victories, and finally lost them all.

5. Cæsar, after conquering Gaul, returned with his triumphant legions to Rome, passed the Rubicon, won the battle of Pharsalia, trampled upon the liberties of his country, and expired by the patriot hand of Brutus. But Rome ceased to be free. War and conquest had enervated and corrupted the masses. The spirit of true liberty was extinguished, and a long line of emperors succeeded, some of whom were the most execrable monsters that ever existed in human form.

6. And Napoleon, that most extraordinary man, perhaps, in all history, after subjugating all Continental Europe, occupying almost all its capitals,—seriously threatening proud Albion itself,—and decking the brows of various members of his family with crowns torn from the heads of other monarchs, lived to behold his own dear France itself in possession of his enemies, was made himself a wretched captive, and, far removed from country, family, and friends, breathed his last on the distant and inhospitable rock of St. Helena.

7. The Alps and the Rhine had been claimed as the natural boundaries of France, but even these could not be secured in the treaties to which she was reduced to submit. Do you believe that the people of Macedon or Greece, of Rome, or of France, were benefited, individually or collectively, by the triumphs of their captains? Their sad lot was immense sacrifice of life, heavy and intolerable burdens, and the ultimate loss of liberty itself.   H. CLAY.

---

90. HOHENLINDEN.

[Hohenlinden, a German word meaning *high lime-trees*, is the name of a village in Bavaria, near which the Austrians were defeated by the French, under General Moreau, in December, 1800. A heavy snow-storm had continued through the night, and had hardly ceased when the roar of the cannons announced the opening of the battle.]

ON Linden, when the sun was low,
All bloodless lay the untrodden snow;
And dark as winter was the flow
Of Iser, rolling rapidly.

2. But Linden saw another sight,
   When the drum beat, at dead of night,
   Commanding fires of death to light
   The darkness of her scenery.

3. By torch and trumpet fast arrayed,
   Each horseman drew his battle-blade,
   And furious every charger neighed
   To join the dreadful revelry.

4. Then shook the hills with thunder riven,
   Then rushed the steed to battle driven,
   And louder than the bolts of Heaven
   Far flashed the red artillery.

5. But redder yet that light shall glow
   On Linden's hills of stainéd snow,
   And bloodier yet the torrent flow
   Of Iser, rolling rapidly.

6. 'Tis morn, but scarce yon level sun
   Can pierce the war-clouds, rolling dun,
   Where furious Frank, and fiery Hun,
   Shout in their sulphurous canopy.

7. The combat deepens. On, ye brave,
   Who rush to glory, or the grave!
   Wave, Munich! all thy banners wave,
   And charge with all thy chivalry!

8. Few, few shall part where many meet!
   The snow shall be their winding-sheet,
   And every turf beneath their feet
   Shall be a soldier's sepulchre.

CAMPBELL.

91. VALEDICTORY ADDRESS TO THE SENATE.

FROM 1806, the period of my entrance upon this noble theatre, with short intervals, to the present time, I have been engaged in the public councils, at home or abroad. Of the services rendered during that long and arduous period of my life it does not become me to speak; history, if she deign to notice me, and posterity, if the recollection of my humble actions shall be transmitted to posterity, are the best, the truest, and the most impartial judges. When death has closed the scene, their sentence will be pronounced, and to that I commit myself.

2. My public conduct is a fair subject for the criticism and judgment of my fellow-men; but the motives by which I have been prompted are known only to the great Searcher of the human heart and to myself; and I trust I may be pardoned for repeating a declaration made some thirteen years ago, that, whatever errors, and doubtless there have been many, may be discovered in a review of my public service, I can with unshaken confidence appeal to that Divine Arbiter for the truth of the declaration, that I have been influenced by no impure purpose, no personal motive; have sought no personal aggrandizement; but that, in all my public acts, I have had a single eye directed, and a warm and devoted heart dedicated to what, in my best judgment, I believed the true interests, the honor, the union, and the happiness of my country required.

3. During that long period, however, I have not escaped the fate of other public men, nor failed to incur censure and detraction of the bitterest, most unrelenting, and most malignant character; and, though not always insensible to the pain it was meant to inflict, I have borne it in general with composure, and without disturbance, waiting as I have done, in perfect and undoubting confidence, for the ultimate triumph of justice and of truth, and in the entire persuasion that time would settle all things as they should be, and that whatever

wrong or injustice I might experience at the hands of man, He to whom all hearts are open and fully known, would, by the inscrutable dispensations of His providence, rectify all error, redress all wrong, and cause ample justice to be done.

4. But I have not, meanwhile, been unsustained. Everywhere throughout the extent of this great continent, I have had cordial, warm-hearted, faithful, and devoted friends, who have known me, loved me, and appreciated my motives. To them, if language were capable of fully expressing my acknowledgments, I would now offer all the return I have the power to make for their genuine, disinterested, and persevering fidelity and devoted attachment, the feelings and sentiments of a heart overflowing with never-ceasing gratitude. If, however, I fail in suitable language to express my gratitude to *them* for all the kindness they have shown me, what shall I say, what *can* I say at all commensurate with those feelings of gratitude with which I have been inspired by the State whose humble representative and servant I have been in this chamber?

5. I emigrated from Virginia to the State of Kentucky, now nearly forty-five years ago; I went as an orphan boy who had not yet attained the age of majority; who had never recognized a father's smile, nor felt his warm caresses; poor, penniless, without the favor of the great, with an imperfect and neglected education, hardly sufficient for the ordinary business and common pursuits of life; but scarce had I set my foot upon her generous soil, when I was embraced with parental fondness, caressed as though I had been a favorite child, and patronized with liberal and unbounded munificence.

6. From that period the highest honors of the State have been freely bestowed upon me; and when, in the darkest hour of calumny and detraction, I seemed to be assailed by all the rest of the world, she interposed her broad and impenetrable shield, repelled the poisoned shafts that were aimed for my destruction, and vindicated my good name from every malignant and unfounded aspersion. I return with indescribable

pleasure to linger awhile longer, and mingle with the warm-hearted and whole-souled people of that State; and when the last scene shall forever close upon me, I hope that my earthly remains will be laid under her green sod with those of her gallant and patriotic sons.

7. In the course of a long and arduous public service, especially during the last eleven years in which I have held a sea in the Senate, from the same ardor and enthusiasm of character, I have no doubt, in the heat of debate, and in an honest endeavor to maintain my opinions against adverse opinions alike honestly entertained, as to the best course to be adopted for the public welfare, I may have often inadvertently and unintentionally, in moments of excited debate, made use of language that has been offensive, and susceptible of injurious interpretation towards my brother Senators.

8. If there be any here who retain wounded feelings of injury or dissatisfaction, produced on such occasions, I beg to assure them that I now offer the most ample apology for any departure on my part from the established rules of parliamentary decorum and courtesy. On the other hand, I assure Senators, one and all, without exception and without reserve, that I retire from this chamber without carrying with me a single feeling of resentment or dissatisfaction to the Senate or any of its members.

9. I go from this place under the hope that we shall mutually consign to perpetual oblivion whatever personal collisions may at any time unfortunately have occurred between us; and that our recollections shall dwell in future only on those conflicts of mind with mind, those intellectual struggles, those noble exhibitions of the powers of logic, argument and eloquence, honorable to the Senate and to the nation, in which each has sought and contended for what he deemed the best mode of accomplishing one common object, the interest and the best happiness of our beloved country. To these thrilling and delightful scenes it will be my pleasure and my pride to look back, on my retirement, with unmeasured satisfaction.

10. In retiring, as I am about to do, forever from the Senate, suffer me to express my heartfelt wishes that all the great and patriotic objects of the wise framers of our Constitution may be fulfilled; that the high destiny designed for it may be fully answered; and that its deliberations, now and hereafter, may eventuate in securing the prosperity of our beloved country, in maintaining its rights and honor abroad, and upholding its interests at home.

11. I retire, I know, at a period of infinite distress and embarrassment. I wish I could take my leave of you under more favorable auspices; but, without meaning at this time to say whether on any, or on whom reproaches for the sad condition of the country should fall, I appeal to the Senate and to the world to bear testimony to my earnest and continued exertions to avert it, and to the truth that no blame can justly attach to me.

12. May the most precious blessings of Heaven rest upon the whole Senate and each member of it, and may the labors of every one redound to the benefit of the nation and the advancement of his own fame and renown. And, when you shall retire to the bosom of your constituents, may you receive that most cheering and gratifying of all human rewards,—their cordial greeting of "Well done, good and faithful servants." And now, Mr. President and Senators, I bid you all a long, a lasting, and a friendly farewell. CLAY.

92. FREEDOM OF DISCUSSION.

[PRESTON holds a distinguished rank among American orators; not even second to Clay, Calhoun, or Webster.]

THE gentleman has referred to the contest to be fought between liberty and power; and I say, that if the contest did not originate here, it is made when we are not permitted to speak of the administration in terms that we believe true, without being denounced for it.

2. The President of the United States certainly demands a degree of forbearance from his political opponents; but am I to be told that one can only allude to him in the humble language of a degraded Roman Senate, speaking of the emperor with his prætorian guards surrounding the capitol?

3. Am I to be told, when he came into power on principles of reform, after "keeping the word of promise to our ear, and breaking it to our hope," am I to be told that I must close my lips, or be denounced for want of decorum? Am I to be told, when he promised to prevent official influence from interfering with the freedom of elections, that I must not speak of the broken promise, under pain of the displeasure of his friends?

4. Am I to be told, when he came into power as a judicious tariff man, after advocating his principles and aiding in his election, believing at the time in his integrity, though I did not believe him possessed of intellectual qualifications,—am I to be told, after pledges that have been violated, promises that have been broken, and principles that have been set at naught, that I must not speak of these things as they are, for fear of being denounced for want of courtesy to the constituted authorities?

5. Why, to what pass are we come! Are we to be gagged —reduced to silence? If nothing else is left to us, the liberty of speech is left; and it is our duty to cry aloud, and spare not, when the undenied, admitted and declared fact before us is, that these pledges have been made and have been violated.

6. This administration is about to end; and if gentlemen can succeed in preventing us from complaining of being deceived, if they can reduce us to abject slavery, they will also have to expunge the history of the country, the President's written and recorded communications to Congress, and the most ardent professions of his friends, when fighting his battles, before they can conceal the recorded fact, that he has made pledges which he has violated, and promises which he has repeatedly broken.

7. If they succeed in reducing us to slavery, and close our lips against speaking of the abuses of this administration, thank God, the voice of history, trumpet-tongued, will proclaim these pledges, and the manner in which they have been violated, to future generations!

8. Neither here nor elsewhere will I use language, with regard to any gentleman, that may be considered indecorous; and the question, not easily solved, is, how far shall we restrain ourselves in expressing a just and necessary indignation; and whether the expression of such indignation may be considered a departure from courtesy?

9. That indignation, that reprobation, I shall express on all occasions. But those who have taken upon themselves the guardianship of the Grand Lama, who is surrounded by a light which no one can approach;—about whom no one is permitted to speak without censure,—have extended that guardianship to the presiding officer of this house.

10. Gentlemen are not permitted to speak of the qualifications of that officer for the highest office in the government. Shall we, sir, because he is here as presiding officer of this body, keep silent when he is urged upon the people, who are goaded and driven to his support, lest we be guilty of an indecorum against those who are the constituted authorities of the country? Thank God, it is not my practice to "crook the pliant hinges of the knee, that thrift may follow fawning!"

11. This aggression of power upon our liberties, sir, and this tame submission to aggression, forbode evil to this nation. "Coming events cast their shadows before them," deepening and darkening; and as the sun sets, the shadows lengthen It may be the going down of the great luminary of the Republic, and that we all shall be enveloped in one universal political darkness!

W. C. PRESTON.

93. THE MEXICAN WAR.

[T. CORWIN, at the bar and in Congress, earned the title of a popular and eloquent speaker.]

I ASK, Mr. President, what has Mexico got from you for parting with two-thirds of her domain? She has given you ample redress for every injury of which you have complained. She has submitted to the award of your commissioners, and up to the time of the rupture with Texas, faithfully paid it. And for all that she has lost (not through or by you, but which loss has been your gain) what requital do we, her strong, rich, robust neighbor, make?

2. Do we send our missionaries there, "to point the way to heaven?" Or do we send the schoolmasters to pour daylight into her dark places, to aid her infant strength to conquer freedom, and reap the fruit of the independence herself alone had won?

3. No, no; none of this do we. But we send regiments, storm towns, and our colonels prate of liberty in the midst of the solitudes their ravages have made. They proclaim the empty forms of social compact to a people bleeding and maimed with wounds received in defending their hearth-stones against the invasion of these very men who shoot them down, and then exhort them to be free.

4. Your chaplain of the navy throws aside the New Testament and seizes a bill of rights. He takes military possession of some town in California, and instead of teaching the plan of the atonement and the way of salvation to the poor, ignorant Celt, he presents Colt's pistol to his ear, and calls on him to take "trial by jury and *habeas corpus*," or nine bullets in his head. Oh! Mr. President, are you not the lights of the earth, if not its salt?

5. What is the territory, Mr. President, which you propose to wrest from Mexico? It is consecrated to the heart of the Mexican by many a well-fought battle with his old Castilian

master. His Bunker Hills, and Saratogas, and Yorktowns are there!

6. The Mexican can say, "There I bled for liberty! and shall I surrender that consecrated home of my affections to the Anglo-Saxon invaders? What do they want with it? They have Texas already. They have possessed themselves of the territory between the Nueces and the Rio Grande. What else do they want? To what shall I point my children as memorials of that independence which I bequeath to them, when those battle-fields shall have passed from my possession?"

7. Sir, had one come and demanded Bunker Hill of the people of Massachusetts—had England's lion ever showed himself there, is there a man over thirteen and under ninety who would not have been ready to meet him? Is there a river on this continent that would not have run red with blood? Is there a field but would have been piled high with the unburied bones of slaughtered Americans, before these consecrated battle-fields of liberty should have been wrested from us?

T. Corwin.

---

94. RETRIBUTIVE JUSTICE.

[Extract from a speech on the Mexican question.]

SIR, I have heard much, and read somewhat of this gentleman, Terminus. Alexander, of whom I have spoken, was a devotee of this divinity. We have seen the end of him and his empire. It was said to be an attribute of this god, that he must always advance, and never recede. So both republican and imperial Rome believed. It was, as they said, their destiny; and for awhile it did seem to be even so.

2. Roman Terminus did advance. Under the eagles of Rome he was carried from his home on the Tiber to the furthest east on the one hand, and to the far west, among the then barbarous tribes of Western Europe, on the other. But at length the time came when retributive justice had become "a destiny."

3. The despised Gaul calls out to the contemned Goths, and Attila, with his Huns, answers back the battle-shout to both. The "blue-eyed nations of the north," in succession, are united, pour their countless hosts of warriors upon Rome and Rome's always advancing god, Terminus.

4. And now the battle-axe of the barbarian strikes down the conquering eagle of Rome. Terminus at last recedes, slowly at first, but finally he is driven to Rome, and from Rome to Byzantium. Whoever would know the further fate of this Roman deity, may find ample gratification of his curiosity in the luminous pages of Gibbon's "Decline and Fall."

5. Such will find that Rome thought as you now think, that it was her destiny to conquer provinces and nations; and no doubt she sometimes said as you say, "I will conquer in peace."

6. And where is she now, the mistress of the world? The spider weaves his web in her palaces, and the owl sings his watch-song in her towers. Teutonic power now lords it over the servile remnant—the miserable memento of old and once omnipotent Rome.

7. Sad, very sad, are the lessons which time has written for us. Through and in them all I see nothing but the inflexible execution of that old law which ordains as eternal that cardinal rule, "Thou shalt not covet thy neighbor's goods, nor any thing that is his."

8. Since I have lately heard so much about the dismemberment of Mexico, I have looked back to see how in the course of events, which some call "Providence," it has fared with other nations who engaged in this work of dismemberment.

9. I see that in the latter half of the eighteenth century three powerful nations—Russia, Austria, and Prussia—united in the dismemberment of Poland. They said, too, as you say, "It is our destiny." They "wanted room." Doubtless each of them thought, with his share of Poland his power was too strong ever to fear invasion, or even insult.

10. One had his California, another his New Mexico, and a

third his Vera Cruz. Did they remain untouched and incapable of harm? Alas! no; far, very far from it. Retributive justice must fulfil its destiny too.

11. A very few years pass off, and we hear of a new man, a Corsican lieutenant, the self-named "armed soldier of democracy"—Napoleon. He ravages Austria, covers her land with blood, drives the northern Cæsar from his capital, and sleeps in his palace. Austria may now remember how her power trampled upon Poland. Did she not pay dear, very dear, for her California?

T. CORWIN.

---

95. THE CAUSE OF THE UNION.

[ROBERT C. WINTHROP, born 1807. During his public life Mr. Winthrop was a leading member of the Whig party. He spoke frequently upon the great questions of the day, and his speeches always commanded attention from their logical and eloquent style.]

"UNION for the sake of the Union;" "our country, our whole country, and nothing but our country;" these are the mottoes, old, stale, hackneyed, and threadbare, as they may have seemed when employed as the watchwords of an electioneering campaign, but clothed with a new power, a new significance, a new gloss, and a new glory, when uttered as the battle-cries of a nation struggling for existence; these are the only mottoes which can give a just and adequate expression to the cause in which you have enlisted.

2. Sir, I thank Heaven that the trumpet has given no uncertain sound while you have been preparing yourselves for the battle.

3. This is the Cause which has been solemnly proclaimed by both branches of Congress, in resolutions passed at the instance of those true-hearted sons of Tennessee and Kentucky,—Johnson and Crittenden,—and which, I rejoice to remember at this hour, received your own official sanction as a senator of the United States.

4. This is the Cause which has been recognized and avowed by the President of the United States, with a frankness and a fearlessness which have won the respect and admiration of us all.

5. This is the Cause which has been so fervently commended to us from the dying lips of a Doug.as, and by the matchless living voices of a Holt and an Everett.

6. And this, finally, is the Cause which has obliterated, as no other cause could have done, all divisions and distinctions of party, nationality, and creed; which has appealed alike to Republican, Democrat, and Union Whig, to native citizen and adopted citizen; and in which not the sons of Massachusetts, or of New England, or of the North alone, not the dwellers on the Hudson, the Delaware, and the Susquehanna only, but so many of those, also, on the Potomac and the Ohio, the Mississippi and the Missouri, on all the lakes, and in all the vast Mesopotamia of the mighty West,—yes, and strangers from beyond the seas, Irish and Scotch, German, Italian and French,—the common emigrant, and those who have stood nearest to a throne,—brave and devoted men from almost every nation under heaven,—men who have measured the value of our country to the world by a nobler standard than the cotton crop, and who realize that other and more momentous destinies are at stake upon our struggle than such as can be wrought upon any mere material looms and shuttles,—all, all are seen rallying beneath a common flag, and exclaiming with one heart and voice: "The American Union, it must be and shall be preserved!"

7. And we owe it, sir, to the memory of our fathers, we owe it to the hopes of our children, we owe it to the cause of free institutions, and of good government of every sort throughout the world, to make the effort, cost what it may of treasure or of blood, and, with God's help, to accomplish the result.

8. I have said enough, and more than enough, to manifest the spirit in which this flag is now committed to your charge. It is the national ensign, pure and simple, dearer to all our

hearts at this moment, as we lift it to the gale, and see no other sign of hope upon the storm-cloud which rolls and rattles above it, save that which is reflected from its own radiant hues.—dearer, a thousand-fold dearer to us all, than ever it was before, while gilded by the sunshine of prosperity and playing with the zephyrs of peace. It will speak for itself far more eloquently than I can speak for it.

9. Behold it! Listen to it! Every star has a tongue; every stripe is articulate. There is no language or speech where their voices are not heard. There is magic in the web of it. It has an answer for every question of duty. It has a solution for every doubt and every perplexity. It has a word of good cheer for every hour of gloom or of despondency.

10. Behold it! Listen to it! It speaks of earlier and of later struggles. It speaks of victories, and sometimes of reverses, on the sea and on the land. It speaks of patriots and heroes among the living and among the dead; and of him, the first and greatest of them all, around whose consecrated ashes this unnatural and abhorrent strife has so long been raging,— "the abomination of desolation, standing where it ought not."

11. But, before all and above all other associations and memories,—whether of glorious men, or glorious deeds, or glorious places,—its voice is ever of Union and Liberty, of the Constitution and the Laws.

12. Behold it! Listen to it! Let it tell the story of its birth to these gallant volunteers, as they march beneath its folds by day, or repose beneath its sentinel-stars by night.

13. Let it recall to them the strange, eventful history of its rise and progress; let it rehearse to them the wondrous tale of its trials and its triumphs, in peace as well as in war; and whatever else may happen to it, or to them, it will never be surrendered to rebels, never be ignominiously struck to treason, nor ever be prostituted to any unworthy and unchristian purpose of revenge, depredation, or rapine.

14. And may a merciful God cover the head of each one of its brave defenders in the hour of battle! R. C. WINTHROP.

96. DUTY OF AMERICAN CITIZENS.

[DOUGLAS, as a political speaker and pleader at the bar, possessed brilliant natural powers, and had he lived, would undoubtedly have become one of the most distinguished American orators.]

BUT this is no time for a detail of causes. The conspiracy is now known. Armies have been raised, war is levied to accomplish it. There are only two sides to the question. Every man must be for the United States or against it. There can be no neutrals in this war: *only patriots or— traitors.*

2. We cannot close our eyes to the sad and solemn fact that war does exist. The Government must be maintained, its enemies overthrown; and the more stupendous our preparations the less the bloodshed, and the shorter the struggle will be. But we must remember certain restraints on our action, even in time of war. We are a Christian people, and the war must be prosecuted in a manner recognized by Christian nations.

3. We must not invade constitutional rights. The innocent must not suffer, nor women and children be the victims. Savages must not be let loose. But while I sanction no war on the rights of others, I will implore my countrymen not to lay down their arms until our own rights are recognized.

4. The Constitution and its guarantees are our birthright, and I am ready to enforce that inalienable right to the last extent. We cannot recognize secession. Recognize it once, and you have not only dissolved government, but you have destroyed social order, and upturned the foundations of society. You have inaugurated anarchy in its worst form, and will shortly experience all the horrors of the French Revolution.

5. Then we have a solemn duty,—to maintain the Government. The greater our unanimity, the speedier the day of peace. We have prejudices to overcome from a fierce party contest waged a few short months since. Yet these must be

allayed. Let us lay aside all criminations and recriminations as to the origin of these difficulties. When we shall have again a country, with the United States flag floating over it, and respected on every inch of American soil,—it will then be time enough to ask who and what brought all this upon us.

6. I have said more than I intended to say. It is a sad task to discuss questions so fearful as civil war: but sad as it is, bloody and disastrous as I expect the war will be, I express it as my conviction, before God, that it is the duty of every American citizen to rally round the flag of his country.

DOUGLAS.

---

97. THE FOUNDATION OF NATIONAL CHARACTER.

[EDWARD EVERETT's style is rich and glowing, but always under the control of sound judgment and good taste. He was in Congress twelve years, and in 1841 was appointed Minister to the Court of St. James. Mr. Everett had one of the most cultivated minds of the day.]

HOW is the spirit of a free people to be formed, and animated, and cheered, but out of the storehouse of its historic recollections? Are we to be eternally ringing the changes upon Marathon and Thermopylæ; and going back to read in obscure texts of Greek and Latin, of the exemplars of patriotic virtue?

2. I thank God that we can find them nearer home, in our own country, on our own soil;—that strains of the noblest sentiment that ever swelled in the breast of man, are breathing to us out of every page of our country's history, in the native eloquence of our mother-tongue,—that the colonial and provincial councils of America exhibit to us models of the spirits and character which gave Greece and Rome their name and their praise among nations.

3. Here we ought to go for our instruction;—the lesson is plain, it is clear, it is applicable. When we go to ancient history, we are bewildered with the difference of manners and

institutions. We are willing to pay our tribute of applause to the memory of Leonidas, who fell nobly for his country in the face of his foe.

4. But when we trace him to his home, we are confounded at the reflection, that the same Spartan heroism, to which he sacrificed himself at Thermopylæ, would have led him to tear his own child, if it had happened to be a sickly babe,—the very object for which all that is kind and good in man rises up to plead,—from the bosom of its mother, and carry it out to be eaten by the wolves of Taygetus.

5. We feel a glow of admiration at the heroism displayed at Marathon, by the ten thousand champions of invaded Greece; but we cannot forget that the tenth part of the number were slaves, unchained from the workshops and door-posts of their masters, to go and fight the battles of freedom.

6. I do not mean that these examples are to destroy the interest with which we read the history of ancient times; they possibly increase that interest by the very contrast they exhibit. But they do warn us, if we need the warning, to seek our great practical lessons of patriotism at home; out of the exploits and sacrifices of which our own country is the theatre; out of the characters of our own fathers.

7. Them we know,—the high-souled, natural, unaffected, the citizen heroes. We know what happy firesides they left for the cheerless camp. We know with what pacific habits they dared the perils of the field. There is no mystery, no romance, no madness, under the name of chivalry, about them. It is all resolute, manly resistance for conscience and liberty's sake, not merely of an overwhelming power, but of all the force of long-rooted habits and native love of order and peace.

8. Above all, their blood calls to us from the soil which we tread; it beats in our veins; it cries to us not merely in the thrilling words of one of the first victims in this cause—"My sons, scorn to be slaves!"—but it cries with a still more moving eloquence—"My sons, forget not your fathers!"

EVERETT.

PART IV.

MISCELLANEOUS.

1. ON BEING FOUND GUILTY OF HIGH TREASON.

[On the 23d of June, 1803, a rebellion against the Government broke out in Dublin, in which Robert Emmet, at the time only twenty-three years of age, was a principal actor. It proved a failure. Emmet was arrested, having missed the opportunity of escape, it is said, by lingering to take leave of a daughter of Curran, the gifted orator. He was tried for high treason at the Sessions House, Dublin, before Lord Norbury, one of the Chief Judges of the King's Bench, and others; was found guilty, and executed the next day. Through his counsel, he had asked, at the trial, that the judgment of the Court might be postponed until the next morning. This request was not granted. The Clerk of the Crown read the indictment, and announced the verdict found, in the usual form. He then concluded thus: "What have you, therefore, now to say, why judgment of death and execution should not be awarded against you, according to law?" Standing forward in the dock, in front of the Bench, Emmet made the following impromptu address. At his execution, Emmet displayed fortitude worthy of him and his cause. As he was passing out of his cell, on his way to the gallows, he met the turnkey, who had become much attached to him. Being fettered, Emmet could not give his hand; so he kissed the poor fellow on the cheek, who, overcome by the mingled condescension and tenderness of the act, fell senseless at the feet of the youthful victim, and did not recover till the latter was no longer among the living.]

WHAT have I to say why sentence of death should not be pronounced on me, according to law? I have nothing to say which can alter your predetermination, or that it would become me to say with any view to the mitigation of that sentence which you are here to pronounce, and which I must abide. But I have that to say which interests me more than life, and which you have labored—as was necessarily your office in the present circumstances of this oppressed country—to destroy.

2. I have much to say why my reputation should be rescued from the load of false accusation and calumny which has been heaped upon it. I do not imagine that, seated where you are, your minds can be so free from impurity as to receive the least impression from what I am going to utter. I have no hope that I can anchor my character in the breast of a court constituted and trammelled as this is.

3. I only wish, and it is the utmost I expect, that your lordships may suffer it to float down your memories, untainted by the foul breath of prejudice, until it finds some more hospitable harbor, to shelter it from the rude storm by which it is at present buffeted.

4. Were I only to suffer death, after being adjudged guilty by *your* tribunal, I should bow in silence, and meet the fate that awaits me, without a murmur. But the sentence of the law which delivers my body to the executioner will, through the ministry of that law, labor, in its own vindication, to consign my *character* to obloquy: for there must be guilt somewhere,—whether in the sentence of the court, or in the catastrophe, posterity must determine.

5. A man in my situation, my lords, has not only to encounter the difficulties of fortune, and the force of power over minds which it has corrupted or subjugated, but the difficulties of established prejudice:—the man dies, but his memory lives: that mine may not perish, that it may live in the respect of my countrymen, I seize upon this opportunity to vindicate myself from *some* of the charges alleged against me.

6. When my spirit shall be wafted to a more friendly port,—when my shade shall have joined the bands of those martyred heroes who have shed their blood, on the scaffold and in the field, in defence of their country and of virtue,—this is my hope: I wish that my memory and name may animate those who survive me, while I look down with complacency on the destruction of that perfidious Government which upholds its

dominion by blasphemy of the Most High,—which displays its power over man as over the beasts of the forest,—which sets man upon his brother, and lifts his hand, in the name of God, against the throat of his fellow, who believes or doubts a little more, or a little less, than the Government standard,— a Government which is steeled to barbarity by the cries of the orphans and the tears of the widows which it has made *

II.

7. I appeal to the immaculate God,—to the throne of Heaven, before which I must shortly appear,—to the blood of the murdered patriots who have gone before,—that my conduct has been, through all this peril, and through all my purposes, governed only by the convictions which I have uttered, and by no other view than that of the emancipation of my country from the superinhuman oppression under which she has so long and too patiently travailed; and that I confidently and assuredly hope that, wild and chimerical as it may appear, there is still union and strength in Ireland to accomplish this noblest enterprise.

8. Of this I speak with the confidence of intimate knowledge, and with the consolation that appertains to that confidence. Think not, my lords, I say this for the petty gratification of giving you a transitory uneasiness; a man who never yet raised his voice to assert a lie will not hazard his character with posterity by asserting a falsehood on a subject so important to his country, and on an occasion like this. Yes, my lords; a man who does not wish to have his epitaph written until his country is liberated, will not leave a weapon in the power of envy, nor a pretence to impeach the probity which he means to preserve even in the grave to which tyranny consigns him.†

---

* Here Lord Norbury said: "The weak and wicked enthusiasts who feel as you feel are unequal to the accomplishment of their wild designs."

† He was here interrupted by Lord Norbury, who said: "You proceed to unwarrantable lengths, in order to exasperate and delude the unwary, and circulate opinions of the most dangerous tendency, for the purposes of mischief."

9. Again I say, that what I have spoken was not intended for your lordships, whose situation I commiserate rather than envy;—my expressions were for my countrymen; if there is a true Irishman present, let my last words cheer him in the hour of his affliction—*

10. I have always understood it to be the duty of a judge, when a prisoner has been convicted, to pronounce the sentence of the law; I have also understood that judges sometimes think it their duty to hear with patience, and to speak with humanity; to exhort the victim of the laws, and to offer, with tender benignity, opinions of the motives by which he was actuated in the crime of which he had been adjudged guilty.

11. That a judge has thought it his duty so to have done, I have no doubt; but where is the boasted freedom of your institutions,—where is the vaunted impartiality, clemency, and mildness of your courts of justice,—if an unfortunate prisoner whom your policy, and not justice, is about to deliver into the hands of the executioner, is not suffered to explain his motives sincerely and truly, and to vindicate the principles by which he was actuated?

12. My lords, it may be a part of the system of angry justice to bow a man's mind, by humiliation, to the purposed ignominy of the scaffold; but worse to me than the scaffold's shame, or the scaffold's terrors, would be the shame of such foul and unfounded imputations as have been laid against me in this court. You, my lord, are a judge. I am the supposed culprit. I am a man,—you are a man also. By a revolution of power, we might change places, though we never could change characters.

13. If I stand at the bar of this court, and dare not vindicate my character, what a farce is your justice! If I stand at this bar, and dare not vindicate my character, how dare you calumniate it? Does the sentence of death, which your unhallowed policy inflicts on my body, also condemn my tongue

---

* Lord Norbury here interrupted the speaker with,—"What you have hitherto said confirms and justifies the verdict of the jury."

to silence, and my reputation to reproach? Your executioner may abridge the period of my existence; but, while I exist, I shall not forbear to vindicate my character and motives from your aspersions.

14. As a man to whom fame is dearer than life, I will make the last use of that life in doing justice to that reputation which is to live after me, and which is the only legacy I can leave to those I honor and love, and for whom I am proud to perish. As men, my lord, we must appear, on the great day, at one common tribunal; and it will then remain for the Searcher of all hearts to show a collective universe who are engaged in the most virtuous actions, or actuated by the purest motives,—my country's oppressors or—*

15. My lord, shall a dying man be denied the legal privilege of exculpating himself, in the eyes of the community, of an undeserved reproach thrown upon him during his trial, by charging him with ambition, and attempting to cast away, for a paltry consideration, the liberties of his country? Why, then, insult me? or, rather, why insult justice, in demanding of me why sentence of death should not be pronounced?

16. I know, my lord, that form prescribes that you should ask the question; the form also presumes the right of answering! This, no doubt, may be dispensed with; and so might the whole ceremony of the trial, since sentence was already pronounced at the Castle before your jury was impannelled. Your lordships are but the priests of the oracle, and I submit to the sacrifice; but I insist on the whole of the forms.†

III.

17. I am charged with being an emissary of France. An emissary of France!—and for what end? It is alleged that I wished to sell the independence of my country! And for what end? Was this the object of my ambition? and is this the

---

* here Lord Norbury exclaimed: "Listen, sir, to the sentence of the law."

† Here Mr. Emmet paused, and the Court desired him to proceed.

mode by which a tribunal of justice reconciles contradictions? No! I am no emissary. My ambition was to hold a place among the deliverers of my country,—not in power, nor in profit, but in the glory of the achievement.

18. Sell my country's independence to France! And for what? For a change of masters? No; but for ambition! O, my country! was it personal ambition that could influence me? Had it been the soul of my actions, could I not, by my education and fortune, by the rank and consideration of my family, have placed myself among the proudest of your oppressors?

19. My country was my idol. To it I sacrificed every selfish, ever endearing sentiment; and for it I now offer up my life! O God! No! my lord; I acted as an Irishman, determined on delivering my country from the yoke of a foreign and unrelenting tyranny, and from the more galling yoke of a domestic faction, its joint partner and perpetrator in the patricide, whose reward is the ignominy of existing with an exterior of splendor, and a consciousness of depravity. It was the wish of my heart to extricate my country from this doubly riveted despotism. I wished to place her independence beyond the reach of any power on earth. I wished to exalt her to that proud station in the world which Providence had fitted her to fill.

20. Connection with France was, indeed, intended; but only as far as mutual interest would sanction or require. Were the French to assume any authority inconsistent with the purest independence, it would be the signal for their destruction. We sought aid of them; and we sought it, as we had assurance we should obtain it,—as auxiliaries in war, and allies in peace. Were the French to come as invaders or enemies, uninvited by the wishes of the people, I should oppose them to the utmost of my strength.

21. Yes, my countrymen, I would meet them on the beach, with a sword in one hand and a torch in the other. I would meet them with all the destructive fury of war; and I would

animate you to immolate them in their boats, before they had contaminated the soil. If they succeeded in landing, and if we were forced to retire before superior discipline, I would dispute every inch of ground, raze every house, burn every blade of grass before them, and the last intrenchment of liberty should be my grave. What I could not do myself, if I should fall, I would leave in charge to my countrymen to accomplish; because I should feel conscious that life, more than death, is unprofitable, when a foreign nation holds my country in subjection.

22. But it was not as an enemy that the succors of France were to land. I looked, indeed, for the assistance of France; but I wished to prove to France, and to the world, that Irishmen deserved to be assisted; that they were indignant at slavery, and ready to assert the independence and liberty of their country! I wished to procure for my country the guarantee which Washington procured for America—to procure an aid which, by its example, would be as important as by its valor,—allies disciplined, gallant, pregnant with science and experience; who would preserve the good and polish the rough points of our character; who would come to us as strangers, and leave us as friends, after sharing our perils and elevating our destiny.

23. These were my objects; not to receive new taskmasters, but to expel old tyrants. These were my views, and these only become Irishmen. It was for these ends I sought aid from France, because France, even as an enemy, could not be more implacable than the enemy already in the bosom of my country.*

IV.

24. I have been charged with that importance, in the efforts to emancipate my country, as to be considered the *key-stone* of the combination of Irishmen, or, as your lordship expressed it, "the life and blood of the conspiracy." You do me honor

---

* Here he was interrupted by the Court.

overmuch. You have given to the subaltern all the credit of a superior. There are men engaged in this *conspiracy* who are not only superior to me, but even to your own conceptions of yourself, my lord;—men, before the splendor of whose genius and virtues I should bow with respectful deference, and who would think themselves dishonored to be called your friends,— who would not disgrace themselves by shaking your blood-stained hands.*

25. What, my lord, shall you tell me, on the passage to the scaffold which that tyranny, of which you are only the intermediate minister, has erected for my murder, that I am accountable for all the blood that has been and will be shed, in this struggle of the oppressed against the oppressor? Shall you tell me this, and must I be so very a slave as not to repel it? I, who fear not to approach the Omnipotent Judge, to answer for the conduct of my short life,—am I to be appalled here, before a mere remnant of mortality?—by you, too, who, if it were possible to collect all the innocent blood that you have caused to be shed, in your unhallowed ministry, in one great reservoir, your lordship might swim in it.]†

26. Let no man dare, when I am dead, to charge me with dishonor. Let no man attaint my memory by believing that I could have engaged in any cause but that of my country's liberty and independence, or that I could have become the pliant minion of power in the oppression and the miseries of my countrymen. The proclamation of the Provisional Government speaks for my views. No inference can be tortured from it to countenance barbarity or debasement at home, or subjection, humiliation, or treachery from abroad. I would not have submitted to a foreign oppressor, for the same reason that I would resist the domestic tyrant.

27. In the dignity of freedom I would have fought upon the threshold of my country, and its enemy should enter only by passing over my lifeless corpse. And am I, who lived but for

---

* Here he was interrupted by Lord Norbury.
† Here the judge interfered.

my country,—who have subjected myself to the dangers of the jealous and watchful oppressor, and now to the bondage of the grave, only to give my countrymen their rights, and my country her independence,—am I to be loaded with calumny, and not suffered to resent it? No! God forbid!*

28. If the spirits of the illustrious dead participate in the concerns and cares of those who were dear to them in this transitory life, O, ever dear and venerated shade of my departed father, look down with scrutiny upon the conduct of your suffering son, and see if I have, even for a moment, deviated from those principles of morality and patriotism which it was your care to instil into my youthful mind, and for which I am now to offer up my life!

29. My lords, you seem impatient for the sacrifice. The blood for which you thirst is not congealed by the artificial terrors which surround your victim;—it circulates, warmly and unruffled, through the channels which God created for nobler purposes, but which you are bent to destroy, for purposes so grievous that they cry to Heaven. Be ye patient! I have but a few words more to say. I am going to my cold and silent grave. My lamp of life is nearly extinguished. My race is run. The grave opens to receive me,—and I sink into its bosom!

30. I have but one request to ask, at my departure from this world;—it is the charity of its silence. Let no man write my epitaph; for, as no man who knows my motives dare *now* vindicate them, let not prejudice or ignorance asperse them. Let them and me repose in obscurity and peace, and my tomb remain uninscribed, until other times and other men can do justice to my character. When my country takes her place among the nations of the earth,—then, and not till then,—let my epitaph be written! I have done. ROBERT EMMET.

---

* Here Lord Norbury told the prisoner that his principles were treasonable and subversive of government, and his language unbecoming a person in his situation; and that his father, the late Dr. Emmet, was a man who would not have countenanced such sentiments.

2. AARON BURR.

[WILLIAM WIRT was one of the most celebrated advocates and writers of the nineteenth century; he died in 1834. In the celebrated trial of Aaron Burr, Mr. Wirt, who was retained as counsel for the State, displayed a degree of learning and eloquence which drew forth the encomiums of the judges, the press and the people. This success established his reputation; his arguments were read with delight, and his name enrolled among the ablest men of the country. At the bar of the Supreme Court he found, says his biographer, the highest forensic theatre in the country, and perhaps there never was one in any country that presented a more splendid array of learning and talent conjoined. In the causes, too, which it is the official duty of the Attorney-General to prosecute or defend, the most conspicuous counsel of that bar are commonly combined against him. In how many conflicts he sustained these odds against him with a vigor always adequate to the occasion, is well known.]

LET us put the case between Burr and Blannerhassett; let us compare the two men, and settle this question of precedence between them. Who Aaron Burr is, we have seen in part already. I will add that, beginning his operations in New York, he associated with him men whose wealth is to supply the necessary funds.

2. Possessed of the main-spring, his personal labor supplies all the machinery. Parading the continent, from New York to New Orleans, he draws into his plan, by every allurement which he can contrive, men of all ranks and descriptions. To youthful ardor he presents danger and glory; to ambition, ranks, and titles, and honors; to avarice, the mines of Mexico. To each person whom he addresses he presents the object adopted to his taste.

3. His recruiting officers are appointed; men are engaged throughout the continent. Civil life is indeed quiet upon its surface, but in its bosom this man has contrived to deposit the materials which, with the slightest touch of his match, would produce an explosion that must shake a continent. All this his restless ambition has contrived, and in the autumn of 1806 he goes forth, for the last time, to apply his match. On this occasion he meets with Blannerhassett. WILLIAM WIRT.

8. WHO IS BLANNERHASSETT?

[From a speech on the trial of Aaron Burr.]

WHO is Blannerhassett? A native of Ireland, a man of letters, who fled from the storms of his own country to find quiet in ours. His history shows that war is not the natural element of his mind. If it had been, he never would have changed Ireland for America.

2. So far is an army from furnishing the society natural and proper to Mr. Blannerhassett's character, that on his arrival in America he retired even from the population of the Atlantic States, and sought quiet and solitude in the bosom of our Western forests.

3. But he carried with him taste, and science, and wealth, and lo, the desert smiled! Possessing himself of a beautiful island in the Ohio, he rears upon it a palace, and decorates it with every romantic embellishment of fancy. A shrubbery that Shenstone might have envied, blooms around him. Music that might have charmed Calypso and her nymphs, is his.

4. An extensive library spreads its treasures before him. A philosophical apparatus offers to him all the secret mysteries of nature. Peace, tranquillity and innocence shed their mingled delights around him.

5. And to crown the enchantment of the scene, a wife who is said to be lovely even beyond her sex, and graced with every accomplishment that can render it irresistible, had blessed him with her love and made him the father of several children. The evidence would convince you that this is but a faint picture of the real life.

6. In the midst of all this peace, this innocent simplicity, and this tranquillity, this feast of the mind, this pure banquet of the heart, the destroyer comes; he comes to change this paradise into a hell. Yet the flowers do not wither at his approach. No monitory shuddering through the bosom of their unfortunate possessor warns him of the ruin that is coming upon him.

7. A stranger presents himself. Introduced to their civilities by the high rank which he had lately held in his country, he soon finds his way to their hearts by the dignity and elegance of his demeanor, the light and beauty of his conversation, and the seductive and fascinating power of his address.

8. The conquest was not difficult. Innocence is ever simple and credulous. Conscious of no design itself, it suspects none in others. It wears no guard before its breast. Every door, and portal, and avenue of the heart is thrown open, and all who choose it, enter.

9. Such was the state of Eden when the serpent entered its bowers. The prisoner, in a more engaging form, winding himself into the open and unpractised heart of the unfortunate Blannerhassett, found but little difficulty in changing the native character of that heart and the objects of its affection.

10. By degrees he infuses into it the poison of his own ambition. He breathes into it the fire of his own courage; a daring and desperate thirst for glory, and ardor panting for great enterprises—for all the storm, and bustle, and hurricane of life.

11. In a short time the whole man is changed, and every object of his former delight is relinquished. No more he enjoys the tranquil scene; it has become flat and insipid to his taste. His books are abandoned; his retort and crucible are thrown aside; his shrubbery blooms and breathes its fragrance upon the air in vain; he likes it not.

12. His ear no longer drinks the rich melody of music; it longs for the trumpet's clangor and the cannon's roar. Even the prattle of his babes, once so sweet, no longer affects him; and the angel smile of his wife, which hitherto touched his bosom with ecstasy so unspeakable, is now unseen and unfelt.

13. Greater objects have taken possession of his soul. His imagination has been dazzled by visions of diadems, of stars and garters, and titles of nobility. He has been taught to burn with restless emulation at the names of great heroes and conquerors.

14. His enchanted island is destined soon to relapse into a wilderness; and in a few months we find the beautiful and tender partner of his bosom, whom he lately "permitted not the winds of" summer "to visit too roughly," we find her shivering at midnight on the winter banks of the Ohio, and mingling her tears with the torrents that froze as they fell.

15. Yet this unfortunate man, thus deluded from his interest and his happiness, thus seduced from the paths of innocence and peace, thus confounded in the toils that were deliberately spread for him, and overwhelmed by the mastering spirit and genius of another—this man, thus ruined and undone, and made to play a subordinate part in this grand drama of guilt and treason, this man is to be called the principal offender, while he by whom he was thus plunged in misery is comparatively innocent—a mere accessory!

16. Is this reason? Is it law? Is it humanity? Sir, neither the human heart nor the human understanding will bear a perversion so monstrous and absurd! so shocking to the soul! so revolting to reason!

17. Let Aaron Burr, then, not shrink from the high destination which he has courted; and, having already ruined Blannerhassett in fortune, character, and happiness forever, let him not attempt to finish the tragedy by thrusting that ill-fated man between himself and punishment. WILLIAM WIRT.

---

4. THE HABEAS CORPUS ACT.

[JOHN PHILPOT CURRAN, in the case of the King against Mr. Justice Johnson, February 4th, 1805, before Chief Baron Lord Avonmore and the other Barons, in the Court of Exchequer.]

I NOW address you on a question the most vitally connected with the liberty and well-being of every man within the limits of the British Empire;—which being decided one way, he may be a freeman; which being decided the other, he must be a slave. I refer to the maintenance of that sacred security for the freedom of Englishmen—so justly called the second Magna Charta of British liberty—the Habeas Corpus Act; the spirit and letter of which is, that the party arrested shall, without a moment's delay, be bailed, if the offence be bailable.

2. What was the occasion of the law? The arbitrary transportation of the subject beyond the realm; the base and malignant war which the odious and despicable minions of power are forever ready to wage against all those who are honest and bold enough to despise, to expose, and to resist them.

3. Such is the oscitancy of man, that he lies torpid for ages under these aggressions, until, at last, some signal abuse— the violation of Lucrece, the death of Virginia, the oppression of William Tell—shakes him from his slumber. For years had those drunken gambols of power been played in England; for years had the waters of bitterness been rising to the brim; at last, a single drop caused them to overflow,—the oppression of a single individual raised the people of England from their sleep.

4. And what does that great statute do? It defines and asserts the right, it points out the abuse; and it endeavors to secure the right, and to guard against the abuse, by giving redress to the sufferer, and by punishing the offender. For years had it been the practice to transport obnoxious persons out of the realm into distant parts, under the pretext of punishment, or of safe custody. Well might they have been said to be sent "to that undiscovered country from whose bourn no traveller returns;" for of these wretched travellers how few ever did return!

5. But of that flagrant abuse this statute has laid the axe to the root. It prohibits the abuse; it declares such detention or removal illegal; it gives an action against all persons concerned in the offence, by contriving, writing, signing, countersigning, such warrant, or advising or assisting therein.

6. Are bulwarks like these ever constructed to repel the

incursions of a contemptible enemy? Was it a trivial and ordinary occasion which raised this storm of indignation in the Parliament of that day? Is the ocean ever lashed by the tempest, to waft a feather, or to drown a fly? By this act you have a solemn legislative declaration, "that it is incompatible with liberty to send any subject out of the realm, under pretence of any crime supposed or alleged to be committed in a foreign jurisdiction, except that crime be capital."

7. Such were the bulwarks which our ancestors placed about the sacred temple of liberty—such the ramparts by which they sought to bar out the ever-toiling ocean of arbitrary power; and thought (generous credulity!) that they had barred it out from their posterity forever. Little did they foresee the future race of vermin that would work their way through those mounds, and let back the inundation!

CURRAN.

5. CURRAN'S APPEAL TO LORD AVONMORE.

I AM not ignorant, my lords, that the extraordinary construction of law against which I contend has received the sanction of another court, nor of the surprise and dismay with which it smote upon the general heart of the bar. I am aware that I may have the mortification of being told, in another country, of that unhappy decision; and I foresee in what confusion I shall hang down my head, when I am told it.

2. But I cherish, too, the consolatory hope, that I shall be able to tell them that I had an old and learned friend, whom I would put above all the sweepings of their hall, who was of a different opinion; who had derived his ideas of civil liberty from the purest fountains of Athens and of Rome; who had fed the youthful vigor of his studious mind with the theoretic knowledge of their wisest philosophers and statesmen; and who had refined that theory into the quick and exquisite sensibility of moral instinct, by contemplating the practice of their most illustrious examples,—by dwelling on the sweet-

souled piety of Cimon, on the anticipated Christianity of Socrates, on the gallant and pathetic patriotism of Epaminondas, on that pure austerity of Fabricius, whom to move from his integrity would have been more difficult than to have pushed the sun from his course.

3. I would add, that if he had seemed to hesitate, it was but for a moment; that his hesitation was like the passing cloud that floats across the morning sun, and hides it from the view, and does so for a moment hide it, by involving the spectator, without even approaching the face of the luminary.

4. And this soothing hope I draw from the dearest and tenderest recollections of my life; from the remembrance of those attic nights and those refections of the gods which we have partaken with those admired, and respected, and beloved companions, who have gone before us,—over whose ashes the most precious tears of Ireland have been shed.*

5. Yes, my good lord, I see you do not forget them; I see their sacred forms passing in sad review before your memory; I see your pained and softened fancy recalling those happy meetings, where the innocent enjoyment of social mirth, became expanded into the nobler warmth of social virtue, and the horizon of the board became enlarged into the horizon of man; where the swelling heart conceived and communicated the pure and generous purpose; where my slenderer and younger taper imbibed its borrowed light from the more matured and redundant fountain of yours. Yes, my lord, we can remember those nights, without any other regret than that they can never more return; for,

> "We spent them not in toys, or lust, or wine;
> But search of deep philosophy,
> Wit, eloquence, and poesy;
> Arts which I loved, for they, my friend, were thine.'
>
> CURRAN.

---

* Here, according to the original report, Lord Avonmore could not refrain from bursting into tears. In the midst of Curran's legal argument, "this most beautiful episode," says Charles Phillips, "bloomed

4. GREAT MINDS IN THEIR RELATIONS TO CHRISTIANITY.

[THOMAS ERSKINE, of Scotland, was made Lord Chancellor in England in 1806. He was one of the greatest advocates who have graced the Bar; and, in serious forensic oratory, has never been surpassed. It has been said of him, that no man that ever lived better elevated and honored his calling.]

IN running the mind along the long list of sincere and devoted Christians, I cannot help lamenting that Newton had not lived to this day, to have had his shallowness filled up with this new flood of light, poured upon the world by Mr. Thomas Paine. But the subject is too awful for irony. I will speak plainly and directly.

2. Newton was a Christian!—Newton, whose mind burst forth from the fetters cast by nature upon our finite conceptions;—Newton, whose science was truth, and the foundations of whose knowledge of it was philosophy: not those visionary and arrogant presumptions which too often usurp its name, but philosophy resting upon the basis of mathematics, which, like figures, cannot lie;—Newton, who carried the line and rule to the uttermost barrier of creation, and explored the principles by which, no doubt, all created matter is held together and exists.

3. But this extraordinary man, in the mighty reach of his mind, overlooked, perhaps, what a minuter investigation of the created things on this earth might have taught him, of the essence of his Creator. What, then, shall be said of the great Mr. Boyle, who looked into the organic structure of all

---

like a green spot amid the desert. Mr. Curran told me himself, that when the court rose, the tip-staff informed him he was wanted immediately in chamber by one of the judges of the Exchequer. He, of course, obeyed the judicial mandate; and the moment he entered, poor Lord Avonmore, whose cheeks were still wet with the tears extorted by this heart-touching appeal, clasped him to his bosom." A coolness caused by political differences, which had for some time existed between them, gave place to a renewal of friendship, which was not again interrupted.

matter, even to the brute inanimate substances which the foot treads on? Such a man may be supposed to have been equally qualified, with Mr. Paine, to look up through nature to nature's God; yet the result of all his contemplation was the most confirmed and devout belief in all which the other holds in contempt, as despicable and drivelling superstition.

4. But this error might, perhaps, arise from a want of due attention to the foundations of human judgment, and the structure of that understanding which God has given us for the investigation of truth. Let that question be answered by Mr. Locke, who was, to the highest pitch of devotion and adoration, a Christian;—Mr. Locke, whose office was to detect the errors of thinking, by going up to the fountains of thought, and to direct into the proper track of reasoning the devious mind of man, by showing him its whole process, from the first perceptions of sense to the last conclusions of ratiocination, putting a rein upon false opinions by practical rules for the conduct of human judgment. But these men were only deep thinkers, and lived in their closets, unaccustomed to the traffic of the world, and to the laws which practically regulate mankind.

5. Gentlemen, in the place where we now sit to administer the justice of this great country, above a century ago, the never-to-be-forgotten Sir Matthew Hale presided, whose faith in Christianity is an exalted commentary upon its truth and reason, and whose life was a glorious example of its fruits in man, administering human justice with wisdom and purity, drawn from the pure fountain of the Christian dispensation, which has been, and will be, in all ages, a subject of the highest reverence and admiration. But it is said by the author that the Christian fable is but the tale of the more ancient superstitions of the world, and may be easily detected by a proper understanding of the mythologies of the heathens.

6. Did Milton understand those mythologies? Was he less versed than Mr. Paine in the superstitions of the world?

No; they were the subject of his immortal song; and though shut out from all recurrence to them, he poured them forth from the stores of a memory rich with all that man ever knew, and laid them in their order, as the illustration of real and exalted faith,—the unquestionable source of that fervid genius which cast a sort of shade upon all the other works of man. But it was the light of the body only that was extinguished; —"the celestial light shone inward, and enabled him to justify the ways of God to man."

7. Thus you find all that is great, or wise, or splendid, or illustrious, amongst created beings,—all the minds gifted beyond ordinary nature, if not inspired by its universal Author for the advancement and dignity of the world,— though divided by distant ages, and by clashing opinions, distinguishing them from one another, yet joining, as it were, in one sublime chorus to celebrate the truths of Christianity, and laying upon its holy altars the never-failing offerings of their immortal wisdom. ERSKINE.

---

7. GUILT CANNOT KEEP ITS OWN SECRET.

AN aged man, without an enemy in the world, in his own house, and in his own bed, is made the victim of a butcherly murder, for mere pay. The fatal blow is given! and the victim passes, without a struggle or a motion, from the repose of sleep to the repose of death! It is the assassin's purpose to make sure work. He explores the wrist for the pulse. He feels for it, and ascertains that it beats no longer! It is accomplished. The deed is done. He retreats retraces his steps to the window, passes out through it as he came in, and escapes. He has done the murder;—no eye has seen him, no ear has heard him. The secret is his own,—and it is safe!

2. Ah! gentlemen, that was a dreadful mistake. Such a secret can be safe nowhere. The whole creation of God has

neither nook nor corner where the guilty can bestow it, and say it is safe. Not to speak of that eye which glances through all disguises, and beholds every thing as in the splendor of noon, such secrets of guilt are never safe from detection, even by men. True it is, generally speaking, that "murder will out." True it is, that Providence hath so ordained, and doth so govern things, that those who break the great law of Heaven, by shedding man's blood, seldom succeed in avoiding discovery. Especially, in a case exciting so much attention as this, discovery must come, and will come, sooner or later.

3. A thousand eyes turn at once to explore every man, every thing, every circumstance, connected with the time and place; a thousand ears catch every whisper; a thousand excited minds intensely dwell on the scene, shedding all their light, and ready to kindle the slightest circumstance into a blaze of discovery.

4. Meantime, the guilty soul cannot keep its own secret. It is false to itself; or, rather, it feels an irresistible impulse of conscience to be true to itself. It labors under its guilty possession, and knows not what to do with it. The human heart was not made for the residence of such an inhabitant. It finds itself preyed on by a torment, which it dares not acknowledge to God nor man. A vulture is devouring it, and it can ask no sympathy or assistance, either from Heaven or earth.

5. The secret which the murderer possesses soon comes to possess him; and, like the evil spirits of which we read, it overcomes him, and leads him whithersoever it will. He feels it beating at his heart, rising to his throat, and demanding disclosure. He thinks the whole world sees it in his face, reads it in his eyes, and almost hears its workings in the very silence of his thoughts. It has become his master. It betrays his discretion, it breaks down his courage, it conquers his prudence.

6. When suspicions, from without, begin to embarrass him,

and the net of circumstance to entangle him, the fatal secret struggles, with still greater violence, to burst forth. It *must* be confessed;—it *will* be confessed;—there is no refuge from confession but suicide—and suicide is confession!

DANIEL WEBSTER.

8. AN APPEAL TO THE JURY.

[PHILLIPS is one of the most brilliant orators of the age.]

OH! gentlemen, am I this day only the counsel of my client? No, no; I am the advocate of humanity—of yourselves, your homes, your wives, your families, your little children. I am glad that this case exhibits such atrocity; unmarked as it is by any mitigatory feature, it may stop the frightful advance of this calamity; it will be met now, and marked with vengeance.

2. If it be not, farewell to the virtues of your country; farewell to all confidence between man and man; farewell to that unsuspicious and reciprocal tenderness without which marriage is but a consecrated curse. If oaths are to be violated, laws disregarded, friendship betrayed, humility trampled, national and individual honor stained, and if a jury of fathers and husbands will give such miscreancy a passport to their homes, and wives, and daughters, farewell to all that yet remains of Ireland!

3. But I will not cast such a doubt upon the character of my country. Against the sneer of the foe and the skepticism of the foreigner, I will still stand and point to the domestic virtues, that no perfidy could barter, and no bribery can purchase; that with a Roman usage at once embellish and consecrate households, giving to the society of the hearth all the purity of the altar; that, lingering alike in the palace and the cottage, are still to be found scattered over this land—the relic of what she was—the source, perhaps, of what she may be—the lone, the stately, and the magnificent memorials that, rearing their majesty amidst surrounding ruins, serve at once as the landmarks of departed glory, and the models by which the future may be erected.

4. Preserve those virtues with a vestal fidelity; mark this day, by your verdict, your horror of their profanation; and believe me, when the hand which records that verdict shall be dust, and the tongue which asks it traceless in the grave, many a happy home will bless its consequences, and many a mother teach her little child to hate the impious treason of adultery.

PHILLIPS.

9. IRELAND.

I DO not despair of my poor old country, her peace, her liberty, her glory. For that country I can do no more than bid her hope. To lift this island up, to make her a benefactor instead of being the meanest beggar in the world, to restore to her her native powers and her ancient constitution, this has been my ambition, and this ambition has been my crime.

2. Judged by the law of England, I know this crime entails the penalty of death, but the history of Ireland explains this crime, and justifies it. Judged by that history I am no criminal; you are no criminal; I deserve no punishment; we deserve no punishment. Judged by that history, the treason of which I stand convicted loses all its guilt, is sanctified as a duty, will be ennobled as a sacrifice.

3. With these sentiments, my lord, I await the sentence of the court, having done what I felt to be my duty, having spoken what I felt to be the truth, as I have done on every other occasion of my short career. I now bid farewell to the country of my birth, my passion and my death—the country whose misfortunes have invoked my sympathies, whose factions I have sought to still, whose intellect I have prompted to a lofty aim, whose freedom has been my fatal dream.

4. I offer to that country, as a proof of the love I bear her, and the sincerity with which I thought and spoke and struggled for her freedom, the life of a young heart; and with that life, all the hopes, the honors, the endearments of an honorable home.

5. Pronounce, then, my lords, the sentence which the law directs, and I will be prepared to hear it. I trust I shall be prepared to meet its execution. I hope to be able, with a pure heart and a perfect composure, to appear before a higher tribunal—a tribunal where a Judge of infinite goodness, as well as of justice, will preside, and where, my lords, many, many of the judgments of this world will be reversed.   T. F. MEAGHER.

10. ADHERBAL AGAINST JUGURTHA.

FATHERS! it is known to you, that King Micipsa, my father, on his death-bed, left in charge to Jugurtha his adopted son, conjointly with my unfortunate brother Hiempsel and myself, the children of his own body, the administration of the kingdom of Numidia, directing us to consider the Senate and the people of Rome as proprietors of it. He charged us to use our best endeavors to be serviceable to the Roman commonwealth; assuring us, that your protection would prove a defence against all enemies; and would be instead of armies, fortifications, and treasures.

2. While my brother and I were thinking of nothing but how to regulate ourselves according to the directions of our deceased father—Jugurtha—the most infamous of mankind!—breaking through all ties of gratitude and of common humanity, and trampling on the authority of the Roman commonwealth, procured the murder of my unfortunate brother; and has driven me from my throne and native country, though he knows I inherit, from my grandfather Massinissa, and my father Micipsa, the friendship and alliance of the Romans.

3. For a prince to be reduced, by villainy, to my distressful circumstances, is calamity enough; but my misfortunes are heightened by the consideration that I find myself obliged to solicit your assistance, fathers, for the services done you by my ancestors, not for any I have been able to render you in my own person. Jugurtha has put it out of my power to de-

serve any thing at your hands; and has forced me to be burdensome, before I could be useful to you.

4. And yet, if I had no plea, but my undeserved misery—a once powerful prince, the descendant of a race of illustrious monarchs, now, without any fault of my own, destitute of every support, and reduced to the necessity of begging foreign assistance, against an enemy who has seized my throne and my kingdom,—if my unequalled distresses were all I had to plead,—it would become the greatness of the Roman commonwealth, to protect the injured, and to check the triumph of daring wickedness over helpless innocence.

5. But to provoke your resentment to the utmost, Jugurtha has driven me from the very dominions which the Senate and people of Rome gave to my ancestors; and from which my grandfather, and my father, under your umbrage, expelled Syphax and the Carthaginians.

6. Thus, fathers, your kindness to our family is defeated; and Jugurtha, in injuring me, throws contempt upon you. Oh wretched prince! Oh cruel reverse of fortune! Oh father Micipsa! Is this the consequence of thy generosity: that he whom thy goodness raised to an equality with thy own children, should be the murderer of thy children? Must, then, the royal house of Numidia always be a scene of havoc and blood?

7. While Carthage remained, we suffered, as was to be expected, all sorts of hardships from their hostile attacks; our enemy near; our only powerful ally, the Roman commonwealth, at a distance. When that scourge of Africa was no more, we congratulated ourselves on the prospect of established peace. But, instead of peace, behold the kingdom of Numidia, drenched with royal blood! and the only surviving son of its late king, flying from an adopted murderer, and seeking that safety in foreign countries which he cannot command in his own kingdom.

8. Whither—Oh! whither shall I fly? If I return to the royal palace of my ancestors, my father's throne is seized by

the murderer of my brother. What can I there expect, but that Jugurtha should hasten to imbrue, in my blood, those hands which are now reeking with my brother's? If I were to fly for refuge, or for assistance, to any other court, from what prince can I hope for protection, if the Roman commonwealth give me up? From my own family or friends I have no expectations.

9. My royal father is no more. He is beyond the reach of violence, and out of hearing of the complaints of his unhappy son. Were my brother alive, our mutual sympathy would be some alleviation. But he is hurried out of life, in his early youth, by the very hand which should have been the last to injure any of the royal family of Numidia. The bloody Jugurtha has butchered all whom he suspected to be in my interest. Some have been destroyed by the lingering torment of the cross. Others have been given a prey to wild beasts; and their anguish made the sport of men more cruel than wild beasts. If there be any yet alive, they are shut up in dungeons, there to drag out a life more intolerable than death itself.

10. Look down, illustrious senators of Rome! from that height of power to which you are raised, on the unexampled distresses of a prince, who is, by the cruelty of a wicked intruder, become an outcast from all mankind. Let not the crafty insinuations of him who returns murder for adoption prejudice your judgment. Do not listen to the wretch who has butchered the son and relations of a king, who gave him power to sit on the same throne with his own sons.

11. I have been informed that he labors by his emissaries to prevent your determining any thing against him in his absence; pretending that I magnify my distress, and might, for him, have staid in peace in my own kingdom. But, if ever the time comes, when the due vengeance from above shall overtake him, he will then dissemble as I do. Then he who, now hardened in wickedness, triumphs over those whom his violence laid low, will, in his turn, feel distress, and suffer for

his impious ingratitude to my father, and his blood-thirsty cruelty to my brother.

12. Oh murdered, butchered brother! Oh dearest to my heart,—now gone forever from my sight! But why should I lament his death? He is, indeed, deprived of the blessed light of heaven, of life, and kingdom, at once, by the very person who ought to have been the first to hazard his own life, in defence of any one of Micipsa's family. But, as things are, my brother is not so much deprived of these comforts, as delivered from terror, from flight, from exile, and the endless train of miseries which render life to me a burden.

13. He lies full low, gored with wounds, and festering in his own blood. But he lies in peace. He feels none of the miseries which rend my soul with agony and distraction, while I am set up a spectacle to all mankind, of the uncertainty of human affairs. So far from having it in my power to punish his murderer, I am not master of the means of securing my own life. So far from being in a condition to defend my kingdom from the violence of the usurper, I am obliged to apply for foreign protection for my own person.

14. Fathers! Senators of Rome! the arbiters of nations! to you I fly for refuge from the murderous fury of Jugurtha. By your affection for your children; by your love for your country; by your own virtues; by the majesty of the Roman commonwealth: by all that is sacred, and all that is dear to you,—deliver a wretched prince from undeserved, unprovoked injury; and save the kingdom of Numidia, which is your own property, from being the prey of violence, usurpation, and cruelty.

SALLUST.

---

11. ALARIC THE VISIGOTH.

[The Visigoths were a race of barbarians occupying Middle Europe, who made war upon the Roman Emperor Arcadius, ravaging Greece and Italy. Their leader, Alaric, boasted that where his hosts trod, the grass never grew. He besieged and plundered Rome, A. D. 400. Afterwards, feeling his end approaching, he ordered that the Busentius, a river of Italy, should be diverted from its channel, that his body might be interred in its bed. Mr. Everett has made this dying injunction the subject of his fine verses.]

WHEN I am dead, no pageant train
   Shall waste their sorrows at my bier,
Nor worthless pomp of homage vain
   Stain it with hypocritic tear;
For I will die as I did live,
Nor take the boon I cannot give.

2. Ye shall not raise a marble bust
   Upon the spot where I repose;
Ye shall not fawn before my dust
   In hollow circumstance of woes:
Not sculptured clay, with lying breath,
Insult the clay that moulds beneath.

3. Ye shall not pile, with servile toil,
   Your monuments upon my breast;
Nor yet within the common soil
   Lay down the wreck of power to rest;
Where man can boast that he has trod
On him that was the scourge of God.

4. But ye the mountain stream shall turn,
   And lay its secret channel bare,
And hollow, for your sovereign's urn,
   A resting-place forever there:
Then bid its everlasting springs
Flow back upon the King of kings;
And never be the secret said,
Until the deep give up his dead.

5. My gold and silver ye shall fling
   Back to the clods that gave them birth;
The captured crowns of many a king,
   The ransom of a conquered earth:
For e'en though dead, will I control
The trophies of the capitol.

6. But when beneath the mountain tide
    Ye've laid your monarch down to rot,
  Ye shall not rear upon its side
    Pillar or mound to mark the spot;
  For long enough the world has shook
  Beneath the terrors of my look;
  And now that I have run my race,
  The astonished realms shall rest a space.

7. My course was like a river deep,
    And from the northern hills I burst,
  Across the world in wrath to sweep;
    And where I went the land was cursed;
  Nor blade of grass again was seen,
  Where Alaric and his hosts had been.

8. See how the haughty barriers fail
    Beneath the terror of the Goth,—
  Their iron-breasted legions quail
    Before my ruthless sabaoth;
  And low the queen of empires kneels,
  And grovels at my chariot-wheels.

9. Not for myself did I ascend,
    In judgment, my triumphal car;
  'T was God alone on high did send
    The avenging Scythian to the war,
  To shake abroad, with iron hand,
  The appointed scourge of his command.

10. With iron hand that scourge I reared,
    O'er guilty king and guilty realm;
  Destruction was the ship I steered,
    And Vengeance sat upon the helm;
  When launched in fury on the flood,
  I ploughed my way through seas of blood,
  And in the stream their hearts had spilt,
  Washed out the long arrears of guilt.

11. Across the everlasting Alp
    I poured the torrent of my *powers*,
And feeble Cæsars shrieked for help
    In vain within their seven-hilled towers;
I quenched in blood the brightest gem
That glittered in their diadem;
And struck a darker, deeper die,
In the purple of their majesty;
And bade my northern banners shine
Upon the conquered Palatine.

12. My course is run, my errand done;
    I go to Him from whence I came;
But never yet shall set the sun
    Of glory that adorns my name;
And Roman hearts shall long be sick,
When men shall think of Alaric.

13. My course is run, my errand done,—
    But darker ministers of fate,
Impatient round the eternal throne,
    And in the caves of vengeance, wait;
And soon mankind shall blench away
Before the name of Attila.
                              EVERETT.

---

12. SPEECH OF SALATHIEL IN FAVOR OF RESISTING THE ROMAN POWER.

WHAT! must we first mingle in the cabals of Jerusalem, and rouse the frigid debaters and disputers of the Sanhedrim into action? Are we first to conciliate the irreconcilable, to soften the furious, to purify the corrupt? If the Romans are to be our tyrants till we can teach patriotism to faction, we may as well build the dungeon at once; for to the dungeon we are consigned for the longest life among us.

2. Death or glory for me. There is no alternative between, not merely the half-slavery that we now live in and independence, but between the most condign suffering and the most illustrious security. If the people would rise, through the pressure of public injury, they must have risen long since; if from private violence, what town, what district, what family, has not its claims of deadly retribution? Yet, here the people stand, after a hundred years of those continued stimulants to resistance, as unresisting as in the day when Pompey marched over the threshold of the temple.

3. I know your generous friendship, Eleazer, and fear that your anxiety to save me from the chances of the struggle may bias your better judgment. But here I pledge myself, by all that constitutes the honor of man, to strike at all risks a blow upon the Roman crest that shall echo through the land.

4. What! commit our holy cause into the nursing of those pampered hypocrites, whose utter baseness of heart you know still more deeply than I do? Linger, till those pestilent profligates raise their price with Florus by betraying a design, that will be the glory of every man who draws a sword in it?

5. Vainly, madly, ask a brood that, like the serpent, engender and fatten among the ruins of their country, to discard their venom, to cast their fangs, to feel for human feelings? As well ask the serpent itself to rise from the original curse.

6. It is the irrevocable nature of faction to be base till it can be mischievous; to lick the dust until it can sting; to creep on its belly until it can twist its folds round the victim. No! let the old pensionaries, the bloated hangers-on in the train of every governor, the open sellers of their country for filthy lucre, betray me when I leave it in their power. To the field, I say! once and for all, to the field!

13. EXTRACT FROM RODERICK, THE LAST OF THE GOTHS.

A CHRISTIAN woman spinning at her door
Beheld him, and, with sudden pity touch'd,
She laid her spindle by, and running in
Took bread, and following after, call'd him back,
And placing in his passive hands the loaf,
She said, "Christ Jesus, for his mother's sake,
Have mercy on thee!" With a look that seem'd
Like idiocy he heard her, and stood still,
Staring awhile; then bursting into tears
Wept like a child, and thus relieved his heart,
Till even to bursting else with swelling thoughts

2. So through the streets, and through the northern gate
Did Roderick, reckless of a resting-place,
With feeble yet with hurried step pursue
His agitated way; and when he reach'd
The open fields, and found himself alone
Beneath the starry canopy of heaven,
The sense of solitude, so dreadful late,
Was then repose and comfort. There he stopt
Beside a little rill, and brake the loaf;
And shedding o'er that unaccustomed food
Painful but quiet tears, with grateful soul
He breathed thanksgiving forth; then made his bed
On heath and myrtle.   SOUTHEY.

14. SALATHIEL TO TITUS.

SON of Vespasian, I am at this hour a poor man, as I may in the next be an exile or a slave: I have ties to life as strong as ever were bound round the heart of man: I stand here a suppliant for the life of one whose loss would embitter mine! Yet, not for wealth unlimited, for the safety of my family, for the life of the noble victim that is now standing at the place of torture, dare I abandon, dare I think the impious thought of abandoning the cause of the City of Holiness.

2. Titus! in the name of that Being to whom the wisdom of the earth is folly, I adjure you to beware. Jerusalem is sacred. Her crimes have often wrought her misery—often has she been trampled by the armies of the stranger. But she is still the City of the Omnipotent; and never was blow inflicted on her by man, that was not terribly repaid.

3. The Assyrian came, the mightiest power of the world he plundered her temple, and led her people into captivity. How long was it before his empire was a dream, his dynasty extinguished in blood, and an enemy on his throne? The Persian came: from her protector, he turned into her oppressor; and his empire was swept away like the dust of the desert! The Syrian smote her: the smiter died in agonies of remorse; and where is his kingdom now? The Egyptian smote her: and who now sits on the throne of the Ptolemies?

4. Pompey came: the invincible, the conqueror of a thousand cities, the light of Rome; the lord of Asia, riding on the very wings of victory. But he profaned her temple; and from that hour he went down—down like a millstone plunged into the ocean! Blind counsel, rash ambition, womanish fears, were upon the great statesman and warrior of Rome. Where does he sleep? What sands were covered with his blood?

5. The universal conqueror died a slave, by the hand of a slave! Crassus came at the head of the legions: he plundered the sacred vessels of the sanctuary. Vengeance followed him, and he was cursed by the curse of God. Where are the bones of the robber and his host? Go, tear them from the jaws of the lion and the wolf of Parthia,—their fitting tomb!

6. You, too, son of Vespasian, may be commissioned for the punishment of a stiff-necked and rebellious people. You may scourge our naked vice by force of arms; and then you may return to your own land exulting in the conquest of the fiercest enemy of Rome. But shall you escape the common fate of the instrument of evil? Shall you see a peaceful old

age? Shall a son of yours ever sit upon the throne? Shall not rather some monster of your blood efface the memory of your virtue, and make Rome, in the bitterness of her soul, curse the Flavian name?

---

15. SEMPRONIUS' SPEECH FOR WAR.

MY voice is still for war.
Gods! can a Roman senate long debate,
Which of the two to choose, slavery or death?
No,—let us rise at once, gird on our swords,
And, at the head of our remaining troops,
Attack the foe, break through the thick array
Of his thronged legions, and charge home upon him.

2. Perhaps some arm more lucky than the rest
May reach his heart, and free the world from bondage.
Rise, fathers, rise! 'tis Rome demands your help:
Rise, and revenge her slaughtered citizens,
Or share their fate! The corpse of half her Senate
Manure the fields of Thessaly, while we
Sit here, deliberating in cold debates,
If we should sacrifice our lives to honor,
Or wear them out in servitude and chains.

3. Rouse up, for shame! Our brothers of Pharsalia
Point out their wounds, and cry aloud—"To battle!"
Great Pompey's shade complains that we are slow,
And Scipio's ghost walks unrevenged among us.
ADDISON.

---

16. CAIUS MARIUS TO THE ROMANS.

YOU have committed to my conduct, O Romans, the war against Jugurtha. The patricians are offended at this. "He has no family statues," they exclaim. "He can point to no illustrious line of ancestors!" What then? Will dead ancestors, will motionless statues help fight your battles? Will it avail your general to appeal to these, in the perilous hour?

2. Rare wisdom would it be, my countrymen, to intrust the command of your army to one whose only qualification for it would be the virtue of his forefathers! to one untried and unexperienced, but of most unexceptionable family! who could not show a solitary scar, but any number of ancestral statues! who knew not the first rudiments of war, but was very perfect in pedigrees! Truly I have known of such holiday heroes,—raised, because of family considerations, to a command for which they were not fitted,—who, when the moment for action arrived, were obliged, in their ignorance and trepidation, to give to some inferior officer—to some despised plebeian—the ordering of every movement.

3. I submit to you, Romans,—is patrician pride or plebeian experience the safer reliance? The actions of which my opponents have merely read, I have achieved or shared in. What they have seen written in books, I have seen written on battle-fields with steel and blood.

4. They object to my humble birth. They sneer at my lowly origin. Impotent objection! Ignominious sneer! Where but in the spirit of a man (bear witness, gods!),—where but in the spirit, can his nobility be lodged? and where his dishonor, but in his own cowardly inaction, or his unworthy deeds? Tell these railers at my obscure extraction, their haughty lineage could not make *them* noble—my humble birth could never make *me* base!

5. I profess no indifference to noble descent. It is a good thing to number great men among one's ancestry. But when a descendant is dwarfed in the comparison, it should be accounted a shame rather than a boast. These patricians cannot despise me, if they would, since their titles of nobility date from ancestral services similar to those which I myself have rendered.

6. And what if I can show no family statues? I can show

the standards, the armor, and the spoils, which I myself have wrested from the vanquished. I can show the scars of many wounds received in combating the enemies of Rome. These are my statues! These the honors I can boast of! Not an accidental inheritance, like theirs; but earned by toil, by abstinence, by valor; amid clouds of dust and seas of blood; scenes of action in which these effeminate patricians, who would now depreciate me in your esteem, have never dared to appear,—no, not even as spectators!

7. Here, Romans, are my credentials; here, my titles of nobility; here, my claims to the generalship of your army! Tell me, are they not as respectable, are they not as valid, are they not as deserving of your confidence and reward, as those which any patrician of them all can offer?

PARAPHRASE FROM SALLUST.

17. BRUTUS ON THE DEATH OF CÆSAR.

ROMANS, countrymen and lovers! hear me for my cause, and be silent that you may hear. Believe me for mine honor, and have respect to mine honor that you may believe. Censure me in your wisdom, and awake your senses, that you may the better judge.

2. If there be any in this assembly, any dear friend of Cæsar's, to him I say, that Brutus' love to Cæsar was no less than his. If, then, that friend demand why Brutus rose against Cæsar, this is my answer: Not that I loved Cæsar less, but that I loved Rome more.

3. Had you rather Cæsar were living, and die all slaves, than that Cæsar were dead, to live all freemen? As Cæsar loved me, I weep for him; as he was fortunate, I rejoice at it; as he was valiant, I honor him; but as he was ambitious—I slew him. There are tears for his love, joy for his fortune, honor for his valor, and death for his ambition.

4. Who is here so base that would be a bondman? If any, speak; for him have I offended. Who is here so rude,

that would not be a Roman? If any, speak; for him have I offended. Who is here so vile, that would not love his country? If any, speak; for him have I offended. I pause for a reply——

5. None! Then none have I offended. I have done no more to Cæsar than you should do to Brutus. The question of his death is enrolled in the capitol—his glory not extenuated, wherein he was worthy; nor his offences enforced, for which he suffered death.

6. Here comes his body, mourned by Mark Antony, who, though he had no hand in his death, shall receive the benefit of his dying, a place in the commonwealth; as which of you shall not? With this I depart—that as I slew my best lover for the good of Rome, I have the same dagger for myself, when it shall please my country to need my death.

18. THE SPARTANS' MARCH.

[The Spartans used not the trumpet in their march into battle, says Thucydides, because they wished not to excite the rage of their warriors. Their charging step was made to the Dorian mood of flutes and soft recorders.]

'TWAS morn upon the Grecian hills, where peasants
    dressed the vines;
Sunlight was on Cithæron's hills, Arcadia's rocks and pines;
And brightly, through his reeds and flowers, Eurotas wan-
    dered by,
When a sound arose from Sparta's towers of solemn harmony.
Was it the hunter's choral strain, to the woodland goddess
    poured?
Did virgin hands, in Pallas' fane, strike the full-sounding chord?

II.

But helms were glancing on the stream, spears ranged in close
    array,
And shields flung back a glorious beam to the morn of a fearful
    day!

And the mountain echoes of the land swelled through the deep-
    blue sky,
While to soft strains moved forth a band of men that moved
    to die.
They marched not with the trumpet's blast, nor bade the horn
    peal out ;
And the laurel groves, as on they passed, rung with no battle-
    shout !

III.

They asked no clarion's voice to fire their souls with an impulse
    high,
But the Dorian reed and the Spartan lyre, for the sons of
    liberty !
And still sweet flutes, their path around, sent forth Æolian
    breath ;
They needed not a sterner sound to marshal them for death !
So moved they calmly to their field, thence never to return,
Save bringing back the Spartan shield, or on it proudly borne !

                                                  FELICIA HEMANS

---

19. THE DEATH OF LEONIDAS.

IT was the wild midnight—a storm was on the sky ;
   The lightning gave its light, and the thunder echoed by.
The torrent swept the glen, the ocean lashed the shore ;
Then rose the Spartan men, to make their bed in gore !
Swift from the deluged ground three hundred took the shield ;
Then in silence gathered round the leader of the field !

II.

All up the mountain's side, all down the woody vale,
All by the rolling tide waved the Persian banners pale.
And foremost from the pass, among the slumbering band,
Sprang King Leonidas, like the lightning's living brand,
Then double darkness fell, and the forest ceased its moan ;
But there came a clash of steel, and a distant dying groan.

III.

Anon a trumpet blew, and a fiery sheet burst high,
That o'er the midnight threw a blood-red canopy.
A host glared on the hill; a host glared by the bay;
But the Greeks rushed onward still, like leopards in their play.
The air was all a yell, and the earth was all a flame,
Where the Spartan's bloody steel on the silken turbans came;
And still the Greek rushed on, where the fiery torrent rolled,
Till, like a rising sun, shone Xerxes' tent of gold.

IV.

They found a royal feast, his midnight banquet there,
And the treasures of the East lay beneath the Doric spear.
Then sat to the repast the bravest of the brave!
That feast must be their last, that spot must be their grave.
Up rose the glorious rank, to Greece one cup poured high;
Then hand in hand they drank, "To immortality!"

V.

Fear on King Xerxes fell, when, like spirits from the tomb,
With shout and trumpet knell, he saw the warriors come.
But down swept all his power, with chariot and with charge;
Down poured the arrows' shower, till sank the Spartan targe.
Thus fought the Greek of old! thus will he fight again!
Shall not the self-same mould bring forth the self-same men?

CROLY.

---

20. THE FLIGHT OF XERXES.

I SAW him on the battle-eve,
  When like a king he bore him:
Proud hosts were there in helm and greave,
  And prouder chiefs before him.
The warrior, and the warrior's deeds,—
The morrow, and the morrow's meeds,—
  No daunting thought came o'er him;
He looked around him, and his eye
Defiance flashed to earth and sky!

2. He looked on ocean,—its broad breast
    Was covered with his fleet;
On earth,—and saw, from east to west,
    His bannered millions meet;
While rock, and glen, and cave, and ocean,
Shook with the war-cry of that host,
    The thunder of their feet!
He heard the imperial echoes ring:
He heard,—and felt himself a king!

3. I saw him next alone; nor camp
    Nor chief his steps attended;
Nor banner blazed, nor courser's tramp
    With war-cries proudly blended.
He stood alone, whom fortune high
So lately seemed to deify:
    He who with Heaven contended,
Fled, like a fugitive and slave!
Behind,—the foe; before,—the wave!

4. He stood; fleet, army, treasure, gone,—
    Alone, and in despair!
While wave and wind swept ruthless on,
    For *they* were monarchs there;
And Xerxes, in a single bark,
Where late his thousand ships were dark,
    Must all their fury dare:
What a revenge, a trophy, this,
For thee, immortal Salamis! *Miss Jewsbury.*

---

21. SCIPIO TO HIS ARMY.

[Before the battle of Ticinus, b. c. 218, in which the Carthaginians, under Hannibal, were victorious. The speech of the latter, on the same occasion, follows.]

NOT because of their courage, O soldiers, but because an engagement is now inevitable, do the enemy prepare for battle. Two-thirds of their infantry and cavalry have been lost in the passage of the Alps. Those who survive hardly equal in number those who have perished. Should any one say, "Though few, they are stout and irresistible," I reply,— Not so! They are the veriest shadows of men; wretches, emaciated with hunger, and benumbed with cold; bruised and enfeebled among the rocks and crags; their joints frost-bitten, their sinews stiffened with the snow, their armor battered and shivered, their horses lame and powerless.

2. Such is the cavalry, such the infantry, against which you have to contend;—not enemies, but shreds and remnants of enemies! And I fear nothing more, than that when you have fought Hannibal, the Alps may seem to have been beforehand, and to have robbed you of the renown of a victory. But perhaps it was fitting that the Gods themselves, irrespective of human aid, should commence and carry forward a war against a leader and a people who violate the faith of treaties; and that we, who next to the Gods have been most injured, should complete the contest thus commenced, and nearly finished.

3. I would, therefore, have you fight, O soldiers, not only with that spirit with which you are wont to encounter other enemies, but with a certain indignation and resentment, such as you might experience if you should see your slaves suddenly taking up arms against you. We might have slain these Carthaginians, when they were shut up in Eryx, by hunger, the most dreadful of human tortures. We might have carried over our victorious fleet to Africa, and, in a few days, have destroyed Carthage, without opposition.

4. We yielded to their prayers for pardon; we released them from the blockade; we made peace with them when conquered; and we afterwards held them under our protection, when they were borne down by the African war. In return for these benefits, they come, under the leadership of a hot-brained youth, to lay waste our country. Ah! would that the contest on your side were now for glory, and not for safety!

5. It is not for the possession of Sicily and Sardinia, but for Italy, that you must fight: nor is there another army behind, which, should we fail to conquer, can resist the enemy: nor are there other Alps, during the passage of which, fresh forces may be procured.

6. Here, soldiers, here we must make our stand. Here we must fight, as if we fought before the walls of Rome! Let every man bear in mind, it is not only his own person, but his wife and children, he must now defend. Nor let the thought of them alone possess his mind. Let him remember that the Roman Senate—the Roman People—are looking, with anxious eyes, to our exertions; and that, as our valor and our strength shall this day be, such will be the fortune of Rome—such the welfare—nay, the very existence, of our country!   LIVY.

---

22. HANNIBAL TO HIS ARMY.

HERE, soldiers, you must either conquer or die. On the right and left two seas enclose you; and you have no ship to fly to for escape. The river Po around you,—the Po, larger and more impetuous than the Rhone,—the Alps behind, scarcely passed by you when fresh and vigorous, hem you in. Here Fortune has granted you the termination of your labors; here she will bestow a reward worthy of the service you have undergone. All the spoils that Rome has amassed by so many triumphs will be yours.

2. Think not that, in proportion as this war is great in name, the victory will be difficult. From the Pillars of Hercules, from the ocean, from the remotest limits of the world, over mountains and rivers, you have advanced victorious through the fiercest nations of Gaul and Spain. And with whom are you now to fight? With a raw army, which this very summer was beaten, conquered, and surrounded; an army unknown to their leader, and he to them.

3. Shall I compare myself, almost born, and certainly bred

in the tent of my father, that illustrious commander,—myself, the conqueror, not only of the Alpine Nations, but of the Alps themselves,—myself, who was the pupil of you all, before I became your commander,—to this six months' general? or shall I compare *his* army with *mine?*

4. On what side soever I turn my eyes, I behold all full of courage and strength:—a veteran infantry; a most gallant cavalry; you, our allies, most faithful and valiant; you, Carthaginians, whom not only your country's cause, but the justest anger, impels to battle. The valor, the confidence of invaders, are ever greater than those of the defensive party.

5. As the assailants in this war, we pour down, with hostile standards, upon Italy. We bring the war. Suffering, injury and indignity, fire our minds. First they demanded me, your leader, for punishment; and then all of you, who had laid siege to Saguntum. And, had we been given up, they would have visited us with the severest tortures.

6. Cruel and haughty nation! Every thing must be *yours*, and at *your* disposal! You are to prescribe to us with whom we shall have war, with whom peace! You are to shut us up by the boundaries of mountains and rivers, which we must not pass! But you—*you* are not to observe the limits yourselves have appointed! "Pass not the Iberus!"—What next? "Saguntum is on the Iberus. You must not move a step in any direction!"—Is it a small thing that you have deprived us of our most ancient provinces, Sicily and Sardinia? Will you take Spain also? Should we yield Spain, you will cross over into Africa. *Will* cross, did I say? They have sent the two Consuls of this year, one to Africa, the other to Spain!

7. Soldiers, there is nothing left to us, in any quarter, but what we can vindicate with our swords. Let those be cowards who have something to look back upon; whom, flying through safe and unmolested roads, their own country will receive. There is a necessity for *us* to be brave. There is no alternative but victory or death; and, if it must be *death,* who

would not rather encounter it in battle than in flight? The immortal gods could give no stronger incentive to victory. Let but these truths be fixed in your minds, and once again I proclaim, you are conquerors! LIVY.

---

28. REGULUS TO THE ROMAN SENATE.

ILL does it become *me*, O Senators of Rome!—ill does it become Rugulus—after having so often stood in this venerable assembly clothed with the supreme dignity of the Republic, to stand before you a captive—the captive of Carthage! Though outwardly I am free,—though no fetters encumber the limbs, or gall the flesh,—yet the heaviest of chains,—the pledge of a Roman Consul,—makes me the bondsman of the Carthaginians.

2. They have my promise to return to them, in the event of the failure of this their embassy. My life is at their mercy. My honor is my own;—a possession which no reverse of fortune can jeopard; a flame which imprisonment cannot stifle, time cannot dim, death cannot extinguish.

3. Of the train of disasters which followed close on the unexampled successes of our arms,—of the bitter fate which swept off the flower of our soldiery, and consigned me, your general, wounded and senseless, to Carthaginian keeping,—I will not speak. For five years, a rigorous captivity has been my portion. For five years, the society of family and friends, the dear amenities of home, the sense of freedom, and the sight of country, have been to me a recollection and a dream,—no more!

4. But during that period Rome has retrieved her defeats. She has recovered under Metellus what under Regulus she lost. She has routed armies. She has taken unnumbered prisoners. She has struck terror to the hearts of the Carthaginians; who have now sent me hither with their ambas-

sadors, to sue for peace, and to propose that, in exchange for me, your former Consul, a thousand common prisoners of war shall be given up.

5. You have heard the ambassadors. Their intimations of some unimaginable horror—I know not what—impending over myself, should I fail to induce you to accept their terms, have strongly moved your sympathies in my behalf.

6. Another appeal, which I would you might have been spared, has lent force to their suit. A wife and children, threatened with widowhood and orphanage, weeping and despairing, have knelt at your feet, on the very threshold of the Senate-chamber. Conscript Fathers! Shall not Regulus be saved? Must he return to Carthage to meet the cruelties which the ambassadors brandish before our eyes?

7. With one voice you answer, No! Countrymen! Friends! For all that I have suffered—for all that I may have to suffer—I am repaid in the compensation of this moment! Unfortunate, you may hold me; but, O, not undeserving! Your confidence in my honor survives all the ruin that adverse fortune could inflict. You have not forgotten the past. Republics are not ungrateful! May the thanks I cannot utter bring down blessings from the Gods on you and Rome!

8. Conscript Fathers! There is but one course to be pursued. Abandon all thought of peace. ' Reject the overtures of Carthage! Reject them wholly and unconditionally! What! Give back to her a thousand able-bodied men, and receive in return this one attenuated, war-worn, fever-wasted frame,—this weed, whitened in a dungeon's darkness, pale and sapless, which no kindness of the sun, no softness of the summer breeze, can ever restore to health and vigor?

9. It must not—it shall not be! O! were Regulus what he was once, before captivity had unstrung his sinews and enervated his limbs, he might pause,—he might proudly think he were well worth a thousand of the foe;—he might say, "Make the exchange! Rome shall not lose by it!"

10. But now—alas! now 'tis gone,—that impetuosity of

strength, which could once make him a leader indeed, to penetrate a phalanx or guide a pursuit. His very armor would be a burden now. His battle-cry would be drowned in the din of the onset. His sword would fall harmless on his opponent's shield. But, if he cannot *live*, he can at least *die*, for his country! Do not deny him this supreme consolation. Consider: every indignity, every torture, which Carthage shall heap on his dying hours, will be better than a trumpet's call to your armies.

11. They will remember only Regulus, their fellow-soldier and their leader. They will forget his defeats. They will regard only his services to the Republic. Tunis, Sardinia, Sicily,—every well-fought field, won by *his* blood and *theirs*,—will flash on their remembrance, and kindle their avenging wrath. And so shall Regulus, though dead, fight as he never fought before against the foe.

12. Conscript Fathers! There is another theme. My family —forgive the thought! To you, and to Rome, I confide them. I leave them no legacy but my name,—no testament but my example.

13. Ambassadors of Carthage! I have spoken; though not as you expected. I am your captive. Lead me back to whatever fate may await me. Doubt not that you shall find, to Roman hearts, country is dearer than life, and integrity more precious than freedom!

24. LEÓNIDAS TO HIS THREE HUNDRED.

YE men of Sparta, listen to the hope with which the Gods inspire Leonidas! Consider how largely our death may redound to the glory and benefit of our country. Against this barbarian king, who, in his battle array, reckons as many nations as our ranks do soldiers, what could united Greece effect?

2. In this emergency there is need that some unexpected power should interpose itself;—that a valor and devotion,

unknown hitherto, even to Sparta, should strike, amaze, confound, this ambitious despot! From our blood, here freely shed to-day, shall this moral power, this sublime lesson of patriotism, proceed. To Greece it shall teach the secret of her strength; to the Persians, the certainty of their weakness.

3. Before our scarred and bleeding bodies, we shall see the great king grow pale at his own victory, and recoil affrighted Or, should he succeed in forcing the pass of Thermopylæ, he will tremble to learn, that, in marching upon our cities, he will find ten thousand, after us, equally prepared for death.

4. Ten thousand, do I say? O, the swift contagion of a generous enthusiasm! Our example shall make Greece all fertile in heroes. An avenging cry shall follow the cry of her affliction.

5. Country! Independence! From the Messenian Hills to the Hellespont, every heart shall respond; and a hundred thousand heroes, with one sacred accord, shall arm themselves, in emulation of our unanimous death.

6. These rocks shall give back the echo of their oaths. Then shall our little band,—the brave these hundred,—from the world of shades, revisit the scene; behold the haughty Xerxes, a fugitive, recross the Hellespont in a frail bark; while Greece, after eclipsing the most glorious of her exploits, shall hallow a new Olympus in the mound that covers our tombs.

7. Yes, fellow-soldiers, history and posterity shall consecrate our ashes. Wherever courage is honored, through all time, shall Thermopylæ and the Spartan three hundred be remembered. Ours shall be an immortality such as no human glory has yet attained.

8. And when ages shall have swept by, and Sparta's last hour shall have come, then, even in her ruins, shall she be eloquent. Tyrants shall turn away from them, appalled; but the heroes of liberty—the poets, the sages, the historians of all time—shall invoke and bless the memory of the gallant three hundred of Leonidas!

25. SPEECH OF GALGACUS TO THE CALEDONIANS.

[GALGACUS was by far the bravest and the noblest of all the native chieftains of Britain, that met and resisted the encroachments of the Romans under Agricola. He is represented by Tacitus, a Roman historian, as addressing his followers,—a vast multitude encamped on the Grampian Hills, and eager for battle,—in the following forcible and spirited strain:]

AS often as I reflect on the origin of the war, and our necessities, I feel a strong conviction that this day, and your will, are about to lay the foundations of British liberty. For we have all known what slavery is, and no place of retreat lies behind us. The sea even is insecure when the Roman fleet hovers around.

2. Thus arms and war, ever coveted by the brave, are now the only refuge of the cowardly. In former actions in which the Britons fought with various success against the Romans, our valor was a resource to look to; for we, the noblest of all the nations, and, on that account, placed in its inmost recesses, unused to the spectacle of servitude, had our eyes even inviolate from its hateful sight.

3. We, the last of the earth, and of freedom, unknown to fame, have been hitherto defended by our remoteness; now the extreme limits of Britain appear, and the unknown is ever regarded as the magnificent. No refuge is behind us; naught but the rocks and the waves, and the deadlier Romans,—men whose pride you have in vain sought to depreciate by moderation and subservience.

4. The robbers of the globe, when the land fails, they scour the sea. Is the enemy rich? they are avaricious; is he poor? they are ambitious; the East and the West are unable to satiate their desires. Wealth and poverty are alike coveted by their rapacity. To carry off, massacre, seize on false pretences, they call empire; and, when they make a desert, they call it peace.

5. Nature has made children and relations dearest to all: they are carried off by levies to serve elsewhere. Our goods and fortunes they seize on as tribute, our corn as supplies;

our very bodies and hands they wear out, amid strife and contumely, in fortifying stations in the woods and marshes.

6. Serfs born in servitude are once bought, and ever after fed by their masters; Britain alone daily buys its slavery, daily feeds it. As in families the last slave purchased is often a laughing-stock to the rest, so we, the last whom they have reduced to slavery, are the first to be agonized by their contumely, and reserved for destruction.

7. We have neither fields, nor minerals, nor harbors, in working which we can be employed: the valor and fierceness of the vanquished are obnoxious to the victors: our very distance and obscurity, as they render us the safer, make us the more suspected. Laying aside, therefore, all hope of pardon, assume the courage of men to whom salvation and glory are alike dear.

8. The Trinobantes, under a female leader, had courage to burn a colony and storm castles; and, had not their success rendered them negligent, they would have cast off the yoke. We, untouched and unconquered, nursed in freedom, shall we not show, on the first onset, what men Caledonia has nursed in her bosom?

9. Do not believe the Romans have the same prowess in war as lust in peace. They have grown great on our divisions; they know how to turn the vices of men to the glory of their own army. As it has been drawn together by success, so disaster will dissolve it, unless you suppose that the Gauls and the Germans, and, I am ashamed to say, many of the Britons, who now lend their blood to a foreign usurpation, and in their hearts are rather enemies than slaves, can be etained by faith and affection.

10. Fear and terror are but slender bonds of attachment; when you remove them, as fear ceases, terror begins. All the incitements of victory are on our side: no wives inflame the Romans; no parents are there, to call shame on their flight; they have no country, or it is elsewhere. Few in number, fearful from ignorance, gazing on unknown woods and seas,

the Gods have delivered them, shut in and bound, into your hands. Let not their vain aspect, the glitter of silver and gold, which neither covers nor wounds, alarm you.

11. In the very line of the enemy we shall find our friends; the Britons will recognize their own cause; the Gauls will recollect their former freedom; the other Germans will desert them, as lately the Usipii have done. No objects of terror are behind them; naught but empty castles, age-ridden colonies, dissension between cruel masters and unwilling slaves, sick and discordant cities.

12. Here is a leader, an army; there are tributes and payments, and the badges of servitude, which to bear forever, or instantly to avenge, lies in your arms. Go forth, then, into the field, and think of your ancestors and your descendants

TACITUS.

---

26. TITUS QUINTIUS AGAINST QUARRELS BETWEEN THE SENATE AND THE PEOPLE.

THOUGH I am conscious of no fault, O Romans, it is yet with the utmost shame I have come forward to your Assembly. You have seen it—posterity will know it—that, in my fourth consulate, the Æquans and Volscians came in arms to the very gates of Rome, and went away unchastised! Had I foreseen that such an ignominy had been reserved for my official year,—that Rome might have been taken while I was Consul,—I would have shunned the office, either by exile or by death.

2. Yes; I have had honors enough,—of life more than enough! I should have died in my third consulate. Whom did these most dastardly enemies despise?—us, Consuls, or you, citizens? If we are in fault, depose us,—punish us as we deserve. If you, Romans, are to blame, may neither Gods nor men make you suffer for your offences!—only may you repent.

3. No, Romans, the confidence of our enemies is not from a belief in their own courage, or in your cowardice. They have been too often vanquished, not to know both themselves and you. Discord, discord amongst ourselves, is the ruin of this city. The eternal disputes between the Senate and the People are the sole cause of our misfortune.

4. In the name of Heaven, what is it, Romans, you would have? You desired Tribunes of the commons For the sake of concord, we granted Tribunes. You were eager to have Decemvirs. We suffered them to be created. You grew weary of Decemvirs. We compelled them to abdicate. You insisted on the restoration of the Tribuneship. We yielded. You invaded our rights. We have borne, and still bear.

5. What termination is there to be to these dissensions? When shall we have a united city? When one common country? With the enemy at our gates,—with the Volscian foe scaling your rampart,—there is no one to hinder it. But against *us* you are valiant,—against us you diligently take up arms!

6. Come on, then. Besiege the Senate-house. Make a camp of the Forum. Fill the jails with our chief nobles. Then sally out with the same determined spirit against the enemy. Does your resolution fail? Look, then, to see your lands ravaged, your houses plundered and in flames, the whole country laid waste with fire and sword.

7. Extinguish, O Romans, these fatal divisions! Break the spell of this enchantment, which renders you powerless and inactive! If you will but summon up the ancient Roman courage, and follow your Consuls to the field, I will submit to any punishment, if I do not rout and put to flight these ravagers of our territories, and transfer to their own cities the terror of war.

LIVY.

27. RICHARD TO THE PRINCES OF THE CRUSADE.

AND is it even so? And are our brethren at such pains to note the infirmities of our natural temper, and the rough precipitance of our zeal, which may have sometimes urged us to issue commands when there was little time to hold council? I could not have thought that offences, casual and unpremeditated, like mine, could find such deep root in the hearts of my allies in this most holy cause, that for my sake they should withdraw their hand from the plough when the furrow was near the end; for my sake turn aside from the direct path to Jerusalem which their swords have opened.

2. I vainly thought that my small services might have outweighed my rash errors; that if it were remembered that I pressed to the van in an assault, it would not be forgotten that I was ever the last in the retreat; that if I elevated my banner upon conquered fields of battle, it was all the advantage I sought, while others were dividing the spoil. I may have called the conquered city by my name, but it was to others that I yielded the dominion.

3. If I have been headstrong in urging bold counsels, I have not, methinks, spared my own blood, or my people's, in carrying them into as bold execution; or if I have, in the hurry of march or battle, assumed a command over the soldiers of others, such have ever been treated as my own, when my wealth purchased the provisions and medicines which their own sovereigns could not procure.

4. But it shames me to remind you of what all but myself seem to have forgotten. Let us rather look forward to our future measures; and believe me, brethren, you shall not find the pride, or the wrath, or the ambition of Richard, a stumbling-block of offence in the path to which religion and glory summon you, as with the trumpet of an archangel!

5. O, no, no! Never would I survive the thought that my frailties and infirmities had been the means to sever this goodly fellowship of assembled princes. I would cut off my left hand

with my right, could my doing so attest my sincerity. I will yield up, voluntarily, all right to command in the host even mine own liege subjects.

6. They shall be led by such sovereigns as you may nominate; and their king, ever but too apt to exchange the leader's baton for the adventurer's lance, will serve under the banner of Beauseant among the Templars—aye, or under that of Austria, if Austria will name a brave man to lead his forces.

7. Or, if ye are yourselves aweary of this war, and feel your armor chafe your tender bodies, leave but with Richard some ten or fifteen thousand of your soldiers to work out the accomplishment of your vow; and when Zion is won—when Zion is won—we will write upon her gates, *not* the name of Richard Plantagenet, but of those generous princes who intrusted him with the means of conquest! SIR WALTER SCOTT.

---

28. ALFRED THE GREAT TO HIS MEN.

MY friends, our country must be free! The land
Is never lost that has a son to right her—
And here are troops of sons, and loyal ones!
Strong in her children should a mother be.
Shall ours be helpless, that has sons like us?
God save our native land, whoever pays
The ransom that redeems her! Now, what wait we?
2. For Alfred's word to move upon the foe?
Upon him, then! Now think ye on the things
You most do love! Husbands and fathers, on
Their wives and children; lovers, on their beloved;
And *all*, upon their COUNTRY! When you use
Your weapons, think on the beseeching eyes,
To whet them, could have lent you tears for water!
O, now be men, or never! From your hearths
Thrust the unbidden feet, that from their nooks
Drove forth your aged sires—your wives and babes!

3. The couches your fair-handed daughters used
To spread, let not the vaunting stranger press,
Weary from spoiling you! Your roofs, that hear
The wanton riot of the intruding guest,
That mocks their masters—clear them for the sake
Of the manhood to which all that's precious clings,
Else perishes. The land that bore you—O!
Do honor to her! Let her glory in
Your breeding! Rescue her! Revenge her—or
Ne'er call her mother more! Come on, my friends!
4 And where you take your stand upon the field,
However you advance, resolve on this—
That you will ne'er recede, while from the tongues
Of age, and womanhood, and infancy,
The helplessness whose safety in you lies,
Invokes you to be strong! Come on! Come on!
I'll bring you to the foe! And when you meet him,
Strike hard! Strike home! Strike while a dying blow
Is in an arm! Strike till you're free, or fall!

KNOWLES.

---

29. THE BATTLE.

HEAVY and solemn,
   A cloudy column,
     Thro' the green plain they marching came!
Measureless spread, like a table dread,
For the wild grim dice of the iron game.
The looks are bent on the shaking ground,
And the heart beats loud with a knelling sound;
Swift by the breasts that must bear the brunt
Gallops the Major along the front,—
     "Halt!"
And fettered they stand at the stark command,
And the warriors, silent, halt!

II.

Proud in the blush of morning glowing,
What on the hill-top shines in flowing!
"See you the foeman's banners waving?"
"We see the foeman's banners waving!"

III.

God be with ye—children and wife!
Hark to the music—the trump and the fife,
How they ring through the ranks which they rouse to the
  strife!
Thrilling they sound with their glorious tone,
Thrilling they go through the marrow and bone!
Brothers, God grant when this life is o'er,
In the life to come that we meet once more!

IV.

See the smoke, how the lightning is clearing asunder!
Hark the guns, peal on peal, how they boom in their
  thunder!
From host to host, with kindling sound,
The shouting signal circles round;
Aye, shout it forth to life or death—
Freer already breathes the breath!
The war is waging, slaughter raging,
And heavy through the reeking pall
The iron death-dice fall!

V.

Nearer they close—foes upon foes—
"Ready!"—from square to square it goes.
Down on the knee they sank,
And the fire comes sharp on the foremost rank;
Many a man to the earth is sent,
Many a gap by the balls is rent—
O'er the corpse before springs the hinder man,
That the line may not fail to the fearless van.

To the right, to the left, and around and around,
Death whirls in its dance on the bloody ground.
God's sunlight is quenched in the fiery fight,
Over the host falls a brooding night!
Brothers, God grant when this life is o'er,
In the life to come that we meet once more!

VI.

The dead men lie bathed in the weltering blood,
And the living are blent in the slippery flood,
And the feet, as they reeling and sliding go,
Stumble still on the corpses that sleep below.
"What, Francis! Give Charlotte my last farewell."
As the dying man murmurs, the thunders swell—
"I'll give—O God! are the guns so near?
Ho! comrades!—yon volley!—look sharp to the rear!—
I'll give thy Charlotte thy last farewell.
Sleep soft! where death thickest descendeth in rain,
The friend thou forsakest thy side shall regain!"
Hitherward—thitherward reels the fight,
Dark and more darkly day glooms into night!
Brothers, God grant when this life is o'er,
In the life to come that we meet once more!

VII.

Hark to the hoofs that galloping go!
The adjutants flying—
The horsemen press hard on the panting foe,
Their thunder booms in dying—
    Victory!
The terror has seized on the dastards all,
And their colors fall!
    Victory!
Closed in the brunt of the glorious fight,
And the day, like a conqueror, burst on the night,

Trumpet and fife swelling choral along,
The triumph already sweeps marching in song.
Farewell, fallen brothers, though this life be o'er,
There's another in which we shall meet you once more!

SCHILLER.

---

80. BEFORE VICKSBURG.

["HEAD-QUARTERS 15TH ARMY CORPS,
"CAMP ON BIG BLACK RIVER, August 8, 1863.

"*To the Hon. Secretary of War:—*

"SIR:—I take the liberty of asking through you that something be done for a lad named Orion P. Howe, of Waukegan, Illinois, who belongs to the 55th Illinois, but at present at home wounded. I think he is too young for West Point, but would be the very thing for a midshipman.

"When the assault at Vicksburg was at its height, on the 19th of May, and I was in front near the road, which formed my line of attack, this young lad came up to me, wounded and bleeding, with a good, healthy boy's cry, 'General Sherman, send some cartridges to Colonel Malmborg: the men are nearly all out.' 'What is the matter, my boy?' 'They shot me in the leg, sir; but I can go to the hospital. Send the cartridges right away.' Even where we stood the shot fell thick, and I told him to go to the rear at once, I would attend to the cartridges; and off he limped. Just before he disappeared on the hill, he turned, and called, as loud as he could, 'Calibre 54.' I have not seen the lad since, and his colonel (Malmborg), on inquiry, gives me the address as above, and says he is a bright, intelligent boy, with a fair preliminary education.

"What arrested my attention then was—and what renewed my memory of the fact now is—that one so young, carrying a musket-ball through his leg, should have found his way to me on that fatal spot, and delivered his message, not forgetting the very important part, even, of the calibre of his musket,—54,—which, you know, is an unusual one.

"I'll warrant that the boy has in him the elements of a man, and I commend him to the Government as one worthy the fostering care of some one of its national institutions.

"I am, with respect, your obedient servant,
"W. T. SHERMAN, *Major-General Commanding.*"]

WHILE Sherman stood beneath the hottest fire,
 That from the lines of Vicksburg gleamed,
And bomb-shells tumbled in their smoky gyre,
 And grape-shot hissed, and case-shot screamed;
  Back from the front there came,
  Weeping and sorely lame,

The merest child, the youngest face
Man ever saw in such a fearful place.

2. Stifling his tears, he limped his chief to meet;
But when he paused, and tottering stood,
Around the circle of his little feet
There spread a pool of bright, young blood.
Shocked at his doleful case,
Sherman cried, "Halt! front face!
Who are you? Speak, my gallant boy!"
"A drummer, sir:—Fifty-fifth Illinois."

3. "Are you not hit?" "That's nothing. Only send
Some cartridges: our men are out;
And the foe press us." "But, my little friend—"
"Don't mind me! Did you hear that shout?
What if our men be driven;
O, for the love of Heaven,
Send to my Colonel, General dear!"
"But you?" "O, I shall easily find the rear."

4. "I'll see to that," cried Sherman; and a drop,
Angels might envy, dimmed his eye,
As the boy, toiling towards the hill's hard top,
Turned round, and with his shrill child's cry
Shouted, "O, don't forget!
We'll win the battle yet!
But let our soldiers have some more,
More cartridges, sir,—calibre fifty-four!"

---

31. THE ALARM—APRIL 19, 1775.

DARKNESS closed upon the country and upon the town, but it was no night for sleep. Heralds on swift relays of horses transmitted the war-message from hand to hand, till village repeated it to village; the sea to the backwoods; the plains to the highlands; and it was never suffered to droop, till it had been borne North, and South, and East, and West, throughout the land.

2. It spread over the bays that receive the Saco and the Penobscot. Its loud reveille broke the rest of the trappers of New Hampshire, and ringing like bugle-notes from peak o peak, overleapt the Green Mountains, swept onward to Montreal, and descended the ocean river, till the responses were echoed from the cliffs of Quebec. The hills along the Hudson told to one another the tale.

3. As the summons hurried to the South, it was one day at New York; in one more at Philadelphia; the next it lighted a watch-fire at Baltimore; thence it waked an answer at Annapolis. Crossing the Potomac near Mount Vernon, it was sent forward without a halt to Williamsburg. It traversed the Dismal Swamp to Nansemond, along the route of the first emigrants to North Carolina.

4. It moved onwards and still onwards through boundless groves of evergreen to Newbern and to Wilmington. "For God's sake, forward it by night and by day," wrote Cornelius Harnett, by the express which sped for Brunswick. Patriots of South Carolina caught up its tones at the border and dispatched it to Charleston, and through pines and palmettos and moss-clad live oaks, further to the South, till it resounded among the New England settlements beyond the Savannah

5. Hillsborough and the Mecklenburg district of North Carolina rose in triumph, now that their wearisome uncertainty had its end. The Blue Ridge took up the voice and made it heard from one end to the other of the valley of Virginia. The Alleghanies, as they listened, opened their barriers that the "loud call" might pass through to the hardy riflemen on the Holston, the Watauga and the French Broad.

6. Ever renewing its strength, powerful enough even to create a commonwealth, it breathed its inspiring word to the first settlers of Kentucky; so that the hunters who made their halt in the matchless valley of Elkhorn commemorated

the nineteenth day of April, by naming their encampment LEXINGTON.

7. With one impulse the colonies sprung to arms ; with one spirit they pledged themselves to each other "to be ready for the extreme event ;" with one heart the continent cried " Liberty or death !" BANCROFT.

---

82. PAUL REVERE'S RIDE.

LISTEN, my children, and you shall hear
Of the midnight ride of Paul Revere,
On the eighteenth of April, in Seventy-Five :
Hardly a man is now alive
Who remembers that famous day and year.

2. He said to his friend,—" If the British march
By land or sea from the town to-night,
Hang a lantern aloft in the belfry-arch
Of the North-Church tower, as a signal-light,—
One if by land, and two if by sea ;
And I on the opposite shore will be,
Ready to ride and spread the alarm
Through every Middlesex village and farm,
For the country-folks to be up and to arm."

3. Then he said good-night, and with muffled oar
Silently rowed to the Charlestown shore,
Just as the moon rose over the bay,
Where swinging wide at her moorings lay
The Somerset, British man-of-war :
A phantom ship, with each mast and spar
Across the moon, like a prison-bar,
And a huge, black hulk, that was magnified
By its own reflection in the tide.

4. Meanwhile, his friend, through alley and street
Wanders and watches with eager ears,

Till in the silence around him he hears
The muster of men at the barrack-door,
The sound of arms, and the tramp of feet,
And the measured tread of the grenadiers
Marching down to their boats on the shore.

5. Then he climbed to the tower of the church,
Up the wooden stairs, with stealthy tread,
To the belfry-chamber overhead,
And startled the pigeons from their perch
On the sombre rafters, that round him made
Masses and moving shapes of shade,—
Up the light ladder, slender and tall,
To the highest window in the wall,
Where he paused to listen and look down
A moment on the roofs of the town,
And the moonlight flowing over all.

6. Beneath, in the church-yard, lay the dead
In their night-encampment on the hill,
Wrapped in silence so deep and still,
That he could hear, like a sentinel's tread,
The watchful night-wind, as it went
Creeping along from tent to tent,
And seeming to whisper, "All is well!"
A moment only he feels the spell
Of the place and the hour, the secret dread
Of the lonely belfry and the dead;
For suddenly all his thoughts are bent
On a shadowy something far away,
Where the river widens to meet the bay,—
A line of black, that bends and floats
On the rising tide, like a bridge of boats.

7. Meanwhile, impatient to mount and ride,
Booted and spurred, with a heavy stride,

On the opposite shore walked Paul Revere.
Now he patted his horse's side,
Now gazed on the landscape far and near,
Then impetuous stamped the earth,
And turned and tightened his saddle-girth;
But mostly he watched with eager search
The belfry-tower of the old North Church,
As it rose above the graves on the hill,
Lonely, and spectral, and sombre, and still.

8. And lo! as he looks, on the belfry's height,
A glimmer, and then a gleam of light!
He springs to the saddle, the bridle he turns,
But lingers and gazes, till full on his sight
A second lamp in the belfry burns!

9. A hurry of hoofs in a village-street,
A shape in the moonlight, a bulk in the dark,
And beneath from the pebbles, in passing, a spark
Struck out by a steed that flies fearless and fleet:
That was all! And yet, through the gloom and the light,
The fate of a nation was riding that night;
And the spark struck out by that steed, in his flight,
Kindled the land into flame with its heat.

10. It was twelve by the village-clock,
When he crossed the bridge into Medford town:
He heard the crowing of the cock,
And the barking of the farmer's dog,
And felt the damp of the river-fog,
That rises when the sun goes down.

11. It was one by the village-clock,
When he rode into Lexington.
He saw the gilded weathercock
Swim in the moonlight as he passed,
And the meeting-house windows, blank and bare,
Gaze at him with a spectral glare,

As if they already stood aghast
At the bloody work they would look upon.

12. It was two by the village-clock,
When he came to the bridge in Concord town.
He heard the bleating of the flock,
And the twitter of birds among the trees,
And felt the breath of the morning-breeze
Blowing over the meadows brown.
And one was safe and asleep in his bed
Who at the bridge would be first to fall,
Who that day would be lying dead,
Pierced by a British musket-ball.

13. You know the rest. In the books you have read
How the British regulars fired and fled,—
How the farmers gave them ball for ball,
From behind each fence and farm-yard wall,
Chasing the red-coats down the lane,
Then crossing the fields to emerge again
Under the trees at the turn of the road,
And only pausing to fire and load.

14. So through the night rode Paul Revere;
And so through the night went his cry of alarm
To every Middlesex village and farm,—
A cry of defiance, and not of fear,—
A voice in the darkness, a knock at the door,
And a word that shall echo for evermore !
For, borne on the night-wind of the Past,
Through all our history, to the last,
In the hour of darkness and peril and need,
The people will waken and listen to hear
The hurrying hoof-beat of that steed,
And the midnight-message of Paul Revere.

LONGFELLOW.

83. MACBRIAR'S SPEECH TO THE SCOTCH INSURGENTS.

SET up a standard in the land; blow a trumpet upon the mountains; let not the shepherd tarry by his sheepfold, nor the seedsman continue in the ploughed field, but make the watch strong, sharpen the arrows, burnish the shields, name ye the captains of thousands, and captains of hundreds, of fifties, and of tens; call the footmen like the rushing of winds, and cause the horsemen to come up like the sound of many waters; for the passages of the destroyers are stopped, their rods are burned, and the face of their men of battle hath been turned to flight.

2. Heaven has been with you, and has broken the bow of the mighty; then let every man's heart be as the heart of the valiant Maccabeus,—every man's hand as the hand of the mighty Samson,—every man's sword as that of Gideon, which turned not back from the slaughter; for the banner of Reformation is spread abroad in the mountains in its first loveliness, and the gates of hell shall not prevail against it.

3. Well is he this day that shall barter his house for a helmet, and sell his garment for a sword, and cast in his lot with the children of the Covenant, even to the fulfilling of the promise; and woe, woe unto him, who, for carnal ends and self-seeking, shall withhold himself from the great work; for the curse shall abide with him, even the bitter curse of Meroz, because he came not to the help of the Lord against the mighty.

4. Up, then, and be doing; the blood of martyrs, recking upon scaffolds, is crying for vengeance; the bones of saints, which lie whitening in the highways, are pleading for retribution; the groans of innocent captives from desolate isles of the sea, and from the dungeons of the tyrant's high place, cry for deliverance; the prayers of persecuted Christians, sheltering themselves in dens and deserts, from the swords of their persecutors, famished with hunger, starving with cold lacking fire food, shelter and clothing, because

they serve God rather than man,—all are with you pleading, watching, knocking, storming the gates of Heaven in your behalf.

5. Heaven itself shall fight for you, as the stars in their courses fought against Sisera. Then, whoso will deserve immortal fame in this world, and eternal happiness in that which is to come, let them enter into God's service, and take arles at the hand of the servant,—a blessing, namely, upon him and his household, and his children, to the ninth generation,—even the blessing of the promise, forever and ever.

SCOTT.

84. SPANISH WAR SONG

I.

FLING forth the proud banner of Leon again;
Let the watchword, Castile, go resounding through Spain!
And thou, free Asturias, encamped on the height,
Pour down thy dark sons to the vintage of fight;
Wake! wake! the old soil where our warriors repose
Rings hollow and deep to the trampling foes.

II.

The voices are mighty that swell from the past,
With Aragon's cry on the shrill mountain blast;
The ancient Sierras give strength to our tread,
Their pines murmur song where bright blood hath been shed.
Fling forth the proud banner of Leon again,
And shout ye, "Castile! to the rescue for Spain!"

85. SPARTACUS TO THE GLADIATORS

IT had been a day of triumph in Capua. Lentulus, returning with victorious eagles, had amused the populace with the sports of the amphitheatre, to an extent hitherto unknown, even in that luxurious city. The shouts of revelry had died away; the roar of the lion had ceased; the last loiterer had retired from the banquet, and the lights in the palace of the victor were extinguished.

2. The moon, piercing the tissue of fleecy clouds, silvered the dew-drop on the corselet of the Roman sentinel, and tipped the dark waters of Volturnus with wavy, tremulous light. It was a night of holy calm, when the zephyr sways the young spring leaves, and whispers among the hollow reeds its dreamy music. No sound was heard but the last sob of some weary wave, telling its story to the smooth pebbles of the beach, and then all was still as the breast when the spirit has departed.

3. In the deep recesses of the amphitheatre a band of gladiators were crowded together,—their muscles still knotted with the agony of conflict, the foam upon their lips, and the scowl of battle yet lingering upon their brows,—when Spartacus, rising in the midst of that grim assemblage, thus addressed them:

4. "Ye call me chief, and ye do well to call him chief, who, for twelve long years, has met upon the arena every shape of man or beast that the broad empire of Rome could furnish, and yet never has lowered his arm. And if there be one among you who can say that ever, in public fight or private brawl, my actions did belie my tongue, let him step forth and say it. If there be three in all your throng dare face me on the bloody sand, let them come on!

5. "Yet, I was not always thus, a hired butcher, a savage chief of savage men. My father was a reverent man, who feared great Jupiter, and brought to the rural deities his offerings of fruits and flowers. He dwelt among the vine-clad rocks and olive groves at the foot of Helicon. My early life

ran quiet as the brook by which I sported. I was taught to prune the vine, to tend the flock; and then, at noon, I gathered my sheep beneath the shade, and played upon the shepherd's flute. I had a friend, the son of our neighbor; we led our flocks to the same pasture, and shared together our rustic meal.

6. "One evening, after the sheep were folded, and we were all seated beneath the myrtle that shaded our cottage, my grandsire, an old man, was telling of Marathon and Leuctra, and how, in ancient times, a little band of Spartans, in a defile of the mountains, withstood a whole army. I did not then know what war meant; but my cheeks burned, I knew not why; and I clasped the knees of that venerable man, till my mother, parting the hair from off my brow, kissed my throbbing temples, and bade me go to rest, and think no more of those old tales and savage wars.

7. "That very night the Romans landed on our shore, and the clash of steel was heard within our quiet vale. I saw the breast that had nourished me trampled by the iron hoof of the war-horse; the bleeding body of my father flung amid the blazing rafters of our dwelling.

8. "To-day I killed a man in the arena, and when I broke his helmet clasps, behold! it was my friend! He knew me,— smiled faintly,—gasped,—and died. The same sweet smile that I had marked upon his face, when, in adventurous boyhood, we scaled some lofty cliff to pluck the first ripe grapes, and bear them home in childish triumph.

9. "I told the Prætor he was my friend, noble and brave, and I begged his body, that I might burn it upon the funeral pile, and mourn over it. Ay, on my knees, amid the dust and blood of the arena, I begged that boon, while all the Roman maids and matrons, and those holy virgins they call vestal, and the rabble, shouted in mockery, deeming it rare sport, forsooth, to see Rome's fiercest gladiator turn pale, and tremble like a very child, before that piece of bleeding clay; but the Prætor drew back as if I were pollution, and sternly said,

10. "'Let the carrion rot! There are no noble men but Romans!' And he, deprived of funeral rites, must wander a helpless ghost, beside the waters of that sluggish river, and look—and look—and look in vain to the bright Elysian fields where dwell his ancestors and noble kindred. And so must you, and so must I, die like dogs!

11. "O Rome! Rome! thou hast been a tender nurse to me! Ay, thou hast given to that poor, gentle, timid shepherd lad, who never knew a harsher sound than a flute-note, muscles of iron, and a heart of flint; taught him to drive the sword through rugged brass and plaited mail, and warm it in the marrow of his foe! to gaze into the glaring eyeballs of the fierce Numidian lion, even as a smooth-cheeked boy upon a laughing girl. And he shall pay thee back till thy yellow Tiber is red as frothing wine, and in its deepest ooze thy life-blood lies curdled!

12. "Ye stand here now like giants, as ye are! the strength of brass is in your toughened sinews; but to-morrow some Roman Adonis, breathing sweet odors from his curly locks, shall come, and with his lily fingers pat your brawny shoulders, and bet his sesterces upon your blood! Hark! Hear ye yon lion roaring in his den? 'Tis three days since he tasted meat; but to-morrow he shall break his fast upon your flesh; and ye shall be a dainty meal for him!

13. "If ye are brutes, then stand here like fat oxen waiting for the butcher's knife; if ye are men, follow me! strike down yon sentinel, and gain the mountain passes, and there do bloody work as did your sires at old Thermopylæ! Is Sparta dead? Is the old Grecian spirit frozen in your veins, that ye do crouch and cower like base-born slaves, beneath your master's lash? O! comrades! warriors! Thracians! if we must fight, let us fight for ourselves; if we must slaughter, let us slaughter our oppressors; if we must die, let us die under the open sky, by the bright waters, in noble, honorable battle."

86. THE BATTLE HYMN.

[KARL THEODORE KÖRNER was born September 23, 1791, at Dresden, Saxony, and was killed in battle against the French, August 26, 1813. He wrote dramas and lyrical poems,—of which latter, many are full of patriotic feeling and warlike spirit. In Germany, when the whole people are called upon to take arms in defence of their country, the name of Landsturm is given o the military force thus raised.]

I.

FATHER of earth and Heaven! I call thy name!
  Round me the smoke and shout of battle roll;
My eyes are dazzled with the rustling flame;
  Father, sustain an untried soldier's soul.
  Or life, or death, whatever be the goal
That crowns or closes round this struggling hour,
  Thou knowest, if ever from my spirit stole
One deeper prayer, 'twas that no cloud might lower
On my young fame!—O hear! God of eternal power!

II.

God! thou art merciful! The wintry storm,
  The cloud that pours the thunder from its womb,
But show the sterner grandeur of thy form;
  The lightnings, glancing through the midnight gloom,
  To Faith's raised eye, as calm, as lovely come,
As splendors of the autumnal evening star,
  As roses shaken by the breeze's plume,
When like cool incense comes the dewy air,
And on the golden wave the sunset burns afar.

III.

God! thou art mighty! At thy footstool bound,
  Lie gazing to thee, Chance, and Life, and Death;
Nor in the Angel-circle flaming round,
  Nor in the million worlds that blaze beneath,
  Is one that can withstand thy wrath's hot breath.
Woe in thy frown—in thy smile victory!
  Hear my last prayer! I ask no mortal wreath;

Let but these eyes my rescued country see,
Then take my spirit, All Omnipotent, to thee.

IV.

Now for the fight—now for the cannon peal—
  Forward—through blood, and toil, and cloud, and fire!
Glorious the shout, the shock, the crash of steel,
  The volley's roll, the rocket's blasting spire;
  They shake—like broken waves their squares retire,—
On them, hussars! Now give them rein and heel;
  Think of the orphaned child, the murdered sire:—
Earth cries for blood:—in thunder on them wheel!
This hour to Europe's fate shall set the triumph-seal!

                      K. T. KÖRNER.

---

87. FLODDEN FIELD.

[In the following extract from "Marmion," in which Scott describes the battle of Flodden Field, 1513, the English, under the Earl of Surrey, defeated with great slaughter the Scotch. Lord Jeffrey, in his able review of "Marmion," says: "Of all the poetical battles which have been fought from the days of Homer to those of Mr. Southey, there is none, in our opinion, at all comparable for interest and animation, for breadth of drawing and magnificence of effect, with this."]

BLOUNT and Fitz Eustace rested still,
  With Lady Clara upon the hill;
On which (for far the day was spent)
The western sunbeams now were bent.
The cry they heard, its meaning knew,
Could plain their distant comrades view:
2. Sadly to Blount did Eustace say,
    "Unworthy office here to stay!
No hope of gilded spurs to-day.
But see! look up—on Flodden bent,
The Scottish foe has fired his tent."
    And sudden, as he spoke,
From the sharp ridges of the hill,

    All downward to the banks of Till,
      Was wreathed in sable smoke.
3. Volumed and fast, and rolling far,
    The cloud enveloped Scotland's war,
      As down the hill they broke;
    Nor martial shout, nor minstrel tone,
    Announced their march; their tread alone,
    At times one warning trumpet blown,
      At times a stifled hum,
    Told England, from his mountain-throne
      King James did rushing come.
4. Scarce could they hear or see their foes,
    Until at weapon-point they close.
    They close, in clouds of smoke and dust,
    With sword-sway, and with lance's thrust;
      And such a yell was there,
    Of sudden and portentous birth,
    As if men fought upon the earth,
      And fiends in upper air;
    O life and death were in the shout,
    Recoil and rally, charge and rout,
      And triumph and despair.
5. Long look'd the anxious squires; their eye
    Could in the darkness naught descry.
    At length the freshening western blast
    Aside the shroud of battle cast;
    And, first, the ridge of mingled spears
    Above the brightening cloud appears;
    And in the smoke the pennons flew,
    As in the storm the white sea-mew.
6. Then mark'd they, dashing broad and far,
    The broken billows of the war,
    And pluméd crests of chieftains brave,
    Floating like foam upon the wave;
      But naught distinct they see.
    Wide raged the battle on the plain;

Spears shook, and falchions flash'd amain;
Fell England's arrow-flight like rain;
Crests rose, and stoop'd, and rose again,
    Wild and disorderly.

7. Far on the left, unseen the while,
Stanley broke Lennox and Argyle;
Though there the western mountaineer
Rushed with bare bosom on the spear,
And flung the feeble targe aside,
And with both hands the broadsword plied,
'Twas vain:—But Fortune, on the right,
With fickle smile, cheered Scotland's fight.

8. Then fell that spotless banner white,
    The Howard's lion fell;
Yet still Lord Marmion's falcon flew
With wavering flight, while fiercer grew
    Around the battle-yell.
The Border slogan rent the sky.
A Home! a Gordon! was the cry;
    Loud were the changing blows;
Advanced,—forced back,—now low, now high
    The pennon sunk and rose;
As bends the bark's mast in the gale,
When rent are rigging, shrouds, and sail,
    It wavered 'mid the foes.

9. No longer Blount the view could bear:
    "By Heaven and all its saints! I swear
    I will not see it lost!
Fitz Eustace, you, with Lady Clare,
May bid your beads, and patter prayer,—
    I gallop to the host."
And to the fray he rode amain,
Followed by all the archer train.

10. The fiery youth, with desperate cnarge,
Made, for a space, an opening large,—
    The rescued banner rose,—

But darkly closed the war around,
Like pine-tree, rooted from the ground,
   It sank among the foes.
Then Eustace mounted too;—yet staid,
As loath to leave the helpless maid,
   When, fast as shaft can fly,

11. Blood-shot his eyes, his nostrils spread,
The loose rein dangling from his head,
Housing and saddle bloody red,
   Lord Marmion's steed rushed by;
And Eustace, maddening at the sight,
A look and sign to Clara cast,
To mark he would return in haste,
   Then plunged into the fight.

12. Ask me not what the maiden feels,
   Left in that dreadful hour alone:
Perchance her reason stoops, or reels;
   Perchance a courage, not her own,
   Braces her mind to desperate tone.
The scatter'd van of England's wheels;—
She only said, as loud in air
The tumult roar'd, "Is Wilton there?"—
They fly, or, madden'd by despair,
Fight but to die,—"Is Wilton there?"   SCOTT.

---

88. FLODDEN FIELD—(CONCLUDED.)

WITH that, straight up the hill there rode,
   Two horsemen drench'd with gore,
And in their arms, a helpless load,
   A wounded knight they bore.
His hand still strain'd the broken brand;
His arms were smear'd with blood and sand:
Dragg'd from among the horses' feet,
With dinted shield, and helmet beat,

The falcon-crest and plumage gone:
2. Can that be haughty Marmion!—
When, doff'd his casque, he felt free air,
Around 'gan Marmion wildly stare:—
   "Where's Harry Blount? Fitz Eustace where?
Linger ye here, ye hearts of hare!
Redeem my pennon,—charge again!
Cry—'Marmion to the rescue!'—vain!
Last of my race, on battle-plain
That shout shall ne'er be heard again!—
3. Yet my last thought is England's—fly,
   To Dacre bear my signet-ring:
   Tell him his squadrons up to bring.
Fitz Eustace, to Lord Surrey hie;
Tunstall lies dead upon the field.
His life-blood stains the spotless shield:
Edmund is down:—my life is reft;
The Admiral alone is left.
Let Stanley charge with spur of fire,—
With Chester charge and Lancashire,
Full upon Scotland's central host,
Or victory and England's lost.
4. Must I bid twice?—hence, varlets! fly!
Leave Marmion here, alone—to die!"
They parted, and alone he lay:
Clare drew her from the sight away,
Till pain wrung forth a lowly moan,
And half he murmured,—"Is there none
   Of all my halls have nurst,
Page, squire, or groom, one cup to bring
Of blesséd water from the spring
   To slake my dying thirst!"
5. O, woman! in our hours of ease,
Uncertain, coy, and hard to please,
And variable as the shade
By the light quivering aspen made;

When pain and anguish wring the brow,
A ministering angel thou!—
6. Scarce were the piteous accents said,
When, with the Baron's casque, the maid
 To the nigh streamlet ran:
Forgot were hatred, wrongs, and fears;
The plaintive voice alone she hears,
 Sees but the dying man.
7. She fill'd the helm, and back she hied,
And with surprise and joy espied
 A monk supporting Marmion's head;
A pious man whom duty brought
To dubious verge of battle fought,
 To shrive the dying, bless the dead.
8. The war, that for a space did fail,
Now trebly thundering swell'd the gale,
 And—Stanley! was the cry;—
A light on Marmion's visage spread,
 And fired his glazing eye:
9. With dying hand, above his head,
He shook the fragment of his blade,
 And shouted, "Victory!—
Charge, Chester, charge! On, Stanley, on!"
Were the last words of Marmion.
By this, though deep the evening fell,
Still rose the battle's deadly swell,
For still the Scots, around their king,
Unbroken, fought in desperate ring.
10. The English shafts in volleys hail'd,
In headlong charge their horse assail'd,
Front, flank, and rear, the squadrons sweep,
To break the Scottish circle deep,
 That fought around their king.
But yet, though thick the shafts as snow,
Though charging knights like whirlwinds go,
Though billmen ply the ghastly blow,
 Unbroken was the ring;

11. The stubborn spearmen still made good
　　Their dark impenetrable wood,
　　　Each stepping where his comrade stood,
　　　　The instant that he fell.
　　No thought was there of dastard flight;
　　Link'd in the serried phalanx tight,
　　Groom fought like noble, squire like knight,
　　　　As fearlessly and well;
　　Till utter darkness closed her wing
　　O'er their thin host and wounded king.

12. Then skilful Surrey's sage commands
　　Led back from strife his shattered bands;
　　　And from the charge they drew,
　　As mountain-waves, from wasted lands,
　　　Sweep back to ocean blue.
　　Then did their loss his foemen know;
　　Their king, their lords, their mightiest, low,
　　They melted from the field as snow,
　　When streams are swoln, and south winds blow,
　　　　Dissolves in silent dew.

13. Tweed's echoes heard the ceaseless plash,
　　　While many a broken band,
　　Disorder'd, through her currents dash,
　　　To gain the Scottish land;
　　To town and tower, to down and dale,
　　To tell red Flodden's dismal tale,
　　And raise the universal wail.
　　Tradition, legend, time and song,
　　Shall many an age that wail prolong;
　　Still from the sire the son shall hear
　　Of the stern strife and carnage drear
　　　　Of Flodden's fatal field,
　　Where shivered was fair Scotland's spear,
　　　　And broken was her shield.

89. EDINBURGH AFTER FLODDEN.

[Mr. AYTOUN is not inferior to Scott in his description of the heart-breaking sorrow with which the news of this battle was received in Edin'urgh.]

NEWS of battle!—news of battle!
  Hark! 'tis ringing down the street;
And the archways and the pavement
  Bear the clang of hurrying feet.
News of battle!—who hath brought it?
  News of triumph!—who should bring
Tidings from our noble army,
  Greetings from our gallant king?

2. All last night we watched the beacons
  Blazing on the hills afar,
Each one bearing, as it kindled,
  Message of the opened war.
All night long the northern streamers
  Shot across the trembling sky:
Fearful lights, that never beacon
  Save when kings or heroes die.

3. News of battle!—who hath brought it?
  All are thronging to the gate;
"Warder—warder! open quickly!
  Man—is this a time to wait?"
And the heavy gates are opened:
  Then a murmur long and loud,
And a cry of fear and wonder,
  Bursts from out the bending crowd.

4. For they see in battered harness
  Only one hard-stricken man;
And his weary steed is wounded,
  And his cheek is pale and wan:

Spearless hangs a bloody banner
  In his weak and drooping hand—
God! can that be Randolph Murray,
  Captain of the city band?

5. Round him crush the people, crying,
  "Tell us all—O, tell us true!
Where are they who went to battle,
  Randolph Murray, sworn to you?
Where are they, our brothers—children,—
  Have they met the English foe?
Why art thou alone, unfollowed?
  Is it weal or is it woe?

6. Like a corpse the grisly warrior
  Looks from out his helm of steel;
But no word he speaks in answer—
  Only with his arméd heel
Chides his weary steed, and onward
  Up the city streets they ride;
Fathers, sisters, mothers, children,
  Shrieking, praying by his side.

7. "By the God that made thee, Randolph!
  Tell us what mischance hath come."
Then he lifts his riven banner,
  And the asker's voice is dumb.
The elders of the city
  Have met within their hall—
The men whom good King James had charged
  To watch the tower and wall.

8. Then in came Randolph Murray,—
  His step was slow and weak,
And as he doffed his dinted helm,
  The tears ran down his cheek:

They fell upon his corselet,
  And on his mailéd hand,
As he gazed around him wistfully,
  Leaning sorely on his brand.

9. And none who then beheld him
    But straight were smote with fear;
  For a bolder and a sterner man
    Had never couched a spear.
  Ay! ye may well look upon it—
    There is more than honor there,
  Else be sure, I had not brought it
    From the field of dark despair.

10. Never yet was royal banner
      Steeped in such a costly dye;
    It hath lain upon a bosom
      Where no other shroud shall lie.
    Sirs! I charge you, keep it holy,
      Keep it as a sacred thing,
    For the stain ye see upon it
      Was the life-blood of your king!

11. Woe, woe, and lamentation!
      What a piteous cry was there!
    Widows, maidens, mothers, children,
      Shrieking, sobbing in despair!
    Through the streets the death-word rushes,
      Spreading terror, sweeping on—
    Jesu Christ! Our king has fallen;
      O, great God! King James is gone!

12. Holy Mother Mary, shield us!
      Thou, who erst didst lose thy Son!
    Oh, the blackest day for Scotland
      That she ever knew before!

Oh our king—the good, the noble,
  Shall we see him never more?

13. Woe to us, and woe to Scotland,
  Oh, our sons, our sons and men!
Surely some have 'scaped the Southron,
  Surely some will come again,
Till the oak that fell last winter
  Shall uprear its shattered stem:
Wives and mothers, Dunedin,
  Ye may look in vain for them!

WILLIAM EDMONDSTOUNE AYTOUN.

---

40. THE LIGHT BRIGADE.

[This spirited poem describes a gallant and desperate charge made at the battle of Balaklava, during the war in the Crimea in 1854. It is supposed that the order to charge was given under a mistake; but of this nothing definite is known, as Captain Nolan, who gave the order, was the first man who fell. Six hundred and thirty rushed to the charge, and only one hundred and fifty ever returned.]

HALF a league, half a league,
  Half a league onward,
All in the valley of Death
  Rode the six hundred.
"Forward, the Light Brigade!
Charge for the guns!" he said:
Into the valley of *Death*
  Rode the six hundred.

2. "Forward, the Light Brigade!"
Was there a man dismay'd?
Not tho' the soldier knew
  Some one had blunder'd:
Theirs not to make reply,
Theirs not to reason why,

Theirs but to do and die:
Into the valley of Death
　Rode the six hundred.

3. Cannon to right of them,
Cannon to left of them,
Cannon in front of them
　Volley'd and thunder'd:
Storm'd at with shot and shell,
Boldly they rode and well,
Into the jaws of Death,
Into the mouth of Hell,
　Rode the six hundred.

4. Flash'd all their sabres bare,
Flash'd as they turn'd in air,
Sabring the gunners there,
Charging an army, while
　All the world wonder'd:
Plunged in the battery-smoke,
Right thro' the line they broke;
Cossack and Russian
Reel'd from the sabre-stroke,
　Shatter'd and sunder'd.
Then they rode back, but not,
　Not the six hundred.

5. Cannon to right of them,
Cannon to left of them,
Cannon behind them
　Volley'd and thunder'd:
Storm'd at with shot and shell,
While horse and hero fell,
They that had fought so well
Came thro' the jaws of Death
Back from the mouth of Hell,

All that was left of them,
  Left of six hundred.

6. When can their glory fade?
  Oh the wild charge they made!
  All the world wonder'd.
  Honor the charge they made!
  Honor the Light Brigade,
    Noble Six Hundred!   TENNYSON.

---

41. THE CLAIMS OF ITALY.

I WILL leave antiquity out of the question, and speak only of modern times. Is it not a striking spectacle to see Italy always give the signal to the world, always open the way to great things? The first modern epic poet is an Italian—Dante; the first lyric poet is an Italian—Petrarch; the first poet of chivalry is an Italian—Boccaccio; the first painter in the world is an Italian—Raffaelle; the first statuary is an Italian—Michael Angelo; the first vigorous statesman and historian of the revival is an Italian—Machiavelli; the first philosophical historian is an Italian—Nico; the discoverer of the New World is an Italian—Christopher Columbus; and the first demonstrator of the laws of the heavenly worlds is an Italian—Galileo.

2. You will find a son of Italy standing on every step of the temple of genius ever since the twelfth century. Then, in times nearer to our own, while all other nations are working at the continuation of this immortal gallery, Italy from time to time collects her strength, and presents to the world a colossus surpassing all. Now, even now, the greatest of living artists—the only one, perhaps, who deserves, solely as an artist, the title of a great man—is he not an Italian—Rossini? And lastly, was he not also a son of Italy—that giant who towered above the whole cen-

tury, and covered all around him with his light or his shade—Napoleon?

8. In fact, it would seem that when Providence wanted a guide or a leader for humanity, it strikes this favored soil, and a great man springs forth

---

42. NAPOLEON TO THE ARMY OF ITALY.

[In modern times Napoleon is perhaps the greatest master of military oratory. After numerous victories in his first campaign in Italy he addressed his troops in a brilliant speech, of which we give the following extract:]

"SOLDIERS: You have, in fifteen days, gained six victories, taken twenty-one standards, fifty pieces of cannon, several fortresses, made fifteen hundred prisoners, and killed or wounded more than ten thousand men! You have equaled the conquerors of Holland and the Rhine.

2. "Destitute of all necessaries, you have supplied all your wants. Without cannon, you have gained battles!—without bridges, you have crossed rivers!—without shoes, you have made forced marches!—without brandy, and often without bread, you have bivouacked! Republican phalanxes, soldiers of Liberty, alone could have survived what you have suffered!

3. "Thanks to you, soldiers!—your grateful country has reason to expect great things of you! You have still battles to fight, towns to take, rivers to pass. Is there one among you whose courage is relaxed? Is there one who would prefer to return to the barren summits of the Apennines and the Alps, to endure patiently the insults of these soldier-slaves?

4. "No!—there is none such among the victors of Montenotte, of Millesimo, of Dego, and of Mondovi! My friends, I promise you this glorious conquest; but be the liberators, and not the scourges, of the people you subdue!"

43. NAPOLEON TO THE SOLDIERS AT FONTAINEBLEAU.

THE disastrous campaign of Russia was ended, and Napoleon, by prodigies of genius and courage, had in vain attempted to dispute the possession of France with the Allied Powers. Masters of Paris itself, they imposed upon him the obligation of abdicating, and to receive, in exchange for the throne of France, the Isle of Elba.

2. His farewell to his Old Guard, at the moment of leaving Fontainebleau, is the most touching recorded in history. He looked for a moment upon the troops arrayed in form of battle in the Court of Honor, and on the immense crowds from the neighboring cities who had assembled to assist at this moment of history, and hand it down to their children.

3. The silence reigned supreme; all heads were bowed, and tears coursed down cheeks hardened by the exposure of many battles. If the drums had been draped in mourning, it would have passed as the funeral obsequies of their general.

4. Napoleon, after a keen martial glance on his battalions and old troops, seemed much affected. How many days of battles, of glory and power, this army recalled to him! Where were those who composed it when it swept through Europe, Africa, and Asia? Where were now those countless hosts? And yet those who remained were faithful, and he was going to separate himself from them forever.

5. The army—it was himself! When he would be gone what would it be? He owed all to the sword, and in losing the sword he lost all. For a moment he paused as if he would re-enter the palace. Then he descended the steps, and advanced towards the soldiers. The drums proclaimed military honors; but, imposing silence, he advanced in front of the battalions, and made a sign that he wished to speak.

6. The silence was instantaneous; respiration even seemed suspended while listening to that voice whose full volume seemed concentrated, and deepened, and re-echoed by the high

walls of the palace, until its lowest notes reached the last rank of the Guard.

7. "Officers, sub-officers, and soldiers of my Old Guard, I bid you farewell. During twenty years I have constantly found you on the road of honor and glory. In these latter days, as in those of our prosperity, you have never ceased to be models of fidelity and bravery. With men such as you, our cause had not been lost; but the war would have been interminable; it would have been civil war, and France would have become more unhappy.

8. "I, then, sacrifice my interests to those of my country. I go: you, my friends, continue to love France; her honor was my only thought; it will always be the object of my heart. Do not deplore my condition. If I have consented to live, it is in order still to continue your glory. I wish to write those great things we have accomplished together. Farewell, my children. I would love to press you all to my heart. Let me at least embrace your general and your flag."

9. These words overcame the soldiers, and ran trembling through the crowd. General Petit, who commanded the Old Guard, advanced, and Napoleon held him a long time in his embrace. The two captains sobbed audibly, and deep sobbing was heard through all the ranks. The grenadiers wiped their eyes with the back of their hands.

10. "Let the eagles be brought," exclaimed Napoleon. The grenadiers brought him the eagles of the regiments. He took those signs so dear to soldiers, pressed them against his heart, and touched them to his lips. "Dear eagle," he exclaimed, in an accent at once manly and broken, "may this last kiss be impressed on the hearts of all my soldiers. Once more farewell, my old companions."

11. The entire army melted into tears, and nothing was heard but the loud and heavy sobbing of the troops.

LAMARTINE.

44. NAPOLEON'S RETURN.

[These lines commemorate the removal of the remains of Napoleon Bonaparte from the Island of St. Helena to France in 1840, in a ship of war commanded by the Prince de Joinville, a son of Louis Philippe, then king of France.]

A BARK has left the sea-girt isle,
   A prince is at the helm;
She bears the exile emperor
   Back to his ancient realm.
No joyous shout bursts from her crew,
   As o'er the waves they dance,
But silently, through foam and spray,
   Seek they the shores of France.

2. A soldier comes! Haste, comrades, haste!
   To greet him on the strand;
'Tis long since by his side ye fought
   For glory's chosen land.
A leader comes! Let loud huzzas
   Burst from the extended line,
And glancing arms and helmets raised
   In martial splendor shine.

3. A conqueror comes! Fly, Austrian, fly!
   Before his awful frown;
Kneel, Lombard, kneel! That pallid brow
   Has worn the iron crown!
The eagles wave! the trumpet sounds!
   Amid the cannon's roar,
Ye victors of a hundred fields,
   Surround your chief once more!

4. A monarch comes! From royal arms
   Remove the envious rust;
A monarch comes! the triple crown
   Is freed from gathering dust.

Guard him not to the halls of State,
  His diadem is riven;
But bear him where yon hallow'd spire
  Is pointing up to heaven;
And with the requiem's plaintive swell,
  With dirge and solemn prayer,
Enter the marble halls of death,
  And throne your monarch there!

5. Napoleon comes! Go speak that word
  At midnight's awful hour,
In Champ de Mars; will it not prove
  A spell of fearful power?
Will not a shadowy host arise
  From field and mountain ridge,
From Waterloo, from Austerlitz,
  From Lodi's fatal bridge,
And wheel in airy échelon,
  From pass, and height, and plain,
To form, upon that ancient ground,
  Their scattered ranks again?

6. Go speak it in the Louvre's halls,
  'Mid priceless works of art;
Will not each life-like figure from
  The glowing canvas start?
Go to Versailles, where heroes frown,
  And monarchs live in stone;
Across those chiselled lips will not
  A startling murmur run?
No, no, the marble still may be
  Cold, cold and silent—so is he.
The pencil's living hues may bloom,
But his have faded in the tomb,
And warriors in their narrow homes
Sleep, reckless that their leader comes.

7. Napoleon comes! but Rhine's pure flood
   Rolls on without a tinge of blood;
   The Pyramids still frown in gloom
   And grandeur, o'er an empty tomb;
   And sweetly now the moonbeam smiles
   Upon the fair Venetian isles.

8. Napoleon comes! but Moscow's spires
   Have ceased to glow with hostile fires;
   No spirit, in a whisper deep,
   Proclaims it where the Cæsars sleep,
   No sigh from column, tower, or dome—
   A man that once was feared at Rome—
   For life and power have passed away,
   And he is here, a king of clay.

9. He will not wake at war's alarms,
     Its music or its moans;
   He will not wake when Europe hears
     The crash of crumbling thrones—
   And institutions gray with age
     Are numbered with forgotten things,
   And privilege and "right divine"
     Rest with the people, not their kings.

10. Now raise the imperial monument,
      Fame's tribute to the brave;
    The warrior's place of pilgrimage
      Shall be Napoleon's grave.
    France, envying long his island tomb
      Amid the lonely deep,
    Has gained at last the treasured dust;
      Sleep! mighty mortal, sleep!

                              MISS WALLACE.

45. THE SOLDIER'S FUNERAL.

THE muffled drum rolled on the air,
Warriors with stately step were there;
On every arm was the black crape bound,
Every carbine was turned to the ground;
Solemn the sound of their measured tread,
As silent and slow they followed the dead.
The riderless horse was led in the rear,
There were white plumes waving over the bier;
Helmet and sword were laid on the pall,
For it was a soldier's funeral.

2. That soldier had stood on the battle-plain,
Where every step was over the slain;
But the brand and the ball had passed him by,
And he came to his native land to die!
'Twas hard to come to that native land,
And not clasp one familiar hand!
'Twas hard to be numbered amid the dead,
Or ere he could hear his welcome said!
But 'twas something to see its cliffs once more,
And to lay his bones on his own loved shore;
To think that the friends of his youth might weep
O'er the green grass turf of the soldier's sleep.

3. The bugles ceased their wailing sound,
As the coffin was lowered into the ground;
A volley was fired, a blessing said,
One moment's praise—and they left the dead!
I saw a poor and an agéd man,
His step was feeble, and his lip was wan;
He knelt him down on the new-raised mound,
His face was bowed on the cold, damp ground;
He raised his head, his tears were done—
The FATHER had prayed o'er his only son. LANDON.

46. PRESS ON.

PRESS on! surmount the rocky steeps,
　Climb boldly o'er the torrent's arch:
He fails alone who feebly creeps,
　He wins who dares the hero's march.
Be thou a hero! let thy might
　Tramp on eternal snows its way,
And, through the ebon walls of night,
　Hew down a passage unto day.

2. Press on! if once and twice thy feet
　Slip back and stumble, harder try;
From him who never dreads to meet
　Danger and death, they're sure to fly.
To coward ranks the bullet speeds,
　While on their breasts who never quail,
Gleams, guardian of chivalric deeds,
　Bright courage, like a coat of mail

3. Press on! if Fortune play thee false
　To-day, to-morrow she'll be true;
Whom now she sinks, she now exalts,
　Taking old gifts and granting new.
The wisdom of the present hour
　Makes up for follies past and gone:
To weakness strength succeeds, and power
　From frailty springs—Press on! press on!

4. Therefore, press on! and reach the goal,
　And gain the prize, and wear the crown:
Faint not! for to the steadfast soul
　Come wealth, and honor, and renown.
To thine own self be true, and keep
　Thy mind from sloth, thy heart from soil;
Press on! and thou shalt surely reap
　A heavenly harvest for thy toil! PARK BENJAMIN.

47. DEATH AND THE WARRIOR.

"AY, warrior, arm! and wear thy plume
On a proud and fearless brow!
I am the lord of the lonely tomb,
And a mightier one than thou!
Bid thy soul's love farewell, young chief,
Bid her a long farewell!
Like the morning's dew shall pass that grief,—
Thou comest with me to dwell!

2. "Thy bark may rush through the foaming deep,
Thy steed o'er the breezy hill;
But they bear thee on to a place of sleep,
Narrow, and cold, and chill!"
"Was the voice I heard *thy* voice, O Death!
And is thy day so near?
Then on the field shall my life's last breath
Mingle with victory's cheer!

3. "Banner shall float, with the trumpet's note,
Above me as I die!
And the palm-tree wave o'er my noble grave,
Under the Syrian sky.
High hearts shall burn in the royal hall,
When the minstrel names that spot;
And the eyes I love shall weep my fall,—
Death, death! I fear thee not!"

4. "Warrior, thou bearest a haughty heart!
But I can bend its pride!
How should'st thou know that thy soul will part
In the hour of victory's tide?
It may be far from thy steel-clad bands
That I shall make thee mine;
It may be lone on the desert's sands
Where men for fountains pine!

5 "It may be deep, amidst heavy chains,
  In some strong Paynim hold;
  I have slow, dull steps, and lingering pains,
  Wherewith to tame the bold!"
  "Death, death! I go to a doom unblest,
  If this indeed must be;
  But the *Cross* is bound upon my breast,
  And I may not shrink from thee!

6. "Sound, clarion, sound!—for my vows are given
  To the cause of the holy shrine;
  I bow my soul to the will of Heaven,
  O Death! and not to thine!" HEMANS.

---

48. KING RICHARD'S MEDITATION ON KINGS.

NO matter where; of comfort no more speak;
Let's talk of graves, of worms, and epitaphs;
Make dust our paper, and with rainy eyes
Write sorrow on the bosom of the earth.
Let's choose executors, and talk of wills:
And yet not so,—for what can we bequeath,
Save our deposéd bodies to the ground?
Our lands, our lives, and all are Bolingbroke's,
And nothing can we call our own, but death;
And that small model of the barren earth,
Which serves as paste and cover to our bones.
For Heaven's sake, let us sit upon the ground,
And tell sad stories of the death of kings:—
How some have been deposed, some slain in war;
Some haunted by the ghosts they have deposed;
Some poisoned by their wives, some sleeping killed;
All murdered:—for within the hollow crown,
That rounds the mortal temples of a king,
Keeps Death his court: and there the antic sits,
Scoffing his state, and grinning at his pomp;

Allowing him a breath, a little scene
To monarchize, be feared, and kill with looks;
Infusing him with self and vain conceit,—
As if this flesh, which walls about our life,
Were brass impregnable; and, humored thus,
Comes at the last, and with a little pin
Bores through his castle wall, and—farewell, king!
Cover your heads, and mock not flesh and blood
With solemn reverence; throw away respect,
Tradition, form, and ceremonious duty,
For you have but mistook me all this while:
I live with bread like you, feel want, taste grief,
Need friends:—subjected thus,
How can you say to me—I am a king? SHAKSPEARE.

49. WELCOME TO GENERAL LAFAYETTE.

WELCOME, friend of our fathers, to our shores. Happy are our eyes that behold those venerable features. Enjoy a triumph, such as never conqueror or monarch enjoyed,—the assurance that, throughout America, there is not a bosom which does not beat with joy and gratitude at the sound of your name. You have already met and saluted, or will soon meet, the few that remain, of the ardent patriots, prudent counsellors, and brave warriors with whom you were associated in achieving our liberties. But you have looked round in vain for the faces of many who would have lived years of pleasure on a day like this, with their old companion in arms and brother in peril.

2. Lincoln, and Greene, and Knox, and Hamilton are gone! The heroes of Saratoga and Yorktown have fallen before the only foe they could not meet! Above all, the first of heroes and of men, the friend of your youth, the more than friend of his country, rests in the bosom of the soil he redeemed. On the banks of his Potomac he lies in glory and peace. You

will revisit the hospitable shades of Mount Vernon; but him whom you venerated, as we did, you will not meet at its door. His voice of consolation, which reached you in the Austrian dungeons, cannot now break its silence to bid you welcome to his own roof.

3. But the grateful children of America will bid you welcome in his name. Welcome, thrice welcome to our shores; and whithersoever throughout the limits of the continent your course shall take you, the ear that hears you shall bless you; the eye that sees you, shall bear witness to you; and every tongue exclaim with heartfelt joy, "WELCOME, WELCOME, LAFAYETTE!"
EDWARD EVERETT.

---

50. ROLLA'S ADDRESS.

MY brave associates, partners of my toils, my feelings, and my fame. Can Rolla's words add vigor to the virtuous energies which inspire your hearts? No, you have judged as I have, the foulness of the crafty plea by which these bold invaders would delude ye. Your generous spirit has compared, as mine has, the motives which in a war like this can animate their minds and ours.

2. They, by a strange frenzy driven, fight for power, for plunder, and extended rule; we—for our country, our altars, and our homes! They follow an adventurer whom they fear, and obey a power which they hate; we serve a country which we love—a God whom we adore. Where'er they move in anger, desolation tracks their progress; where'er they pause in amity, affliction mourns their friendship.

3. They boast they come but to improve our state, enlarge our thoughts, and free us from the yoke of error. Yes, they will give enlightened freedom to our minds, who are themselves the slaves of passion, avarice, and pride. They offer us their protection; yes, such protection as vultures give to lambs, covering and devouring them. They call on us to bar

ter all of good we have inherited and proved, for the desperate chance of something better which they promise.

4. Be our plain answer this: The throne we honor is the people's choice; the laws we reverence are our brave fathers' legacy; the faith we follow, teaches us to live in bonds of charity with all mankind and die—with hope of bliss beyond the grave. Tell your invaders this, and tell them, too, we seek no change, and least of all, such change as they would bring us.

51. ADDRESS TO THE SUN.

O THOU that rollest above, round as the shield of my fathers! Whence are thy beams, O sun! thy everlasting light? Thou comest forth, in thy awful beauty, and the stars hide themselves in the sky; the moon, cold and pale, sinks in the western wave. But thou thyself movest alone: who can be a companion of thy course?

2. The oaks of the mountains fall; the mountains themselves decay with years; the ocean shrinks and grows again; the moon herself is lost in heaven; but thou art forever the same, rejoicing in the brightness of thy course. When the world is dark with tempests; when thunder rolls, and lightning flies, thou lookest in thy beauty from the clouds, and laughest at the storm.

3. But to Ossian, thou lookest in vain; for he beholds thy beams no more, whether thy yellow hair flows on the eastern clouds, or thou tremblest at the gates of the west. But thou art, perhaps, like me, for a season, and thy years will have an end. Thou shalt sleep in thy clouds, careless of the voice of the morning. Exult then, O sun, in the strength of thy youth!

4. Age is dark and unlovely; it is like the glimmering light of the moon, when it shines through broken clouds, and the mist is on the hills; the blast of the north is on the plain, the traveller shrinks in the midst of his journey. OSSIAN.

52. ENGLAND'S DOOM.

ON that great and dreadful Day of the Lord, when nations as well as individuals shall be placed at the bar of God to be judged according to their works, England will have an awful account to render of her stewardship. Her impoverished and downtrodden population within her own borders, the crushed and degraded millions whom she has enslaved in India, and the widows and orphans whom she has made throughout the world, in her reckless career of ambition, will all rise up in judgment against her.

2. The nations of the civilized earth will stand up too, and will bear evidence to her hard-hearted and relentless avarice, to her utter disregard of the most solemn promises and treaties, to her all-grasping spirit of aggrandizement, and to her entire recklessness as to the means by which her ends were to be attained.

3. And on that awful day of final reckoning, the voice of poor crushed and bleeding Ireland shall be heard pleading, with all the earnest eloquence of truth, that justice, swift and terrible, may at length fall on the head of that unnatural stepdame, to whose wanton cruelty, griping avarice, and iron policy she owes most of the wrongs which have weighed her down for centuries.

4. What will England say, when all these terrible witnesses shall appear against her, and when the ghosts of her countless murdered victims shall glare at her "with their fiery eyeballs?" What answer shall she give when the long and dark roll of her iniquities towards Ireland shall be unfolded before the judgment-seat of the most just, omnipotent, and all-seeing God of heaven and earth? Will her diplomacy then profit her any thing?

5. Will those cunning devices and that political *legerdemain* by which, on this earth, she has so often succeeded in making "the worse appear the better cause," then avail her

aught? No, no. The Lord will then tear from her brow the veil of hypocrisy which has so long concealed her hideous deformities; He will strip her of all disguise, and exhibit her as she is before the assembled world; for on that day "He will reveal the hidden things of darkness, and manifest the counsels of hearts."

6. And then shall proud England be humbled even unto the lust, and poor bleeding Ireland, which has been downtrodden by her for nearly seven centuries, be raised up from her lowliness to the lofty eminence to which her noble virtues and her long sufferings have entitled her. This is no mere flight of elevated fancy; it is a solemn and sober religious view of a subject invested with an all-absorbing interest.

ABP. SPALDING.

---

53. A NATIONAL MONUMENT TO WASHINGTON.

FELLOW-CITIZENS: let us seize this occasion to renew to each other our vows of allegiance and devotion to the American Union, and let us recognize in our common title to the name and the fame of Washington, and in our common veneration for his example and his advice, the all-sufficient centripetal power which shall hold the thick clustering stars of our confederacy in one glorious constellation forever! Let the column which we are about to construct be at once a pledge and an emblem of perpetual union!

2. Let the foundations be laid, let the superstructure be built up and cemented, let each stone be raised and riveted in a spirit of national brotherhood! And may the earliest ray of the rising sun,—till that sun shall set to rise no more,—draw forth from it daily, as from the fabled statue of antiquity, a strain of national harmony which shall strike a responsive chord in every heart throughout the republic!

3. Proceed, then, fellow-citizens, with the work for which you have assembled. Lay the corner-stone of a monument

which shall adequately bespeak the gratitude of the whole American people to the illustrious Father of his country! Build it to the skies; you cannot outreach the loftiness of his principles! Found it upon the massive eternal rock; you cannot make it more enduring than his fame! Construct it of the peerless Parian marble; you cannot make it purer than his life! Exhaust upon it the rules and principles of ancient and of modern art; you cannot make it more proportionate than his character.

4. But let not your homage to his memory end here. Think not to transfer to a tablet or a column the tribute which is due from yourselves. Just honor to Washington can only be rendered by observing his precepts and imitating his example. He has built his own monument. We, and those who come after us, in successive generations, are its appointed, its privileged guardians. The wide-spread republic is the future monument to Washington.

5. Maintain its independence. Uphold its Constitution. Preserve its union. Defend its liberty. Let it stand before the world in all its original strength and beauty, securing peace, order, equality, and freedom to all within its boundaries, and shedding light, and hope, and joy upon the pathway of human liberty throughout the world,—and Washington needs no other monument. Other structures may fully testify our veneration for him; this, this alone, can adequately illustrate his services to mankind.

6. Nor does he need even this. The republic may perish; the wide arch of our ranged Union may fall; star by star, its glories may expire; stone by stone, its columns and its capitol may molder and crumble; all other names which adorn its annals may be forgotten, but as long as human hearts shall anywhere pant, or human tongue shall anywhere plead for a true, rational, constitutional liberty, those hearts shall enshrine the memory, and those tongues prolong the fame, of GEORGE WASHINGTON. R. C. WINTHROP.

54. WASHINGTON'S FAREWELL TO HIS ARMY.

THE chieftain gazed with moistened eyes upon the veteran band,
Who with him braved the battle's storm for God and native land;
At last the parting hour had come—from prairie, mount, and sea,
The glad shout burst from countless hearts: "Our land—our land is free!"

II.

Then up from every altar rose a hymn of praise to God,
Who nerved the patriot hearts and arms to free their native sod;
The stormy strife of grief and gloom, of blood and death, was o'er—
The heroes who survived its wrath might seek their homes once more.

III.

With bared heads bowed, and swelling hearts, they gathered round their chief;
The parting day to them was one of mingled joy and grief;
They thought of all his love and care, his patience sorely tried,
Of how he shared their wants and woes, and with them death defied.

IV.

They looked back to that fearful night when 'mid the storm he stood,
Beside the icy Delaware, to guide them o'er its flood—
Back to red fields where, thick as leaves upon an autumn day,
The tawny savage warriors and British foemen lay.

V.

They thought of many a cheerless camp, where lay the sick and dead,
Where oft that form was bent o'er many a sufferer's bed;

Well had he won the deathless love of all that patriot band—
Their friend and guide, their nation's hope, the savior of their land.

VI.

He, too, saw all they had endured to break their country's chains—
Their naked footprints stamped in blood on Jersey's frozen plains;
The gloomy huts at Valley Forge, where winter's icy breath
Froze many a brave heart's crimson flow, chained many an arm in death.

VII.

And looking on their war-thinned ranks, he sighed for those who fell;
It stirred the depths of his great heart to say the word "farewell:"
He saw strong men, who, facing death, had never thought of fear,
Dash from their scarred and sun-browned cheeks the quickly-gushing tear.

VIII.

He stood in the receding boat, his noble brow laid bare,
And the wild fingers of the breeze tossing his silv'ry hair;
While to his trusty followers, the sternly tried and true,
Whose sad eyes watched him from the shore, he waved a last adieu.

IX.

Earth showed no laurelled conqueror so truly great as he
Who laid the sword and power aside when once his land was free—
Who calmly sought his quiet home when freedom's fight was won,
While with one voice the nation cried: "God bless our WASHINGTON!"

UNA.

55. THE SPIRIT OF DEMOCRACY IN AMERICA AND IN EUROPE.

[ABBE LECORDAIRE, born in 1802, obtained a brilliant eminence at the bar in France, when, to the astonishment of all, he renounced the most flattering prospecst to become a priest of the Order of St. Dominic, and devoted his rare talents to his celebrated Conferences at Nôtre Dame. Father Lecordaire was also a member of the French Academy, where he represents Christian eloquence in the most elevated and perfect sense.]

THE American who respects the law of God respects also the law of man; and if he believes it unjust, he reserves himself to obtain the repeal of it some day, not by violence, but in making for himself a peaceful and sure arm of all those means of persuasion which intelligence gives a man, and by the still more powerful means which he is able to possess from a tried devotion to the cause of justice.

2. To the European democrat I may say still, with necessary exceptions, the law is only a decree rendered by force, and which force has the right to overthrow. Was it an entire people who had given their assent and their sanction, he pretends that a minority, or even a single man, has the right to oppose to it the protestation of the sword, and to tear in blood a paper which has no other value than the want of power to replace it by another.

3. The American, come from a land where the aristocracy of birth always enjoyed a considerable part in public affairs, has cast away from his institutions the hereditary nobility, and reserved to personal merit the honor of governing.

4. But at the same time that he is passionately devoted to the equality of conditions, whether he considers it in a point of view derived from God, or in the point of view of a man, he does not estimate liberty at a less price, and, if the occasion presented itself for choosing between one and the other, he would do as the mother did in the judgment of Solomon: he would say to God and the world, "Do not separate them, because they have but one life in my soul; and I will die the day that one dies."

5. The European democrat does not understand it thus. In

his eyes equality is the grand and supreme law, that which prevails over all others, and to which all should be sacrificed. Equality in servitude appears preferable to him to liberty sustained by a hierarchy of ranks. He likes much better Tiberius ruling a multitude which no longer possess either rights or a name, to the Roman people governed by a patrician class, and receiving from it the impulse which makes them free with the reign which makes them strong.

6. The American leaves nothing to the mercy of an arbitrary power. He understands that, commencing with his soul, all that belongs to and surrounds him should be free—family, commerce, province, association for letters or science, for the worship of his God or the well-being of his body.

7. The European democrat, idolater of what he calls the State, takes the man from his infancy to offer him as a holocaust to public omnipotence.

8. He pretends that the infant, before seeing the property of the family, is the property of the city, and the city—that is, the people represented by those who govern it—has the right to form his intellect on a uniform and equal model. He pretends that the commune, the province, and every acsociation, even the most indifferent, depend on the State, and can neither act, speak, sell, buy, nor, in fine, exist without the intervention of the State, and only within the bonds determined by it, making thus the most absolute civil servitude the vestibule and foundation of political liberty.

9. The American gives to the unity of the country only just what is necessary to make it a body; the European democrat oppresses every man in order to create for him, under the name of country, a narrow prison.

10. If, finally, gentlemen, we compare the results, American democracy has founded a great people—religious, powerful, respected; free, in fine, although not without trials and perils. European democracy has broken the ties that connect the present with the past, buried abuses in ruins, raised up here and there a precarious liberty, agitated the world by events

much more than it has renewed it by institutions; and, incontestable master of the future, it prepares for us, if not instructed, the frightful alternative of a demagogy without foundations, or a despotism without curb. LECORDAIRE.

---

56. THE DEATH OF O'CONNELL.

THERE is sad news from Genoa. An aged and weary pilgrim, who can travel no further, passes beneath the gate of one of her ancient palaces, saying with pious resignation as he enters its silent chambers, "Well, it is God's will that I shall never see Rome. I am disappointed. But I am ready to die. It is all right." The superb though fading queen of the Mediterranean holds anxious watch, through ten long days, over that majestic stranger's wasting frame. And now death is there—the Liberator of Ireland has sunk to rest in the Cradle of Columbus.

2. Coincidence beautiful and most sublime! It was the very day set apart by the elder daughter of the Church for prayer and sacrifice throughout the world, for the children of the sacred island, perishing by famine and pestilence in their homes and in their native fields, and on their crowded paths of exile, on the sea and in the havens, and on the lakes, and along the rivers of this far-distant land. The chimes rung out by pity for his countrymen were O'Connell's fitting knell; his soul went forth on clouds of incense that rose from altars of Christian charity; and the mournful anthems which recited the faith, and the virtue, and the endurance of Ireland, were his becoming requiem.

3. It is a holy sight to see the obsequies of a soldier, not only of civil liberty, but of the liberty of conscience—of a soldier, not only of freedom, but of the Cross of Christ—of a benefactor, not merely of a race of people, but of mankind. The vault lighted by suspended worlds is the temple within which the great solemnities are celebrated. The nations of

the earth are mourners ; and the spirits of the just made perfect, descending from their golden thrones on high, break forth into songs.

4. Behold now a nation which needeth not to speak its melancholy precedence. The lament of Ireland comes forth from palaces deserted, and from shrines restored ; from Boyne's dark water, witness of her desolation, and from Tara's lofty hill, ever echoing her renown. But louder and deeper yet that wailing comes from the lonely huts on mountain and on moor, where the people of the greenest island of all the seas and expiring in the midst of insufficient though world-wide charities. Well indeed may they deplore O'Connell, for they were his children ; and he bore them

> " A love so vehement, so strong, so pure,
> That neither age could change nor art could cure."
>
> W. H. SEWARD.

---

57. THE EXECUTION OF MONTROSE, 1645.

[There is no ingredient of fiction in the historical incidents recorded in the following ballad. The perfect serenity of Montrose, the "Great Marquis," as he was called, in the hour of trial and death,—the courage and magnanimity which he displayed to the last,—have been dwelt upon, with admiration, by writers of every class.]

COME hither, Evan Cameron; come, stand beside my knee,—
I hear the river roaring down towards the wintry sea.
There's shouting on the mountain-side, there's war within the blast :
Old faces look upon me,—old forms go trooping past.
I hear the pibroch wailing amidst the din of fight,
And my dim spirit wakes again, upon the verge of night.

II.

'Twas I that led the Highland host through wild Lochaber's snows,
What time the plaided clans came down to battle with Montrose.

I've told thee how the Southrons fell beneath the broad claymore,
And how we smote the Campbell clan by Inverlochy's shore.
I've told thee how we swept Dundee, and tamed the Lindsays' pride;
But never have I told thee yet how the Great Marquis died.

III.

A traitor sold him to his foes;—O, deed of deathless shame!
I charge thee, boy, if e'er thou meet with one of Assynt's name,
Be it upon the mountain's side, or yet within the glen,
Stand he in martial gear alone, or backed by arméd men,
Face him, as thou wouldst face the man who wronged thy sire's renown;
Remember of what blood thou art, and strike the caitiff down!

IV.

They brought him to the Watergate, hard bound with hempen span,
As though they held a lion there, and not a 'fenceless man.
But when he came, though pale and wan, he looked so great and high,
So noble was his manly front, so calm his steadfast eye,
The rabble rout forbore to shout, and each man held his breath;
For well they knew the hero's soul was face to face with death.

V.

Had I been there, with sword in hand, and fifty Camerons by
That day, through high Dunedin's streets, had pealed the slogan-cry.
Not all their troops of trampling horse, nor might of mailéd men,
Not all the rebels in the South, had borne us backwards then!

Once more his foot on Highland heath had trod as free as air,
Or I, and all who bore my name, been laid around him there!

VI.

It might not be. They placed him next within the solemn hall,
Where once the Scottish kings were throned amidst their nobles all.
But there was dust of vulgar feet on that polluted floor,
And perjured traitors filled the place where good men sate before.
With savage glee came Warriston, to read the murderous doom;
And then uprose the great Montrose in the middle of the room.

VII.

"Now, by my faith as belted knight, and by the name I bear,
And by the bright Saint Andrew's cross that waves above us there,—
Yea, by a greater, mightier oath,—and O, that such should be!
By that dark stream of royal blood that lies 'twixt you and me,—
I have not sought in battle-field a wreath of such renown,
Nor hoped I on my dying day to win the martyr's crown!

VIII.

"There is a chamber far away where sleep the good and brave,
But a better place ye've named for me than by my fathers' grave.
For truth and right, 'gainst treason's might, this hand hath always striven,
And ye raise it up for a witness still in the eye of earth and heaven:

Then nail my head on yonder tower,—give every town a limb,—
And God who made shall gather them: I go from you to Him!"

IX.

The morning dawned full darkly; like a bridegroom from his room,
Came the hero from his prison to the scaffold and the doom.
There was glory on his forehead, there was lustre in his eye,
And he never walked to battle more proudly than to die;
There was color in his visage, though the cheeks of all were wan,
And they marvelled as they saw him pass, that great and goodly man.

X.

Then radiant and serene he stood, and cast his cloak away,
For he had ta'en his latest look of earth, and sun, and day.
He mounted up the scaffold, and he turned him to the crowd;
But they dared not trust the people,—so he might not speak aloud.
But he looked upon the heavens, and they were clear and blue,
And in the liquid ether the eye of God shone through:

XI

A beam of light fell o'er him, like a glory round the shriven,
And he climbed the lofty ladder as it were the path to heaven.
Then came a flash from out the cloud, and a stunning thunder-roll;
And no man dared to look aloft; fear was on every soul.
There was another heavy sound,—a hush, and then a groan;
And darkness swept across the sky,—the work of death was done!

AYTOUN.

57.* A STORM AT SEA.

O GOD! have mercy in this dreadful hour
   On the poor mariner! in the comfort here,
Safe sheltered as I am, I almost fear
The blast that rages with resistless power.
   What were it now to toss upon the waves,
The maddened waves and know no succor near!
The howling of the storm alone to hear,
   And the wild sea that to the tempest raves;
To gaze amid the horrors of the night
   And only see the billows' ghostly light,
   And in the dread of death to think of her
Who, as she listens sleepless to the gale,
Puts up a silent prayer and waxes pale!
   O God! have mercy on the mariner!

SOUTHEY.

---

58. "HOW THEY BROUGHT THE GOOD NEWS FROM GHENT TO AIX," 16—.

I SPRANG to the stirrup, and Joris, and he;
  I galloped, Dirck galloped, we galloped all three;
"Good speed!" cried the watch, as the gate-bolts undrew;
"Speed!" echoed the wall to us galloping through;
Behind shut the postern, the lights sank to rest,
And into the midnight we galloped abreast.

II.

Not a word to each other; we kept the great pace
Neck by neck, stride for stride, never changing our place;

I turned in my saddle and made its girths tight,
Then shortened each stirrup, and set the pique right,
Rebuckled the cheek-strap, chained slacker the bit,
Nor galloped less steadily Roland, a whit.

III.

'Twas moonset at starting; but while we drew near
Lokeren, the cocks crew, and twilight dawned clear;
At Boom, a great yellow star came out to see;
At Duffeld, 'twas morning as plain as could be;
And from Mecheln church-steeple we heard the half-chime,
So Joris broke silence with, "Yet there is time!"

IV.

At Aerschot, up leaped of a sudden the sun,
And against him the cattle stood black every one,
To stare through the mist at us galloping past,
And I saw my stout galloper Roland, at last,
With resolute shoulders, each butting away
The haze, as some bluff river headland its spray.

V.

And his low head and crest, just one sharp ear bent back
For my voice, and the other pricked out on his track;
And one eye's black intelligence,—ever that glance
O'er its white edge at me, his own master, askance!
And the thick heavy spume-flakes which aye and anon
His fierce lips shook upwards in galloping on.

VI.

"By Hasselt!" Dirck groaned; and cried Joris, "Stay spur!
Your Roos galloped bravely, the fault's not in her,
We'll remember at Aix"*—for one heard the quick wheeze
Of her chest, saw the stretched neck and staggering knees,
And sunk tail, and horrible heave of the flank,
As down on her haunches she shuddered and sank.

---

* The *x* in this word is not sounded.

VII.

So we were left galloping, Joris and I,
Past Looz and past Tongres, no cloud in the sky;
The broad sun above laughed a pitiless laugh,
'Neath our feet broke the brittle bright stubble like chaff;
Till over by Dalhem a dome-spire sprang white,
And "Gallop," gasped Joris, "for Aix is in sight!"

VIII.

"How they'll greet us!"—and all in a moment his roan,
Rolled neck and croup over, lay dead as a stone;
And there was my Roland to bear the whole weight
Of the news which alone could save Aix from her fate,
With his nostrils like pits full of blood to the brim,
And with circles of red for his eye-sockets' rim.

IX.

Then I cast loose my buffcoat, each holster let fall,
Shook off both my jack-boots, let go belt and all,
Stood up in the stirrup, leaned, patted his ear,
Called my Roland his pet-name, my horse without peer;
Clapped my hands, laughed and sang, any noise, bad or good,
Till at length into Aix Roland galloped and stood.

X.

And all I remember is, friends flocking round
As I sate with his head 'twixt my knees on the ground,
And no voice but was praising this Roland of mine,
As I poured down his throat our last measure of wine,
Which (the burgesses voted by common consent)
Was no more than his due who brought good news from Ghent.

ROBERT BROWNING.

59. CATO ON THE SOUL'S IMMORTALITY.

[CATO is seated with Plato's treatise in his hand, and beside him his sword. The expression should be solemn, and the declamation of a lofty and dignified character.]

IT must be so! Plato, thou reasonest well:
Else whence this fond desire, this pleasing hope,
This longing after immortality?
Or whence this secret dread, and inward horror
Of falling into naught? Why shrinks the soul
Back on herself, and shudders at destruction?
'Tis the divinity that stirs within us;
'Tis heaven itself that points out a hereafter,
And intimates eternity to man!—
Eternity! thou pleasing, dreadful thought!—
Through what variety of untried being,
Through what new forms and changes must we pass?
The wide, the unbounded prospect lies before me;
But shadows, clouds, and darkness rest upon it.
Here will I hold:—If there's a Power above,—
And that there is all Nature cries aloud
Through all her works,—He must delight in virtue;
And that which He delights in must be happy:
But when? or how? This world was made for Cæsar.
I'm weary of conjectures; this must end 'em!

[*Taking up the sword.*]

Thus am I doubly arm'd: my life and death,
My bane and antidote, are both before me.
This, in a moment, brings me to an end;
But this assures me I shall never die!
The soul, secure in her existence, smiles
At the drawn dagger, and defies its point.
The stars shall fade away, the Sun himself
Grow dim with age, and Nature sink in years,—
Thou still shalt flourish in eternal youth,
Unhurt amidst the war of elements,
The wreck of matter and the crush of worlds!

ADDISON.

60. MARC ANTONY'S APOSTROPHE TO CÆSAR'S BODY.

[This apostrophe is a fine practice in intonation and powerful and impassioned declamation. The speaker should commence in the deep, solemn tone of grief; making a burst of passion as he prophesies the curse that is to follow; and increase in energy till he reach the climax at the close.]

O PARDON me, thou bleeding piece of earth,
That I am meek and gentle with these butchers;
Thou art the ruins of the noblest man
That ever lived in the tide of times!
Woe to the hand that shed this costly blood!
Over thy wounds now do I prophesy,—
Which, like dumb mouths, do ope their ruby lips,
To beg the voice and utterance of my tongue,
A curse shall light upon the limbs of men;
Domestic fury and fierce civil strife
Shall cumber all the parts of Italy;
Blood and destruction shall be so in use,
And dreadful objects so familiar,
That mothers shall but smile, when they behold
Their infants quarter'd with the hands of war;
All pity chok'd with custom of fell deeds;—
And Cæsar's spirit, ranging for revenge,
With Até by his side, come hot from hell,
Shall in these confines, with a monarch's voice,
Cry Havoc, and let slip the dogs of war;
That this foul deed shall smell above the earth
With carrion men groaning for burial!

SHAKSPEARE.

61. SCENE FROM JULIUS CÆSAR.

BRUTUS—CASSIUS.

Cas. Will you go see the order of the course?
Bru. Not I.
Cas. I pray you, do.

Bru. I am not gamesome; I do lack some part
Of that quick spirit that is in Antony.
Let me not hinder, Cassius, your desires;
I'll leave you.

Cas. Brutus, I do observe you now of late;
I have not from your eyes that gentleness
And show of love, as I was wont to have:
You bear too stubborn and too strange a hand
Over your friend that loves you.

Bru. Cassius,
Be not deceived: If I have veil'd my look,
I turn the trouble of my countenance
Merely upon myself. Vexed I am,
Of late, with passions of some difference,
Conceptions only proper to myself,
Which give some soil, perhaps, to my behaviors;
But let not therefore my good friends be grieved;
Among which number, Cassius, be you one;
Nor construe any further my neglect,
Than that poor Brutus, with himself at war,
Forgets the shows of love to other men.

Cas. Then, Brutus, I have much mistook your passion;
By means whereof, this breast of mine hath buried
Thoughts of great value, worthy cogitations.——
Tell me, good Brutus, can you see your face?

Bru. No, Cassius, for the eye sees not itself,
But by reflection, by some other things.

Cas. 'Tis just:
And it is very much lamented, Brutus,
That you have no such mirror, as will turn
Your hidden worthiness into your eye,
That you might see your shadow. I have heard,
Where many of the best respect in Rome—
Except immortal Cæsar—speaking of Brutus,—
And groaning underneath this age's yoke,
Have wished that noble Brutus had his eyes.

Bru. Into what dangers would you lead me, Cassius,
That you would have me seek into myself
For that which is not in me?

Cas. Therefore, good Brutus, be prepared to hear:
And, since you know you cannot see yourself
So well as by reflection, I, your glass,
Will modestly discover to yourself
That of yourself which you yet know not of.
And be not jealous of me, gentle Brutus:
Were I a common laugher, or did use
To stale with ordinary oaths my love
To every new protester: if you know
That I do fawn on men, and hug them hard,
And, after, scandal them: or if you know
That I profess myself in banqueting
To all the rout, then hold me dangerous.

Bru. What means this shouting? I do fear the people
Choose Cæsar for their king.

Cas. Ay, do you fear it?
Then must I think, you would not have it so.

Bru. I would not, Cassius; yet I love him well:—
But wherefore do you hold me here so long?
What is it that you would impart to me?
If it be aught towards the general good,
Set honor in one eye, and death i' the other,
And I will look on both indifferently:
For let the gods so speed me, as I love
The name of honor more than I fear death.

Cas. I know that virtue to be in you, Brutus,
As well as I do know your outward favor.
Well, honor is the subject of my story.—
I cannot tell what you and other men
Think of this life; but, for my single self,
I had as lief not be, as live to be
In awe of such a thing as I myself.
I was born free as Cæsar; so were you;

We both have fed as well; and we can both
Endure the winter's cold as well as he;
For once, upon a raw and gusty day,
The troubled Tiber chafing with his shores,
Cæsar said to me, "Dar'st thou, Cassius, now,
Leap in with me into this angry flood,
And swim to yonder point?"—Upon the word,
Accoutred as I was, I plunged in,
And bade him follow; so, indeed, he did.
The torrent roar'd; and we did buffet it
With lusty sinews, throwing it aside,
And stemming it with hearts of controversy.
But, ere we could arrive the point proposed,
Cæsar cried, "Help me, Cassius, or I sink."
I—as Æneas, our great ancestor,
Did from the flames of Troy, upon his shoulder,
The old Anchises bear, so, from the waves of Tiber,
Did I the tired Cæsar. And this man
Is now become a god; and Cassius is
A wretched creature, and must bend his body,
If Cæsar carelessy but nod on him.
He had a fever when he was in Spain,
And when the fit was on him, I did mark
How he did shake; 'tis true, this god did shake;
His coward lips did from their color fly;
And that same eye, whose bend doth awe the world,
Did lose its lustre: I did hear him groan:
Ay, and that tongue of his, that bade the Romans
Mark him, and write his speeches in their books,
Alas, it cried, "Give me some drink, Titinius,"
As a sick girl. Ye gods! it doth amaze me,
A man of such a feeble temper should
So get the start of the majestic world,
And bear the palm alone.

Bru. Another general shout!
I do believe that these applauses are

For some new honors that are heap'd on Cæsar.

Cas. Why, man, he doth bestride the narrow world
Like a Colossus; and we, petty men,
Walk under his huge legs, and peep about,
To find ourselves dishonorable graves.
Men at some times are masters of their fates:
The fault, dear Brutus, is not in our stars,
But in ourselves, that we are underlings.
Brutus and Cæsar: What should be in that Cæsar?
Why should that name be sounded more than yours?
Write them together, yours is as fair a name;
Sound them, it does become the mouth as well;
Weigh them, it is as heavy; conjure with 'em,
Brutus will start a spirit as soon as Cæsar.—
Now, in the names of all the gods at once,
Upon what meat doth this our Cæsar feed,
That he hath grown so great? Age, thou art shamed:
Rome, thou hast lost the breed of noble bloods!
When went there by an age, since the great flood,
But it was famed with more than with one man!
When could they say, till now, that talked of Rome,
That her wide walls encompass'd but one man?
Oh! you and I have heard our fathers say,
There was a Brutus once that would have brook'd
The eternal devil to keep his seat in Rome,
As easily as a king.

Bru. That you do love me, I am nothing jealous;
What you would work me to I have some aim:
How I have thought of this, and of these times,
I shall recount hereafter; for this present
I would not—so with love I might entreat you—
Be any further moved. What you have said
I will consider; what you have to say
I will with patience hear; and find a time
Both meet to hear and answer such high things.
Till then, my noble friend, chew upon this;

Brutus nad rather be a villager,
Than to repute himself a son of Rome,
Under these hard conditions as this time
Is like to lay upon us.   SHAKSPEARE.

---

62. PETER PLYMLEY'S LETTERS.

[During one of the periodical anti-Catholic excitements which were so common in England in the early part of the present century, Sydney Smith, under the assumed name of P. Plymley, wrote a series of papers abounding in good sense, sound logic, and brilliant wit and humor.]

DEAR ABRAHAM: A worthier and better man than yourself does not exist; but I have always told you, from the time of our boyhood, that you were a bit of a goose.

2. Your parochial affairs are governed with exemplary order and regularity; you are as powerful in the vestry as Mr. Perceval in the House of Commons,—and, I must say, with much more reason; nor do I know any church where the faces and smock-frocks of the congregation are so clean, or their eyes so uniformly directed to the preacher.

3. There is another point upon which I will do you ample justice; and that is, that the eyes so directed towards you are wide open; for the rustic has, in general, good principles, though he cannot control his animal habits; and however loud he may snore, his face is perpetually turned towards the fountain of orthodoxy.

4. Having done you this act of justice, I shall proceed, according to our ancient intimacy and familiarity, to explain to you my opinions about the Catholics, and to reply to yours. In the first place, my sweet Abraham, the Pope is not landed, nor are there any curates sent out after him; nor has he been hid at St. Alban's, by the Dowager Lady Spencer, nor dined privately at Holland House, nor been seen near Dropmore.

5. If these fears exist (which I do not believe), they exist only in the mind of the Chancellor of the Exchequer; they

emanate from his zeal for the Protestant interest; and though they reflect the highest honor upon the delicate irritability of his faith, must certainly be considered as ambiguous proofs of the sanity and vigor of his understanding.

6. By this time, however, the best informed clergy in the neighborhood of the metropolis are convinced that the rumor is without foundation; and, though the Pope is probably hovering about our coast, in a fishing smack, it is most likely he will fall a prey to the vigilance of our cruisers; and it is certain he has not yet polluted the Protestantism of our soil.

7. Exactly in the same manner, the story of the wooden gods seized at Charing Cross, by an order from the Foreign Office, turns out to be without the shadow of a foundation; instead of the angels and archangels, mentioned by the informer, nothing was discovered but a wooden image of Lord Mulgrave, going down to Chatham as a head-piece for the Spanker gun-vessel; it was an exact resemblance of his lordship in his military uniform, and, therefore, as little like a god as can well be imagined. Having set your fears at rest as to the extent of the conspiracy formed against the Protestant religion, I will now come to the argument itself.

8. You say these men interpret the Scriptures in an orthodox manner; and that they eat their God. Very likely. All this may seem very important to you, who live fourteen miles from a market town and, from long residence upon your living, are become a kind of holy vegetable; and, in a theological sense, it is highly important.

9. But I want soldiers and sailors for the State; I want to make a greater use than I now can do of a poor country full of men; I want to render the military service popular among the Irish; to check the power of France; to make every possible exertion for the safety of Europe, which, in twenty years' time, will be nothing but a mass of French slaves; and then you, and ten thousand other such bodies as you, call out: "For God's sake, do not think of raising cavalry and infantry in Ireland! . . . . They interpret the Epistle to Timothy in a

different manner from what we do! .... They eat a bit of wafer every Sunday, which they call their God!"

10. I wish to my soul they would eat you, and such reasoners as you are. What! when Turk, Jew, heretic, infidel, Catholic, Protestant, are all combined against this country; when men of every religious persuasion, and no religious persuasion; when the population of half the globe is up in arms against us, are we to stand examining our generals and armies as a bishop examines a candidate for holy orders? and to suffer no one to bleed for England who does not agree with you about the 2d of Timothy?

11. You talk about the Catholics! If you and your brotherhood have been able to persuade the country into a continuation of this grossest of all absurdities, you have ten times the power which the Catholic clergy ever had in their best days. Louis XIV., when he revoked the Edict of Nantes, never thought of preventing the Protestant from fighting his battles, and gained, accordingly, some of his most splendid victories by the talents of his Protestant generals.

12. No power in Europe, but yourselves, has ever thought, for these hundred years past, of asking whether a bayonet is Catholic, or Presbyterian, or Lutheran; but whether it is sharp and well-tempered. A bigot delights in public ridicule, for he begins to think he is a martyr. I can promise you the full enjoyment of this pleasure, from one extremity of Europe to the other.
SYDNEY SMITH.

---

63. THE REFORM BILL.

[The writings of the late Rev. Sydney Smith, an Episcopal clergyman of England, are characterized by brilliant wit and rich humor, that were always under the control of a warm and good heart. The following is an extract from a speech delivered in consequence of the rejection by the House of Lords of a reform bill which had been passed by the House of Commons:]

I HAVE spoken so often on this subject, that I am sure both you and the gentlemen here present will be obliged to me for saying but little, and that favor I am as willing to confer as you can be to receive it. I feel most deeply the event which has taken place, because, by putting the two Houses of Parliament in collision with each other, it will impede the public business and diminish the public prosperity.

2. I feel it as a churchman, because I cannot but blush to see so many dignitaries of the Church arrayed against the wishes and happiness of the people. I feel it, more than all, because I believe it will sow the seeds of deadly hatred between the aristocracy and the great mass of the people.

3. The loss of the bill I do not feel, and for the best of all possible reasons—because I have not the slightest idea that it is lost. I have no more doubt, before the expiration of the winter, that this bill will pass, than I have that the annual tax bills will pass; and greater certainty than this no man can have, for Franklin tells us there are but two things certain in this world—death and taxes.

4. As for the possibility of the House of Lords preventing, ere long, a reform of Parliament, I hold it to be the most absurd notion that ever entered into human imagination. I do not mean to be disrespectful, but the attempt of the Lords to stop the progress of reform reminds me very forcibly of the great storm of Sidmouth, and of the conduct of the excellent Mrs. Partington on that occasion.

5. In the winter of 1824 there set in a great flood upon that town—the tide rose to an incredible height—the waves rushed in upon the houses, and every thing was threatened with destruction. In the midst of this sublime and terrible storm, Dame Partington, who lived upon the beach, was seen at the door of her house, with mop and feathers, trundling her mop, squeezing out the sea-water, and vigorously pushing away the Atlantic Ocean.

6. The Atlantic was roused; Mrs. Partington's spirit was up; but I need not tell you that the contest was unequal. The Atlantic Ocean beat Mrs. Partington. She was excellent at a slop, or a puddle, but she should not have meddled with a

tempest. Gentlemen, be at your ease—be quiet and steady. You will beat Mrs. Partington. SYDNEY SMITH.

64. TAXES THE PRICE OF GLORY.

JOHN BULL can inform Jonathan what are the inevitable consequences of being too fond of glory—TAXES! Taxes upon every article which enters into the mouth, or covers the back, or is placed under the foot; taxes upon every thing which it is pleasant to see, hear, feel, smell, or taste; taxes upon warmth, light, and locomotion; taxes on every thing on earth, and the waters under the earth; on every thing that comes from abroad, or is grown at home; taxes on the raw material; taxes on every fresh value that is added to it by the industry of man; taxes on the sauce which pampers man's appetite, and the drug that restores him to health; on the ermine which decorates the judge, and the rope which hangs the criminal; on the poor man's salt, and the rich man's spice; on the brass nails of the coffin, and the ribbons of the bride;—at bed or board, couchant or levant, we must pay.

2. The school-boy whips his taxed top; the beardless youth manages his taxed horse, with a taxed bridle, on a taxed road;—and the dying Englishman, pouring his medicine, which has paid seven per cent., into a spoon that has paid fifteen per cent., flings himself back upon his chintz-bed, which has paid twenty-two per cent., makes his will on an eight-pound stamp, and expires in the arms of an apothecary, who has paid a license of a hundred pounds for the privilege of putting him to death. His whole property is then immediately taxed from two to ten per cent. Besides the probate, large fees are demanded for burying him in the chancel; his virtues are handed down to posterity on taxed marble; and he is then gathered to his fathers,—to be taxed no more. SYDNEY SMITH.

65. THE UNION

["Liberty and Union, now and forever, one and inseparable!"—WEBSTER.]

THE Union! The Union! The hope of the free!
Howsoe'er we may differ, in this we agree:—
Our glorious banner no traitor shall mar,
By effacing a stripe, or destroying a star!
Division! No, never! The Union forever!
And cursed be the hand that our country would sever!

II.

The Union! The Union! 'Twas purchased with blood!
Side by side, to secure it, our forefathers stood:—
From the North to the South, through the length of the land,
Ran the war-cry which summon'd that patriot band!
Division! No, never! The Union forever!
And cursed be the hand that our country would sever!

III.

The Union! The Union! At Lexington first,
Through the clouds of oppression, its radiance burst:—
But at Yorktown roll'd back the last vapory crest,
And, a bright constellation, it blazed in the West!
Division! No, never! The Union forever!
And cursed be the hand that our country would sever!

IV.

The Union! The Union! Its heavenly light
Cheers the hearts of the nations who grope in the night,—
And, athwart the wide ocean, falls, gilding the tides,
A path to the country where Freedom abides!
Division! No, never! The Union forever!
And cursed be the hand that our country would sever!

V.

The Union! The Union! In God we repose!
We confide in the power that vanquish'd our foes!

The God of our fathers,—Oh, still may He be
The strength of the Union, the hope of the free!
Division! No, never! The Union forever!
And cursed be the hand that our country would sever!

DR. HARR JANVIER.

---

66. THE DESTINY OF AMERICA.

WE stand the latest, and, if we fail, probably the last, experiment of self-government by the people. We have begun it under circumstances of the most auspicious nature. We are in the vigor of youth. Our growth has never been checked by the oppressions of tyranny. Our constitutions have never been enfeebled by the vices or luxuries of the Old World. Such as we are, we have been from the beginning: simple, hardy, intelligent, accustomed to self-government and self-respect. The Atlantic rolls between us and any formidable foe.

2. Within our own territory, stretching through many degrees of latitude and longitude, we have the choice of many products, and many means of independence. The government is mild. The press is free. Religion is free. Knowledge reaches, or may reach, every home. What fairer prospects of success could be presented! What means more adequate to accomplish the sublime end? What more is necessary than for the people to preserve what they themselves have created?

3. Already has the age caught the spirit of our institutions. It has already ascended the Andes, and snuffed the breezes of both oceans. It has infused itself into the life blood of Europe, and warmed the sunny plains of France, and the lowlands of Holland. It has touched the philosophy of Germany and the North, and, moving onward to the South, has opened to Greece the lessons of her better days.

4. Can it be that America, under such circumstances, can betray herself? that she is to be added to the catalogue of republics, the inscription upon whose ruins is, "They were,

but they are not?" Forbid it, my countrymen! forbid it, Heaven!

5. The Old World has already revealed to us, in its unsealed books, the beginning and end of all its own marvellous struggles in the cause of liberty. Greece, lovely Greece, "the land of scholars and the nurse of arms," where sister republics in fair procession chanted the praises of liberty and the gods,—where and what is she?

6. For two thousand years the oppressor has bound her to the earth. Her arts are no more. The last sad relics of her temples are but the barracks of a ruthless soldiery; the fragments of her columns and her palaces are in the dust, yet beautiful in ruin. She fell not when the mighty were upon her.

7. Her sons were united at Thermopylæ and Marathon; and the tide of her triumph rolled back upon the Hellespont. She was conquered by her own factions. She fell by the hands of her own people. The man of Macedonia did not the work of destruction. It was already done, by her own corruptions, banishments, and dissensions.

8. Rome, republican Rome, whose eagles glanced in the rising and setting sun,—where and what is she? The Eternal City yet remains, proud even in her desolation, noble in her decline, venerable in the majesty of religion, and calm as in the composure of death. The malaria has but travelled in the paths worn by her destroyers.

9. More than eighteen centuries have mourned over the loss of her empire. A mortal disease was upon her vitals before Cæsar had crossed the Rubicon. The Goths, and Vandals, and Huns, the swarms of the North, completed only what was already begun at home. Romans betrayed Rome. The legions were bought and sold, but the people offered the tribute-money.

10. When we reflect on what has been, and is, how is it possible not to feel a profound sense of the responsibleness of this republic to all future ages! What vast motives press

upon us for lofty efforts! What brilliant prospects invite our enthusiasm! What solemn warnings at once demand our vigilance and moderate our confidence!

STORY.

---

67. REPUBLICS.

THE name of REPUBLIC is inscribed upon the most imperishable monuments of the species, and it is probable that it will continue to be associated, as it has been in all past ages, with whatever is heroic in character, and sublime in genius, and elegant and brilliant in the cultivation of arts and letters. It would not be difficult to prove that the base hirelings who have so industriously inculcated a contrary doctrine, have been compelled to falsify history and abuse reason.

2. It might be asked, triumphantly, what land has ever been visited with the influences of liberty, that has not flourished like the spring? What people has ever worshipped at her altars without kindling with a loftier spirit and putting forth more noble energies? Where has she ever acted that her deeds have not been heroic? Where has she ever spoken, that her eloquence has not been triumphant and sublime?

3. With respect to ourselves, would it not be enough to say that we live under a form of government and in a state of society to which the world has never yet exhibited a parallel? Is it then nothing to be free? How many nations, in the whole annals of human kind, have proved themselves worthy of being so? Is it nothing that we are republicans?

4. Were all men as enlightened, as brave, as proud as they ought to be, would they suffer themselves to be insulted with any other title? Is it nothing, that so many independent sovereignties should be held together in such a confederacy as ours? What does history teach us of the difficulty of instituting and maintaining such a polity, and of the glory that, of consequence, ought to be given to those who enjoy its advantages in so much perfection and on so grand a scale?

5. For, can any thing be more striking and sublime, than the idea of an imperial republic, spreading over an extent of territory more immense than the empire of the Cæsars, in the accumulated conquest of a thousand years—without præfects, or proconsuls, or publicans—founded in the maxims of common sense—employing within itself no arms but those of reason—and known to its subjects only by the blessings it bestows or perpetuates, yet capable of directing, against a foreign foe, all the energies of a military despotism,—a republic, in which men are completely insignificant, and principles and laws exercise, throughout its vast dominion, a peaceful and irresistible sway, blending in one divine harmony such various habits and conflicting opinions, and mingling in our institutions the light of philosophy with all that is dazzling in the associations of heroic achievement and extended domination, and deep-seated and formidable power.   LEGARE.

---

68. CATO'S SPEECH OVER HIS DEAD SON.

[With a heroic but dignified expression.]

THANKS to the gods! my boy has done his duty.—
Welcome, my son! Here set him down, my friends
Full in my sight; that I may view at leisure
The bloody corse, and count those glorious wounds.
How beautiful is death, when earn'd by virtue!
Who would not be that youth?—what pity is it
That we can die but once to serve our country!
Why sits this sadness on your brow, my friends?
I should have blush'd if Cato's house had stood
Secure, and flourish'd in a civil war.—
Porcius, behold thy brother! and remember,
Thy life is not thy own when Rome demands it!
When Rome demands!—but Rome is now no more!
The Roman empire's fall'n!—(Oh! curs'd ambition!)—
Fall'n into Cæsar's hands! Our great forefathers

Had left him naught to conquer but his country.—
Porcius, come hither to me!—Ah! my son,
Despairing of success,
Let me advise thee to withdraw, betimes,
To our paternal seat, the Sabine field,
Where the great censor toil'd with his own hands,
And all our frugal ancestors were bless'd
In humble virtues and a rural life.
There live retired: content thyself to be
Obscurely good.
When vice prevails, and impious men bear sway,
The post of honor is a private station!
Farewell, my friends! If there be any of you
Who dare not trust the victor's clemency,
Know, there are ships prepared by my command—
Their sails already op'ning to the winds,—
That shall convey you to the wish'd-for port.
The conqueror draws near—once more, farewell!
If e'er we meet hereafter, we shall meet
In happier climes, and on a safer shore,
Where Cæsar never shall approach us more!
There, the brave youth with love of virtue fired,
Who greatly in his country's cause expired,
Shall know he conquer'd! The firm patriot there,
Who made the welfare of mankind his care,
Tho' still by faction, vice and fortune cross'd,
Shall find the generous labor was not lost.

ADDISON.

69. WHO IS THERE TO MOURN?

IN the spring of the year 1774, a robbery was committed by some Indians on certain land adventurers on the river of Ohio. The whites undertook to punish this outrage in a summary way. They attacked travelling and hunting parties of the Indians, having their women and children with them, and murdered many. Among these were the family of Logan, a chief celebrated in peace and war, and long distinguished as the friend of the whites. This unworthy return provoked his vengeance.

2. He accordingly signalized himself in the war which ensued. The Indians were defeated, and sued for peace. Logan, however, disdained to be seen among the suppliants. But, lest the sincerity of a treaty should be distrusted, from which so distinguished a chief absented himself, he sent, by a messenger, the following speech to be delivered to Lord Dunmore.

3. Of this speech Jefferson says:—"I may challenge the whole orations of Demosthenes and Cicero, and of any more eminent orator, if Europe has furnished more eminent, to produce a single passage superior to the speech of Logan, a Mingo chief."

4. "I appeal to any white man to say if ever he entered Logan's cabin hungry, and he gave him not meat; if ever he came cold and naked and he clothed him not. During the course of the last long and bloody war, Logan remained idle in his cabin, an advocate for peace. Such was my love for the whites, that my countrymen pointed as they passed, and said, 'Logan is the friend of white men.'

5. "I had even thought to have lived with you, but for the injuries of one man. Colonel Cresap, the last spring, in cold blood, and unprovoked, murdered all the relations of Logan, not even sparing my women and children. There runs not a drop of my blood in the veins of any living creature. This called on me for revenge. I have sought it: I have killed many: I have fully glutted my vengeance. For my country, I rejoice at the beams of peace: but do not harbor a thought that mine is the joy of fear: Logan never felt fear: he will not turn on his heel to save his life. Who is there to mourn for Logan? Not one."

LOGAN.

70. BLACK HAWK'S ADDRESS TO GENERAL STREET.

YOU have taken me prisoner, with all my warriors. I am much grieved, for I expected, if I did not defeat you, to hold out much longer, and give you more trouble before I surrendered. I tried hard to bring you into ambush, but your last general understands Indian fighting. I determined to rush on you, and fight you face to face. I fought hard. But your guns were well aimed. The bullets flew like birds in the air, and whizzed by our ears like the wind through the trees in winter.

2. My warriors fell around me: it began to look dismal: I saw my evil day at hand. The sun rose dim on us in the morning, and at night it sank in a dark cloud, and looked like a ball of fire. That was the last sun that shone on Black Hawk. His heart is dead, and no longer beats quick in his bosom. He is now a prisoner to the white men. They will do with him as they wish. But he can stand torture, and is not afraid of death. He is no coward. Black Hawk is an Indian.

3. He has done nothing for which an Indian ought to be ashamed. He has fought for his countrymen, the squaws and pappooses, against white men, who came, year after year, to cheat them and take away their lands. You know the cause of our making war. It is known to all white men. They ought to be ashamed of it. The white men despise the Indians, and drive them from their homes. They smile in the face of the poor Indians to cheat them. They shake them by the hand to gain their confidence, to make them drunk, and to deceive them.

4. We told them to let us alone, and keep away from us; but they followed on, and beset our paths, and they coiled themselves among us, like the snake. They poisoned us by their touch. We were not safe. We lived in danger. We looked up to the Great Spirit. We went to our father. We

were encouraged. His great council gave us fair words and big promises; but we got no satisfaction: things were growing worse. There were no deer in the forest. The opossum and beaver were fled. The springs were drying up, and our squaws and pappooses without victuals to keep them from starving.

5. We called a great council, and built a large fire. The spirit of our fathers arose and spoke to us to avenge our wrongs or die. We set up the war-whoop, and dug up the tomahawk; our knives were ready, and the heart of Black Hawk swelled high in his bosom when he led his warriors to battle. He is satisfied. He will go to the world of spirits contented. He has done his duty. His father will meet him there, and commend him.

6. Farewell, my nation! Black Hawk tried to save you, and avenge your wrongs. He drank the blood of some of the whites. He has been taken prisoner, and his plans are stopped. He can do no more. He is near his end. His sun is setting, and he will rise no more. Farewell to Black Hawk!

71. THE INDIAN HUNTER.

WHEN the summer harvest was gather'd in,
    And the sheaf of the gleaner grew white and thin,
And the ploughshare was in its furrow left,
Where the stubble land had been lately cleft,
An Indian hunter, with unstrung bow,
Look'd down where the valley lay stretch'd below.

II.

He was a stranger, and all that day
Had been out on the hills, a perilous way,
But the foot of the deer was far and fleet,
And the wolf kept aloof from the hunter's feet,
And bitter feelings passed o'er him then,
As he stood by the populous haunts of men.

III.

The winds of autumn came over the woods
As the sun stole out from their solitudes,
The moss was white on the maple's trunk,
And dead from its arms the pale vine shrunk,
And ripen'd the mellow fruit hung, and red
Were the tree's wither'd leaves round it shed.

IV.

The foot of the reaper moved slow on the lawn,
And the sickle cut down the yellow corn—
The mower sung loud by the meadow side,
Where the mists of evening were spreading wide,
And the voice of the herdsman came up the lea,
And the dance went round by the greenwood tree.

V.

Then the hunter turn'd away from that scene,
Where the home of his fathers once had been,
And heard by the distant and measured stroke
That the woodman hew'd down the giant oak,
And burning thoughts flash'd o'er his mind
Of the white man's faith and love unkind.

VI.

The moon of the harvest grew high and bright,
As her golden horn pierced the cloud of white—
A footstep was heard in the rustling brake,
Where the beach o'ershadowed the misty lake,
And a mourning voice and a plunge from shore;—
And the hunter was seen on the hills no more.

VII.

When years had pass'd on, by that still lake-side
The fisher look'd down through the silver tide,
And there, on the smooth yellow sand display'd,
A skeleton wasted and white was laid,

And 'twas seen as the waters moved deep and slow,
That the hand was still grasping a hunter's bow.
                                        LONGFELLOW.

---

72. RIGHTS OF THE INDIANS DEFENDED

THINK of the country for which the Indians fought! Who can blame them? As Philip looked down from his seat on Mount Hope, that glorious eminence, that

> "————————throne of royal state, which far
> Outshone the wealth of Ormus or of Ind,
> Or where the gorgeous east, with richest hand,
> Showers on her kings barbaric pomp and gold,"—

as he looked down and beheld the lovely scene which spread beneath at a summer sunset,—the distant hill-tops blazing with gold, the slanting beams streaming along the waters, the broad plains, the island groups, the majestic forest,—could he be blamed, if his heart burned within him, as he beheld it all passing, by no tardy process, from beneath his control into the hands of the stranger?

2. As the river chieftains—the lords of the waterfalls and the mountains—ranged this lovely valley, can it be wondered at, if they beheld with bitterness the forest disappearing beneath the settler's axe—the fishing-place disturbed by his saw-mills?

3. Can we not fancy the feelings with which some strong-minded savage, in company with a friendly settler, contemplating the progress already made by the white man, and marking the gigantic strides with which he was advancing into the wilderness, would fold his arms and say, "White man, there is eternal war between me and thee! I quit not the land of my fathers, but with my life.

4. "In those woods, where I bent my youthful bow, I will still hunt the deer; over yonder waters I will still glide un-

restrained in my bark canoe. By those dashing waterfalls I will still lay up my winter's store of food; on these fertile meadows I will still plant my corn.

5. "Stranger, the land is mine. I understand not these paper rights. I gave not my consent, when, as thou sayest, these broad regions were purchased for a few baubles, of my fathers. They could sell what was theirs; they could sell no more. How could my father sell that which the Great Spirit sent me into the world to live upon? They knew not what they did.

6. "The stranger came, a timid suppliant, and asked to lie down on the red man's bear-skin, and warm himself at the red man's fire, and have a little piece of land, to raise corn for his women and children; and now he is become strong, and mighty, and bold, and spreads out his parchment over the whole, and says, 'It is mine.'

7. "Stranger, there is not room for us both. The Great Spirit has not made us to live together. There is poison in the white man's cup; the white man's dog barks at the red man's heels. If I should leave the land of my fathers, whither shall I fly? Shall I go to the south, and dwell among the graves of the Pequots? Shall I wander to the west?—the fierce Mohawk—the man-eater—is my foe. Shall I fly to the east?—the great water is before me.

8. "No, stranger; here I have lived, and here will I die; and if here thou abidest, there is eternal war between me and thee. Thou hast taught me thy arts of destruction; for that alone I thank thee; and now take heed to thy steps; the red man is thy foe.

9. "When thou goest forth by day, my bullet shall whistle by thee; when thou liest down at night, my knife is at thy throat. The noonday sun shall not discover thy enemy, and the darkness of midnight shall not protect thy rest. Thou shalt plant in terror, and I will reap in blood; thou shalt sow the earth with corn, and I will strew it with ashes; thou shalt go forth with the sickle, and I will follow after with the scalp-

ing-knife ; thou shalt build, and I will burn,—till the white
man or the Indian shall cease from the land. Go thy way for
this time in safety ; but remember, stranger, there is eternal
war between me and thee !"

EVERETT.

---

73. LINES TO A FALLEN LEAF

THOU little, yellow, floating atom,
   Thou waiting-maid on lovely autumn,
Thou harbinger of winter sprays,
Thou leave-taker of summer days—
How oft, in brooding o'er the past,
(For memory's dream must always last,)
I've gazed on thee, as on the storm
And howling blast you're by me borne,
And thought thee like the many gone—
The friends who leave us here alone,
This day—bright and free from sorrow,
Dead, cold, and buried on the morrow!

Thou little atom, I've thee seen
In all thy prime, in all thy green ;
Ere severed from the parent stem,
Thou wert a lovely, blooming gem ;
When the wild, roving honey-bee
Would rest its wing and light on thee.
Now thou art an outcast, driven
By every breath of wind from Heaven.
Oh, is it not too often thus,
Thou little fallen leaf, with us ?
At first we're blooming, bright, and green,
Again—the shade of what we've been.

RICHARD TERNAN.

74. DRYBURGH ABBEY.

[In the following beautiful poem of Dryburgh Abbey, all the principal characters that figure in the wonderful creations of Scott are pertinently and appropriately introduced. Henry Giles, in his "Illustrations of Genius," also pays a glowing tribute to the great novelist's fame.]

HE has left that which nothing can take from him except that which sweeps letters from the earth—a fame which lies in all that is lovable—a fame which gathers its applause from the grateful friendship of civilized generations.

The consolation that he has administered to desponding spirits; the cheerfulness with which he has banished care; the mirth with which he has banished sadness; the tragic grandeur by which he has drowned individual sorrow; the stirring events by which he has shaken the torpor of indolence; the gentle, the gay, the heroic, the humane emotions with which he has agitated so many souls,—these are things which are deathless and which are priceless.

There is no standard of exchange by which the gifts of genius can be balanced with the goods of earth; and though such goods should attend on genius in every variety that men desire, they could never be taken for its wages or its equivalent. No temporal station could have added to Scott's dignity; and all factitious contrivances for posthumous importance, if perfectly successful, would have been nullified by the compass of his true immortality.

His name is to us above the proudest of the Pharaohs; and we would not give the least of his romances for the greatest of the Pyramids.

'TWAS morn—but not the ray which falls
 The summer boughs among,
When Beauty walks in gladness forth,
 With all her light and song;
'Twas morn—but mist and cloud hung deep
 Upon the lonely vale,

    And shadows like the wings of death
      Were out upon the gale.

2. For he whose spirit woke the dust
      Of nations into life,
   That o'er the waste and barren earth
      Spread flowers and fruitage rife,—
   Whose genius, like a sun, illumed
      The mighty realms of mind,
   Had fled forever from the fame,
      Love, friendship of mankind!

3. To wear a wreath in glory wrought,
      His spirit swept afar,
   Beyond the soaring wings of thought,
      The light of moon or star;
   To drink immortal waters, free
      From every taint of earth,—
   To breathe before the shrine of life
      The source whence worlds had birth.

4. There was wailing on the early breeze,
      And darkness in the sky,
   When with sable plume, and cloak, and pall,
      A funeral train swept by.
   Methought—St. Mary, shield us well!—
      That other forms moved there,
   Than those of mortal brotherhood,—
      The noble, young, and fair.

5. Was it a dream?—how oft in sleep
      We ask, "Can this be true?"
   Whilst warm Imagination paints
      Her marvels to our view.
   Earth's glory seems a tarnish'd crown
      To that which we behold,

When dreams enchant our sight with things
   Whose meanest garb is gold.

6. Was it a dream?—Methought
   The "dauntless Harold" passed me by,—
The proud "Fitz-James" with martial step,
   And dark, intrepid eye.
That "Marmion's" haughty crest was there,
   A mourner for his sake,
And she,—the bold, the beautiful,
   Sweet "Lady of the Lake."

7. The "Minstrel" whose *last lay* was o'er,
   Whose broken heart lay low,
And with him glorious "Waverley,"
   With glance and step of woe;
And "Stuart's" voice was there, as when
   'Mid fate's disastrous war,
He led the bold, ambitious, proud,
   And brave "Vich Ian Vohr."

8. Next, marvelling at his sable suit,
   The "Dominie" stalk'd past,
With "Bertram,"—"Julia" by his side,
   Whose tears were flowing fast;
"Guy Mannering," too, moved there, o'erpower'd
   By that afflicting sight;
And "Merrilies," as when she wept
   On Ellangowan's height.

9. Solemn and grave "Monkbarns" approach'd,
   Amidst that burial line,
And "Ochiltree" leant on his staff,
   And mourn'd for "Auld Lang Syne."
Slow march'd the gallant "McIntyre,"
   While "Lovel" mused alone,
For once "Miss Wardour's" image left
   That bosom's faithful throne.

10. With coronach, and arms revers'd,
   Forth came "McGregor's" clan,
  "Red Dougal's" cry peal'd shrill and wild,—
   "Rob Roy's" bold brow look'd wan,
   And fair "Diana" kiss'd her cross,
   And blessed its sainted ray;
   And "Wae is me," tho "Bailie" sigh'd,
   "That I should see this day!"

11. Next rode, in melancholy guise,
   With sombre vest and scarf,
   Sir Edward, Laird of Ellieslaw,
   The far-renown'd "Black Dwarf!"
   Upon his left, in bonnet blue,
   And white locks flowing free,
   The pious sculptor of the grave,—
   Stood "Old Mortality."

12. "Balfour of Burley,"—"Claverhouse,"—
   "The Lord of Evandale,"—
   And stately "Lady Margaret,"
   Whose woe might not avail;
   Fierce "Bothwell" on his charger black,
   As from the conflict won;
   And pale "Habakkuk Mucklewrath,"
   Who cried "God's will be done!"

13. And like a rose, a young white rose,
   That blooms 'mid wildest scene,
   Pass'd she—the modest, eloquent,
   And virtuous "Jeanie Deane;"
   And "Dumbidikes," that silent laird,
   With love *too deep to smile*,
   And "Effie" with her noble friend,
   The good "Duke of Argyle."

14. With lofty look and bearing high,
   Dark "Ravenswood" advanced

Who on the false "Lord Keeper's" mien
    With eye indignant glanced;—
Whilst graceful as a lonely fawn
    'Neath covert close and sure,
Approached the beauty of all hearts,
    The "Bride of Lammermoor!"

15. Then "Annot Lyle," the fairy queen
        Of light and sun, stepp'd near
    The "Knight of Ardenvoir," and *he*,
        The gifted Highland seer;
    "Dalgetty,"—"Duncan,"—"Lord Monteith,"—
        And "Ranald" met my view,—
    The hapless "Children of the Mist,"
        And bold "Mac Connel-Dhu."

16. On swept "Bois Guilbert,"—"Front de Bœuf,"—
        "De Tracey's" plume of woe;
    And "Cœur de Lion's" crest shone near
        The valiant "Ivanhoe."
    While, soft as glides a summer cloud,
        "Rowena" closer drew,
    With beautiful "Rebecca," peerless
        Daughter of a Jew!

17. Still onward like the gathering night
        Advanced that funeral train,
    Like billows when the tempest sweeps
        Across the shadowy main.
    Where'er the eager gaze might reach
        In noble ranks were seen
    Dark plume, and glittering mail, and crest,
        And woman's beauteous mien.

18. A sound thrill'd thro' that length'ning host;—
        Methought the vault was closed,
    Where, in his glory and renown,
        Fair Scotia's bard reposed.

A sound thrill'd thro' that length'uing host!—
And from my vision fled:—
But ah! that mournful dream proved true—
The immortal Scott was dead!

         CHARLES SWAIN.

---

75. MARIUS IN PRISON.

THE peculiar sublimity of the Roman mind does not express itself, nor is it at all to be sought in their poetry. Poetry, according to the Roman ideal of it, was not an adequate organ for the grander movements of the national mind. Roman sublimity must be looked for in Roman acts and in Roman sayings. Where, again, will you find a more adequate expression of the Roman majesty, than in the saying of Trajan: —*Imperatorem oportere stantem mori*—that Cæsar ought to die standing; a speech of imperatorial grandeur!

2. Implying that he, who was "the foremost man of all this world,"—and, in regard to all other nations, the representative of his own, should express its characteristic virtue in his farewell act—should die *in procinctu*—and should meet the last enemy as the first, with a Roman countenance and in a soldier's attitude. If this had an imperatorial—what follows had a consular majesty, and is almost the grandest story upon record.

3. Marius, the man who rose to be seven times consul, was in a dungeon, and a slave was sent in with commission to put him to death. These were the persons,—the two extremities of exalted and forlorn humanity, its vanward and its rearward man, a Roman consul and an abject slave.

4. But their natural relations to each other were, by the caprice of fortune, monstrously inverted: the consul was in chains; the slave was for a moment the arbiter of his fate. By what spells, what magic, did Marius reinstate himself in his natural prerogatives?

5. By what marvels drawn from heaven or from earth, did he, in the twinkling of an eye, again invest himself with the purple, and place between himself and his assassin a host of shadowy lictors? By the mere blank supremacy of great minds over weak ones. He *fascinated* the slave, as a rattle-snake does a bird.

6. Standing, "like Teneriffe," he smote him with his eye, and said, "*Tune, homo, audes occidere C. Marium?*"—Dost thou, fellow, presume to kill Caius Marius? Whereat, the reptile, quaking under the voice, nor daring to affront the consular eye, sank gently to the ground—turned round upon his hands and feet—and, crawling out of the prison like any other vermin, left Marius standing in solitude as steadfast and immovable as the Capitol. DE QUINCEY.

76. MARIUS.

[Suggested by a painting of MARIUS seated among the ruins of Carthage. By VANDERLYAR.]

PILLARS are fallen at thy feet,
   Fanes quiver in the air,
A prostrate city is thy seat—
   And thou alone art there.

2. No change comes o'er thy noble brow,
   Though ruin is around thee;
Thine eye-beam burns as proudly now
   As when the laurel crowned thee.

3. It cannot bend thy lofty soul,
   Though friends and fame depart;
The car of fate may o'er thee roll,
   Nor crush thy Roman heart.

4. And genius hath electric power,
   Which earth can never tame;

Bright suns may scorch, and dark clouds lower—
  Its flash is still the same.

5. The dreams we loved in early life
    May melt like mists away;
  High thoughts may seem 'mid passion's strife
    Like Carthage in decay.

6. And proud hopes in the human heart
    May be to ruin hurled,
  Like mouldering monuments of art,
    Heaped on a sleeping world.

7. Yet there is something will not die,
    Where life hath once been fair;
  Some towering thoughts still rear on high,—
    Some Roman lingers there.

LYDIA MARIA CHILD.

77. A LEGEND OF BREGENZ.

GIRT round with rugged mountains,
  The fair Lake Constance lies;
In her blue heart reflected
  Shine back the starry skies.
And watching each white cloudlet
  Float silently and slow,
You think a piece of heaven
  Lies on our earth below!!

2. Midnight is there; and silence,
    Enthroned in heaven, looks down
  Upon her own calm mirror,
    Upon a sleeping town;
  For Bregenz, that quaint city
    Upon the Tyrol shore,
  Has stood above Lake Constance
    A thousand years and more.

3. Her battlements and towers,
    From off their rocky steep,
Have cast their trembling shadow
    For ages on the deep;
Mountain, and lake, and valley,
    A sacred legend know
Of how the town was saved one night,
    Three hundred years ago.

4. Far from her home and kindred
    A Tyrol maid had fled,
To serve in the Swiss valleys,
    And toil for daily bread;
And every year that fleeted
    So silently and fast,
Seemed to bear farther from her
    The memory of the Past.

5. She served kind, gentle masters,
    Nor asked for rest or change;
Her friends seemed no more new ones,
    Their speech seemed no more strange.
And when she led her cattle
    To pasture every day,
She ceased to look and wonder
    On which side Bregenz lay.

6. She spoke no more of Bregenz
    With longing and with tears;
Her Tyrol home seemed faded
    In a deep mist of years;
She heeded not the rumors
    Of Austrian war and strife;
Each day she rose contented
    To the calm toils of life.

7. Yet, when her master's children
    Would, clustering, round her stand,

She sang them ancient ballads
 Of her own native land;
And when, at morn and evening,
 She knelt before God's throne,
The accents of her childhood
 Rose to her lips alone.

8. And so she dwelt; the valley
 More peaceful year by year;
When, suddenly, strange portents
 Of some great deed seemed near.
The golden corn was bending
 Upon its fragile stalk;
While farmers, heedless of their fields,
 Paced up and down in talk.

9. The men seemed stern and altered,
 With looks cast on the ground;
With anxious faces, one by one,
 The women gathered round.
All talk of flax or spinning,
 Or work was put away;
The very children seemed afraid
 To go alone to play.

10. One day out in the meadow
 With strangers from the town,
Some secret plan discussing,
 The men walked up and down;
Yet now and then seemed watching
 A strange, uncertain gleam,
That looked like lances 'mid the trees,
 That stood below the stream.

11. At eve they all assembled,
 Then care and doubt were fled;
With jovial laugh they feasted;
 The board was nobly spread.

The elder of the village
  Rose up, his glass in hand,
And cried: "We drink the downfall
  Of an accursèd land!

12. "The night is growing darker;
  Ere one more day is flown,
Bregenz, our foemen's stronghold,
  Bregenz shall be our own!"
The women shrank in terror
  (Yet Pride, too, had her part);
But one poor Tyrol maiden
  Felt death within her heart.

13. Before her stood fair Bregenz;
  Once more her towers arose;
What were the friends beside her?
  Only her country's foes!
The faces of her kinsfolk,
  The days of childhood flown,
The echoes of her mountains
  Reclaimed her as their own!

14. Nothing she heard around her
  (Though shouts rang forth again);
Gone were the green Swiss valleys,
  The pasture and the plain;
Before her eyes one vision,
  And in her heart one cry,
That said: "Go forth, save Bregenz,
  And then, if need be, die!"

15. With trembling haste, and breathless,
  With noiseless step she sped;
Horses and weary cattle
  Were standing in the shed:
She loosed the strong white charger,
  That fed from out her hand;

She mounted, and she turned his head
　　Towards her native land.

16. Out—out into the darkness—
　　Faster and still more fast;
The smooth grass flies behind her,
　　The chestnut wood is past:
She looks up; clouds are heavy!
　　Why is her steed so slow?
Scarcely the wind beside them
　　Can pass them as they go.

17. "Faster," she cries; "O faster!"
　　Eleven the church-bells chime;
"O God," she cries, "help Bregenz,
　　And bring me there in time!"
But louder than bells' ringing,
　　Or lowing of the kine,
Grows nearer in the midnight
　　The rushing of the Rhine.

18. Shall not the roaring waters
　　Their headlong gallop check?
The steed draws back in terror;
　　She leans upon his neck
To watch the flowing darkness:
　　The bank is high and steep;
One pause,—he staggers forward,
　　And plunges in the deep.

19. She strives to pierce the blackness,
　　And looser throws the rein;
Her steed must breast the waters
　　That dash above his mane.
How gallantly, how nobly,
　　He struggles through the foam!
And see, in the far distance
　　Shine out the lights of home!

20. Up the steep banks he bears her,
    And now they rush again
Towards the heights of Bregenz,
    That tower above the plain.
They reach the gate of Bregenz
    Just as the midnight rings,
And out come serf and soldier
    To meet the news she brings.

21. Bregenz is saved! Ere daylight
    Her battlements are manned:
Defiance greets the army
    That marches on the land;
And if to deeds heroic
    Should endless fame be paid,
Bregenz does well to honor
    The noble Tyrol maid.

22. Three hundred years are vanished,
    And yet upon the hill
An old stone gateway rises
    To do her honor still.
And there, when Bregenz women
    Sit spinning in the shade,
They see in quaint old carving
    The charger and the maid.

23. And when to guard old Bregenz,
    By gateway, street, and tower,
The warder paces all night long,
    And calls each passing hour:
"Nine," "ten," "eleven," he cries aloud,
    And then (O crown of Fame!)
When midnight pauses in the skies,
    He calls the maiden's name!

Miss A. A. Proctor.

78. THE FIRE-WORSHIPPERS.—(From "Lalla Rookh.")

BUT see—he starts—what heard he then?
That dreadful shout!—across the glen
From the land side it comes, and loud
Rings through the chasm; as if the crowd
Of fearful things that haunt that dell,
Its ghouls and dives, and shapes of hell,
Had all in one dread howl broke out,
So loud, so terrible that shout!
"They come—the Moslems come!"—he cries,
His proud soul mounting to his eyes :—
"Now, spirits of the brave, who roam
Enfranchised through yon starry dome,
Rejoice—for souls of kindred fire
Are on the wing to join your choir!"
He said—and, light as bridegrooms bound
  To their young loves, re-climb'd the steep
And gain'd the shrine—his chiefs stood round—
  Their swords, as with instinctive leap,
Together, at that cry accurst,
Had from their sheaths, like sunbeams, burst.
And hark!—again—again it rings;
Near and more near its echoings
Peal through the chasm. Oh! who that then
Had seen those listening warrior-men,
With their swords grasped, their eyes of flame
Turn'd on their chief—could doubt the shame,
Th' indignant shame with which they thrill
To hear those shouts, and yet stand still?

2. He read their thoughts—they were his own—
  "What! while our arms can wield these blades,
Shall we die tamely—die alone?
  Without one victim to our shades,
One Moslem heart where, buried deep,
The sabre from its toil may sleep?

No—God of Iran's burning skies!
Thou scorn'st th' inglorious sacrifice.
No—though of all earth's hope bereft,
Life, swords, and vengeance still are left.
We'll make yon valley's reeking caves
   Live in the awe-struck minds of men,
Till tyrants shudder when their slaves
   Tell of the Ghebers' bloody glen.
Follow, brave hearts!—this pile remains
Our refuge still from life and chains;
But his the best, the holiest bed,
Who sinks entomb'd in Moslem dead!"

MOORE.

79. THE IRISH EMIGRANT'S MOTHER.

"O COME! my mother, come away, across the sea-green water;
O! come with me, and come with him, the husband of thy daughter;
O! come with us, and come with them, the sister and the brother,
Who, prattling, climb thine aged knees, and call thy daughter—mother.

"O! come, and leave this land of death—this isle of desolation—
This speck upon the sun-bright face of God's sublime creation,
Since now o'er all our fatal stars the most malign hath risen,
When Labor seeks the Poorhouse, and Innocence the Prison.

"'Tis true o'er all the sun-brown fields the husky wheat is bending;
'Tis true God's blessed hand at last a better time is sending;
'Tis true the island's aged face looks happier and younger,

But in the best of days we've known the sickness and the
    hunger.

"When health breathed out in every breeze, too oft we've
    known the fever—
Too oft, my mother, have we felt the hand of the bereaver;
Too well remember many a time the mournful task that brought
    him,
When freshness fanned the Summer air, and cooled the glow
    of Autumn.

"But then the trial, though severe, still testified our patience,
We bowed with mingled hope and fear, to God's wise dispen
    sations;
We felt the gloomiest time was both a promise and a warning;
Just as the darkest hour of night is herald of the morning.

"But now through all the black expanse no hopeful morning
    breaketh—
No bird of promise in our hearts the gladsome song awaketh;
No far-off gleams of good light up the hills of expectation—
Naught but the gloom that might precede the world's annihi-
    lation.

"So, mother, turn thine aged feet, and let our children lead 'em
Down to the ship that wafts us soon to plenty and to freedom;
Forgetting naught of all the past, yet all the past forgiving;
Come, let us leave the dying land, and fly unto the living.

"They tell us, they who read and think of Ireland's ancient story
How once its Emerald Flag flung out a Sunburst's fleeting glory;
O! if that sun will pierce no more the dark clouds that efface it,
Fly where the rising Stars of Heaven commingle to replace it.

"So, come, my mother, come away, across the sea-green
    water;

O! come with us, and come with him, the husband of thy
    daughter;
O! come with us, and come with them, the sister and the
    brother,
Who, prattling, climb thine aged knees, and call thy daughter—
    mother."

"Ah! go, my children, go away—obey this inspiration;
Go, with the mantling hopes of health and youthful expecta-
    tion;
Go, clear the forests, climb the hills, and plough the expectant
    prairies;
Go, in the sacred name of God, and the Blessed Virgin Mary's.

"But though I feel how sharp the pang from thee and thine to
    sever,
To look upon these darling ones the last time and for ever;
Yet in this sad and dark old land, by desolation haunted,
My heart has struck its roots too deep ever to be transplanted.

"A thousand fibres still have life, although the trunk is dying—
They twine around the yet green grave where thy father's
    bones are lying;
Ah! from that sad and sweet embrace no soil on earth can
    loose 'em,
Though golden harvests gleam on its breast, and golden sands
    in its bosom.

"Others are twined around the stone, where ivy blossoms
    smother
The crumbling lines that trace thy names, my father and my
    mother;
God's blessing be upon their souls—God grant, my old heart
    prayeth,
Their names be written in the Book whose writing ne'er
    decayeth.

"Alas! my prayers would never warm within those great
    cold buildings,
Those grand cathedral churches, with their marbles and their
    gildings;
Far fitter than the proudest dome that would hang in splendor
    o'er me,
Is the simple chapel's white-washed wall, where my people
    knelt before me.

"No doubt it is a glorious land to which you now are going,
Like that which God bestowed of old, with milk and honey
    flowing;
But where are the blessed saints of God, whose lives of his
    law remind me,
Like Patrick, Brigid, and Columbkille, in the land I'd leave
    behind me?

"So leave me here, my children, with my old ways and old
    notions;
Leave me here in peace, with my memories and devotions;
Leave me in sight of your father's grave, and as the heavens
    allied us.
Let not, since we were joined in life, even the grave divide us.

"There's not a week but I can hear how you prosper better
    and better,
For the mighty fireships o'er the sea will bring the expected
    letter;
And if I need aught for my simple wants, my food or my
    winter firing,
Thou'lt gladly spare from thy growing store a little for my
    requiring.

"Remember with a pitying love the hapless land that bore
    you;
At every festal season be its gentle form before you;

When the Christmas candle is lighted, and the holly and ivy
    glisten,
Let your eye look back for a vanished face—for a voice that
    is silent, listen!

"So go, my children, go away—obey this inspiration;
Go, with the mantling hopes of health and youthful expecta-
    tion;
Go, clear the forests, climb the hills, and plough the expectant
    prairies;
Go, in the sacred name of God, and the blessed Virgin Mary's."

D. F. M'CARTHY.

---

80. ENGLAND'S PRESENT.

FOR nearly two hundred years, until within the present century, she has not met her match on lake or ocean, gun to gun and man to man—and certainly not yet among the nations of Europe.

2. She has consequently rested for ages secure from the devastations of war. Since the Norman invasion no hostile foreign force has found footing on her shores. The jutting cliff which she presents as her nearest point to Europe,

    "That pale and white-faced shore,
      Whose foot spurns back the raging ocean's tides,"

is typical of the defensive power of this island people. But her power, beyond her own rock-bound coast, is on the sea alone:

    "Her march is on the mountain wave,
      Her home is on the deep;"

and though there, on her own proper element, she is all-powerful, yet on land, in the wars of Europe, she has, except in two memorable instances, acted but a secondary part.

3. Her merchant and coasting ships employ great numbers of sailors, and out of these she supplies abundantly her navy with men whose lives have been on the ocean, and who know no home but the deck. She never lacks sailors.

4. But her miners and manufacturers, who live and work under shelter, are not fit for service in the open field; and her agricultural laborers have no taste for military adventure. Shakspeare, with his instinctive appreciation of character, gives in the second part of his King Henry IV. a just measure of the military predilection of the English boor.

5. His Mouldy and Bull Calf may be fairly taken, then and at the present time, as representatives of the class to which they belong. When drafted as soldiers, one begs to be released, for if he go, "his old dame will be undone for some one to do her husbandry and her drudgery;" and the other "would as lief be hanged as to go."

6. And at no time, down to the present day, has the British peasant panted for the tented field, or been eager to advance to "the imminent deadly breach." He has always preferred, and still prefers, his old dame's "husbandry and drudgery," with the home comforts of the English cottage, to the laurels to be won, and the limbs to be lost, at Waterloo or Sebastopol. For his "own part, he would as lief be hanged as to go."

7. Ireland has supplied much the larger contingent of soldiers for the British service. Her sons have been starved into the ranks of the army; and there is more truth than poetry in the doggerel triplet of Daniel O'Connell:

> "At famous Waterloo,
> Duke Wellington would have looked blue,
> If Paddy had not been there too."

But Irishmen, though fond of war, have no love for the British service. They enter it only from necessity; and since the natural increase has been kept down by emigration, the ranks of the army can no longer be filled in Ireland.

8. Great Britain, therefore, cannot raise an army for continental service; but has been compelled to resort to the employment of foreign troops, and to enlistments in foreign countries. Her necessities drove her to try even ours; and with all her boundless wealth, and with the spindles which conquered Buonaparte quadrupled, she is able to bear but an nferior part in the present conflict of mighty nations.

9. It is evident, therefore, that Great Britain, powerful as she is on the ocean, is comparatively feeble everywhere off her own soil, and out of the range of the guns of her men-of-war. "Her home is on the deep." There, too, was the home of her predecessors, Tyre, and Carthage, and Venice. Like them in the days of their prosperity, she has foreign possessions quite disproportioned to the power of her own people; and like them she must trust to foreign mercenaries to defend those possessions, and to hold them in subjection.

10. Besides her inability to raise men, her military arm is paralyzed by a vice inherent in her system. Her armies are not well officered. Commissions, up to a certain grade, are the subject of purchase and sale, not the reward of merit. By this the *morale* of the army suffers, and that too even to the highest in command; for the General-in-Chief himself, if he have military experience, must be selected from those who have bought their way, instead of those who have fought their way, to high military rank.

11. Her soldiers are as brave as any on the face of the earth; but all who have attended to the details of the war in the Crimea, must have felt the great superiority of the French over the English organization and command. The French commissariat has from the first been better; their medical staff better; their corps of engineers better; and fewer mistakes have been committed by their officers.

12. All this is perceived and felt, and the proud spirit of the British nation is wounded and revolts at the contrast; and the ministry is censured for what is inherent in the system, and not under their control. Great Britain had in times past

a Marlborough and a Wellington, but there was a century between them, and those great commanders are but exceptions: they were great in spite of the vices of the system under which they rose.

13. Her military power is now less than it was fifty years ago during the wars consequent on the French Revolution though within that time she has more than doubled her population, and trebled her manufactures and commerce.

EWING.

81. THE BIBLE.

[DONOSO CORTES is a popular philosopher and a brilliant poet. The following extract is from a speech delivered in Madrid on the occasion of his reception as a member of the Royal Spanish Academy of Languages.]

THERE is a book, the treasure of a nation, which has now become the fable and the reproach of the world, though in former days the star of the East, to whose pages all the great poets of the Western world have gone to drink in divine inspiration, and from which they have learned the secret of elevating our hearts and transporting our souls with superhuman and mysterious harmonies. This book is the Bible—the Book of books. In it Dante saw his terrific visions; from it Petrarch learned to modulate the voice of his complainings; from that burning forge the poet of Sorrentum drew for the splendid brightness of his songs.

2. In the Bible are written the annals of heaven, of earth, and of the human race. In it, as in the Divinity itself, is contained that which was, which is, and which is to come. In its first page is recorded the beginning of time and of all things—in its last, the end of all things, and of time. It begins with Genesis, which is an idyl; it finishes with the Apocalypse of St. John, which is a funeral hymn.

3. Genesis is beautiful as the first breeze which refreshed the world, as the first flower which budded forth in the fields, as the first tender word which humanity pronounced, as the

first sun that rose in the East. The Apocalypse is sad, like the last throb of nature, like the last ray of light, like the last glance of the dying; and between that funeral hymn and that idyl we behold all generations pass, one after another, before the sight of God, and one after another, all nations.

4. There all catastrophes are related or predicted, and therefore immortal models for all tragedies are to be found there. There we find the narration of all human griefs, and therefore the Biblical harps resound mournfully, giving the tone to all lamentations and to all elegies. Who will again moan like Job, when, driven to the earth by the mighty hand that afflicted him, he fills with his groanings and waters with his tears the valleys of Idumea?

5. Who will again lament as Jeremiah lamented, wandering around Jerusalem, and abandoned of God and men? Who will be mournful and gloomy, with the gloom and mournfulness of Ezekiel, the poet of great woes and tremendous punishments, when he gave to the winds his impetuous inspiration, the terror of Babylon? Who shall again sing like Moses, when, after crossing the Red Sea, he chanted the victory of Jehovah, the defeat of Pharaoh, the liberty of his people?

6. Who shall again chant a hymn of victory like that which was sung by Deborah, the sybil of Israel, the amazon of the Hebrews, the strong woman of the Bible? And if from hymns of victory you pass to hymns of praise, what temple shall ever resound like that of Israel, when those sweet harmonious voices arose to heaven, mingled with the soft perfume of the roses of Jericho, and with the aroma of Oriental incense?

7. If you seek for models of lyric poetry, what lyre shall we find comparable to the harp of David, the friend of God, who listened to the sweet harmonies and caught the soft tones of the harps of angels? or to that of Solomon, the wisest and most fortunate of monarchs, the inspired writer of the song of songs; he who put his wisdom into sentences and proverbs, and finished by pronouncing that all was vanity?

8. If you seek for models of bucolic poetry, where will you

find them so fresh and so pure as in the Scriptural era of the patriarchate, when the woman and the fountain and the flower were friends, because they were all united—each one by itself the symbol of primitive simplicity and of candid innocence?

9. A prodigious book that, gentlemen, in which the human race began to read thirty-three centuries ago, and although reading it every day, every night, and every hour, have not yet finished its perusal. A prodigious book that, in which all is computed, before the science of calculation was invented; in which, without the study of the languages, we are informed of the origin of languages; in which, without astronomical studies, the revolutions of the stars are computed; in which, without historical documents, we are instructed in history; in which, without physical studies, the laws of nature are revealed.

10. A prodigious book that, which sees all and knows all; which knows the thoughts that arise in the heart of man, and those which are present to the mind of God; which views that which passes in the abysses of the sea, and that which takes place in the bosom of the earth; which relates or predicts all the catastrophes of nations, and in which are contained and heaped together all the treasures of mercy, all the treasures of justice, and all the treasures of vengeance.

11. A book, in short, gentlemen, which, when the heavens shall fold together like a gigantic scroll, and the earth shall faint away, and the sun withdraw its light, and the stars grow pale, will remain alone with God, because it is his eternal word, and shall resound eternally in the heavens.

Donoso Cortes.

---

82. INFLUENCE OF PAGAN CLASSICS ON RELIGION.

WHEN it is the object of an enemy to take possession of a strong place, he begins by occupying a favorable position, whence he destroys the outworks which protect the heart of the fortress; and such are the tactics employed by paganism, which seeks to take revenge upon Christianity.

2. Established on the most favorable ground, that of education, we have seen it batter literature, philosophy, the arts and sciences; then, under the pretext of regeneration, animate them with its spirit, enroll them under its banner, and march upon Christianity itself, which is the heart of the place, the true aim of all its attacks.

3. To prove the progress of the enemy on this point, and to show that classic paganism tends to the entire ruin of Christianity, is the important matter upon which we shall enter.

4. Classic paganism ruins Christianity in causing it to be forgotten, to be contemned, to be altered. Let us examine things as they are. From the family, where, generally speaking, he has received but a superficial knowledge of Christianity, the child enters an establishment for public instruction, where he remains for seven or eight years. If not the first, at least the second Latin or Greek book put into his hands is pagan; the third is pagan, the fourth is pagan, and, in fact, all are pagan, to the end of his studies.

5. His daily and hourly occupation is to read, to translate, and to commit to memory all the doings of paganism, from the exploits of the gods to those of the warriors, the orators, and the philosophers. In the classes nothing is heard but the names of Romans and Carthaginians. To identify the students more completely with these models, the classes are divided into two camps, and the youth is either Greek or Roman,— Scipio or Annibal.

6. The explanations of the professors never, or very rarely, furnish him with Christian notions. He lives in the midst of paganism; his horizon never, except by some unusual circumstance, extends beyond the limits of Greece and Italy. The Holy Mountain, the Palatine, Thebes, Sparta, Marathon, the Thermopylæ, the Tribune, the Capitol, the Areopagus, the Forum, are the only places upon which his thoughts, his imagination and his memory dwell.

7. In giving our full tribute of praise to the zeal and virtue of our masters, we cannot help protesting loudly against the pagan system, under which our childhood was formed, and the ignorance in matters of religion that was the result of it. On leaving college, we knew by heart the names, the history, the attributes, the adventures of the gods and goddesses of fable; we knew the Danaides and the Parcæ, Ixion and his wheel, Tantalus with his torment, the feathered tribe of the Capitol and of Claudius.

8. Without a single mistake, we could have given the biography of Minos, of Æacus, of Rhadamanthus, of Codrus and of Tarquin, of Epaminondas, of Scipio and of Annibal, of Cicero and of Demosthenes, without counting that of Alexander and of Cæsar, of Ovid, of Sallust, of Virgil and of Homer. Lycurgus, Socrates, Plato, the Flamens, the Circus and the Amphitheatre, the sacrifices, the feasts, all were familiar to us.

9. In a word, we knew all that was desirable in young men of distinction in Rome and Athens, the offshoots of Brutus and of Gracchus, candidates for the glories of the Forum, adorers or future priests of Jupiter and of Saturn.

10. But if we had been transported into the arena of Christianity, and called upon to name the twelve Apostles, or the numbers of the Epistles; if we had been interrogated on our saints and martyrs, on our heroes and our glories, our Chrysostoms, our Augustines, our Athanasiuses, and our Ambroses, on these kings of Christian eloquence and philosophy, these fathers of the modern world, these masters of the science of life; if we, their children, and the children of the Church and of the martyrs, had been asked the date of their birth, what were the combats they sustained, the works they composed, the actions that commanded the admiration, the veneration of future ages, it would have been as an unknown tongue to us.

11. The blush on our cheek and the silence of our lips would have excited the pity of a man of sense, and convinced us of the nakedness of our classical studies. Such is our history, as it is doubtless that of many others.

12. Will it be said that this deplorable ignorance on matters of religion is to be dissipated later? Alas! how many young people, men of ripe age, in the various conditions of life, do we know, who, from the time they left college, have devoted *twenty-four hours* to the study of religion!

13. How many, on the contrary, may we not cite, who, so far from developing what little they knew of religion, have long, long since, lost even the elementary notions of the Catechism! Thus we have shown that classic paganism condemns the immense majority of *instructed* men to an eternal ignorance in matters of religion.

GAUME.

---

83. PAGAN AND CHRISTIAN CLASSICS.

IT has often been a subject of astonishment and complaint, that a direction almost exclusively classical should be given to the studies of youth in modern times; and though it might not be difficult to detect the real cause which has operated to produce this partiality, which certainly must be sought elsewhere than in the supposed barrenness and barbarism of the ancient Christian literature, it may be sufficient here to bear testimony to the justice of such complaints.

2. For, in fact, what can be more unreasonable than to maintain that an acquaintance with the histories and manners of the ancient Greeks and Romans is more essential to complete the instruction of Christians than the like knowledge of the habits and institutions of their own national ancestors and fathers in the faith; that an English student should be familiar with Livy without having ever even heard of Ingulphus or a William of Malmesbury; that he should know by heart the sentences of Demosthenes, without being aware that St. Chrysostom was, perhaps, his equal in eloquence and grandeur; and that he should be afraid of corrupting his Latinity by looking into St. Jerome, of whom Erasmus said, that if he had a prize to award between him and Cicero, he should

be tempted to give it to the Christian father rather than to the great orator of Rome.

3. Ah! could these mighty spirits of the ancient world give utterance to the conviction which now possesses them in answer to the multitude of voices which continually are raised from earth to speak their praise, they would counsel their fond admirers to place their affection upon diviner models; they would speak in words like those of the shade of Virgil, when he first meets Dante: "We lived in times of false and lying gods: we sung of earthly conquests, but why dost thou return to this fatal region? why not scale this delicious mountain, which is the beginning and the cause of all joy?"

4. "——————— At Rome my life was past,
Beneath the mild Augustus, in the time
Of fabled Deities and false. A bard
Was I, and made Anchises' upright son
The subject of my song, who came from Troy,
When the flame preyed on Ilium's haughty towers.
But thou, say wherefore to such perils past
Return'st thou? Wherefore not this pleasant mount
Ascendest, cause and source of all delight?"

. . . .

5. Now it is not certainly too much to affirm, that the customs and manners of the Middle Ages are deserving of quite as much attention from us, as that Homeric way of life, and those Pythagorean manners spoken of by Socrates, that their literature might supply most interesting variety to those who may very well think that they have heard enough of the hard Eurystheus and the altars of the illaudible Busiris, and the other verses which continue to arrest so many vacant minds; and that these our domestic antiquities would furnish ample matter to exercise, with the greatest advantage, all our diligence and research, though we had the industry of a Chrysippus, who was so curious, as Cicero says, in collecting various examples from all history.

. . . .

6. In whatever direction, on that blessed shore, we turn our steps, we shall find inexhaustible riches of every virtue, of wisdom and learning, of beauty and grandeur; to cheer the sage, who may then detect the truth of things in an abyss of radiance, clear and lofty; to ravish that imagination of the young which is kindled by the splendor of eternal light; and to satisfy in all

"The increate perpetual thirst, that draws
Towards the realm of God's own form."

. . . .

7. But if a description of the armor of one hero could justly occupy so many verses as those of Homer and Virgil, in explaining that of Achilles and of Æneas, what indulgence may not be granted to him who should endeavor to place before men's eyes the grandeur and holiness of the lives and deaths of men under the ancient Catholic state?

. . . .

8. Guizot, who, in such a question, is an authority not to be suspected, says of the writers of the Middle Ages, who recorded the deeds and thoughts of holy men, "If we consider them in a purely literary point of view, we shall find their merit no less brilliant and no less varied. Nature and simplicity are not wanting in them; they are devoid of affectation and free from pedantry."

9. A slight acquaintance with them will, with most minds, generate a distaste for those innumerable books of later times which bear undoubted signs of having been written by men who were full of themselves, and who, in composing them, were really no otherwise occupied than in worshipping their own miserable image.　　　　　　　　　　　DIGBY.

---

84. CHRISTIAN ORATORS.—FATHERS OF THE CHURCH.

THE eloquence of the Fathers of the Church has in it something that overawes; something energetic, something royal, as it were, and whose authority at once confounds and subdues. You are convinced that their mission comes from on high, and that they teach by the express command of the Almighty. In the midst of these inspirations, however, their genius retains its majesty and serenity.

2. St. Ambrose is the Fénélon of the Latin Fathers. He is flowery, smooth, and rich; and, with the exception of a few defects, which belonged to the age in which he lived, his works are equally entertaining and instructive. To be convinced of this, the reader need only turn to the "Treatise on Virginity," and the "Praise of the Patriarchs." St. Jerome is particularly distinguished for a vigorous imagination, which his immense learning was incapable of extinguishing.

3. The collection of his letters is one of the most curious monuments of patristic literature. He loves to dwell on the nature and delights of solitude. From the recess of his cell at Bethlehem he beheld the fall of the Roman Empire. What a vast subject of reflection for a holy anchorite! Accordingly, death and the vanity of human life are ever present to his view.

4 "We are dying, we are changing every hour," says he, in a letter to one of his friends, "and yet we live as if we were immortal. The very time which it takes to pen these lines must be retrenched from my day. We often write to one another, my dear Heliodorus; our letters traverse the seas, and, as the ship scuds along, so life flies: a moment passes with every wave." As Ambrose is the Fénélon of the Fathers, so Tertullian is the Bossuet.

5. Part of his vindication of religion might, even at the present day, be of service to the same cause. How wonderful that Christianity should now be obliged to defend herself before her own children, as she formerly defended herself before her executioners, and that the "Apology to the Gentiles" should have become the "Apology to the Christians!"

6. The most remarkable feature of this work is the intellectual development which it displays. You are ushered into a new order of ideas; you feel that what you hear is not the

language of early antiquity, or the scarcely articulate accents of man.

7. Tertullian speaks like a modern; the subjects of his eloquence are derived from the circle of eternal truths, and not from the reasons of passion and circumstance employed in the Roman tribune, or in the public place at Athens. This progress of the genius of philosophy is evidently the effect of our holy religion.

8. Had not the false deities been overthrown, and the true worship of God been established, man would have continued in endless infancy; for, persevering in error in regard to the first principle of all other notions, would have been more or less tinctured with the fundamental vice. The other tracts of Tertullian, particularly those on "Patience," the "Shows," the "Martyrs," the "Ornaments of Women," and the "Resurrection of the Body," contain numberless beautiful passages.

9. "I doubt," says the orator, reproaching the Christian females with their luxury, "I doubt whether hands accustomed to bracelets will be able to endure the weight of chains; whether feet adorned with fillets will become habituated to galling fetters. I much question whether a head covered with a network of pearls and diamonds would not yield to the sword."

10. These words, addressed to the women who were daily conducted to the scaffold, glow with courage and with faith. Among the fathers of the Greek Church, two only are highly eloquent—SS. Chrysostom and Basil. The homilies of the former on "Death," and the "Disgrace of Eutropius," are real masterpieces.   CHATEAUBRIAND.

---

85. "LET THE WATERS BE GATHERED TOGETHER."

[ST. BASIL occupies a distinguished rank among the great bishops who rendered illustrious not only the Church, but their age, and humanity itself. As a model of eloquence, he now particularly interests us. Erasmus affirms that in the art of oratory he has no rival. Rollin, who closely studied his principles of elocution, proposes him to youth as one of the most skilful masters of eloquence. Photius says, "Whoever wishes to become an accomplished orator has no need of Plato nor of Demosthenes, if he takes Basil as a model." There is no writer whose style is purer, more beautiful, or more energetic; he reunites all that can convince or charm the mind; his style, always natural, flows with the same rapidity as the stream gushes from its source. The discourse on the text, "Let the waters be gathered together in one place," is full of delicate imagery, grand and elevated thoughts, and happy comparisons, which show in the orator a profound knowledge of the sciences. This discourse is one of a number delivered by St. Basil on the 1st chapter of Genesis. It is said that the most simple understood them, and the most learned were delighted and astonished with them. It is deeply to be regretted that no able pen and intelligent pious mind has undertaken the translation of the Fathers into English. Still more is it to be regretted that they do not enter into the classic course of our colleges.]

THE waters have received the order to flow, and, always obedient, they never exhaust their source. I speak of those which are in movement—the fountains and rivers. When seated by the fountain from which the bright waters gush spontaneously, have you never asked yourself, Why it springs from the earth? Who has caused it? Where is the reservoir from whence it flows? Where will the course of its term be checked? Why does it not stop of itself? Why does not that sea, into which all the waters pour themselves, overflow its bounds?

2. This word of the Gospel answers all. There is the history of all the waters on the face of the earth: "Let the waters be gathered together in one place," for fear that, overflowing the space assigned them and passing from one place to another, they would inundate the entire continent.

3. Thus we frequently see the ocean agitated by tempests, elevating its waters to a stupendous height; scarcely do they touch the shore when all this impetuosity is reduced to foam, and the waters return to their channel. "Will you not fear me, saith the Lord? I have set the land the bound for the sea."

4. What would prevent the Red Sea from overflowing Egypt, which is lower than is its bed, and uniting its waters with those of the Indian Ocean, if it was not chained in its

bed by the order of its Sovereign Master? Sesostris and Darius, the Mede, attempted it, but without success. Their power was overthrown by the power of Him who, in collecting the waters in such a place, decided that they should not pass the bounds which he assigned for them.*

5. *And God saw that it was good!* Ah! without doubt the sea presents a beautiful spectacle when in its calm repose, its surface rippled by gentle winds, delicately tinted with purple or azure, beats not with violence against the neighboring earth, but seems to come with gentle caresses. Yes, God judged this work good, in its connection with others.

6. The waters of the ocean are the common source of all the humidity on the earth, which it distributes by imperceptible channels. Good, because, being the reservoir of our rivers, from all parts it receives waters without ever passing its bounds. Good, in furnishing the vapors which are converted into refreshing showers for the earth; because it enriches the islands, of which it is at the same time the ornament and the rampart; because it unites the most distant countries by the advantages of navigation and commerce; it enriches history; furnishes abundantly all the necessaries of life, and, by transporting different productions into other countries, replaces what is needed in some, by the superabundance of others.

. . . .

7. But is it possible to understand and fathom the beauties of the sea, with the same eye as he who made them sees them? If they obtain the approbation of the Lord, how by much more should this Christian assembly, where the united voices of men, women, and children, like the murmuring of the waves which break against the shore, carry, even to heaven, the prayers which we address to the Most High!

8. A profound calm shelters you from the tempests. The peace which reigns among you has not been troubled by the

---

* Nieuwentl has made a most luminous application of this argument in his beautiful "Treatise on the Existence of God."

perverse doctrines which the spirit of heresy has spread elsewhere. Merit, then, the praises of the Lord by the faithful practice of the duties of your state, through the grace of our Lord Jesus Christ, to whom be glory and power in all ages.

ST. BASIL.

---

86. "IN THE BEGINNING WAS THE WORD."

[BOSSUET says: "One of the most forcible discourses, although one of the shortest, upon this text of St. John, is that of St. Basil. One must be deeply prejudiced, not to feel with what force the Arians were refuted by it."]

THE simplest words of the Gospel surpass in depth and magnificence all the other oracles which the Holy Ghost has diffused throughout the Scriptures. Elsewhere it is the servants who speak to us; here it is the Master of the prophets himself. But among the holy evangelists, the one whose voice sounds with the greatest effect—the one who has revealed to us mysteries most sublime and elevated above all intelligence, is John, the son of thunder, whose words you have just heard. "In the beginning was the Word, and the Word was with God, and the Word was God."

2. I know more than one writer, a great stranger to the true doctrine, and solely desirous of the glory resulting from human wisdom, who, in his admiration for this opening, has dared to appropriate it, and to insert it in his works. These are the accustomed larcenies of the devil, who has robbed us of our riches to adorn his own lies.

3. And if mere human wisdom has testified so high an admiration for these words, how much should not we, the disciples of the Holy Ghost, esteem them! But if it is easy to admire beautiful passages, it is not so easy to fathom them. One needs only eyes to recognize the beauty of the heavenly orb that enlightens us with his rays; but try to fix your gaze upon him, and your dazzled vision will soon lose the power of contemplating him. Such is the effect produced by meditation on these words, "In the beginning was the Word."

4. The evangelist, wishing to teach us what pertains to the knowledge of the Son of God, takes us back to the principle of all that exists. The Holy Ghost knew well those who would attack one day the glory of the only Son of God; he saw in futurity the sophisms by which certain men would seek to overthrow the faith of Christians.

5. "If he was begotten," they say, "he did not exist before;" and again, "Would that which did not exist have given him birth?" The Holy Ghost has foreseen all these objections; he answers all by this one sentence: "In the beginning was the Word." And if they tell you, If he was begotten, he did not exist before, answer, "In the beginning he was." Before being begotten, what was he? Reflect on this word, "In the beginning."

6. Why speak of the beginning, since there is question of that which has no beginning? "It is to say that in the beginning, from the origin of things, *he was;* he did not begin—*he was.* He was not created—he was not made—*he was.* *Non prius factus est, sed erat.**

7. "There was nothing before this beginning. Go back to the beginning of all things; stretch your thoughts as far as you can; go to the first day—farther still—to the beginning—before all that has ever begun—*he was.*" And if he was at the beginning, at what time was he not?

8. "But what was he? He was the Word. What does this mean? He who was at the beginning was the Word, the inward utterance, thought, reason, intelligence, wisdom, interior speech, *sermo;* speech which is substantially all truth, and which is truth itself.

9. Where was the Word? Not in a certain place; for that which is limitless cannot occupy a determined position. He was with God. *Verbum erat apud Deum,*†—equally infinite. Seek throughout all space; everywhere you will find God who fills it; everywhere, likewise, is the Son, himself as immense.

---

* He was not made, but he was first.
† The Word was with God.

"The Word was with God"—*apud Deum;* that is to say, that he was not something inherent in God—something that affects God—but something that dwells in him as subsisting in him as being a person in God, and another person than that God in whom he is; and this person was divine; it was God.

ST. BASIL.

87. LETTER OF ST. BASIL, DESCRIBING HIS HERMITAGE, TO ST. GREGORY NAZIANZEN.

I BELIEVE I may at last flatter myself with having found the end of my wanderings. The hopes of being united with thee—or, I should rather say, my dreams for hopes have been justly termed the waking dreams of men—have remained unfulfilled.

2. God has suffered me to find a place, such as has often flitted before our imaginations; for that which fancy has shown us from afar is now made manifest to me. A high mountain, clothed with thick woods, is watered to the north by fresh and ever-flowing streams. At its foot lies an extended plain, rendered fruitful by the vapors with which it is moistened. The surrounding forest, crowded with trees of different kinds, encloses one as in a strong fortress.

3. This wilderness is bounded by two ravines: on the one side the river, rushing in foam down the mountain, forms an almost impassable barrier, while on the other all access is impeded by a broad mountain ridge. My hut is so situated on the summit of the mountain that I can overlook the whole plain, and follow throughout its course the Iris, which is more beautiful, and has a more abundant body of water than the Strymon, near Amphipolis.

4. The river of my wilderness, which is more impetuous than any other that I know of, breaks against the jutting rocks, and throws itself foaming into the abyss below—an object of admiration to the mountain wanderer, and a source of

profit to the natives from the numerous fishes that are found in its waters.

5. Shall I describe to thee the fructifying vapors that rise from the moist earth, or the cool breezes wafted over the rippled face of the waters? Shall I speak of the sweet song of the birds, or of the rich luxuriance of the flowering plants? What charms me beyond all else is the calm repose of the spot.

6. It is only visited occasionally by huntsmen; for my wilderness nourishes herds of deer and wild goats, but not bears and wolves. What other spot could I exchange for this? Alcmæan, when he had found the Echinades, would not wander farther.

7. When I see every ledge of rock, every valley and plain covered with new-born verdure, the varied beauty of the trees, and the lilies at my feet decked by Nature with the double charm of perfume and color; when in the distance I see the ocean, towards which the clouds are borne onward, my spirit is overpowered by a sadness not wholly devoid of enjoyment.

8. When in autumn the fruits have passed away, the leaves have fallen, and the branches of the trees, dried and shrivelled, are everlasting and regular change in Nature, to feel the harmony of the wondrous powers pervading all things—he who contemplates them with the eye of the soul, feels the littleness of man among the grandeur of the universe.

ST. BASIL.

---

88. THOU ART BEAUTIFUL, O SEA!

THE Sea offers us a lovely spectacle when its surface is bright, or when, rippling gently under the wind, it is tinted with purple and green; when, without beating violently upon the shore, it surrounds the earth, and caresses her with its wild embraces. But it is not this which constitutes, in the eyes of God, the grace and beauty of the Sea: it is its works which makes it beautiful.

2. See here the immense reservoir of water which irrigates and fertilizes the earth, and which penetrates into her bosom to reappear in rivers, in lakes, and in refreshing fountains; for in traversing the earth it loses its bitterness, and is almost civilized by the distance it travels.

3. Thou art beautiful, O Sea! because in thy vast bosom thou receivest all the rivers, and remainest between thy shores without ever overleaping them. Thou art beautiful, because the clouds rise from thee. Thou art beautiful, with thine isles spread over thy surface, because thou unitest, by commerce, the most distant countries—because, instead of separating them, thou joinest the nations, and bearest to the merchant his wealth, and to life its resources.

4. But if the Sea is beautiful before men and before God, how much more beautiful is that multitude, that human sea, which has its sounds and murmurs, voices of men, of women, and of children, resounding and rising up to the throne of God!

St. Basil.

89. VENERABLE BEDE.

BLIND with old age, the Venerable Bede
Ceased not, for that, to preach and publish forth
The news from Heaven—the tidings of great joy.
From town to town—through all the villages—
With trusty guidance roamed the aged saint,
And preached the Word with all the fire of youth.

2. One day, his boy had led him to a vale
That lay all thickly sowed with mighty rocks.
In mischief, more than malice, spake the boy:
"Most reverend father, there are many men
Assembled here, who wait to hear thy voice."
The blind old man, so bowed, straightway rose up,

Chose him his text, expounded, then applied;
Exhorted, warned, rebuked, and comforted,
So fervently, that soon the gushing tears
Streamed thick and fast down to his hoary beard.

3. When, at the close, as seemeth always meet,
He prayed, " Our Father," and pronounced aloud,
"Thine is the kingdom and the power, thine
The glory now and through eternity,"
At once there rang, through all that echoing vale,
A sound of many voices, crying,
"Amen! most reverend sire, Amen! Amen!"

4. Trembling with terror and remorse, the boy
Knelt down before the saint, and owned his sin;
"Son," said the old man, "hast thou, then, ne'er read,
'When men are dumb, the stones shall cry aloud?'—
Henceforward, mock not, son, the word of God!
Living it is, and mighty, cutting sharp,
Like a two-edged sword. And when the heart
Of flesh grows hard and stubborn like the stone,
A heart of flesh shall stir in stones themselves."

---

90. TO THE CHRISTIANS OF ROME.

[ST. IGNATIUS OF ANTIOCH:—This holy bishop governed the Church of Antioch for forty years. Having escaped the cruel persecution of Domitian, he obtained the crown of martyrdom in the pacific one under the reign of Trajan.

This emperor, so lauded by Pliny, his panegyrist, and by modern writers, cruelly commanded the martyrdom of the holy bishop, whom he sent from Antioch to Rome under the escort of soldiers more ferocious even than the animals for whom Ignatius was destined; we may conclude from such an example what was the tolerance of philosophic writers. Although Trajan issued no edict against the Christians, yet he permitted their persecution.

The most celebrated epistle of Ignatius is addressed to the Christians of Rome, to persuade them not to obtain the revocation of the sentence of martyrdom pronounced upon him. How often are the last words of Socrates quoted! Why should not the noble eloquence of an Ignatius and a Polycarp be household words amongst us?]

THE commencement is well; if I am permitted to obtain the portion reserved for me, *all* will be well. But, alas! I fear your too tender compassion for me! You will supplicate the Almighty for me, and He will hear your prayers; He will spare me because you ask it, and then I must commence anew my course.

2. But remember! *I* also wish to please God as you please Him; if you love me with a true charity, you will let me go to enjoy my God.

3. Never shall I have a more favorable occasion to be united to Him; nor you to honor Him by a *good* work. If you speak not of me to Him, I shall go to God; but if, yielding to a false compassion for this miserable flesh, you bring me back to the labor of this life, what is it but to double the length and multiply the cares of my soul's journey towards her home?

4. Ah! can you procure me a greater blessing than to be immolated to God when the altar is prepared? I ask you only to unite yourselves to my sacrifice with canticles of thanksgiving in honor of the Father and of Jesus Christ His Son, whilst I offer the victim. You are forbidden to envy in aught,—envy not, then, my felicity; you have instructed others,—be faithful to your own precepts.

5. Occupy yourselves solely with this thought—to obtain for me by your prayers courage to overcome the enemy within and the enemy without, that I may thus wear truly and in very deed, not merely the name, but the reality of a Christian and a Bishop. I declare now to all the churches, that, provided you place no obstacles in the way, I shall with joy embrace the martyr's crown. I shall serve as food to lions and bears, but oh! how speedy such a path to heaven!

6. I am the wheat of God; would that, being ground between the teeth of beasts, I might become bread worthy to be offered to Christ. Pray with me that the beasts may tear me

to pieces, that they may become my tomb, leaving no fragment of my body unconsumed. I do not command you,— Peter and Paul could do so, for they were apostles; but what am I, *save* one condemned by wicked men? They were free, but I am yet a slave.

7. If I suffer, *then* shall *I* be a freedman of Christ, then shall I arise to true liberty. Now, in my chains, I desire nothing in this world—only that the beasts may be eager for their prey. If they shrink, as they have often done heretofore, I myself will urge them to the attack; I will seek to arouse their native violence.

8. Forgive me, but I know my own interests; the price of victory is Jesus Christ; what higher reward can be bestowed? Now only do I commence to be his disciple; all created things in the visible or invisible world are indifferent to me; my only desire is to possess my Saviour.

9. What, then, is there to dread in the scorching fire, in the slow and cruel death of the Cross; in the jaws of the famished tigers, in the lions of the amphitheatre; what though my bones be scattered, my limbs mangled, my body broken; what though demons exhaust upon me their rage? I am ready for all torments, provided I enjoy my Jesus.

10. Ah! what would it serve me to possess all the riches, all the grandeur of the earth? It is more glorious to die for my God, than to reign over the whole world. I seek Him who died for me; I desire Him who rose again for my sake.

11. Leave me liberty to imitate the sufferings of my God; do not snatch me from life in seeking to save me from death; let me run towards that pure and vivid light. He whose heart is already filled with this light will comprehend my desire, and *he will* have compassion on me, for he knows the strength of the bonds which draw me to my Beloved.

12. The fire which animates and impels me can suffer no diminution; rather He who liveth and speaketh in me calls me continually: *Hasten thou; come to my Father.* If, before you, I shrink from the array of torments, sustain my courage.

Think only of what I now write—now, when I write in full liberty of spirit, aspiring only to die.

13. All the bread I need is the adorable body of my Jesus; all the wine I crave is His most precious blood—that celestial wine which excites within the soul the fire of an incorruptible, an undying charity. I cling no more to earth, no longer do I regard myself as living among men.

14. Forget not, in your prayers, the Church of Syria, who, deprived of her pastors, turns her hopes towards Him who is the Sovereign Pastor of all churches. May Jesus Christ deign to direct it during my absence; I confide it to His providence and to your charity.

---

91. JULIAN THE APOSTATE.

[ST. GREGORY OF NAZIANZEN. The Church, by enrolling Gregory in the number of her saints, and adding to his name the title of theologian, has rendered the most magnificent of all testimonies to his virtues and learning. This title of theologian he shares with St. John alone; so that his name and title are, as it were, synonymous. Pagans and heretics crowded to his discourses; they even forced the balustrades which separated them from the sanctuary, and they frequently broke out into applause and acclamation, so great was their admiration of his wonderful powers of eloquence. He is equally renowned as a poet and orator. In his famous invectives against Julian the Apostate, we recognize oratory equal to that which was opposed to Philip and Catiline. And the exordium is remarkable for an enthusiasm which recalls the language of prophecy. These invectives were called forth by an edict of Julian prohibiting Christians access to the schools of Greece, under the flimsy pretext that, as Christians, all worldly acquirements must be in their estimation of little value.]

YE people, be attentive while I address you! Ye who inhabit the earth, hearken to my words! I call unto you as from a high mountain in the midst of the world, from whence I would that my voice should reach to the ends of the earth. Hearken unto me people, and tribes, and tongues, men of all conditions and of every age; ye who dwell now upon the earth, or ye whom future ages shall bring forth!

2. Let my voice stretch yet further, even unto the heavens, amidst the choirs of angels who have exterminated the tyrant. He whom their hands are about to immolate is not a Sihon, king of the Amorrhites, nor an Og, king of Bashan, feeble monarchs holding under the yoke the land of Juda, a little country lost in the immensity of the earth; it is the tortuous serpent, it is the apostate, that great and rare genius, that scourge alike of Israel and the world; whose fury and whose menaces have everywhere left deep traces, and whose insolent tongue has dared to attack even the Most High.

3. Awaken! ashes of the great Constantine! If some feeling yet dwelleth in the tomb, O heroic soul, hearken to my words. Arouse at my voice, O ye faithful servants of Jesus Christ, who before him ruled the empire. Thou, O great prince, who didst most extend the heritage of Jesus Christ, who didst surpass in glory all thy predecessors, how wert thou mistaken in thy choice of the man who was to succeed thee! Thus a Christian emperor didst nourish, without knowing it, the mortal enemy of Christ; and thy generosity, blinded and deceived, was lavished on him who of all men merited it least.

4. Although the cultivation of the mind is a right common to all who are endowed with reason, he wished to reserve to himself this privilege, alleging this ridiculous pretext—that the Greek letters belong only to those who follow the Greek religion (that is, paganism). By this astounding assertion, he exhibits us as taking that which in nowise belongs to us. This, for a man as literary as he pretends to be, is indeed the strangest of mistakes!

5. He imagined that we would not suspect his secret, and that he would not appear to be depriving us of a very considerable gift, considering the trifling importance we attach to these human letters. His true motive was an apprehension lest we should use them to refute his impiety; as if our blows derived their force from the elegance of words and the artifices of language, rather than from solid reasoning supplied by

truth. It is as impossible to attack us in this manner, as it is to prevent us from praising God while we have a tongue. Julian thus only manifests his weakness.

6. Certainly he would not have forbidden us to speak, if he had believed that his religion was incontrovertible, and could be corroborated by discussion. An athlete who would merit the glory of surpassing all others, and who demands that the public should acknowledge his superiority by universal suffrage, would show timidity rather than courage, by objecting to the strongest and most generous descending into the arena to prove his prowess. Crowns are for the combatants, and not for the spectators; for him who exercises all the energies of his strength, not for him who carries about but a maimed body.

7. You fear the contest, then you acknowledge your conqueror—you avow your inferiority. I have conquered without combating, since your whole effort is to avoid the combat.

---

92. MARTYRDOM OF ST. THEODOSIA.

I.

THEY sought the noble, high-born dame, the daughter of Amiens;
They drag her from love's sheltering arms and home's endearing scenes;
And to the temple of their gods they bear her rudely on—
The brazen censer stands aloft upon the altar-stone;
They bid her throw the spices in, and gently whisper, "Live,—
Live for thy spouse,—thy babe,—thy sons,—thy life is thine to give."
Perchance she wavered then awhile, as from her blue-veined breast
Flowed the white stream, where erst the lips of her fair babe had pressed;
Her dark-haired daughters and her sons—her spouse—her stricken home—

Her sunny youth in old Amiens, in memory's flood-tides come!
"Deny thy Christ—burn incense here," again they rudely cry—
"Never, Oh tempters of my soul!—Never, Oh Christ most high!
Perish my body!—break my heart!—break every earthly link!—
But Christ, the Son of God adored—adored on death's dark brink—
Is my eternal hope and gain—ho! it will soon be ended,
And this poor life, immortal grown, will with His own be blended.
His side was pierced," she murmured low: "Oh, joy to be like Him!
But lo! it brightens round me now, while earth grows cold and dim.
All hail, sweet Lord, and angels fair!" The crimson tide flowed fast;
She waves her hands in triumph high—and lo! the conflict's past—
The palm is won—the glorious hosts of martyrs greet her now;
And He for whom she died lifts up the crown upon her brow.

II.

Midnight hangs o'er imperial Rome, and through the murky gloom
A little band with stealthy steps move towards the Catacomb.
They bear upon their trembling arms a pale and shrouded one;
On—on—through all the winding ways—through many an arch of stone,
They glide in tears and silence, and with many a whisper'd prayer
Lay down the noble martyr's dust, by the red torches' glare.
The sculptured stone, the crystal vase, stained with its crimson dyes,
Told where the daughter of Amiens had slept for centuries.
'Tis she!—sought out in that low crypt, far in the Catacomb,
Raised up with honor—touched with awe—borne from death's stilly gloom

Back to her vine-clad, sunny land,—in regal splendor now
She shines, the fairest gem that France wears on her lofty brow !
Yes, bend the knee, ye countless throngs—the martyr's triumph tell,
Until from sea to sea the notes of Alleluia swell !

Mrs. A. H. Dawson.

---

98. ST. CECILIA BEFORE THE ROMAN PREFECT

Almachius. Young girl, what is thy name?

Cecilia. Men call me Cecilia; but my most beautiful name is Christian.

Al. What is thy condition?

Ce. A Roman citizen, of an illustrious and noble race.

Al. It is of thy religion I question thee; we know the nobility of thy family.

Ce. Your inquiry, then, was not exact, since it requires two answers.

Al. From whence comes this assurance before me?

Ce. From a pure conscience and a sincere faith.

Al. Are you, then, ignorant of my authority and power?

Ce. You speak of your power—and you yourself have not the slightest idea of it; but if you question me on the subject, I can, with clear proofs, reply to it.

Al. Speak, then, for I am anxious to hear thee.

Ce. You seldom pay attention to those things not agreeable to you. Nevertheless, listen. The power of man is like a leathern bag filled with wind—at the mere prick of a needle it shrinks into nothing; all that is solid disappears.

Al. Thy speech, from the beginning, has been marked by insolence.

Ce. Is it insolence to assert what is true? Show where I have violated the truth, then I will admit that I have been insolent; otherwise, the reproach you make is a calumny.

Al. (Changing the discourse.) Dost thou not know that our masters, the invincible emperors, have decreed that those who will not deny that they are Christians are punished, and those who deny it are acquitted?

Ce. How deceived are your emperors and your excellency also! The laws of which you speak only prove your cruelty and our innocence. For, if the name of Christian is a crime, then it would be our place to deny it, and you should oblige us by tortures to confess it.

Al. Nay, it is in their clemency that the emperors have so decreed; wishing, by this means, to assure you of a means of saving your life.

Ce. Could there be more impious conduct, or acts more fatal to the innocent, than yours? You employ tortures to force criminals to confess their guilt—the place, the time, and their accomplices; now, with respect to us, all our crime consists in the name of Christian. And you are satisfied if we deny that name! But we know too well all the beauty of that sacred name, and we cannot deny it. Better die and be happy, than live to be miserable. You wish us to utter a falsehood; and in proclaiming the truth, we inflict a greater torment on you than you can possibly make us suffer.

Al. Let us end this discussion. I give you two chances for your life—sacrifice to the gods, or simply deny that you are a Christian, and you may retire in peace.

Ce. (Smiling.) What a humiliating situation for a magistrate—to persuade me to deny the title by which my innocence is proved, and to become guilty of a falsehood! He consents to spare me, in order to show more clearly his cruelty. If you admit the accusation, why make these efforts to force me to deny that with which I am accused? If you wish to pardon me, why not at least order means to be taken for it?

Al. Behold your accusers. They testify that you are a Christian. I repeat, then—deny this, and the accusation shall immediately be dismissed; but, if you persist in your denial, you will recognize your folly when called to undergo the sentence.

Ce. The accusation is my triumph, and the torture will be my victory. Do not tax me with folly—rather apply this reproach to yourself, for having thought for an instant that you could make me deny Christ.

Al. Unhappy woman, knowest thou not that the power of life and death is placed in my hands by our invincible princes? How, then, darest thou speak to me with such pride?

Ce. Pride is different from firmness. I speak not with pride, but with firmness—for this vice we hold in horror. If you fear not to hear me again speak truth to you, I will show you wherein thou hast just spoken falsely.

Al. Let us hear, then, in what I have spoken falsely.

Ce. You pronounced a falsehood when you said that your princes had conferred on you the power of life and death.

Al. (With astonishment.) I lied in saying that!

Ce. Yes; and if you will permit me, I can prove to you that you lied against the evidence itself.

Al. (With confusion.) Explain—explain yourself.

Ce. Did you not say that your princes had conferred on you the power of life and death? And you well know that you only have the power of death. You can, I admit, take life from those who enjoy it. But can you restore it to those who are dead? Say, then, that your emperors have made you the minister of death, but nothing more; if you add any thing to it, you lie without any advantage.

Al. (Concealing the shame of his affront with assumed calmness.) Lay aside this audacity and sacrifice to the gods (pointing to the statues which filled the prætorium).

Ce. It seems that you have lost the use of your eyes. I, and all those who can see clearly, find nothing here but stones, brass, and lead.

Al. My philosophy makes me despise thy insults when directed against myself; but I cannot support thy insults against the gods.

Ce. You have not uttered one word but I have shown you either its injustice or its folly. Now, that nothing may be wanting, you are convicted of having lost your sight. You call gods these objects which we see are stones—and the most useless stones; touch them, and you will feel what they are. Why do you so ridiculously expose yourself to the people? Every one knows that God is in heaven. These statues of stone might be of some service if you would throw them into a furnace and convert them into lime; they are wearing out in their idleness, and are incapable of defending themselves from the flames. Christ alone can save from death, and deliver guilty man from the punishment of fire.

These were Cecilia's last words before the judge. But Almechius, fearing to brave the murmurs of the patricians of Rome by condemning so illustrious a person to public execution, ordered her to be reconducted to her own home, where she could be put to death quietly. By his orders she was to be confined in the vapor-bath, and a hot fire kindled, by which she would be suffocated to death.

But this cowardly expedient was not successful. Cecilia entered the place of her martyrdom with the most lively joy, and passed the day and night without being in the slightest affected by the burning atmosphere. In vain did the cruel ministers of Almechius heat the furnace to its utmost power. In vain did the burning steam fill the close, air-tight bath. Cecilia was invulnerable, calmly waiting until her celestial spouse would open another route for her to ascend to him. This wonder frustrated the hope Almechius entertained of causing death without being forced to the extremity of shedding the blood of this high-born Roman lady.

He found it impossible to do so. A lictor was accordingly dispatched to behead Cecilia in the place where she seemed to be sporting with death. Cecilia saw him enter, and joyfully knelt to receive the martyr's crown.

The lictor brandished his sword, and, after three strokes, left the virgin extended on the ground, bathed in blood; yet, wonderful to relate, she remained three days in this state.

94. THE SECOND COMING OF JESUS CHRIST.

[ST. EPHREM holds the same relation to the Church of Syria as St. John Chrysostom does to the Greek and St. Augustine to the African Church. Among those men of lofty genius whom God has given to his Church on earth, corresponding to the archangels and seraphs who lead the choirs of blessed spirits surrounding his throne in heaven, St. Ephrem will ever hold distinguished rank. His sublime writings present to our admiration the most persuasive and profound pathos, united with an unfailing unction which charms and penetrates at every line. No one can compare with him in combining pomp of expression and depth of sentiment. Even the weakness of translation does not deprive his thoughts of the grandeur, his images of the vivacity, which animates them. He writes as he spoke, in the presence of God and his angels, in the presence of the tombs, sad witnesses of our mortality. These aspects, which his mind so powerfully conceives, impress on the abounding flow of his language an elevation and a fire unequalled by any other writer, leaving you overpowered by the weight of a sombre and terrible majesty, enveloping the soul as it were in a cloud seamed with the lightning and the thunder. He depicts with as much energy as variety the fragility of life, the nothingness of terrestrial goods, the terrors of death and of judgment. "You already behold," says St. Gregory of Nyssa, "the last scene which will accompany the consummation of the world. You see Jesus Christ appear, borne upon the clouds of heaven. You arouse from your supineness, even as the dead arise from their tombs at the sound of the trumpet; nothing is wanting to the picture but the actual presence of Him who is to judge the living and the dead." It is in these descriptions that his style is elevated to all the sublimity of poetry. The writers of his nation call St. Ephrem, with truth, *the prophet of the last judgment*.]

LEND an attentive ear to what I am going to tell you of the formidable coming of our Lord. In thinking of it I am paralyzd with fear! Ah, who can relate without shuddering the dreadful events connected with this coming? What human language, what tongue can describe this mournful scene?

2. The King of kings, seated on a throne brilliant with light, descends from the highest heavens. In the face of all the universe, as Judge, he calls mankind to the foot of his tribunal!

3. At the thought of this scene my strength fails me; the most violent agitation overwhelms my poor body; my limbs

refuse to support me, my eyes fill with tears, my tongue is paralyzed, my lips tremble, my voice, interrupted by sobs, stops, and there remains nothing in my ideas but disorder and confusion.

4. If a clap of thunder which breaks suddenly upon the ear excites terror in the heart, what will then be the effect of the sound of that trumpet, a thousand times more powerful than the noise of the thunder? It will be heard even in the depths of the tombs, awakening all men, the just and the sinner, who have existed since the creation of the world.

5. The entire human race, reunited at the same time, will appear before the bar of the Sovereign Judge! He speaks, and the trembling earth sends forth the dead whom she had entombed. The ocean restores those it had ingulfed in its abyss, and those who had been a prey of ferocious beasts appear in their proper forms.

6. A torrent of fire, flowing from the Source which gave birth to the sun, with the impetuosity of a sea in fury, pours itself upon the earth, covering mountain and valley, and consuming the entire universe.

7. No more smiling landscapes, no more refreshing fountains, no more streams nor rivers, bearing afar the abundance of their waters; the air is burning, the stars fall from the heavens, the sun is destroyed and the moon changed into blood.

8. A short time and all has disappeared; the heavens rolled back as a scroll; the angels have received the order to assemble the faithful servants of God from one extremity to the other, and they execute it in a moment. A new heaven and a new earth replace the destroyed heaven and earth.

9. Suddenly the majestic throne advances, the sign of the Son of Man appears resplendent as the sun, and its brilliancy fills an immense horizon. All mankind have recognized the royal sceptre of the terrible Monarch. How can they present themselves before Jesus Christ and enter into judgment with him?

10. Overwhelmed by the remembrance of his sins and void of good works, the sinner stands naked and trembling, in fearful anticipation of the sentence to be rendered against him.

11. Each one reads the tablet of his entire life. Those who have walked in the narrow way, those who have effaced their sins by sincere repentance, and those who have shown mercy to the poor and the stranger, await, full of confidence and blessed hope, the glorious coming of the great God-Saviour, our Lord Jesus Christ.

12. It is the day of their triumph. Behold, not coming from the earth, but descending from heaven, He appears as the lightning cutting the air. Hear the cry—"Behold, the Spouse arrives; behold, the Judge comes to pronounce the sentence; the God of the universe comes to judge the world and render to every one according to his works."

13. All hearts, at this cry, are seized with trembling. Universal consternation prevails. The firmament becomes one blaze of light; the choirs of archangels advance; the cherubim and seraphim chant the hymn of glory. Holy, holy, holy is the Lord God of Hosts, who is, who was, and who comes in His omnipotence.

14. And the heavens and the earth reply, "*Blessed be He who comes in the name of the Lord.*" The opened heavens display the King of kings, the Sovereign Ruler of all powers, clothed in glory and majesty. All eyes see Him. Those who nailed Him to the cross recognize Him, and the ancient inhabitants of the earth weep with them, bewailing their blindness. The Prophet Evangelist marks His coming in these words:

15. Alas, sinners that we are, what will then become of us? The Son of Man is seated on His throne of glory; the books are opened according to the prophecy of Daniel; those books wherein are written not only our works, good and bad, but our words and our most secret thoughts.

16. What then will become of those sinners who now refuse

to do penance? *This* is no time, they say, to pray, to fast, and to give alms. Then the voice of the Judge will be heard in tones of thunder, "Show me what have been your works and receive the reward they deserve."

17. Alas, how do we deceive ourselves! Ah, my brethren, what tears should we continually shed in anticipation of that terrible day!

18. Behold all men assembled with pallid faces and downcast eyes, suspended as it were between life and death, heaven and hell: before that redoubtable tribunal each one hears himself called—cited by name to undergo a rigorous examination. Woe is me! I would explain the rest, but my voice is mute.

19. All then is examined — discussed — judged in the presence of angels and of men. Every Christian is examined on the promises of his baptism; on the deposit of faith; on the renunciation he has made of the devil and all his works, without exception. Happy he who has faithfully fulfilled these engagements!

20. The examination over, the good are separated from the bad, the sheep from the goats. To the first is said, "*Come, ye blessed of My Father, possess the kingdom prepared for you;*" to the second, "*Depart from me, ye cursed, into everlasting fire!*"

21. You who were without charity, enemies of God and of your brethren—you were without mercy, I shall be without pity—deaf to the voice of my gospel. I say to you now, I know you not! And the division is made for eternity. To the wicked, hell, with its everlasting torments; to the just, heaven, with its immortal rewards.

22. The torments of hell! Exterior darkness—tortures—wailing and gnashing of teeth, the worm that never dies—the pool of fire—the fiery, exhaustless furnace—and to all of these torments are assigned particular victims corresponding with the sins of which they were guilty. All banished forever from the presence of God! All abandoned to despair! All delivered to everlasting death, who makes them his prey!

[Here Ephrem, weeping bitterly and striking his breast,

suspended his discourse. His congregation with one voice begged him to continue.]

23. You wish it? I will then speak, but only with my tears and deep sighs.

24. Oh, my brethren, what do you wish to learn? Oh dreadful day! Woe is me! woe is me! You who have tears, weep with me! Let those who have them not learn what fate awaits them. Ah, let them not forget their salvation.

25. Cruel separation—the false priest—the prince and the monarch, who abuse their power; the worldly Christian fathers and mothers who forget their duties, are separated forever from the faithful priest, from their brothers, their sons, their friends, without regard to their anguish—without one to plead for them.

26. In vain do they implore aid; vain are now their riches and their flatterers. The angels with lashes chase them before them and force them into the abyss. Unfortunate beings! they look backward, imploring pity; they arrive at the brink of the abode of eternal torments; "No more hope!" they scream, in plunging in. Oh, why were we carried away by the seductions of the flesh? what good has it been for us to have served the world? where are the parents from whom we received life? Where are our children and our friends?

27. Where our riches and our pleasures? Adieu, adieu forever, Saints and just, the blessed souls whose example we refused to follow! Adieu parents, friends, children, whom we shall never again see! Adieu holy apostles, prophets, and martyrs of the Lord!

28. August Mother of the God-Saviour—oh, you who united us to penance, you who entreated us with such tender prayers to think of our salvation—oh, why did we refuse to listen to you? Farewell, delights of Paradise, the Celestial Jerusalem! Farewell, immortal Kingdom of Heaven!

St. Ephrem of Edessa, Doctor.

95. MY GOD! I LOVE THEE!

[St. Augustine, born in Africa, 354, was one of the most eloquent writers of the Latin Church. According to Bossuet, Augustine is one of the most renowned orators, and one of the most extraordinary men who have been given to the world.]

MY God! I love Thee! Thou hast struck my heart with Thy Word, and I have loved Thee! Heaven and earth, and all things that are in them, tell me to love Thee; nor do they cease to say the same to all men, that they may be inexcusable.

2. But what do I love when I love Thee? Not the beauty of the body; not the graceful revolutions of time; not the dazzling brilliancy of light, so enchanting to our eyes; not the sweet melodies of dulcet sounds of every description; not the aromatic fragrance of flowers and of perfumes; not manna, and not honey. It is not these I love when I love my God; and yet I do love light, and harmony, and fragrance; I do enjoy the pleasures of food and of endearment; but when I love my God, light, harmony, fragrance, food, endearments, speak to my inward being; a light shines on my soul which is not hemmed in by space.

3. Harmonies are there which time interrupts not: fragrance not to be dissipated by a breath of wind; pleasures of taste not to be diminished by indulgence of the palate; abiding caresses, endearments, over which satiety has no power to produce disgust. This is what I love when I love my God. And what is God? I asked of Earth, and it answered me: "It is not I!" And all the creatures she contains within her bosom made the same acknowledgment.

4. I asked the Sea, and the deep abyss, the reptiles alike, and the animals which live within their depths, and they answered me: "We are not thy God; search thou above what we are." I asked the atmosphere we breathe, and the vast encircling air, with all its inhabitants, thus answered me: "Anaximenes was wrong—I am not thy God." I asked the

azure sky, the sun, the moon, the stars, and they replied: "Neither are we the God whom thou dost seek."

5. Then said I to all objects exterior to my body, and which surround me: "Speak to me of my God, which you are not; tell me something concerning Him." And they exclaimed with a loud voice—"HE MADE US."

6. I interrogated them by the intention framed within my soul. They answered me: "By their beauty." I then addressed me to myself, and questioned: "What art Thou?" And I answered: "A Man!"—a being in whom a body and soul are conjoined, the one exterior, the other interior. "In which of these ought I now to seek my God, whom I had already sought by means of my bodily senses, throughout all earth, up to the heavens themselves, wherever I could send my eyes as messengers to gather light?"

7. But far better speaks the interior sense, since all exterior objects refer to that in judging and appreciating the several responses of earth and heaven, and of all which are contained within them, saying: "We are not God, but He it was who made us." The interior man knows this by the ministry of his exterior organization; I myself know these things, by my inward sense; I, *i. e.*, my soul, receive impressions through the senses of my body. I have interrogated Matter concerning God, and it answered me: "I am not He, but He made me."

ST. AUGUSTINE.

---

96. DEFENCE OF EUTROPIUS.

[ST. JOHN, Archbishop of Constantinople, was surnamed Chrysostom, or "Golden-Mouthed," on account of his wonderful gift of oratory and success in the ministry of preaching. The entire East, Christians and Pagans, called him the Divine Orator. Christian eloquence never achieved more brilliant victories, or reigned with more triumphant sway, than from the pulpit of St. Chrysostom. The people hastened in crowds to hear him. His regular audience in the city of Antioch was a hundred thousand. Heretics, Jews, even Pagans, mingling with Catholics at the feet of this man, the worthy Ambassador of the Supreme Judge of the living and the dead, presented an image of the future concourse of the human race on that day when he shall come in the clouds of heaven to open the portals of eternity. Chrysostom's words carried conviction to every mind, persuasion to every heart, so well did he ally the most powerful reasoning and the tenderest pathos. Involuntary acclamations, universal plaudits, extorted by irrepressible admiration, ordinarily interrupted his discourses. The modesty and piety of the holy Archbishop complained of this, and his complaints only called forth renewed acclamations. Other more decisive manifestations testified to his powers. A mournful silence, sobs that could not be restrained, remarkable conversions, and permanent reformations, accompanied his instructions.

Seditious Antioch, on the eve of falling under the wrath of Theodosius, owed her salvation to the eloquence of Chrysostom. But nowhere is the Saint more sublime than in the defence of Eutropius.

As a favorite of Arcadius, Eutropius had been elevated to the highest dignities of the empire. His great excesses and abuses excited the populace and army against him, and the Emperor, as weak in sustaining his ministers as he was imprudent in selecting them, found himself obliged to forsake his favorite. Utterly abandoned, Eutropius fled to the portals of the Church he had so cruelly persecuted. He sought an asylum at the foot of the altar which he had labored to abolish. The public hatred eagerly pursued him; a furious populace, sustained by an undisciplined military force, surrounded and filled the church, demanding the life of Eutropius. At this moment the Archbishop of Constantinople made his way through the infuriated crowd, and sheltering by his presence the poor victim, who clung to the altar in all the agony of despair, saved for the time being the unfortunate Eutropius.

This discourse of St. Chrysostom is universally regarded as one of the most sublime specimens of the inspiration of human eloquence; he literally quelled at his feet the unchained passions of the enraged crowd. The proud courtier, the powerful favorite of the Emperor, fallen from the pinnacle of prosperity to the last excess of misery, insulted in his flight by the same people who the evening before offered him their homage as the idol of fortune—now obliged to beg an asylum in the temple of the God whose minister he had persecuted—the ferocious multitude ready to drag him from this asylum. Such was the scene.]

IN every season of our lives, but most especially in the present, we may exclaim, "Vanity of vanities! all is vanity!" Where now are the costly insignia of the consulship, and where the blaze of torches? Where now is the enthusiasm of applause, and the crowded hall, and the sumptuous banquet, and the midnight revelry? Where is the tumult that echoed through the city, the acclamations which resounded in the hippodromes, and the flattery of the spectators? All these are fled.

2. The first tempestuous gale hath scattered the rich foliage on the ground, presenting to our eyes the naked tree, reft of its blossoms, and bowed inglorious to the earth. So wild hath been the storm, so infuriate the blast, that it threatened to tear up the very roots from their proud foundation, and to rend the nerves and vitals of the tree.

3. Where now are the fictitious friends? Where is the swarm of parasites, the streaming goblets of exhaustless wine, the arts which administered to luxury, the worshippers of the imperial purple, whose words and actions were the slaves of interest?

4. They were the vision of a night and the illusion of a dream, but when the day returned they were blotted from existence; they were flowers of the spring, but when the spring departed they were all withered; they were a shadow, and it passed away; they were a smoke, and it was dissolved; they were bubbles of water, and they were broken; they were a spider's web, and it was torn.

5. Wherefore, let us proclaim this spiritual saying, incessantly repeating, "Vanity of vanities! all is vanity!" This is a saying which should be inscribed on our garments, in the Forum, in the houses, in the highways, on the doors, and on the thresholds; but far more should it be engraven on each man's conscience, and be made the theme of ceaseless meditation.

6. Since fraud, and dissimulation, and hypocrisy, are all sanctioned in the commerce of the world, it behooves each man, on each passing day, at supper, and at dinner, and in the public meetings, to repeat unto his neighbor, and to bear his neighbor repeating unto him, "Vanity of vanities! all things are vanity!" Did I not continually say to you that wealth is a fugitive slave? but my words were not endured. Did I not perpetually remind you that it is a servant void of gratitude? but you were not willing to be convinced.

7. Lo! experience hath proved to thee that it is not only a fugitive slave, not only an ungrateful servant, but likewise a destroyer of man. It is this which hath undone thee, which

hath abased thee in the dust. Did I not frequently observe that the wound inflicted by a friend is more worthy of regard than the kisses of an enemy? If thou hadst endured the wounds my hands inflicted, perchance their kisses had not engendered this death to thee.

8. For my wounds are the ministers of health, but their isses are the harbingers of disease. Where now are thy laves and cup-bearers? Where are they who walked insolently through the Forum, obtruding upon all their encomiums of thee? They have taken the alarm; they have renounced thy friendship; they have made thy downfall the foundation of their security. Far different our practice.

9. In the full climax of thy enormities we braved thy fury; and now that thou art fallen, we cover thee with our mantle, and tender thee our service. The Church, unrelentingly besieged, hath spread wide her arms and pressed thee to her bosom; while the theatres, those idols of thy soul, which so oft have drawn thy vengeance upon us, have betrayed thee, have abandoned thee.

10. And yet, how often did I exclaim, Impotent is thy rage against the Church; thou seekest to overturn her from her lofty eminence, and thy incautious steps will be hurried down the precipice; but all was disregarded. The Hippodromes having consumed thy riches, sharpen their swords against thee, while the Church—poor suffering victim of thy wrath—traverses the mountains, valleys, woods, panting to rescue thee from the snare.

11. I speak not these things to trample on a prostrate foe, but more firmly to establish the upright. I am not to lacerate a wound yet bleeding, but to insure sweet health to those who are unwounded. I wish not to bury in an abyss of waters him who is half drowned already, but to caution those whose bark glides smoothly on the ocean, lest they should be wrecked at last. And how shall they be preserved? Let them meditate on the vicissitudes of mortals. This very man, had he but feared a change, had not experienced a change.

12. But, since neither foreign nor domestic examples could reclaim him, ye at least, who are enshrined in wealth from his calamity, should derive instruction. Nothing is more imbecile or more empty than the affairs of men; therefore, whatever terms I might employ to denote their vileness, my illustration would be insufficient. To call them a blade of grass, a smoke, a flower, would be to stamp a dignity on them; for they are less than nothing.

13. That they are not only visionary and unsubstantial, but likewise pregnant with disaster, is manifest from hence. Was ever man more elevated, more august than he? Did he not surpass the universe in wealth? Did he not ascend the meridian of dignities? Did not all men tremble and bend before him? Lo! he is become more necessitous than the slave, more miserable than the captive, more indigent than the beggar wasted with excess of hunger; each day doth he behold swords waving, gulfs yawning, the lictus and the passage to the grave.

14. Were this moment to be his last, he would be utterly unconscious; he regards not the sun's fair beam, but, standing in meridian day, and though he were enveloped in tenfold darkness, his sight and feelings are extinct. But wherefore do I attempt to delineate those sufferings, which he himself, in glowing colors, depicts unto us? Even yesterday, when soldiers from the imperial palace came to drag him to his fate, with what a speed, with what an agitation did he rush unto the altar! Pale was his countenance, as though he were an inmate of the tomb; his teeth chattered, his whole frame trembled, his speech was broken, his tongue was motionless; ye would have thought his very heart had been congealed to stone.

15. Believe me, I relate not this to insult and triumph in his fall, but that I may soften your heart's rough surface; may infuse one drop of pity, and persuade you to rest satisfied with his present anguish, since there are persons in this assembly who reproach my conduct in admitting him to the altar; to smooth

the asperity of their hearts, I unfold the history of his woes. Wherefore, O my friend, art thou offended? Because, thou wilt reply, that man is sheltered by the Church, who waged an incessant war on it.

16. This is the special reason for which we should glorify our God, because He hath permitted him to stand in so awful a necessity as to experience both the power and the clemency of the Church:—the power of the Church, because his continued persecutions have drawn down this thunderbolt on his head; and her clemency, because, still bleeding from her wounds, she extends her shield as a protection; she covers him with her wings; she places him in an impregnable security, and, forgetting every past circumstance of ill, she makes her bosom his asylum and repose.

17. No illustrious conquest, no high-raised trophy, could reflect so pure a splendor; this is a triumph which might cover the infidel with shame, and raise even the blushes of a Jew. It is this which irradiates her face with smiles, and lights up her eye with exultation.

18. She hath received, she hath cherished, a fallen enemy; and when all besides abandoned him to his fate, she alone, like a tender mother, hath covered him with her garment, and withstood at once the indignation of the prince, the fury of the people, and a spirit of inextinguishable hatred.

19. This is the glory, the pride, of our religion! What glory is there, you will exclaim, in receiving an iniquitous wretch unto the altar? Ah! speak not thus, since even a harlot took hold of the feet of Christ—a harlot utterly impure; yet no reproach proceeded from Jesus' lips; He approved, He praised her; the impious did not contaminate the holy, but the pure and spotless Jesus rendered by His touch the impure harlot pure. O man, remember not thine injuries; are we not the servants of a crucified Redeemer, who said, as he was expiring: "Forgive them, for they know not what they do?"

20. But He interdicted this asylum, you will say, by His decrees and His laws. Lo! He now perceives the nature of

what He did, and is Himself the first to dissolve the laws which He enacted. He is become a spectacle to the world, and, though silent, from hence He admonisheth the nations. Do not such things as I have, lest you should suffer what I suffer.

21. Illustrated by this event, the altar darts forth an unprecedented splendor, and shines a warning beacon to the earth. How tremendous, how august doth it appear, since it holds this lion in chains and crouching at your feet! ST. CHRYSOSTOM.

---

97. SUPPLICATION.
FROM THE GREEK OF ST. CLEMENT OF ALEXANDRIA.

CURB for the stubborn steed,
    Making its will give heed;
Wing that directest right
The wild-bird's wandering flight;
Helm for the ships that keep
Their pathway o'er the deep;
Shepherd of sheep that own
Their Master on the throne—
Stir up thy children meek
With guileless lips to speak,
In hymn and song, thy praise,
Guide of their infant ways.
O King of Saints, O Lord,
Mighty, all-conquering Word:
Son of the highest God,
Wielding His Wisdom's rod,
Our stay when cares annoy,
Giver of endless joy;
Of all our mortal race
Saviour, of boundless grace,
        O Jesus, hear!

2. "Shepherd and Sower thou,
　　Now helm, and bridle now,
　　Wing for the heavenward flight
　　Of flock all pure and bright;
　　Fisher of men, the blest,
　　Out of the world's unrest,
　　Out of sin's troubled sea,
　　Taking us, Lord, to thee;
　　Out of the waves of strife
　　With bait of blissful life,
　　With choicest fish good store,
　　Drawing thy nets to shore—
　　Lead us, O Shepherd true,
　　Thy mystic sheep, we sue.
　　Lead us, O Holy Lord,
　　Who from thy sons dost ward,
　　With all-prevailing charm,
　　Peril, and curse, and harm;
　　O Path where Christ has trod,
　　O Way that leads to God,
　　O Word, abiding aye,
　　O endless Light on high,
　　Mercy's fresh-springing blood,
　　Worker of all things good,
　　O glorious life of all
　　That on their Maker call,
　　　　　　Christ Jesus, hear!

3. "O Milk of Heaven, that pressed
　　From full, o'erflowing breast
　　Of her, the mystic Bride,
　　Thy Wisdom hath supplied;
　　Thine infant children seek,
　　With baby lips all weak,
　　Filled with the Spirit's dew
　　From that dear bosom true,

Thy praises pure to sing,
Hymns meet for Thee, our King,—
For Thee, the Christ;

4. "Our holy tribute this,
For wisdom, life, and bliss,
Singing in chorus meet,
Singing in concert sweet,
The Almighty Son.

5. "We, heirs of peace unpriced,
We who are born in Christ,
A people pure from stain,
Praise we our God again,
Lord of our Peace."

---

98. APPEAL FOR THE CRUSADES, TO THE PEOPLE OF FRANCONIA.

[ST. BERNARD, at the age of twenty-three, entered the Monastery of Cityaux. To this extraordinary man was given in a moment the power to rule the minds of man. He passed from the depths of the cloister to the midst of the Court, as thoroughly a monk in one place as in the other. Scarcely a year of his life is unmarked by some great event. From his poor cell he governed all Europe. Nations and kings chose him to arbitrate their differences. Ambassadors were sent to his cloister. All the Orders of the West submitted themselves to the wisdom of his counsels. Pious bishops, learned men, with the sons of kings, placed themselves under his direction. Pope Eugenius called upon Bernard to preach the Crusades throughout France and Germany. Everywhere his appeal was received as an oracle, and men of every grade and every age enrolled themselves in this pious expedition.]

I SPEAK to you of the interests of Christ, whereon depends your salvation. The authority of the Lord, and the consideration of your own benefit, will excuse the unworthiness of him who addresses you. I am indeed of little consequence, but I earnestly desire that you be saved by the merits of Jesus Christ. Behold the time of salvation ; the universe is moved, the whole world trembled because the God of Heaven is about to lose the land which was his abiding-place—the land where as man he passed more than thirty years with the children of men; a land illustrated by his miracles, consecrated by his blood; a land wherein the first flowers of the Resurrection appeared.

2. To-day, on account of our sins, the enemies of the Cross have lifted their sacrilegious heads; they ravage this Holy Land, this Land of Promise, and none resist them; they throw themselves upon the city even of the living God; they overturn the monuments of our redemption; they desecrate the holy places, reddened with the blood of the spotless Lamb.

3. O Grief! their impious zeal burns to invade the very sanctuary of Christianity, to trample under foot the mysterious resting-place where Jesus, our Life, slept for us in the bosom of Death.

4. And you, brave men, you servants of the faith, will you thus deliver holy things to dogs, thus cast pearls before swine? Ah! how many confessing their sins with tears, have there obtained pardon since your fathers' swords purged away the Pagan hosts! The enemy of the human race saw it, and trembled with rage; he stirred up the vessels of iniquity, and he will leave no trace, no vestige of so great a piety, if he succeed (which God forbid!) in making himself master of the Holy of Holies. What an inconsolable grief for all ages, for the loss will be irreparable!

5. But above all, what confusion, what eternal reproach for this perverse generation! Meanwhile, my brethren, what shall we think! That the hand of God is shortened, that His arm is powerless, that He calls worms of the earth to defend His inheritance? Could He not send legions of angels, or merely say the word, and the Holy Land would be free? He can do whatsoever He wills. But I say to you, the Lord your God wishes to prove you. He looks to the children of men, to see whether any will take part in His grief; for the Lord has mercy upon His people.

6. He prepares means of salvation for those who have abandoned Him. See with what artifice He endeavors to save you. Sinners, consider the depth of His tenderness for you,

and take confidence. He wishes not your death, but only that you be converted and live; it is for this that He seeks an occasion, not against you, but for you. What better opportunity, and who but God could have found it, than this by which He recalls to His service, as if they had always practised justice, ravishers, homicides, perjurers, and all who have covered themselves with crimes?

7. Doubt not, sinners, the Lord is indulgent. If He wished to punish you, not only would He not demand your service, but He would refuse it when offered. I repeat it, think on the treasures of the Most High, reflect on His mercy. While He desires to come to your succor, He feigns to need yours for Himself; He wishes to appear as your debtor, that He may reward your service by the forgiveness of your sins, and the recompense of eternal glory.

8. Happy generation! I say unto you, who live in a time so rich in indulgence. Since your land is fertile in brave men, in robust youth; since your glory and the fame of your valor have filled the world, let your zeal for the Christian name hasten you to take up those arms which have ever been crowned with victory. Yes! soldiers! press forward to the combat—press onward to the battle!

9. O noble and valiant warriors, to-day a war offers itself wherein you have every thing to gain, and nothing to fear; your triumph is a true glory; your fall a real good. And you, busied in amassing the treasures of this world, beware, lest you permit the treasures now offered you to escape. Take up the Cross, and you will obtain the pardon of all the sins you have confessed with a contrite heart.

10. This Cross is a little thing in itself, but if you carry it with devotion, it will purchase for you the kingdom of God. Those who already bear this celestial sign have done well; those who now follow their example will receive the same reward. But beware of too much precipitation in this enterprise. Choose from among you experienced and able chieftains; let the Army of the Lord move forward together, that thus in

their first expedition they may be able to overcome. May God, who is blessed forever, preserve you. Amen.

ST. BERNARD.

99. BOSSUET AS AN ORATOR.

BUT what shall we say of Bossuet as an orator? To whom shall we compare him? And which of the harangues of Cicero and Demosthenes are not eclipsed by his *Funeral Orations?* The *Christian* orator seems to be indicated in those words of a *King:*—" There is gold and a multitude of jewels; but the lips of knowledge are a precious vessel."

2. Looking always upon the grave, and bending as it were over the gulf of futurity, Bossuet is incessantly dropping the awful words of *time* and death, which are re-echoed in the silent abyss of eternity. He gathers around him an indescribable sadness; he becomes merged in sorrows inconceivable. The heart, after an interval of more than a century, is yet struck with that celebrated exclamation:—" The Princess is dying—the Princess is dead!"

3. Did monarchs ever receive such lessons? Did philosophy ever express itself with greater independence? The diadem is as nothing in the eyes of the preacher; by him the poor are raised to an equality with the monarch, and the most absolute potentate in the world must submit to be told, before thousands of witnesses, that all his grandeur is but vanity; that his power is but a dream, and himself is but dust.

4. There are three things continually succeeding one another in Bossuet's discourses:—the stroke of genius or of eloquence; the quotation so admirably blended with the text, as to form but one piece with it; lastly, the reflection, on the survey taken with eagle eye, of the causes of the event of which he treats.

5. Often, too, does this star of the Church throw a light upon discussions in the most abstruse metaphysics, or the most sublime theology. To him nothing is obscure. He has cre

ated a language employed by himself alone, in which frequently the simplest term and the loftiest idea, the most common expression and the most tremendous image, serve, as in Scripture, to produce the most striking effect.

6. Thus, when pointing to the coffin of the Duchess of Orleans, he exclaims:—"*There you see, notwithstanding her great heart, that Princess so admired, so beloved! There you behold her, such as death has made her!* Why do we shudder at the simple expression, *such as death has made her?* 'Tis on account of the opposition between that *great heart*—that *Princess so admired*, and the inevitable stroke of death, which laid her low as the meanest of mankind."

7. 'Tis because the *verb*, make, applied to death, which unmakes all, produces a contradiction in the words, and a clashing of the ideas which agitate the whole soul, as if, to describe an event so sudden and so afflicting, the terms had changed their signification, and the language itself were thrown into confusion as well as the heart. CHATEAUBRIAND.

---

100. THE GREAT CONDE.

[Never was BOSSUET more eloquent; never did he excite so deep an enthusiasm among his audience, than in the funeral oration of the "Prince of Condé." The orator identified himself with the greatness of his hero; we might say that he did not relate, but conceived the plans himself; he is on the field of battle — sees all — prepares for all — commands the movement — he unites and paints at the same time the past, the present, and the future.

The last part is the most wonderful mingling of the sublime and pathetic. In the touching peroration we see the orator himself appear upon the scene. The imposing idea of the venerable orator, who mourns the great man ; those white hairs—that wonderful voice, now trembling and growing weak—the retrospect of the past—the firm, sad glance into the future—and, finally, the death of the orator, make an impression never to be effaced.]

COME, then, inhabitants of the earth! Come, rather should I say, come princes and lords! You who rule the earth, and you who open to man the gates of heaven ; and you, more than all the rest, princes and princesses, noble scions of so many kings—lights of France—but to-day obscured and covered with sorrow, as with a cloud.

2. Come and see the little that remains to us of so august a birth, of so much grandeur, of so much glory. Cast your eyes on all sides; behold all that magnificence and piety can give to honor—a hero! Titles, inscriptions, vain marks of that which no longer exists, figures which seem to weep around a tomb, and the frail images of a grief which time carries away with all the rest.

3. These columns, which seem to wish to elevate even to the heavens—the magnificent evidence of our nothingness; nothing is wanted in all these honors, except him to whom they are rendered.

4. Weep, then, over these feeble remains of human life, weep over this sad immortality which we give to heroes; approach, in particular, O ye who run with so much ardor in the career of glory—warlike and intrepid souls, who was more worthy to command you? Where have you found so noble a chief? Weep, then, for this great captain, and say, in sighing: Behold him who led us through perils; under whom so many renowned captains were formed; so many renowned captains who have been elevated, by his example, to the first honors of the camp—his shadow might yet have gained some battles.

5. Behold his silence—his name even animates us, and warns us that if in death we wish to find some repose after our labors, and hope to reach happily our eternal residence, we must, while serving the kings of the earth, also serve the King of Heaven. Serve, then, this Immortal King, so full of mercy, who will reward you for even a cup of cold water given in His name, more than all the others for all the blood you shed for them, and commence to count your services as useful from the day you give yourselves to so generous a Master.

6. And you—will you not come to this sad monument; you, I say, whom he loved to rank among his friends? All together, in whatever degree of confidence he has received you—sur-

round this tomb; give him your tears and your prayers, and, admiring in this prince a friendship so generous, an intercourse so sweet, preserve the memory of a hero whose goodness equalled his courage. May he ever be to you a dear remembrance, and may you profit by his virtues; and may his death, which you deplore, serve, at the same time, as a consoation and an example.

7. For myself, if I am permitted, after all the others, to come and render my last tribute at his tomb, O Prince, the worthy object of our praises and our regrets, you will live eternally in my memory; your image will there be impressed, not with that air of triumph which promises victory—no; I wish to see nothing which death can efface—you will have in that image only those traits which are immortal. I shall see you such as you were on that last day, under the hand of God, when his glory commenced to appear in you.

8. There I shall see you more triumphant than at Fribourg, or at Rocroy, and, ravished at so beautiful a triumph, I shall exclaim in thanksgiving with the beloved apostle: "The true victory is that which places under our feet the entire world,"—in this is faith.

9. Enjoy, then, O Prince, this glory; enjoy it eternally, by the immortal virtue of this sacrifice. Accept these last efforts of a voice which was well known to you; you have put an end to all its words, instead of deploring the death of others. O great Prince, I shall learn from you to make mine holy; happy, if warned by these white hairs of the account I must soon render of my administration. I reserve for the flock that I must nourish with the words of life the remainder of my failing voice and weakened strength. BOSSUET.

---

101. CHRIST OUR LIGHT.

"Then shall the eyes of the blind be opened."—ISA., XXXV., 5.

A THOUSAND years have fleeted,
And, Saviour, still we see

Thy deed of love repeated
　On all who come to Thee:
As he who sat benighted,
　Afflicted, poor and blind,
So now thy word is plighted,—
　Say, light and peace I find.

2. Dark gloom my spirit filling,
　Beside the way I sat;
Desire my heart was thrilling,
　But anguish more than that.
To me no ray was granted,
　Although I heard the psalms
The faithful sweetly chanted,
　And felt the waving palms.

3. With grief my heart was aching,
　O'erwhelming were my woes,
Till Heaven-born courage taking,
　To Thee my cry arose:
O David's Son, relieve me,
　My bitter anguish quell,
Thy promised succor give me,
　And this dark night dispel!

4. With tears that fast were flowing,
　I sought Thee through the crowd,
My heart more tender growing,
　Until I wept aloud:
O! then my grief diminished,
　For then they cried to me,
"Blind man, thy woe is finished;
　Arise! He calleth thee!"

5. I came with steps that faltered,
　Thy course I felt the check;
Then straight my mind was altered,
　And bowed my stubborn neck.

Thou saids't, "What art thou seeking?"
"O! Lord! that I may see;"
O! then I heard thee speaking,
"Believe, and it shall be."

6. Our hope, Lord, faileth never;
    When thou thy word dost plight,
My fears then ceased forever,
    And all my soul was light.
Thou gav'st me then Thy blessing,
    From former guilt set free;
Now heavenly joy possessing,
    O Lord! I follow Thee.

DE LA MOTTE FOUQUÉ.

---

102. FUNERAL ORATION OF HENRIETTA OF ENGLAND.

[BOSSUET (JAMES BENIGNE), born in Dijon, 1627, was scarcely sixteen, when he sustained his first thesis with such brilliancy, that the *literati* of Paris desired to hear the young orator at the Hôtel Rambouillet. There, in the presence of the renowned characters of the age, he extemporized a sermon, which delighted and astonished his auditors.

His funeral orations, particularly those of the Queen of England, the Duchess of Orleans, the Great Condé, and the Princess Palatine, are unrivalled in any language. Bossuet, Bishop of Meaux, died in 1704.

This oration was delivered in the Church of Chaillot, near Paris, where the head of the queen, the wife of the unfortunate Charles the First, was deposited.]

HE who reigns in heaven, and from whom all empires proceed, to whom belongs all glory, majesty, and independence, is alone the only one to whom it belongs to make laws for kings, and to give them, when it pleases Him, great and terrible lessons.

2. Whether in raising thrones or in overthrowing them, in communicating His power to princes, or in withdrawing it, and leaving them to their own weakness, He teaches them their duties in a sovereign manner worthy of Himself; for, in

giving them His power, He commands them to use it as He would Himself, for the good of the world; and, by withdrawing it, he convinces them that all their power is only borrowed, and although seated on thrones, they are no less under His hand and supreme authority. It is not by words and discourses alone that He instructs princes, but still more by events and examples.

3. Christians, let the memory of a great queen, daughter, wife, and mother of powerful and sovereign kings in the three kingdoms, speak on all sides at this sad ceremony. This discourse will give you one of those awful examples which displays to the eyes of the world its entire vanity.

4. You will see in a single life the extremes of all things human—joys without bounds, as well as miseries; a long and peaceful enjoyment of one of the most noble crowns in the universe; every thing which could give the greatest glory to birth and rank, adorning a head which was afterwards exposed to all the outrages of misfortune.

5. The good cause, at first followed by good success—then sudden reverses; unheard-of changes; rebellion, checked for a long time, but finally mastering all order; unbridled license; laws abolished; the majesty of the throne violated by outrages, until then unknown; usurpation and tyranny under the name of liberty; a fugitive queen, who could find no retreat in the three kingdoms, and to whom her native land was only a place of exile;—nine voyages by sea, undertaken by this princess, in spite of tempests;—the astonished ocean saw itself traversed so many times, under so many different circumstances, and for such opposite causes; a throne overthrown with ignominy, and again miraculously re-established:

6. Behold, the lesson God gives to kings, showing at the same time to the world, the nothingness of their pomp and magnificence. If words fail us, if expressions are powerless to describe a subject so vast and elevated, the subject will speak for itself.

7. The heart of a great queen, formerly exalted by a long

succession of prosperities, and then suddenly plunged into an abyss of misery, will speak sufficiently loud. And if it is not permitted to private individuals to give lessons to princes on events so strange, a king lends me his words to say to them, "Listen, O ye great of the earth!—Be instructed, O ye arbiters of the world!"

BOSSUET.

---

108. FUNERAL ORATION OF THE DUCHESS OF ORLEANS.

[HENRIETTA OF ORLEANS was the youngest child of Charles I. of England. When quite young, she married the Duke of Orleans, brother of Louis XIV. She was distinguished by her talents and great personal attractions; she died after an illness of a few hours, at the age of twenty-six, at a period when she had rendered herself most popular in France by the delicate tact and wonderful prudence with which she effected a good understanding between her brother Charles II. and Louis XIV., on the subject of the invasion of Holland.]

"VANITY of vanity, and all is vanity!" Again am I destined to render the funeral service to the high and powerful Princess Henrietta of England. She who was so attentive while I rendered this duty to her mother, so soon to become the subject of a similar discourse!

2. Oh vanity! Oh nothingness! Oh mortals, ignorant of their destiny! Would she have believed it ten months ago? And you, gentlemen, could you have believed, while she shed so many tears in this place, that you would so soon be reassembled to weep for her? Princess! worthy object of the admiration of two great kingdoms! was it not enough for England to weep your absence, without being reduced to weep your death?

3. And France, who with such joy saw you return, surrounded with new splendor, had she no other pomp, no other triumph for you on the return from this famous voyage—bearing with you so much glory, so many beautiful hopes? Vanity of vanities, and all is vanity! This is the only word left for me. • • • • • • • • •

4. No; after what we have just seen, health is but a name, life but a dream, glory but a phantom, graces and pleasures but dangerous amusements. All is vain in us but the sincere avowal we make to God of our vanity and nothingness.

5. Consider the mighty ones of the earth! God strikes them as a warning to us. . . . God spares them so little that he fears not to sacrifice them for the instruction of mankind. . . . We must be convinced of our nothingness— and if our hearts, enchanted by the world, require sudden shocks, surely the present is sufficiently great and terrible.

6. Oh disastrous night! Oh terrible night! when suddenly, like a clap of thunder, was heard this astounding news—The Princess is dying! The Princess is dead!

7. What, then—she must die so soon! Death ordinarily prepares the greater part of mankind for its last stroke. The princess passed from morning until evening like the flower of the field. In the morning she bloomed with what grace you all know! In the evening we saw her withered; and these strong expressions by which the Sacred Writings exaggerate the inconstancy of human things became for this princess exact and literal.

8. Alas! we composed her history as the most glorious that can be imagined—the past and the present guaranteed a brilliant future. But in place of the history of such a beautiful life, we are compelled to give the history of an admirable but lamented death.

9. Behold her, notwithstanding her great heart, this princess, so admired, so beloved; behold her, such as death has made her! A little while, and all will disappear; this shadow of glory will vanish; we will see her stripped even of its sad decorations!

10. She will descend to those gloomy places, to that subterraneous abode, to sleep in dust with the great ones of the earth, among those dead kings and princes, where scarcely can room be found for her, so closely crowded are their ranks, and so prompt is death to fill these places.

11. But here our imagination deceives us again; death does not even leave us enough of the body to occupy any place, and we only see the tombs. The flesh soon changes its nature; the body takes another name—while something human yet remains of it—but even this soon passes; it becomes—I know not what—it has no name in any language. So true it is that all dies in it, even to the terms by which we could designate its unfortunate remains.

12. In this way does the Divine Power, justly irritated against our pride, destroy it; and in order to render all conditions equal forever, reduces us all to the same dust. Can any one build on such ruins? Can any one erect great monuments on such inevitable decay? BOSSUET.

---

104. THE DEATH OF THE SINNER.

[MASSILLON (JOHN BAPTIST) was born in Provence, 1663. At the age of eighteen, he was admitted into the congregation of the Oratory. His success was so brilliant on his first appearance in the pulpit, that in his humility he sought a retreat in one of the most retired houses of the Order, to escape, as he said, "*the demon of Pride.*" All critics have awarded him a pre-eminent place among the small number who are naturally eloquent. He is frequently styled the Racine of the Chair and the Cicero of the Pulpit. After one of his sermons before the Court of Versailles, Louis XIV. said to him:—"Father, I have heard great orators in my chapel, and I was always *exceedingly satisfied* with them; but when I hear you, I am always *exceedingly dissatisfied* with myself."]

THEN, the dying sinner, finding nothing in the remembrance of the past but regrets which overwhelm him—nothing in all objects that are presented to his eyes, but sights which afflict him, and in the thought of the future, only horrors which terrify. Not knowing where to turn or on whom to call, for creatures fly from him, and the world is fast disappearing; men cannot deliver him from death. A declared enemy of God —from Him no indulgence can be expected—writhes in the horrors he has created for himself; every thought is a torment. Oh, could he but fly from death, which seizes him; or, at least, could he only fly from himself!

2. His dying eyes glare gloomily and savagely, expressing all the terror of his soul. From his depths of misery he utters words so interrupted by sobs, that half cannot be understood, and no one knows whether they are the expression of despair or of repentance. He casts on a crucified God frightful looks, which leave a doubt in the minds of those who surround him as to whether it is fear or hope, hatred or love, which they express.

3. He is seized with horrible convulsions, and they know not if it is the dissolution of the body or the soul which feels the approach of its judge. He sighs profoundly, and they know not if it is the remembrance of his crimes which draw these sighs, or despair at leaving life.

4. At length, in the midst of the most painful agony, his eyes become glazed, his features change, his face is distorted, his livid mouth half opens of itself, his whole frame is convulsed; and with this last effort, his unfortunate soul, drawn from its earthly tabernacle, falls into the hands of God, and stands alone at the foot of His awful tribunal. MASSILLON.

---

105. ON THE SMALL NUMBER OF THE ELECT.

IMAGINE that it is now your last hour, and the end of the world; that the heavens are about to open above your heads, and Jesus Christ in all His glory to appear in the middle of this temple; that you are only assembled as trembling criminals, and, in an instant, the sentence of pardon or of eternal condemnation will be pronounced for you.

2. In vain do you flatter yourselves, for you will die such as you are to-day; all the desires of a change or a future conversion which deceive you to-day, will deceive you on your death-bed. This is the experience of all ages. All that you will then find new in yourselves will be an account, perhaps, still greater than the one you would have to render to-day; and by what you would be, were you to be judged this mo-

ment, you can almost decide what will be your fate when life will end.

3. Now I ask you, and as I ask you, I am overwhelmed with terror—for I do not separate my own fate from yours—and placing myself in the same condition that I so earnestly wish for you; I ask you, then—If Jesus Christ were to appear in this temple, in the midst of this assembly, the most august in the universe, to pass sentence of judgment—to make the terrible distinction between the sheep and the goats; do you believe that the greatest number of you who are around me would be placed on the right? Do you even believe that there would be an equal number on both sides? Do you believe that He would find the ten just and holy persons that the Lord in former times could not find in five entire cities? I ask this question—you cannot answer it; neither can I. Thou only, O my God, knowest those who belong to Thee!

4. But if we know not who are His, we at least know that sinners do not belong to Him. Now, who are the faithful here assembled? Titles and dignities must be counted as nothing; you will be stripped of all of them before Jesus Christ.

5. Again I ask, Who are here? Many sinners who do not wish to be converted; many more who wish their conversion, but who defer it; many others who only reform in order to fall back into their former state; and, finally, a great number who believe they have no need of conversion. Behold the number of the reprobates! Take, then, these four sorts of sinners from this holy assembly, for they will be assuredly cut off on that great day.

6. Appear, now, O ye just—where are ye? Remnant of Isreal, pass to the right. Wheat of Jesus Christ, separate yourself from this straw destined for the flames! Oh, God, where are Thy elect, and what remains for Thy portion?

MASSILLON.

106. EXORDIUM AT ST. SULPICE.

[PÈRE BRIDAINE is one of those apostolic missionaries, endowed with a bold and vigorous imagination, who knows no other success than conversions, no other applause than tears. No one ever possessed in a higher degree the rare talent of arresting the attention of an assembled multitude than the Abbé Bridaine. He had so fine a voice as to render credible all the wonders which history relates of the declamation of the ancients; for he was as easily heard y ten thousand people in the open fields, as if he had spoken under the most esounding arch. He preached in the Church of St. Sulpice, 1751. The *élite* the Capital went out of curiosity to hear the man who had created such sensation in the province. Père Bridaine perceived among the congregation many nobles and persons of the first rank, as well as a vast number of ecclesiastics. The sight, far from intimidating, suggested to him the following exordium, not unworthy of Bossuet or Demosthenes: In apologizing, so to speak, for having preached upon hell in the villages, he boldly assumed all the authority over his audience which belonged to his office, and prepared their hearts for the awful truths which he intended to announce. This exordium gave him a right to say every thing.]

UNTIL now I have proclaimed the righteousness of the Most High in churches covered with thatch. I have preached the rigors of penance to the unfortunate who wanted bread. I have declared to the good inhabitants of the country the most awful truths of my religion. Unhappy man! what have I done? I have made sad the poor, the best friends of my God! I have conveyed terror and grief into those simple and honest souls, whom I ought to have pitied and consoled! It is here only where I behold the great, the rich, the oppressors of suffering humanity, or sinners daring and hardened. Ah! it is here only where the sacred Word should be made to resound with all the force of its thunder; and where I should place with me in this pulpit, on the one side, Death which threatens you, and on the other, my great God, who is about to judge you. I hold to-day your sentence in my hand. Tremble, then, in my presence, ye proud and disdainful men who hear me!

2. The necessity of salvation, the certainty of death, the uncertainty of that hour, so terrifying to you, final impenitence, the last judgment, the number of the elect, hell, and, above all, eternity! Eternity! These are the subjects upon

which I am come to discourse, and which I ought, doubtless, to have reserved for you alone. Ah! what need have I of your commendation, which perhaps might damn me without saving you? God is about to rouse you while his unworthy minister speaks to you! for I have had a long experience of his mercies. Penetrated with a detestation of your past iniquities, and shedding tears of sorrow and repentance, you will then throw yourselves into my arms, and by this remorse you will prove that I am sufficiently eloquent.

3. Maury, after citing this exordium of Father Bridaine as one of the master-pieces of pulpit eloquence, proceeds with these remarks:—Every thing, then, is in the orator's power, when he has thus won his audience; and he ought to take advantage of this power, which is given to him temporarily, to complete his work, and to develop and organize in the minds of the listeners the idea to which he has given birth: this is the third stage of his undertaking.

4. Strike the iron while it is hot, says the proverb. In the present instance, there is something more than iron, and better than iron, to forge and fashion. Eloquence would miss its aim, if it failed to lead the hearer by some act by which the idea is to be realized. It is in this last stage, then, that the practical part of the discourse should be placed along with the application of the deductions. In these must the speaker reap the fruits of his labor. After having imparted his feelings and thoughts to the listener, he must also make them partakers of his will. He must imprint his personality upon them, fashion them in his resemblance, so that they shall feel, think, and will as he does, in the interest of that truth and excellence of which he has brought home to them the manifestation.

5. He must not take leave of his audience till he has touched, convinced, and carried it away. It is in the peroration, as we are about to see, that the seal must be set to the work, and that it must receive its plenary completeness.

107. SONG OF THE ANGELS OVER THE SKEPTIC'S CONVERSION.

HAIL to the Spirit
That all shall inherit
By childlike belief!
Hail to the mortal,
Now safe through the portal
That hideth from grief!

2. Crown him with roses,
As glad he reposes
In the garden of love;
No longer forbidden,
The apples of Eden
He findeth above.

3. Angels caress him,
For Jesus doth bless him
With grace freely given;
Seraphs, keep ringing
Your harps, sweetly singing
His welcome to heaven.

4. Tempests have tossed him,
Lower loves crossed him,
Nearly we lost him;
Hardly he won
Escape from the burning;
Hail his returning,
The prodigal son!

5. Show him the river
Where life wells forever,
As grand as the Giver
He now doth adore;
Fling round him denser
Perfumes from the censer,

Till his faith burns intenser
Into light evermore.

6. Clothe him with pinions
To scale the dominions
Of vision unknown;
Bid him soar higher
An Angel of fire,
Still higher and nigher,
Till he faints with desire
At the foot of the throne.

FROM AN UNPUBLISHED POEM BY JUDGE ARRINGTON.

---

108. CHARACTER OF CHAMPLAIN.

WHAT we esteem most of all other features in the life of our Founder, is that chief virtue of all eminent men—his indomitable fortitude; and next to that we revere the amazing versatility and resources of the man. Originally a naval officer, he had voyaged to the West Indies and to Mexico, and had written a memoir, lately discovered at Dieppe, and edited both in France and England, advocating among other things the artificial connection of the Atlantic and Pacific Oceans. From the quarter-deck we trace him to the counting-rooms of the merchants of Rouen and Saint Malo, who first intrusted him, in 1603, with the command of a commercial enterprise of which Canada was the field. From the service of the merchants of Rouen, Dieppe, and Saint Malo, we trace him to the service of his sovereign—Henry IV.

2. For several successive years we find his flag glancing at all points along the rock-bound coast on which we are now assembled, from Port Royal to Massachusetts Bay. Whenever we do not find it here, we may be certain it has advanced into the interior, that it is unfurled at Quebec, at Montreal, or towards the sources of the Hudson and the Mohawk. We will find that this versatile sailor has become in time a founder of

cities, a negotiator of treaties with barbarous tribes, an author, a discoverer. As a discoverer, he was the first European to ascend the Richelieu, which he named after the patron of his latter years—the all-powerful Cardinal. He was the first to traverse that beautiful lake, now altogether your own, which makes his name so familiar to Americans; he was the first to ascend our great central river, the Ottowa, as far north as Lake Nippising, and he was the first to discover what he very justly calls "the fresh-water sea" of Lake Ontario.

3. His place as an American discoverer is, therefore, among the first; while his claims as a colonizer rest on the firm foundations of Montreal and Quebec, and his project—extraordinary for the age—of uniting the Atlantic with the Pacific by an artificial channel of communication. As a legislator, we have not yet recovered, if we ever shall recover, the ordinances he is known to have promulgated; but as an author we have his narrative of transactions in New France, his voyage to Mexico, his treatise on navigation, and some other papers. As a diplomatist, we have the Franco-Indian alliances, which he founded, and which lasted a hundred and fifty years on this continent, and which exercised so powerful an influence, not only on American, but on European affairs. To him also it was mainly owing that Canada, Acadia, and Cape Breton were reclaimed by, and restored to France under the treaty of Saint Germain-en-Laye, in 1632.

4. As to the moral qualities, our Founder was brave almost to rashness. He would cast himself with a single European follower in the midst of savage enemies, and more than once his life was endangered by the excess of his confidence and his courage. He was eminently social in his habits—as his order of *le bon temps*—in which every man of his associates was for one day host to all his comrades, and commanded in turn in those agreeable encounters of which we have just had a slight skirmish here. He was sanguine as became an adventurer, and self-denying as became a hero. He served under De Monts, who for a time succeeded to his honors and

office, as cheerfully as he had ever acted for himself, and in the end he made a friend of his rival. He encountered, as Columbus and many others had done, mutiny and impatience in his own followers, but he triumphed over the bad passions of men as completely as he triumphed over the ocean and the wilderness.

5. He touched the extremes of human experience among diverse characters and nations. At one time he sketched plans of civilized aggrandizement for Henry IV. and Richelieu; at another, he planned schemes of wild warfare with Huron chiefs and Algonquin braves. He united, in a most rare degree, the faculties of action and reflection, and like all highly reflective minds, his thoughts, long cherished in secret, ran often into the mould of maxims, and some of them would form the fittest possible inscriptions to be engraven upon his monument.

6. When the merchants of Quebec grumbled at the cost of fortifying that place, he said:—"It is best not to obey the passions of men; they are but for a season; it is our duty to regard the future." With all his love of good-fellowship and society, he was, what seems to some inconsistent with it, sincerely and enthusiastically religious; among his maxims are these two—that "The salvation of one soul is of more value than the conquest of an empire;" and, that "Kings ought not to think of extending their authority over idolatrous nations, except for the purpose of subjecting them to Jesus Christ."

THOMAS D'ARCY MCGEE.

109. HEROISM OF THE HOSPITAL AND THE PRISON.

THERE is a sort of sanctity about the very idea of a Christian hospital, second only to that we associate with a church; and one can well understand that both the proud Templars, and the gallant Knights of Malta, both bound to works of corporal mercy, owed much of their early prestige to their origin upon the very spot where our Lord was believed to have appeared to his Apostles, and where Ananias and Sapphira gave up the ghost, according to the doom denounced on them by the first Apostle. One of the chief glories of every civilized country is in its hospitals. Bishops consecrate them; kings endow them; artists adorn them; science seeks them out; travellers celebrate their praises; Parliaments and Congresses have issued commissions to improve and enlarge their operations.

2. Unquestionably the greatest organizer of this class of institutions the world has ever seen came out of Gascony, in the first years of the seventeenth century, from a rank of life answering to that of our ordinary *habitant*—you all know, I am sure, to whom I allude,—St. Vincent de Paul, the founder of the Lazarists, and of the Sisters of Charity. There have been many orders of hospitallers in the Catholic Church in former ages, but none near our own time, at all to compare in efficiency and renown with the daughters of Vincent de Paul.

3. Their extraordinary founder was not what the world would call a man of genius—he was not more than ordinarily learned, as a priest; he was not nobly born; he was at all times poor in this world's wealth. Yet, in the sixty years of his priestly office (1600 to 1660), he became the founder of the General Hospital at Paris; the Foundling Asylum in the same city; the Hospital of St. Reine, the Hospital for Galley Slaves at Marseilles, with the numerous progeny of these institutions all over Christendom, brought into existence during the great organizer's lifetime.

4. In sending the first Sisters of Charity forth on their trying task, to mingle with the world, in all its grossness and all its weaknesses, yet be not of it, the high-hearted Gascon said:—"Your Monasteries are the houses of the sick; your cell is a hired room; your cloister the streets of the city or the wards of the hospital. Let obedience be your solitude, and a strict and holy modesty your only veil."

5. I shall not presume to sketch the sixty years passed by

St. Vincent in the service of all the heroic charities; we may measure his achievements by the fact that at this day—more than two centuries after his death—more money is paid in alms, in the name of this humbly-born Gascon, more food and clothing are given, more criminals are reformed, more sick are nursed, more foundlings are adopted, more deserted dead are decently buried, than is done by the governmental expenditure of the greatest prince or government in Christendom.

6. Of the mere monetary value of those gratuitous and undaunted nurses of the sick—the Sisters of his Order—I leave those to form an estimate who have seen them in the military hospitals, after a battle or a siege, who have seen them face to face with pestilence in its most violent forms, or who have had the assistance of their gentle and ever-ready hands in the most trying surgical operations. An order of women, dedicated from girlhood to God, who should consider the daily labor of their lives to be to dress wounds, to serve the fallen and the unfortunate, to harbor the harborless, to heal the bruised spirit; such an Order was a conception possible only for a Christian.

7. Not that I would deny the possession of a spirit of admirable benevolence to those who are not Christians. Among all the Mussulman nations the natural virtue of charity has had many beautiful illustrations, and I remember reading some years ago an account of a magnificent Parsee merchant who built in an interior city of India a hospital open to all strangers, whether Christians, or Moslems, or believers in Bramah or in Buddah—which himself he could never dare to enter. The only joy, but not, let us hope, the only recompense of this good Parsee, was to watch from a distant station the numbers who departed healed, and the numbers who presented themselves to be cured at the gates of the great establishment he had founded—where the founder's name was never spoken, and across whose threshold his footsteps could never pass! That was the disinterestedness inseparable from heroism; that was a degree of spiritual self-denial seldom attained even among Christians.

8. One of the main helps to success received by St. Vincent de Paul in all his enterprises, was the cordial co-operation in his plans of women of every grade of society. Ladies of the city or the court, like Madame de Legnas and Madame de Miramion, gave their wealth, their presence, their prayers and their time to second all his charitable undertakings; others volunteered for service in pestilential places, in besieged cities, and even among the galley-slaves.

9. If the follies and weaknesses of the sex were conspicuously exhibited at the court of Louis XIV., never had the moral courage and the pure self-sacrifice of woman more splendid illustrations than in that same age and country. We should be ungrateful, indeed, in Canada, for the sound basis of Christian civilization which we enjoy here, if we were to overlook that fact; if we were not to recall that we were speaking of the age and country of Madame d'Aiguillon, of Madame d'Youville, of Mademoiselle Manse, and of that glorious pioneer of religious education on this island—Sister Marguerritte Bourgeoys!

McGEE.

---

110. MENTAL AND MORAL DESTITUTION OF DEAF-MUTES.

BUT the peculiar merit of this charity is to be estimated, not merely by quantity, but also by quality. Usually, the visit is a penalty for the violation of some natural law, such as the intermarriage of cousins; and sometimes it swallows up a whole family; we have had here three and four sisters all similarly afflicted. But it is not alone that the natural avenues to the heart and brain are closed against the sufferers—that they can never hear a mother's voice, or the prattle of playmates, or the measured breathings of sweet music, or the voice of psalm, or organ, or sermon, or vespers; but it is, that this which Johnson calls "one of the most desperate of human calamities," leaves those on whom it falls, mentally and morally, mere savages, while born in the midst of civilisation, they feel the physical wants, and are subject to the temptations of civilized life.

2. It is a melancholy fact, that of all the deaf-mutes who have been examined, after instruction, as to their previous state, not one in ten thousand had any previous idea of the existence of a God. As to the history of man's redemption, of course they knew nothing of it whatever. Some, who had observed speaking people pray, thought they prayed to the sun or the sky. With the exception of Mussieu, the celebrated pupil of Abbé Sicard—a man of uncommon genius—there is hardly a case in which a deaf-mute, so born, had the faintest natural idea of God. Those, therefore, who rescue one such creature from the darkness of the soul, find their heathen in the midst of civilization, and make a conquest not less glorious than if they had sought proselytes at the ends of the earth.

3. It may show us how much we ought to value and reverence language—the ripener, if not the sower of ideas,—the conductor, if not the producer of thought,—that it was only when a substitute was found for language—or, perhaps I should say, when the sign-language was invented for the relief of the deaf and dumb, that they began to be conscious of such ideas as God, heaven, hell, soul, judgment, right and wrong. So that those who devote themselves to the education of deaf-mutes, do not, as other teachers do, improve upon Nature, by making the most of the materials at hand; they actually create their own materials; they rescue so many Christian children—by seven years' painful seeking and striving—for it takes seven years—from a forlorn state of interior savagery, in which no God reigns, and no law binds.

4. In ancient times, even in the palmy days of Roman civilization, the born mute was outcast and outlawed as a monster beyond the pale of law; in modern times, until recently, they had in most countries—France excepted—no protection whatever, as to their natural rights, from the civil law: but it will be one of the purest glories of the eighteenth century

that it produced such men as the Abbé de l'Epée and Abbe Sicard, who sought out the victims of this calamity, so to speak, in the cradle, and filled the darkened chambers of their minds with the glorious images of God and His Saviour Son before the dangerous days of puberty and passion came upon them.

5. In this heroic charity, I say it not aggressively nor in a spirit of controversy, but I say it thankfully, as a Catholic, that we find the Church always in the van, from the old Spanish Benedictine, De Buce, to the living French Jesuit, Castel, the inventor of the *clavier oculaire*, the Catholic clergy have been among the most studious, most constant, and most successful instructors of the deaf and the dumb. They have wrought miracles in this behalf—not, indeed, by supernatural means—but miracles of patience, of industry, and of perseverance in well-doing!
McGee.

111. PARADISE.

O PARADISE! O Paradise!
    Who doth not crave for rest?
Who would not seek the happy land
    Where they that loved are blessed;
Where loyal hearts and true
    Stand ever in the light,
All rapture, through and through,
    In God's most holy sight?

2. O Paradise! O Paradise!
    The world is growing old;
Who would not be at rest and free
    Where love is never cold;
Where loyal hearts and true
    Stand ever in the light,

    All rapture, through and through,
      In God's most holy sight?

3. O Paradise! O Paradise!
    Wherefore doth death delay;—
  Bright death, that is the welcome dawn
    Of our eternal day;
  Where loyal hearts and true
    Stand ever in the light,
  All rapture, through and through,
    In God's most holy sight?

4. O Paradise! O Paradise!
    'Tis weary waiting here:
  I long to be where Jesus is,
    To feel, to see Him near;
  Where loyal hearts and true
    Stand ever in the light,
  All rapture, through and through,
    In God's most holy sight.

5. O Paradise! O Paradise!
    I want to sin no more:
  I want to be as pure on earth
    As on thy spotless shore,
  Where loyal hearts and true
    Stand ever in the light,
  All rapture, through and through,
    In God's most holy sight.

6. O Paradise! O Paradise!
    I greatly long to see
  The special place my dearest Lord
    Is destining for me;
  Where loyal hearts and true
    Stand ever in the light,
  All rapture, through and through,
    In God's most holy sight.

7. O Paradise! O Paradise!
   I feel 'twill not be long:
   Patience! I almost think I hear
   Faint fragments of thy song;
   Where loyal hearts and true
   Stand ever in the light,
   All rapture, through and through,
   In God's most holy light.

FABER.

---

112. THE SONG OF THE COSSACK.

[Rev. Francis Mahony is a native of Cork, and after some years spent in the ministry as a Catholic clergyman, devoted himself to literature, and was long a prized contributor to English magazines and journals, where his keen wit, his intimate acquaintance with ancient and modern literature, no less than great versatility of power, made his articles of the greatest interest. His renderings of modern poems into Latin and Greek are inimitable, and those into English, like the following from Beranger, are distinguished by ease and grace, retaining all the vigor of the original.]

COME, arouse thee up, my gallant horse, and bear thy rider on!
The comrade thou, and the friend, I trow, of the dweller on the Don.
Pillage and Death have spread their wings! 'tis the hour to hie thee forth,
And with thy hoofs an echo wake to the trumpets of the North!
Nor gems nor gold do men behold upon thy saddle-tree;
But earth affords the wealth of lords for thy master and for thee.
Then fiercely neigh, my charger gray!—thy chest is proud and ample;
Thy hoofs shall prance o'er the fields of France, and the pride of her heroes trample!

Europe is weak—she hath grown old—her bulwarks are laid
  low;
She is loath to hear the blast of war—she shrinketh from a
  foe!
Come, in our turn, let us sojourn in her goodly haunts of
  joy—
In the pillared porch to wave the torch, and her palace
  destroy!
Proud as when first thou slakedst thy thirst in the flow of
  conquered Seine,
Aye shalt thou lave, within that wave, thy blood-red flanks
  again.
Then fiercely neigh, my gallant gray!—thy chest is strong
  and ample!
Thy hoofs shall prance o'er the fields of France, and the pride
  of her heroes trample!

Kings are beleaguered on their thrones by their own vassal
  crew;
And in their den quake noblemen, and priests are bearded
  too;
And loud they yelp for the Cossack's help to keep their
  bondsmen down,
And they think it meet, while they kiss *our* feet, to wear a
  tyrant's crown!
The sceptre now to my lance shall bow, and the crosier and
  the cross
Shall bend alike, when I lift my pike, and aloft THAT SCEPTRE,
  toss!
Then proudly neigh, my gallant gray!—thy chest is broad
  and ample;
Thy hoofs shall prance o'er the fields of France, and the pride
  of her heroes trample!

In a night of storm I have seen a form!—and the figure was
  A GIANT,

And his eye was bent on the Cossack's tent, and his look
    was all defiant;
Kingly his crest—and towards the West with his battle-axe
    he pointed;
And the "form" I saw *was* ATTILA! of this earth the scourge
    anointed.
From the Cossack's camp let the horseman's tramp the com
    ing crash announce;
Let the vulture whet his beak sharp set, on the carrion field
    to pounce;
And proudly neigh, my charger gray!—Oh! thy chest is
    broad and ample;
Thy hoofs shall prance o'er the fields of France, and the pride
    of her heroes trample!

What boots old Europe's boasted fame, on which she builds
    reliance,
When the North shall launch its *avalanche* on her works of
    art and science?
Hath she not wept her cities swept by our hordes of tramp-
    ling stallions?
And tower and arch crushed in the march of our barbarous
    battalions?
Can *we* not wield our father's shield? the same war-hatchet
    handle?
Do our blades want length, or the reapers' strength, for the
    harvest of the Vandal?
Then proudly neigh, my gallant gray, for thy chest is strong
    and ample;
And thy hoofs shall prance o'er the fields of France, and the
    pride of her heroes trample!

                      FRANCIS MAHONY.

118. IRELAND AND THE IRISH.

MUCH there is in Ireland that we most dearly love. We love its music, sweet and sad, and low and lonely; it comes with a pathos, a melancholy, a melody, on the pulses of the heart, that no other music breathes, and while it grieves, it soothes.

2. It seems to flow with long complaint over the course of ages, or to grasp with broken sobs through the ruins and fragments of historic thought. We are glad with the humor of Ireland, so buoyant and yet so tender, quaint with smiles, quivering with sentiment, pursing up the lips while it bedews the eyelids.

3. We admire the bravery of Ireland, which may have been broken, but never has been bent,—which has often been unfortunate, but which never has been craven. We have much affection for the Irish character. We give unfeigned praise to that purity of feeling which surrounds Irish women in the humblest class, and amidst the coarsest occupations, with an atmosphere of sanctity.

4. We acknowledge with heartfelt satisfaction that kindred love in the Irish poor, that no distance can weaken, and that no time can chill. We feel satisfied with our humanity, when we see the lowly servant girl calling for her wages, or drawing on the savings' bank for funds, to take tears from the eyes of a widowed mother in Connaught, or fears from the soul of an aged father in Munster.

5. We behold a radiance of grandeur around the head of the railroad laborer, as he bounds, three thousand miles away, at the sound of repeal, at the name of O'Connell, and yet more as his hand shakes, as he takes a letter from the post-office, which, rude as it may be in superscription, is a messenger from the cot in which his childhood lay, is an angel from the fields, the hills, the streams, the mountains, and the moors wherein his boyhood sported.

6. We remember, with many memories of delight, too, the beauties of Ireland's scenery. We recollect the fields that are ever green; the hills that bloom to the summit; the streamlets that in sweetness seem to sing her legends; the valleys where the fairies play; the voices among her glens, that sound from her winds as with the spirits of her bards; the shadows of her ruins at moonlight, that in pale and melancholy splendor appear like the ghosts of her ancient heroes.

HENRY GILES.

THE END.